THE GLOBAL AGENDA

ISSUES AND PERSPECTIVES

FIFTH EDITION

EDITED BY

Charles W. Kegley, Jr.
University of South Carolina

Eugene R. Wittkopf
Louisiana State University

Boston, Massachusetts   Burr Ridge, Illinois   Dubuque, Iowa
Madison, Wisconsin   New York, New York
San Francisco, California   St. Louis, Missouri

McGraw-Hill

A Division of The McGraw-Hill Companies

THE GLOBAL AGENDA: Issues and Perspectives

Copyright © 1998 by The McGraw-Hill Companies, Inc. All rights reserved. Previous editions © 1984, 1988, 1992 and 1995. Printed in the United States of America. Except as permitted under the United States Copyright Act of 1976, no part of this publication may be reproduced or distributed in any form or by any means, or stored in a data base or retrieval system, without the prior written permission of the publisher.

This book is printed on acid-free paper.

1 2 3 4 5 7 8 9 0   DOC/DOC   9 0 9 8 7

ISBN 0–07–034329–2

Publisher: *Jane Vaicunas*
Sponsoring editor: *Leslye Jackson*
Marketing manager: *Annie Mitchell*
Editorial coordinator: *Stephanie Cappiello*
Project manager: *Robert A. Preskill*
Production supervisor: *Scott Hamilton*
Senior designer: *Crispin Prebys*
Compositor: *Shepherd Incorporated*
Typeface: *10/12 Times Roman*
Printer: *R. R. Donnelley & Sons Company*

Library of Congress Cataloging-in Publication Data

The global agenda: issues and perspectives / edited by Charles W.
  Kegley, Jr., Eugene R. Wittkopf.—5th ed.
        p. cm.
     ISBN 0–07–034329–2
     1. International relations. 2. International economic relations.
  I. Kegley. Charles W.   II. Wittkopf, Eugene R., 1943–
  JX1395.G575   1997
  327.1'01—dc21   97–1315

http://www.mhhe.com

ABOUT
THE EDITORS

CHARLES W. KEGLEY, JR., is Pearce Professor of International Relations at the University of South Carolina. President of the International Studies Association (1993–1994), Kegley has held appointments at Georgetown University, the University of Texas, Rutgers University, and the People's University of China. He is the editor of *Controversies in International Relations Theory: Realism and the Neoliberal Challenge* (St. Martin's Press, 1995) and *The Long Postwar Peace* (HarperCollins, 1991). With Gregory A. Raymond, Kegley is the coauthor of *A Multipolar Peace? Great-Power Politics in the Twenty-First Century* (St. Martin's Press, 1994) and *When Trust Breaks Down: Alliance Norms and World Politics* (University of South Carolina Press, 1990).

EUGENE R. WITTKOPF is R. Downs Poindexter Professor of Political Science at Louisiana State University. A past president of the Florida Political Science Association and of the International Studies Association/South, he has also held appointments at the University of Florida and the University of North Carolina at Chapel Hill. Wittkopf is the author of *Faces of Internationalism: Public Opinion and American Foreign Policy* (Duke University Press, 1990) and the editor of *The Future of American Foreign Policy* (St. Martin's Press, 1994) and *The Domestic Sources of American Foreign Policy* (St. Martin's Press, 1994).

Together, Kegley and Wittkopf have coauthored and edited many texts, including *World Politics: Trend and Transformation,* sixth edition (1997) and *American Foreign Policy: Pattern and Process,* fifth edition (1996).

For Jeannie
— CWK

For Barbara, Debra, and Jonathan
— ERW

CONTENTS

PREFACE

There is no scientific antidote [to the atomic bomb], only education. You've got to change the way people think. I am not interested in disarmament talks between nations. . . . What I want to do is to disarm the mind. After that, everything else will automatically follow. The ultimate weapon for such mental disarmament is international education.

—Albert Einstein

On the threshold of the 21st century, with discussion centered throughout the world on the likely character of international affairs in the new millennium, there is much uncertainty. The many recently and rapidly unfolding trends observable have generated new issues, new cleavages, and a new international landscape. Nonetheless, both change and constancy alongside the prospect of revolutionary transformation are evident in contemporary international politics, and each of these can obscure from vision an accurate description of international realities. Perhaps this is why, in the wake of the Cold War, a consensus has not yet emerged about the defining character of world politics, even though the era of transition between the past epoch and the future one has understandably made for much speculation. Our period of history does not yet have a name or label, and in the absence of agreement about its properties, it has become conventional to postpone definitions by referring to it simply as "post–Cold War."

Whatever the international system's ultimate nature, the potential for great changes has opened up a Pandora's Box of new controversies and unfamiliar developments. Simultaneously, traditional controversies continue to color countries' relations. This condition presents an intellectual challenge because the study of contemporary international politics must consider the factors that produce change as well as those that promote continuities in relations among political actors on the global stage.

Because change is endemic to international politics, it is not surprising that many new issues on the global agenda and fresh perspectives on their analysis have emerged since the fourth edition of this book was published. Our purpose in preparing a fifth edition is to provide a basis for making an informed assessment of international relations by bringing information up to date and by presenting current commentary on the dominant issues in contemporary international politics and the rival analytical perspectives constructed to understand them. But the overarching goals that motivated the first four editions remain: to make available to students what we, as editors, believe to be the best introductions to the issues that underlie contemporary world politics and to introduce the major analytical perspectives and organizing concepts that scholars have fashioned to make these issues comprehensible. It seems to us that, to a greater or lesser degree, coverage of both these elements is missing in standard texts (by design and necessity) and that a supplementary anthology is the logical place for them.

The Global Agenda: Issues and Perspectives categorizes essays into four "baskets" that build on the distinction between "high politics" (peace and security issues) and "low politics" (nonmilitary issues). The criteria that guided the selection of particular articles within each part and the rationale that underlies the organization of the book are made explicit in our introductions to each part. These introductions are further designed to help students connect individual essays to common themes.

The organization of the book is intended to capture the diversity of global issues and patterns of interaction that presently dominate the attention of world political actors and precipitate policy responses. This thematic organization allows treatment of the breadth of global issues and of the analytical perspectives that give them meaning, ranging from classic theoretical formulations to the newer analytical foci and concepts that have arisen to account for recent developments in world affairs. In preparing the volume in this manner, we have proceeded from the assumption that there is a need for educational materials that treat description and theoretical exposition in a balanced manner and expose a variety of normative interpretations without advocating any particular one.

Several people have contributed to the development of this book. We wish especially to acknowledge the contributions of Ole R. Holsti, Christopher C. Joyner, Jack S. Levy, Dennis Pirages, Donald J. Puchala, James N. Rosenau, Marvin Soroos, and Christina Payne. The helpful suggestions of a number of reviewers are also gratefully acknowledged: Peter D. Feaver, Duke University; Lloyd Jensen, Temple University; Douglas Lemke, Florida State University; Karrin Scapple, Southwest Missouri State University; Suisheng Zhao, Colby College. We additionally thank Jeannie Weingarth and Fernando Jimenez for their assistance. At McGraw-Hill we are indebted to Lyn Uhl, Bertrand W. Lummus, Fred Burns, Monica Freedman, Leslye Jackson, Stephanie Cappiello, and Robert Preskill for their support and professional assistance.

Charles W. Kegley, Jr.

Eugene R. Wittkopf

PART ONE

ARMS AND INFLUENCE

The contemporary international political system began to acquire its present shape and definition more than three centuries ago, with the emergence of a state system in Europe after the highly destructive Thirty Years War. As the Westphalian treaties in 1648 brought that war to an end and as political, economic, and social intercourse grew among the states of Europe, new legal norms were embraced in an effort to regulate interstate behavior. The doctrine of state sovereignty, according to which no legal authority is higher than the state, emerged supreme. Thus the nascent international system was based on the right of states to control their internal affairs without interference from others and to manage their relations with other states with whom they collaborated or competed as they saw fit. Foremost in this system was the belief, reinforced by law, that the state possessed the right—indeed, the obligation—to take whatever measures it deemed necessary to ensure its preservation.

Although the international system and patterns of interaction among its political actors have changed profoundly since the birth of the state system, contemporary world politics remains significantly colored by its legacy: it continues to be conducted in an atmosphere of anarchy. As in the past, the system remains fragmented and decentralized, with no higher authority above nation-states, which, as the principal actors in world politics, remain free to behave toward one another as they choose.

This is not meant to imply either that states exercise their freedom with abandon or that they are unconstrained in the choices they make. The political, legal, moral, and circumstantial constraints on states' freedom of choice are formidable. Moreover, states' national interests are served best when states act in a manner that does not threaten the stability of their relations with others or of the global system that protects their autonomy. Hence, the international system, as the British political scientist Hedley Bull reminds us, may be an anarchical society, but it is one of "ordered anarchy" nonetheless.

The world has grown increasingly complex, interdependent, and "globalized" as contact, communication, and exchange have increased among the actors in the state system and as the number of nation-states and other non-state international actors has grown. Expanded interaction enlarges the range of potential mutually beneficial exchanges between and among transnational actors. But just as opportunities for cooperation have expanded, so have the possible sources of disagreement. That we live in an age of conflict is a cliché that contains elements of truth because differences of opinion and efforts to resolve disputes to one's advantage, often at the expense of others, are part of any long-term relationship. Thus, as the world has grown smaller and the barriers once provided by borders between states have eroded, the mutual dependence of transnational political actors on one another has grown and the number of potential rivalries, antagonisms, and disagreements has increased correspondingly. Friction and tension therefore appear to be endemic to international relations; the image of world politics conveyed in newspaper headlines does not suggest that a shrinking world will necessarily become a more peaceful one. Instead, even as memory of the Cold War from 1947 through 1989 fades, competition and conflict persist, as demonstrated by the ubiquitous eruption of ethnic conflicts, civil wars, and religious disputes throughout the world and the inability to prevent their outbreak in many flash points across the globe.

Given the persistent characteristics of contemporary world politics, the number of *issues* that are at any one time in dispute among nation-states and other global actors appears to have increased greatly. The multitude of disagreements and controversies renders the *global agenda*—the list of issues that force their way into consideration and command that they be addressed, peacefully or not—more crowded and complex. Because the responses that are made to address the issues on the global agenda shape our lives both today and into the future, it is appropriate that we direct attention to those matters that animate world politics and stimulate the attention and activities of decision makers. At the same time, as different state and nonstate actors view global political issues from widely varying vantage points, it is fitting that we remain sensitive to the various perceptual lenses through which the items on the global agenda are viewed. Accordingly, *The Global Agenda: Issues and Perspectives* seeks to focus on the range of issues that dominates world politics as well as on the multitude of analytical and interpretive perspectives from which those issues are viewed.

The issues and perspectives discussed in *The Global Agenda* are grouped into four broad, somewhat overlapping, but analytically distinct issue areas: (1) arms and influence, (2) discord and collaboration, (3) politics and markets, and (4) ecology and politics. The first two issue areas deal with states' security interests, often referred to as matters of *high politics.* The latter two deal with the nonsecurity issues, often referred to as matters of *low politics,* on which world political actors increasingly have concentrated their attention. In all four issue areas, we seek to convey not only the range of issues now facing those responsible for political choices, but also the many vantage points from which they are typically viewed.

We begin in Part One with consideration of a series of issues appropriately subsumed under the collective rubric "Arms and Influence." As the term "high politics" suggests, the issues and perspectives treated here focus on the prospects for peace and security in a world of competitive nation-states armed with increasingly diverse arsenals of lethal and "nonlethal" weapons with which to coerce and/or destroy adversaries, or both.

ARMS AND INFLUENCE

It is often argued that states strive for power, security, and domination in a global environment punctuated by the threat of violence and death. This viewpoint flows naturally from the characteristics of the international political system, which continues to be marked by the absence of central institutions empowered to authoritatively manage and resolve conflict. Hence, preoccupation with preparations for defense becomes understandable, for the fear persists that one adversary might use force against another to realize its goals or to vent its frustrations, and the threat of separatist revolts and civil rebellions to sever minority populations from existing sovereign states has become a major concern. In such an environment, arms are widely perceived as useful not only to enhance security but also as a means to realize and extend one's influence. Hence, countries frequently see their interests best served by a search for power, by whatever means. Understandably, therefore, *power* and *influence* remain the core concepts in the study of world politics.

Appropriately, our first essay, "Power, Capability, and Influence in International Politics," by K. J. Holsti, provides a thoughtful discussion of the meaning of power, capability, and influence in the foreign policy behavior of states in contemporary world politics. The essay provides insights important not only for evaluating the subsequent essays in this book but also for evaluating the use to which these necessary but ambiguous terms are often incorporated into other interpretations of global issues. For almost invariably such discussions make reference, implicitly or explicitly, to the interrelationships among power, capability, and influence.

If the purpose of statecraft is the pursuit of political power, then a critical question is: What are the most appropriate means through which states might rise to a position of prominence in the international hierarchy? In "From Military Strategy to Economic Strategy: The Rise of the 'Virtual State' and the New Paths to Global Influence," Richard Rosecrance provides a reinterpretation of the factors that are most likely to enable states to travel that path successfully in the future. Arguing that a technological revolution in knowledge and direct investment is underway, he contends that it is transforming the classical meanings of the nature of power, its sources, and the purposes and functions of the state. Whereas in the past the acquisition of military might for territorial conquest was habitually seen as the best path to national power and leadership over competitors, today the military struggle for territory no longer holds the promise that once was widely ascribed to it. Although the struggle for influence through arms clearly continues, the key to global power in the future will lie primarily in leadership in the new technologies rather than in the pursuit of territorial control by force; as Rosecrance puts it, "a nation's economic strategy is now at least as important as its military strategy; its ambassadors have become foreign trade and investment representatives."

Rosecrance predicts that global leadership is destined to pass to the states that recognize that territorial conquest is no longer a cost-efficient means to economic growth and political power, because with technology and globalization states can readily produce goods overseas for the foreign market. The "virtual state," "a state that has downsized its territorially based production capability," will lead internationally because it can better compete for a share of world trade. Hence, the rise of the virtual state presages the advent of an age in which the bases of and strategies for national power have been transformed. The thesis is disquieting that as territory is becoming passé, the dangers of armed conflict are declining and war over territory is becoming quaint. It challenges vested interests that have a stake in the continuation of preparations for war as a strategy for national power and prominence. For that reason, many find it threatening. And to maintain that virtual states investing in people rather than amassing land, capital, and labor "hold the competitive key to greater wealth in the 21st century" is to challenge the strategies on which most states historically have relied to gain wealth and stature.

At issue are basic controversies: *how* security can best be attained and welfare assured, and how people should most accurately conceive of the sources of global power in the future. Perhaps precisely because the world is rapidly changing, Rosecrance's provocative prescriptions about the most viable strategies to both national prosperity and international influence must be given serious attention. These questions deserve a high place on the global agenda because they concern choices regarding national strategies for development no policy maker can dare ignore.

The interpretation, predictions, and prescriptions advanced by Rosecrance are, of course, subject to theoretical and empirical questioning from other perspectives. In the next essay, "A Revolution in Warfare: The Changing Face of

Force," Eliot A. Cohen takes exception to the view that military force no longer plays a decisive role in world politics. He maintains that even with the end of the Cold War and the declining incidence of war between states, military capabilities will continue to matter greatly among the factors that will enable states to exercise international influence. Cohen avers that military power will continue to play a central, maybe even growing, role in international politics because the tools and techniques for waging war never stand still and the countries that succeed in their development are certain to gain a competitive advantage over their rivals. He sees a revolution in military affairs underway that is as momentous as the revolutions produced by the railroad and airplane, and he claims that this new revolution is a result of developments in civilian society such as the information revolution and postindustrial capitalism. The creation of such revolutionary technologies as satellite imagery, smart bombs, and a variety of so-called nonlethal weapons that destroy and incapacitate their targets without killing, Cohen maintains, will transform the forms and conduct of combat and armies, even though personnel and politics, as always, will remain as crucial as technological innovation in the ways military power is translated in political influence on the world stage.

Cohen's thesis is compelling. However, the picture and prescriptions it presents must be interpreted in light of the changing relationship of arms to decisions regarding war and peace. Against the backdrop of revolutionary changes in the tools and techniques for waging war, careful consideration needs to be given to the sources or determinants of war. Because arms both threaten and protect, a congeries of rival hypotheses can be advanced about the causes of armed conflict and of peace in the 21st century. In "Towards a New Millennium: Structural Perspectives on the Causes of War," Jack S. Levy summarizes leading ideas embedded in the assumptions of contending theories to which we might refer to explain the role of force in world politics and the means to preserve peace.

Levy notes that the outbreak of war derives from a wide range of circumstantial and causal factors, some internal to individual states and many external to them, that combine to influence its occurrence. Focusing primarily on "systemic" or "structural" factors—attributes of the international system writ large—Levy reviews three major structural explanations for the continuing outbreak of war: (1) international anarchy and the security dilemma it creates, (2) theories of international equilibrium such as the balance of power and the questionable operation of a successful balance of power under the emerging conditions of multipolarity, and (3) "power transition" theories and their most important variant, "long cycle" theories. This review suggests that, because war clearly has multiple potential causes, it is difficult to control, inasmuch as control depends on a varied combination of tangible and intangible factors. Moreover, this reading selection warns that "the changing structures of power in international and regional systems that have influenced decisions for war or peace so often in the past will continue to play a central role in such decisions in the future."

Achieving international security is often confounded by changes in global conditions. One potential change underway that prompts fresh thinking is the growing evidence about a profoundly important long-term world political achievement: Since World War II the great powers have experienced the longest period of uninterrupted peace since the advent of the territorial state system in 1648. In this category of analysis, we can claim that the disappearance of wars between the great powers truly *has* transformed the character of international politics, without risking the accusation that the claim is exaggerated. However, whether weapons produced this remarkable outcome—or whether this long post–World War II peace occurred despite these weapons—deserves consideration.

In "The Obsolescence of Major War," John Mueller explores the policy and moral implications of this accomplishment, in which war between states has passed from a noble institution to one in which it is now widely regarded as illegal, immoral, and counterproductive. The steps to this global awakening are traced in his account, which sees the contribution of nuclear weapons as essentially irrelevant to the preservation of the long peace among the great powers that has persisted since World War II. Noting that although "war in the developed world . . . has not become impossible" and war in the Third World remains frequent and increasingly lethal, Mueller nonetheless sees hope for the future in the fact that "peoples and leaders in the developed world—where war was once endemic—have increasingly found war to be disgusting, ridiculous, and unwise." "If war begins in the minds of men, as the UNESCO Charter insists," then, Mueller maintains, "it can end there." That would indeed alter the way the world has conventionally thought about arms, influence, and peace. In such a world (Cohen's account of the revolutionary changes in military capabilities notwithstanding), the utility of armed force as an instrument of influence would be certain to command far less respect than in the past.

Nuclear weapons are doubtless the most lethal form of power and hence the most threatening instruments of influence. How to avoid their use has dominated strategic thinking ever since the atomic age began in 1945. *Deterrence*—preventing a potential adversary from launching a military attack—has dominated strategic thinking about nuclear weapons since their creation. The failure of deterrence, particularly in a war between nuclear powers, could, of course, ignite a global conflagration culminating in the destruction of humanity, which means that the entire world has a stake in the operation of a successful deterrent strategy.

For many years great faith was placed in the ability of nuclear weapons to keep the peace. Indeed, the most popular theory of the avoidance of general war since 1945 is the claim that nuclear weapons have made general war obsolete. But others endorse John Mueller's thesis that nuclear weapons are "essentially irrelevant" in the prevention of major war. As argued at length in his well-known 1989 book, *Retreat from Doomsday,* the growing aversion to war in general, in conjunction with the inhibiting fear of another major *conventional* war in particular, explain the obsolescence of war in the developed world.

Kenneth N. Waltz, a neorealist, disagrees. In "Nuclear Myths and Political Realities," Waltz contends that nuclear weapons have had a pacifying impact on the course of world affairs since World War II. In a comprehensive review of thinking about nuclear weapons that outlines the evolution of nuclear doctrines, the efforts to construct a foolproof strategic defense, and efforts to bring about nuclear disarmament, Waltz advances the controversial conclusion that nuclear weapons have been "a tremendous force for peace" that "afford nations who possess them the possibility of security at reasonable cost." Without them, the post–World War II world would likely have been far less stable. But, Waltz warns, scholars and policy makers have not understood the true strategic implications of nuclear weaponry, with the result that the advantages of nuclear weapons have not been properly appreciated.

A key variable in the future of global peace is the possibility that the number of members of the "nuclear club" could increase dramatically in the future. This makes worldwide control over weapons of mass destruction at once imperative and at the same time increasingly difficult. As argued by former U.S. Undersecretary of Defense Fred Charles Iklé in 1997, the "second coming of the nuclear age" is on the horizon. Thus managing *nuclear proliferation* is a major political issue.

In "The Changing Proliferation Threat," John F. Sopko shows why the complex nuclear issue has not receded in importance. The overwhelming deterrent forces that worked during the Cold War will not provide protection against the new military dangers the arms race poses on the threshold of the 21st century. Despite recent breakthroughs in the negotiated reduction of the superpowers' arsenals, many states and non-state actors have powerful incentives to join the nuclear club and are actively pursuing the development of nuclear capabilities. The proliferation threat has changed, Sopko shows, and for the worse. "Plans for making weapons of mass destruction, including nuclear devices, can now be accessed on the Internet, through catalogs, and at the local library." This ready availability of weaponry raises the stakes; the formidable array of new technologies for destruction puts control over the fate of millions in the possession of lunatics, fanatics, and terrorists throughout the globe who have no qualms about using them for their narrow and evil purposes.

The grim prospects for deterrence to safeguard civilization are exacerbated, Sopko warns, by the widespread presumption that aggressors will continue to abide by the doctrine of "no first use" of weapons of mass destruction. Wishful thinking about the low probability of a nuclear calamity has inhibited the great powers' planning for the international control of annihilating weapons. The strategic mindsets and theories of deterrence of the past half century are still being applied to the new threats; tactics have failed to keep pace with technology, and defense strategies have not changed to deal with the emergent proliferation threats. Because many "either do not believe that there is a new proliferation threat or consider it a low priority," Sopko warns that the dangers have escalated as "traditional Cold War approaches to nonproliferation do little to deter groups or individuals bent on procuring crude weapons of mass destruction." Responding to these new challenges necessitates overcoming the conceptual, bureaucratic, intergovernmental and tactical barriers that are interfering with the peace-loving democracies' ability to effectively address these new kinds of threats. Inventorying the problems and prospects confronting the world community on this global issue, Sopko not only finds the existing obstacles to the further expansion of nuclear capabilities insufficient, but also insists that to contain their spread, far-reaching disarmament that shuts down test sites and devises solutions for the disposal of fissionable materials will be required. As the risks expand, the control of proliferation is destined, Sopko's reasoning suggests, to become a key issue on the 21st century global agenda.

Sopko is one among many proponents who advocate that meaningful steps can be taken to control the problem of the spread of weapons systems by building a comprehensive arms control regime. However, as noted, other analysts argue just the opposite: that weapons *increase* national security and that the most lethal arms deter their use. Nonetheless, and consistent with Sopko's thesis, new forms of violence—often referred to as "low-intensity conflict"—are unlikely to decline as the spread of these new instruments of destruction continues.

The widespread incidence of low-intensity violence draws attention to perhaps its most conspicuous and threatening form: international terrorism. In "Postmodern Terrorism," Walter Laqueur offers a timely and illuminating discussion of international terrorism, recent trends in its occurrence, its old and new causes, and its probable future impact. Laqueur doubts that this terrifying force can be brought under control in the new millennium, despite the recent decline in the frequency of acts of terrorism as they were practiced during the Cold War and in the years following its end. Accordingly, he contends that efforts to grapple with the terrorism of the future must begin with a sober account of its diverse purposes and changing character, and of the reasons why terrorism is likely to continue to be an issue of great importance in the politics within nations and in relations between them.

Laqueur's depiction of the terrorist of the future portrays a set of actors likely to remain, like the terrorists of the past, intent on achieving political objectives by the threat of violence. However, he sees the new terrorists as different from those of the past: less ideological, more likely to harbor ethnic grievances, perhaps fired by apocalyptic visions, and harder to distinguish from others outside the law. Armed with new weapons and experimenting with others, and willing to use them more indiscriminately, the "postmodern" future terrorists have at their disposal a wider range of methods, because now a political wing of a terrorist group can openly raise funds, run schools, and contest elections, and the loner with a grudge, who may be the computer hacker next door, can be included in the category of those who have turned to terror. At the other end of the scale, Lacqueur predicts, state-sponsored terrorism will take the place of warfare. He concludes with the warning that the destructive power of terrorism is on the rise, and that the most advanced societies are the most vulnerable.

Terrorism is practiced by weak actors in order to attempt to influence strong actors (and, often, through "state terrorism," by powerful governments to repress the powerless within their own countries). More commonly, on many occasions states have engaged in another practice by which they hope to change the behavior of a target by methods short of the actual use of force: what in diplomatic practice and international law are termed *sanctions.* Ranging from economic methods of punishment such as trade embargoes to collective international censorship to ostracize the target, the purpose of sanctions is generally the same: to modify the target's conduct so as to persuade it to do something it would not otherwise do (such as ceasing to pursue nuclear armament) or to convince it to stop some action in which it is currently engaging (such as persecution of minorities).

In "Asphyxiation or Oxygen? The Sanctions Dilemma," Franklin L. Lavin evaluates the use of sanctions as a set of methods to attempt to influence another actor's actions. Summarizing the substantial body of literature that examines the effectiveness of economic instruments of nonmilitary coercive diplomacy, Lavin distinguishes two general approaches. The first, termed an "oxygen" strategy, emphasizes rewards for compliance on the part of the sanctioned target; it includes economic policies that "can reduce trade barriers such as tariffs and quotas and adopt more active measures such as loans, credits, trade and investment missions, and foreign aid." In contrast, the second alternative, an "asphyxiation" strategy, relies on punishment to coerce the sanctioned state; its arsenal of methods includes "impeding exports to, or imports from, the targeted country and restricting financial flows." The essay then assesses the rationale for, and the record of performance of, these two approaches, against a variety of legal, moral, and political criteria of evaluation. A number of cases are examined to uncover patterns that explain successes and failures—that is, to discover the conditions under which sanctions work. This leads to a series of astute observations about the power and the limitations of these alternative sanction strategies. Showing that "sanctions are not always economic, not necessarily peaceful, not silent, and deadly only at the margin . . . and over the long run," Lavin concludes that "sometimes they do the trick," even though neither strategy "is a terribly effective response to aggression." Inasmuch as "either strategy can work, given the circumstances," the "challenge for the policy maker, as always, is to avoid a dogmatic approach and choose the right tool for the job."

Finally, Part One concludes with an assessment of power and influence in light of the 1990s' turbulent transformations. In "The Changing Nature of World Power," Joseph S. Nye, Jr., provides us with the tools to evaluate how the relationships between arms, influence, and world leadership are likely to change in the waning days of the 20th century. Here, he comprehensively surveys and critiques current thinking and theorizing about the changing sources of power, the balance of power, and hegemony in modern history. And, in comparing rival models (for example, realist interpretations of hegemonic transitions, the neo-Marxist view of hegemony, and the long-cycle theory of world leadership), Nye provides a theoretical foundation for predicting the future of American power and evaluating the risks of world war as we approach the 21st century.

The issues discussed in the 10 essays in Part One—capabilities and influence, trade power, the changing face of armed force, the causes of war, the frequency of war, the effects of nuclear weapons and effectiveness of strategies of nuclear deterrence, the changing weapons proliferation threat, terrorism, sanctions as a mode of coercive diplomacy, and the evolving nature of world power—do not exhaust the range of security problems on the global agenda. However, in focusing attention on some of the many issues relating to the role of arms and influence in a world of interdependent and often competitive states, they offer insight into the complexities of the issues of high politics with which national decision makers must grapple. Part Two, in which we shift attention to the nature of discord and collaboration in world politics, will add further insight into the politics of peace and security.

1

POWER, CAPABILITY, AND INFLUENCE IN INTERNATIONAL POLITICS

K. J. Holsti

In this essay K. J. Holsti clarifies the meaning of three concepts crucial to the conduct of international politics—power, capability, and influence—and examines the complexities of each as it relates to states' efforts to realize their foreign policy objectives. Holsti is professor of political science at the University of British Columbia. His publications include *The State, War, and the State of War* (1996).

. . . [A foreign policy] act is basically a form of communication intended to change or sustain the behavior of those upon whom the acting government is dependent for achieving its own goals. It can also be viewed as a "signal" sent by one actor to influence the receiver's image of the sender.[1] In international politics, acts and signals take many different forms. The promise of granting foreign aid is an act, as are propaganda appeals, displays of military strength, wielding a veto in the Security Council, walking out of a conference, organizing a conference,

---

From K. J. Holsti, *International Politics: A Framework for Analysis,* 4th ed. (Englewood Cliffs, N.J.: Prentice-Hall) pp. 114–59. © 1983. Reprinted by permission of the author. Some footnotes have been deleted.

[1]A comprehensive treatment of how governments "signal" each other is in Robert Jervis, *The Logic of Images in International Relations* (Princeton, N.J.: Princeton University Press, 1970).

issuing a warning in a diplomatic note, sending arms and money to a liberation movement, instituting a boycott on the goods of another state, or declaring war. These types of acts and signals, and the circumstances in which they are likely to succeed, will be discussed. . . . Our organizing principle will be the amount of threat involved in the various techniques of influence. Diplomatic persuasion seemingly involves the least amount of threat; economic pressures, subversion, intervention, and various forms of warfare involve increasingly great amounts of threat and punishment. To help understand what all these types of action or techniques of influence have in common, however, we will discuss in a more abstract manner the behavior governments show when they turn toward each other to establish orientations, fulfill roles, or achieve and defend objectives.

The international political process commences when any state—let us say state A—seeks through various acts or signals to change or sustain the behavior (for instance, the acts, images, and policies) of other states. Power can thus be defined as the general capacity of a state to control the behavior of others. This definition can be illustrated as follows, where the solid line represents various acts:

A seeks to influence B because it has established certain objectives that cannot be achieved (it is perceived) unless B (and perhaps many other states as well) does X. If this is the basis of all international political processes, the capacity to control behavior can be viewed in several different ways:

1 Influence (an aspect of power) is essentially a *means* to an end. Some governments or statesmen may seek influence for its own sake, but for most it is instrumental, just like money. They use it primarily for achieving or defending other goals, which may include prestige, territory, souls, raw materials, security, or alliances.

2 State A, in its acts toward state B, uses or mobilizes certain *resources*. A resource is any physical or mental object or quality available as an instrument of inducement to persuade, reward, threaten, or punish. The concept of resource may be illustrated in the following example. Suppose an unarmed robber walks into a bank and asks the clerk to give up money. The clerk observes clearly that the robber has no weapon and refuses to comply with the order. The robber has sought to influence the behavior of the clerk, but has failed. The next time, however, the robber walks in armed with a pistol and threatens to shoot if the clerk does not give up the money. This time, the clerk complies. In this instance, the robber has mobilized certain resources or capabilities (the gun) and succeeds in influencing the clerk to comply. But other less tangible resources may be involved as well. The appearance of the person, particularly facial expression, may convey determination, threat, or weakness, all of which may subtly influence the behavior of the clerk. In international politics, the diplomatic gestures and words accompanying actions may be as important as the acts themselves. A government that places troops on alert but insists that it is doing so for domestic reasons will have an impact abroad quite different from the government that organizes a similar alert but accompanies it with threats to go to to war. "Signals" or diplomatic "body language" may be as important as dramatic actions such as alerts and mobilizations.

3 The act of influencing B obviously involves a *relationship* between A and B, although, as will be seen later, the relationship may not even involve overt communication. If the relationship covers any period of time, we can also say that it is a *process*.

4 If A can get B to do something, but B cannot get A to do a similar thing, then we can say that A has more power than B regarding that particular issue. Power, therefore, can also be viewed as a *quantity,* but as a quantity it is only meaningful when compared to the power of others. Power is therefore relative.

To summarize, power may be viewed from several aspects: It is a means; it is based on resources; it is a relationship and a process; and it can be measured, at least crudely.

We can break down the concept of power into three distinct analytic elements: power comprises (1) the *acts* (process, relationship) of influencing other states; (2) the *resources* used to make the wielding of influence successful; and (3) the *responses* to the acts. The three elements must be kept distinct. Since this definition may seem too abstract, we can define the concept in the more operational terms of policy makers. In formulating policy and the strategy to achieve certain goals, they would explicitly or implicitly ask the five following questions:

1 Given our goals, what do we wish B to do or not to do? (X)

2 How shall we get B to do or not to do X? (implies a relationship and process)

3 What resources are at our disposal so that we can induce B to do or not to do X?

4 What is B's probable response to our attempts to influence its behavior?

5 What are the *costs* of taking actions 1, 2, or 3—as opposed to other alternatives?

Before discussing the problem of resources and responses, we have to fill out our model of the influence act to account for the many patterns of behavior that may be involved in an international relationship. First, the exercise of influence implies more than merely A's ability to *change* the behavior of B. Influence may also be seen when A attempts to get B to *continue* a course of action or policy that is useful to, or in the interests of, A.[2] The exercise of influence does not always cease, therefore, after B does X. It is often a continuing process of reinforcing B's behavior.

Second, it is almost impossible to find a situation where B does not also have some influence over A. Our model has suggested that influence is exercised only in one direction, by A over B. In reality, influence is multilateral. State A, for example, would seldom seek a particular goal unless it has been influenced in a particular direction by the actions of other states in the system. At a minimum, there is the problem of feedback in any relationship: If B complies with A's wishes and does X, that behavior may subsequently prompt A to change its own behavior, perhaps in the interest of B. The phenomenon of feedback may be illustrated as follows:

Third, there is the type of relationship that includes "anticipated reaction."[3] This is the situation where B, anticipating rewards or punishments from A, changes his behavior, perhaps even before A makes any "signals" about possible action. Deterrence theory clearly assumes that B—the potential aggressor against A—will not attack (where it might, were there no deterrent), knowing that an unacceptable level of punishment would surely result. A similar situation, but in reverse, is also common in international politics. This is where A might wish B to do X, but does not try to influence B for fear that B will do Y instead, which is an unfavorable response from A's point of view. In a hypothetical situation, the government of India might wish to obtain arms from the United States to build up its own defenses, but does not request such arms because it fears that the United States would insist on certain conditions for the sale of arms that might compromise India's nonalignment. This anticipated reaction may also be multilateral, where A wishes B to do X, but will not try to get B to do it because it fears that C, a third state, will do Y, which is unfavorable to A's interests. India wants to purchase American arms, but does not seek to influence the United States to sell them for fear that Pakistan (C) will then build up its own armaments and thus

[2]J. David Singer, "Inter-Nation Influence: A Formal Model," *American Political Science Review* 57 (1963), pp. 420–30. State A might also wish state B to do W, Y, and Z, which may be incompatible with the achievement of X.

[3]Herbert A. Simon, "Notes on the Observation and Measurement of Political Power," *Journal of Politics* 15 (1953), pp. 500–16. For further analysis, see David A. Baldwin, "Inter-Nation Influence Revisited," *Journal of Conflict Resolution* 15 (December 1971), pp. 478–79.

accelerate the arms race between the two countries. In this situation, Pakistan (C) has influence over the actions of the Indian government even though it has not deliberately sought to influence India on this particular matter or even communicated its position in any way. The Indian government has simply perceived that there is a relatively high probability that if it seeks to influence the United States, Pakistan will react in a manner contrary to India's interests.

Fourth, power and influence may be measured by scholars, but what is important in international politics is the *perceptions* of influence and capabilities held by policy makers and the way they interpret another government's signals. The reason that governments invest millions of dollars for gathering intelligence is to develop a reasonably accurate picture of other states' capabilities and intentions. Where there is a great discrepancy between perceptions and reality, the results to a country's foreign policy may be disastrous. To take our example of the bank robber again, suppose that the person held a harmless toy pistol and threatened the clerk. The clerk perceived the gun to be real and deduced the robber's intention to use it. As a result, the clerk complied with the demand. In this case, the robber's influence was far greater than the "objective" character of the robber's capabilities and intentions; and distorted perception by the clerk led to an act that was unfavorable to the bank.

Finally, as our original model suggests, A may try to influence B *not to do* X. Sometimes this is called negative power, or deterrence, where A acts in a manner to *prevent* a certain action it deems undesirable to its interests. This is a typical relationship in international politics. By signing the Munich treaty, the British and French governments hoped to prevent Germany from invading Czechoslovakia; Israeli attacks on PLO facilities in Lebanon [were] designed to demonstrate that PLO guerrilla operations against Israel [would] be met by vast punishments, the costs of which to the PLO would far outweigh the gains of the terrorist acts. Such a cost-benefit analysis, the Israelis [hoped], would deter the PLO from undertaking further operations. The reader should keep in mind the distinction between compellence and deterrence.

RESOURCES

The second element of the concept of power consists of those resources that are mobilized in support of the acts taken to influence state B's behavior. It is difficult to assess the general capacity of a state to control the actions and policies of others unless we also have some knowledge of the capabilities involved.[4] Nevertheless, it should be acknowledged that social scientists do not understand all the reasons why some actors—whether people, groups, governments, or states—wield influence successfully, while others do not.

---

[4]We might assess influence for historical situations solely on the basis of whether A got B to do X, without our having knowledge of either A's or B's capabilities.

It is clear that, in political relationships, not everyone possesses equal influence. In domestic politics, it is possible to construct a lengthy list of capabilities and attributes that seemingly permit some to wield influence over large numbers of people and important public decisions. Robert Dahl lists such tangibles as money, wealth, information, time, political allies, official position, and control over jobs, and such intangibles as personality and leadership qualities.[5] But not everyone who possesses these capabilities can command the obedience of other people. What is crucial in relating resources to influence, according to Dahl, is that one *mobilize them for one's political purposes* and possess the skill to mobilize them. One who uses wealth, time, information, friends, and personality for political purposes will probably be able to influence others on public issues. A person, on the other hand, who possesses the same capabilities but uses them to invent a new mousetrap is not apt to be important in politics. The same propositions also hold true in international politics. The amount of influence a state wields over others can be related to the capabilities *mobilized* in support of *specific* foreign-policy objectives. To put this proposition in another way, we can argue that resources do not determine the uses to which they will be put. Nuclear power can be used to provide electricity or to deter and perhaps destroy other nations. The use of resources depends less on their quality and quantity than on the external objectives a government formulates for itself.

The *variety* of foreign-policy instruments available to a nation for influencing others is partly a function of the quantity and quality of capabilities. What a government seeks to do—the type of objectives it formulates—and how it attempts to do it will depend at least partially on the resources it finds available. A country such as Thailand, which possesses relatively few resources, cannot, even if it would desire, construct intercontinental ballistic missiles with which to intimidate others, establish a worldwide propaganda network, or dispense several billion dollars annually for foreign aid to try to influence other countries. We can conclude, therefore, that how states use their resources depends on their external objectives, but the choice of objectives and the instruments to achieve those objectives are limited or influenced by the quality and quantity of available resources.

THE MEASUREMENT OF RESOURCES

For many years, students of international politics have made meticulous comparisons of the potential capabilities of various nations, assuming that a nation was powerful, or capable of achieving its objectives, to the extent that it possessed certain "elements of power." Comparative data relating to production of iron ore, coal, and hydroelectricity, economic growth rates, educational levels, population growth rates, military resources, transportation systems, and sources of raw materials are presented as indicators of a nation's power. Few have acknowledged

[5]Robert A. Dahl, *Who Governs?* (New Haven, Conn.: Yale University Press, 1961).

that these comparisons do not measure a state's power or influence but only its potential capacity to wage war. Other resources, such as diplomatic or propaganda skills, are seldom measured; but surely they are as important as war-making potential. Measurements and assessments are not particularly useful anyway unless they are related to specific foreign-policy issues. Capability is always the capability to do something; its assessment is most meaningful when carried on within a framework of certain foreign-policy objectives.

The deduction of actual influence from the quantity and quality of potential and mobilized capabilities may, in some cases, give an approximation of reality, but historically there have been too many discrepancies between the basis of power and the amount of influence to warrant adopting this practice as a useful approach to international relations. One could have assumed, for example, on the basis of a comparative study of technological and educational levels and general standards of living in the 1920s and 1930s that the United States would have been one of the most influential states in international politics. A careful comparison of certain resources, called the "great essentials,"[6] revealed the United States to be in an enviable position. In the period 1925 to 1930, it was the only major country in the world that produced from its own resources adequate supplies of food, power, iron, machinery, chemicals, coal, iron ore, and petroleum. If actual diplomatic influence had been deduced from the quantities of "great essentials" possessed by the major nations, the following ranking of states would have resulted: (1) United States, (2) Germany, (3) Great Britain, (4) France, (5) Russia, (6) Italy, (7) Japan. However, the diplomatic history of the world from 1925 to 1930 would suggest that there was little correlation between the resources of these countries and their *actual influence.* If we measure influence by the impact these states made on the system and by the responses they could invoke when they sought to change the behavior of other states, we would find for this period quite a different ranking, such as the following: (1) France, (2) Great Britain, (3) Italy, (4) Germany, (5) Russia, (6) Japan, (7) United States.

Indeed, many contemporary international relationships reveal how often the "strong" states do not achieve their objectives—or at least have to settle for poor substitutes—even when attempting to influence the behavior of "weak" states. How, for instance, did Marshal Tito's Yugoslavia effectively resist all sorts of pressures and threats by the powerful Soviet Union after it was expelled from the Communist bloc? Why, despite its overwhelming superiority in capabilities, was the United States unable in the 1960s to achieve its major objectives against a weak Cuba and North Vietnam? How have "small" states gained trading privileges and all sorts of diplomatic concessions from those nations with great economic wealth and military power? The ability of state A to change the behavior of state B is, we would assume, enhanced if it possesses physical resources to

---

[6]Frank H. Simonds and Brooks Emeny, *The Great Powers in World Politics* (New York: American Book, 1939).

use in the influence act; but B is by no means defenseless or vulnerable to diplomatic, economic, or military pressures because it fails to own a large modern army, raw materials, and money for foreign aid. The successful exercise of influence is also dependent upon such factors as personality, perceptions, friendships, and traditions, and, not being easy to measure, these factors have a way of rendering power calculations and equations difficult. . . .

VARIABLES AFFECTING THE EXERCISE OF INFLUENCE

One reason that gross quantities of resources cannot be equated with effective influence relates to the distinction between a state's overall capabilities and the *relevance* of resources to a particular diplomatic situation. A nuclear force, for example, is often thought to increase the diplomatic influence of those who possess it. No doubt nuclear weaponry is an important element in a state's general prestige abroad and may be an effective deterrent against a strategic attack on its homeland or "core" interests. Yet the most important aspect of a nuclear capability—or any military capability—is not its possession, but its relevance and the ability to signal one's determination to use it. Other governments must know that the capability is not of mere symbolic significance. The government of North Vietnam possessed a particular advantage over the United States (hence, influence) because it knew that in almost no circumstances would the American government use strategic nuclear weapons against its country. It therefore effectively broke through the significance of the American nuclear capability as far as the Vietnam War was concerned. A resource is useless unless it is both mobilized in support of foreign-policy objectives and made credible. Likewise, nuclear weapons would be irrelevant in negotiations on cultural exchanges, just as the Arab countries' vast oil resources could not be effectively mobilized to influence the outcome of international negotiations on satellite communications. Influence is always specific to a particular issue, and resources must be relevant to that issue.

A second variable that determines the success or failure of acts of influence is the extent to which there are *needs* between the two countries in any influence relationship. In general, a country that needs something from another is vulnerable to its acts of influence. This is the primary reason that states that are "weak" in many capabilities can nevertheless obtain concessions from "strong" countries. Consider the case of France and Germany and some of the "weak" states in the Middle East. Both European countries are highly dependent upon Arab lands for oil supplies. They have an important need, which only the Arab countries can satisfy at a reasonable cost. On the other hand, the Middle Eastern countries that control these oil resources may not be so dependent upon Germany and France, particularly if they can sell their oil easily elsewhere. Because, in this situation, needs are not equal on both sides, the independent states (in terms of needs) can make demands (or resist demands made against them) on the dependent great powers and obtain important concessions. The German and French governments know that if they do not make these concessions or if they press their own demands too hard, the Arab states can threaten to cut off oil supplies. Their dependence thus makes them vulnerable to the demands and influence acts of what would otherwise be considered "weak" states. To the Arab states, oil is much more important as a capability than military forces—at least in their relations with major powers. In the form of a general hypothesis, we can suggest that, regardless of the quantity, quality, and credibility of a state's capabilities, the more state B needs, or is dependent upon, state A, the more likely that state A's acts—threats, promises, rewards, or punishments—will succeed in changing or sustaining B's behavior.

A third variable that has assumed increasing importance in the past several decades, and one that can be considered an important resource, is level of technical expertise. An increasing number of issues on the international and foreign-policy agendas are highly technical in nature: law of the sea, satellite broadcasting, international monetary matters, and the like. Many of these issues are discussed in international fora, where leadership often depends more on knowledge of the technical issues than on other types of resources. Those governments that come armed with technical studies, have a full command of the nature of the problem, and are prepared to put forth realistic solutions are more likely to wield influence than are governments that have only rudimentary knowledge of the problem and no scientific studies to back their national positions. A number of recent case studies have demonstrated conclusively that the outcomes of negotiations on technical questions cannot be predicted from the gross power of the participants and that knowledge, among other factors, accounts for more than raw capabilities.[7]

Understanding the dynamics of power relationships at the international level would be relatively easy if resource relevance, credibility, need, and knowledge were the only variables involved. Unfortunately, political actions do not always conform to simple hypotheses, because human characteristics of pride, stubbornness, prestige, and friendship enter into all acts of influence as well. A government may be highly dependent upon some other state and still resist its demands; it may be willing to suffer all sorts of privations, and even physical destruction and loss of independence, simply for the sake of pride. The government of North Vietnam was willing to accept a very high level of destruction of lives and productive facilities by American bombers rather than make diplomatic or military concessions to the United States.

Additional variables affecting the exercise of influence can be observed in the situation where two small states of approximately equal capabilities make similar demands upon a "major" power and neither of the small states is dependent

---

[7]See, for example, the case studies in Robert O. Keohane and Joseph S. Nye, *Power and Interdependence: World Politics in Transition* (Boston: Little, Brown and Company, 1977). See also David Baldwin's strong emphasis on the relevance of resources to particular situations in "Power Analysis and World Politics," *World Politics* 31 (January 1979), pp. 161–94.

upon the large—or vice versa. Which will achieve its objectives? Will both exercise influence equally? Hypothetically, suppose that the ambassadors of Norway and Albania go to the British Foreign Office on the same day and ask the British government to lower tariffs on bicycles, a product that the two countries would like to export to England. Assume that the quality and price of the bicycles are approximately the same and that the British government does not wish to allow too many imports for fear of damaging the domestic bicycle industry. Assume further that both the Norwegian and Albanian ambassadors offer roughly equal concessions if the British will lower their tariffs on bicycles. Both claim they will lower their own tariffs on English automobiles. Which ambassador is most likely to succeed—that is, to achieve his government's objectives? Chances are that the British government would favor the request of the Norwegian ambassador and turn down the representation by the diplomat from Tirana. The explanation of this decision can probably not be found in the resources of either of the small countries (both offered approximately equal rewards) or in need, since in this hypothetical situation Britain needs neither of the small countries' automobile markets. Norway would get the favorable decision because British policy makers are more *responsive* to Norwegian interests than to those of . . . a Communist state whose government normally displays through its diplomacy and propaganda strong hostility toward England.

After relevant resources, need, and knowledge, the fourth variable that determines the effectiveness of acts of influence is thus the ephemeral quality of responsiveness.[8] Responsiveness can be seen as a disposition to receive another's requests with sympathy, even to the point where a government is willing to sacrifice some of its own values and interests in order to fulfill those requests; responsiveness is the willingness to be influenced. In one study, it was shown that members of the State Department in the United States may take considerable pains to promote the requests and interests of other governments among their superiors and in other government agencies, provided that the requesting government feels that the issue is important or that the need must be fulfilled.[9] In our hypothetical case, if the quality of responsiveness is present in the case of the Norwegian request, members of the British Foreign Office would probably work for the Norwegians and try to persuade other government agencies concerned with trade and commerce to agree to a lowering of the tariff on bicycles. In the British reaction to the Albanian request, it is not likely that the government would display much responsiveness. Suspicion, traditional animosities, lack of

---

[8]The concept of responsiveness is introduced by Karl W. Deutsch et al., *Political Community and the North Atlantic Area* (Princeton, N.J.: Princeton University Press, 1957); developed by Dean G. Pruitt, "National Power and International Responsiveness," *Background* 7 (1964), pp. 165–78. See also Dean G. Pruitt, "Definition of the Situation as a Determinant of International Action," in *International Behavior: A Social-Psychological Analysis,* ed. Herbert C. Kelman (New York: Holt, Rinehart & Winston, 1965), pp. 393–432.

[9]Pruitt, "National Power," pp. 175–76.

trust, and years of unfavorable diplomatic experience would probably prevent the development of much British sympathy for Albania's needs or interests. . . . When the other variables, such as resources or need, are held constant or made equal, the degree of responsiveness will determine the success or failure of acts taken to influence other states' behavior.

If effective influence cannot be deduced solely from the quantity and quality of physical capabilities, how do we proceed to measure influence? If we want to assess a situation that has already occurred, the easiest way to measure influence is to study the *responses* of those in the influence relationship.[10] If A can get B to do X, but C cannot get B to do the same thing, then in that particular issue, A has more influence. If B does X despite the protestations of A, then we can assume that A, in this circumstance, did not enjoy much influence over B. It is meaningless to argue that the Soviet Union [may have been] more powerful than the United States unless we cite how, for what purposes, and in relation to whom the Soviet Union and the United States [were] exerting influence. . . .

HOW INFLUENCE IS EXERCISED

Social scientists have noted several fundamental techniques that individuals and groups use to influence each other. In a political system that contains no one legitimate center of authority that can command the members of the group or society, bargaining has to be used among the sovereign entities to achieve or defend their objectives. Recalling that A seeks one of three courses of conduct from B (B to do X in the future, B not to do X in the future, or B to continue doing X), it may use six different tactics, involving acts of:

1. PERSUASION. By persuasion we mean simply initiating or discussing a proposal with another and eliciting a favorable response without explicitly holding out the possibility of rewards or punishments. We cannot assume that the exercise of influence is always *against* the wishes of others and that there are only two possible outcomes of the act, one favoring A, the other favoring B. For example, state A asks B to support it at a coming international conference on the control of narcotics. State B might not originally have any particular interest in the conference or its outcome; but it decides, on the basis of A's initiative, that something positive might be gained, not only by supporting A's proposals, but also by attending the conference. In this case, B might also expect to gain some type of reward in the future, although not necessarily from A. Persuasion would also include protests and denials that do not involve obvious threats.

2. THE OFFER OF REWARDS. This is the situation where A promises to do something favorable to B if B complies with the wishes of A. Rewards may be of almost any type in international relations. To gain the diplomatic support of B

---

[10]Robert A. Dahl, "The Concept of Power," *Behavioral Science,* 2 (1957), pp. 201–15.

at the narcotics conference, A may offer to increase foreign-aid payments, lower tariffs on goods imported from B, support B at a later conference on communications facilities, or promise to remove a previous punishment. The last tactic is used often by negotiators. After having created an unfavorable situation, they promise to remove it in return for some concessions by their opponents.

3 THE GRANTING OF REWARDS. In some instances, the credibility of a government is not very high, and state B, before complying with A's wishes, may insist that A actually give the reward in advance. Frequently, in armistice negotiations neither side will unilaterally take steps to demilitarize an area or demobilize troops until the other shows evidence of complying with the agreements. One of the clichés of . . . diplomacy holds that deeds, not words, are required for the granting of rewards and concessions.

4 THE THREAT OF PUNISHMENT. Threats of punishment may be further subdivided into two types: (a) positive threats, where, for example, state A threatens to increase tariffs, institute a boycott or embargo against trade with B, or use force; and (b) threats of deprivation, where A threatens to withdraw foreign aid or in other ways withhold rewards or other advantages that it already grants to B.

5 THE INFLICTION OF NONVIOLENT PUNISHMENT. In this situation, threats are carried out in the hope of altering B's behavior, which, in most cases, could not be altered by other means. The problem with this tactic is that it often results in reciprocal measures by the other side, thus inflicting damage on both, and not necessarily bringing about a desired state of affairs. If, for example, A threatens to increase its military capabilities if B does X and then proceeds to implement the threat, it is not often that B will comply with A's wishes, because it, too, can increase its military capabilities. In this type of situation, both sides indulge in the application of punishments that may escalate into more serious forms unless the conflict is resolved. Typical acts of nonviolent punishment include breaking diplomatic relations, raising tariffs, instituting boycotts and embargoes, holding hostages, organizing blockades, closing frontiers, or walking out of a diplomatic conference.

6 FORCE. In previous eras, when governments did not possess the variety of foreign-policy instruments available today, they frequently had to rely upon the use of force in the bargaining process. Force and violence were not only the most efficient tactics, but in many cases the only means possible for influencing. Today, the situation is different. As technological levels rise and dependencies develop, other means of inducement become available and can serve as substitutes for force.

PATTERNS OF INFLUENCE
IN THE INTERNATIONAL SYSTEM

Most governments at some time use all their techniques for influencing others, but probably over 90 percent of all relations between states are based on simple persuasion and deal with relatively unimportant technical matters. Since such interactions seldom make the headlines, we often assume that most relations between states involve the making or carrying out of threats. But whether a government is communicating with another over an unimportant technical matter or over a subject of great consequence, it is likely to use a particular type of tactic in its attempts to influence, depending on the past tradition of friendship or hostility between those two governments and the amount of compatibility between their objectives and interests. Allies, for example, seldom threaten each other with force or even make blatant threats of punishment, but governments that disagree over a wide range of policy objectives and hold attitudes of suspicion and hostility toward each other are more likely to resort to threats and imposition of punishments. The methods of exerting influence between Great Britain and the United States are, typically, persuasion and rewards, whereas the methods of exerting influence between the Soviet Union and the United States in the early post–World War II era were typically threatening and inflicting punishments of various types. . . .

To summarize this analysis of power, we can suggest that power is an integral part of all political relationships; but in international politics we are interested primarily in one process: how one state influences the behavior of another in its own interests. The act of influencing becomes a central focus for the study of international politics, and it is from this act that we can best deduce a definition of power. If we observe the act of influencing, we can see that power is a process, a relationship, a means to an end, and even a quantity. Moreover, we can make an analytical distinction among the act of influencing, the basis, or resources, upon which the act relies, and the response to the act. Resources are an important determinant of how successful the wielding of influence will be, but they are by no means the only determinant. The nature of a country's foreign-policy objectives, the skill with which a state mobilizes its capabilities for foreign-policy purposes, its needs, responsiveness, costs, and commitments are equally important. Acts of influencing may take many forms, the most important of which are the offer and granting of rewards, the threat and imposition of punishments, and the application of force. The choice of means used to induce will depend, in turn, upon the general nature of relations between any two given governments, the degree of involvement between them, and the extent of their mutual responsiveness. . . .

2

FROM MILITARY STRATEGY TO ECONOMIC STRATEGY: THE RISE OF THE "VIRTUAL STATE" AND THE NEW PATHS TO GLOBAL INFLUENCE

Richard Rosecrance

Throughout history, states have pursued power through the acquisition of military capabilities and the use of force. This convention, argues Richard Rosecrance, has been challenged since World War II by the growing evidence that "trading states," nations such as Japan and Germany that gave up territorial conquest through military strategies in favor of economic approaches to world power and global influence, have been the most successful in attaining prosperity and preeminence on the world stage. This will accelerate, he predicts, because war over territory is becoming quaint, and what the world is witnessing now is the rise of the "virtual state." As more corporations farm out production and land becomes less valuable than technology, knowledge, and portfolio investment, the state will further shift its efforts from amassing productive capacity to choosing industries and investing in people. Rosecrance is professor of political science and director of the Center for International Relations at the University of California at Los Angeles. Among his many books are *America's Economic Resurgence* **(1990).**

From "The Rise of the Virtual State," by Richard Rosecrance. Reprinted by permission of *Foreign Affairs,* July/August 1996. Copyright © 1996 by the Council on Foreign Relations, Inc. The article has been abridged and footnotes have been deleted.

TERRITORY BECOMES PASSÉ

Amid the supposed clamor of contending cultures and civilizations, a new reality is emerging. The nation-state is becoming a tighter, more vigorous unit capable of sustaining the pressures of worldwide competition. Developed states are putting aside military, political, and territorial ambitions as they struggle not for cultural dominance but for a greater share of world output. Countries are not uniting as civilizations and girding for conflict with one another. Instead, they are downsizing—in function if not in geographic form. Today and for the foreseeable future, the only international civilization worthy of the name is the governing economic culture of the world market. Despite the view of some contemporary observers, the forces of globalization have successfully resisted partition into cultural camps.

Yet the world's attention continues to be mistakenly focused on military and political struggles for territory. In beleaguered Bosnia, Serbian leaders sought to create an independent province with an allegiance to Belgrade. In 1990 Iraqi leader Saddam Hussein aimed to corner the world oil market through military aggression against Kuwait and, in all probability, Saudi Arabia; oil, a product of land, represented the supreme embodiment of his ambitions. In Kashmir, India and Pakistan are vying for territorial dominance over a population that neither may be fully able to control. Similar rivalries beset Rwanda and Burundi and the factions in Liberia.

These examples, however, look to the past. Less developed countries, still producing goods that are derived from land, continue to covet territory. In economies where capital, labor, and information are mobile and have risen to predominance, no land fetish remains. Developed countries would rather plumb the world market than acquire territory. The virtual state—a state that has downsized its territorially based production capability—is the logical consequence of this emancipation from the land.

In recent years the rise of the economic analogue of the virtual state—the virtual corporation—has been widely discussed. Firms have discovered the advantages of locating their production facilities wherever it is most profitable. Increasingly, this is not in the same location as corporate headquarters. Parts of a corporation are dispersed globally according to their specialties. But the more important development is the political one, the rise of the virtual state, the political counterpart of the virtual corporation.

The ascent of the trading state preceded that of the virtual state. After World War II, led by Japan and Germany, the most advanced nations shifted their efforts from controlling territory to augmenting their share of world trade. In that period, goods were more mobile than capital or labor, and selling abroad became the name of the game. As capital has become increasingly mobile, advanced nations have come to recognize that exporting is no longer the only means to economic growth; one can instead produce goods overseas for the foreign market.

As more production by domestic industries takes place abroad and land becomes less valuable than technology, knowledge, and direct investment, the function of the state is being further redefined. The state no longer commands resources as it did in mercantilist yesteryear; it negotiates with foreign and domestic capital and labor to lure them into its own economic sphere and stimulate its growth. A nation's economic strategy is now at least as important as its military strategy; its ambassadors have become foreign trade and investment representatives. Major foreign trade and investment deals command executive attention as political and military issues did two decades ago. The frantic two weeks in December 1994 when the White House outmaneuvered the French to secure for Raytheon Company a deal worth over $1 billion for the management of rain forests and air traffic in Brazil exemplifies the new international crisis.

Timeworn methods of augmenting national power and wealth are no longer effective. Like the headquarters of a virtual corporation, the virtual state determines overall strategy and invests in its people rather than amassing expensive production capacity. It contracts out other functions to states that specialize in or need them. Imperial Great Britain may have been the model for the 19th century, but Hong Kong will be the model for the 21st.

The virtual state is a country whose economy is reliant on mobile factors of production. Of course it houses virtual corporations and presides over foreign direct investment by its enterprises. But more than this, it encourages, stimulates, and to a degree even coordinates such activities. In formulating economic strategy, the virtual state recognizes that its own production does not have to take place at home; equally, it may play host to the capital and labor of other nations. Unlike imperial Germany, czarist Russia, and the United States of the Gilded Age—which aimed at 19th century omnicompetence—it does not seek to combine or excel in all economic functions, from mining and agriculture to production and distribution. The virtual state specializes in modern technical and research services and derives its income not just from high-value manufacturing, but from product design, marketing, and financing. The rationale for its economy is efficiency attained through productive downsizing. Size no longer determines economic potential. Virtual nations hold the competitive key to greater wealth in the 21st century. They will likely supersede the continent-sized and self-sufficient units that prevailed in the past. Productive specialization will dominate internationally just as the reduced instruction set, or "RISC," computer chip has outmoded its more versatile but slower predecessors.

THE TRADING STATE

In the past, states were obsessed with land. The international system with its intermittent wars was founded on the assumption that land was the major factor in both production and power. States could improve their position by building empires or invading other nations to seize territory. To acquire land was a boon: a conquered province contained peasants and grain supplies, and its inhabitants rendered tribute to the new sovereign. Before the age of nationalism, a captured principality willingly obeyed its new ruler. Hence the Hapsburg monarchy, Spain, France, and Russia could become major powers through territorial expansion in Europe between the 16th and 19th centuries.

With the Industrial Revolution, however, capital and labor assumed new importance. Unlike land, they were mobile ingredients of productive strength. Great Britain innovated in discovering sophisticated uses for the new factors. Natural resources—especially coal, iron, and, later, oil—were still economically vital. Agricultural and mineral resources were critical to the development of the United States and other fledgling industrial nations like Australia, Canada, South Africa, and New Zealand in the 19th century. Not until late in the 20th century did mobile factors of production become paramount.

By that time, land had declined in relative value and become harder for nations to hold. Colonial revolutions in the Third World since World War II have shown that nationalist mobilization of the population in developing societies impedes an imperialist or invader trying to extract resources. A nation may expend the effort to occupy new territory without gaining proportionate economic benefits.

In time, nationalist resistance and the shift in the basis of production should have an impact on the frequency of war. Land, which is fixed, can be physically captured, but labor, capital, and information are mobile and cannot be definitively seized; after an attack, these resources can slip away like quicksilver. Saddam Hussein ransacked the computers in downtown Kuwait city in August 1990 only to find that the cash in bank accounts had already been electronically transferred. Even though it had abandoned its territory, the Kuwaiti government could continue to spend billions of dollars to resist Hussein's conquest.

Today, for the wealthiest industrial countries such as Germany, the United States, and Japan, investment in land no longer pays the same dividends. Since mid-century, commodity prices have fallen nearly 40 percent relative to prices of manufactured goods. The returns from the manufacturing trade greatly exceed those from agricultural exports. As a result, the terms of trade for many developing nations have been deteriorating, and in recent years the rise in prices of international services has outpaced that for manufactured products. Land prices have been steeply discounted.

Amid this decline, the 1970s and 1980s brought a new political prototype: the trading state. Rather than territorial expansion, the trading state held trade to be its fundamental purpose. This shift in national strategy was driven by the declining value of fixed productive assets. Smaller states—those for which, initially at any rate, a military-territorial strategy was not feasible—also adopted trade-oriented strategies. Along with small European and East Asian states, Japan and West Germany moved strongly in a trading direction after World War II.

Countries tend to imitate those that are most powerful. Many states followed in the wake of Great Britain in the 19th century; in recent decades, numerous states seeking to improve their lot in the world have emulated Japan. Under Mikhail Gorbachev in the 1980s, even the Soviet Union sought to move away from its emphasis on military spending and territorial expansion.

In recent years, however, a further stimulus has hastened this change. Faced with enhanced international competition in the late 1980s and early 1990s, corporations have opted for pervasive downsizing. They have trimmed the ratio of production workers to output, saving on costs. In some cases productivity increases resulted from pruning of the work force; in others output increased. These improvements have been highly effective. . . . The most efficient corporations are those that can maintain or increase output with a steady or declining amount of labor. Such corporations grew on a worldwide basis.

Meanwhile, corporations in Silicon Valley recognized that cost-cutting, productivity, and competitiveness could be enhanced still further by using the production lines of another company. The typical American plant at the time, such as Ford Motor Company's Willow Run factory in Michigan, was fully integrated, with headquarters, design offices, production workers, and factories located on substantial tracts of land. This comprehensive structure was expensive to maintain and operate; hence, a firm that could employ someone else's production line could cut costs dramatically. Land and machines did not have to be bought, labor did not have to be hired, medical benefits did not have to be provided. These advantages could result from what are called economies of scope, with a firm turning out different products on the same production line or quality circle. Or they might be the result of small, specialized firms' ability to perform exacting operations, such as the surface mounting of miniaturized components directly on circuit boards without the need for soldering or conventional wiring. In either case, the original equipment manufacturer would contract out its production to other firms. . . .

Thus was born the virtual corporation, an entity with research, development, design, marketing, financing, legal, and other headquarters functions, but few or no manufacturing facilities: a company with a head but no body. It represents the ultimate achievement of corporate downsizing, and the model is spreading rapidly from firm to firm. It is not surprising that the virtual corporation should catch on. "Concept" or "head" corporations can design new products for a range of different production facilities. Strategic alliances between firms, which increase specialization, are also very profitable. According to the October 2, 1995, *Financial Times,* firms that actively pursue strategic alliances are 50 percent more profitable than those that do not.

TOWARD THE VIRTUAL STATE

In a setting where the economic functions of the trading state have displaced the territorial functions of the expansionist nation, the newly pruned corporation has led to the emerging phenomenon of the virtual state. Downsizing has become an index of corporate efficiency and productivity gains. Now the national economy is also being downsized. Among the most efficient economies are those that possess limited production capacity. The archetype is Hong Kong, whose production facilities are now largely situated in southern China. This arrangement may change after 1997 with Hong Kong's reversion to the mainland, but it may not. It is just as probable that Hong Kong will continue to govern parts of the mainland economically as it is that Beijing will dictate to Hong Kong politically. The one country–two systems formula will likely prevail. In this context, it is important to remember that Britain governed Hong Kong politically and legally for 150 years but it did not dictate its economics. Nor did this arrangement prevent Hong Kong Chinese from extending economic and quasi-political controls to areas outside their country.

The model of the virtual state suggests that political as well as economic strategy push toward a downsizing and relocation of production capabilities. The trend can be observed in Singapore as well. The successors of Lee Kuan Yew keep the country on a tight political rein but still depend economically on the inflow of foreign factors of production. Singapore's investment in China, Malaysia, and elsewhere is within others' jurisdictions. The virtual state is in this sense a negotiating entity. It depends as much or more on economic access abroad as it does on economic control at home. Despite its past reliance on domestic production, Korea no longer manufactures everything at home, and Japanese production (given the high yen) is now increasingly lodged abroad. In Europe, Switzerland is the leading virtual nation; as much as 98 percent of Nestlé's production capacity, for instance, is located abroad. Holland now produces most of its goods outside its borders. England is also moving in tandem with the worldwide trend; according to the Belgian economic historian Paul Bairoch in 1994, Britain's foreign direct investment abroad was almost as large as America's. A remarkable 20 percent of the production of U.S. corporations now takes place outside the United States.

A reflection of how far these tendencies have gone is the growing portion of GDP consisting of high-value-added services, such as concept, design, consulting, and financial services. Services already constitute 70 percent of American GDP. Of the total, 63 percent are in the high-value category. Of course manufacturing matters, but it matters much less than it once did. As a proportion of foreign direct investment, service exports have grown strikingly in most highly industrialized economies. According to a 1994 World Bank report, *Liberalizing International Transactions in Services,* "The reorientation of [foreign direct investment] towards the services sector has occurred in almost all developed market economies, the principal exporters of services capital: in the most important among them, the share of the services sector is around 40 percent of the stock of outward FDI, and that share is rising."

Manufacturing, for these nations, will continue to decline in importance. If services productivity increases as much as it has in recent years, it will greatly strengthen U.S. competitiveness abroad. But it can no longer be assumed that services face no international competition. Efficient high-value services will be as important to a nation as the manufacturing of automobiles and electrical equipment once were. Since 1959, services prices have increased more than three times as rapidly as industrial prices. This means that many nations will be able to prosper without major manufacturing capabilities.

Australia is an interesting example. Still reliant on the production of sheep and raw materials (both related to land), Australia has little or no industrial sector. Its largest export to the United States is meat for hamburgers. On the other hand, its service industries of media, finance, and telecommunications—represented most notably by the media magnate Rupert Murdoch—are the envy of the world. Canada represents a similar amalgam of raw materials and powerful service industries in newspapers, broadcast media, and telecommunications.

As a result of these trends, the world may increasingly become divided into "head" and "body" nations, or nations representing some combination of those two functions. While Australia and Canada stress the headquarters or head functions, China will be the 21st-century model of a body nation. Although China does not innately or immediately know what to produce for the world market, it has found success in joint ventures with foreign corporations. China will be an attractive place to produce manufactured goods, but only because sophisticated enterprises from other countries design, market, and finance the products China makes. At present China cannot chart its own industrial future.

Neither can Russia. Focusing on the products of land, the Russians are still prisoners of territorial fetishism. Their commercial laws do not yet permit the delicate and sophisticated arrangements that ensure that "body" manufacturers deliver quality good for their foreign "head." Russia's transportation network is also primitive. These, however, are temporary obstacles. In time Russia, with China and India, will serve as an important locus of the world's production plant. . . .

THE REDUCED DANGER OF CONFLICT

As nations turn to the cultivation of human capital, what will a world of virtual states be like? Production for one company or country can now take place in many parts of the world. In the process of downsizing, corporations and nation-states will have to get used to reliance on others. Virtual corporations need other corporations' production facilities. Virtual nations need other states' production capabilities. As a result, economic relations between states will come to resemble nerves connecting heads in one place to bodies somewhere else. Naturally, producer nations will be working quickly to become the brains behind emerging industries elsewhere. But in time, few nations will have within their borders all the components of a technically advanced economic existence.

To sever the connections between states would undermine the organic unit. States joined in this way are therefore less likely to engage in conflict. In the past, international norms underlying the balance of power, the Concert of Europe, or even rule by the British Raj helped specify appropriate courses of action for parties in dispute. The international economy also rested partially on normative agreement. Free trade, open domestic economies, and, more recently, freedom of movement for capital were normative notions. In addition to specifying conditions for borrowing, the International Monetary Fund is a norm-setting agency that inculcates market economics in nations not fully ready to accept their international obligations.

Like national commercial strategies, these norms have been largely abstracted from the practices of successful nations. In the 19th century many countries emulated Great Britain and its precepts. In the British pantheon of virtues, free trade was a norm that could be extended to other nations without self-defeat. Success for one nation did not undermine the prospects for others. But the acquisition of empire did cause congestion for other nations on the paths to industrialization and growth. Once imperial Britain had taken the lion's share, there was little left for others. The inability of all nations to live up to the norms Britain established fomented conflict between them.

In a similar vein, Japan's current trading strategy could be emulated by many other countries. Its pacific principles and dependence on world markets and raw materials supplies have engendered greater economic cooperation among other countries. At the same time, Japan's insistence on maintaining a quasi-closed domestic economy and a foreign trade surplus cannot be successfully imitated by everyone; if some achieve the desired result, others necessarily will not. In this respect, Japan's recent practice and norms stand athwart progress and emulation by other nations.

[U.S.] President [Bill] Clinton rightly argues that the newly capitalist developmental states, such as Korea and Taiwan, have simply modeled themselves on restrictionist Japan. If this precedent were extended to China, the results would endanger the long-term stability of the world economic and financial system. Accordingly, new norms calling for greater openness in trade, finance, and the movement of factors of production will be necessary to stabilize the international system. Appropriate norms reinforce economic incentives to reduce conflict between differentiated international units. . . .

So long as the international system of nation-states lasts, there will be conflict among its members. States see events from different perspectives, and competition and struggle between them are endemic. The question is how far conflicts will proceed. Within a domestic system, conflicts between individuals need not escalate to the use of physical force. Law and settlement procedures usually reduce outbreaks of hostility. In international relations, however, no sovereign, regnant authority can discipline feuding states. International law sets a standard, but it is not always obeyed. The great powers constitute the executive committee of nation–states and can intervene from time to time to set things right. But, as Bosnia shows, they often do not, and they virtually never intervene in the absence of shared norms and ideologies.

In these circumstances, the economic substructure of international relations becomes exceedingly important. That structure can either impel or retard conflicts between nation–states. When land is the major factor of production, the temptation to strike another nation is great. When the key elements of production are less tangible, the situation changes. The taking of real estate does not result in the acquisition of knowledge, and aggressors cannot seize the needed capital. Workers may flee from an invader. Wars of aggression and wars of punishment are losing their impact and justification. . . .

Small nations have attained peak efficiency and competitiveness, and even large nations have begun to think small. If durable access to assets elsewhere can be assured, the need to physically possess them diminishes. Norms are potent reinforcements of such arrangements. Free movement of capital and goods, substantial international and domestic investment, and high levels of technical education have been the recipe for success in the industrial world of the late 20th century. Those who depended on others did better than those who depended only on themselves. Can the result be different in the future? Virtual states, corporate alliances, and essential trading relationships auger peaceful times. They may not solve domestic problems, but the economic bonds that link virtual and other nations will help ease security concerns.

THE CIVIC CRISIS

Though peaceful in its international implications, the rise of the virtual state portends a crisis for democratic politics. Western democracies have traditionally believed that political reform, extension of suffrage, and economic restructuring could solve their problems. In the 21st century none of these measures can fully succeed. Domestic political change does not suffice because it has insufficient jurisdiction to deal with global problems. The people in a particular state cannot determine international outcomes by holding an election. Economic restructuring in one state does not necessarily affect others. And the political state is growing smaller, not larger.

If ethnic movements are victorious in Canada, Mexico, and elsewhere, they will divide the state into smaller entities. Even the powers of existing states are becoming circumscribed. In the United States, if Congress has its way, the federal government will lose authority. In response to such changes, the market fills the vacuum, gaining power.

As states downsize, malaise among working people is bound to spread. Employment may fluctuate and generally decline. President Clinton observed [in 1995] that the American public has fallen into a funk. The economy may temporarily be prosperous, but there is no guarantee that favorable conditions will last. The flow of international factors of production—technology, capital, and labor—will swamp the stock or economic power at home. The state will become just one of many players in the international marketplace and will have to negotiate directly with foreign factors of production to solve domestic economic problems. Countries must induce foreign capital to enter their domain. To keep such investment, national economic authorities will need to maintain low inflation, rising productivity, a strong currency, and a flexible and trained labor force. These demands will sometimes conflict with domestic interests that want more government spending, larger budget deficits, and more benefits. That conflict will result in continued domestic insecurity over jobs, welfare, and medical care. Unlike the remedies applied in the insulated and partly closed economies of the past, purely domestic policies can no longer solve these problems.

THE NECESSITY OF INTERNATIONALIZATION

The state can compensate for its deficient jurisdiction by seeking to influence economic factors abroad. The domestic state therefore must not only become a negotiating state but must also be internationalized. This is a lesson already learned in Europe, and well on the way to codification in East Asia. Among the world's major economies and polities, only the United States remains, despite its potent economic sector, essentially introverted politically and culturally. Compared with their counterparts in other nations, citizens born in the United States know fewer foreign languages, understand less about foreign cultures, and live abroad reluctantly, if at all. In recent years, many English industrial workers who could not find jobs migrated to Germany, learning the language to work there. They had few American imitators.

The virtual state is an agile entity operating in twin jurisdictions: abroad and at home. It is as prepared to mine gains overseas as in the domestic economy. But in large countries, internationalization operates differently. Political and economic decision makers have begun to recast their horizons, but middle managers and workers lag behind. They expect too much and give and learn too little. That is why the dawn of the virtual state must also be the sunrise of international education and training. The virtual state cannot satisfy all its citizens. The possibility of commanding economic power in the sense of effective state control has greatly declined. Displaced workers and business people must be willing to look abroad for opportunities. . . .

3

A REVOLUTION IN WARFARE: THE CHANGING FACE OF FORCE

Eliot A. Cohen

This essay questions the proposition that military power is of diminishing importance as an element of national power and in world politics. Eliot A. Cohen predicts that war will remain a central concern because we are now in the early days of a revolution in military affairs. This transformation in the tools and techniques for waging war is a consequence of the information revolution and postindustrial capitalism; Cohen foresees the satellite imagery and smart bombs produced by these developments changing the forms of combat and armies and making leadership in the next generation of weaponry a key to power. Cohen is professor and director of Strategic Studies at the Paul H. Nitze School of Advanced International Studies, the Johns Hopkins University. He has co-authored (with John Gouch) *Military Misfortunes: The Anatomy of Failure in War* (1990).

From "A Revolution in Warfare," by Elliot A. Cohen. Reprinted by permission of *Foreign Affairs,* March/April 1996. Copyright © 1996 by the Council on Foreign Relations, Inc. The essay has been abridged and footnotes have been deleted.

TECHNOLOGY STRIKES AGAIN

For almost a decade . . . defense planners have foreseen an impending revolution in military affairs, sometimes described as the military-technical revolution. Such a transformation would open the way for a fundamental reordering of . . . defense posture[s]. It might lead, for example, to a drastic shrinking of the military, a casting aside of old forms of organization and creation of new ones, a slashing of current force structure, and the investment of unusually large sums in research and development.

Such a revolution would touch virtually all aspects of the military establishment. Cruise missiles and unmanned aerial vehicles would replace fighter planes and tanks as chess pieces in the game of military power. Today's military organizations—divisions, fleets, and air wings—could disappear or give way to successors that would look very different. And if the forces themselves changed, so too would the people, as new career possibilities, educational requirements, and promotion paths became essential. New elites would gain in importance: "information warriors," for example, might supplant tankers and fighter pilots as groups from which the military establishment draws the bulk of its leaders.

The proponents of this view have turned to history to illustrate—and in some measure to create—their theory of radical change. It is, therefore, proper to ask whether the historical record substantiates their claims.

Most soldiers, in their heart of hearts, would agree with Cyril Falls, a military historian of an older generation, who noted in his 1953 work *A Hundred Years of War, 1850–1950:*

> Observers constantly describe the warfare of their own age as marking a revolutionary breach in the normal progress of methods of warfare. Their selection of their own age ought to put readers and listeners on their guard. . . . It is a fallacy, due to ignorance of technical and tactical military history, to suppose that methods of warfare have not made continuous and, on the whole, fairly even progress.

The cautious military historian (and even more cautious soldier) looks askance at prophets of radical change, although by no means at change itself. Unquestionably, military technology has never stood still. In the 18th century, for example, minor improvements in the design and manufacture of gun barrels and carriages, coupled with the standardization of cannon calibers, laid the groundwork for the vastly improved cannonades of the armies of the French Revolution and Empire. At the same time, on closer inspection the apparently rapid rate of change in modern warfare may prove deceptive. Despite the attention the press lavished on "smart" bombs during the 1991 Persian Gulf War, for example, most of the ordnance in that conflict consisted of 1950s-technology unguided bombs dropped by aircraft developed in the 1960s or in some cases 1970s. This being so, whence comes the contention that . . . a revolution [is underway] in military affairs?

THE RUSSIANS SAW IT COMING

Beginning in the early 1980s Soviet observers led by Marshal Nikolai Ogarkov, then chief of the general staff, advanced the notion of an imminent technical revolution that would give conventional weapons a level of effectiveness in the field comparable to that of small tactical nuclear weapons. Armor on the march might find itself detected and attacked by conventional missiles showering self-guided antitank weapons, in an operation conducted from a distance of several hundred miles and with as little as 30 minutes between detection and assault. The Soviets found their reading of the military future profoundly disheartening, since it promised to thwart their strategy in case of war in Western Europe, which rested on the orderly forward movement of massed echelons of tanks and armored vehicles. They realized, moreover, that their country, incapable of manufacturing a satisfactory personal computer, could not possibly keep up in an arms race driven by the information technologies.

Soviet conceptions of a military-technical revolution seeped into the West, chiefly through the U.S. Department of Defense and its Office of Net Assessment. It gradually became clear that the Soviets had portrayed the revolution too narrowly. They had focused on one type of warfare in a single theater—armored conflict in Central Europe—and concentrated almost exclusively, as befitted the materialism of Marxist-Leninist thought, on technology and weapons rather than the organizational dimension of warfare. With the groundwork laid for an American assessment, the 1991 war with Iraq crystallized awareness among military planners in the United States on this momentous issue.

Many exponents of air power declared that in the Persian Gulf War the technology had finally caught up with the promise of air operations, first articulated in the period between the world wars; the revolution, they said, was in the realization of the 50-year quest for the decisive application of air power in war. Yet the conduct of the war against Iraq had very little to do with the kinds of operations envisaged by the original theorists of air warfare. No theorist in the 1920s imagined it would be possible to take down telecommunications systems or to conduct extensive attacks in densely populated areas without killing many civilians. The Gulf War showed air power off to great advantage but in extremely favorable circumstances: the United States brought to bear a force sized and trained to fight the Soviet Union in a global war, obtained the backing of almost every major military and financial power, and chose the time and place at which combat would begin in a theater ideally suited to air operations. Knowledgeable observers remained skeptical that a revolution had taken place.

A third version of the revolution has come from the American military. Admiral William Owens, vice chairman of the Joint chiefs of Staff, has written of a "system of systems"—a world in which the many kinds of sensors, for satellites to shipborne radar, from unmanned aerial vehicles to remotely planted acoustic devices, will provide information to any military user who needs it. Thus a helicopter might launch a missile at a tank a dozen miles away based on information derived from airborne radar or satellite imagery. In this view the revolution in military affairs consists of the United States' astounding and unprecedented ability to amass and evaluate enormous quantities of information about any given battle arena—Owens has referred to a 200-mile-by-200-mile box—and make near-instantaneous use of it.

Ground soldiers are particularly dubious about the system of systems. They wonder whether any technologist can disperse what Carl von Clausewitz called the fog of war and ask what will happen when an opponent attempts to conceal its force or attacks the information systems that observe it. Even in naval warfare, where the system of systems originated, sea and storm can make it difficult to know all that goes on in a box of the kind described by Owens. The admiral's version of the military revolution focuses almost entirely on technology rather than on the less tangible aspects of warfare. As yet, it bespeaks an aspiration, not a reality, and it is predicated on the inability of other countries to systematically deny the United States the information its weapons systems need.

The Soviet, air power, and Owens versions of the revolution in military affairs all offer only partial insights into a larger set of changes. A revolution has indeed begun. But it will be shaped by powerful forces emanating from beyond the domain of warfare. It will, moreover, represent the culmination in modern military organizations of a variety of developments, some of them dating back decades. To understand it, one must begin with its origins.

REVOLUTION FROM THE OUTSIDE

From time to time dramatic changes in warfare occur as a consequence of forces endogenous to war. Military research and development programs gave birth to the nuclear revolution, and although space exploration has many civilian spin-offs, military resources drove it in its early phases. Submarine warfare, which gave weaker naval powers a tremendously potent tool against stronger ones, also originated in the military. Just as often, however, the driving forces behind a change in the conduct of war lie in the realms of political and economic life.

The transformation of warfare in the 19th century offers a particularly useful analogy for contemporary strategists. Describing the posture of Austria and Prussia at the outset of the French Revolution, Clausewitz noted in *On War* that the two countries resorted to the kind of limited war that the previous century had made familiar in Europe. However,

> they soon discovered its inadequacy. . . . People at first expected to have to deal only with a seriously weakened French army; but in 1793 a force appeared that beggared all imagination. Suddenly war again became the business of the people—a people of thirty millions, all of whom considered themselves to be citizens. . . . The resources and efforts now available for use surpassed all conventional limits; nothing now impeded the vigor with which war could be waged, and consequently the opponents of France faced the utmost peril.

The advent of broadly based conscription greatly enlarged armies and increased their durability. The secret of the success of the French revolutionary armies lay not in their skill on the battlefield—the reviews there are mixed—but in the new regime's ability to replenish its forces repeatedly after defeat and in the opening of military advancement to all classes of citizen. The age of the mass army had arrived.

Civilian technologies have also brought revolutionary change in warfare. The mass-produced rifle of the 19th century complicated the task of military tacticians enormously, while the appearance of the railroad and telegraph altered war even more. Generals could shuttle armies from one theater to another in weeks, a feat demonstrated in spectacular fashion during the Civil War when the Union shifted 25,000 troops, with artillery and baggage, over 1,100 miles of rail lines from Virginia to Chattanooga, Tennessee, in less than 12 days. Furthermore, the railroad, in conjunction with the mass army, made mobilization at the outset of war a critical element in the efficiency of a military organization.

The telegraph affected not only armies and governments but newspapers. It helped general staffs coordinate rapid mobilization and launch large military movements. Even more important, the rapid dissemination of news transformed the nature of civil-military relations in wartime, creating new opportunities for tension. Politicians discovered, to their consternation, that the literate publics of modern states could learn of events on the battlefield almost immediately from mass circulation newspapers. At the same time, generals discovered that political leaders could now communicate with them in the field, and would gladly do so. During the Civil War the Union established a military telegraph system, laying some 15,000 miles of wires, but placed it under civilian control rather than the Army Signal Corps'; Secretary of War Edwin M. Stanton made certain the lines terminated in his office, not that of the army's senior general. With knowledge came intervention—or interference, as many a Union general keenly felt it. As the wars of German unification went on, Field Marshal Helmuth Graf von Moltke felt the same way about the suggestions Bismarck telegraphed his subordinates, and attempted to restrict the information flowing over the wires to higher headquarters.

The contemporary revolution in military affairs, like those of the 19th century, has its origins in the civilian world, and in two developments in particular. The first is the rise of information technologies, which have transformed economic and social life in ways that hardly need elaboration. The consequences for military organizations are numerous; the development of intelligent weapons that can guide themselves to their targets is only one, and not necessarily the most important. The variety of ever-expending capabilities of intelligence-gathering machines and the ability of computers to bring together and distribute to users the masses of information from these sources stem from the information revolution. Small wonder that a group of senior Marine Corps officers, led by the assistant commandant of the corps, visited the New York Stock Exchange recently to learn how brokers absorb, process, and transmit the vast quantities of perishable information that are the lifeblood of the financial markets.

The efflorescence of capitalism in the United States and abroad constitutes a second driving force. In the years after World War II, even Western nations spent a great deal of their national wealth on defense and created vast state bureaucracies to provide for every military need and function. Today very few states can successfully resist the pressures of postindustrial capitalism. Military dimensions include the sale of government-owned defense industries around the world and the increasing privatization of military functions; private contractors, for instance, handled much of the logistics for the U.S. operations in Haiti and Somalia. In a world where commercial satellites can deliver images of a quality that only a few years ago was the prerogative of the superpowers, military organizations are more and more willing to use civilian systems for military communications and even intelligence gathering rather than spend to develop their own. Furthermore, the end of the Cold War has freed up the markets in military goods and services. Countries can gain access to a wide spectrum of military capabilities for ready cash, including the services of skilled personnel to maintain and perhaps operate high-technology weapons. For much of this century armed forces could ignore the market, practicing a kind of military socialism in a sea of capitalism; no longer.

To know what the revolution in military affairs will look like, we need the answers to four questions. Will it change the appearance of combat? Will it change the structure of armies? Will it lead to the rise of new military elites? Will it alter countries' power position? Reflection on each of these suggests that this is the eve of a far-reaching change in warfare whose outlines are only dimly visible but real nonetheless.

THE FORMS OF COMBAT

A transformation of combat means change in the fundamental relationship between offense and defense, space and time, fire and maneuver. The advent of carrier-based warfare provides an example. Warfare in the age of battleships took place within visual range, between tightly drilled formations of ships of the line that battered each other with their big guns. Once carriers came on the scene, fleets struck at one another from hundreds of miles away, and their blows were not repeated salvos but massed air aids; fighting now depended on "one large pulse of firepower unleashed upon the arrival of the air wing at the target," as Wayne Hughes put it in his 1986 *Fleet Tactics*. The firepower revolution of the late 19th century rested on the adoption of the rifle and subsequent improvement of the weapon with smokeless powder, breechloading, and metal cartridges. In short order the densely packed battlefield of the early American Civil War gave way to the empty battlefield of modern times, in which small groups of soldiers scurry from shellhole to shellhole, eschewing the massed rush that dominated tactics for almost two centuries.

Today the forms of combat have begun a change no less dramatic. A military cliché has it that what can be seen on the modern battlefield can be hit, and what can be hit will be destroyed. Whereas at the beginning of the century this applied with deadly certainty only to frontline infantrymen, it now holds not only for machines on the front lines but for supporting forces in the rear. The introduction of long-range precision weapons, delivered by plane or missile, together with the development of intelligent mines that can be activated from a remote location, means that sophisticated armies can inflict unprecedented levels of destruction on any large armored force on the move. Fixed sites are also increasingly vulnerable.

The colossal maneuvers of the coalition armies in the deserts of Kuwait and Iraq in 1991 may in retrospect appear, like the final charges of cavalry in the 19th century, to be an anomaly in the face of modern firepower. Future warfare may be more a gigantic artillery duel fought with exceptionally sophisticated munitions than a chesslike game of maneuver and positioning. As all countries gain access to the new forms of air power (space-based reconnaissance and unmanned aerial vehicles), hiding large-scale armored movements or building up safe rear areas chock-a-block with ammunition dumps and truck convoys will gradually become impossible.

From the middle of the 19th century until very recently, platforms dominated warfare: the newest ship, plane, or tank outclassed its rivals and in most cases speedily rendered them obsolete. But this was not always the case. Until the 1830s, for example, naval technology remained roughly where it had been since the mid-18th century. Nelson's *Victory* was laid down in 1759, launched in 1765, served brilliantly at Trafalgar in 1805, and was paid off only in 1835—a service life of 70 years. Steam propulsion and metal construction changed all that, and a period of near-constant technological change ensued, in which naval superiority seemed to shift rapidly from power to power depending on who had the most recently built warship.

The wheel has now turned again. The platform has become less important, while the quality of what it carries—sensors, munitions, and electronics of all kinds—has become critical. A modernized 30-year-old aircraft armed with the latest long-range air-to-air missile, cued by an airborne warning plane, can defeat a craft a third its age but not so equipped or guided. In a world dominated by long-range, intelligent precision weapons, the first blow can prove decisive; the collapse of the Iraqi air defense system in 1991 within a few hours of a sophisticated air attack is a case in point. As a result, incentives for preemption may grow. For two duelists armed with swords approaching each other from a dozen yards' distance, it makes little difference who unsheathes his weapon first. Give them pistols, however, and all odds favor the man quicker on the draw.

Furthermore, the nature of preemption itself may change. To the extent that information warfare, including the sabotage of computer systems, emerges as a new type of combat, the first blow may be covert, a precursor to more open and conventional hostilities. Such attacks—to which an information-dependent society like the United States is particularly vulnerable—could have many purposes: blinding, intimidating, diverting, or simply confusing an opponent. They could carry as well the threat of bringing war to a country's homeland and people, and thus even up the balance for countries that do not possess the conventional tools of long-range attack, such as missiles and bombers. How such wars initiated by information strikes would play themselves out is a matter of tremendous uncertainty.

THE STRUCTURE OF MILITARY ORGANIZATIONS

It is not merely the tools of warfare but the organizations that wield them that make for revolutionary change in war. . . . The new military will be an increasingly joint force—or perhaps, one might say, less and less a traditional, service-oriented force. In militaries around the world the traditional division into armies, navies, and air forces (and in only a few countries, marine corps) has begun to break down. Not only have air operations become inseparable from almost any action on the ground, but naval forces increasingly deliver fire against a wide range of ground targets. Quasi services have begun to emerge. In all militarily sophisticated countries special forces have grown, imitating the highly successful models of the British Special Air Service and its American and Israeli counterparts. Even regular infantry formations have adopted the tactics of special forces—very small units, dispersion, and the extensive use of fire brought to bear from the air or rear areas. Other quasi services include organizations oriented toward space and information warfare and the horde of civilian contractors who fix airplanes, build bases, pay the troops, operate mess halls, and analyze operations.

Another structural change looms. Tack an organizational chart of an army corps on a wall, and next to it place a similar chart for a leading corporation of the 1950s—General Motors, say—and the similarities stand out. One would see in both cases a classical pyramid, small units reporting up to progressively smaller numbers of larger organizations. The organization of a corps has not changed much since then, but the cutting-edge corporation of today is not GM but Microsoft or Motorola, neither of which much resembles an army corps. The modern corporation has stripped out layers of middle management, reduced or even eliminated many of the functional and social distinctions between management and labor that dominated industrial organizations, and largely abolished the old long-term tenure and compensation systems, including company-based pensions. By and large, military organizations have not done this. "Management" still consists of commissioned and noncommissioned officers, and although the latter play a role quite different from that of even their World War II counterparts, they still operate within rank, deference, and pay structures of a bygone time. The radical revision of these structures will be the last manifestation of a revolution in military affairs, and the most difficult to implement.

THE NATURE OF COMMAND

In a period of revolutionary change in the conduct of war, different kinds of people—not simply the same people differently trained—rise to the top of armed services. For instance, air power gave birth to entirely new kinds of military organizations; unlike armies and navies, air forces consist of a tiny percentage of officer-warriors backed by an elaborate array of enlisted technicians. To take another example: in the late 19th century it became clear that the increasingly complex problem of mobilizing reservists and deploying them over a country's railroad network required a corps of technocratic experts. The American Civil War and the Franco-Prussian War demonstrated that dash and bravura could not compete with skill at scheduling large numbers of locomotives, handling loading manifests, and repairing damaged track. The logistical manager had become an indispensable member of a general staff and a well-trained general staff an essential feature of a military establishment.

A similar evolution is under way today. Even in the U.S. Air Force, an organization dominated by pilots (bomber pilots in the 1950s and 1960s, fighter pilots thereafter), the number of general officers in important positions who are not combat aviators has risen. The new technologies will increasingly bring to the fore the expert in missile operations, the space general, and the electronic warfare wizard—none of them a combat specialist in the old sense and a fair percentage of them, sooner or later, female. Military organizations still need, and will always need, specialists in direct combat. Indeed, both the lethality of direct combat and its physical and intellectual demands have grown. But the number of such fighters in military organizations, both in absolute terms and in proportion to the overall size of the militaries, has declined steadily since the beginning of the century and will continue to do so. The cultural challenge for military organizations will be to maintain a warrior spirit and the intuitive understanding of war that goes with it, even when their leaders are not, in large part, warriors themselves.

Different eras in warfare give rise to characteristic styles of military leadership. The age of industrial warfare has ended, and with it a certain kind of supreme command. Shortly after the mobilization against Austria in 1866, an aide found the Prussian chief of the general staff, Helmuth Graf von Moltke, lying on a sofa reading a novel. On the evening before D-Day, General Dwight D. Eisenhower, supreme commander of Allied forces, could be found on his sofa doing precisely the same thing. Despite the 80 intervening years, some features of supreme command remained constant: the general in chief and his staff assembled a vast force, planned its intricate movements, and then spent the next day or two letting the machine conduct its initial operations on virtual autopilot.

Today, an aide would more likely find a field marshal pacing back and forth in an electronic command post, fiddling with television displays, talking to pilots or tank commanders on the front line by radio, and perhaps even peeking over their shoulders through remote cameras.

That the modern field marshal can sit invisibly in the cockpit with a pilot or perch cybernetically in the hatch of a tank commander raises a profound problem of centralization of authority. Although all military organizations pay lip service to delegation of maximum authority to the lowest levels of command, few military leaders can resist the temptation to dabble in their subordinates' business. The easier it is for them to find out what that business is, even though they are 10,000 miles away, the more likely they are to do so. Political leaders will have the same capability, and although for the moment most of them show little inclination to meddle, one can imagine situations in which they would choose otherwise.

THE POWER OF STATES

Few subjects exercise historians of early modern Europe more than the military revolution of the 16th and early 17th centuries. Yet all would agree that that period's remarkable set of changes profoundly altered the relative balance of power between Europe and the rest of the world in Europe's favor. The creation of modern military organizations—that is, armies led by professional officers, trained and organized according to impersonal standards of discipline and behavior—coupled with the appearance of governments that could mobilize both soldiers and financial resources, changed the international system. The rise of Holland and the decline of the Ottoman Empire represent the opposite extremes of the consequences of the revolution.

The contemporary revolution in military affairs offers tremendous opportunities to countries that can afford to acquire expensive modern weaponry and the skills to use it properly. An accurate measurement of Israel's power potential relative to its Arab neighbors, for example, would probably show a steep rise since 1973. Taiwan, Singapore, and Australia, to take just three examples, can do far more against potential opponents than would have been thinkable 30 years ago. As we have seen, the military leadership of the Soviet Union believed the revolutionary changes it saw coming would put it at a disadvantage. Indeed, only the United States, with its vast accumulation of military capital, better than four times the defense budget of the next leading power, and an unsurpassed ability to integrate large, complicated technological systems, can fully exploit this revolution.

Transformation in one area of military affairs does not, however, mean the irrelevance of all others. Just as nuclear weapons did not render conventional power obsolete, this revolution will not render guerrilla tactics, terrorism, or weapons of mass destruction obsolete. Indeed, the reverse may be true: where unconventional bypasses to conventional military power exist, any country confronting the United States will seek them out. The phenomenon of the persistence of older systems in the midst of revolutionary change occurs even at a tactical level. After the arrival of the carrier as the capital ship of naval warfare, for example, the venerable battleship did not disappear but instead acquired two important roles: shore bombardment platform and vast floating air defense battery. Battleships were part of the American fleet as recently as the Persian Gulf War, almost half a century after their day as the queens of naval warfare had passed.

To the extent that the revolution proceeds from forces in the civilian world, the potential will exist for new military powers to emerge extremely rapidly. A country like Japan or, in a few years, China will quickly translate civilian technological power into its military equivalent. An analogy might be Germany's acquisition of a modern air force in the space of less than a decade in the 1930s. At a time when civilian and military aviation technologies did not diverge too greatly, Germany could take the strongest civilian aviation industry in Europe and within a few years convert it into enormous military power, much as the United States would do a few years later with its automobile industry. After a long interval during the Cold War when military industry became an exotic and separate entity, the pendulum has begun to swing back, and economic strength may again prove easily translatable into military power.

THE CHANGING ORDER

Revolutionary change in the art of war stems not simply from the ineluctable march of technology but from an adaptation of the military instrument to political purposes. The subject of armored warfare languished in Great Britain and France between the world wars because those governments saw little need for an operationally offensive force on the continent. The powers that contemplated offensives to regain lost territories or to seize new ones—the Soviet Union and Germany—developed the armored instrument more fully than other states.

The United States may drive the revolution in military affairs, but only if it has a clear conception of what it wants military power for—which it does not now have. Indeed, when the Clinton administration formulated its defense policy in 1993 it came up with the Bottom-Up Review, which provided for a force capable of fighting simultaneously two regional wars assumed to resemble the Gulf War of 1991. By structuring its analysis around enemy forces similar to those of Iraq in that year—armor-heavy, with a relatively large conventional but third-rate air force—it guaranteed a conservatism in military thought at odds with the thorough reexamination promised by the administration early in its tenure. For this reason, among others, the revolution will take far longer to consummate than the Soviets predicted in the 1980s. Barring the pressure of a severe competition between the United States and some state capable of posing a real challenge to it, even available technologies are unlikely to be exploited fully. Military institutions in peacetime will normally evolve rather than submit to radical change.

World politics will also shape the revolution. One feature will certainly be the predominance of conventional warfare for limited objectives. Until the end of the Cold War, the possibility of total war, as in the great struggles of the first half of this century, dominated the planning of the American and Soviet military establishments, and perhaps others as well. With some exceptions, military action for limited ends seems more likely in the years ahead.

The most useful metaphor for the future military order may be a medieval one. During the middle Ages, as at present, sovereignty did not reside exclusively in states but was diffused among political, civic, and religious bodies—states, but also sub- and supra-state entities. Warfare was not, as it has been in the modern period, an affair almost exclusively of states, but one that also involved private entities such as religious orders and other associations. Then, unlike during the past two centuries, military technology varied widely among combatants—an army of English bowmen and knights fought very differently from the Arab warriors of Saladin or the Mongol cavalry of Genghis Khan or the pike-wielding peasantry of Switzerland. Militaries defied comparison; their strength varied greatly depending on where and whom they were fighting.

Opacity in the matter of military power may prove one of the most troubling features of the current revolution. The wildly inaccurate predictions of casualties in the Gulf War from responsible and experienced observers (including military estimators, let it be noted) reflected not conservatism or incompetence but a disjunction between the realities of military power and conventional means of measuring it. Numbers of tanks, airplanes, and soldiers and more elaborate firepower-based measurements of military might were always questionable, but now they say almost nothing about real military effectiveness. As platforms become less important and the quality of munitions and, above all, the ability to handle information become more so, analysts will find it ever more difficult to assess the military balance of opposing sides. If Admiral Owens is right, the revolution in military affairs may bring a kind of tactical clarity to the battlefield, but at the price of strategic obscurity.

In the 19th and early 20th centuries, God may not always have been on the side of the bigger battalions, as the saying went, but victory usually was. Future technologies, however, may create pockets of military capability that will allow very small states to hold off larger ones, much as companies of Swiss pikemen could stop armies sweeping through their mountain passes or a single, well-fortified castle could hold immensely larger forces at bay for months. Herein lies a potential challenge even for the United States, which will find itself attempting to project military power for limited purposes and at a low cost in material and lives. Other parties may well decide to inflict some hard, if not fatal, blows to stave off American intervention. For stymieing the America advantage in the megasystems of modern military power—fantastically expensive and effective aircraft carriers or satellites, for example—the microsystems of modern military technology, such as the cruise missile, may prove sufficient.

The predominance of warfare for limited objectives, the availability of vast quantities of centralized information, and the obscurity of military power may combine to make civil-military relations more awkward. Politicians will seek to use means they can readily see, as it were, but do not understand; generals will themselves be handling forces they do not fully comprehend and will be divided on the utility of various forms of military power.

In every previous period of revolutionary change in the conduct of war, military leaders made large mistakes. The human toll on European armies coming to terms with modern firepower in World War I reflected not only, or even primarily, the incompetence of generals but their bafflement in the face of new conditions of warfare. Less costly but no less time-consuming was the difficulty the U.S. Navy had developing the multicarrier task forces that would ultimately enable it to sweep the Pacific clear of Japanese forces in World War II. The lesson of the 1942 Battle of Midway had appeared to be that the massing of carriers offered great advantages but posed no lesser vulnerabilities, should the defending side by caught while rearming its strike aircraft. As a result, the transformation of naval warfare by the carrier could not be realized until one side either felt overwhelming pressure to mass carriers despite the risks—the case in the early part of the war—or had enough carriers to make the risks bearable. For the United States the latter did not occur until almost two years after it entered the war, when the naval building program had produced the sheer numbers of vessels adequate for large-scale carrier operations.

A revolution in military affairs is under way. It will require changes of a magnitude that military people still do not completely grasp and political leaders do not fully imagine. For the moment, it appears to offer the United States the prospect of military power beyond that of any other country on the planet, now and well into the next century. Small wonder, then, that by and large American theorists have embraced the idea of a revolution in warfare as an opportunity for their country, as indeed it is. But revolution implies rapid, violent, and, above all, unpredictable change. Clio has a number of lessons to teach Mars, but perhaps none is more important than that.

4

TOWARDS A NEW MILLENNIUM: STRUCTURAL PERSPECTIVES ON THE CAUSES OF WAR

Jack S. Levy

In this essay Jack S. Levy examines several theories that trace the roots of war to underlying structural forces in the international system. His analysis highlights the sources of continuity as well as change in the international system. Levy is professor of political science at Rutgers University and author of *War in the Modern Great Power System, 1495–1975* (1983).

As we move towards a new millennium, after a century that witnessed two world wars, the development of nuclear weapons, the end of the Cold War, and the collapse of the Soviet Union, many scholars and intellectuals have begun to speculate about a fundamental change in the dynamics of international politics and the nature of warfare.[1] Hypotheses regarding the obsolescence of war among advanced industrial states following the nuclear revolution[2] have been reinforced by arguments about the pacifying effects of increasing economic

---

This essay was written especially for this book.

[1]Jack S. Levy, Thomas C. Walker, and Martin S. Edwards, "Continuity and Change in the Evolution of Warfare," paper presented at a conference on "War in a Changing World," Jaffee Center for Strategic Studies, Tel Aviv, Israel, November 1996.

[2]John Lewis Gaddis, *The Long Peace* (New York: Oxford University Press, 1987); Robert Jervis, *The Meaning of the Nuclear Revolution* (Ithaca: Cornell University Press, 1989).

interdependence,[3] the end of the Cold War, the "end of history,"[4] changing attitudes toward war in the West,[5] and the rapid spread of democratic political systems.[6]

There has indeed been a "long peace" since World War II,[7] but this peace has been confined to advanced industrial states while war continues to ravage much of the rest of the world. These trends reflect a dramatic shift, beginning in 1945, in the concentration of war from Europe to other regional subsystems and from international wars to civil wars.[8] Although many informed observers expected that the end of the Cold War would result in a reduction in the frequency of warfare around the world, these hopes were shattered first by the Iraqi invasion of Kuwait, and then, after fleeting forecasts of a new world order and a new generation of peace, by the outbreak of frequent and brutal ethnic conflicts in the former Soviet Union, in central Africa, and elsewhere. These ethnic conflicts, combined with the prospect for increasingly serious resource scarcities and environmental pressures, will continue to generate major refugee flows, additional suffering, and the potential for more domestic and international violence.[9]

The areas of the world in which war is most likely to be fought and the types of states that are most likely to fight these wars may have changed, but there is little evidence to suggest that war itself will soon cease to exist as a regular pattern of behavior in world politics. Nor can we dismiss the potential seriousness of these wars, in light of the increasingly sophisticated weapons systems available to many states throughout the world and the real possibility of the proliferation of chemical, biological, and nuclear weapons systems.

Most of us would like to eliminate war or at least to control its destructive consequences, but that requires that we first understand its causes. Although philosophers, historians, social theorists, and others have been trying to understand why wars occur ever since Thucydides' account of the Peloponnesian War

---

[3]Robert O. Keohane and Joseph S. Nye, *Power and Interdependence* (Boston: Little Brown, 1977); Richard Rosecrance, *The Rise of the Trading State* (New York: Basic Books, 1986).

[4]Francis Fukuyama, *The End of History and the Last Man* (New York: Free Press, 1992).

[5]James Lee Ray, "The Abolition of Slavery and the End of International War," *International Organization* 43 (Summer 1989), pp. 405–39; John Mueller, *Quiet Cataclysm: Reflections on the Recent Transformation of World Politics* (New York: HarperCollins, 1995).

[6]Bruce Russett, *Grasping the Democratic Peace: Principles for a Post–Cold War World* (Princeton: Princeton University Press, 1993); James Lee Ray, *Democracy and International Conflict:* (Columbia: University of South Carolina Press, 1995).

[7]Gaddis, *The Long Peace.*

[8]J. David Singer, "Peace in the Global System: Displacement, Interregnum, or Transformation?" in Charles W. Kegley, Jr., ed., *The Long Postwar Peace* (New York: HarperCollins, 1991), pp. 56–84; Levy, Walker, and Edwards, "Continuity and Change in the Evolution of Warfare."

[9]On ethno-national, demographic, and environmental sources of international conflict see Sean M. Lynn-Jones and Steven E. Miller, eds., *Global Dangers: Changing Dimensions of International Security* (Cambridge, Mass.: MIT Press, 1995); Chester Crocker and Fen Hampson with Pamela Aall, eds., *Managing Global Chaos: Sources of and Responses to International Conflict* (Washington, D.C.: United States Institute of Peace, 1996).

between Athens and Sparta nearly 25 centuries ago, no consensus has emerged regarding the answer to this vital question.[10]

Some scholars argue that the underlying causes of war can be found in the structure of power and alliances in the international system or in the way that structure changes over time.[11] Others trace the roots of war to political, economic, social, and psychological factors internal to the nation-state. Immanuel Kant and many liberal theorists argue that liberal democratic regimes are inherently peaceful whereas authoritarian regimes are more warlike.[12] Marxist-Leninists argue that war results primarily from the tendencies of capitalist states to expand in search of external markets, investment opportunities, and raw materials.[13] War has also been traced to attempts by political leaders to solve their internal political problems through the adoption of hostile foreign policies, on the assumption that external conflict will promote internal harmony.[14] Some theorists argue that war results from misperception, the effects of stress on crisis decision making, bureaucratic rigidities, and other flaws in the decision-making process that prevent the selection of those policies most likely to advance the national interest.[15] Others insist that decisions for war are based on very careful cost-benefit calculations incorporating interests, constraints, and uncertainties.[16]

Scholars disagree on other things besides the identity of the most important causes of war. Some argue that a single theory (usually their own) explains all wars. Others argue that each war is unique and has a unique set of causes, or that there are several different causal sequences leading to war and that these arise under different and often unpredictable circumstances. Some theorists say that because of the enormous changes from one historical era to the next in military technology and forms of social and political organization, the causes of war have changed over time. Others argue that patterns of international behavior in general and of war in particular have demonstrated a profound continuity over time,

---

[10]Thucydides, *History of the Peloponnesian War,* trans. by Rex Warner (New York: Penguin, 1954).

[11]The leading proponents of a "structural" theory of international politics include Hans Morgenthau, *Politics Among Nations,* 4th ed. (New York: Knopf, 1967) and Kenneth N. Waltz, *Theory of International Politics* (Reading, Mass.: Addison-Wesley, 1979).

[12]Immanuel Kant, "Eternal Peace," in C. J. Friedrich, ed., *The Philosophy of Kant* (New York: Modern Library, 1949).

[13]V. I. Lenin, *Imperialism: The Highest Stage of Capitalism* (New York: International Publishers, 1939).

[14]Jack S. Levy, "The Diversionary Theory of War: A Critique," in Manus I. Midlarsky, ed., *Handbook of War Studies* (London: Unwin-Hyman, 1989), pp. 259–88.

[15]Robert Jervis, *Perception and Misperception in International Politics* (Princeton, N.J.: Princeton University Press, 1976); Richard Ned Lebow, *Between Peace and War* (Baltimore: Johns Hopkins, 1981), chaps. 5–7; Robert Jervis, Richard Ned Lebow, and Janis Gross Stein, *Psychology and Deterrence* (Baltimore: Johns Hopkins, 1985); Jack S. Levy, "Organizational Routines and the Causes of War," *International Studies Quarterly* 30 (June 1986), pp. 193–222.

[16]Bruce Bueno de Mesquita, *The War Trap* (New Haven, Conn.: Yale University Press, 1981); Bruce Bueno de Mesquita and David Lalman, *War and Reason* (New Haven, Conn.: Yale University Press, 1992).

and that the causes of war in the nuclear era are no different from the causes of war in the age of Thucydides. These disagreements apply not only to the question of the causes of war in general but also to the question of the causes of particular wars. Historians are nearly as divided regarding the origins of individual wars as political scientists are regarding an explanation for the general phenomenon of war.

It will not be possible to examine all of the theories of the causes of war in this essay or to reach a definitive conclusion as to which is most consistent with the historical record.[17] Instead, we will focus on "structural realist" theories, which assume that the key actors are sovereign states who act rationally to advance their security, power, and wealth in an anarchic and threatening international system.[18] A central hypothesis is that the distribution of power between two or more states is the primary determinant of international outcomes, though different conceptions of power and of the nature of the system lead to different theories and different predictions about what those specific outcomes are. Two of the leading theories are balance-of-power theory and power transition theory, but before we examine these theories it would first be useful to look at the consequences of international anarchy, which refer to the absence of a centralized political authority in the global system.

ANARCHY AND THE SECURITY DILEMMA

Whereas in domestic political systems there exists a government with the legitimate authority and the power to regulate the disputes between individual citizens within the state, there is no such institution to regulate disputes between individual states in the international system. In the absence of a higher authority, sovereign states are forced to rely on themselves to provide for their security and other interests, so that each state is the ultimate judge and ultimate protector of its own interests. Force is the final arbiter of disputes, and in this sense wars occur because of the absence of anything to prevent them. States might usually prefer to settle their disputes peacefully; but since it is possible that any state might use force, all others must be prepared to use force or be willing to suffer the consequences of weakness. In such a high-threat environment, the maintenance of a minimal level of security tends to become the primary goal of states, one that must be satisfied before attention can be directed to other goals. The

---

[17]For more thorough discussions of the causes of war see Geoffrey Blainey, *The Causes of War* (New York: Free Press, 1973); Jack S. Levy, "The Causes of War: A Review of Theories and Evidence," in Philip E. Tetlock, Jo L. Husbands, Robert Jervis, Paul C. Stern, and Charles Tilly, eds., *Behavior, Society, and Nuclear War*, vol. 1 (New York: Oxford University Press, 1989), pp. 209–333; and "Contending Theories of International Conflict: A Levels-of-Analysis Approach," in Crocker et al., *Managing Global Chaos*, pp. 3–24; and John A. Vasquez, *The War Puzzle* (Cambridge: Cambridge University Press, 1993).

[18]Waltz, *Theory of International Politics;* Robert O. Keohane, ed., *Neorealism and Its Critics* (New York: Columbia University Press, 1986).

main means by which states provide for their security is the accumulation of military power and economic strength and the formation of alliances. The problem is that power and security tend to be relative rather than absolute. As Jean-Jacques Rousseau once argued,

> The state . . . always feels itself weak if there is another that is stronger. Its security and preservation demand that it make itself more powerful than its neighbors. It can increase, nourish and exercise its power only at their expense. . . . Because the grandeur of the state is purely relative it is forced to compare itself to that of the others. . . . It becomes small or great, weak or strong, according to whether its neighbor expands or contracts, becomes stronger or declines.[19]

Thus there is no natural limit to the pursuit of power and security, and therefore states, and particularly the leading states in the system, engage in a continuous effort to increase or at least maintain their power and influence relative to their rivals. This contributes to the processes leading to war by generating conflicting and sometimes mutually incompatible interests between states. Because a purely fortress defense is not viable, states attempt to maintain an extended defense through the control of territory, resources, strategic areas, and vital sea lanes beyond their own borders. The external defense requirements of two or more states may be in direct conflict, however, and this is particularly likely for contiguous states. The conflict is especially serious if the political authorities of one state believe that their external security requirements include the control over part of the territory within another state, as illustrated by the current Israeli occupation of the Syrian Golan Heights. A related problem is that states often try, if they can, to minimize threats to their security by attempting to influence or even control the internal political processes of other states, especially those on their borders. This often takes the form of attempting to assure the ideological compatibility of adjacent states, as illustrated by the Soviet Union in Eastern Europe during much of the post–World War II era. Intervention in the internal affairs of other states is a major source of conflict between great powers and secondary states, and since the latter have an incentive to secure protection through an alliance with another great power, these conflicts sometimes escalate to great–power confrontations. Great powers' perceptions of their security interests tend to expand even further, however, to include the maintenance of a balance of power, which prevents any rival from achieving such a dominant position that it is able to interfere with one's own ability to maintain an extended defense beyond one's borders. These conflicts between the concrete strategic interests of rival states trying to provide for their own security in an anarchic state system have undoubtedly been one of the most important causes of war.

The relativity of security and the continuous pursuit of power would be mitigated if it were possible for statesmen to distinguish between the aggressive and

---

[19]Quoted in Robert Gilpin, *U.S. Power and the Multinational Corporation* (New York: Basic Books, 1975), pp. 34–35.

defensive intentions of others and between offensive and defensive weapons systems. But most weapons can serve offensive as well as defensive functions, and most actions of other states are inherently ambiguous. Even if the political leadership of the adversary were fully trusted, there is no guarantee how long they would be in power or that they would necessarily be succeeded by others with equally benign intentions. Given this uncertainty, political leaders prefer to err on the side of safety and to engage in worst-case analysis. They recognize that false pessimism regarding the adversary's intentions might lead unnecessarily to a further escalation of tensions, but they fear that the consequences of a false optimism would be even worse. Thus even actions that are purely defensive in intent are often perceived as threatening by another state and lead it to take defensive countermeasures, which in turn are perceived as threatening by the first state, and so on. This action-reaction cycle or conflict spiral that often results from sincere attempts to increase one's security without threatening others may in fact decrease the security of oneself as well as one's adversaries. This classic "security dilemma" is extremely important, because it explains how states with primarily defensive motivations can be induced by the structure of the system to take actions that leave all states worse off than before.[20] Under certain conditions, the security dilemma can lead directly to war. If the nature of military technology is such as to give a major advantage to the state that strikes first in a crisis, states can be induced to initiate a preemptive attack even though both states would prefer to avoid war. The origins of World War I, for example, are often traced to the offensive war plans and rapid mobilization schedules that created strong incentives for both Germany and Russia to act preemptively.[21] Similarly, Israel was led by worst-case logic to act preemptively against Egypt in the 1967 war. Thus, while limited political objectives may decrease the likelihood of war, they do not guarantee that war will be avoided.

Although international anarchy and the security dilemma help explain the generally high level of conflict in the international system, they cannot explain the many extended periods of peace. More specific theories are needed to specify the conditions under which the continuous struggle for power and security is most likely to trigger an irreconcilable conflict of vital interests or a conflict spiral, and the conditions under which these escalate to war. Let us now turn to two of these theories.

BALANCE-OF-POWER THEORY

Balance-of-power theory is not a well-articulated theory but, instead, a weakly integrated collection of propositions regarding the behavior of the leading states

---

[20]Robert Jervis, "Cooperation under the Security Dilemma," *World Politics* 30 (January 1978), pp. 167–214.

[21]Steven E. Miller, Sean M. Lynn-Jones, and Stephen Van Evera, eds., *Military Strategy and the Origins of the First World War,* rev. ed. (Princeton, N.J.: Princeton University Press, 1991).

in an anarchic international system and the conditions for stability in such a system. Although the key concepts are ambiguous and some of the propositions inconsistent, the "theory" has had a tremendous impact on the study of international relations for the past century. In spite of their disagreements on a number of specific issues, most balance-of-power theorists share a common set of general assumptions: that states define their interests primarily in terms of security, that they attempt to maximize their power, and that power is defined mainly in terms of military strength. The primary means by which states increase their power is through the formation of alliances, internal increases in their military capabilities and the economic foundations of military potential, and, if necessary, territorial compensations and the threat or use of military force for intervention or war. The balance-of-power system is said to function effectively or to be "stable" if no single state achieves a dominant position, if the independence of the great powers is assured, and if major wars are avoided, though there is some disagreement regarding the relative importance of these different criteria.[22]

One key proposition on which all balance-of-power theorists agree is that if any single state threatens to achieve a position of "hegemony" from which it could dominate over the other states in the system, a military coalition of nearly all the other great powers will form to block it and a general or "hegemonic war" is likely to follow in order to restore equilibrium to the system. There are several historical cases that appear to fit this hypothesis, including the wars against Philip II of Spain in the late 16th century, wars involving Louis XIV of France in the late 17th century, the French Revolution and the Napoleonic wars a century later, and the two world wars with Germany in this century. Blocking coalitions are also likely to emerge if one state threatens to establish dominance over a regional system, as illustrated by the response to Saddam Hussein of Iraq in 1990.

This hypothesis regarding antihegemonic coalitions is an extension of the common balance-of-power hypothesis that a relatively equal distribution of military capabilities among the great powers is conducive to the avoidance of a major war, whereas the concentration of capabilities tends to be destabilizing. An alternative to this "parity hypothesis" is the "power preponderance" hypothesis, which asserts that parity only tempts aggressors whereas preponderance reinforces deterrence and stability, as illustrated by the periods of peace enforced by ancient Rome and by 19th-century Britain. Whereas preponderance theorists argue that war is too risky for weaker states and unnecessary for the dominant state, balance-of-power theorists are more skeptical of the peaceful intentions of dominant states. They believe in the corrupting effects of power and in the tendency for a state's expansionist ambitions to increase along with its strength; therefore they fear the consequences of the absence of countervailing power.

---

[22]Inis L. Claude, Jr., *Power and International Relations* (New York: Random House, 1962); Edward Vose Gulick, *Europe's Classical Balance of Power* (New York: Norton, 1955).

The parity/preponderance question is related to the debate over whether multipolar systems, characterized by several leading great powers, are more stable than bipolar systems, characterized by only two leading powers. In the context of the end of the Cold War, these conflicting hypotheses have generated an interesting debate about whether the current transformation of the international system from bipolarity to multipolarity will lead to an increase in the instability of the system.[23]

Balance-of-power theorists also emphasize the role of alliances, though they generally make a distinction between relatively permanent peacetime alliances and "ad hoc" alliances. Ad hoc alliances, which form in response to specific threats of aggression or to dangerous shifts in the distribution of power in the system, are necessary to maintain an equilibrium in the system and are considered to be stabilizing. Permanent alliances, on the other hand, are said to be destabilizing because they limit the "flexibility" of the system to respond to threats of aggression by reducing the number of coalitions that might form against a potential aggressor (since some states are already committed). Permanent alliances are particularly destabilizing if they become polarized, creating two rival alliance blocs. These tend to increase tensions, reduce possibilities for compromise because states must defend their allies' interests as well as their own, and increase both the probability of war and of its expansion into a general conflict involving all of the major states. World War I is considered a classic case of the destabilizing effects of a polarized alliance system.[24]

POWER-TRANSITION THEORY

A. F. K. Organski and Jacek Kugler argue that balance-of-power theory's focus on territory, armaments, and allies as the basis of power and security is too narrow. It ignores the importance of internal development in general and industrialization in particular as a source of the changing military power and potential of states. Organski and Kugler's power-transition theory emphasizes that industrialization leads to uneven rates of economic growth and therefore to changing distributions of power in the international system, and that these changing power differentials between states have been the primary cause of war between the great powers for the past two centuries. Organski and Kugler conceive of

---

[23]On the greater stability of multipolar systems, see Morgenthau, chap. 21; Claude, chaps. 2–3. On the stability of bipolarity, particularly when combined with nuclear weapons, see Waltz, chap. 8; Gaddis, *The Long Peace,* chap. 8; John J. Mearsheimer, "Back to the Future: Instability in Europe After the Cold War," *International Security* 15 (Summer 1990): 5–56. See also Charles W. Kegley, Jr., and Gregory A. Raymond, *A Multipolar Peace? Great-Power Politics in the Twenty-first Century* (New York: St. Martin's Press, 1994).

[24]Balance-of-power theorists also suggest other conditions affecting international stability and peace, but those involving the distribution of power in the system and the pattern of alliances are the most important.

the international system as consisting of one dominant state at the top of the power hierarchy, a handful of rival great powers directly below, and a number of weaker states. As some great powers begin to grow in strength as a result of industrialization, they become increasingly dissatisfied with the existing international system and their own role in it and wish a share of the benefits and influence in the system commensurate with their newly acquired power. They also become an increasing military threat to the dominant state in the system. Organski and Kugler argue that the likelihood of a major war is highest when the military power of a rising great power begins to approach that of the leading state in the system. The rising but still weaker challenger has an incentive to initiate a war in order to accelerate the power transition and secure the benefits to which it feels entitled by virtue of its military power. The underlying cause of World War I, in this view, was the rise of Germany and its challenge to the dominant position of Britain. It should be noted that in power-transition theory, in contrast to balance-of-power theory, alliances play very little role either as a factor affecting the distribution of power in the system or as a factor in the dynamic processes leading to major war.[25]

One curious element in power-transition theory is the fact that the rising challenger initiates a war against the dominant state while it is still militarily inferior, rather than waiting until the underlying trends in economic and military power thrust it into a stronger position. This has led some scholars to argue that the more likely mechanism by which power transitions lead to war is the initiation of a "preventive war" by the dominant state in a desperate attempt to block or retard the rise of the challenger before it is surpassed in strength. The declining leader has an incentive to fight a war now rather than risk a war under worsening circumstances later. Robert Gilpin suggests that preventive war is often perceived as the best option by a leading state in decline, and numerous historical cases have been interpreted as preventive wars. Many have argued that World War I was an attempt by Germany to secure its position before an increasingly powerful Russia had achieved a position of equality with Germany (which the latter expected to happen by 1917).[26]

Regardless of who initiates the war, differential rates of growth and the power transition are important phenomena in international relations. It is not necessary, however, to restrict the scope of the theory to the modern industrial era, as Organski and Kugler do. In fact, Thucydides argued with respect to the Peloponnesian War that "What made war inevitable was the growth of Athenian power and the fear which this caused in Sparta," suggesting that differential rates of

---

[25]A. F. K. Organski and Jacek Kugler, *The War Ledger* (Chicago: University of Chicago Press, 1980), chap 1.

[26]Robert Gilpin, *War and Change in World Politics* (Cambridge, Eng.: Cambridge University Press, 1981), p. 191; Jack S. Levy, "Declining Power and the Preventive Motivation for War," *World Politics* 40 (October 1987), pp. 82–107. On the preventive motivation in World War I, see Jack S. Levy, "Preferences, Constraints, and Choices in July 1914," *International Security* 15 (Winter 1990–91), pp. 151–86.

growth, power transitions, and preventive war were important long before the industrial revolution. Several scholars have elaborated on the power-transition model and integrated it into more general theories of world politics. Gilpin has analyzed the general economic, social, and political dynamics contributing to hegemonic wars and transitions in any historical era, and Paul Kennedy has provided a detailed historical analysis of the rise and fall of great powers since 1500. Modelski and Thompson have developed a theory of long cycles of global leadership, global war, and leadership succession in world politics over the last 500 years, based on naval power (combined with air power in the 20th century) and the economic strength that supports it.[27]

IMPLICATIONS FOR THE FUTURE OF WAR

This essay has focused on a particular type of causes of war: the structure of power at the level of the international system, how that power is distributed among the various states in the system, and how that distribution changes over time. Although these structural theories were originally developed to explain the behavior of the great powers in international politics, we should not underestimate their applicability to other states as well. Theories of balance of power and power transition apply not only at the level of the international system but also at the level of regional systems that operate within the larger international system. Thucydides' comment about Sparta's fear of the rising power of Athens applies equally well to Israel's decision to launch a preventive strike against Iraq's nuclear reactor in 1981 in order to block the rising power of Iraq. It applies also to the United States in the Persian Gulf War, in that American concerns about Iraq's development of a biological and nuclear capability and its consequences for the regional balance of power and the security of world oil supplies contributed significantly to its decision to go to war to expel Iraq from Kuwait and in the process destroy much of Iraq's growing military capability.

Balance-of-power calculations also played a central role in the foreign policy decisions of Arab states. Many of these states aligned (diplomatically and economically) with Iraq in the Iran-Iraq War of 1980–88 because they perceived the primary threat to their interests as deriving from Iran and from Iranian efforts to spread its revolutionary doctrines throughout the Persian Gulf region (much like the European great powers formed a military coalition against

---

[27]Thucydides, *History of the Peloponnesian War,* p. 49; Gilpin, *War and Change in World Politics;* Paul Kennedy, *The Rise and Fall of the Great Powers* (New York: Random House, 1987); George Modelski, "The Long Cycle of Global Politics and the Nation-State." *Comparative Studies in Society and History* 20 (April 1978), pp. 214–35; William R. Thompson, *On Global War* (Columbia: University of South Carolina Press, 1988). For a summary and critique of various theories of hegemonic transitions and hegemonic wars, see Jack S. Levy, "Long Cycles, Hegemonic Transitions, and the Long Peace," in Kegley, *The Long Postwar Peace,* pp. 147–76. For recent empirical research on power transition theories, see Jacek Kugler and Douglas Lemke, eds., *Parity and War* (Ann Arbor: University of Michigan Press, 1996).

revolutionary France in 1792). With the end of that war and the growth of Iraqi power, however, all the major Arab states except Jordan (and the PLO) shifted their alignments and joined a military coalition against Iraq in order to contain the growing Iraqi threat, even if it meant that they had implicitly aligned with their hated Israeli enemy.

The politics of regional systems can also be directly affected by shifts in military power at the global level. The end of the Cold War has had a profound impact on the Middle East, for example. If Iraq had invaded Kuwait several years earlier, at a time when Soviet power rivaled that of the United States and when both superpowers competed for influence in the Middle East, it is extremely unlikely that the United States would have intervened with military force to expel Iraq from Kuwait, for fear of a provoking a direct military confrontation with the Soviet Union.[28]

The end of the Cold War and the diplomatic realignment in the Middle East in the aftermath of the Persian Gulf War also contributed significantly to the breakthrough in the peace process involving Israel and the PLO and other Arab states. These developments deprived the PLO of its major sources of economic support, and a weakened PLO needed a dramatic action in order to restore its diminishing influence in Middle Eastern and Palestinian politics. Similarly, Arab states such as Syria could no longer threaten war against Israel in the absence of a superpower backer whose protection might limit their losses in worst-case war scenarios by deterring Israeli escalation. This example is illuminating in another sense, however, because the deterioration of the peace process after the assassination of Israeli Prime Minister Rabin and the rise of the Likud party to power demonstrate the importance of individual and domestic political variables and the limitations of purely structural theories.

One cannot deny that there have been fundamental changes in international politics as a result of the enormous technological, social, economic, and political changes in the world in the past half century in general and the past half decade in particular. At the same time, however, it is clear that the changing structures of power in international and regional systems that have influenced decisions for war or peace so often in the past will continue to play a central role in such decisions in the future.

---

[28]Admittedly, it is less likely that Iraq would have invaded Kuwait under such conditions. A more powerful Soviet Union would have helped ease the desperate economic conditions that largely drove Saddam Hussein's aggressive policies, and Soviet fears of a confrontation with the United States would have led it to put pressures on Saddam for military restraint. In addition, a viable Soviet balancer against what Saddam perceived as the unmitigated and unconstrained hostility of the United States would have further reduced Saddam's sense of desperation about the future. See Lawrence Freedman and Efraim Karsh, *The Gulf Conflict, 1990–91* (Princeton, N.J.: Princeton University Press, 1993).

5

THE OBSOLESCENCE OF MAJOR WAR

John Mueller

Observing the virtual absence of war between the great powers since World War II (alongside its continuation in the same period among the powerful and the weak in the Third World), John Mueller explores the various reasons why the probability of another major or general world war appears to have receded and the consequences of the end of the Cold War for this "imperfect" but prolonged postwar peace. Mueller is professor of political science at the University of Rochester, where he serves as director of the Watson Center for the Study of International Peace and Cooperation. He is author of *Quiet Cataclysm: Reflections on the Recent Transformation of World Politics* (1995).

In discussing the causes of international war, commentators have often found it useful to group theories into what they term levels of analysis. In his classic work, *Man, the State and War,* Kenneth N. Waltz organizes the theories according to whether the cause of war is found in the nature of man, in the nature of the

From Mueller, John (1990), "The Obsolescence of Major War," Bulletin of Peace Proposals, vol. 21(3), pp. 321–28. Reprinted by permission of Sage Publications Ltd.

state, or in the nature of the international state system. More recently Jack Levy, partly setting the issue of human nature to one side, organizes the theories according to whether they stress the systemic level, the nature of state and society, or the decision-making process.[1]

In various ways, these level-of-analysis approaches direct attention away from war itself and toward concerns that may influence the incidence of war. However, war should not be visualized as a sort of recurring outcome that is determined by other conditions, but rather as a phenomenon that has its own qualities and appeals. And over time these appeals can change. In this view, war is merely an idea, an institution, like dueling or slavery, that has been grafted onto human existence. Unlike breathing, eating, or sex, war is not something that is somehow required by the human condition, by the structure of international affairs, or by the forces of history.

Accordingly, war can shrivel up and disappear, and this may come about without any notable change or improvement on any of the level-of-analysis categories. Specifically, war can die out without changing human nature, without modifying the nature of the state or the nation-state, without changing the international system, without creating an effective world government or system of international law, and without improving the competence or moral capacity of political leaders. It can also go away without expanding international trade, interdependence, or communication; without fabricating an effective moral or practical equivalent; without enveloping the earth in democracy or prosperity; without devising ingenious agreements to restrict arms or the arms industry; without reducing the world's considerable store of hate, selfishness, nationalism, and racism; without increasing the amount of love, justice, harmony, cooperation, good will, or inner peace in the world; without establishing security communities; and without doing anything whatever about nuclear weapons.

Not only *can* such a development take place: it *has* been taking place for a century or more, at least within the developed world, once a cauldron of international and civil war. Conflicts of interest are inevitable and continue to persist within the developed world. But the notion that war should be used to resolve them has increasingly been discredited and abandoned there. War is apparently becoming obsolete, at least in the developed world: in an area where war was once often casually seen as beneficial, noble, and glorious, or

---

[1]Kenneth N. Waltz, *Man, the State and War* (New York: Columbia University Press, 1959); Jack S. Levy, "The Causes of War: A Review of Theories and Evidence," in Philip E. Tetlock, Jo L. Husbands, Robert Jervis, Paul C. Stern, and Charles Tilly, eds., *Behavior, Society, and Nuclear War,* vol. 1 (New York: Oxford University Press, 1989), pp. 209–333. See also J. David Singer, "The Levels of Analysis Problem in International Relations," in Klaus Knorr and Sydney Verba, eds., *The International System* (Princeton, NJ: Princeton University Press, 1961), pp. 77–92; and James N. Rosenau, "Pretheories and Theories of Foreign Policy," in R. B. Farrell, ed., *Approaches to Comparative and International Politics* (Evanston, IL: Northwestern University Press, 1966), pp. 27–92.

at least as necessary or inevitable, the conviction has now become widespread that war would be intolerably costly, unwise, futile, and debased.[2]

Some of this may be suggested by the remarkable speed with which the Cold War ended in the late 1980s. The dangers of a major war in the developed world clearly declined remarkably: yet this can hardly be attributed to an improvement in human nature, to the demise of the nation-state, to the rise of a world government, or to a notable improvement in the competence of political leaders.

TWO ANALOGIES: DUELING AND SLAVERY

It may not be obvious that an accepted, time-honored institution that serves an urgent social purpose can become obsolescent and then die out because many people come to find it obnoxious. But the argument here is that something like that has indeed been happening to war in the developed world. To illustrate the dynamic, [consider] two analogies: the processes by which the once-perennial institutions of dueling and slavery have all but vanished from the face of the earth.

Dueling

In some important respects, war in the developed world may be following the example of another violent method for settling disputes, dueling. Up until a century ago dueling was common practice in Europe and the USA among a certain class of young and youngish men who liked to classify themselves as gentlemen.[3] Men of the social set that once dueled still exist, they still get insulted, and they are still concerned about their self-respect and their standing among their peers. But they no longer duel. However, they do not avoid dueling today because they evaluate the option and reject it on cost-benefit grounds. Rather, the option never percolates into their consciousness as something that is available. That is, a form of violence famed and fabled for centuries has now sunk from thought as a viable, conscious possibility.

The Prussian strategist, Carl von Clausewitz, opens his famous 1832 book, *On War,* by observing that "War is nothing but a duel on a larger scale." If war, like dueling, comes to be viewed as a thoroughly undesirable, even ridiculous, policy, and if it can no longer promise gains, or if potential combatants come no longer to value the things it can gain for them, then war can fade away as a coherent possibility even if a truly viable substitute or "moral equivalent" for it were never formulated. Like dueling, it could become unfashionable and then obsolete.

---

[2]For a further development of these arguments, see John Mueller, *Retreat from Doomsday: The Obsolescence of Major War* (New York: Basic Books, 1989).

[3]For other observations of the analogy between war and dueling, see Bernard Brodie, *War and Politics* (New York: Macmillan, 1973), p. 275; Norman Angell, *The Great Illusion* (London: Heinemann, 1914), pp. 202–03; G. P. Gooch, *History of Our Time, 1885–1911* (London: Williams & Norgate, 1911), p. 249; J. E. Cairnes, "International Law," *Fortnightly Review* 2, 1 November 1865, p. 650 n.

Slavery

From the dawn of prehistory until about 1788 slavery, like war, could be found just about everywhere in one form or another, and it flourished in every age. Around 1788, however, the anti-slavery forces began to argue that the institution was repulsive, immoral, and uncivilized: and this sentiment gradually picked up adherents. . . .

. . . The abolitionists were up against an institution that was viable, profitable, and expanding, and moreover one that had been uncritically accepted for thousands—perhaps millions—of years as a natural and inevitable part of human existence. To counter this powerful and time-honored institution, the abolitionists' principal weapon was a novel argument: it had recently occurred to them, they said, that slavery was no longer the way people ought to do things.

As it happened, this was an idea whose time had come. The abolition of slavery required legislative battles, international pressures, economic travail, and, in the United States, a cataclysmic war (but it did *not* require the fabrication of a functional equivalent or the formation of an effective supranational authority). Within a century slavery, and most similar institutions like serfdom, had been all but eradicated from the face of the globe. Slavery became controversial and then obsolete.

War

Dueling and slavery no longer exist as effective institutions; they have largely faded from human experience except as something we read about in books. While their reestablishment is not impossible, they show after a century of neglect no signs of revival. Other once-popular, even once-admirable, institutions in the developed world have been, or are being, eliminated because at some point they began to seem repulsive, immoral, and uncivilized: bearbaiting, bareknuckle fighting, freak shows, casual torture, wanton cruelty to animals, burning heretics, flogging, vendetta, deforming corsetting, laughing at the insane, the death penalty for minor crimes, eunuchism, and public cigarette smoking.

War may well be in the process of joining this list of recently discovered sins and vices. War is not, of course, the same as dueling or slavery. Like war, dueling is an institution for settling disputes; but it was something of a social affectation and it usually involved only matters of "honor," not ones of physical gain. Like war, slavery was nearly universal and an apparently inevitable part of human existence, but it could be eliminated area by area: a country that abolished slavery did not have to worry about what other countries were doing, while a country that would like to abolish war must continue to be concerned about those that have kept it in their repertory.

On the other hand, war has against it not only substantial psychic costs, but also obvious and widespread physical ones. Dueling brought death and destruction but, at least in the first instance, only to a few people who had specifically volunteered to participate. And while slavery may have brought moral destruction, it generally was a considerable economic success.

In some respects then, the fact that war has outlived dueling and slavery is curious. But there are signs that, at least in the developed world, it too has begun to succumb to obsolescence.

TRENDS AGAINST WAR BEFORE 1914

There were a number of trends away from war in the developed world before World War I. Two of these deserve special emphasis.

The Hollandization Phenomenon

As early as 1800 a few once-warlike countries in Europe, like Holland, Switzerland, and Sweden, quietly began to drop out of the war system. While war was still generally accepted as a natural and inevitable phenomenon, these countries found solace (and prosperity) in policies that stressed peace. People who argue that war is inherent in nature and those who see war as a recurring, cyclic phenomenon need to supply an explanation for these countries. Switzerland, for example, has avoided all international war for nearly 200 years. If war is inherent in human nature or if war is some sort of cyclic inevitability, surely the Swiss ought to be roaring for a fight by now.

The Rise of an Organized Peace Movement

While there have been individual war opponents throughout history, the existence of organized groups devoted to abolishing war from the human condition is quite new. The institution of war came under truly organized and concentrated attack only after 1815, and this peace movement did not develop real momentum until the end of the century. . . .

Peace advocates were a noisy gadfly minority by 1900, and they had established a sense of momentum. Their arguments were inescapable, but, for the most part they were rejected and derided by the majority, which still held to the traditional view that war was noble, natural, thrilling, progressive, manly, redemptive, and beneficial. Up until 1914, as Michael Howard has observed, war "was almost universally considered an acceptable, perhaps an inevitable and for many people a desirable way of settling international differences."

THE IMPACT OF WORLD WAR I

The holocaust of World War I turned peace advocates into a pronounced majority in the developed world and destroyed war romanticism. As Arnold Toynbee points out, this war marked the end of a "span of five thousand years during which war had been one of mankind's master institutions." Or, as Evan Luard observes, "the First World War transformed traditional attitudes toward war. For the first time there was an almost universal sense that the deliberate launching of a war could now no longer be justified."

World War I was, of course, horrible. But horror was not invented in 1914. History had already had its Carthages, its Jerichos, its wars of 30 years, of 100 years. Seen in historic context, in fact, World War I does not seem to have been all that unusual in its duration, destructiveness, grimness, political pointlessness, economic consequences, breadth, or intensity. However, it does seem to be unique in that it was the first major war to be preceded by substantial, organized antiwar agitation, and in that, for Europeans, it followed an unprecedentedly peaceful century during which Europeans had begun, perhaps unknowingly, to appreciate the virtues of peace.[4]

Obviously, this change of attitude was not enough to prevent the wars that have taken place since 1918. But the notion that the institution of war, particularly war in the developed world, was repulsive, uncivilized, immoral, and futile—voiced only by minorities before 1914—was an idea whose time had come. It is one that has permeated most of the developed world ever since.

WORLD WAR II

It is possible that enough war spirit still lingered, particularly in Germany, for another war in Europe to be necessary to extinguish it there. But analysis of opinion in the interwar period suggests that war was viewed with about as much horror in Germany as any place on the continent. To a remarkable degree, major war returned to Europe only because of the astoundingly successful machinations of Adolf Hitler, virtually the last European who was willing to risk major war. As Gerhard Weinberg has put it: "Whether any other German leader would indeed have taken the plunge is surely doubtful, and the very warnings Hitler received from some of his generals can only have reinforced his belief in his personal role as the one man able, willing, and even eager to lead Germany and drag the world into war." That is, after World War I a war in Europe could only be brought about through the maniacally dedicated manipulations of an exceptionally lucky and spectacularly skilled entrepreneur; before World War I, any dimwit—e.g. Kaiser Wilhelm—could get into one.

The war in Asia was, of course, developed out of the expansionary policies of distant Japan, a country that neither participated substantially in World War I nor learned its lessons. In World War II, Japan got the message most Europeans had received from World War I.

---

[4]For a further development of this argument, see John Mueller, "Changing Attitudes Toward War: The Impact of World War I," *British Journal of Political Science* 21 (January 1991), pp. 1–28.

THE COLD WAR, THE LONG PEACE, AND NUCLEAR WEAPONS

Since 1945 major war [was] most likely to develop from the Cold War that . . . dominated postwar international history. The hostility of the era mostly [derived] from the Soviet Union's ideological—even romantic—affection for revolution and for revolutionary war. While this ideology [was] expansionistic in some respects, it . . . never visualized major war in the Hitler mode as a remotely sensible tactic.

East and West [were] never . . . close to major war, and it seems unlikely that nuclear weapons [were] important determinants of this—insofar as a military deterrent [was] necessary, the fear of escalation to a war like World War I or II [supplied] it. Even allowing considerably for stupidity, ineptness, miscalculation, and self-deception, a large war, nuclear or otherwise, has never been remotely in the interest of the essentially contented, risk-averse, escalation-anticipating countries that have dominated world affairs since 1945. This is not to deny that nuclear war is appalling to contemplate and mind-concentratingly dramatic, particularly in the speed with which it could bring about massive destruction. Nor is it to deny that decision makers, both in times of crisis and in times of noncrisis, are well aware of how cataclysmic a nuclear war could be. It is simply to stress that the horror of repeating World War II is not all that much less impressive or dramatic, and that leaders essentially content with the status quo will strive to avoid anything that they feel could lead to either calamity. A jump from a 50th-floor window is probably quite a bit more horrible to contemplate than a jump from a 5th-floor one, but anyone who finds life even minimally satisfying is extremely unlikely to do either.[5]

In general the wars that have involved developed countries since World War II have been of two kinds, both of them declining in frequency and relevance. One of these concerns lingering colonial responsibilities and readjustments. Thus the Dutch got involved in (but did not start) a war in Indonesia, the French in Indochina and Algeria, the British in Malaya and the Falklands.

The other kind [related] to the Cold War contest between East and West. The communists . . . generally sought to avoid major war, not so much because they necessarily [found] such wars to be immoral, repulsive, or uncivilized, but because they [found] them futile—dangerous, potentially counter-productive, wildly and absurdly adventurous. However, for decades after 1945 they retained a dutiful affection for what they came to call wars of national liberation—smaller wars around the world designed to further the progressive cause of world revolution. The West [saw] this threat as visceral and as one that [had to] be

---

[5]For a further development of this argument, see John Mueller, "The Essential Irrelevance of Nuclear Weapons: Stability in the Postwar World," *International Security* 13 (No. 2, Fall 1988), pp. 55–79.

countered even at the cost of war if necessary. Wars fought in this context, such as those in Korea and Vietnam, [were] essentially . . . seen [as] preventive—if communism [was] countered there, it [would] not have to be countered later, on more vital, closer turf.

The lesson learned (perhaps overlearned) from the Hitler experience is that aggressive threats must be dealt with by those who abhor war when the threats are still comparatively small and distant; to allow the aggressive force to succeed only brings nearer the day when a larger war must be fought. Thus some countries that abhor war have felt it necessary to wage them in order to prevent wider wars.

CONSEQUENCES OF THE END OF THE COLD WAR

Because of economic crisis and persistent ideological failure, . . . the Cold War . . . ended as the Soviet Union, following the lead of its former ideological soulmate, China, [has abandoned] its quest for ideological expansion, questing instead after prosperity and a quiet, normal international situation. Unless some new form of conflict emerges, war participation by developed countries is likely to continue its decline.

As tensions have lapsed between the two sides in what used to be known as the Cold War, there is a natural tendency for the arms that backed that tension, and in a sense measured it, to atrophy. Both sides have begun what might be called a negative arms race. . . .

The end of the Cold War should also facilitate further expansion of international trade and interdependence. Trade and interdependence may not lead inexorably to peace, but peace does seem to lead to trade, interdependence, and economic growth—or, at any rate, it facilitates them. That is, peace ought to be seen not as a dependent but rather as an independent variable in such considerations. The 1992 economic unity of Europe and the building of a long-envisioned Channel tunnel are the consequences of peace, not its cause.

Left alone, enterprising business people will naturally explore the possibilities of investing in other countries or selling their products there. Averse to disastrous surprises, they are more likely to invest if they are confident that peace will prevail. But for trade to flourish, governments must stay out of the way not only by eschewing war, but also by eschewing measures that unnaturally inhibit trade.

Furthermore, if nations no longer find it sensible to use force or the threat of force in their dealings with one another, it may be neither necessary nor particularly desirable to create an entrenched international government or police force (as opposed to ad hoc arrangements and devices designed to meet specific problems). Indeed, an effective international government could be detrimental to economic growth since, like domestic governments, it could be manipulated to reward the inefficient, coddle the incompetent, and plague the innovative.

WAR IN THE THIRD WORLD

War has not, of course, become fully obsolete. While major war—war among developed countries—seems to be going out of style, war obviously continues to flourish elsewhere. The end of the Cold War suggests that the United States and [Russia], in particular, are likely to involve themselves less in these wars. Moreover, it is possible that the catastrophic Iran-Iraq war [has sobered] people in the Third World about that kind of war. And it does seem that much of the romance has gone out of the concept of violent revolution as Third World countries increasingly turn to the drab, difficult, and unromantic task of economic development.

Thus it is possible that the developed world's aversion to war may eventually infect the rest of the world as well (international war, in fact, has been quite rare in Latin America for a century). But this development is not certain, nor is its pace predictable. As slavery continued to persist in Brazil even after it had been abolished elsewhere, the existence of war in some parts of the world does not refute the observation that it is vanishing, or has vanished, in other parts.

IMPERFECT PEACE

War, even war within the developed world, has not become impossible—nor could it ever do so. When it has seemed necessary, even countries like the United States and Britain, which were among the first to become thoroughly disillusioned with war, have been able to fight wars and to use military force—often with high morale and substantial public support, at least at first. The ability to make war and the knowledge about how to do so can never be fully expunged—nor, for that matter, can the ability or knowledge to institute slavery, eunuchism, crucifixion, or human sacrifice. War is declining as an institution not because it has ceased to be possible or fascinating, but because peoples and leaders in the developed world—where war was once endemic—have increasingly found war to be disgusting, ridiculous, and unwise.

The view presented in this [chapter] is based upon the premise that, in some important respects, war is often taken too seriously. War, it seems, is merely an idea. It is not a trick of fate, a thunderbolt from hell, a natural calamity, or a desperate plot contrivance dreamed up by some sadistic puppeteer on high. If war begins in the minds of men, as the UNESCO charter insists, it can end there as well. Over the centuries, war opponents have been trying to bring this about by discrediting war as an idea; the argument here is that they have been substantially successful at doing so. The long peace since World War II is less a product of recent weaponry than the culmination of a substantial historical process. For the last two or three centuries, major war has gradually moved toward terminal disrepute because of its perceived repulsiveness and futility.

It could also be argued that, to a considerable degree, people have tended to take peace too seriously as well. Peace is merely what emerges when the institution of war is neglected. It does not mean that the world suddenly becomes immersed in those qualities with which the word "peace" is constantly being associated: love, justice, harmony, cooperation, brotherhood, and good will. People still remain contentious and there still remain substantial conflicts of interest. The difference is only that they no longer resort to force to resolve their conflicts, any more than young men today resort to formal dueling to resolve their quarrels. A world at peace would not be perfect, but it would be notably better than the alternative.

6

NUCLEAR MYTHS AND POLITICAL REALITIES

Kenneth N. Waltz

In this essay, Kenneth N. Waltz theorizes about the role that nuclear weapons and the deterrence strategies and doctrines governing their use have played in preventing great-power conflicts from escalating to war. Contrasting the logic of conventional and nuclear weaponry and tracing the history of the doctrines the superpowers have constructed to govern their use, Waltz evaluates why the age of nuclear "overkill" may provide a better foundation for the prevention of war than that afforded by reliance on conventional weapons. Waltz is professor of political science at the University of California, Berkeley, and has served as president of the American Political Science Association. He is the author of *Theory of International Politics* (1979).

Nuclear weapons have been given a bad name. . . . Uneasiness over nuclear weapons and the search for alternative means of security stem in large measure from widespread failure to understand the nature and requirements of deterrence.

From "Nuclear Myths and Political Realities," by Kenneth N. Waltz, *The American Political Science Review*, vol. 84, Sept. 1990. Reprinted by permission. This article has been abridged and references have been deleted.

Not unexpectedly, the language of strategic discourse has deteriorated over the decades. This happens whenever discussion enters the political arena, where words take on meanings and colorations reflecting the preferences of their users. Early in the nuclear era *deterrence* carried its dictionary definition, dissuading someone from an action by frightening that person with the consequences of the action. To deter an adversary from attacking, one need have only a force that can survive a first strike and strike back hard enough to outweigh any gain the aggressor had hoped to realize. Deterrence in its pure form entails no ability to defend; a deterrent strategy promises not to fend off an aggressor but to damage or destroy things the aggressor holds dear. Both defense and deterrence are strategies that a status quo country may follow, hoping to dissuade a state from attacking. They are different strategies designed to accomplish a common end in different ways, using different weapons differently deployed. Wars can be prevented, as they can be caused, in various ways.

Deterrence antedates nuclear weapons, but in a conventional world deterrent threats are problematic. . . . Nuclear weapons purify deterrent strategies by removing elements of defense and war-fighting. Nuclear warheads eliminate the necessity of fighting and remove the possibility of defending, because only a small number of warheads need to reach their targets.

Ironically, as multiplication of missiles increased the ease with which destructive blows can be delivered, the distinction between deterrence and defense began to blur. Early in President Kennedy's administration, Secretary McNamara began to promote a strategy of Flexible Response, which was halfheartedly adopted by NATO in 1967. Flexible Response calls for the ability to meet threats at all levels from irregular warfare to conventional warfare to nuclear warfare. In the 1970s and 1980s more and more emphasis was placed on the need to fight and defend at all levels in order to "deter." The melding of defense, war-fighting, and deterrence overlooks a simple truth about nuclear weapons proclaimed in the title of a book edited by Bernard Brodie in 1946: Nuclear weapons are absolute. Nuclear weapons can carry out their deterrent task no matter what other countries do. If one nuclear power were able to destroy almost all of another's strategic warheads with practical certainty or defend against all but a few strategic warheads coming in, nuclear weapons would not be absolute. But because so much explosive power comes in such small packages, the invulnerability of a sufficient number of warheads is easy to achieve and the delivery of fairly large numbers of warheads impossible to thwart, both now and as far into the future as anyone can see. The absolute quality of nuclear weapons sharply sets a nuclear world off from a conventional one.

WHAT DETERS?

Most discussions of deterrence are based on the belief that deterrence is difficult to achieve. In the Eisenhower years "massive retaliation" was the phrase popularly used to describe the response we would supposedly make to a Soviet Union attack. Deterrence must be difficult if the threat of massive retaliation is required to achieve it. As the Soviet Union's arsenal grew, MAD (mutual assured destruction) became the acronym of choice, thus preserving the notion that deterrence depends on being willing and able to destroy much, if not most, of a country.

That one must be able to destroy a country in order to deter it is an odd notion, though of distinguished lineage. During the 1950s emphasis was put on the *massive* in *massive retaliation*. Beginning in the 1960s the emphasis was put on the *assured destruction* in the doctrine of MAD. Thus viewed, deterrence becomes a monstrous policy, as innumerable critics have charged. One quotation can stand for many others. In a warning to NATO defense ministers that became famous, Henry Kissinger counseled the European allies not to keep "asking us to multiply strategic assurances that we cannot possibly mean or if we do mean, we should not want to execute because if we execute, we risk the destruction of civilization." . . . The notion that the failure of deterrence would lead to national suicide or to mutual annihilation betrays a misunderstanding of both political behavior and nuclear realities.

Introducing the Eisenhower administration's New Look policy in January of 1954, John Foster Dulles gave the impression that aggression anywhere would elicit heavy nuclear retaliation. Just three months later, he sensibly amended the policy. Nuclear deterrence, Dulles and many others quickly came to realize, works not against minor aggression at the periphery, but only against major aggression at the center of international politics. Moreover, to deter major aggression, Dulles now said, "the probable hurt" need only "outbalance the probable gain." . . . Like Brodie before him, Dulles based deterrence on the principle of proportionality: "Let the punishment fit the crime."

What would we expect the United States to do if . . . a major conventional attack [were launched] against vital U.S. interests—say, in Western Europe? Military actions have to be related to an objective. Because of the awesome power of nuclear weapons, the pressure to use them in ways that achieve the objective at hand while doing and suffering a minimum of destruction would be immense. It is preposterous to think that if [an] attack [had broken] through NATO's defenses, the United States would strike thousands of [the aggressor's] military targets or hundreds of [its] cities. Doing so would serve no purpose. Who would want to make a bad situation worse by launching wantonly destructive attacks on a country that can strike back with comparable force, or, for that matter, on a country that could not do so? In the event, we might strike a target or two—military or industrial—chosen to keep casualties low. If the [aggressor] had run the preposterous risk of attacking the center of Europe believing it could escape retaliation, we would thus show them that they were wrong while conveying the idea that more would follow if they persisted. Among countries with abundant nuclear weapons, none can gain an advantage by striking first. The purpose of demonstration shots is simply to remind everyone—should anyone forget—that catastrophe threatens. Some people purport to believe that if a few warheads go off, many will follow. This would seem to be the least likely of all the unlikely possibilities. That no country gains by destroying another's cities and then seeing a comparable number of its own destroyed in return is obvious to everyone.

Despite widespread beliefs to the contrary, deterrence does not depend on destroying cities. Deterrence depends on what one *can* do, not on what one *will* do. What deters is the fact that we can do as much damage to them as we choose, and they to us. The country suffering the retaliatory attack cannot limit the damage done to it; only the retaliator can do that.

With nuclear weapons, countries need threaten to use only a small amount of force. This is so because once the willingness to use a little force is shown, the adversary knows how easily more can be added. This is not true with conventional weapons. Therefore, it is often useful for a country to threaten to use great force if conflict should lead to war. The stance may be intended as a deterrent one, but the ability to carry the threat through is problematic. With conventional weapons, countries tend to emphasize the first phase of war. Striking hard to achieve a quick victory may decrease the cost of war. With nuclear weapons, political leaders worry not about what may happen in the first phase of fighting but about what may happen in the end. As Clausewitz wrote, if war should ever approach the absolute, it would become "imperative . . . not to take the first step without considering what may be the last. . . ."

Since war now approaches the absolute, it is hardly surprising that President Kennedy echoed Clausewitz's words during the Cuban Missile Crisis of 1962. "It isn't the first step that concerns me," he said, "but both sides escalating to the fourth and fifth step—and we don't go to the sixth because there is no one around to do so. . . ." In conventional crises, leaders may sensibly seek one advantage or another. They may bluff by threatening escalatory steps they are in fact unwilling to take. They may try one stratagem or another and run considerable risks. Since none of the parties to the struggle can predict what the outcome will be, they may have good reason to prolong crises, even crises entailing the risk of war. A conventional country enjoying military superiority is tempted to use it before other countries right the military balance. A nuclear country enjoying superiority is reluctant to use it because no one can promise the full success of a disarming first strike. As Henry Kissinger retrospectively said of the Cuban Missile Crisis, the Soviet Union had only "60–70 truly strategic weapons while we had something like 2,000 in missiles and bombs." But, he added, "with some proportion of Soviet delivery vehicles surviving, the Soviet Union could do horrendous damage to the United States." . . . In other words, we could not be sure that our 2,000 weapons would destroy almost all of their 60 or 70. Even with numbers immensely disproportionate, a small force strongly inhibits the use of a large one.

The catastrophe promised by nuclear war contrasts sharply with the extreme difficulty of predicting outcomes among conventional competitors. This makes one wonder about the claimed dependence of deterrence on perceptions and the alleged problem of credibility. In conventional competitions, the comparative qualities of troops, weaponry, strategies, and leaders are difficult to gauge. So complex is the fighting of wars with conventional weapons that their outcomes have been extremely difficult to predict. Wars start more easily because the uncertainties of their outcomes make it easier for the leaders of states to entertain illusions of victory at supportable cost. In contrast, contemplating war when the use of nuclear weapons is possible focuses one's attention not on the probability of victory but on the possibility of annihilation. Because catastrophic outcomes of nuclear exchanges are easy to imagine, leaders of states will shrink in horror from initiating them. With nuclear weapons, stability and peace rest on easy calculations of what one country can do to another. Anyone—political leader or man in the street—can see that catastrophe lurks if events spiral out of control and nuclear warheads begin to fly. The problem of the credibility of deterrence, a big worry in a conventional world, disappears in a nuclear one. . . .

WHY NUCLEAR WEAPONS DOMINATE STRATEGY

Deterrence is easier to contrive than most strategists have believed. With conventional weapons, a number of strategies are available, strategies combining and deploying forces in different ways. Strategies may do more than weapons to determine the outcomes of wars. Nuclear weapons are different; they dominate strategies. As [Bernard Brodie] clearly saw, the effects of nuclear weapons derive not from any particular design for their employment in war but simply from their presence. . . . Indeed, in an important sense, nuclear weapons eliminate strategy. If one thinks of strategies as being designed for defending national objectives or for gaining them by military force and as implying a choice about how major wars will be fought, nuclear weapons make strategy obsolete. Nevertheless, the conviction that the only reliable deterrent force is one able to win a war or at least end up in a better position than the [adversary] is widespread. . . .

NATO policy well [illustrated] the futility of trying to transcend deterrence by fashioning war-fighting strategies. The supposed difficulties of extending deterrence to cover major allies . . . led some to argue [during the Cold War] that we require nuclear superiority, that we need nuclear war-fighting capabilities, and that we must build up our conventional forces. Once the Soviet Union achieved nuclear parity, confidence in our extended deterrent declined in the West. One wonders whether it did in the East. Denis Healey once said that one chance in a hundred that a country will retaliate is enough to deter an adversary, although not enough to reassure an ally. Many have repeated his statement; but none, I believe, has added that reassuring allies is unnecessary militarily and unwise politically. Politically, allies who are unsure of one another's support have reason to work harder for the sake of their own security. Militarily, deterrence requires only that conventional forces be able to defend long enough to determine that an attack is a major one and not merely a foray. For this, a trip wire force as envisioned in the 1950s, with perhaps 50,000 U.S. troops in Europe, would be sufficient. Beyond that, deterrence requires only that forces be invulnerable and that the area protected be of manifestly vital interest. West European countries can be counted on to maintain forces of trip wire capability.

Nuclear weapons strip conventional forces of most of their functions. Bernard Brodie pointed out that in "a total war" the army "might have no function at all." . . . Herman Kahn cited "the claim that in a thermonuclear war it is important to keep the sea lanes open" as an example of the "quaint ideas" still held by the military. . . . Conventional forces have only a narrow role in any confrontation between nuclear states over vital interests, since fighting beyond the trip wire level serves no useful purpose. Enlarging conventional capabilities does nothing to strengthen deterrence. Strategic stalemate does shift military competition to the tactical level. But one must add what is usually omitted: nuclear stalemate limits the use of conventional forces and reduces the extent of the gains one can seek without risking devastation. For decades U.S. policy . . . nevertheless aimed at raising the nuclear threshold in Europe. Stronger conventional forces would presumably have enabled NATO to sustain a longer war in Europe at higher levels of violence. At some moment in a major war, however, one side or the other—or perhaps both—would believe itself to be losing. The temptation to introduce nuclear weapons might then prove irresistable, and they would be fired in the chaos of defeat with little chance of limited and discriminant use. Early use would promise surer control and closer limitation of damage. In a nuclear world a conventional war-fighting strategy would appear to be the worst possible one, more dangerous than a strategy of relying on deterrence.

Attempts to gain escalation dominance, like efforts to raise the nuclear threshold, betray a failure to appreciate the strategic implications of nuclear weapons. Escalation dominance, so it is said, requires a "seamless web of capabilities" up and down "the escalation ladder." Earlier, it had been thought that the credibility of deterrence would be greater if some rungs of the escalation ladder were missing. The inability to fight at some levels would make the threat to use higher levels of force easy to credit. But again, since credibility is not a problem, this scarcely matters militarily. Filling in the missing rungs neither helps nor hurts. Escalation dominance is useful for countries contending with conventional weapons only. Dominance, however, is difficult to achieve in the absence of a decisive weapon. Among nuclear adversaries the question of dominance is pointless because one second-strike force cannot dominate another. Since strategic nuclear weapons will always prevail, the game of escalation dominance cannot be played. Everyone knows that anyone can quickly move to the top rung of the ladder. Because anyone can do so, all of the parties in a serious crisis have an overriding incentive to ask themselves one question: How can we get out of this mess without nuclear warheads exploding? Deescalation, not escalation, becomes the problem that the presence of nuclear weapons forces them to solve.

To gain escalation dominance, if that were imaginable, would require the ability to fight nuclear wars. War-fighting strategies imply that nuclear weapons are not absolute but relative, so that the country with more and better nuclear weapons could in some unspecified way prevail. No one, however, has shown how such a war could be fought. Indeed, Desmond Ball [in 1981] . . . argued that a nuclear war could not be sustained beyond the exchange of strategic warheads numbered not in the hundreds but in the tens. . . . After a small number of exchanges no one would know what was going on or be able to maintain control. Yet nuclear weapons save us from our folly: fanciful strategies are irrelevant because no one will run the appalling risk of testing them.

Deterrence has been faulted for its lack of credibility, its dependence on perceptions, its destructive implications, and its inability to cover interests abroad. The trouble with deterrence, however, lies elsewhere: The trouble with deterrence is that it can be implemented cheaply. The claim that we need a seamless web of capabilities in order to deter does serve one purpose: It keeps military budgets wondrously high. Efforts to fashion a defensive and war-fighting strategy . . . are pointless because deterrence prevails and futile because strategy cannot transcend the military conditions that nuclear weapons create.

NUCLEAR ARMS AND DISARMAMENT

The probability of major war among states having nuclear weapons approaches zero. But the "real war" may, as William James claimed, lie in the preparation for waging it. The logic of deterrence, if followed, circumscribes the causes of "real wars." . . . Nuclear weapons make it possible for a state to limit the size of its strategic forces as long as other states are unable to achieve disarming first-strike capabilities by improving their forces. . . .

Many who urge us to build ever more strategic weapons in effect admit the military irrelevance of additional forces when, as so often, they give political rather than military reasons for doing so; spending less, it is said, would signal weakness of will. Yet militarily, only one perception counts, namely, the perception that a country has second-strike forces. Nuclear weapons make it possible for states to escape the dynamics of arms racing; yet [during the Cold War] the United States and the Soviet Union . . . multiplied their weaponry far beyond the requirements of deterrence. Each . . . obsessively measured its strategic forces against the other's. The arms competition between them [arose] from failure to appreciate the implications of nuclear weapons for military strategy and, no doubt, from internal military and political pressures in both countries.

Many of the obstacles to arms reduction among conventional powers disappear or dwindle among nuclear nations. For the former, the careful comparison of the quantities and qualities of forces is important. Because this is not so with nuclear weapons, the problem of verifying agreements largely disappears. Provisions for verification may be necessary in order to persuade [a legislature] to ratify an agreement, but the possibility of noncompliance is not very worrisome. Agreements that reduce one category of conventional weapons may shift competition to other types of weapons and lead to increases in their numbers and capabilities. Because with nuclear weapons sufficiency is easily defined, there is no military reason for reductions in some weapons to result in increases in others. Conventionally, multiparty agreements are hard to arrive at because each party has to consider how shifting alignments may alter the balance of forces if agreements are reached to reduce them. In a world of second-strike nuclear forces, alliances have little effect on the strategic balance. The Soviet Union's failure to insist that British, French, and Chinese forces be counted in strategic arms negotiations may [have reflected] its appreciation of this point. Finally, conventional powers have to compare weapons of uncertain effectiveness. Arms agreements are difficult to reach because their provisions may bear directly on the prospects for victory or defeat. Because in a nuclear world peace is maintained by the presence of deterrent forces, strategic arms agreements do not have military, but economic and political, significance. They can benefit countries economically and help to improve their relations.

A minority of U.S. military analysts have understood the folly of maintaining more nuclear weapons than deterrence requires. In the [former] Soviet Union, Mikhail Gorbachev and some others . . . put forth the notion of "reasonable sufficiency," defined as having a strategic force roughly equal to ours and able to inflict unacceptable damage in retaliation. [In 1989] Edward Warner [pointed] out that some civilian analysts have gone further, "suggesting that as long as the USSR had a secure second-strike capability that could inflict unacceptable damage, it would not have [had] to be concerned about maintaining approximate numerical parity with U.S. strategic nuclear forces." . . . If leaders in both countries [came] to accept the minority view—and [had they] also [realized] that a deterrent force [would have] greatly [reduced] conventional requirements on central fronts—both countries [could have enjoyed] security at much lower cost.

STRATEGIC DEFENSE

Strategic defenses would radically change the propositions advanced here. The Strategic Defense Initiative, in Reagan's vision, was to provide an area defense that would protect the entire population of the United States. Strategic defenses were to pose an absolute defense against what have been absolute weapons, thus rendering them obsolete. The consequences that would follow from mounting such a defense boggle the mind. That a perfect defense against nuclear weapons could be deployed and sustained is inconceivable.

First, nuclear weapons are small and light; they are easy to move, easy to hide, and easy to deliver in a variety of ways. Even an unimaginably perfect defense against ballistic missiles would fail to negate nuclear weapons. Such a defense would instead put a premium on the other side's ability to deliver nuclear weapons in different ways: firing missiles on depressed trajectories, carrying bombs in suitcases, placing nuclear warheads on freighters to be anchored in American harbors. Indeed, someone has suggested that [a nuclear adversary of the United States] can always hide warheads in bales of marijuana, knowing we cannot keep them from crossing our borders. To have even modestly effective defenses we would, among other things, have to become a police state. We would have to go to extraordinary lengths to police our borders and exercise control within them. Presumably, [a totalitarian state] does these things better than we do. It is impossible to imagine that an area defense can be a success because there are so many ways to thwart it. In no way can we prevent [another nuclear power] from exploding nuclear warheads on or in the United States if it is determined to do so.

Second, let us imagine for a moment that an airtight defense, however defined, is about to be deployed by one country or the other. The closer one country came to deploying such a defense, the harder the other would work to overcome it. When he was secretary of defense, Robert McNamara argued that the appropriate response to a Soviet defensive deployment would be to expand our deterrent force. More recently, Caspar Weinberger and Mikhail Gorbachev . . . made similar statements. Any country deploying a defense effective for a moment cannot expect it to remain so. The ease of delivering nuclear warheads and the destructiveness of small numbers of them make the durability of defenses highly suspect.

The logic of strategic defense is the logic of conventional weaponry. Conventional strategies pit weapons against weapons. That is exactly what a strategic defense would do, thereby recreating the temptations and instabilities that have plagued countries armed only with conventional weapons. If the United States and another nuclear power deploy defensive systems, each will worry—no doubt excessively—about the balance of offensive and defensive capabilities. Each will fear that the other may score an offensive or defensive breakthrough. If one side should do so, it might be tempted to strike in order to exploit its temporary advantage. The dreaded specter of the hair trigger would reappear. Under such circumstances a defensive system would serve as the shield that makes the sword useful. An offensive-defensive race would introduce many uncertainties. A country enjoying a momentary defensive advantage would be tempted to strike in the forlorn hope that its defenses would be able to handle a ragged and reduced response to its first strike. [Great-power rivals] would prepare to launch on warning while obsessively weighing the balance between offensive and defensive forces. . . . Strategic considerations should dominate technical ones. In a nuclear world defensive systems are predictably destabilizing. It would be folly to move from a condition of stable deterrence to one of unstable defense.

CONCLUSION

Nuclear weapons dissuade states from going to war more surely than conventional weapons do. In a conventional world, states going to war can at once believe that they may win and that, should they lose, the price of defeat will be bearable. World Wars I and II called the latter belief into question before atomic bombs were ever dropped. If the United States and [Russia] were now armed only with conventional weapons, the lesson of those wars would be strongly remembered—especially by Russia, since she has suffered more in war than [the United States has]. If the atom had never been split, the United States and [the other great powers] would still have much to fear from each other. The stark opposition of countries of continental size armed with ever-more-destructive conventional weapons would strongly constrain them. Yet in a conventional world even forceful and tragic lessons have proved to be exceedingly difficult for states to learn. Recurrently in modern history one great power or another has looked as though it might become dangerously strong: Louis XIV's and Napolean's France, Wilhelm II's and Hitler's Germany. Each time, an opposing coalition formed, if belatedly, and turned the expansive state back. The lesson would seem to be clear: in international politics, success leads to failure. The excessive accumulation of power by one state or coalition of states elicits the opposition of others. . . .

How can we perpetuate peace without solving the problem of war? This is the question that states with nuclear weapons must constantly answer. Nuclear states continue to compete militarily. With each state tending to its security interests as best it can, war is constantly possible. Although the possibility of war remains, nuclear weapons have drastically reduced the probability of its being fought by the states that have them. Wars that might bring nuclear weapons into play have become extraordinarily hard to start. Over the centuries great powers have fought more wars, and lesser states have fought fewer; the frequency of war has correlated less closely with the attributes of states than with the international standing. Yet because of a profound change in military technology, waging war has more and more become the privilege of poor and weak states. Nuclear weapons have reversed the fates of strong and weak states. Never since the Treaty of Westphalia in 1648, which conventionally marks the beginning of modern history, have great powers enjoyed a longer period of peace than we have known since the Second World War. One can scarcely believe that the presence of nuclear weapons does not greatly help to explain this happy condition.

7

THE CHANGING PROLIFERATION THREAT

John F. Sopko

The spread of armaments to countries throughout the globe and technological innovations that increase their accuracy, transportability, and destructiveness affect substantially the distribution of military power and the prospects for regional and global security. In this essay, John F. Sopko describes the speed and magnitude of these trends, which have increased the threat of proliferation by making weapons of mass destruction and the means of their delivery readily available to rogue states, terrorists, and organized crime. Sopko concludes with warnings about the failure of the international community to recognize the growing danger and its failure to construct programs to control it. Sopko is deputy chief council to U.S. Senator Sam Nunn (D-Georgia) on the Permanent Subcommittee on Investigations.

If you listen, the dead do speak. Perhaps especially in the area of national security, we can learn from the mistakes of those who have gone before us. They warn of tactics that failed to keep pace with technology and strategies that did not change with evolving threats. . . .

From "The Changing Proliferation Threat," by John F. Sopko. Reprinted with permission from *Foreign Policy* 105, Winter 1996–97. Copyright © 1996 by the Carnegie Endowment for International Peace. This essay has been abridged.

Technological advances and new adversaries with new motives have reduced the relevancy and effectiveness of the nonproliferation [strategies] that [were] developed during the Cold War. The Cold War's end and the breakup of the Soviet Union have created new proliferation dangers even as they have reduced others. The familiar balance of nuclear terror that linked the superpowers and their client states for nearly 50 years in a choreographed series of confrontations has given way to a much less predictable situation, where weapons of unthinkable power appear within the grasp of those more willing to use them. Rogue nations and "clientless" states, terrorist groups, religious cults, ethnic minorities, disaffected political groups, and even individuals appear to have joined a new arms race toward mass destruction. The following recent events suggest the new trend . . . . :

• *December 1995.* A man with alleged ties to survivalist groups is charged with attempting to smuggle 130 grams of ricin into the United States for use as a weapon. A small amount of ricin can kill in minutes if ingested, inhaled, or absorbed through the skin. A mere speck of ricin, daubed on the tip of an umbrella, was used by Soviet agents to kill a Bulgarian defector in London in 1978.

• *November 1995.* Chechen rebels threaten to detonate radiological devices in and around Moscow.

• *November 1995.* Jordanian officials seize sophisticated missile guidance systems from dismantled Soviet intercontinental ballistic missiles on their way to Iraq. The following month, similar components are pulled out of the Tigris River by U.N. inspectors.

• *Summer 1995.* Iraqi defectors reveal the extent of Iraq's massive chemical and biological weapons program, which has been in existence since before the Persian Gulf war and includes bombs and missiles capable of carrying anthrax, botulinum, sarin, and VX, the most lethal form of nerve gas.

• *May 1995.* A sometime member of the white-supremacist Aryan Nations organization is arrested in Ohio after ordering freeze-dried bubonic plague bacteria for "research purposes."

• *March 1995.* The Japanese doomsday cult, Aum Shinrikyo, releases deadly sarin nerve gas into the Tokyo subway system at the height of morning rush hour, killing 12 people and hospitalizing more than 5,000.

• *March 1995.* Two members of a militia-style organization called the Minnesota Patriots Council are convicted of planning to use ricin to assassinate federal agents and other federal employees.

• *December 1994.* Prague police seize 2.72 kilograms of weapons-grade highly enriched uranium (HEU) and arrest a Czech, a Russian, and a Byelorussian with ties to the nuclear industry. Later, a Czech police officer is arrested as well. According to Czech authorities, these individuals dealt with suppliers in Russia who claimed they could deliver 40 kilograms of HEU.

• *August 1994.* German authorities seize 363 grams of Pu 239 from a Lufthansa flight arriving in Munich from Moscow. According to German authorities, the material had come from a nuclear facility in Obninsk, and the smugglers had claimed they could supply 11 kilograms of plutonium.

• *May 1994.* The sentencing judge in the World Trade Center case announces that the defendants had placed sodium cyanide in their explosives package with the intent of creating a poisonous cyanide gas cloud.

The kind of threat represented by these and other such incidents and the policy challenges they create call for rapid and serious consideration by . . . national security specialists.

NEW TOOLS FOR TERRORISTS: GAS, BUGS, AND THUGS

The bombings in Oklahoma City and Saudi Arabia, the arrests in Arizona of several members of a fanatic militia group, and the recent conviction of Ramsi Yousef for attempting to simultaneously blow up dozens of U.S. jumbo jets are but examples of the changing face of the proliferation threat.

One notable difference in the proliferation threat is that the actors themselves have changed. The cast of proliferation characters has gradually expanded beyond the initial five nuclear weapons nations and a few outlaw states such as Iran, Iraq, Libya, and North Korea to include regional powers; religious, ethnic, and nationalist groups; other politically disaffected groups and nonstate actors; terrorists; and, possibly, criminal organizations. Few of these actors attracted attention in past analyses of proliferation.

Indeed, even individuals have come to be viewed as potential key actors in what was once a national or state-sponsored affair. The December 1995 attempt by Thomas Lewis Lavy to smuggle 130 grams of ricin across the Canadian border is a case in point: The fact that the man was an alleged white supremacist with alleged ties to survivalist groups, that the quantity of ricin was enough to kill thousands of people, and that U.S. and Canadian authorities believe there was no legitimate reason for him to amass this quantity of ricin raises questions of "mass destruction" not seen in the past. When he was stopped at the Canadian border, Lavy was carrying four guns, 20,000 rounds of ammunition, and several pieces of "survivalist literature," including *The Poisoner's Handbook* and *Silent Death.*

The efforts of another white supremacist to "experiment" with potential weapons of mass destruction (WMD) suggest a trend toward nonstate actors becoming proliferation threats. In this case, Larry Wayne Harris, a former member of the Aryan Nations, successfully ordered three vials of freeze-dried bubonic plague bacteria (*Yersinia pestis*) from the American Type Culture Collection, the world's largest distributor of microorganisms. Harris paid $240 for three vials of a pure strain of bubonic plague that he ordered through the mail. When he was later arrested, Harris claimed that he was working on an antidote for plague and was "concerned about an imminent invasion from Iraq of super–germ-carrying rats."

Organized crime has also become one of the new additions to the proliferation game. Russian and U.S. officials alike—including Russian prime minister Viktor Chernomyrdin, former Russian minister of internal affairs Viktor Yerin, FBI director Louis Freeh, and CIA director John Deutch—have expressed concern that organized crime groups may gain access to poorly secured nuclear weapons and materials in the former Soviet Union. These groups have established smuggling networks and close connections to government officials who reportedly might be willing to provide them with access to nuclear weapons and weapons-grade materials. Most specialists view organized crime in the former USSR in broader terms—as a number of interlocking networks consisting of criminals, politicians, bureaucrats, military personnel, and intelligence and security officers that could easily divert such material without alerting Western intelligence agencies. In that sense, the threat posed by organized crime becomes more immediate.

Some analysts argue that criminal groups are unlikely to smuggle weapons and materials of mass destruction, because they can make more than enough money from traditional activities, and even they believe that these markets are beyond the pale of acceptable behavior. This reasoning is flawed. Organized crime in the former Soviet Union is not monolithic: It has various structures that, though sometimes hierarchical, are generally quite "unorganized." While some groups and individuals may find the smuggling of weapons of mass destruction abhorrent, others do not. History disproves the notion that certain misconduct is taboo even for organized crime syndicates. Money talks louder than ethical strictures. It is worth recalling that it was once a widely held belief in the United States that organized crime would not deal in narcotics.

The second aspect of the changing face of proliferation regards the types of materials involved. Although a massive nuclear missile exchange remains an important concern, the threat . . . has expanded to include crude nuclear devices, chemical and biological weapons, and radiological devices.

At the beginning of the Gulf war, for example, Iraq was capable of producing more than 1,000 tons of chemical agents per year, including nerve and mustard gas. The main chemical production site was equipped with state-of-the-art facilities, as was the biological production site. According to Rolf Ekeus, chairman of the U.N. Special Commission on Iraq (UNSCOM), the full extent of the Iraqi WMD threat was generally unknown until late 1995, when the United States learned, among other things, that Iraq had deployed at least 150 to 200 bombs and 25 warheads filled with anthrax, botulinum, and other toxins. Ekeus noted that most of Iraq's arsenal was produced from dual-use or outdated technologies acquired legally under export laws of the time.

Radiological devices likewise pose a new threat. The CIA . . . has warned that even radioactive waste, when used with a conventional explosive, can become a weapon of mass destruction in an urban environment. Others have pointed out that if a simple radiological device had been used in conjunction with the World Trade Center explosive, large areas of lower Manhattan would still be uninhabitable. A tragedy in Goiana, Brazil, in 1987 demonstrated the extensive consequences of even an inadvertent release from a radiological device. In that instance, two adults unwittingly broke open a cesium source found in an abandoned clinic and allowed children to play with the glowing material found inside. Only 17 grams of cesium powder were released, yet four persons were killed within a few days, 249 others were contaminated. The incident resulted in public hysteria. Thousands of cubic meters of soil had to be removed and decontaminated.

The third aspect of the changing proliferation threat involves the means of delivery, which are no longer limited to traditional methods, such as bombers and sophisticated ballistic missiles. Rather, highly destructive devices can be transported on small trucks, in cargo containers, or even in a lunch box. It is not necessary to possess a large number of battlefield-ready weapons in order to create mass terror. Especially with a chemical or biological device, a crude dispersal system may be enough to kill thousands and cripple a major metropolitan area.

The [U.S.] Congressional Office of Technology Assessment reported in 1993 that a crop-duster carrying a mere 100 kilograms of anthrax spores could deliver a fatal does to up to 3 million residents in the Washington, D.C., metropolitan area. Likewise, tests conducted by the U.S. military in the 1960s in the New York City subway system showed that even a crude dispersal of anthrax spores from the rear compartment of moving trains would claim hundreds of thousands of lives.

Indeed, the delivery system used in Tokyo by the Aum Shinrikyo consisted of plastic bags of sarin punctured by the tips of umbrellas. Although it would never meet military specifications for dissemination purposes, this crude weapon still killed 12 and injured 5,000. Likewise, the plan of an alleged Minnesota terrorist group was simple and, some experts believe, potentially devastating. They hoped to mix ricin with a solvent—to allow its absorption into the bloodstream—and to rub the mixture onto the doorknobs of federal buildings and the door handles and steering wheels of cars. And in Oregon in 1984, followers of cult leader Bhagwan Shree Rajneesh simply sprinkled their homemade salmonella bacteria from a bottle onto the salad bars of various restaurants in order to influence the outcome of a local election, in which several candidates were sect supporters.

The fourth feature of this new threat is the relative ease with which the technical know-how, materials, and equipment to make chemical, biological, and radiological weapons can be acquired. Traditionally, our working assumption has been that only nation-states have the resources and expertise to develop or acquire weapons of mass destruction. Today, it appears, terrorist and other groups or individuals can develop massively destructive capabilities. Plans for making weapons of mass destruction, including nuclear devices, can now be accessed on the Internet, through catalogs, and at the local public library.

The dual-use nature of many of the products used in chemical manufacturing and biotechnology only complicates this problem. The same technologies and organisms that are used to produce pesticides, solvents, vaccines, medicines, and even beer can easily be diverted to produce chemical and biological weapons. Indeed, the ingredients that go into some of the most dangerous chemical weapons can often be found under the kitchen sink or in the garden shed of most suburban households.

Bubonic plague bacteria, deadly viruses, and toxins can either be obtained directly from mail-order catalogs or stolen from laboratories and hospitals. What can be used to kill a man on the battlefield is currently being used by others to cure him in hospitals. For example, highly toxic materials such as ricin, botulinum, and diphtheria toxin, once thought to be devoid of any practical use, are now being used or considered for medical therapies. In fact, approximately 1 million patients per year in the United States and Europe receive botulinum toxin injections as therapy for a variety of diseases. These deadly toxins, as well as the research that supports their use, can easily be accessed by would-be proliferants or terrorists without attracting the attention of most intelligence sources.

Larry Wayne Harris' success in obtaining bubonic plague bacteria in 1995 was possible because at that time the only internal control on the purchase of human pathogens imposed by the American Type Culture Collection, a clearinghouse for microbiological samples, was to require that the purchaser provide a copy of the letterhead of the organization that was ultimately responsible for the shipment. Harris did so by fax. It was accidental that Harris was even arrested. His repeated calls concerning the delay in the delivery aroused suspicions. Ironically, at the time of his arrest there was no criminal penalty for the possession of bubonic plague or other more dangerous pathogens such as anthrax, ricin, and botulinum toxins; only the weaponized versions of such materials violated federal criminal law. Prosecutors were forced to charge Harris with wire and mail fraud for false claims he made about the ultimate recipient of the bacteria. He subsequently pleaded guilty to one count and was sentenced to probation.

Weapons-grade uranium and plutonium are still beyond the reach of most proliferants and terrorists, but the disintegration of the Soviet Union made accessing these materials and sophisticated nuclear know-how far easier than in the past. Despite Western efforts to address these problems, large surpluses of weapons- and bomb-grade material stockpiles still remain poorly protected. In addition, some of the world's most highly trained scientists still suffer economically, and they may be induced to work for proliferants if the price is right. One Russian military prosecutor who was investigating a spate of diversions from Russian naval facilities stated that "potatoes were guarded better" than weapons-usable nuclear fuel.

Equally disconcerting is the overwhelming evidence that the governments of the Soviet successor states do not even know how much weapons-grade material they are supposed to have. Senior Russian and Ukrainian officials have admitted that they do not know how much is located at their civilian facilities; that their inventories were kept in terms of "ruble value," not weight; and that inventories may be over- or understated by a matter of tons. Russian nuclear inspectors have revealed that there have been instances when they have opened sealed containers purportedly holding nuclear material only to find them empty. It was not unusual in the Soviet era, Russian officials explained, for nuclear facility managers to withhold some nuclear material from their official accounting system. By withholding excess material, managers could, if necessary at a later time, compensate for any shortfalls in their production quotas. As a result, many nuclear facilities in the former Soviet Union may have large, unaccounted-for caches of nuclear materials. As one former Soviet nuclear regulator wryly explained, "what's never been 'counted' can never be 'missed.' "

Serious customers are attempting to link up with this potential proliferation supermarket. That few diversion cases have been discovered to date may not indicate that the problem is small so much as the fact that our ability to apprehend these smugglers remains weak. The 1996 investigations subcommittee hearings held by Senator Sam Nunn documented that Iran, Iraq, and other countries have sought such materials and have attempted to recruit nuclear specialists and advanced-weapons designers. Investigators produced a copy of an advertisement that was confirmed by U.S. officials as having been circulated in the Middle East in 1993 by the Hong Kong Sun Shine Industrial Company. The company claimed it had Chinese weapons for sale, including rockets, amphibious tanks, and middle- and short-range guided missiles. The advertisement also stated that "we have detailed files of hundreds of former Soviet Union experts in the field of rocket, missile, and nuclear weapons. These weapons experts are willing to work in a country which needs their skills and can offer reasonable pay."

Finally, the motivation for using these weapons of mass destruction also seems to have changed. New Proliferants do not necessarily acquire such weapons to deter aggressors; they more likely acquire them to use them. Terrorist attacks at Lockerbie, the World Trade Center, Tokyo, and Oklahoma City, as well as the Cali cartel's destruction of an airliner over Colombia, demonstrate that religious, ethnic, nationalist, criminal, or simply politically disaffected groups have become more aggressive in seeking to further their aims by using weapons that cause large-scale casualties.

For years it was thought that terrorist groups imposed some self-restraint. As espoused by terrorism experts, terrorists or their state sponsors did not want to cause too many casualties, as [that] would destroy sympathy and support for their cause. By contrast, the new terrorists—whether religious, political, or individual—appear to care little for garnering public sympathy or support. They are more interested in the "biggest bang for their buck." Experts such as retired ambassador Morris Busby, the former counterterrorism coordinator for the U.S. government, have warned that, for the foreseeable future, rogue states and subnational groups may be inclined to use weapons of mass destruction solely to punish America. They may want to inflict significant loss of life and property damage. The World Trade Center bombing as well as Ramsi Yousef's plan to destroy dozens of jumbo jets over the Pacific may be evidence of this trend.

THE AUM SHINRIKYO: SHIVA MEETS SARIN

One of the most telling illustrations of the changing proliferation threat is provided by the Aum Shinrikyo. A nonstate actor, in this case a Japanese Buddhist sect, easily acquired the technology and know-how to develop and use weapons of mass destruction. Their purpose was to bring about their version of Armageddon. This one group combined the religious zealotry of the Branch Dividians, the antigovernmental agenda of the U.S. militia movement, and the technical know-how of Doctor Strangelove. It was a deadly mix.

On the morning of March 20, 1995, the Aum attempted to murder tens of thousands of people in Tokyo; their goal was to create unimaginable disorder and chaos. At the height of the morning rush hour, several members of the cult placed 11 sarin-filled bags wrapped in newspapers on five subway trains. The attack targeted a station in the heart of the city that served major agencies of the Japanese government. In all, 15 stations and three separate subway lines were affected by the dispersal of the sarin. Twelve people were killed and more than 5,000 were hospitalized. With this act, members of the Aum Shinrikyo gained the distinction of becoming the first people, other than a nation during wartime, to use chemical weapons on a major scale. The act also signaled that the world had crossed into a new era of history, marked by greater militarization and technical sophistication on the part of terrorists.

Some observers believe that the Aum is an aberration and that its Tokyo attack was an isolated incident unlikely to be repeated. But others believe that the incident illustrates a fundamental change in the proliferation threat: the ease with which such groups can acquire and deploy WMD capabilities undetected. The Aum recruited scientists and technical experts in Japan, Russia, and elsewhere in order to develop and acquire weapons of mass destruction. Ultimately, they boasted more than 30,000 members in Russia alone—more than in Japan. They actively sought equipment and technologies in Russia, including chemical weapons and nuclear warheads. They purchased property to mine uranium and test chemical weapons in Australia.

Beginning in 1987, the Aum also had an active purchasing program in the United States to acquire materials relevant to their WMD programs—including air-filtration equipment, molecular modeling software, sophisticated lasers, and other high-tech necessities. The group's activities did not arouse suspicion in the United States because most of its purchases were dual-use technologies requiring no special export licenses or government approvals. Individually, many of the purchases appeared benign—if unusual for a religious sect. Only after the 1995 Tokyo subway attack did these purchases reveal a more deadly purpose.

The Aum constructed its own chemical manufacturing complex under the guise of producing fertilizer. It produced chemical weapons, including toxic chemical agents such as sarin, VX, phosgene, and sodium cyanide. These substances were successfully deployed a year before the 1995 Tokyo subway incident. In June 1994, in an attempt to kill three judges who were presiding over a civil trial against them, the Aum sprayed an apartment complex in Matsumoto, Japan, with sarin. Although the judges fell ill as a result of the attack, they survived; seven other residents of the complex died, however, and more than 500 were injured.

The Aum's deadly practices did not end in Tokyo. On two occasions following the subway attack, the Aum attempted to release hydrogen cyanide gas in Tokyo. These attempts were unsuccessful, although one device was discovered and disarmed just seconds before it would have dispersed its deadly gas into a crowded subway station in Tokyo.

The Aum also attempted to develop a biological weapons program, again under the guise of a legitimate purpose—in this case, the production of herbal medicines, vitamins, and teas. The Nunn investigation revealed a sustained research effort by the Aum to manufacture biological agents, including the ebola virus, anthrax, and the botulinum toxin, for weapons use. Japanese authorities have confirmed the Aum's acquisition of these substances and some details of its weapons program. Several Aum facilities contained biological materials and dual-use equipment that could be used to manufacture such agents. One facility, for example, contained preserved yeast, freeze-drying equipment, large quantities of the medium used for cultivating bacteria, incubators, and liquid nitrogen containers in which to preserve cells.

Aum scientists also experimented with the genetic engineering of anthrax bacteria before the Tokyo incident and the cloning of anthrax bacteria into other bacilli. The subcommittee discovered that the Aum tested dispersal techniques on at least three occasions between 1990 and 1995 to assess the effectiveness of their toxins on humans. On one occasion, the Aum tried unsuccessfully to disseminate anthrax from the top floor of its headquarters in Tokyo over a period of eight hours. In all, the Aum conducted at least three biological and five chemical attacks.

Could it happen again? Could another nonstate group, whether religious or political, quietly develop WMD capabilities and then launch an attack on an unsuspecting urban population? Some say it has already happened here in the United States. U.S. District Court judge Kevin Duffy, the sentencing judge in the World Trade Center bombing case, stated that he was certain the defendants had laced their truck bomb with deadly sodium cyanide in an attempt to generate cyanide gas. "Thank God the sodium cyanide burned instead of vaporizing . . . [or] everybody in the north tower would have been killed," he said.

. . . [Efforts] to respond to these new challenges will need to overcome conceptual, bureaucratic, intergovernmental, and tactical problems. Old ways of thinking coupled with bureaucratic and jurisdictional barriers and difficulties in working with foreign governments all hamper [the] ability to address these new threats effectively.

Conceptually, traditional Cold War approaches to nonproliferation do little to deter groups or individuals bent on procuring crude weapons of mass destruction. Such approaches to arms control, for example, have for the most part assumed large state efforts with detectable weapons-production and other manufacturing programs. Additional methods of keeping proliferation in check include export controls, sanctions, treaties, and deterrence efforts—none of which may be effective against nonstate actors. . . .

Traditional arms control measures assume that the threat of retaliation will act as a deterrent. The public threat of massive retaliation may have deterred Iraq from using its CBW arsenal on coalition forces. Yet retaliation is only useful as a deterrent if responsibility for an attack can be assigned. Unlike ballistic missiles, the launching of which is more easily observed, the alternative delivery methods for deploying biological and chemical weapons usually leave few clues to identify who is responsible. Likewise, past assumptions that those in possession of weapons of mass destruction are rational, informed opponents who calculate the risks and benefits before using such force do not apply when these groups are driven by "divine intervention," messianic leadership, or suicidal instincts. As one FBI terrorist specialist noted, "it is extremely difficult to deal with someone not playing with a full deck of cards."

Many in the U.S. government either do not believe that there is a new proliferation threat or consider it a low priority. . . . [And] observers in and out of government disagree on how to define the problem. Previously distinct issues— proliferation, terrorism, arms control, and organized crime—are now merging; the roles of organized crime and foreign corruption are especially neglected by most policy analysts who work on the proliferation issue. . . .

Today, the initial challenge is to develop a framework that will aid in the analysis of these new national security threats. Government officials and members of the nonproliferation community must intensify their focus on the various aspects of proliferation, including international terrorism, the leakage of nuclear and other advanced arms and materials from the former Soviet Union, the foreign policy implications of organized crime, the motives of various religious cults, and so forth. Equally important, funding commensurate with the threat must be directed to those agencies that are charged with defending [targets] from the myriad aspects of this new threat. . . .

A thorough assessment of these new security threats, similar to those that resulted in the Manhattan Project and the Marshall Plan, should be conducted not only by the "usual suspects" but by government bodies that traditionally have not collaborated closely on these issues. The defense, law enforcement, intelligence, health, and foreign policy agencies should participate, as should the nongovernmental community. Smaller-scale, piecemeal reviews have occurred in recent panels on intelligence and defense, but what is needed is a [thorough] analysis with a broad mandate for addressing [the] national security challenges into the next century. . . .

Of perhaps greatest importance is the need to encourage informed discussion among the public at large regarding these new threats and how to respond soberly and effectively. . . . In the past, government officials, scientists, and journalists have been torn about what to disseminate and what to withhold. Would publicizing information sow unnecessary fear or provide important knowledge to terrorists? Or is public ignorance on these issues even worse? Some kind of understanding must be reached as to what is important and what is unnecessary to disseminate. For the public must be able to hold officials accountable, take part in the debate over the use of resources to combat these threats and, ultimately, respond to possible attacks in a productive way. . . .

8

POSTMODERN
TERRORISM

Walter Laqueur

In this essay, Walter Laqueur examines the nature of the "terrorist menace" of our time. With terrorism representing a relatively successful strategy for many political actors (including some national governments), and the global environment providing unprecedented opportunities for terrorist activities, much of the global political agenda has become dominated by the search for ways to confront this threatening practice. Here, the author defines the essence of terrorism and predicts the new rules by which future terrorists will play the old game of terrorism, including reliance on new weapons and a willingness to use them more indiscriminately. In the postmodern age, state-sponsored terrorism is predicted to replace warfare, and with the destructive power of terrorism rising the most advanced societies are becoming the most vulnerable. Laqueur is Chairman of the International Research Council at the Center for Strategic and International Studies in Washington, D.C., and has recently authored *Fascism: Past, Present, and Future* (1996) and *The End of the Century* (1996).

NEW RULES FOR AN OLD GAME

As the 19th century ended, it seemed no one was safe from terrorist attack. In 1894 an Italian anarchist assassinated French President Sadi Carnot. In 1897 anarchists fatally stabbed Empress Elizabeth of Austria and killed Antonio Cánovas, the Spanish prime minister. In 1900 Umberto I, the Italian king, fell in yet another anarchist attack; in 1901 an American anarchist killed William McKinley, president of the United States. Terrorism became the leading preoccupation of politicians, police chiefs, journalists, and writers from Dostoevsky to Henry James. If in the year 1900 the leaders of the main industrial powers had assembled, most of them would have insisted on giving terrorism top priority on their agenda, as President Clinton did at the Group of Seven meeting after the June bombing of the U.S. military compound in Dhahran, Saudi Arabia.

From this perspective the recent upsurge of terrorist activity is not particularly threatening. According to the State Department's annual report on the subject, fewer people died [in 1995] in incidents of international terrorism (165) than the year before (314). Such figures, however, are almost meaningless, because of both the incidents they disregard and those they count. Current definitions of terrorism fail to capture the magnitude of the problem worldwide.

Terrorism has been defined as the substate application of violence or threatened violence intended to sow panic in a society, to weaken or even overthrow the incumbents, and to bring about political change. It shades on occasion into guerrilla warfare (although unlike guerrillas, terrorists are unable or unwilling to take or hold territory) and even a substitute for war between states. In its long history terrorism has appeared in many guises; today society faces not one terrorism but many terrorisms.

Since 1900, terrorists' motivation, strategy, and weapons have changed to some extent. The anarchists and the left-wing terrorist groups that succeeded them, down through the Red Armies that operated in Germany, Italy, and Japan in the 1970s, have vanished; if anything, the initiative has passed to the extreme right. Most international and domestic terrorism these days, however, is neither left nor right, but ethnic-separatist in inspiration. Ethnic terrorists have more staying power than ideologically motivated ones, since they draw on a larger reservoir of public support.

The greatest change in recent decades is that terrorism is by no means militants' only strategy. The many-branched Muslim Brotherhood, the Palestinian Hamas, the Irish Republican Army (IRA), the Kurdish extremists in Turkey and Iraq, the Tamil Tigers of Sri Lanka, the Basque Homeland and Liberty (ETA) movement in Spain, and many other groups that have sprung up in this century have had political as well as terrorist wings from the beginning. The political arm provides social services and education, runs businesses, and contests elections, while the "military wing" engages in ambushes and assassinations. Such division of labor has advantages: the political leadership can publicly disassociate itself when the terrorists commit a particularly outrageous act or something goes wrong. The claimed lack of control can be quite real because the armed wing tends to become independent; the men and women with the guns and bombs often lose sight of the movement's wider aims and may end up doing more harm than good.

Terrorist operations have also changed somewhat. Airline hijackings have become rare, since hijacked planes cannot stay in the air forever and few countries today are willing to let them land, thereby incurring the stigma of openly supporting terrorism. Terrorists, too, saw diminishing returns on hijackings. The trend now seems to be away from attacking specific targets like the other side's officials and toward more indiscriminate killing. Furthermore, the dividing line between urban terrorism and other tactics has become less distinct, while the line between politically motivated terrorism and the operation of national and international crime syndicates is often impossible for outsiders to discern in the former Soviet Union, Latin America, and other parts of the world. But there is one fundamental difference between international crime and terrorism: mafias have no interest in overthrowing the government and decisively weakening society; in fact, they have a vested interest in a prosperous economy.

Misapprehensions, not only semantic, surround the various forms of political violence. A terrorist is not a guerrilla, strictly speaking. There are no longer any guerrillas engaging in Maoist-style liberation of territories that become the base of a counter-society and a regular army fighting the central government—except perhaps in remote places like Afghanistan, the Philippines, and Sri Lanka. The term "guerrilla" has had a long life partly because terrorists prefer the label, for its more positive connotations. It also persists because governments and media in other countries do not wish to offend terrorists by calling them terrorists. The French and British press would not dream of referring to their countries' native terrorists by any other name but call terrorists in other nations militants, activists, national liberation fighters, or even "gun persons."

The belief has gained ground that terrorist missions by volunteers bent on committing suicide constitute a radical new departure, dangerous because they are impossible to prevent. But that is a myth, like the many others in which terrorism has always been shrouded. The bomber willing and indeed eager to blow himself up has appeared in all eras and cultural traditions, espousing politics ranging from the leftism of the Baader-Meinhof Gang in 1970s Germany to rightist extremism. When the Japanese military wanted kamikaze pilots at the end of World War II, thousands of volunteers rushed to offer themselves. The young Arab bombers on Jerusalem buses looking to be rewarded by the virgins in Paradise are a link in an old chain.

State-sponsored terrorism has not disappeared. Terrorists can no longer count on the Soviet Union and its Eastern European allies, but some Middle Eastern and North African countries still provide support. Tehran and Tripoli, however, are less eager to argue that they have a divine right to engage in terrorist operations outside their borders; the 1986 U.S. air strike against Libya and the various boycotts against Libya and Iran had an effect. No government today boasts about surrogate warfare it instigates and backs.

On the other hand, Sudan, without fanfare, has become for terrorists what the Barbary Coast was for pirates of another age: a safe haven. Politically isolated and presiding over a disastrous economy, the military government in Khartoum, backed by Muslim leaders, believes that no one wants to become involved in Sudan and thus it can get away with lending support to terrorists from many nations. Such confidence is justified so long as terrorism is only a nuisance. But if it becomes more than that, the rules of the game change, and both terrorists and their protectors come under great pressure.

OPPORTUNITIES IN TERRORISM

History shows that terrorism more often than not has little political impact, and that when it has an effect it is often the opposite of the one desired. Terrorism in the 1980s and 1990s is no exception. The 1991 assassination of Rajaiv Gandhi as he campaigned to retake the prime ministership neither hastened nor inhibited the decline of India's Congress Party. Hamas' and Hezbollah's stepped-up terrorism in Israel undoubtedly influenced the outcome of Israeli elections in May, but while it achieved its immediate objective of setting back the peace process on which Palestine Authority President Yasir Arafat has gambled his future, is a hard-line Likud government really in these groups' interests? On the other side, Yagal Amir, the right-wing orthodox Jewish student who assassinated Prime Minister Yitzhak Rabin [in 1995] because he disapproved of the peace agreement with the Palestinians, might well have helped elect Rabin's dovish second-in-command, Shimon Peres, to a full term had the Muslim terrorists not made Israeli security an issue again.

Terrorists caused disruption and destabilization in other parts of the world, such as Sri Lanka, where economic decline has accompanied the war between the government and the Tamil Tigers. But in Israel and in Spain, where Basque extremists have been staging attacks for decades, terrorism has had no effect on the economy. Even in Algeria, where terrorism has exacted the highest toll in human lives, Muslim extremists have made little headway since 1992–93, when many predicted the demise of the unpopular military regime.

Some argue that terrorism must be effective because certain terrorist leaders have become president or prime minister of their country. In those cases, however, the terrorists had first forsworn violence and adjusted to the political process. Finally, the common wisdom holds that terrorism can spark a war or, at least, prevent peace. That is true, but only where there is much inflammable material: as in Sarajevo in 1914, [or] in the Middle East and elsewhere today. Nor can one ever say with certainty that the conflagration would not have occurred sooner or later in any case.

Nevertheless, terrorism's prospects, often overrated by the media, the public, and some politicians, are improving as its destructive potential increases. This has to do both with the rise of groups and individuals that practice or might take up terrorism and with the weapons available to them. The past few decades have witnessed the birth of dozens of aggressive movements espousing varieties of nationalism, religious fundamentalism, fascism, and apocalyptic millenarianism, from Hindu nationalists in India to neofascists in Europe and the developing world to the Branch Davidian cult of Waco, Texas. The earlier fascists believed in military aggression and engaged in a huge military buildup, but such a strategy has become too expensive even for superpowers. Now, mail-order catalogs tempt militants with readily available, far cheaper, unconventional as well as conventional weapons—the poor man's nuclear bomb, Iranian President Ali Akbar Hashemi Rafsanjani called them.

In addition to nuclear arms, the weapons of mass destruction include biological agents and man-made chemical compounds that attack the nervous system, skin, or blood. Governments have engaged in the production of chemical weapons for almost a century and in the production of nuclear and biological weapons for many decades, during which time proliferation has been continuous and access ever easier. The means of delivery—ballistic missiles, cruise missiles, and aerosols—have also become far more effective. While in the past missiles were deployed only in wars between states, recently they have played a role in civil wars in Afghanistan and Yemen. Use by terrorist groups would be but one step further.

Until the 1970s most observers believed that stolen nuclear material constituted the greatest threat in the escalation of terrorist weapons, but many now think the danger could lie elsewhere. An April 1996 Defense Department report says that "most terrorist groups do not have the financial and technical resources to acquire nuclear weapons but could gather materials to make radiological dispersion devices and some biological and chemical agents." Some groups have state sponsors that possess or can obtain weapons of the latter three types. Terrorist groups themselves have investigated the use of poisons since the 19th century. The Aum Shinrikyo cult staged a poison gas attack in March 1995 in the Tokyo subway; exposure to the nerve gas sarin killed 10 people and injured 5,000. Other, more amateurish attempts in the United States and abroad to experiment with chemical substance and biological agents for use in terrorism have involved the toxin that cause botulism, the poisonous protein rycin (twice), sarin (twice), bubonic plague bacteria, typhoid bacteria, hydrogen cyanide, vx (another nerve gas), and possibly the Ebola virus.

TO USE OR NOT TO USE?

If terrorists have used chemical weapons only once and nuclear material never, to some extent the reasons are technical. The scientific literature is replete with the technical problems inherent in the production, manufacture, storage, and delivery of each of the three classes of unconventional weapons.

The manufacture of nuclear weapons is not that simple, nor is delivery to their target. Nuclear material, of which a limited supply exists, is monitored by the U.N.-affiliated International Atomic Energy Agency. Only governments can legally procure it, so that even in this age of proliferation investigators could trace those abetting nuclear terrorists without great difficulty. Monitoring can overlook a more primitive nuclear weapon: nonfissile but radioactive nuclear material. Iranian agents in Turkey, Kazakhstan, and elsewhere are known to have tried to buy such material originating in the former Soviet Union.

Chemical agents are much easier to produce or obtain but not so easy to keep safely in stable condition, and their dispersal depends largely on climatic factors. The terrorists behind [the 1995] attack in Tokyo chose a convenient target where crowds of people gather, but their sarin was apparently dilute. The biological agents are far and away the most dangerous: they could kill hundreds of thousands where chemicals might kill only thousands. They are relatively easy to procure, but storage and dispersal are even trickier than for nerve gases. The risk of contamination for the people handling them is high, and many of the most lethal bacteria and spores do not survive well outside the laboratory. Aum Shinrikyo reportedly released anthrax bacteria—among the most toxic agents known—on two occasions from a building in Tokyo without harming anyone.

Given the technical difficulties, terrorists are probably less likely to use nuclear devices than chemical weapons, and least likely to attempt to use biological weapons. But difficulties could be overcome, and the choice of unconventional weapons will in the end come down to the specialties of the terrorists and their access to deadly substances.

The political arguments for shunning unconventional weapons are equally weighty. The risk of detection and subsequent severe retaliation or punishment is great, and while this may not deter terrorists it may put off their sponsors and suppliers. Terrorists eager to use weapons of mass destruction may alienate at least some supporters, not so much because the dissenters hate the enemy less or have greater moral qualms but because they think the use of such violence counterproductive. Unconventional weapon strikes could render whole regions uninhabitable for long periods. Use of biological arms poses the additional risk of an uncontrollable epidemic. And while terrorism seems to be tending toward more indiscriminate killing and mayhem, terrorists may draw the line at weapons of superviolence likely to harm both foes and large numbers of relatives and friends—say, Kurds in Turkey, Tamils in Sri Lanka, or Arabs in Israel.

Furthermore, traditional terrorism rests on the heroic gesture, on the willingness to sacrifice one's own life as proof of one's idealism. Obviously there is not much heroism in spreading botulism or anthrax. Since most terrorist groups are as interested in publicity as in violence, and as publicity for a mass poisoning or nuclear bombing would be far more unfavorable than for a focused conventional attack, only terrorists who do not care about publicity will even consider the applications of unconventional weapons.

Broadly speaking, terrorists will not engage in overkill if their traditional weapons—the submachine gun and the conventional bomb—are sufficient to continue the struggle and achieve their aims. But the decision to use terrorist violence is not always a rational one; if it were, there would be much less terrorism, since terrorist activity seldom achieves its aims. What if, after years of armed struggle and the loss of many of their militants, terrorist groups see no progress? Despair could lead to giving up the armed struggle, or to suicide. But it might also lead to a last desperate attempt to defeat the hated enemy by arms not tried before. As one of Racine's heroes said of himself, their "only hope lies in their despair."

APOCALYPSE SOON

Terrorist groups traditionally contain strong quasi-religious, fanatical elements, for only total certainty of belief (or total moral relativism) provides justification for taking lives. That element was strong among the prerevolutionary Russian terrorists and the Romanian fascists of the Iron Guard in the 1930s, as it is among today's Tamil Tigers. Fanatical Muslims consider the killing of the enemies of God a religious commandment, and believe that the secularists at home as well as the State of Israel will be annihilated because it is Allah's will. Aum Shinrikyo doctrine held that murder could help both victim and murderer to salvation. Sectarian fanaticism has surged during the past decade, and in general, the smaller the group, the more fanatical.

As humankind approaches the end of the second millennium of the Christian era, apocalyptic movements are on the rise. The belief in the impending end of the world is probably as old as history, but for reasons not entirely clear, sects and movements preaching the end of the world gain influence toward the end of a century, and all the more at the close of a millennium. Most of the preachers of doom do not advocate violence, and some even herald a renaissance, the birth of a new kind of man and woman. Others, however, believe that the sooner the reign of the Antichrist is established, the sooner this corrupt world will be destroyed and the new heaven and earth foreseen by St. John in the Book of Revelation, Nostradamus, and a host of other prophets will be realized.

Extreme millenarians would like to give history a push, helping create world-ending havoc replete with universal war, famine, pestilence, and other scourges. It is possible that members of certain Christian and Jewish sects that believe in Armageddon or Gog and Magog or the Muslims and Buddhists who harbor related extreme beliefs could attempt to play out a doomsday scenario. A small group of Israeli extremists, for instance, firmly believes that blowing up Temple Mount in Jerusalem would bring about a final (religious) war and the beginning of redemption with the coming of the Kingdom of God. The visions of Shoko

Asahara, the charismatic leader of Aum Shinrikyo, grew increasingly apocalyptic, and David Koresh proclaimed the Last Day's arrival in the Branch Davidians' 1994 confrontation with Bureau of Alcohol, Tobacco, and Firearms agents.

Those who subscribe to such beliefs number in the hundreds of thousands and perhaps millions. They have their own subcultures, produce books and CDs by the thousands, and build temples and communities of whose existence most of their contemporaries are unaware. They have substantial financial means at their disposal. Although the more extreme apocalyptic groups are potentially terrorist, intelligence services have generally overlooked their activities; hence the shock over the subway attack in Tokyo and Rabin's assassination, to name but two recent events.

Apocalyptic elements crop up in contemporary intellectual fashions and extremist politics as well. For instance, extreme environmentalists, particularly the so-called restoration ecologists, believe that environmental disasters will destroy civilization as we know it—no loss, in their view—and regard the vast majority of human beings as expendable. From such beliefs and values it is not a large step to engaging in acts of terrorism to expedite the process. If the eradication of smallpox upset ecosystems, why not restore the balance by bringing back the virus? The motto of *Chaos International,* one of many journals in this field, is a quotation from Hassan I Sabbah, the master of the Assassins, a medieval sect whose members killed Crusaders and others in a "religious" ecstasy; everything is permitted, the master says. The premodern world and postmodernism meet at this point.

FUTURE SHOCK

Scanning the contemporary scene, one encounters a bewildering multiplicity of terrorist and potentially terrorist groups and sects. The practitioners of terrorism as we have known it to this point were nationalists and anarchists, extremists of the left and the right. But the new age has brought new inspiration for the users of violence along with the old.

In the past, terrorism was almost always the province of groups of militants that had the backing of political forces like the Irish and Russian social revolutionary movements of 1900. In the future, terrorists will be individuals or like-minded people working in very small groups, on the pattern of the technology-hating Unabomber, who apparently worked alone sending out parcel bombs over two decades, or the perpetrators of the 1995 bombing of the federal building in Oklahoma City. An individual may possess the technical competence to steal, buy, or manufacture the weapons he or she needs for a terrorist purpose; he or she may or may not require help from one or two others in delivering these weapons to the designated target. The ideologies such individuals and mini-groups espouse are likely to be even more aberrant than those of larger groups.

And terrorists working alone or in very small groups will be more difficult to detect unless they make a major mistake or are discovered by accident.

Thus at one end of the scale, the lone terrorist has appeared, and at the other, state-sponsored terrorism is quietly flourishing in these days when wars of aggression have become too expensive and too risky. As the century draws to a close, terrorism is becoming the substitute for the great wars of the 1800s and early 1900s.

Proliferation of the weapons of mass destruction does not mean that most terrorist groups are likely to use them in the foreseeable future, but some almost certainly will, in spite of all the reasons militating against it. Governments, however ruthless, ambitious, and ideologically extreme, will be reluctant to pass on unconventional weapons to terrorist groups over which they cannot have full control; the governments may be tempted to use such arms themselves in a first strike, but it is more probable that they would employ them in blackmail than in actual warfare. Individuals and small groups, however, will not be bound by the constraints that hold back even the most reckless government.

Society has also become vulnerable to a new kind of terrorism, in which the destructive power of both the individual terrorist and terrorism as a tactic are infinitely greater. Earlier terrorists could kill kings or high officials, but others only too eager to inherit their mantle quickly stepped in. The advanced societies of today are more dependent every day on the electronic storage, retrieval, analysis, and transmission of information. Defense, the police, banking, trade, transportation, scientific work, and a large percentage of the government's and private sector's transactions are on-line. That exposes enormous vital areas of national life to mischief or sabotage by any computer hacker, and concerted sabotage could render a country unable to function. Hence the growing speculation about infoterrorism and cyberwarfare.

An unnamed U.S. intelligence official has boasted that with $1 billion and 20 capable hackers, he could shut down America. What he could achieve, a terrorist could too. There is little secrecy in the wired society, and protective measures have proved of limited value—teenage hackers have penetrated highly secret systems in every field. The possibilities for creating chaos are almost unlimited even now, and vulnerability will almost certainly increase. Terrorists' targets will change: why assassinate a politician or indiscriminately kill people when an attack on electronic switching will produce far more dramatic and lasting results? The switch at the Culpeper, Virginia, headquarters of the Federal Reserve's electronic network, which handles all federal funds and transactions, would be an obvious place to hit. If the new terrorism directs its energies toward information warfare, its destructive power will be exponentially greater than any it wielded in the past—greater even than it would be with biological and chemical weapons.

Still, the vulnerability of states and societies will be of less interest to terrorists than to ordinary criminals and organized crime, disgruntled employees of big corporations, and, of course, spies and hostile governments. Electronic thieves, whether engaged in credit card fraud or industrial espionage, are part of the system, using it rather than destroying it; its destruction would cost them their livelihood. Politically motivated terrorist groups, above all separatists bent on establishing states of their own, have limited aims. The Kurdish Workers Party, the IRA, the Basque ETA, and the Tamil Tigers want to weaken their enemies and compel them to make far-reaching concessions, but they cannot realistically hope to destroy them. It is also possible, however, that terrorist groups on the verge of defeat or acting on apocalyptic visions may not hesitate to apply all destructive means at their disposal.

All that leads well beyond terrorism as we have known it. New definitions and new terms may have to be developed for new realities, and intelligence services and policy makers must learn to discern the significant differences among terrorists' motivations, approaches, and aims. The Bible says that when the Old Testament hero Samson brought down the temple, burying himself along with the Philistines in the ruins, "the dead which he slew at his death were more than he slew in his life." The Samsons of a society have been relatively few in all ages. But with the new technologies and the changed nature of the world in which they operate, a handful of angry Samsons and disciples of apocalypse would suffice to cause havoc. Chances are that of 100 attempts at terrorist superviolence, 99 would fail. But the single successful one could claim many more victims, do more material damage, and unleash far greater panic than anything the world has yet experienced.

9

ASPHYXIATION OR OXYGEN? THE SANCTIONS DILEMMA

Franklin L. Lavin

This essay examines the advantages and disadvantages of alternative strategies for using economic and other types of sanctions for purposes of exercising influence over targets. Examining a series of cases and the checkered record of this method of coercive diplomacy since World War II, Lavin dispels a number of myths about this policy instrument and pinpoints the conditions under which sanctions are most likely to succeed. Lavin is the Executive Director of the Asia Pacific Policy Center in Washington, D.C., and served from 1991 to 1993 as Deputy Assistant Secretary for East Asia and the Pacific in the U.S. Department of Commerce.

One of Aesop's fables concerns a wager between the wind and the sun as to who is more powerful. The sun spies a man walking down a path and challenges the wind to remove the man's coat. The wind begins blowing. But the harder it tries to blow off the coat, the more the man grasps the wrap tightly in his hands. Finally, the sun steps in to try. The wind subsides and the sun warms up the day. Feeling the noon heat, the man begins to sweat and takes off his coat. The sun wins the bet.

From "Asphyxiation or Oxygen? The Sanctions Dilemma," by Franklin L. Lavin. Reprinted with permission from *Foreign Policy* 104, Fall 1996. Copyright © 1996 by the Carnegie Endowment for International Peace. This essay has been abridged.

International politics does not neatly follow fables, but this story does illustrate that there are sometimes two very different ways to attempt to influence another's actions. In U.S. foreign policy, for example, a fundamental question is whether American interests are best advanced by promoting more extensive economic relations with a particular country or by diminishing those relations. This question is frequently asked when the issues of human rights or military intervention come up, and one need only look at recent headlines to see its relevance. Whether regarding Bosnia, China, Haiti, Iran, Iraq, or North Korea, the economic dimension of foreign policy figures into virtually every issue the United States faces.

The economic role of foreign policy continues to attract considerable interest. Woodrow Wilson summed up the appeal of economic sanctions, stating that they are an "economic, peaceful, silent, deadly enemy." First, the use of economic policy to advance foreign policy goals is perceived to be cost free, or at least low cost. Second, it is less brutal and thus more acceptable than military conflict. Third, it is a normal human desire to want to be aware of the moral consequences and propriety of one's actions. If the United States is going to undertake business activities in a foreign country, Americans would like to be assured that such actions are "helpful," or at the least that they are not unwittingly bolstering distasteful policies.

A substantial body of literature examines the effectiveness of economic sanctions as well as the subject of economic growth, particularly foreign aid. On one side—call it an "oxygen" strategy—economic policy can reduce trade barriers such as tariffs and quotas and adopt more active measures such as loans, credits, trade and investment missions, and foreign aid. On the other—call it an "asphyxiation" strategy—options include impeding exports to, or imports from, the targeted country and restricting financial flows. More serious sanctions can include degrading trade by withdrawing most-favored-nation (MFN) or Generalized System of Preferences privileges, blocking International Monetary Fund or World Bank projects, or imposing a trade blockade or embargo.

The economic dimension of foreign policy is a difficult subject to analyze, because international events are usually the product of several causes, and the economic factors cannot always be separated from related politico-military ones. In addition, inconsistency has at times characterized the American approach to sanctions, with the advocates' own political orientation seeming to determine which course is followed.

Thus in the two most celebrated uses of sanctions of the 1980s—against Cuba and South Africa—conservatives tended to favor "asphyxiation" for Cuba and "oxygen" for South Africa. Liberals, on the other hand, advocated strangulation for South Africa; some even favored a tougher trade line toward South Africa than toward the Soviet Union. Although few analysts advocated engagement with Cuba in the 1980s, those who did were on the Left. Both approaches should be assessed without regard for ideological considerations.

OXYGEN

The "oxygen" school is backed by several arguments. The most common one holds that greater economic activity will lead to positive political consequences. [Editorialized] the *Economist,* ". . . nothing on earth but fast economic growth has the power to shift whole societies for the better more or less overnight."

Asia scholar Robert Scalapino, writing in the July 1993 *Journal of Democracy,* sees three reasons for this connection. First, growth stabilizes the traditional order by creating "increased diversity—of occupations and status. . . . Thus neither highly centralized rule nor self-sufficient localism is any longer adequate; authority must be divided and shared in complex ways." Second, prosperity creates a group that seeks greater political freedoms. And third, development ends isolation.

A fourth development from economic progress is that government no longer holds a monopoly over socioeconomic mobility. The government loses some of its appeal and legitimacy as an employer or a benefactor, because alternatives emerge. Advancement is no longer determined by the degree to which people follow a party line or a government's dictates.

Oxygen supporters argue that, beyond prosperity, familiarity can be gained and mutual benefits dramatized through economic activity. Autocratic governments can be induced to behave better by the successful demonstration of open economic arrangements. Trade is a confidence-building measure. Finally, the school notes that the oxygen approach is more humane since it is likely to improve the day-to-day lives of people in the subject country.

ASPHYXIATION

The "asphyxiation" school also has its points. First, attaching an economic cost to bad behavior acts as a disincentive. Second, the economic cost of sanctions can directly ameliorate the problem by limiting the government's capacity to engage in the offending practices. That was the logic behind America's most famous attempt at asphyxiation: Franklin Roosevelt's decision to discontinue the sale of American scrap metals and fuel oil to Japan. Since Japan was heavily dependent on imported fuel and metals, Roosevelt thought an embargo of those goods could halt the Japanese war effort.

Third, if pushed to extremes, economic sanctions could even topple a government through mass discontent or unhappiness within a leadership faction, thereby ending the bad behavior. Fourth, asphyxiation has a certain appeal over oxygen because it is an active step, while oxygen is essentially passive. If governments need to demonstrate they are "doing something," then asphyxiation fits the bill. A sanction might be an empty gesture according to economic criteria, but it could send a clear political message. The Soviet Union once toppled a Finnish government it deemed too conservative through a series of trade actions that sent a clear political signal. Thus, sanctions can operate on a symbolic level by serving as a prelude to a more serious move.

Even supposedly "empty" trade sanctions can be useful political tools. The 50-year-old Arab economic boycott of Israel has had minimal economic impact, but it has promoted Arab solidarity and served an important domestic political role. In general, asphyxiation is more effective than oxygen in making a political statement, because government policy can more readily disrupt market forces of trade and investment than encourage them.

SUCCESSES AND FAILURES

Successful examples of either approach can be found. Many scholars point to the Reagan administration's determination in restricting the Soviet Union's access to international funding as a factor that exacerbated its economic problems. In the end, Soviet leader Mikhail Gorbachev had to come to terms with the West, this theory holds, because he had no economic option except to reduce military expenditures.

South Africa is also held up as an example of a government against which sanctions were used successfully. After years of economic stagnation, the South African business establishment realized that apartheid was increasingly untenable and that their prospects for preserving their position lay in changing the status quo rather than preserving it. They shifted to favoring majority rule not so much from a democratic impulse but so that the boycott would be ended.

In the oxygen camp, most analysts of South Korea and Taiwan conclude that their moves toward democracy and a Western-style human rights standard were facilitated by their prosperity in the 1980s. The autocratic leadership in these two countries could relax political controls with a fair amount of confidence in continued domestic stability as the countries were enjoying substantial economic success. Economic growth promoted the establishment of an educated middle class that sought and received more political freedoms.

Similarly, detractors find failed examples of each approach. Economic sanctions against Serbia were not airtight, but they still impoverished Serbia and drove inflation to 2,000 percent a month—which compounds to about 410 quadrillion percent a year. Nonetheless, for years Serbia was not hindered in its ability to meddle in Bosnia. Economic sanctions against Cuba have existed as long as the 37-year-old Castro regime, yet Fidel Castro remains unchallenged.

More dramatic examples of the limits of asphyxiation might be both the Allies' blockade of the Central Powers during World War I and the Union's blockade of the Confederacy during the American Civil War. As with Serbia, both actions helped cripple the targeted economies, but neither degraded the adversaries' ability to wage war until a number of years had passed.

On the oxygen side, the East European country that interacted most frequently with the West was East Germany because of its special relationship with

West Germany. West Germany's *Ostpolitik* employed a deliberate policy of economic engagement, or *Osthandel.* Nonetheless, of all the former Warsaw Pact countries, East Germany was also the most Stalinist in structure and the most enduringly loyal to the Soviet Union. Thus, economic interaction by itself does not seem to guarantee a political opening. Indeed, many would argue that the West's economic activity with the Soviet bloc served to prolong the Soviet system by subsidizing a system in decline. Further, because the East German leadership was aware that interaction with the West might infect the body politic, they erected a massive security apparatus.

When Do Sanctions Work?

With examples of success and failure in each school, . . . policy makers must understand the particular circumstances at play. Four criteria must be met for the policy of asphyxiation to succeed: sufficiency, economics, confluence, and cohesion/proportionality.

First, the sanction must reach a level of sufficiency, as the League of Nations discovered when it attempted to take action against Italy in 1935–36 for its invasion of Ethiopia. A total blockade is not necessary, but the sanctions must be harsh enough to have an impact. A blockade that covers 90 percent of the border might in the end exert zero impact on imports. The United States discovered during the Vietnam War that mining Haiphong harbor could disrupt the North Vietnamese economy, but it never impaired the North's ability to wage war given its geographic contiguity with then-ally China. U.N. sanctions against Libya have been ineffective because they do not apply to Libya's oil exports, leaving Libya's economy largely unscathed.

Sufficiency is determined by the degree to which the flow of goods is restricted. In cases such as North Vietnam, a partial success in closing the border is no success in restricting the flow of goods. Two core determinants of sufficiency are geography and alliance solidarity. A country that is landlocked or has few neighbors will be more vulnerable than one that is littoral or extensive. Geography is a given; solidarity is dependent on allies sharing the same perception of a problem and the same prescription. Otherwise, countries will agree to subscribe to the proposed economic sanctions only when the costs are so low as to make their participation essentially symbolic, such as Japan's support for the U.S. blockade of Haiti. Thus the most important requirements for successful sanctions are largely outside the control of policy makers.

Second, the economic dimension of the proposal is also important and is substantially dependent on the target country and its economic relations with the United States. Here there are several vital components. The first is a country's susceptibility to sanctions, which is contingent upon the ability to interdict three critical items: fuel (what military people call POL, for petroleum, oil, and lubricants), hard currency, and high-technology weaponry. Though the interdiction of food, water, and medicine would inflict hardship on the general population, there is a practical political objection: the opprobrium a country using these morally questionable tactics is likely to receive from the international community would harm its standing. It is not surprising that states have violated these prohibitions only during life-and-death struggles, such as Germany's blockade of Great Britain during World War II.

Asphyxiation strategy has to assess the extent to which a country's susceptibility to sanctions can be manipulated, so specialists spend time modeling the target country's autarky, its gasoline storage and consumption rates, the percentage of its gross domestic product that is derived from exports, and so forth.

Iraq, after its seizure of Kuwait, stands out as an example where sanctions at first worked, then did not. The U.N. Security Council ordered broad economic sanctions. They succeeded on one level, in that geography and alliance solidarity were sufficient for a near-total economic blockade of Iraq, involving fuel, hard currency, and high-tech weaponry. But the sanctions did not induce Iraq to withdraw from Kuwait, nor did they have a particular impact on the war itself. Unlike World War I or the American Civil War, the Persian Gulf War was not a war of attrition; the denial of weaponry to Iraq was of little military significance because Iraq had stockpiled all the weapons it needed.

The assessment of sanctions' impact should go beyond these criteria for disrupting the target country's economy to consider the *relative* disruption: Will the target country be hurt more than the implementer or the implementing alliance? There is a Newtonian dynamic to sanctions: Every action has an equal and opposite reaction that can make it less cost-effective than a military attack. A $1 million cruise missile can paralyze a target country's communication network, causing maybe $100 million worth of damage. But in order to deprive the target country of $1 million worth of petroleum, it could cost the implementer $1 million in foregone profits. Economically, sanctions can hurt the target country less than the implementing country. When the United States imposed a grain embargo on the Soviet Union in 1980, the Soviets easily found other suppliers, but the United States found no alternative buyers. Disrupting trade hurts all of the target country's trading partners as well. It is easy for the United States to support an economic blockade against Serbia, but it is much more difficult for the neighboring states of Bulgaria, Greece, Hungary, or Romania to do so. Yet without their support the blockade is meaningless. Therefore, one key to analyzing the relative disruption of sanctions is to compare the size of the target country's economy with that of the implementer. A smaller country will have difficulty enduring economic disruption.

Third, beyond the question of sufficiency and economics comes the issue of confluence: Asphyxiation can raise the cost of actions and exacerbate economic problems but is rarely successful by itself. South Africa and Nicaragua both eventually changed policies while being subjected to trade sanctions, but the asphyxiation simply brought to the surface more serious preexisting problems:

Each government lacked popular support and was engaged in a costly counterinsurgency campaign. Proponents of a continued embargo of Cuba argue that the policy will be effective now that the Soviet Union is gone and Russia can no longer subsidize the Cuban economy. Since sanctions frequently exert only a marginal impact on a country, one of the keys to success is to target countries already burdened by other problems.

A fourth determinant of success relates to the issues of national cohesion, internal political structure, presentation of the sanctions, and proportionality of the actions. Jim Hoagland, a *Washington Post* columnist, asks, "Does Saddam Hussein care that Iraqi children go to bed hungry and sick? Does Gen. Raoul Cédras fret about Haitian citizens being deprived of work because he clings to power? How much does Moammar Gadhafi care that Libyans cannot travel abroad easily, even in emergencies?" Trade sanctions can function like a neutron bomb, destroying the economy, wreaking misery on the general population, but leaving the political establishment intact. Worse, trade sanctions can even bolster support for the targeted government by appearing to be a heavy-handed impingement upon sovereign prerogatives. U.N. and British sanctions against the white minority–run government of Rhodesia from 1965 to 1979 stand out as an example where a government's domestic position was actually strengthened by sanctions.

More recently, the 1991 massacre at Dili in East Timor, in which Indonesian troops fired on unarmed protesters, prompted angry reactions. Though Indonesia apologized and punished some of the officers involved in the incident, the response was not sufficient for Western countries: The Netherlands publicly criticized the Indonesian government (and the Indonesians responded by rejecting Dutch foreign aid); Portugal blocked an Association of South East Asian Nations—European Union economic cooperation agreement; and the United States suspended military training and blocked certain weapons sales. All of these actions took place after Indonesia had undertaken its most in-depth response ever to such a human rights issue, and they simply caused discord between the Indonesian government and the West.

This episode illustrates the principle of proportionality. The implementer of sanctions must keep the tools in line with the foreign policy goal. Economic sanctions have been attempted in efforts to fulfill a range of foreign policy goals, such as winning a war, toppling a government, punishing a country for support of terrorism, or encouraging it to change some policy. But if the other fundamentals of sanctions noted above are not in order, they will be successful in pursuit of only modest goals.

The above example also shows the link between proportionality and presentation. Because sanctions are a marginal tool, they are most effective when applied to marginal issues such as technical trade matters. The goals outsiders sought in Rhodesia and Indonesia were vastly disproportional to the economic tools employed. The goal in Rhodesia was to overthrow the government. The goal in Indonesia was nothing less than a radical change in Indonesia's policy toward East

Timor, a former Portuguese colony seized by Indonesia. Core issues of sovereignty cannot be addressed successfully by sanctions. What country would choose national humiliation over economic hardship? Since even seemingly minor issues—a fishing dispute, for example—can be perceived as a test of the sovereignty and integrity of a government, sanctions must be implemented in such a way as to not back the target country into a corner. Presentation becomes important so as to ensure that the threat of sanctions is not perceived as a challenge to a country's sovereign integrity. Peculiarly, political sensitivities make sanctions a more effective tool in dealing with friendly countries than with unfriendly ones, for with the former there is no issue of sovereignty at stake. The prospect of sanctions can be held out with regret, and not as a threat.

Sanctions have a moral dimension. Asphyxiation is premised on a philosophy of making things worse before they get better and of inflicting hardship on a broad population. Just as Nicaragua and South Africa might stand as examples of countries where economic manipulation worked, they might also be reminders that crippled economies do not recover easily. Although the initial political problems that prompted the economic sanctions have been rectified, the economic hardship will be felt for years. Indeed, in the case of South Africa, lingering economic underperformance, combined with weighty popular expectations, might prove harmful to the new majority government of Nelson Mandela. Although U.S.–backed sanctions were imposed on Haiti for only three years, the economic disruptions will remain long after the political dispute has ended—and long after Haiti has been forgotten.

When to Engage

Under what circumstances will the policy of oxygen be successful? There is one critical criterion: The country in question must have some openness that will allow the economic benefits to flow broadly to the general population. It will do little good for the international side of a country's economy to be open if the domestic side is closed. Even in their most authoritarian days, for example, both South Korea and Taiwan permitted broad economic freedoms, including private property, inheritance rights, and the right to choose professions and engage in a wide variety of economic activities. East Germany, by contrast, offered little of this. Economic activity in Taiwan undercut the government; in East Germany it was a mechanism of government control. . . .

SANCTIONS: A SELECTIVE INSTRUMENT

Wilsonians and liberal internationalists stand as paramount supporters of asphyxiation; the business community as the paramount supporter of oxygen. The Wilsonians are inherently pessimists and activists, viewing the international situation as a series of problems that are in need of correction. The business community is inherently optimistic and skeptical of political activism, viewing problems as transitory and best ameliorated by normal economic growth.

But oxygen is not merely the opposite of asphyxiation. As difficult as it is for a government to *disrupt* another country's economic activity, it is still easier than stimulating it. To the dismay of government planners, and in complete disregard for the views and desires of U.S. policy makers, economic activity thrives around the world—or fails to do so—for a series of complicated reasons, and not generally because of U.S. policy. As a Turkish saying puts it, "The dog barks and the caravan rolls on."

Moreover, for as long as asphyxiation can take, an oxygen strategy may take even longer. The full emergence of a middle class can take decades, and only then does pressure begin to build on the authorities to relax an authoritarian political structure.

Some observers argue that sanctions simply don't work or alternatively, that engagement doesn't work. It is true that one rarely finds examples of economic activity working quickly; the mechanisms are slow and indirect. But to argue that economic measures—be they positive or negative—do not work is to argue that foreign policy does not work, for economic strategy is simply applied incentives and disincentives. Countries might not react quickly, or they might not react the way they are desired to act, making a very different calculus of self-interest than that for which the implementer of sanctions had hoped. But, over the long run, countries—even odious ones—tend to act rationally.

Unfortunately, the idea of using economic policy as an instrument of foreign policy has been degraded through misapplication. Sanctions have become the lazy man's foreign policy, viewed as an instant and painless way of advancing national interests. Both sanctions and economic assistance are frequently invoked like a mantra. If the [sanctioning state] approves of another country's actions, the country receives a check; if it disapproves, a bill.

Economic policies need to be viewed as a selective instrument of foreign policy that is most often successful when specific circumstances prevail. Sanctions can make a political statement, but they will be useful as a foreign policy tool only when the criteria discussed above are met.

To take Wilsons' four adjectives, history has shown that sanctions are not always economic, not necessarily peaceful, not silent, and deadly only at the margin (in conjunction with other factors) and over the long run. But sometimes they do the trick. Similarly, engagement offers no automatic prospect of success, but sometimes it, too, is the right formula. Sanctions tend to be more effective in response to trade issues, and engagement in response to human rights problems. Neither is a terribly effective response to aggression. Either strategy can work, given the circumstances. The challenge for the policy maker, as always, is to avoid a dogmatic approach and choose the right tool for the job.

10

THE CHANGING NATURE
OF WORLD POWER

Joseph S. Nye, Jr.

This essay draws fundamental distinctions among three concepts—power,
the balance of power, and hegemony—and evaluates, in light of several
theoretical perspectives, how the revolutionary changes sweeping the world
in the 1990s are changing their meaning. The author, Joseph S. Nye, Jr., is
the former Chairman of the National Intelligence Council and Assistant
Secretary of Defense for International Affairs in the Clinton administration,
and now serves as Dean of the John F. Kennedy School of Government at
Harvard University. His many publications include *Understanding
International Conflict* (1992).

THE CHANGING SOURCES OF POWER

. . . Some observers have argued that the sources of power are, in general,
moving away from the emphasis on military force and conquest that marked

From "The Changing Nature of American Power," by Joseph S. Nye, Jr., *Political Science Quarterly,* vol. 105, No. 2, Summer, 1990, pp. 177–182. This article draws on material from Joseph S. Nye, Jr., *Bound to Lead: The Changing Nature of American Power* (New York: Basic Books, 1990). Some footnotes have been deleted and others have been renumbered to appear in consecutive order. Reprinted with permission from *Political Science Quarterly.*

earlier eras. In assessing international power today, factors such as technology, education, and economic growth are becoming more important, whereas geography, population, and raw materials are becoming less important. Kenneth Waltz argues that a five percent rate of economic growth in the United States for three years would add more to American strength than does our alliance with Britain.[1] Richard Rosecrance argues that since 1945, the world has been poised between a territorial system composed of states that view power in terms of land mass, and a trading system "based in states which recognize that self-sufficiency is an illusion." In the past, says Rosecrance, "it was cheaper to seize another state's territory by force than to develop the sophisticated economic and trading apparatus needed to derive benefit from commercial exchange with it."[2]

If so, perhaps we are in a "Japanese period" in world politics. Japan has certainly done far better with its strategy as a trading state after 1945 than it did with its military strategy to create a Greater East Asian Co-Prosperity sphere in the 1930s. But Japan's security vis-à-vis its large military neighbors—China and [Russia]—depends heavily on U.S. protection. In short, even if we can define power clearly, it still has become more difficult to be clear about the relationship of particular resources to it. Thus, we cannot leap too quickly to the conclusion that all trends favor economic power or countries like Japan.

Like other forms of power, economic power cannot be measured simply in terms of tangible resources. Intangible aspects also matter. For example, outcomes generally depend on bargaining, and bargaining depends on relative costs in particular situations and skill in converting potential power into effects. Relative costs are determined not only by the total amount of measurable economic resources of a country but also by the degree of its interdependence in a relationship. If, for example, the United States and Japan depend on each other but one is less dependent than the other, that asymmetry is a source of power. The United States may be less vulnerable than Japan if the relationship breaks down, and it may use that threat as a source of power.[3] Thus, an assessment of Japanese and American power must look not only at shares of resources but also at the relative vulnerabilities of both countries.

Another consideration is that most large countries today find military force more costly to apply than in previous centuries. This has resulted from the dangers of nuclear escalation, the difficulty of ruling nationalistically awakened populations in otherwise weak states, the danger of rupturing profitable relations on other issues, and the public opposition in Western democracies to prolonged

---

[1]Kenneth N. Waltz, *Theory of International Politics* (Reading, Mass.: Addison-Wesley, 1979), p. 172.

[2]Richard N. Rosecrance, *The Rise of the Trading State* (New York: Basic Books, 1986), pp. 16, 160.

[3]Robert O. Keohane and Joseph S. Nye, Jr., *Power and Interdependence* (Boston: Little, Brown, 1977), chap. 1. . . .

and expensive military conflicts. Even so, the increased cost of military force does not mean that it will be ruled out. To the contrary, in an anarchic system of states where there is no higher government to settle conflicts and where the ultimate recourse is self-help, this could never happen. In some cases, the stakes may justify a costly use of force. And, as . . . episodes in Grenada and Libya have shown, not all uses of force by great powers involve high costs.

Even if the direct use of force were banned among a group of countries, military force would still play an important political role. For example, the American military role in deterring threats to allies, or of assuring access to a crucial resource such as oil in the Persian Gulf, means that the provision of protective force can be used in bargaining situations. Sometimes the linkage may be direct; more often it is a factor not mentioned openly but present in the back of statesmen's minds.

In addition, there is the consideration that is sometimes called "the second face of power."[4] Getting other states to change might be called the directive or commanding method of exercising power. Command power can rest on inducements ("carrots") or threats ("sticks"). But there is also an indirect way to exercise power. A country may achieve the outcomes it prefers in world politics because other countries want to follow it or have agreed to a system that produces such effects. In this sense, it is just as important to set the agenda and structure the situations in world politics as it is to get others to change in particular situations. This aspect of power—that is, getting others to want what you want—might be called indirect or co-optive power behavior. It is in contrast to the active command power behavior of getting others to do what you want.[5] Co-optive power can rest on the attraction of one's ideas or on the ability to set the political agenda in a way that shapes the preferences that others express. Parents of teenagers know that if they have structured their children's beliefs and preferences, their power will be greater and will last longer than if they had relied only on active control. Similarly, political leaders and philosophers have long understood the power that comes from setting the agenda and determining the framework of a debate. The ability to establish preferences tends to be associated with intangible power resources such as culture, ideology, and institutions. This dimension can be thought

---

[4]Peter Bachrach and Morton S. Baratz, "Decisions and Nondecisions: An Analytical Framework," *American Political Science Review* 57 (September 1963), pp. 632–42. See also Richard Mansbach and John Vasquez, *In Search of Theory: A New Paradigm for Global Politics* (New York: Columbia University Press, 1981).

[5]Susan Strange uses the term *"structural power,"* which she defines as "power to shape and determine the structures of the global political economy" in *States and Markets* (New York: Basil Blackwell, 1988), p. 24. My term, *"co-optive power,"* is similar in its focus on preferences but is somewhat broader, encompassing all elements of international politics. The term *structural power,* in contrast, tends to be associated with the neorealist theories of Kenneth Waltz.

of as soft power, in contrast to the hard command power usually associated with tangible resources like military and economic strength.[6]

Robert Cox argues that the 19th-century *Pax Britannica* and the 20th-century *Pax Americana* were effective because they created liberal international economic orders, in which certain types of economic relations were privileged over others and liberal international rules and institutions were broadly accepted. Following the insights of the Italian thinker Antonio Gramsci, Cox argues that the most critical feature for a dominant country is the ability to obtain a broad measure of consent on general principles—principles that ensure the supremacy of the leading state and dominant social classes—and at the same time to offer some prospect of satisfaction to the less powerful. Cox identifies Britain from 1845 to 1875 and the United States from 1945 to 1967 as such countries.[7] Although we may not agree with his terminology or dates, Cox has touched a major point: soft co-optive power is just as important as hard command power. If a state can make its power legitimate in the eyes of others, it will encounter less resistance to its wishes. If its culture and ideology are attractive, others will more willingly follow. If it can establish international norms that are consistent with its society, it will be less likely to have to change. If it can help support institutions that encourage other states to channel or limit their activities in ways the dominant state prefers, it may not need as many costly exercises of coercive or hard power in bargaining situations. In short, the universalism of a country's culture and its ability to establish a set of favorable rules and institutions that govern areas of international activity are critical sources of power.[8] These soft sources of power are becoming more important in world politics today.

Such considerations question the conclusion that the world is about to enter a Japanese era in world politics. The nature of power is changing and some of the changes will favor Japan, but some of them may favor the United States even

---

[6]The distinction between hard and soft power resources is one of degree, both in the nature of the behavior and in the tangibility of the resources. Both types are aspects of the ability to achieve one's purposes by controlling the behavior of others. Command power—the ability to change what others *do*—can rest on coercion or inducement. Co-optive power—the ability to shape what others *want*—can rest on the attractiveness of one's culture and ideology or the ability to manipulate the agenda of political choices in a manner that makes actors fail to express some preferences because they seem to be too unrealistic. The forms of behavior between command and co-optive power range along this continuum:

Command power	coercion	inducement	agenda-setting	attraction	Co-optive power

Further, soft power resources tend to be associated with co-optive power behavior, whereas hard power resources are usually associated with command behavior. But the relationship is imperfect. For example, countries may be attracted to others with command power by myths of invincibility, and command power may sometimes be used to establish institutions that later become regarded as legitimate. But the general association is strong enough to allow the useful shorthand reference to hard and soft power resources.

[7]Robert W. Cox, *Production, Power, and World Order* (New York: Columbia University Press, 1987), chaps. 6, 7.

[8]Stephen D. Krasner, *International Regimes* (Ithaca, N.Y.: Cornell University Press, 1983).

TABLE 10-1
LEADING STATES AND MAJOR POWER RESOURCES, 1500s–1900s

Period	Leading State	Major Resources
Sixteenth century	Spain	Gold bullion, colonial trade, mercenary armies, dynastic ties
Seventeenth century	Netherlands	Trade, capital markets, navy
Eighteenth century	France	Population, rural industry, public administration, army
Nineteenth century	Britain	Industry, political cohesion, finance and credit, navy, liberal norms, island location (easy to defend)
Twentieth century	United States	Economic scale, scientific and technical leadership, universalistic culture, military forces and alliances, liberal international regimes, hub of transnational communication

more. In command power, Japan's economic strength is increasing, but it remains vulnerable in terms of raw materials and relatively weak in terms of military force. And in co-optive power, Japan's culture is highly insular and it has yet to develop a major voice in international institutions. The United States, on the other hand, has a universalistic popular culture and a major role in international institutions. Although such factors may change in the future, they raise an important question about the present situation: What resources are the most important sources of power today? A look at the five-century-old modern state system shows that different power resources played critical roles in different periods. (See Table 10-1.) The sources of power are never static and they continue to change in today's world.

In an age of information-based economies and transnational interdependence, power is becoming less transferable, less tangible, and less coercive. However, the transformation of power is incomplete. The 21st century will certainly see a greater role for informational and institutional power, but military force will remain an important factor. Economic scale, both in markets and in natural resources, will also remain important. As the service sector grows within modern economies, the distinction between services and manufacturing will continue to blur. Information will become more plentiful, and the critical resource will be the organizational capacity for rapid and flexible response. Political cohesion will remain important, as will a universalistic popular culture. On some of these dimensions of power, the United States is well endowed; on others, questions arise. But even larger questions arise for the other major contenders—Europe, Japan, [Russia], and China. But first we need to look at the patterns in the distribution of power—balances and hegemonies, and how they have changed over history. . . .

BALANCE OF POWER

International relations is far from a precise science. Conditions in various periods always differ in significant details, and human behavior reflects personal choices. Moreover, theorists often suffer from writing in the midst of events, rather than viewing them from a distance. Thus, powerful theories—those that are both simple and accurate—are rare. Yet political leaders (and those who seek to explain behavior) must generalize in order to chart a path through the apparent chaos of changing events. One of the longest-standing and most frequently used concepts is balance of power, which 18th-century philosopher David Hume called "a constant rule of prudent politics." For centuries, balance of power has been the starting point for realistic discussions of international politics.

To an extent, balance of power is a useful predictor of how states will behave; that is, states will align in a manner that will prevent any one state from developing a preponderance of power. This is based on two assumptions: that states exist in an anarchic system with no higher government and that political leaders will act first to reduce risks to the independence of their states. The policy of balancing power helps to explain why in modern times a large state cannot grow forever into a world empire. States seek to increase their powers through internal growth and external alliances. Balance of power predicts that if one state appears to grow too strong, others will ally against it so as to avoid threats to their own independence. This behavior, then, will preserve the structure of the system of states.

However, not all balance-of-power predictions are so obvious. For example, this theory implies that professions of ideological faith will be poor predictors of behavior. But despite Britain's criticism of the notorious Stalin-Hitler pact of 1939, it was quick to make an alliance with Stalin's Soviet Union in 1941. As Winston Churchill explained at the time, "If I learned that Hitler had invaded Hell, I would manage to say something good about the Devil in the House of Commons." Further, balance of power does not mean that political leaders must maximize the power of their own states in the short run. Bandwagoning—that is, joining the stronger rather than the weaker side—might produce more immediate spoils. As Mussolini discovered in his ill-fated pact with Hitler, the danger in bandwagoning is that independence may be threatened by the stronger ally in the long term. Thus, to say that states will act to balance power is a strong generalization in international relations, but it is far from being a perfect predictor.

Proximity and perceptions of threat also affect the way in which balancing of power is played out. A small state like Finland, for instance, [could not] afford to try to balance Soviet power. Instead, it [sought] to preserve its independence through neutrality. Balance of power and the proposition that "the enemy of my enemy is my friend" help to explain the larger contours of current world politics, but only when proximity and perceptions are considered. The United States was by far the strongest power after 1945. A mechanical application of power balance might seem to predict an alliance against the United States. In fact, Europe and Japan allied with the United States because the Soviet Union, while weaker in overall power, posed a proximate threat to its neighbors. Geography and psychology are both important factors in geopolitics.

The term *balance of power* is sometimes used not as a prediction of policy but as a description of how power is distributed. In the latter case, it is more accurate to refer to the distribution of power. In other instances, though, the term is used to refer to an evenly balanced distribution of power, like a pair of hanging scales. The problem with this usage is that the ambiguities of measuring power make it difficult to determine when an equal balance exists. In fact, the major concerns in world politics tend to arise from inequalities of power, and particularly from major changes in the unequal distribution of power.

HEGEMONY IN MODERN HISTORY

No matter how power is measured, an equal distribution of power among major states is relatively rare. More often the processes of uneven growth, which realists consider a basic law of international politics, mean that some states will be rising and others declining. These transitions in the distribution of power stimulate statesmen to form alliances, to build armies, and to take risks that balance or check rising powers. But the balancing of power does not always prevent the emergence of a dominant state. Theories of hegemony and power transition try to explain why some states that become preponderant later lose that preponderance.

As far back as ancient Greece, observers attempting to explain the causes of major world wars have cited the uncertainties associated with the transition of power. Shifts in the international distribution of power create the conditions likely to lead to the most important wars. However, while power transitions provide useful warning about periods of heightened risk, there is no iron law of hegemonic war. If there were, Britain and the United States would have gone to war at the beginning of this century, when the Americans surpassed the British in economic and naval power in the Western Hemisphere. Instead, when the United States backed Venezuela in its boundary dispute with British Guyana in 1895, British leaders appeased the rising American power instead of going to war with it.

When power is distributed unevenly, political leaders and theorists use terms such as *empire* and *hegemony*. Although there have been many empires in history, those in the modern world have not encompassed all major countries. Even the British Empire at the beginning of this century encompassed only a quarter of the world's population, and Britain was just one of a half-dozen major powers in the global balance of power. The term *hegemony* is applied to a variety of situations in which one state appears to have considerably more power than others. For example, for years China accused the Soviet Union of seeking hegemony in Asia. When Soviet leader Mikhail Gorbachev and Chinese leader Deng Xiaoping met in 1989, they pledged that "neither side will seek hegemony in any form anywhere in the world."

Although the word comes from the ancient Greek and refers to the dominance of one state over others in the system, it is used in diverse and confused ways. Part of the problem is that unequal distribution of power is a matter of degree, and there is no general agreement on how much inequality and what types of power constitute hegemony. All too often, hegemony is used to refer to different behaviors and degrees of control, which obscures rather than clarifies that analysis. For example, Charles Doran cites aggressive military power, while Robert Keohane looks at preponderance in economic resources. Robert Gilpin sometimes uses the terms *imperial* and *hegemonic* interchangeably to refer to a situation in which "a single powerful state controls or dominates the lesser states in the system."[9] British hegemony in the 19th century is commonly cited even though Britain ranked third behind the United States and Russia in GNP and third behind Russia and France in military expenditures at the peak of its relative power around 1870. Britain was first in the more limited domains of manufacturing, trade, finance, and naval power.[10] Yet theorists often contend that "full hegemony requires productive, commercial, and financial as well as political and military power."[11]

Joshua Goldstein usefully defines hegemony as "being able to dictate, or at least dominate, the rules and arrangements by which international relations, political and economic, are conducted. . . . Economic hegemony implies the ability to center the world economy around itself. Political hegemony means being able to dominate the world militarily."[12] However, there are still two important questions to be answered with regard to how the term *hegemony* is used. First, what is the scope of the hegemon's control? In the modern world, a situation in which one country can dictate political and economic arrangements has been extremely rare. Most examples have been regional, such as Soviet power in Eastern Europe [during the Cold War], American influence in the Caribbean, and India's control over its small neighbors—Sikkim, Bhutan, and Nepal. In addition, one can find instances in which one country was able to set the rules and arrangements governing specific issues in world politics, such as the American role in money or trade in the early postwar years. But there has been no global, systemwide hegemon during the past two centuries. Contrary to the myths about *Pax Britannica* and *Pax Americana,* British and American hegemonies have been regional and issue-specific rather than general.

[9]Charles F. Doran, *The Politics of Assimilation: Hegemony and Its Aftermath* (Baltimore: Johns Hopkins University Press, 1971), p. 70; Robert O. Keohane, *After Hegemony* (Princeton, N.J.: Princeton University Press, 1984), p. 32; Robert Gilpin, *War and Change in World Politics* (New York: Cambridge University Press, 1981), p. 29.

[10]Bruce M. Russett, "The Mysterious Case of Vanishing Hegemony; or, Is Mark Twain Really Dead?" *International Organization* 39 (Spring 1985), p. 212.

[11]Robert C. North and Julie Strickland, "Power Transition and Hegemonic Succession," Paper delivered at the meeting of the International Studies Association, Anaheim, Calif., (March–April 1986), p. 5.

[12]Joshua S. Goldstein, *Long Cycles: Prosperity and War in the Modern Age* (New Haven, Conn.: Yale University Press, 1988), p. 281.

Second, we must ask what types of power resources are necessary to produce a hegemonic degree of control. Is military power necessary? Or is it enough to have preponderance in economic resources? How do the two types of power relate to each other? Obviously, the answers to such questions can tell us a great deal about the future world, in which Japan may be an economic giant and a military dwarf while [Russia] may fall into the opposite situation. A careful look at the interplay of military and economic power raises doubt about the degree of American hegemony in the postwar period.

Theories of Hegemonic Transition and Stability

General hegemony is the concern of theories and analogies about the instability and dangers supposedly caused by hegemonic transitions. Classical concerns about hegemony among leaders and philosophers focus on military power and "conflicts precipitated by the military effort of one dominant actor to expand well beyond the arbitrary security confines set by tradition, historical accident, or coercive pressures."[13] In this approach, hegemonic preponderance arises out of military expansion, such as the efforts of Louis XIV, Napoleon, or Hitler to dominate world politics. The important point is that, except for brief periods, none of the attempted military hegemonies in modern times has succeeded. (See Table 10-2.) No modern state has been able to develop sufficient military power to transform the balance of power into a long-lived hegemony in which one state could dominate the world militarily.

More recently, many political scientists have focused on economic power as a source of hegemonic control. Some define hegemonic economic power in terms of resources—that is, preponderance in control over raw materials, sources of capital, markets, and production of goods. Others use the behavioral definition in

[13]Doran, *Politics of Assimilation,* p. 15.

TABLE 10-2
MODERN EFFORTS AT MILITARY HEGEMONY

State Attempting Hegemony	Ensuing Hegemonic War	New Order After War
Hapsburg Spain	Thirty Years War, 1618–1648	Peace of Westphalia, 1648
Louis XIV's France	Wars of Louis XIV	Treaty of Utrecht, 1713
Napoleon's France	1792–1815	Congress of Vienna, 1815
Germany (and Japan)	1914–1945	United Nations, 1945

Source: Charles F. Doran, *The Politics of Assimilation: Hegemony and Its Aftermath* (Baltimore: Johns Hopkins University Press, 1971), pp. 19–20.

which a hegemon is a state able to set the rules and arrangements for the global economy. Robert Gilpin, a leading theorist of hegemonic transition, sees Britain and America, having created and enforced the rules of a liberal economic order, as the successive hegemons since the Industrial Revolution.[14] Some political economists argue that world economic stability requires a single stabilizer and that periods of such stability have coincided with periods of hegemony. In this view, *Pax Britannica* and *Pax Americana* were the periods when Britain and the United States were strong enough to create and enforce the rules for a liberal international economic order in the 19th and 20th centuries. For example, it is often argued that economic stability "historically has occurred when there has been a sole hegemonic power: Britain from 1815 to World War I and the United States from 1945 to around 1970. . . . With a sole hegemonic power, the rules of the game can be established and enforced. Lesser countries have little choice but to go along. Without a hegemonic power, conflict is the order of the day."[15] Such theories of hegemonic stability and decline are often used to predict that the United States will follow the experience of Great Britain, and that instability will ensue. Goldstein, for example, argues that "we are moving toward the 'weak hegemony' end of the spectrum and . . . this seems to increase the danger of hegemonic war."[16]

I argue, however, that the theory of hegemonic stability and transition will not tell us as much about the future of the United States. Theorists of hegemonic stability generally fail to spell out the causal connections between military and economic power and hegemony. As already noted, 19th-century Britain was not militarily dominant nor was it the world's largest economy, and yet Britain is portrayed by Gilpin and others as hegemonic. Did Britain's military weakness at that time allow the United States and Russia, the two larger economies, to remain mostly outside the liberal system of free trade? Or, to take a 20th-century puzzle, did a liberal international economy depend on postwar American military strength or only its economic power? Are both conditions necessary today, or have modern nations learned to cooperate through international institutions?

One radical school of political economists, the neo-Marxists, has attempted to answer similar questions about the relationship between economic and military hegemony, but their theories are unconvincing. For example, Immanuel Wallerstein defines hegemony as a situation in which power is so unbalanced that

> one power can largely impose its rules and its wishes (at the very least by effective veto power) in the economic, political, military, diplomatic, and even cultural arenas. The material base of such power lies in the ability of enterprises domiciled

[14]Keohane, *After Hegemony,* p. 32; Gilpin, *War and Change,* p. 144.
[15]Michael Moffitt, "Shocks, Deadlocks and Scorched Earth: Reaganomics and the Decline of U.S. Hegemony," *World Policy Journal* 4 (Fall 1987), p. 576.
[16]Goldstein, *Long Cycles,* p. 357.

in that power to operate more efficiently in all three major economic arenas—agro-industrial production, commerce, and finance.[17]

According to Wallerstein, hegemony is rare and "refers to that short interval in which there is simultaneously advantage in all three economic domains." At such times, the other major powers become "*de facto* client states." Wallerstein claims there have been only three modern instances of hegemony—in the Netherlands, 1620–1650; in Britain, 1815–1873; and in the United States, 1945–1967. (See Table 10-3.) He argues that "in each case, the hegemony was secured by a thirty-year-long world war," after which a new order followed—the Peace of West-phalia after 1648; the Concert of Europe after 1815; and the United Nations–Bretton Woods system after 1945.[18] According to this theory, the United States will follow the Dutch and the British path to decline.

The neo-Marxist view of hegemony is unconvincing and a poor predictor of future events because it superficially links military and economic hegemony and has many loose ends. For example, contrary to Wallerstein's theory, the Thirty Years War *coincided* with Dutch hegemony, and Dutch decline began with the Peace of Westphalia. The Dutch were not militarily strong enough to stand up to the British on the sea and could barely defend themselves against the French on land, "despite their trade-derived wealth."[19] Further, although Wallerstein argues that British hegemony began after the Napoleonic Wars, he is not clear about how the new order in the balance of power—that is, the 19th-century Concert of Europe—related to Britain's supposed ability to impose a global free-trade system. For example, Louis XIV's France, which many historians view as the dominant military power in the second half of the 17th century, is excluded from Wallerstein's schema altogether. Thus, the neo-Marxist historical analogies seem

TABLE 10-3
A NEO-MARXIST VIEW OF HEGEMONY

Hegemony	World War Securing Hegemony	Period of Dominance	Decline
Dutch	Thirty Years War, 1618–1648	1620–1650	1650–1672
British	Napoleonic Wars, 1792–1815	1815–1873	1873–1896
American	World Wars I and II, 1914–1945	1945–1967	1967–

Source: Immanuel Wallerstein, *The Politics of the World Economy* (New York: Cambridge University Press, 1984), pp. 41–42.

[17]Immanuel M. Wallerstein, *The Politics of the World-Economy: The States, the Movements, and the Civilizations: Essays* (New York: Cambridge University Press, 1984), pp. 38, 41.
[18]Ibid.
[19]Goldstein, *Long Cycles*, p. 317.

TABLE 10-4
LONG CYCLES OF WORLD LEADERSHIP

Cycle	Global War	Preponderance	Decline
1495–1580	1494–1516	Portugal, 1516–1540	1540–1580
1580–1688	1580–1609	Netherlands, 1609–1640	1640–1688
1688–1792	1688–1713	Britain, 1714–1740	1740–1792
1792–1914	1792–1815	Britain, 1815–1850	1850–1914
1914–	1914–1945	United States, 1945–1973	1973–

Source: George Modelski, *Long Cycles in World Politics* (Seattle: University of Washington Press, 1987), pp. 40, 42, 44, 102, 131, 147.

forced into a Procrustean ideological bed, while other cases are left out of bed altogether.

Others have attempted to organize past periods of hegemony into century-long cycles. In 1919, British geopolitician Sir Halford Mackinder argued that unequal growth among nations tends to produce a hegemonic world war about every hundred years. More recently, political scientist George Modelski proposed a hundred-year cyclical view of changes in world leadership. (See Table 10-4.) In this view, a long cycle begins with a major global war. A single state then emerges as the new world power and legitimizes its preponderance with postwar peace treaties. (Preponderance is defined as having at least half the resources available for global order keeping.) The new leader supplies security and order for the international system. In time, though, the leader loses legitimacy, and deconcentration of power leads to another global war. The new leader that emerges from that war may not be the state that challenged the old leader but one of the more innovative allies in the winning coalition (as, not Germany, but the United States replaced Britain). According to Modelski's theory, the United States began its decline in 1973.[20] If his assumptions are correct, it may be Japan and not [Russia] that will most effectively challenge the United States in the future.

Modelski and his followers suggest that the processes of decline are associated with long waves in the global economy. They associate a period of rising prices and resource scarcities with loss of power, and concentration of power with falling prices, resource abundance, and economic innovation.[21] However, in linking economic and political cycles, these theorists become enmeshed in the controversy surrounding long cycle theory. Many economists are skeptical about

[20]George Modelski, "The Long Cycle of Global Politics and the Nation-State," *Comparative Studies in Society and History* 20 (April 1978), pp. 214–35; George Modelski, *Long Cycles in World Politics* (Seattle: University of Washington Press, 1987).

[21]William R. Thompson, *On Global War: Historical Structural Approaches to World Politics* (Columbia: University of South Carolina Press, 1988), chaps. 3, 8.

the empirical evidence for alleged long economic waves and about dating historical waves by those who use the concept.[22]. . .

Vague definitions and arbitrary schematizations alert us to the inadequacies of such grand theories of hegemony and decline. Most theorists of hegemonic transition tend to shape history to their own theories by focusing on particular power resources and ignoring others. Examples include the poorly explained relationship between military and political power and the unclear link between decline and major war. Since there have been wars among the great powers during 60 percent of the years from 1500 to the present, there are plenty of candidates to associate with any given scheme.[23] Even if we consider only the nine general wars that have involved nearly all the great powers and produced high levels of casualties, some of them, such as the Seven Years War (1755–1763), are not considered hegemonic in any of the schemes. As sociologist Pitirim Sorokin concludes, "no regular periodicity is noticeable."[24] At best, the various schematizations of hegemony and war are only suggestive. They do not provide a reliable basis for predicting the future of American power or for evaluating the risk of world war as we enter the 21st century. Loose historical analogies about decline and falsely deterministic political theories are not merely academic: they may lead to inappropriate policies. The real problems of a post–cold-war world will not be new challenges for hegemony, but the new challenges of transnational interdependence.

[22]Richard N. Rosecrance, "Long Cycle Theory and International Relations," *International Organization* 41 (Spring 1987), pp. 291–5. An interesting but ultimately unconvincing discussion can be found in Goldstein, *Long Cycles.*

[23]Jack S. Levy, "Declining Power and the Preventive Motivation for War," *World Politics* 40 (October 1987), pp. 82–107. See also Jack S. Levy, *War in the Modern Great Power System, 1495–1975* (Lexington: University of Kentucky Press, 1983), p. 97.

[24]Pitirim Aleksandrovich Sorokin, *Social and Cultural Dynamics: A Study of Change in Major Systems of Art, Truth, Ethics, Law and Social Relationships* (1957; reprint, Boston: Porter Sargent, 1970), p. 561.

DISCORD AND COLLABORATION

States necessarily must direct their attention and resources toward the quest for security, for the threat of war is an ever-present danger in an anarchical society. Issues relating to arms and influence therefore occupy a prominent place on the foreign policy agendas of nation-states. Indeed, the pursuit of national security is widely perceived to be the very essence of international politics. Hence the issues treated in Part One of *The Global Agenda* appropriately command central importance.

Compelling as is this perspective, which is at the core of realist theories, it is at best a caricature of international politics, because it fails to acknowledge the broad range of issues and objectives that motivate states' behavior, even in their quest for security. The *high politics* of peace and security entails both issues and strategies that lie beyond arms and war, deterrence, and the raw exercise of influence. It also includes activities of states that often have little or nothing to do with armaments or the threat of war; and it includes many actions motivated by the desire to collaborate with others so as to derive mutual benefits.

Indeed, contrary to the harsh realist perspective of the English political theorist Thomas Hobbes, international politics is not accurately described as nothing but a "war of all against all." States are not normally straining at the leash to attack one another. Nor do they devote the bulk of their day-to-day activities to planning the use of force against their perceived adversaries. The texture of world politics is shaped by more varied national interests and activities.

Part Two of *The Global Agenda* directs attention to the other ways that states seek to promote their national interests. Under normal conditions, of course, relations among states are often marked by conflict. Disputes are common because conflict is endemic to politics and hence unavoidable. Nonetheless, we can observe that how states usually respond to conflict does not routinely involve preparations for war and the threat or use of force.

Part Two begins with the assumption that states respond to a perceived need not only for power but also for order. States value a stable international environment. They therefore seek and support not just a strong defense but also institutions and rules that contribute to the creation of a more orderly world. In short, world politics involves both discord and collaboration.

What factors influence whether enmity or amity will dominate the pattern of interaction among states? Clearly, there are many. Underlying all of them, it may be argued, are states' perceptions of reality. Reality is partially subjective—what states perceive it to be, not just what it is. Thus states' behavior is influenced strongly by images of reality as well as by objective facts. Whether states see the world as fearful and hostile or as peaceful and cooperative will influence the postures they assume toward global issues and their reactions to the challenges and options those issues present.

How international politics and the policies of states toward one another are pictured is shaped by our images of the global system's dominant characteristics. To organize perceptions about these subjects, social scientists have developed models that describe and explain various properties of international relations. To assist us in developing a frame of reference, Ole R. Holsti, in "Models of International Relations: Realist and Neoliberal Perspectives on Conflict and Cooperation," describes and summarizes two models that scholars have fashioned to organize research and theorizing on world politics: the classical and modern versions of "realism," and the neoliberal challengers to it who emphasize the interdependent nature of global realities and the prospects for cooperation and change. He elucidates the assumptions and conclusions about international relations suggested by the alternative theoretical orientations. In so doing, he provides a basis for understanding the diverse ways discord and collaboration manifest themselves in world affairs and why the potential for enduring conflict coexists with the potential for cooperation and change.

Models and theories provide a lens through which international realities are interpreted. Their usefulness depends in large part on the accuracy of the assumptions about international realities upon which they are based. Hence, the accuracy of observers' perceptions will matter greatly in determining the ways in which scholars and policy makers respond to the changes unfolding on the eve of the 21st century. In "Disorder and Order in a Turbulent World: The Evolution of Globalized Space," James N. Rosenau trains his eye on the major changes unfolding in international affairs in order to uncover the underlying dynamics that are eroding the long-standing patterns of world politics. From his insightful survey

Rosenau provides us with a vision of international life from which we can inter-pret the prospects for disorder and for order. His picture of contemporary inter-national affairs highlights its essential complexity and dynamism, as captured by the metaphor of *turbulence* so that the great commotion and uncertainty of our age can be appreciated and described. Identifying and defining the most signifi-cant transformations, Rosenau shows how they collectively have given rise to the simultaneous tendencies toward integration and fragmentative tensions that is "the central characteristic of world politics today."

For the compelling reasons Rosenau cites, both cooperative and conflictual processes are simultaneously at work throughout the world. It is likely that in the years ahead we will see at the same time both zones of order and of disorder, with pockets of integration emerging in a sea of disintegration. This is probable because the significance of borders is vanishing, as is the division between do-mestic and foreign affairs. A new "space" has been created, which Rosenau terms "globalized space" to stress the internationalization of the personal agen-das of people throughout the world. Pervasive transformations are underway in international affairs, and the transnationalization of global space has made for hostility and harmony as boundaries have become porous while territoriality is still a central preoccupation of many people. In framing the environment in which world politics will take place in the new millennium, explaining how the major forces and factors will interact, and describing the contradictions that this turbulent set of transformations is causing, Rosenau accounts for the breakup in globalized space of some communities alongside the consolidation of others. Picturing this disarray, he nonetheless concludes on an optimistic note. Suggest-ing that the dynamics of globalization unleashed by technology are the dominant catalyst in world affairs, Rosenau predicts that "the world will manage to move from crisis to crisis without collapsing into calamitous war."

By looking at the prevailing properties of the contemporary global landscape, we gain perspective on the nature and mixture of discord and collaboration that appear destined to govern the future. Which will dominate will not be deter-mined by long-term secular trends that cannot be controlled, even if awareness of the existence of discrepant trajectories leaves the impression, given the myr-iad issues that will occupy the crowded global agenda of the future, that global problems and challenges are likely to overwhelm the capacity of people to suc-cessfully manage them.

Of all the factors that will influence the prospects for global collaboration, how the relationships between the great powers evolve is unquestionably pivotal. The probable character of their relationships is the subject of considerable con-troversy because the intentions and foreign policy priorities of each emerging great power remain ill-defined. For more than four decades, the expectation of superpower discord remained high and the possibilities for lasting cooperation appeared remote, in large measure because of the distrust, ideological rivalry, and misperceptions that fueled the superpowers' animosity during the Cold War.

But in 1989 this chronic antagonism came abruptly to an end. As we look to the future, the likely shape of the great powers' relations with one another inspires hope that accommodation will prevail, and also fears that a new cycle of competition, conflict, and even war will commence.

In "Great-Power Relations in the 21st Century: A New Cold War, or Concert-Based Peace?" Charles W. Kegley, Jr., and Gregory A. Raymond evaluate the diverse ways in which an embryonic set of relationships might develop to cement the great powers' future collaboration with one another. They also explain why a strong potential exists for the emergence of a new wave of rivalry that will destroy these hopes for future harmony.

This assessment takes as its point of departure the growing evidence that the international system is presently undergoing a historic transformation because military and economic capabilities are becoming increasingly diffused among great powers. As China, Japan, and Germany expand their power positions and become rivals to the United States and Russia, as they have for the past decade, the structure of the international system has moved toward a multipolar distribution of power.

Systems composed of many roughly equal great powers have been common throughout history. Some of these systems have been relatively stable. More typically, however, multipower systems gradually break into rigid, antagonistic blocs—followed by the outbreak of a destructive global war. Accordingly, to cope with the welter of transnational security threats that will face the world community in the immediate future, it is imperative that the great powers do not once again become polarized into competitive coalitions, facing each other in a new cold war with each alliance seeking to defend itself by preparing for war against the rivals.

Three avenues are available to cope with such an emerging security threat: the great powers can act alone; they can develop bilateral partnerships; or they can engage in multilateral cooperation. To Kegley and Raymond, neither unilateralism nor special bilateral alliances bode well for the stability of a future multipolar system. Multilateralism, in the form of a two-tiered system of collective security, offers far better prospects for building on the great powers' common interests and for preventing a potentially bitter competition from erupting among them. Reviewing the contribution that might be made by the United Nations, the Organization for Security and Cooperation in Europe (OSCE), the geographically expanding North Atlantic Treaty Organization (NATO), and the Group of Seven (G-7), Kegley and Raymond conclude, in light of the limitations of existing security organizations, that any new multilateral security architecture can be built most constructively through an ad hoc combination of regional bodies tied together by the interlocking concert among the great powers. Without it, great-power rivalry may culminate in intense conflict. Then war cannot be discounted.

That grim fate is not preordained, of course. States have it within their power to cooperate in order to achieve greater prosperity and build a firmer foundation for peace. The best illustration of this is provided by the collaborative links that sovereign states in Europe after World War II purposefully built to pool their sovereignty and create a security community in which the prospects of war have disappeared. This experience illuminates the means and methods by which collaboration among states can supersede discord and attempts to settle disputes by force of arms.

The remarkable progress evident in inter-European cooperation and integration did not occur steadily or smoothly. Advances on the path to integration were often followed by reversals and periods without movement. However, the current phase began to accelerate when, in 1985, the European Community (EC) adopted the Single European Act. This treaty sought boldly to jump-start momentum for the integration of the 12 Western European countries then comprising the EC. The target date for realization of a single continentwide European common market was 1992.

In our next essay, "Building Peace in Pieces: The Promise of European Unity," Donald J. Puchala examines the expectations that led, step by step in a piecemeal integrative process, to the achievement of this goal and, since then, to progress that culminated in the creation of the European Union (EU) and set the stage for the next step in the political and economic unification of Europe. Necessarily the process of creating a single common market and currency involves political decisions designed to remove economic barriers; non-state actors, such as multinational corporations, are also playing an important role in the integrative process. Moving European unity into realms of foreign and defense policy, as envisioned in the Maastricht Treaties, will require rather extraordinary commitments of political will on the part of EU countries. The encouraging advance of integration in Europe inspires hope for international cooperation through institution building, but the problems and obstacles to deeper unification serve as a reminder of just how difficult this kind of progress is to engineer. What a unified and enlarged European Union ultimately portends economically and politically for the rest of the world may, however, be the most important if the most elusive question.

The fact that turmoil and violence plague many regions—and countries within them—throughout the world provides a sobering antidote to those who optimistically expect peace to be at hand and progress through international cooperation to expand. The European Union may be an exception to the global pattern because in many parts of the world peace, domestic stability, and prosperity are absent. The prevalence of discord is the subject of our next essay. In "Communal Conflicts and Global Security," Ted Robert Gurr puts into perspective the most threatening source of tension in the world today: the rise of "ethno-national issues" and the violence that communal conflicts *within* states are inciting.

Ethnic tensions and secession revolts by oppressed minority nationalities have reached epidemic proportions. They now constitute by far the most potent cause of death and greatest threat to international order in the world. As a result, the challenge of resolving conflicts within multiethnic societies has become perhaps *the* most critical issue on the agenda facing the international community. Based on a survey and comparison of 292 politically active communal groups during the 1980s and 1990s undertaken in his *Minorities at Risk* project, Gurr proposes answers to 11 of the most controversial questions about this issue. In so doing, he heightens awareness of the magnitude of the challenge and points to the ethical, legal, and political dilemmas confronting the global community in its quest to protect minority populations who are now the principal victims of flagrant human rights violations. He concludes with some prescriptions about how the global community might best cope with this serious threat to international security.

The zone of turmoil in which most civil rebellions and ethno-national conflicts occur is located primarily in the less-developed countries of the Third World (although many states in the advanced industrialized countries are also afflicted by this problem). It is in the so-called "Global South" where poverty, persecution, and the flight of refugees from their homelands is most pronounced that the issue assumes particular importance. For this reason, how the world's wealthy countries interact with those in the Southern hemisphere who are poor will be a decisive influence on future order or disorder there. Shahram Chubin examines the future of rich-poor relations from the vantage point of the poor countries in "Southern Perspectives on World Order." Surveying "the perspectives and attitudes of leaders in states of the South concerning the emerging international agenda," Chubin provides a searching overview of "the problems of security and development faced by these countries and the changing international context in which leaders of these states make choices." Emphasizing that the end of the Cold War has had "cataclysmic" consequences for the countries of the South, Chubin worries that the North could now treat the Third World not as allies or equals but as objects of antipathy to be manipulated. That conclusion derives from his review of the key issues on the North-South agenda, "namely proliferation, arms control, and collective security." Chubin warns that "the South is under siege—from an international community impatient to meddle in its affairs." By framing the Third World's predicament, problems, and probable policy postures, Chubin shows why the divisive issues between the North and South can only be dealt with productively if they are defined, not as North-South security issues, but as "global security issues, requiring dialogue, compromise, and grand bargains."

Relations between unequal countries comprise but one important dimension of world politics. Another involves the transnational factors that do not define themselves in terms of territorial borders and that influence the global climate writ large. Of these, cultural variables often exert considerable weight, especially when cultures collide.

Throughout the world's history, when distinct cultures have come into contact, the collisions have ignited a combination of communication, cooperation, and conflict. At times, such cultural contact has produced a healthy respect for diversity, as the members of each interacting cultural tradition have learned from each other. On many other occasions, familiarity has bred contempt. When followers have embraced the ethnocentric view that their own group's values are inherently superior, feuds and face-offs have prevailed.

Today, as the ideological contest between communism and capitalism has disappeared, ancient cultural cleavages and hatreds have reappeared. Tribalism, religious fanaticism, and hypernational ethnicity are again rampant. The nasty trend of violent assaults on immigrants and the rise of racial violence cast an ugly shadow across the world. Thus far the consequences have been lethal. Ethnic conflict and secessionist revolts are prevalent, and they are now the world's greatest killers. Hypernationalist beliefs rationalize large-scale violence and the subjugation of other nationalities. "Ethnic cleansing" has accompanied ethnocultural conflict, with the intent being to destroy unprotected subgroups rather than to pursue accommodation and assimilation. Even genocide has resurfaced.

In "The Coming Clash of Civilizations: Or, the West Against the Rest," Samuel P. Huntington argues that world politics is entering a new era, in which cultural conflict will be the fundamental problem. Because cultural conflict derives from cultural divisions, it is neither primarily ideological nor economic. But it will "dominate global politics," according to Huntington, because cultural hostility between civilizations is deeply entrenched. As "the world is becoming smaller," increased globalization through the technological revolution in communications has intensified "civilization consciousness" and the psychological identities that give much of the world meaning. In particular, Huntington predicts that because "the West is at a peak of its power" and engaged in an effort to promote worldwide its values of liberalism and democracy, the hostile resistance of others is likely to grow increasingly intense. Huntington foresees the cultural conflict "along the fault line between Western and Islamic civilizations" as the most likely source of discord in the next millennium. The challenge, he maintains, is learning how to transcend this centuries-old antagonism.

Huntington's warning seems destined to be put to its most severe test, not only globally, but also across and within those particular regions where religious and communal conflicts are the most ubiquitous and explosive. Conflict has been especially recurrent and deadly in the world's most unstable trouble spot, the Middle East, and in that region's relations with actors in other regions operating from different cultural traditions. In "Islam and Liberal Democracy: Muslim Perceptions and Western Reactions," Bernard Lewis provides a focused interpretation of the propositions advanced by Huntington and by the dimensions of the problem of intercommunal strife interpreted by Gurr and described by Chubin.

The Middle East does not enjoy the same level of democratization and stability as much of the rest of the world, and throughout history it has frequently exploded into intense struggles between the Islamic and Western cultural traditions. For 14 centuries an episodic series of attacks and reprisals, jihads and crusades, conquests and reconquests has erupted. Today, as in the past, fundamentalists in the Islamic world are driven by an intensely violent resentment of the West and its institutions, of its imperialism, and of its preferred form of governance founded on popular sovereignty and civil liberties. Lewis' purpose is to explore the question, "Can liberal democracy work in a society inspired by Islamic beliefs and principles and shaped by Islamic experience and tradition?" His explication goes far in enabling us to understand why Muslim religious precepts and memories of a glorious Muslim past now lost, in combination with recollections of humiliation at the hands of the industrialized West, have embittered the Muslim world and made it an inhospitable home for the liberal democratic values of the West.

Although Islam has traditions that are not incompatible with democratic institutions, Muslim resentment of the West's liberalism is deeply rooted, as Lewis explains. Because these differences are intensely felt, they are likely to cast their spell over future relations between the Middle East and the West. Especially worrisome, Lewis submits, is the danger that Western governments will succumb to the twin temptations to either "accept, and even to embrace, the most odious of dictatorships" or "to press Muslim regimes for concessions on human rights . . . and premature democratization." These reactions can be avoided, however, for Lewis believes that "now that the Cold War has ended and the Middle East is no longer a battlefield for rival power blocs, the peoples of the Middle East will have the chance—if they can take it—to make their own decisions and find their own solutions."

Assessments such as those of Gurr, Chubin, Huntington, and Lewis indicate that people's identity—their sentiments of loyalty and sense of membership in a particular group—is an important determinant of their preferences and behavior. Another key influence toward discord or collaboration is *institutional*—the ways groups organize themselves for political action. Throughout most of the modern era, of course, the predominant institution or actor on the international stage has been the independent territorial state, not ethno-national groups, civilizations, or religions. But on the eve of the 21st century, it has become conventional to proclaim that the sovereign nation-state is losing its power and legitimacy in the eyes of many people, and that other actors now compete for people's affiliation and give them their primary identity. The prospects of "vanishing borders" and the erosion of the sovereign authority of the nation-state thus present to the world an unfamiliar issue: whether nation-states, designed to separate countries and control conflict between them, are dying, and, if so, whether the demise of this institutional pillar of the international system will spawn a new era of chaos and disorder.

In "The Institutional Pillars of Global Order: The Nation-State Is Dead; Long Live the Nation-State," the editors of *The Economist* confront the issues surrounding the debate about the survivability of the nation-state and popular speculations about alternatives to it. Summarizing the rival perspectives about the decline of the nation-state, its causes, and its probable consequences, the reading selection maintains that the death of the nation-state should not be expected, and that an obituary is premature. It concludes that "nation-states will be the only pieces on the geopolitical chessboard," and this probability will strongly shape the prospects for both discord and collaboration in world affairs—more so than will multinational corporations, regional actors such as the integrating European Union, world government, or crystallizing transnational religious movements and civilizations based on cultural identities.

A corollary dimension to the debate about the impact of institutions on international discord and collaboration concerns the influence of the *types* of governments that states create to make decisions about domestic and foreign policy. One of the core assumptions of liberal international relations theory is that the types of regimes or institutional arrangements for governance *within* nation-states are an important determinant of their foreign behavior. That theoretical tradition also is predicated on the belief that the growth of liberal democracy exerts a medicinal and stabilizing impact on global politics. Since the dawn of history, reformers have searched for the path by which peaceful coexistence between contentious actors might be achieved. Until recently, however, few students of international conflict (especially those schooled in the realist tradition of theory) paid serious attention to the contribution that democracy might make to the peaceful management of international disputes. This has changed dramatically as a new wave of democratization took root in 1989 at precisely the moment in history when the Cold War conflict began to thaw. For the first time in history, a majority of countries in the world were democratically ruled.

In response to this sea change, researchers and policy makers alike began to explore the proposition advanced by classic liberal theory that democracy could be an antidote to warfare. Much evidence supports the belief that democracies are very unlikely to fight wars with each other. Whereas autocracies have historically been more expansionist and, in turn, more war-prone, democracies in contrast have been steadfastly pacifistic in their relations with one another. In addition, democratic states are not only constrained in their warfare but also are prone to form overwhelming counter-coalitions against expansionist autocracies. Because democracies frequently police territorial expansionism through concerted cooperation to maintain the status quo, democracies have been more likely to win wars against aggressive tyrannies. This augers well for neoliberal theorists' hope that a world of many democratic states will become a peaceful world.

Despite the optimism suggested by democratic peace theory, it is apparent that conflict remains pervasive throughout the world, even in a post–Cold War era populated by many fledgling new democratic states. As we look to the future, will the enlarged community of liberal democratic states approach the issues they face on the global agenda in a collaborative manner? Or will conflict become more common? It is to this question that Bruce Russett brings insight in his informed and provocative interpretative essay. Using the primary structural feature of the international system as his point of reference—namely, that world politics takes place in anarchy, without supranational regulation—Russett shows in "A Community of Peace: Democracy, Interdependence, and International Organization" how cooperation can prevail even under conditions where it might appear most unlikely. In helping us to understand the success of attempts at cooperation in both military-security relations and political-economic relations, Russett highlights the ways in which democratic institutions, the growth of interdependence, and the influence of international organizations have contributed to the development and maintenance of cooperation. Whether discord or collaboration will be greater or lesser ingredients in the future of world politics *will* be influenced considerably, Russett argues, by the extent to which states organize themselves to make foreign policy decisions through democratic processes and procedures that give people a voice in their government's national security policies and limit the freedom of rulers to wage war. The spread of democratic governance, in combination with the rising tide of economic interdependence through global trade and investment and the expanding clout of international institutions, he concludes, can reduce the frequency of war and increase the prospects for international cooperation, despite the continuous reality of anarchy and discord.

How states are likely to respond to the challenge of managing global discord and promoting collaboration is likely influenced not only by the kinds of institutions and governments that nation-states create, but also by the kind of norms the international legal system supports. In the concluding reading selection of Part Two of *The Global Agenda,* "The Reality and Relevance of International Law in the 21st Century," Christopher C. Joyner examines a wide spectrum of viewpoints regarding the functions of international law in world affairs. He concludes that despite its limitations (many of which are exaggerated by those uninformed about its principles and procedures), international law succeeds in doing what states ask of it. Not the least of its functions is facilitating the maintenance of the order, stability, and predictability that states prize. Joyner also predicts that international law's contribution to world order will grow, and that its impact will continue to expand.

As we look to the 21st century, we can gain intellectual leverage by comparing the issues and theoretical perspectives described by the essays in Part Two. Although they differ in coverage and conclusions, together they provide a basis for understanding the roots of discord and the foundations of collaboration in international affairs. They should be read with an eye to studying not just military-security issues in the realm of "high politics," but also political-economic issues in the "low politics" realm of global material well-being. We encourage the reader to apply the concepts and lessons introduced in the essays in Part Two to both categories, in order to better interpret the problems on the global agenda that are examined.

11

MODELS OF INTERNATIONAL RELATIONS: REALIST AND NEOLIBERAL PERSPECTIVES ON CONFLICT AND COOPERATION

Ole R. Holsti

Ole R. Holsti describes two models that have been developed to describe and explain different properties of discordant and accommodative relations in world politics: classical and modern "realism" and the so-called neoliberal elaboration of traditional liberal theories. Holsti is George V. Allen Professor of International Affairs at Duke University and is a former president of the International Studies Association. He is the author of *Public Opinion and American Foreign Policy* (1996), and an editor of *The Encyclopedia of American Foreign Relations* (1997).

The question of how best to understand international relations has been debated since the advent of the international system. This debate between proponents of

Adapted for this edition of this book by Ole R. Holsti, from "Models of International Relations and Foreign Policy," *Diplomatic History* 13, 1 (Winter 1989). Many footnotes were deleted and renumbered to appear in consecutive order. Alexander L. George, Joseph Grieco, Michael J. Hogan, Timothy Lomperis, Roy Melbourne, James N. Rosenau, and Andrew M. Scott kindly provided very helpful comments and suggestions on early drafts of that essay. For an alternate, extended theoretical analysis that also discusses Marxist and decision-making approaches, see also Ole R. Holsti, "Theories of International Relations and Foreign Policy: Realism and Its Challengers" in Charles W. Kegley, ed., *Controversies in International Relations Theory: Realism and the Neoliberal Challenge* (New York: St. Martin's Press, 1995), pp. 35–65. Reprinted by permission of the author and Blackwell Publishers.

alternative theories has customarily grown especially intense in times of profound turmoil and change.

In the 20th century, the cataclysm of World War I resurfaced and intensified the dialogue between liberals, such as Woodrow Wilson, who sought to create a new world order anchored in the League of Nations and realists, exemplified by Georges Clemenceau, who sought to use more traditional means to ensure their countries' security. World War II renewed that debate, but the events leading up to that conflict and the Cold War that emerged almost immediately after the guns had stopped firing in 1945 seemed to provide ample evidence to tip the balance strongly in favor of the realist vision of international relations. In the meantime, the growth of Soviet power, combined with the disintegration of the great colonial empires that gave rise to the emergence of some 100 newly independent countries, gave prominence to still another perspective on world affairs, most variants of which drew to some extent upon the writing of Marx and Lenin.

More recent events, including the disintegration of the Soviet Union, the end of the Cold War, the reemergence of inter- and intranational ethnic conflicts that had been suppressed during the Cold War, the Persian Gulf War, the continuing economic integration of Europe, and the declining international economic position of the United States, have stimulated new debates about the theories of the international relations that can best contribute to understanding the emerging issues on the global agenda of the late 20th century. This essay describes two prominent schools of thought on which contemporary theoretical inquiry presently centers. Although different, they speak to each other and place primary explanatory emphasis on features of the international system. These are the variants of realism and the newly revived liberal theories that challenge one or more of the core premises of both classical and modern realism.

Because "classical realism" is the most venerable and persisting model of international relations, it provides a good starting point and baseline for comparison with competing models. Following a discussion of classical realism, an examination of "modern realism" and "neorealism" identifies the continuities and differences between the two approaches. The essay then turns to an examination of the premises underlying neoliberal theories.

REALISM: CLASSICAL, MODERN, AND ITS NEOREALIST EXTENSION

Robert Gilpin[1] may have been engaging in hyperbole when he questioned whether our understanding of international relations has advanced significantly since Thucydides, but one must acknowledge that the latter's analysis of the Peloponnesian War includes concepts that are not foreign to contemporary students of

---

[1]Robert Gilpin, *War and Change in World Politics* (Cambridge: Cambridge University Press, 1981).

balance-of-power politics. There have always been Americans such as Alexander Hamilton who viewed international relations from a realist perspective, but its contemporary intellectual roots are largely European. Three important figures probably had the greatest impact on American scholarship: the historian E. H. Carr,[2] the geographer Nicholas Spykman, and the political theorist Hans J. Morgenthau. Other Europeans who have contributed significantly to realist thought include John Herz (1959), Raymond Aron (1966), Hedley Bull (1977), and Martin Wight (1973), while notable Americans of this school include scholars Arnold Wolfers (1962) and Norman Graebner (1984), as well as diplomat George F. Kennan (1951), journalist Walter Lippmann (1943), and theologian Reinhold Niebuhr (1945).[3]

Classical Realism

Although classical realists do not constitute a homogeneous school—any more than do proponents of any of the other theories discussed in this essay—most of them share at least five core premises about international relations. To begin with, they consider the central questions to be the causes of war and the conditions of peace. They also regard the structure of the system as a necessary if not always sufficient explanation for many aspects of international relations. According to classical realists, "structural anarchy," or the absence of a central authority to settle disputes, is the essential feature of the contemporary system, and it gives rise to the "security dilemma": in a self-help system one nation's search for security often leaves its current and potential adversaries insecure, any nation that strives for absolute security leaves all others in the system absolutely insecure, and the search for security can provide a powerful incentive for arms races and other types of hostile interactions. Consequently, the question of *relative* capabilities is a crucial factor. Efforts to deal with this central element of the international system constitute the driving force behind the relations of units within the system; those that fail to cope will not survive. Thus, unlike "idealists" or "liberals," classical realists view conflict as a natural state of affairs rather than a consequence

---

[2]E. H. Carr, *Twenty Years Crisis* (London: Macmillan, 1939); Nicholas Spykman, *America's Strategy in World Politics* (New York: Harcourt, Brace, 1942); and Hans Morgenthau, *Politics Among Nations* 5th ed. (New York: Knopf, 1973).

[3] John Herz, *International Politics in the Atomic Age* (New York: Columbia University Press, 1959); Raymond Aron, *Peace and War* (Garden City, N.Y.: Doubleday, 1966); Hedley Bull, *The Anarchical Society: A Study of Order in World Politics* (London: Macmillan, 1977); Martin Wight, "The Balance of Power and International Order," in Alan James, ed., *The Bases of International Order* (London: Oxford University Press, 1973); Arnold Wolfers, *Discord and Collaboration* (Baltimore: Johns Hopkins University Press, 1962); Norman A. Graebner, *America as a World Power: A Realist Appraisal from Wilson to Reagan* (Wilmington, Del.: Scholarly Resources, 1984); George F. Kennan, *American Diplomacy, 1900–1950* (Chicago: University of Chicago Press, 1951); Walter Lippmann, *U.S. Foreign Policy: Shield of the Republic* (Boston: Little, Brown, 1943); and Reinhold Niebuhr, *The Children of Light and the Children of Darkness* (New York: Scribner, 1945).

that can be attributed to historical circumstances, evil leaders, flawed sociopolitical systems, or inadequate international understanding and education.

A third premise that unites classical realists is their focus on geographically based groups as the central actors in the international system. During other periods the primary entities may have been city-states or empires, but at least since the Treaties of Westphalia (1648), nation-states have been the dominant units. Classical realists also agree that state behavior is rational. The assumption behind this fourth premise is that states are guided by the logic of the "national interest," usually defined in terms of survival, security, power, and relative capabilities. To Morgenthau, for example, "rational foreign policy minimizes risks and maximizes benefits."[4] Although the national interest may vary according to specific circumstances, the similarity of motives among nations permits the analyst to reconstruct the logic of policy makers in their pursuit of national interests— what Morgenthau called the "rational hypothesis"—and to avoid the fallacies of "concern with motives and concern with ideological preferences."

Finally, the nation-state can also be conceptualized as a *unitary* actor. Because the central problems for states are starkly defined by the nature of the international system, their actions are primarily a response to external rather than domestic political forces. At best, the latter provide very weak explanations for external policy. According to Stephen Krasner, for example, the state "can be treated as an autonomous actor pursuing goals associated with power and the general interest of the society."[5] However, classical realists sometimes use domestic politics, especially the alleged deficiencies of public opinion, to explain deviations from rational policies.

Realism has been the dominant model of international relations during recent decades, perhaps in part because it seemed to provide a useful framework for understanding World War II and the Cold War. Nevertheless, the classical versions articulated by Morgenthau and others have received a good deal of critical scrutiny. The critics have included scholars who accept the basic premises of realism but who found that in at least four important respects these theories lacked sufficient precision and rigor.

Classical realism has usually been grounded in a pessimistic theory of human nature, either a theological version (e.g., St. Augustine and Reinhold Niebuhr) or a secular one (e.g., Machiavelli, Hobbes, and Morgenthau). Egoism and self-interested behavior are not limited to a few evil or misguided leaders, as the idealists would have it, but are basic to *homo politicus* and thus are at the core of a realist theory. But because human nature, if it means anything, is a constant rather than a variable, it is an unsatisfactory explanation for the full range of international relations. If human nature explains war and conflict, what accounts

---

[4]Morgenthau, *Politics among Nations,* pp. 3, 5.

[5]Stephen Krasner, *Defending the National Interest* (Princeton, N.J.: Princeton University Press, 1978), p. 33.

for peace and cooperation? In order to avoid this problem, most modern realists have turned their attention from human nature to the structure of the international system to explain state behavior.

In addition, critics have noted a lack of precision and even contradictions in the way classical realists use such concepts as "power," "national interest," and "balance of power." They also see possible contradictions between the central descriptive and prescriptive elements of classical realism. On the one hand, as Hans Morgenthau put it, nations and their leaders "think and act in terms of interests defined as power,"[6] but on the other, diplomats are urged to exercise prudence and self-restraint, as well as to recognize the legitimate interests of other nations. Obviously, then, power plays a central role in classical realism. But the correlation between the relative power balance and political outcomes is often less than compelling, suggesting the need to enrich analyses with other variables. Moreover, the distinction between "power as capabilities" and "usable options" is especially important in the nuclear age.

Modern Realism

While classical realists have typically looked to history, philosophy, and political science for insights and evidence, the search for greater precision has led many modern realists to look elsewhere for appropriate models, analogies, metaphors, and insights. The discipline of choice is often economics, from which modern realists have borrowed such tools and concepts as rational choice, expected utility, theories of firms and markets, bargaining theory, and game theory. Contrary to the assertion of some critics, however, modern realists *share* rather than reject the core premises of their classical predecessors.

The quest for precision has yielded a rich harvest of theories and models, and a somewhat less bountiful crop of supporting empirical applications. Drawing in part on game theory, Morton Kaplan described several types of international systems—for example, balance of power, loose bipolar, tight bipolar, universal, hierarchical, and a unit-veto system in which any action requires the unanimous approval of all its members. He then outlined the essential rules that constitute these systems. For example, the rules for a balance-of-power system are "(1) increase capabilities, but negotiate rather than fight; (2) fight rather than fail to increase capabilities; (3) stop fighting rather than eliminate an essential actor; (4) oppose any coalition or single actor that tends to assume a position of predominance within the system; (5) constrain actors who subscribe to supranational organizational principles; and (6) permit defeated or constrained essential actors to re-enter the system."[7]

---

[6]Morgenthau, *Politics among Nations,* p. 5.
[7] Morton Kaplan, *System and Process in International Politics* (New York: Wiley, 1957), p. 23.

Neorealism

Kenneth Waltz's *Theory of International Politics,*[8] the most prominent effort to develop a rigorous and parsimonious model of "neorealist" or "structural" realism, has tended to define the terms of recent theoretical debates. It follows and builds upon another enormously influential book in which Waltz developed the Rousseauian position that a theory of war must include the system level (the "third image") and not just first (theories of human nature) or second (state attributes) images.[9] Why war? Because there is nothing in the system to prevent it.

Theory of International Politics is grounded in analogies from microeconomics: international politics and foreign policy are analogous to markets and firms. Oligopoly theory is used to illuminate the dynamics of interdependent choice in a self-help anarchical system. Waltz explicitly limits his attention to a structural theory of international systems, eschewing the task of linking it to a theory of foreign policy. Indeed, he doubts that the two can be joined in a single theory and is highly critical of many system-level analysts, including Morton Kaplan, Stanley Hoffmann, Richard Rosecrance, Karl Deutsch, J. David Singer, and others, charging them with various errors, including "reductionism," that is, defining the system in terms of the attributes or interactions of the units.

In order to avoid reductionism and to gain rigor and parsimony, Waltz erects his theory on the foundations of three core propositions that define the structure of the international system. The first concentrates on the principles by which the system is ordered. The contemporary system is anarchic and decentralized rather than hierarchial; although they differ in many respects, each unit (state) is formally equal. Because Waltz strives for a universal theory that is not limited to any era, he uses the term "unit" to refer to the constituent members of the system; in the contemporary system these are states, but in order to reflect Waltz's intent more faithfully, the term "unit" is used here. A second defining proposition is the character of the units. An anarchic system is composed of similar sovereign units, and therefore the functions that they perform are also similar rather than different; for example, all have the task of providing for their own security. In contrast, a hierarchical system would be characterized by some type of division of labor, as is the case in domestic politics. Finally, there is the distribution of capabilities among units in the system. Although capabilities are a unit-level attribute, the distribution of capabilities is a system-level concept.

A change in any of these elements constitutes a change in system structure. The first element of structure as defined by Waltz is a quasi-constant because the ordering principle rarely changes, and the second element drops out of the analysis because the functions of units are similar as long as the system remains anarchic. Thus, the last of the three attributes, the distribution of capabilities, plays the central role in Waltz's model.

---

[8] Kenneth W. Waltz, *Theory of International Politics* (Reading, Mass.: Addison Wesley, 1979).
[9] Kenneth W. Waltz, *Man, the State, and War* (New York: Columbia University Press, 1959).

Waltz uses his theory to deduce the central characteristics of international relations. These include some nonobvious propositions about the contemporary international system. For example, with respect to system stability (defined as maintenance of its anarchic character and no consequential variation in the number of major actors), he concludes that because the Cold War's bipolar system reduced uncertainty, it was more stable than alternative structures. Furthermore, he contends that because interdependence has declined rather than increased during the 20th century, this trend has actually contributed to stability; and he argues that the proliferation of nuclear weapons may contribute to rather than erode system stability.[10]

Unlike some system-level models, Waltz's effort to bring rigor and parsimony to realism has stimulated a good deal of further research, but it has not escaped controversy and criticism.[11] Leaving aside highly charged polemics—for example, that Waltz and his supporters are guilty of engaging in a "totalitarian project of global proportions"[12]—most of the vigorous debate has centered on four alleged deficiencies relating to interests and preferences, system change, misallocation of variables between the system and unit levels, and an inability to explain outcomes.

Specifically, a sparse structural approach suffers from an inability to identify adequately the nature and sources of interests and preferences because these are unlikely to derive solely from the structure of the system. Ideology or domestic considerations may often be at least as important. Consequently, the model is also unable to specify how interests and preferences may change. The three defining characteristics of system structure are too general, moreover, and thus they are not sufficiently sensitive to specify the sources and dynamics of system change. The critics buttress their claim that the model is too static by pointing to Waltz's assertion that there has only been a single structural change in the international system during the past three centuries.

Another drawback is the restrictive definition of system properties, which leads to the charge that Waltz misplaces and therefore neglects elements of international relations that properly belong at the system level. Critics have focused on his treatment of the destructiveness of nuclear weapons and interdependence. Waltz labels these as unit-level properties, whereas some of his critics assert that they are in fact attributes of the system.

---

[10] Kenneth W. Waltz, "The Myth of National Interdependence," in Charles P. Kindleberger, ed., *The International Corporation* (Cambridge: M.I.T. Press, 1970), and "The Spread of Nuclear Weapons: More May Be Better," *Adelphi Papers*, no. 171 (1981).

[11] See especially Joseph Grieco, *Between Dependence and Autonomy* (Berkeley: University of California Press, 1984); Robert Keohane, ed., *Neorealism and Its Critics* (New York: Columbia University Press, 1986); David A. Baldwin, ed., *Neorealism and Neoliberalism: The Contemporary Debate* (New York: Columbia University Press, 1993); and Charles W. Kegley, Jr., ed., *Controversies in International Relations Theory: Realism and the Neoliberal Challenge* (New York: St. Martin's Press, 1995).

[12] Richard K. Ashley, "The Poverty of Neo-Realism," *International Organization* 38 (1984), pp. 225–286.

Finally, the distribution of capabilities explains outcomes in international affairs only in the most general way, falling short of answering the questions that are of central interest to many analysts. For example, the distribution of power at the end of World War II would have enabled one to predict the rivalry that emerged between the United States and the Soviet Union (as de Tocqueville did more than a century earlier), but it would have been inadequate for explaining the pattern of relations between these two countries—the Cold War rather than withdrawal into isolationism by either or both, a division of the world into spheres of influence, or World War III. In order to do so, it is necessary to explore political processes *within* states—at minimum within the United States and the USSR—as well as *between* them.

Robert Gilpin shares with Waltz the core assumptions of modern realism, but his study of *War and Change in World Politics* also attempts to cope with some of the criticism leveled at Waltz's theory by focusing on the dynamics of system change. Drawing upon both economic and sociological theory, his model is based on five core propositions.[13] The first is that the international system is stable—in a state of equilibrium—if no state believes that it is profitable to attempt to change it. Second, a state will attempt to change the status quo of the international system if the expected benefits outweigh the costs; that is, if there is an expected net gain for the revisionist state. Related to this is the proposition that a state will seek change through territorial, political, and economic expansion until the marginal costs of further change equal or exceed the marginal benefits. Moreover, when an equilibrium between the costs and benefits of further change and expansion is reached, the economic costs of maintaining the status quo (expenditures for military forces, support for allies, etc.) tend to rise faster than the resources needed to do so. An equilibrium exists when no powerful state believes that a change in the system would yield additional net benefits. Finally, if the resulting disequilibrium between the existing governance of the international system and the redistribution of power is not resolved, the system will be changed and a new equilibrium reflecting the distribution of relative capabilities will be established.

Unlike Waltz, Gilpin includes state-level processes in order to explain change. Differential economic growth rates among nations—a structural-systemic-level variable—play a vital role in his explanation for the rise and decline of great powers, but his model also includes propositions about the law of diminishing returns on investments, the impact of affluence on martial spirits and on the ratio of consumption to investment, and structural change in the economy. Table 11-1 summarizes some key elements of realism. It also contrasts them to a rival system-level model of international relations—the neoliberal model, to which we now turn our attention.

---

[13]Gilpin, *War and Change in World Politics,* pp. 10–11.

TABLE 11-1
TWO MODELS OF THE INTERNATIONAL SYSTEM

	Realism	Neoliberalism
Type of model	Classical: descriptive and normative Modern: deductive	Descriptive and normative
Central problems	Causes of war Conditions of peace	Broad agenda of political, social, economic, and environmental issues arising from gap between demands and resources
Conception of current international system	Structural anarchy	Global society Complex interdependence (structure varies by issue-area)
Key actors	Geographically based units (tribes, city-states, nation-state, etc.)	Highly permeable nation-states *plus* a broad range of non-state actors, including IOs, IGOs, NGOs, and individuals
Central motivations	National interests Security Power	Human needs and wants (including security)
Loyalties	To geographically based groups (from tribes to nation-states)	Loyalties to nation-state declining To emerging global values and institutions that transcend those of the nation-state and/or to subnational groups
Central processes	Search for security and survival	Aggregate effects of decisions by national and non-national actors How units (not limited to nation-states) cope with a growing agenda of threats and opportunities arising from human wants
Likelihood of system transformation	Low (basic structural elements of system have revealed an ability to persist despite many other kinds of changes)	High in the direction of the model (owing to the rapid pace of technological change, etc.)
Sources of theory, insights, and evidence	Politics History Economics (especially "modern" realists)	Broad range of social sciences Natural and technological sciences

NEOLIBERALISM

Just as there are variants of realism, there are several neoliberal theories, but this discussion focuses on two common denominators: they all challenge the first and third core propositions of realism identified earlier, asserting that inordinate attention to the war/peace issue and the nation-state renders it an increasingly anachronistic model of global relations.[14]

The agenda of critical problems confronting states has been vastly expanded during the 20th century. Attention to the issues of war and peace is by no means misdirected according to proponents of a liberal perspective, but concerns for welfare, modernization, the environment, and the like are today no less potent sources of motivation and action. Indeed, many liberals define security in terms that are broader than the geopolitical-military spheres, and they emphasize the potential for cooperative relations among nations. Institution building to reduce uncertainty, information costs, and fears of perfidy; improved international education and communication to ameliorate fears and antagonisms based on misinformation and misperceptions; and the positive-sum possibilities of such activities as trade are but a few of the ways, according to liberals, by which nations may jointly gain and thus mitigate, if not eliminate, the harshest features of international relations emphasized by the realists. Finally, the diffusion of knowledge and technology, combined with the globalization of communications, has vastly increased popular expectations. The resulting demands have outstripped resources and the ability of existing institutions—notably the nation-state—to cope effectively with them. Interdependence arises from an inability of even the most powerful states to cope, or to do so unilaterally or at acceptable levels of cost and risk, with issues ranging from trade to AIDS, and immigration to environmental threats.

Paralleling the widening agenda of critical issues is the expansion of actors whose behavior can have a significant impact beyond national boundaries; indeed, the cumulative effects of their actions can have profound consequences for the international system. Thus, although nation-states continue to be important international actors, they possess a declining ability to control their own destinies. The aggregate effect of actions by multitudes of non-state actors can have potent effects that transcend political boundaries. These may include such powerful or highly visible non-state institutions as Exxon, the Organization of Petroleum Exporting Countries, or the Palestine Liberation Organization. On the other hand, the cumulative effects of decisions by less powerful or less visible actors

---

[14] Robert Keohane and Joseph S. Nye, Jr., *Power and Interdependence* (Boston: Little, Brown, 1977); Edward Morse, *Modernization and the Transformation of International Relations* (New York: Free Press, 1976); James N. Rosenau, *The Study of Global Interdependence* (London: F. Pinter, 1980); and *Turbulence in World Politics* (Princeton, N.J.: Princeton University Press, 1990); Richard Mansbach and John Vasquez, *In Search of Theory: A New Paradigm* (New York: Columbia University Press, 1981); Andrew M. Scott, *The Dynamics of Interdependence* (Chapel Hill: University of North Carolina Press, 1982).

may also have profound international consequences. For example, decisions by thousands of individuals, mutual funds, banks, pension funds, and other financial institutions to sell securities on 19 October 1987 not only resulted in an unprecedented "crash" on Wall Street but within hours its consequences were also felt throughout the entire global financial system. Governments might take such actions as loosening credit or even closing exchanges, but they were largely unable to contain the effects of the panic.

The widening agenda of critical issues, most of which lack a purely national solution, has also led to creation of new actors that transcend political boundaries, for example, international organizations, transnational organizations, nongovernmental organizations, multinational corporations, and the like. Thus, not only does an exclusive focus on the war/peace issue fail to capture the complexities of contemporary international life but it also blinds the analyst to the institutions, processes, and norms that permit cooperation and significantly mitigate some features of an anarchic system. In short, according to emerging new liberal perspectives, an adequate understanding of the proliferating issues in the evolving global system must recognize that no single model is likely to be sufficient for all issues, and that if it restricts attention to the manner in which states deal with traditional security concerns, it is more likely to obfuscate than clarify the realities of contemporary world affairs.

The liberal models have several important virtues. They recognize that international behavior and outcomes arise from a multiplicity of motives, not merely security, at least if security is defined solely in military or strategic terms. They also alert us to the fact that important international processes and conditions originate not only in the actions of nation-states but also in the aggregated behavior of other actors. These models not only enable the analyst to deal with a broader agenda of critical issues but, more importantly, they force one to contemplate a much richer menu of demands, processes, and outcomes than would be derived from power-centered realist models. Stated differently, liberal theories are more sensitive to the possibility that the politics of trade, currencies, immigration, health, the environment, and the like may significantly and systematically differ from those typically associated with security issues.

On the other hand, some liberal analysts underestimate the potency of nationalism and the durability of the nation-state. Two decades ago one of them wrote that "the nation is declining in its importance as a political unit to which allegiances are attached."[15] Objectively, nationalism may be an anachronism, but for better or worse, powerful loyalties are still attached to nation-states. The

---

[15]James N. Rosenau, "National Interest," *International Encyclopedia of the Social Sciences* (New York: Macmillan, 1968), pp. 34–40. See also Richard Rosecrance, *The Rise of the Trading State* (New York: Basic Books, 1986); and John Herz, "The Rise and Demise of the Territorial State," *World Politics* 9 (1957), pp. 473–93, and "The Territorial State Revisited: Reflections on the Future of the Nation-State," *Polity* 1 (1968), pp. 12–34.

suggestion that because even some well-established countries have experienced independence movements among ethnic, cultural, or religious minorities, the sovereign territorial state may be in decline is not wholly persuasive. Indeed, that evidence perhaps points to precisely the opposite conclusion: in virtually every region of the world there are groups that seek to create or restore geographically based entities in which its members may enjoy the status and privileges associated with sovereign territorial statehood. Evidence from Poland to Palestine, Serbia to Sri Lanka, Estonia to Eritrea, Armenia to Afghanistan, Bosnia to Chechnya, and elsewhere seems to indicate that obituaries for nationalism may be somewhat premature.

The notion that such powerful non-national actors as major multinational corporations (MNCs) will soon transcend the nation-state seems equally premature. International drug rings do appear capable of dominating such states as Colombia and Panama. However, the pattern of outcomes in confrontations between MNCs and states, including cases involving major expropriations of corporate properties, indicates that even relatively weak nations are not always the hapless pawns of the MNCs. Case studies by Joseph Grieco and Gary Gereffi, among others, indicate that MNC-state relations yield a wide variety of outcomes.[16]

Underlying the liberal critique of realist models is that the latter are too wedded to the past and are thus incapable of dealing adequately with change. For the present, however, even if global dynamics arise from multiple sources (including non-state actors), the actions of nation-states and their agents would appear to remain the major sources of change in the international system.

THE REALIST-LIBERAL DIALOGUE AND THE FUTURE

A renowned diplomatic historian has asserted that most theories of international relations flunked a critical test by failing to forecast the end of the Cold War.[17] This conclusion speculates on the related question of how well the theories discussed above might help us understand conflict and cooperation in the post–Cold-War world. Dramatic events since the late 1980s appear to have posed serious challenges for several theories, but one should be wary about writing premature obituaries for any of them. The importance of recent developments notwithstanding, one should avoid "naive (single case) falsification" of major theories. Further, in 1997, eight short years after the Berlin Wall came down and only six years after dissolution of the Soviet Union, some caution about declaring that major events and trends are irreversible seems warranted.

Liberal theories have recently regained popularity, especially in efforts to explain relations among the industrial democracies. Progress toward economic

---

[16]Grieco, *Between Dependence and Autonomy;* and Gary Gereffi, *The Pharmaceutical Industry and Dependency in the Third World* (Princeton: Princeton University Press, 1983).

[17]John Lewis Gaddis, "International Relations Theory and the End of the Cold War," *International Security* 17 (1992–93), p. 5–58.

unification of Europe, although not without detours and setbacks, would appear to provide significant support for the liberal view that, even in an anarchic world, major powers may find ways of cooperating and overcoming the constraint of the "relative gains" problem. Moreover, Woodrow Wilson's thesis that a world of democratic nations will be more peaceful has stood the test of time rather well, at least in the sense that democratic nations have not gone to war with each other.[18] Wilson's diagnosis that self-determination also supports peace may be correct in the abstract, but universal application of that principle is neither possible nor desirable, if only because it would result in immense bloodshed; the peaceful divorces of Norway and Sweden in 1905 and of the Czech Republic and Slovakia in 1992 are unfortunately not the norm. Although it appears that economic interests have come to dominate nationalist, ethnic, or religious passions among the industrial democracies, the evidence is far less assuring in other areas, including parts of the former Soviet Union, Central Europe, the Middle East, South Asia, Africa, and elsewhere.

Recent events appear to have created an especially acute challenge to structural realism. Although structural realism provides a parsimonious and elegant theory, its deficiencies are likely to become more rather than less apparent in the post–Cold-War world. Its weaknesses in dealing with questions of system change and in specifying policy preferences other than survival and security are likely to be magnified. Moreover, whereas classical realism espouses a number of attractive prescriptive features (caution, humility, warnings against mistaking one's preferences for the moral laws of the universe), neorealism is an especially weak source of policy-relevant theory.[19] Indeed, some of the prescriptions put forward by neorealists seem reckless, such as the suggestion to let Germany join the nuclear club.[20] In addition to European economic cooperation, specific events that seem inexplicable by structural realism include Soviet acquiescence in the collapse of its empire and peaceful transformation of the system structure. These developments are especially telling because structural realism is explicitly touted as a theory of major powers.[21] Although proponents of realism are not ready to concede that the end of the Cold War has raised some serious questions about its validity,[22] even as distinguished a realist as Robert Tucker has characterized the structural version of realism as "more questionable than ever."

---

[18] Michael Doyle, "Kant, Liberal Legacies, and Foreign Affairs," *Philosophy and Public Affairs* 12 (1983), pp. 205–35, and "Liberalism and World Politics," *American Political Science Review* 80 (1986), pp. 1151–70.

[19] Alexander L. George, *Bridging the Gap: Theory and Practice in Foreign Policy* (Washington: U.S. Institute of Peace, 1993).

[20] John Mearsheimer, "Back to the Future: Instability in Europe after the Cold War," *International Security* 15 (1990), pp. 5–56.

[21] Waltz, *Theory of International Politics.*

[22] Robert W. Tucker, "Realism and the New Consensus," *National Interest* 30 (1992–93), pp. 33–36. See also Paul Schroeder, "Historical Reality vs. Neo-realist theory," *International Security* 19 (1994) pp. 108–48.

More importantly, even though the international system remains anarchic, the possibility of war among major powers cannot wholly be dismissed, and proliferation may place nuclear weapons in the hands of leaders with little stake in maintaining the status quo, as the constraints imposed by systemic imperatives on foreign policy choices are clearly eroding. National interests and even national security have increasingly come to be defined in ways that transcend the military/strategic concerns that are at the core of realist theory. Well before the disintegration of the Soviet Union, an Americans Talk Security survey in 1988 revealed that the perceived threat to national security from "Soviet aggression around the world" ranked in a seventh place tie with the "greenhouse effect" and well behind a number of post–Cold War, nonmilitary threats. Trade, drug trafficking, immigration, the environment, and AIDS are among the nonmilitary issues that regularly appear on lists of top national security threats as perceived by both mass public and elites.

The expanded agenda of national interests, combined with the trend toward greater democracy in many parts of the world, suggests that we are entering an era in which the balance between the relative potency of systemic and domestic forces in shaping and constraining foreign policies is moving toward the latter. Such issues as trade, immigration, and others can be expected to enhance the impact of domestic actors—including public opinion and ethnic, religious, economic, and perhaps even regional pressure groups—while reducing the ability of executives to dominate policy processes on the grounds, so frequently invoked during the Cold War, that the adept pursuit of national security requires secrecy, flexibility, and the ability to act with speed on the basis of classified information. In short, we are likely to see the increasing democratization of foreign policy in the post–Cold-War era. And that brings us back to the point at which we started, for the relationship between democracy and foreign policy is another of the issues on which realists and liberals are in sharp disagreement. Realists such as de Tocqueville, Morgenthau, Lippmann, Kennan, and many others share a profound skepticism about the impact of democratic political processes, and especially of public opinion, on the quality and continuity of foreign policy. In contrast, liberals in the Kant-Wilson tradition maintain that more democratic foreign policy processes contribute to peace and stability in international politics. Thus, if domestic politics do in fact come to play an increasingly important role in shaping post–Cold-War era foreign policies, that development will ensure continuation of the venerable debate between realists and liberals.

12

DISORDER AND ORDER IN A TURBULENT WORLD: THE EVOLUTION OF GLOBALIZED SPACE

James N. Rosenau

The forces of change and continuity are creating unprecedented levels of complexity in world affairs and new challenges to global order. Describing the accelerating pace of change across many dimensions of international affairs, this essay surveys the major diverging trends and underlying dynamics of globalization in an interdependent world that are altering the very texture of history and are simultaneously producing integration and disintegration, cooperation and conflict, and order and disorder. Rosenau is University Professor of International Affairs at George Washington University. His many books include *Along the Domestic-Foreign Frontier: Exploring Governance in a Turbulent World* **(1997) and** *Turbulence in World Politics: A Theory of Change and Continuity* **(1990).**

The original version of this essay was written for an earlier edition of this volume. This essay is from *United Nations in a Turbulent World* by James Rosenau. (Boulder: Lynn Reinner Publishing, 1992). Copyright © 1992 by International Peace Academy. Reprinted by permission of the International Peace Academy. Earlier versions were presented in James N. Rosenau, "Security in a Turbulent World," *Current History* 94 (May 1995), pp. 193–200, and James N. Rosenau, "The Dynamism of a Turbulent World," in Michael Klare and Yogesh Chandrani (eds.), *World Security: Challenges for a New Century,* 3rd ed., (New York : St. Martin's Press, 1998). Several paragraphs have also been drawn from James N. Rosenau, *Along the Domestic-Foreign Frontier: Exploring Governance in a Turbulent World* (Cambridge: Cambridge University Press, 1997), chaps. 1 and 3. The author is grateful to Hongying Wang for helpful reactions to the earlier versions.

More than a few observers have come to recognize that in a rapidly changing interdependent world the separation of national and international affairs is problematic.[1] Some may still cling to the logic that divides domestic from foreign affairs, but most acknowledge that such boundaries are pervasively porous because they do not confine the phenomena, problems, and processes of greatest interest. To separately analyze domestic and foreign affairs is thus more than arbitrary; it is downright erroneous. The two have always been a seamless web and the need to treat them as such is urgent in this time of enormous transformation. Border guards may check passports and customs officials may impose duties, but to conceive of the foreign-domestic distinction in this simple way is to mislead, to mistake surface appearances for underlying patterns, and to underplay the powerful dynamics that are accelerating the pervasive transformations of even the most routine dimensions of daily life. Individuals, groups, and communities are contending with the challenges of expanded horizons, the ambiguities of transnationalization, and the realities of globalization.

This essay presumes that the domestic-foreign arena has yielded to a new political space—here called Globalized Space and capitalized to stress its centrality[2]—in which questions of identity have climbed to the top of personal agendas even as questions of shared norms have climbed to the top of community agendas and the problem of how to mesh personal identities with shared community norms climbs ever higher on political agendas at all levels of organization. The tensions embedded in these questions are closely linked to a multiplicity of contradictions that pervade Globalized Space: The international system is less commanding, but it is still influential. States are changing, but they are not disappearing. Some communities are breaking up and others are consolidating. Governments are weaker, but they can still throw their weight around. Politicians run for office, but they border on becoming irrelevant even when they win.[3] At times publics are more demanding, but they are also more pliable at other times. People are more skillful, but huge numbers also feel more vulnerable to the vicissitudes of globalization. "Home" is no longer so much a place as it is a sense of connectedness, but it remains the center of daily life. Boundaries still keep out intruders, but they are also more porous. Landscapes are giving

---

[1]See, for example, John Agnew and Stuart Corbridge, *Mastering Space: Hegemony, Territory and International Political Economy* (New York: Routledge, 1995), and Hugh De Santis, *Beyond Progress: An Interpretive Odyssey to the Future* (Chicago: University of Chicago Press, 1996).

[2]For an extensive analysis of this emergent space, see Rosenau, *Along the Domestic-Foreign Frontier.*

[3]"While politicians go through the motions of national elections—offering chimerical programs and slogans—world markets, the Internet and the furious pace of trade involve people in a global game in which elected representatives figure as little more than bit players." Roger Cohen, "Global Forces Batter Politics," *New York Times,* November 17, 1996, sec. 4, p. 1.

way to ethnoscapes, mediascapes, ideoscapes, technoscapes, and finanscapes, but territoriality is still a central preoccupation for many people.[4]

Sorting out contradictions such as these poses a number of difficult questions: How do we assess a world in which Globalized Space is continuously shifting and widening, simultaneously undergoing erosion with respect to some issues and cohering with respect to others? How do we reconceptualize politics so as to trace the new or transformed authorities that occupy the new political spaces created by shifting and porous boundaries?[5]

Various responses to such questions are possible. One, the most rigid, is to treat the indicators of change as superficial and to assert that the fundamentals of global life are no different today from what they were in the past. A second is to regard the changes as newly recognized rather than as new phenomena. A third is to perceive the changes as real and powerful, but to assert that they have not altered the basic parameters of world affairs. A fourth response, and the one that guides the ensuing analysis, presumes that the basic parameters that have long underlay world affairs are caught up in deep and pervasive changes. It treats Globalized Space as becoming ever more expansive and, thus, as a widening field of action, as the realm in which world affairs unfold, as the locale to which communities must either adapt or give way to new forms of organization, as the arena in which domestic and foreign issues converge, intermesh, or otherwise become indistinguishable as a seamless web. In effect, it is in Globalized Space and not the nation-state system where people sort and play out the many contradictions presently at work on the world stage.[6]

Such a perspective is not easily addressed. We are so accustomed to thinking of domestic and international politics as separate playing fields that it is difficult to conceptualize any structures and processes that may be superseding them as a new field of play. It is easier to assert what Globalized Space is not than to enumerate its diverse characteristics. It is not a vacuum to which the homeless in the nation-state system have fled. Nor is it a residual category for actors whose missions are not consonant with those of the nation-state system. Rather, it is populated by groups and organizations whose activities transgress the nation-state system and who have thus become increasingly independent of

---

[4]For a discussion of the nature of these diverse "scapes," see Arjun Appadurai, "Disjuncture and Difference in the Global Cultural Economy," *Public Culture* 2 (1990), pp. 1–23.

[5]An extended effort to answer these questions is provided in James N. Rosenau, *Along the Domestic-Foreign Frontier.*

[6]For a similar formulation that focuses on some of the processes considered here to be central to Globalized Space, see Mathias Albert and Luthar Brock, *Debordering the World of States: New Spaces in International Relations* (Frankfurt: World Society Research Group, Working Paper No. 2, 1995). Another formulation that downplays the domestic-foreign boundary—calling it a "nonplace" (p. 260)—is developed in Richard K. Ashley, "Living on Border Lines: Man, Poststructuralism, and War," in James Der Derian and Michael J. Shapiro (eds.), *International/Intertextual Relations* (Lexington, Mass.: Lexington Books, 1989), pp. 259–321.

the nation-state system. In effect, Globalized Space has replaced the international system because all the world's public and private actors are being drawn, some eagerly and others reluctantly, into its confines. The processes of Globalized Space involve the intensification of either boundary-spanning or boundary-contracting activities in response to the multifaceted dynamics of globalization—to the emergence of a world economy, to the communications revolution and the rapid flow of information, to the ease of travel and the vast movements of people, and to the emergence of norms widely shared across traditional boundaries. Put more challengingly, Globalized Space is a terra incognito that sometimes takes the form of a market, sometimes appears as a civil society, sometimes seems to be a fledgling community, often looks like a regional network, sometimes resembles a legislative chamber, periodically is a crowded town square, occasionally is a battlefield, increasingly is traversed by an information highway, and usually looks like a multiring circus in which all these—and many other—activities are unfolding simultaneously.

Given this diversity, Globalized Space is not so much a single political space as it is a host of diverse spheres (even though here it is referred to generically in the singular) that are so new as to confound established patterns and long-standing expectations, with the result that background often becomes foreground, time becomes disjointed, nonlinear patterns predominate, structures bifurcate, societies implode, regions unify, and politics swirl about issues of identity, territoriality, and the interface between long-established institutions and emergent orientations. Globalized Space is thus marked by complex and unfamiliar patterns that fluctuate erratically as different issues widen or alter its terrain and foster corresponding shifts in the distinction between "us" and "them" or—to use a less combative distinction—between Self and Other.

In short, Globalized Space points to an epochal transformation, a new worldview as to the essential nature of human affairs, a new way of thinking about how politics unfold. At the center of the emergent worldview lies an understanding that the order that sustains families, communities, countries, regions, and the world through time rests on contradictions, ambiguities, and uncertainties. Where earlier epochs were conceived in terms of central tendencies and orderly patterns, the present epoch appears to derive its order from contrary trends and episodic patterns. Where the lives of individuals and societies were once seen as moving along linear and steady trajectories, now their movement seems nonlinear and erratic, with equilibria being momentary and continuously punctuated by sudden accelerations or directional shifts.

Accordingly, the long-standing inclination to think in either/or terms has begun to give way to framing challenges as both/and problems. People now understand, emotionally as well as intellectually, that unexpected events are commonplace, that anomalies are normal occurrences, that minor incidents can mushroom into major outcomes, that fundamental processes trigger opposing forces even as they expand their scope, that what was once transitional may now be enduring, and that the complexities of modern life are so deeply rooted as to infuse ordinariness into the surprising development and the anxieties that attach to it.

Being complex, the new conditions that have widened Globalized Space cannot be explained by a single source.[7] The information revolution and other technological dynamics are major stimulants, but so is the breakdown of trust, the shrinking of distances, the globalization of economies, the greater skills of citizens, the explosive proliferation of organizations, the fragmentation of groups and the integration of regions, the surge of democratic practices and the spread of fundamentalism, the cessation of intense enmities and the revival of historic animosities—all of which in turn provoke further reactions that add to the complexity.

Not only does grasping this complexity call on us to locate Globalized Space at the center of the political agenda, but it also requires us to back off from established conceptual premises and be ready to think afresh. It asks that we accept the possibility that the core of political units has shrunk as effective authority has shifted toward and beyond their peripheries. And, not least, it invites us to appreciate that *both* the dynamics of global change and the resistances to them are part and parcel of the human condition as one millennium ends and another begins.

THINKING AFRESH

To break with conventional approaches to any subject demands considerable effort. One must be continuously alert to the danger of slipping back into old analytic habits and, even more, to doing so unknowingly. Even if they are no longer functional, the old habits are comfortable. They worked earlier, one tends to reason, so why abandon them when thinking afresh can as readily lead to dead ends as down paths to greater understanding. Yet, if we do not confront our ways of thinking, talking, and writing about governance in a turbulent world, our analysis will suffer from a reliance on artifacts of the very past beyond which it seeks to move. It will remain plagued by a lack of conceptual tools appropriate to the task of sorting out the underpinnings of political processes sustained by the altered borders, redirected legitimacy sentiments, impaired or paralyzed governments, and new identities that underlie the emergence of new spheres of authority in Globalized Space.

A depleted toolshed suggests that understanding is no longer served by clinging to the notion that boundaries do indeed bind. We have become so accustomed to treating states and national governments as the foundations of politics that we

---

[7]Since repercussions of the end of the Cold War were clearly evident at all levels of organization, it is tempting to treat this development as an epochal turning point. Such an interpretation, however, is misleading; it exaggerates the impact of a single historical moment and does not allow for the possibility that the end of the Cold War was the culmination of underlying and long-standing processes of change that, as stressed here, ushered in a common sense of dynamics and structures that amounted to a new epoch. For an analysis in which the Cold War is seen as having "left so light an impact on the living memory of states and societies that it is already en route to oblivion," see Ian Gambles, "Lost Time—The Forgetting of the Cold War," *National Interest* 41 (Fall 1995), p. 35.

fall back on them when contemplating the dynamics of global change, thereby relegating the shifting boundaries, relocated authorities, and proliferating nongovernmental organizations (NGOs) to the status of new but secondary dimensions of the processes through which communities allocate values and frame policies. To be sure, few observers would dismiss the impact of these dimensions as peripheral. Nonetheless, the predominant tendency is to cling to old ways of thought that accord primacy to states and national governments. Table 12-1 conveys this conventional conception of how politics works. Its vertical columns call attention to the firmness of the boundaries that differentiate the various types of territorial communities, ranging from the least to the most encompassing. Each column represents a governance entity that has responsibility for the issues and qualities of life within its jurisdiction. Likewise, the rows in Table 12-1 depict some of the diverse issues encompassed by any community in the waning epoch. Each row represents an issue area and the concerns that set apart the groups active within it.

If it is accepted, however, that Globalized Space has widened and eroded the boundaries separating domestic and foreign affairs, then Table 12-2 (p. 153) is a more accurate portrayal of the underlying structure of world affairs in the emerging epoch. It suggests that while the same political issues and territorial units are still part of the political scene, they are no longer constrained by firm boundaries. Instead, the table's diagonal spaces highlight some of the nonterritorial actors and networks active in Global Space that interdependently link the issues and units. To be sure, in various parts of the world the long-established boundaries remain fully intact, and it may also be the case that the structure implied in Table 12-2 has yet to surface fully; but here the analysis proceeds from the presumption that, indeed, the diagonal spaces represent common threads sufficiently woven into the fabric of global life to form the foundations of an emergent epoch. The essential argument is that the overlaps among communities depicted by the diagonal spaces have become increasingly salient precisely because they subsume numerous problems that cannot be accounted for, much less managed by, established collectivities. The enormous complexities and interdependencies that have been fostered by a multiplicity of postindustrial dynamics are simply too extensive for the diverse problems of territorial communities not to meld into a larger set of challenges, which in turn foster the evolution of new arrangements for politics in a turbulent world. Among the new arrangements, perhaps none is more crucial than the advent of networks as organizational forms no less central to the conduct of world affairs than are hierarchical structures.[8] It follows that if the in-

[8]Compare Francis Fukuyama, "Social Networks and Digital Networks" (Washington, D.C.: Rand Corporation, 1996, xerox); Dee W. Hock, "Institutions in the Age of Mindcrafting" (San Francisco: Bionomics Annual Conference, 1994, xerox); David Ronfeldt, "Tribes, Institutions, Markets, Networks: A Framework About Societal Evolution" (Santa Monica: Rand Corporation, 1996, xerox). For a succinct discussion of the challenges analysts face in studying networks, see Mustafa Emirbayer and Jeff Goodwin, "Network Analysis, Culture, and the Problem of Agency," *American Journal of Sociology* 99 (May 1994), pp. 1411–54.

TABLE 12-1
GOVERNANCE SUSTAINED BY TERRITORIAL UNITS AND ISSUE AREAS

	Levels of Political Organization				
Issue Areas	Towns	Cities	Provinces	Nation States	International Agencies
Science and technology					
Commerce and trade					
Conservation versus development					
Labor					
Agriculture					
Immigration					
Education					
Human rights					
Religion					
Environmental					
Health and welfare					
Elections					
Constitutional issues					
Etc.					

teractions of sovereign states in an anarchical world constitute the theoretical core of the waning epoch, the theoretical center of the emergent epoch consists of interactions among a diversity of globalizing and localizing forces, of tendencies toward integration and fragmentation that are so simultaneous and interactive as to collapse into erratic but discernible processes.

But how to proceed? How to think afresh with respect to the map of the world depicted in Table 12-2? How to comprehend the responses of individuals and communities to the new epoch? Two innovations, one conceptual and the other theoretical, strike me as adequate to the task. The conceptual innovation provides an overall perspective on the prime dynamic that unfolds in Globalized Space and the theoretical innovation offers a more elaborate framework with which to assess the course of events.

FRAGMEGRATION AS AN ORGANIZING CONCEPT

It does not require much insight to appreciate that a prime characteristic of present-day world affairs is continuing tensions between the forces simultaneously promoting order and those inducing disorder, between the boundary-spanning and boundary-contracting responses to the evolution of Globalized Space—tensions that I have sought to capture through the label of fragmegration, a label that is perhaps grating but that highlights the close, continuous, and causal interactions between the forces fragmenting communities and those integrating communities, between the globalizing and localizing forces that are altering the underlying structures of world affairs.[9] The break-up of the former Yugoslavia and the continuation of unifying processes in the European Union are extreme examples of these two dynamics, but it can readily be argued that all communities fall somewhere between the two extremes, that all communities at every level of organization are responding to the globalization of economies and the information revolution by either lowering or heightening their boundaries, by fragmenting into smaller and more coherent communities or integrating into larger and still forming communities. Most importantly, these contradictory dynamics are causally linked, so much so that it can be said that every increment of integration and globalization gives rise to an increment of fragmentation and localization, and vice versa. Indeed, these fragmegrative dynamics are so pervasive and so inextricably interconnected that I do not hesitate to use them as a basis for labeling the emergent epoch as that of fragmegration. The post–Cold-War world is over; it has been replaced by the era of fragmegration.

---

[9]Development of the fragmegration approach has occurred in fits and starts. See James N. Rosenau, "'Fragmegrative' Challenges to National Security," in Terry L. Heyns (ed.), *Understanding U.S. Strategy: A Reader* (Washington, D.C.: National Defense University, 1983), pp. 65–82; James N. Rosenau, "Distant Proximities: The Dynamics and Dialectics of Globalization," in Bjorn Hettne (ed.), *International Political Economy: Understanding Global Disorder* (London: Zed Books, 1995), pp. 46–64; and James N. Rosenau, *Along the Domestic-Foreign Frontier*, chap. 6.

TABLE 12-2
GOVERNANCE ALONG THE DOMESTIC-FOREIGN DIVIDE

	Levels of Political Organization				
Issue Areas	Towns	Cities	Provinces	Nation States	International Agencies
Science and technology					
Commerce and trade					
Conservation versus development					
Labor					
Agriculture					
Immigration					
Education					
Human rights					
Religion					
Environmental					
Health and welfare					
Housing					
Employment					
Constitutional issues					
Elections					
Etc.					

Diagonal labels across the cells: Arms trade, The internet, International regimes, Market forces, Subnational governments, Transnational organizations, Multinational corporations, Ethnic minorities, Social movements, Professional societies, Humanitarian associations, Church groups, Terrorist organizations, Coalitions of the willing, Miscellaneous NGOs, Political parties, Elite networks, Drug trade, Labor unions, Etc.

TURBULENCE AS A THEORETICAL FRAMEWORK[10]

The transformation of three basic parameters of world affairs constitutes the theoretical foundation of the turbulence framework. These parameters have long been fixed features of world affairs, but the theory conceives of them as having entered into a period of transformation, thereby allowing for the release of enormous and powerful forces for change. Normally the parameters of any human system serve as the sources of constancy, as boundary conditions within which variations may occur but never so greatly as to alter the underlying structures of the system. However, at rare moments in history a system's parameters may undergo enormous stress and change. In effect, they become variables until such time as new boundary conditions emerge. Such is the case for the international system late in the 20th century. The prime parameters that have long bound and sustained world affairs have been overcome by high degrees of complexity and dynamism—that is, Globalized Space is now occupied by increasingly numerous, interdependent, and volatile actors—a condition that is conceived as having moved world politics into a turbulent state.[11] Lest there be any terminological confusion, however, I must stress at the outset that the notion of turbulence is used here as more than a metaphor for great commotion and uncertainty. My purpose is not to wax eloquent about change, but rather to probe its underlying dynamics.

The three parameters this theory conceives to be primary are the distribution of power in world politics through which states, international organizations, NGOs, and other key actors respond to each other (a macro parameter); the authority relationships through which governments, multinational corporations, ethnic groups, and other large collectivities are linked to individual citizens (a macro-micro parameter); and the analytical and emotional skills citizens possess and through which they respond to the course of events (a micro parameter). The enormous transformation of all three parameters (that is, the substantial expansion of their complexity and dynamism outlined below) justifies the conclusion that the world is presently experiencing its first period of turbulence since the birth of the state system some 350 years ago. Perhaps more to the point, the relative simultaneity that marks the impact of much greater complexity and dynamism on all three parameters underlies the fragmegration that is the central characteristic of world politics today. As will be seen, these interactive fragmegrative tensions are especially evident in the transformation of each of the three prime parameters.

---

[10]The turbulence model was first developed at length in James N. Rosenau, *Turbulence in World Politics: A Theory of Change and Continuity* (Princeton: Princeton University Press, 1990), and is further expanded in Rosenau, *Along the Domestic-Foreign Frontier.* For a comparison of the turbulent model and various realist theories, see James N. Rosenau and Mary Durfee, *Thinking Theory Thoroughly: Coherent Approaches to an Incoherent World* (Boulder: Westview Press, 1995).

[11]This definition of turbulence is elaborated in Rosenau, *Turbulence in World Politics,* pp. 59–65.

Incisive insights into the turbulence of world politics depend on an appreciation of the continuing overlap among the three parameters—on recognizing that even as individuals shape the actions and orientations of the collectivities to which they belong, so do the goals, policies, and laws of those collectivities shape the actions and orientations of individuals. Out of such interactions a network of interdependence is fashioned that is so intermeshed as to make it difficult to separate causes from effects. Indeed, much of the rapidity of the transformations at work in world politics can be traced to the ways in which the changes in each parameter stimulate and reinforce the changes in the other two.

A Skill Revolution

The transformation of the micro parameter lies in the shifting capabilities of citizens everywhere. Individuals have undergone a skill revolution. For a variety of reasons—ranging from the advance of communications technology to the greater intricacies of life in an ever more interdependent world—people have become increasingly more competent in assessing where they fit in international affairs and how their behavior can be aggregated into significant collective outcomes.

Put differently, it is an error to assume that citizenries are a constant in politics, that the world has changed rapidly and complexity increased greatly without consequences for individuals everywhere. As long as people were uninvolved in and apathetic about world affairs, it made sense to look at the macro level for explanations of what happens in world politics. Today, however, the skill revolution has expanded the learning capacity of individuals, enriched their cognitive maps, and elaborated the scenarios with which they anticipate the future. It is no accident that late in the 20th century the squares of the world's cities have been filled with large crowds demanding change.

It is tempting to affirm the impact of the skill revolution by pointing to the many restless publics that have protested authoritarian rule and clamored for more democratic forms of governance. While the worldwide thrust toward an expansion of political liberties and a diminution in the central control of economies is certainly linked to citizens and publics having greater appreciation of their circumstances and rights, there is nothing inherent in the skill revolution that leads people in more democratic directions. The change in the micro parameter is not so much one of new orientations as it is an evolution of new capacities. The world's peoples are not so much converging around the same values as they are sharing a greater ability to recognize and articulate their values. This change is global in scope; it enables Islamic fundamentalists, Asian peasants, and Western sophisticates alike to serve better their respective orientations. Thus the convergence of protesters in public squares has not been confined to cities in any particular region of the world. From Seoul to Prague, from Soweto to Beijing, from Paris to the West Bank, from Belgrade to Yangon (Rangoon), from Hong Kong to Toronto, the transformation of the micro parameter has been unmistakably evident.

Equally important, evidence of the skill revolution can be readily discerned by looking at trends in education, television viewing, computer usage, travel, and a host of other situations in which people are called on to employ their analytic and emotional skills. And hardly less relevant, in a number of local circumstances—from traffic jams to water shortages, from budget crises to racial conflicts, from flows of refugees to threats of terrorism—people are relentlessly confronted with social, economic, and political complexities that impel them to forego simplistic premises and replace them with more elaborate conceptions of how to respond to the challenges of daily life.

This is not to say that people everywhere are now equal in the skills they bring to bear on world politics. Obviously, the analytically rich continue to be more skillful than the analytically poor. But while the gap between the two ends of the skill continuum may be no narrower than in the past, the advance in the competencies of those at every point on the continuum is sufficient to contribute to a major transformation in the conduct of world affairs. More important for present purposes, the skill revolution highlights the extent to which scientific and technological advances have facilitated new opportunities for citizens to extend their influence if they seize them.

Let us be more precise as to the foundations of the skill revolution. It consists of two dimensions, analytic skills and emotional skills. The former springs from a growing ability to construct scenarios as to how distant events feed back into people's pocketbooks and living rooms, while the latter involves a deepening capacity for focusing emotions and making judgments as to whether the scenarios are to be welcomed or feared. It follows that the skill revolution does not necessarily entail an increase in information. It is perfectly possible to be well-informed and lacking in analytic and emotional skills, just as wise Vermont farmers or Asian peasants can grasp where they fit in the course of events even if they do not possess extensive and up-to-date information about what is happening. People may not know, for example, the name of the capital of Pakistan even though they understand that an upheaval in that country may have consequences that can circuitously feed back and affect their well-being. Stated differently, the skill revolution derives from an extension of people's working knowledge, from an elaboration of understanding that is not so much memorized or calculated as it is intuitively grasped. In sum, and to use a colloquial phrase, it is a revolution that derives as much from an enlargement of "street smarts" as from an advance in detailed information.

A Relocation of Authority

The macro-micro parameter consists of the orientations, practices, and patterns through which citizens at the micro level are linked to their collectivities at the macro level. In effect, it encompasses the authority structures whereby large aggregations—private organizations as well as public agencies—achieve and sustain the cooperation and compliance of their memberships. Historically these authority structures have been founded on traditional criteria of legitimacy derived from constitutional and legal sources: individuals were habituated to comply with the directives issued by higher authorities. People did what they were told to do because that is what one did. As a result, authority structures remained in place for decades, even centuries, as people tended to yield unquestioningly to the dictates of governments or the leadership of any other organizations with which they were affiliated.

For a variety of reasons, including the expanded analytic skills of citizens, the foundations of this parameter have been eroded. Throughout the world today, in both public and private settings, the sources of authority have shifted from traditional to performance criteria of legitimacy. Where the structures of authority were once in place, in other words, they are now in crisis, with the readiness of individuals to comply with governing directives very much a function of their assessment of the performances of the authorities. The more citizens consider the performance record appropriate—in terms of satisfying needs, moving toward goals, and providing stability—the more they are likely to cooperate and comply. The less they approve of the performance record, the more they are likely to withhold their compliance or otherwise complicate the efforts of the authorities.

As a consequence of the pervasive authority crises, states and governments have become less effective in confronting challenges and implementing policies. They can still maintain public order through their police powers, but their ability to address substantive issues and sole substantive problems is declining as people find fault with their performances and thus question their authority, redefine the bases of their legitimacy, and withhold their cooperation. Such a transformation is being played out dramatically today in Russia, as it was only a few years earlier within all the countries of Eastern Europe. But authority crises in the former communist world are only the more obvious instances of this newly emergent pattern. It is equally evident in every other part of the world, albeit taking different forms in different countries and among different types of private organizations. In Canada the authority crisis is rooted in linguistic, cultural, and constitutional issues as Quebec seeks to secede or otherwise redefine its relationship to the central government. In France the devolution of authority has been legally sanctioned through legislation that privatized several governmental activities and relocated authority away from Paris and toward greater jurisdiction for the provinces. In China the provinces enjoy wider jurisdiction by, in effect, ignoring or defying Beijing. In Yugoslavia a devolution crisis led to violence and civil war. In countries of Latin America the challenge to traditional authority originates with insurgent movements or the drug trade. And in those parts of the world where the shift to performance criteria of legitimacy has not resulted in the relocation of authority, uneasy stalemates prevail in the form of either slim majorities or, more frequently, divided governments. The United States, Israel, Italy, and Japan are but the more obvious examples of governments immersed in continuing policy stalemates and, sometimes, in paralysis. Viewed in this way, it is easier to grasp that the U.S. government closed down twice late in 1995.

Nor are global authority crises confined to states and governments They are also manifest in subnational jurisdictions, international organizations, and nongovernmental transnational entities. Indeed, in some cases the crises unfold simultaneously at different levels. For example, when the issue of Quebec's place in Canada became paramount, the Mohawks in Quebec also pressed for their own autonomy. Similarly, just as Moldava rejected Moscow's authority, so did several ethnic groups within Moldava seek to establish their own autonomy by rejecting Moldava'a authority. And among international and transnational organizations, UNESCO, the PLO, and the Roman Catholic Church have all experienced decentralizing dynamics that are at least partly rooted in the replacement of traditional with performance criteria of legitimacy.

The relocation of authority occurs in several directions. In many instances it has involved "downward" relocation toward subnational groups—toward ethnic minorities, local governments, single-issue organizations, religious and linguistic groupings, political factions, trade unions, and the like. In some cases the relocation process has moved "upward" toward more encompassing collectivities that transcend national boundaries. The beneficiaries of this upward relocation of authority range from supranational organizations like the European Union to intergovernmental organizations like the International Labor Organization, nongovernmental organizations like Greenpeace, professional groups such as Doctors without Borders, multinational corporations like IBM, and inchoate transnational social movements such as environmental or women's groups. These upward and downward relocations reinforce the fragmegrative tensions that underlie the turbulence presently at work in world politics.

Associated with these crises is an undermining of the principle of national sovereignty. To challenge the authority of the state and then to redirect legitimacy sentiments toward supranational or subnational collectivities is to begin to deny states have the right to resort to force. Since authority is layered such that many levels of governance may have autonomy within their jurisdictions, there is no one-to-one relationship between the location of authority and sovereignty. Nevertheless, trends toward the relocation of authority are bound to contribute to the erosion of sovereignty. If a state is thwarted in its efforts to mobilize effective armed forces, then its sovereignty is hardly a conspicuous feature of its existence as an independent collectivity. If it cannot prevent one of its subjurisdictions from seceding, then the reach of its sovereignty is certainly reduced.

It is useful to note that the undermining of the sovereignty principle began with its redefinition during the decolonizing processes of the former European empires after World War II, processes that "amounted to nothing less than an international revolution . . . in which traditional assumptions about the right to sovereign statehood were turned upside down."[12] In using self-determination as the sole criterion for statehood—irrespective of whether a former colony had the consensual foundations and resources to govern—a number of sovereign states were created, recognized, and admitted to the UN even though they were unable to develop economically and manage their internal affairs without external assistance. Sovereignty thus often seemed to be less a source of independence than an invitation to interdependence.

A Bifurcation of Global Structures

For some three centuries the overall structure of world politics—the macro parameter—has been founded on an anarchic system of sovereign nation-states that did not have to answer to any higher authority and that managed conflict through accommodation or war. States were not the only actors on the world stage, but traditionally they were the dominant collectivities that set the rules. The resulting state-centric world evolved its own hierarchy based on the distribution of military, economic, and political power. Depending on how many states had the greatest concentration of power, at different historical moments the overall system was varyingly marked by hegemonic, bipolar, or multipolar structures.

Today the state-centric world no longer predominates. The skill revolution, the worldwide authority crises, and other sources of turbulence (noted below) have led to a bifurcation of the international system into two global structures, one the long-standing state-centric world of sovereign states and the other a complex multicentric world of diverse, relatively autonomous actors replete with structures, processes, and rules of their own in Globalized Space. The actors of the multicentric world consist of NGOs, multinational corporations, ethnic minorities, subnational governments and bureaucracies, professional societies, incipient communities, and the like. Individually, and sometimes jointly, they compete, conflict, cooperate, or otherwise interact with the sovereignty-bound actors of the state-centric world. Table 12-3 delineates the main differences between the multicentric and state-centric worlds.

In sum, and to reiterate, while the bifurcation of world politics has not pushed states to the edge of the global stage, they are no longer the only key actors. Now they are faced with the new task of coping with disparate but formidable rivals from another world as well as the challenges posed by counterparts in their own world.

---

[12]Robert H. Jackson, *Quasi-States: Sovereignty, International Relations and the Third World* (Cambridge: Cambridge University Press, 1990), p. 85.

TABLE 12-3
STRUCTURE AND PROCESS IN THE TWO WORLDS OF WORLD POLITICS

	State-centric world	Multicentric world
Number of essential actors	Fewer than 200	Hundreds of thousands
Prime dilemma of actors	Security	Autonomy
Principal goals of actors	Preservation of territorial integrity, and physical security	Increase in world market shares, maintenance of integration of subsystems
Ultimate resort for realizing goals	Armed force	Withholding of cooperation or compliance
Normative priorities	Processes, especially those that preserve sovereignty and the rule of law	Outcomes, especially those that expand human rights, justice, and wealth
Modes of collaboration	Formal alliances whenever possible	Temporary coalitions
Scope of agenda	Limited	Unlimited
Rules governing interactions among actors	Diplomatic practices	Ad hoc, situational
Distribution of power among actors	Hierarchical by amount of power	Relative equality as far as initiating action is concerned
Interaction patterns among actors	Symmetrical	Asymmetrical
Locus of leadership	Great powers	Innovative actors with extensive resources
Institutionalization	Well established	Emergent
Susceptibility to change	Relatively low	Relatively high
Control over outcomes	Concentrated	Diffused
Bases of decisional structures	Formal authority, law	Various types of authority, effective leadership

Source: James N. Rosenau, *Turbulence in World Politics: A Theory of Change and Continuity* (Princeton: Princeton University Press, 1990), p. 250.

SOURCES OF GLOBAL TURBULENCE

Thus far we have defined turbulence and indicated the sites at which its consequences are likely to be most extensive and enduring, but we have not accounted for the dynamics that underlie the parametric transformations. What drives the turbulence? Although a variety of factors have contributed to its onset, several stand out as particularly salient. Some are external to the processes of world politics and some are internal. Together they go a long way toward explaining why what once seemed to anomalous now appears so patterned.

Proliferation of Actors

The world's population exceeded 2.5 billion in 1950; it is more than 5.5 billion today and is projected to reach 8 billion by 2025. This demographic explosion lies at the heart of many of the world's problems and is also a continual source of the complexity and dynamism that has overwhelmed the parameters of the global system. Ever greater numbers of people have exerted pressure for technological innovations. They have meant larger, more articulate, and increasingly unwieldy publics. They have contributed to the unmanageability of public affairs that has weakened states, stimulated the search for more responsive collectivities, and hastened the advent of paralyzing authority crises. And through the sheer weight of numbers, the population explosion has created new and intractable public issues, of which famines and threats to the environment are only the more conspicuous examples.

But the proliferation of relevant actors is not confined to people. No less important has been the vast increase in the number and types of collective actors whose leaders can clamber onto the global stage and act on behalf of their memberships. Indeed, to note that the mounting complexity of world affairs springs in part from the deepening density of the global system is to stress not so much the unorganized complexity fostered by the population explosion as it is to refer to an organized complexity consisting of millions of factions, associations, parties, organizations, movements, and interest groups that share an aspiration to advance their welfare and a sensitivity to the ways in which a rapidly changing world may require them to network with each other.

The dizzying increase in the density of actors that sustain world politics stems from a variety of sources. In part it is a product of the trend toward ever greater specialization—the hallmark of industrial and postindustrial economies—and the greater interdependence these economies foster. In part it stems from worldwide concerns about the environment and efforts in communities everywhere to concert efforts to meet ecological challenges. In part, too, it is a consequence of widespread dissatisfaction with large-scale collectivities and the performance of existing authorities, a discontent that underlies the turn to less encompassing organizations that are more fully expressive of immediate needs and wants.

Impact of Dynamic Technologies

Where population growth has led to the crowding of geographic space, technology has fostered the narrowing of social and political space: physical distances have been shortened, social distances have been narrowed, and economic barriers have been circumvented. And as people have thus become more interdependent, enormous consequences have followed for the skills of individuals, the conduct of their relations with higher authorities, and the viability of their collectivities. In short, it is highly doubtful whether world politics would have been overtaken by turbulence without the explosion of innumerable technologies.

The nuclear and communications revolutions stand out as especially relevant. The extraordinary advances in military weaponry after World War II, marked by nuclear warheads and the rocketry to deliver them, reduced the probability of a major global war. The nuclear revolution thus had the ironic consequence of depriving states of one of their prime instruments for pursuing and defending their interests. To be sure, the arms race and events like the Cuban missile crisis infused this context with a high degree of volatility that often made it seem fragile. Nevertheless, even as the nuclear context emphasized the extraordinary capacities several states had acquired, it also pointed up the limits of state action and thereby opened the door for challenges to state authority. It is no accident that as states added substantially to their nuclear arsenals, a series of transnational, large-scale, and powerful social movements—in the realms of peace, ecology, and women's rights—acquired momentum and posed serious challenges to governments.

The communications revolution is hardly less central as a source of global turbulence. The rapidity and clarity with which ideas and information now circulate through television, VCRs, the internet, fax machines, satellite hook-ups, fiber-optic telephone circuits, and many other microelectronic devices have rendered national boundaries ever more porous and world politics ever more vulnerable to cascading demands. Today the whole world, its leaders and its citizenries, instantaneously share the same pictures and descriptions (albeit not necessarily the same understandings) of what is occurring in any situation.

Examples of the cascading impact of science and technology through the communications revolution abound. Most conspicuous perhaps is the impact of the Cable News Network (CNN), which is said to be continuously watched in every embassy and every foreign office of every country in the world and which served as the basis for diplomatic and military action on both sides of the conflict during the Gulf War. Hardly less telling is the example of the French journal, *Actuel,* which was so upset by the crackdown in Tiananmen Square that, having compiled a mock edition of the *People's Daily* that contained numerous accounts the Chinese leadership did not want their people to read, sent it to every fax machine in China in the fall of 1989.[13] Or consider the explosive implications of the fact that 5 percent of Brazil's households had television receiving

---

[13]An account of *Actuel*'s efforts can be found in *Europe: Magazine of the European Community* (April 1990), pp. 40–41.

sets when its 1960 presidential election was held and that this figure had swollen to 72 percent at the time of the next presidential contest in 1989.

Given the magnitude of what the communications revolution has wrought, it is not surprising that people everywhere have become more skillful, more ready to challenge authority, and more capable of engaging in collective actions to press their demands. Their information may be skewed and their understanding of the stakes at risk in situations may be loaded with bias, but the stimuli to action are now ever present. Today individuals can literally see how the participation of their counterparts elsewhere can have meaningful consequences. Likewise, the availability of high-tech communications equipment has enabled leaders in the public and private sectors to turn quickly to their memberships and mobilize them.

The Globalization of National Economies

If the communications revolution has been a prime stimulus of the tendencies toward decentralization through the empowering of citizens and subnational groups, the dynamics at work in the economics realm are equally powerful as sources of centralizing tendencies. Starting in the technologically most advanced sectors of the global economy, a new kind of production organization geared to limited orders for a variety of specialized markets began to replace the large plants that produced standardized goods. Consequently, businesses began to restructure capital to be more effective in world markets. And as capital became increasingly internationalized, so did groups of producers and plants in different countries become linked in order to supply markets in many countries, all of which fostered and sustained a financial system global in scope and centered in major cities such as New York, Tokyo, and London.

In short, capital, production, labor, and markets have been globalized and are deeply enmeshed in networks of the world economy that have superseded the traditional political jurisdictions of the state. Such a transformation was bound to affect the established parameters of world politics. It has loosened the ties of producers and workers to their states, expanded the horizons within which citizens ponder their self-interests, and fostered the formation of transnational organizations. The rapid growth and maturation of the multi-centric world can in good part be traced to the extraordinary dynamism and expansion of the global economy. And so can the weakening of the state, which is no longer the manager of the national economy and has become instead an instrument for adjusting the national economy to the exigencies of an expanding world economy.

The Advent of Interdependence Issues

But the evolution of the world economy is not the only source of centralizing tendencies at work in global life. A number of new transnational problems also are crowding high on the world's agenda. Where the political agenda used to consist of issues that governments could cope with on their own or through interstate bargaining, now these issues have been joined by challenges that do not fall exclusively within the jurisdiction of states and their diplomatic institutions. Six current challenges are illustrative: environmental pollution, currency crises, the drug trade, terrorism, AIDS, and the flow of refugees. Each embraces processes that involve participation by large numbers of citizens and that inherently transgress national boundaries. The winds from the nuclear accident at Chernobyl in 1986, for example, carried radioactive pollution into many countries and had immediate and long-term effects on the people living there that made it impossible for governments to treat them as domestic problems or to address them through conventional diplomatic channels.

Since they are essentially the product of dynamic technologies and the shrinking social and geographic distances that separate people, such problems can appropriately be called "interdependence" issues. And, given their origins and scope, they can also be regarded as important centralizing dynamics in the sense that they require cooperation on a transnational scale. Each of the six issues, for instance, is the focus of either transnational social movements or ad hoc international institutions forged to ameliorate, if not to resolve, the boundary-crossing problems they have created.

The advent of interdependence issues has contributed to the present era of turbulence in world politics in several ways. First, they have caused citizens to question that their states are the ultimate problem solvers and, in the case of those who join social movements, they have led people to ponder a restructuring of their loyalties. In doing so, interdependence issues have also fostered the notion that transnational cooperation can be as central to world politics as interstate conflict. Equally important, given their diffuse, boundary-crossing structure, these issues are spawning a range of transnational associations that are likely to further challenge the authority of states.

The Weakening of States and the Restructuring of Loyalties

States have not become peripheral to global affairs; they continue to maintain their world and infuse its international system with vitality and a capacity to adapt to change. Moreover, states have been and continue to be a source of the turbulent changes that are at work. After all, it was the state-centric and not the multicentric world that created multilateral organizations, that contained the nuclear revolution, and that responded to the demands for decolonization by producing the hierarchical arrangements that have enabled the industrial countries to dominate the developing world.

Accordingly, some analysts see states as increasingly robust and explicitly reject the patterns highlighted here. They see the state as so deeply ensconced in the routines and institutions of politics that the erosion of its capabilities and influence is unimaginable. The state has proved itself, the argument goes, by performing vital functions that serve the needs of people, which is why it has been around more than 300 years. During this time the state has overcome all kinds of challenges, many of which are far more severe than the globalization of national economies and the emergence of new types of collectivities. Indeed, the argument concludes, there are many ways in which states may actually be accumulating greater capabilities.

However, it seems just as erroneous to treat states as constants as it is to view the skills of citizens as invulnerable to change. States are not eternal verities; they are as susceptible to variability as any other social system. This includes the possibility of a decline in the sovereignty principle from which they derive their legitimacy as well as an erosion of their ability to address problems.

Viewed from the perspective of vulnerabilities—the growing density of populations, the expanding complexity of the organized segments of society, the globalization of national economies, the constraints of external debts, the relentless pressure of technological innovations, the challenge of subgroups intent on achieving greater autonomy, and the endless array of other intractable problems that comprise the modern political agenda—it seems evident that present circumstances lessen the capacity of states. Their agendas are expanding, but they are short on the will, competence, and resources to expand correspondingly. Consequently, most states are overwhelmed to the point where effective management is largely impossible. And added to these difficulties is the fact that citizenries, through the microelectronic revolution, are continuously exposed to authority crises elsewhere in the world, scenes bound to give rise to doubts and demands in even the most stable of polities and thus to foment a greater readiness to question the legitimacy of government policies. There is considerable evidence, for example, that the collapse of authority in East Germany in the fall of 1989 was stimulated by the televised scenes of authority being challenged in Tiananmen Square several months earlier.

Accordingly, while states may not be about to exit from the political stage, and while they may even continue to occupy the center of the stage, they do seem likely to become increasingly vulnerable and impotent. And as ineffective managers of their own affairs, they also serve as stimuli to turbulence in world politics.

But this argument for diminished state competence is subtle and depends on many intangible processes for which solid indicators are not easily developed. Perhaps most notable in this regard are subtle shifts in loyalties that accompany the globalization of national economies, the decentralizing tendencies toward subgroup autonomy, and the emergence of performance criteria of legitimacy. Such circumstances seem bound to affect loyalties to the state. That is, as transnational and subnational actors in the multicentric world become increasingly active and effective, as they demonstrate a capacity to deal with problems that states have found intractable or beyond their competence, citizens will begin to look elsewhere than the national capital for assistance. As previously noted, most states are presently undergoing authority crises, of which Chechnya is only the most recent example.

It would be a mistake, however, to regard the loyalty problem as confined to multiethnic systems. Relatively homogeneous societies are beset with the same dilemma, as was so clearly evident in European countries during the debates and plebiscites over whether to accept membership in the EU.

This is not to say that traditional national loyalties are being totally abandoned; such attachments do not suddenly collapse. Rather, it is only to take note of subtle processes whereby what was once well established and beyond question is now problematic and undergoing change. It seems reasonable to presume that the diminished competence of states to act decisively, combined with the processes of loyalty transformation, are rendering more complex each of the three prime parameters of world politics.

Subgroupism

Since there is a widespread inclination to refer loosely to "nationalism" as a source of the turbulent state of world politics, it is perhaps useful to be more precise about the collective nature of those pervasive decentralizing tendencies wherein individuals and groups feel readier to challenge authority and reorient their loyalties. As previously noted, the authority crises that result from such challenges can be either "upward" or "downward." In both kinds of relocation, the motivation that sustains them may not be so deeply emotional as to qualify as an "ism." The creation of subnational administrative divisions, for example, can stem from efforts to rationalize the work of a governmental agency or private organization, and the process of implementing the decentralized arrangements can occur in the context of reasoned dialogue and calm decision making. Often, however, intense concerns and powerful attachments can accompany the press for new arrangements—feelings and commitments strong enough to justify regarding the upward relocations as evoking "transnationalism," "supranationalism," or "internationalism." The downward relocations marked by comparable intensities are perhaps best labeled with the generic term, "subgroupism."

Subgroupism refers to those deep affinities that people develop for the associations, organizations, and subcultures with which they have been historically, professionally, economically, socially, or politically linked and to which they attach their highest priorities. Subgroupism values the in-group over the out-group, sometimes treating the two as adversaries and sometimes positing them as susceptible to extensive cooperation. Subgroupism can derive from and be sustained by a variety of sources, not the least being disappointment in—and alienation from—the performances of the whole system in which the subgroup is located. Most of all, its intensities are the product of historical roots that span generations and that get reinforced by the lore surrounding past events in which the subgroup survived.

That subgroupism can be deeply implanted in the consciousness of peoples is manifestly apparent in the resurfacing of strong ethnic identities throughout Eastern Europe and Russia. There the subgroups were historic nations and the accompanying feelings can thus be readily regarded as expressions of nationalism. Not all, or even a preponderance, of these decentralizing tendencies attach to nations, however. Governmental subdivisions, political parties, labor unions, professional societies, and a host of other types of subgroups can also evoke intense attachments, and it would grossly understate the relevance of the decentralizing tendencies at work in world politics to ignore these other forms of ties. Accordingly, it seems preferable to regard the emotional dimensions of the generic decentralizing tendencies as those of subgroupism and to reserve the concept of nationalism for those subgroup expressions that revolve around nations and feelings of ethnicity.

The Spread of Hunger, Poverty, and the Developing World

Underlying the bifurcation of world politics into state- and multicentric worlds has been another split—between industrially developed and underdeveloped countries—that has also contributed substantially to the onset of turbulence. The many and diverse countries of the developing world have added to the complexity and dynamism of global structures; sharpened performance criteria of legitimacy; enriched the skills of the underprivileged; hastened the transnationalization of economies and social movements; limited the authority of developed states over their production facilities; intensified the flow of people from South to North; lengthened the list of interdependence issues; and strengthened the tendencies toward subgroupism.

The impact of the split fostered by the breakup of Europe's colonial empires is perhaps most obvious with respect to the global distribution of power. Decolonialization not only resulted in the proliferation of actors in the state-centric world, it also infused a greater hierarchical rigidity in global structures. The process whereby ever greater power accompanied the emergence of industrial states in the developed world was not matched when statehood came to Africa and Asia. As was noted earlier, the newly established states of the developing world acquired sovereignty and international recognition even though they lacked the internal resources and consensual foundations to provide for their own development, a circumstance that led the states themselves into a deep resentment over their dependence on the industrialized world for trade, technology, and many of the other prerequisites necessary to fulfill their desire for industrial development. Their sovereignty, in effect, is "negative" in that it protects them against outside interference but does not empower them to address their problems successfully. The result has been a pervasive global pattern in which the industrial world has continued to prosper while the developing world has languished, thus endlessly reinforcing the inequities that underlie the hierarchical structures of world politics. And having long remained at or below the poverty line, most of these quasi-states have been keenly aware of the inequities and have sought vainly to overcome them.

Even as the advent of the Third World has rigidified the hierarchical structure of the state-centric world, so has it added to the decentralizing tendencies in the multicentric world. Composed of tribes and ethnic groups artificially brought together under state banners during decolonization, besieged by multinational corporations seeking to extend their operations and markets, and plagued with internal divisions and massive socioeconomic problems, many developing countries have added greatly to the breadth and depth of the multicentric world. Their quasi-sovereignty keeps them active in the state system, but the multicentric world has been hospitable to their fragmenting dynamics and thereby contributed to the process wherein subgroup networks are proliferating.

It must be noted, on the other hand, that a number of developing countries have dramatically raised their productivity and living standards to the point where they are now regarded as forming a new category—that of newly developed countries, or NICs. South Korea, Taiwan, Hong Kong, and Singapore are especially illustrative in this regard, but a few others are also showing signs of increasingly successful development. Once again, in other words, generalization is difficult as contradictions and ambiguities have come to pervade the developing world.

ORDER OR DISORDER?

Where are the conditions of turbulence taking world affairs? Do they add up to a gloomy assessment of the prospects for peace and stability? Or do they point to a trendline wherein shared norms evolve on a global scale that facilitate an eventual decline in upheaval and disarray? Do they portend the emergence of order or the persistence of disorder in Globalized Space?

Surely there are no simple answers to these questions. Positive scenarios in which cooperation among people, communities, societies, and states steadily increase can be as easily constructed as scenarios that envision a continuing breakdown of intergroup relations, deepening authority crises, and a worsening of humankind's lot. The turbulence model suggests that at present the integrating and fragmenting forces are roughly in balance, allowing world affairs to limp from situation to situation, some of which get resolved and others of which persist and fester. Much depends, in the end, on the kind of leaders that come to power in the state-centric and multicentric worlds and the quality of the demands that ever more skillful publics make upon them.[14]

---

[14]For an effort to assess the kind of leadership that conduces to movement in cooperative directions, see James N. Rosenau, "Notes on the Servicing of Triumphant Subgroupism," *International Sociology* 8 (March 1993), pp. 77–90.

In all probability, both scenarios are likely to play out in the years ahead. The turbulence model does not anticipate that the parametric changes will occur at the same pace in the same direction everywhere in the world. Fragmegrative processes are anything but uniform. They are, rather, uneven, with cooperative dynamics prevailing in some regions and conflictual tendencies holding sway in other areas. In an era of ever more skillful and challenging citizenries, however, it seems doubtful that ruthless, conflict-ridden regimes will be able to hold on to power for very long. It may be decades before the world's transformed parameters settle into place and again serve as boundary conditions for the global system, but in the meantime it is likely the world will manage to move from crisis to crisis without collapsing into calamitous war.

13

GREAT-POWER RELATIONS IN THE 21ST CENTURY: A NEW COLD WAR, OR CONCERT-BASED PEACE?

Charles W. Kegley, Jr., and Gregory A. Raymond

Global power is shifting toward a new distribution in which three, four, or five major states will share roughly equal capabilities. Whether their relationships will be cooperative or competitive will depend on the security institutions the great powers create. Exploring the contribution that the United Nations, the OSCE, NATO, and the Group of Seven can make to peace, this chapter argues that a two-tiered, concert-based collective security system provides the best mechanism for preserving global security. Kegley is Pearce Professor of International Relations at the University of South Carolina. Raymond is Professor of Political Science at Boise State University. They have coauthored *A Multipolar Peace? Great-Power Politics in the Twenty-First Century* (1994).

When the Cold War ended, many people believed that a "new world order" would soon emerge. The great powers were expected to replace confrontation with collaboration, empowering institutions such as the United Nations to keep peace through what was then termed "assertive multilateralism." Those hopes promptly began to fade, however. It is now apparent that the great powers have

This essay was written especially for this book.

yet to forge a clear, coherent strategy for promoting global security. Instead, confusion and conflicting impulses abound. From efforts to deal with the civil war in what was once Yugoslavia to coping with tribal genocide in Rwanda, their policies have been characterized by hesitation and false starts. The failure to prevent aggression stemming from long-suppressed ethnic hatreds in hot spots throughout the world has heightened apprehensions about whether the great powers will be able to maintain world order in the new millennium.

To some extent, the prevailing uncertainty about national security policy that provokes frustration and despair is understandable. Creating a global security policy for a chaotic, complex, and confusing post–Cold War world is a formidable challenge. The simple bipolar system of the recent past has already given way to a more complex configuration of power, and the shifting ratio of the great powers' military might and uncertainty about their intentions combine to make crafting a new security strategy difficult.

Nonetheless, one of the properties of the emerging global distribution of power can be foreseen: Military and economic might will be increasingly diffused among the great powers. In contrast to bipolarity, where two superpowers held a preponderance of strength compared to all other countries, the multipolar state system of the future appears destined to contain as many as five roughly equal great powers: the United States, China, Russia, Japan, and either Germany or a European Union with a common defense policy. A "power transition" (see Essay 4, "Towards a New Millennium: Structural Perspectives on the Causes of War," by Jack S. Levy) is well underway, and the changes promise to be fundamental.

The military and economic capabilities of the great powers relative to one another are rapidly changing, with the rise of China in the international hierarchy of power the most dramatic transformation underway. As one expert observes,

> China is the fastest growing economy in the world, with what may be the fastest growing military budget. It has nuclear weapons, border disputes with most of its neighbors, and a rapidly improving army that may within a decade or so be able to resolve old quarrels in its own favor. The United States has possessed the world's largest economy for more than a century, but at present trajectories China may displace it in the first half of the next century and become the number one economy in the world.[1]

Such a revolutionary power shift would fundamentally reorder the global pecking order, especially if Russia fails to exploit its literate population and rich resources to propel economic recovery and if Japan and the European Union close the gap with that of the United States or surpass it (as some projections anticipate). The

---

[1] Nicholas D. Kristof, "The Rise of China," *Foreign Affairs* 70 (no. 1, 1993), p. 59. For evidence that China will far surpass the United States in the rank order of the largest economic powerhouses by the year 2020, see Donald McGranahan, "Measurement of Development," *International Social Science Journal* 143 (March 1995), p. 59.

world will then fundamentally change, and the policies of each of the great powers will necessarily change as a result of movement in the global distribution of power in the direction of approximate parity.

Such a massive reordering of the international hierarchy raises several important questions. Will latent rivalries between any pair of the great powers escalate, producing the advent of a new Cold War? In response to a great-power confrontation between, for example, the United States and China, which great powers might align with one another? Will these alignments be seen as a threat by others and therein stimulate the formation of counteralliances to contain each other's power? Or can a security regime be built to prevent the rise of rival great-power alliances that are primed for war?

THE CHARACTER OF A NEW MULTIPOLAR SYSTEM

The diffusion of strength among the world's leading states demands our attention because some forms of multipolarity have been more war-prone than others. For example, the multipolar system of antagonistic blocs that developed on the eve of World War I became the particularly dangerous tinderbox from which a globalized war ignited. When a world of many great powers splits into rival camps, there is little chance that competitors in one policy arena will emerge as partners somewhere else, so as to reduce the competition. Rather, the gains made by one side will be seen as losses by the other, ultimately causing minor disagreements to grow into larger face-offs from which neither coalition is willing to retreat.

Since the international system of the early 21st century will probably include three or more extremely powerful states whose security interests are global, it is important that they do not become Cold War competitors that draw others into their segregated rival blocs. It is equally important that the great powers build institutions that provide incentives to cooperate in order to provide mutually beneficial rewards, so potential competitors develop a stake in their continued collaboration.

Aside from the danger of armed conflict among the great powers, the security threats of the future will also include such challenges as inter-bloc trade wars, rogue states and failed states, environmental degradation, drug trafficking across borders, resource depletion, the rising tide of refugees, terrorism, and a welter of health concerns ranging from AIDS to multidrug-resistant strains of tuberculosis. None of these global problems can be met without substantial great-power cooperation; they all are truly transnational problems that necessitate global solutions.

Whereas the impact of these nontraditional threats to global welfare promises to be potent, such threats do not necessarily mean geoeconomics or ecopolitics will replace geopolitics. Conflict over political and territorial issues remains much in evidence, as illustrated by Japan's disagreements with the United States, Russia, and China over territorial claims; China's assertiveness in the South China Sea and the Taiwan Straits; and Russia's fears of encirclement and containment as a result of NATO's enlargement to the east. While we can rejoice in the end of Cold War hostility between East and West, differences in the interests of the great powers have not disappeared, and the prospect of coming economic battles looms large if as predicted the major rivals go "head to head" against each other.[2] As former U.S. Secretary of State Lawrence S. Eagleburger has pointed out, we are "returning to a more traditional and complicated time of multipolarity, with a growing number of countries increasingly able to affect the course of events." The primary issues are how well the United States and Russia can adjust to their unequal decline from overwhelming preponderance, and how well China, Japan, and the European Union will adapt to their new-found importance. "The change will not be easy for any of the players, as such shifts in power relationships have never been easy,"[3] Eagleburger wrote. The challenge to be confronted is ensuring that great-power cooperation, not some kind of a rekindled Cold War conflict, becomes institutionalized. At issue is whether the traditional and nontraditional security threats that collectively face the world will be managed through concerted great-power action.

GREAT-POWER OPTIONS IN A MULTIPOLAR FUTURE

As power in the international system becomes more diffused, what can be done to prevent the reemergence of an unstable form of multipolarity? How can the great powers avoid becoming polarized into antagonistic blocs? Three general courses of action exist: they can act unilaterally; they can develop specialized bilateral alliances with another state; or they can engage in some form of broad collaboration with many countries.

Of course, each option has many possible variations, and the foreign policies of most great powers contain a mix of acting single-handedly, joining with a partner, and cooperating globally. What matters for the stability of multipolar systems is the relative emphasis placed on "going it alone" versus "going it with others," and whether joint action is defined in inclusive or exclusive terms.

Unilateral policies, though attractive because they symbolize the nostalgic pursuit of national autonomy and confident self-reliance, are unlikely to be viable in a multipolar future. The end of the Cold War has reduced public anxieties about foreign dangers and, in many countries including the United States, led to calls for a reduction in the scale of foreign commitments. But a retreat from active participation in world affairs by any great power would imperil efforts to deal with the many transnational threats to global security mentioned above that require global activity and engagement.

[2]See Lester C. Thurow, *Head to Head: Coming Economic Battles among Japan, Europe, and America* (New York: William Morrow, 1992).

[3]Lawrence S. Eagleburger, "The 21st Century: American Foreign Policy Challenges," in E.K. Hamilton, ed., *America's Global Interests: A New Agenda* (New York: W.W. Norton, 1989), pp. 244–245.

On the other hand, a surge of unilateral activism by any of the great powers would be equally harmful. None of them holds unquestioned hegemonic status with enough power to override all others. Although the United States is unrivaled in military might, many foreign dangers exist that cannot be managed by the use of military power, and America's offensive capability and unsurpassed military technology are not paralleled by unrivaled financial clout. Like others, the U.S. economy faces problems that constrain and inhibit the projection of American power on a global scale. True, on many issues U.S. Secretary of State Madeleine Albright is accurate when she warns that most threats to peace cannot be managed without U.S. involvement; she and former National Security Adviser Anthony Lake concur in their often-repeated assertion that "America today is the indispensable force for peace in the world, whether in Bosnia, the Middle East or elsewhere."[4] But there exist stubborn budgetary and doctrinal limits on, and strong domestic opposition to, U.S. use of its superb military to police every hot spot. Given the prohibitive costs of shouldering the financial burden of acting alone, and given the probability that other great powers would be unlikely to accept subordinate positions, unilateralism will be problematic in a multipolar future. Countries like Japan, Russia, and Germany "will have to relearn their old great-power roles, and the United States will have to learn a role it has never played before; namely, to coexist and interact with other great powers."[5]

An alternative to acting unilaterally is joining with selected states in a series of special relationships, such as that between Great Britain and the United States throughout this century. On the surface, this option also appears attractive. Yet in a world lacking the stark simplicities of bipolarity, differentiating friend from foe is exceedingly difficult, particularly when allies in the realm of military security are the most likely to be trade competitors in a cut-throat global marketplace. Instead of adding predictability to international affairs, a network of special bilateral relationships would foster a fear of encirclement or containment among those who perceive themselves as the targets of these combinations.

Whether they entail informal cooperative understandings or formal treaties of alliance, all bilateral partnerships have a common drawback: They promote a politics of exclusion that can lead to dangerously polarized forms of multipolarity, in which the competitors align by forming countercoalitions. For example, the formation of a Russo-American alliance would concern many members of the European Union; similarly, construction of a U.S.–Russian–European Union axis stretching from the Atlantic to the Urals would alarm both China and Japan. Instructively, the Russian and Chinese "strategic partnership" agreement prior to the April 1997 Beijing summit was interpreted in Washington and Europe as the first threatening step to offset their influence. The problem with such special relationships is that they inevitably shun those standing outside the charmed circle.

---

[4]Lake, echoing Albright, as quoted in *The State,* December 10, 1996, p. A10.
[5]Kenneth N. Waltz, "The Emerging Structure of International Politics," *International Security* 18 (no. 2, 1993), p. 72.

Resentment, revenge, and revisionist efforts to overturn the status quo are the predictable consequences. The free-wheeling dance of balance-of-power politics typically set in motion by such alignments casts some potential partners aside and thus gives them reasons to break up the whole dance. As a careful student of world politics concludes, balance-of-power alliances can

> hardly be classed as stabilizing manoeuvres or equilibrating processes, and one cannot take seriously any claim of maintaining international stability that does not entail the prevention of such disasters as the Napoleonic wars or World War I. . . . It is not easy to justify the contention that a system for the management of international relations that failed to prevent the events of 1914–1918 deserves high marks as a guardian of stability, or order, or peace. If the balance of power system does not aim at the prevention of world war, then it aims too low; if it offers no hope of maintaining the general peace, then the quest for a better system is fully warranted.[6]

Beyond forming special bilateral alliances, great powers have the option of establishing broad, multilateral associations. Two common variants of this option are concerts and collective security organizations. The former involve regularized consultation among those at the top of the global hierarchy; the latter, full participation by all states. A concert constructed to manage the international system jointly and to prevent disputes from escalating to war offers the benefit of helping control the great-power rivalries that often spawn polarized blocs, though at the cost of ignoring the interests of those not belonging to the elite group. Alternatively, the all-inclusive nature of collective security allows every voice to be heard, but exacerbates the problems of providing a timely response to threatening situations. Moreover, it is exhausting to mobilize all to respond to every threat to peace, and especially to those distant from a particular country's immediate security interests. In addition, under collective security schemes in the past, consensus building has usually proven both difficult and delayed, especially in identifying the culpable party, in choosing an appropriate response, and in implementing the selected course of action. Since all decision-making bodies tend to become unwieldy as their size expands, what may be needed to make multilateralism a viable option for the multipolar future looming on the political horizon is a hybrid that combines elements of a great-power concert with elements of collective security.

A CONCERT-BASED COLLECTIVE SECURITY SYSTEM: RATIONALE AND REQUIREMENTS

Finding a mechanism to preserve peace in a multipolar world will be a serious challenge on the global agenda of the 21st century. Unilateral and bilateral approaches do not offer promising paths to lasting great-power peace. Multilateral

---

[6]Inis L. Claude, Jr., "The Balance of Power Revisited," *Review of International Studies* 15 (January 1989), p. 78. For an alternate critique of the balance of power as a tinderbox for warfare, see Richard Rosecrance, "A New Concert of Powers," *Foreign Affairs* 71 (Spring 1992), pp. 64–82.

approaches provide a better solution for checking great-power competition, should prevailing trends in the strength of each great power relative to the others culminate in the creation of a truly multipolar system. If no single state is stronger than the combination of all other states in a collective security organization, the collectivity could jointly deter—and, if necessary, defeat—an aggressor, provided that the members (1) share a common commitment to maintain peace, (2) agree on which actor is a potential or actual threat to peace, and (3) apply prompt and powerful sanctions against that threat.

Unfortunately, whenever such an organization has existed, some members have sought to maximize their relative gains rather than to minimize their mutual losses. Thinking that they could rely on joint action to resist aggression, they either reduced their own military preparedness so as to "free-ride" on the defense efforts of their companions, or in the spirit of burden sharing they mobilized at the first hint of trouble and thus expanded what might have remained small, local conflicts into larger wars. As political scientist Richard Betts notes, the history of collective security reveals twin deficiencies—it may "not work when needed, or that it would work when it should not."[7]

Even if the post–Cold War environment is more hospitable to collective security than in the past, implementing it will be difficult. A solution to this problem is to create a modified version of collective security, one that is grounded in a *two-tiered, modular design,* and that rests on a shared commitment to cooperation and common security. Under such a scheme, countries at the center of policy deliberations would shift as different kinds of problems arise. The system would be concert based, with some great powers taking a leadership role on certain security issues, and others on a different set of issues. At the same time, this great-power concert would be anchored in a larger collective security framework, where small and medium powers would have a voice in pending matters if their interests were affected or if they possessed expertise in dealing with the issue in question.

What conditions are necessary for such a mechanism to function adequately? For many theorists, common threats are the glue that holds security regimes together.[8] Previous concerts were formed after wars with potential hegemons or after a single, massively armed enemy appeared on the scene to threaten the existence

---

[7]Richard K. Betts, "Systems for Peace or Causes of War? Collective Security, Arms Control, and the New Europe," in S.M. Lynn-Jones and S.E. Miller, eds. *America's Strategy in a Changing World* (Cambridge: The MIT Press, 1992), p. 214.

[8]For examples of recent thinking on the prerequisites for success, see Andrew Bennett and Joseph Lepgold, "Reinventing Collective Security after the Cold War and the Gulf Conflict," *Political Science Quarterly* 108 (no. 2, 1993), pp. 213–237; see also Inis L. Claude, "Collective Security After the Cold War," in I. L. Claude, S. Simon, and D. Stuart, eds., *Collective Security in Europe and Asia* (Carlisle Barracks: U.S. Army War College, Strategic Studies Institute, 1992), pp. 7–28.

of others. The passage of time or the demise of a threat always loosened these bonds. A shared sense of common threat, either from an aggressor bent on world domination or from a nonmilitary challenge (such as global warming) that cannot be managed unilaterally, must arise to preserve the commitment to collective action. Without a threat common to and recognized by all, the chances that great powers will show self-restraint or forgo unilateral advantages predictably declines.

A second correlate of success is said to lie in including defeated or declining powers in the security regime. A dissatisfied great power lacking a voice in security matters will reject the legitimacy of the prevailing order, strive to destroy the status quo, and undermine the organization's capacity to act. Treating a defeated or declining power as an equal and respected member avoids this problem. In this context, including Russia, which presently faces economic difficulties and political instability, as a partner in a democratic and united Europe is crucial to the long-term success of any new security structure.

The third potential contributor to the longevity of a security mechanism of this sort is a rough military balance among its members. The presence of a state that is significantly stronger than all of the other great powers reduces the effectiveness of both concerts and collective security systems, since the preponderant state would be able to withstand any pressures that the others might initiate, and the single superpower would be asked to independently shoulder responsibility for preserving order in failing or fragmenting states where the other powers do not have a direct interest or investment.

A fourth factor affecting the viability of concert-based security systems is a sense of common duty coupled with a statesmanship of self-restraint. During the 19th century, when the Concert of Europe was at its zenith, a "just" equilibrium among the contending great powers meant more than an equal distribution of capabilities; it included recognition of the importance of conferring honor, national rights, and dignity to all. In contrast, when a great power has been isolated and deprived of a place commensurate with its size and importance, the wounded sense of national pride of the pariah has often stimulated aggressive behavior.

Finally, many theorists stress flexibility as a hallmark of effective security regimes. Just as a concert's small, uncomplicated structure makes it more supple and resilient than highly institutionalized collective security organizations, its informal processes of mutual consultation provide an opportunity to tailor solutions to the special requirements of the situation at hand.

Given the advantages of a concert-based collective security system in preventing the emergence of the most unstable types of multipolarity, and given the conditions needed to make it effective, the question remains as to whether any existing multilateral organizations offer a potential home for such a security mechanism.

THE ARCHITECTURE FOR CONCERT-BASED COLLECTIVE SECURITY

Throughout history different types of multipolar systems have existed. Some of these diffused distributions of power were unstable because they contained antagonistic blocs poised on the brink of war. We contend that the key to the stability of any future multipolar system lies in the inclusiveness and transparent decision-making processes of multilateralism. It is not a panacea for all of the world's security problems, but it offers humanity a chance to avoid the kinds of polarized alignment patterns that have proven so destructive in the past.

At the minimum, building a concert-based collective security structure will require an institutional foundation that:

• Enlarges the circle of participation to include all of the emergent great powers in collective decision making.

• Fosters movement away from reliance on strictly national defense, and combines elements of collective defense against a particular potential aggressor with elements of collective security against all threats of aggression.

• Encourages greater security communication and cooperation among the states likely to acquire the most armed strength.

• Copes imaginatively with the security vacuum that has followed the implosion of the Warsaw Pact and the disintegration of the Soviet Union.

• Binds Germany and Japan to the pursuit of multilateral security, providing them with nonnational nuclear deterrents.

• Incorporates representation from the Muslim world in order to include a potential new Islamic power in a web of interdependence with the other great powers.

• Pursues the continuation of long-term efforts to further reduce existing nuclear inventories, and prevents the further proliferation of strategic weapons to regional powers.

• Establishes confidence-building measures among the great powers in East Asia and the Pacific.

• Constructs rules for crisis management, supplemented by conflict-resolution mechanisms with enforcement capabilities.

Creating a new security architecture has seldom proven easy. When seen from the perspective of the late-1990s, all of the existing institutions upon which a concert-based collective security system might be constructed have limitations. Consider, for instance, the case of the United Nations. After the Persian Gulf War, many people assumed that the UN would at long last be able "to take effective collective measures for the prevention and removal of threats to the peace" as originally proclaimed in its charter (Article 1, paragraph 1). Whether hopes for this role are fulfilled in the 21st century will continue to depend on the political dynamics in the Security Council. According to the UN Charter, the Security Council has "primary responsibility for the maintenance of international peace and security" (Article 24, paragraph 1). Of its 15 members, 5 hold permanent seats and possess the right to veto council actions—the United States, Russia, Britain, France, and China. The harmonious veneer witnessed in the immediate wake of the Cold War has already begun to fade, as "peacekeeping fatigue" has set in and morale has declined over the failure of the United States to pay its UN debts. The United Nations in 1997 was nearly bankrupt, and the resentments of the other great powers over their disagreements with the United States about such issues as U.S. opposition in late 1996 to Kofi Annan as a successor to former Secretary-General Boutros Boutros-Ghali have eroded the sense of consensus that formerly prevailed in the Security Council. Moreover, if the Security Council's permanent membership is expanded to include Germany, Japan, and such regional powers as Brazil, India, or Nigeria, reaching agreement for collective action will become even more challenging.

To complicate matters further, there is a pervasive fear among UN members that, despite its waning leadership role, the organization has become a captive of its strongest member at the moment, the United States. Although American influence is resented by many states, they still recognize the need for U.S. leadership if the United Nations is to play a peacekeeping and peacemaking role. This creates a dilemma: "Without U.S. leadership and power, the United Nations lacks muscle. With it, the United Nations loses its independent identity."[9]

Thus an invigorated, independent United Nations would need more resources to carry out its mandate for peacekeeping—a dim prospect since most members owe back dues totaling in the billions and the organization continues to suffer from severe criticism for financial mismanagement and a bloated bureaucracy, Secretary-General Kofi Annan's reform efforts notwithstanding. Attempting to reform the United Nations while simultaneously coping with the exploding demand for UN peacekeepers was described by former Secretary-General Boutros Boutros-Ghali as "trying to repair a car while you are driving at a speed of 120 miles per hour."[10] Undaunted by the difficulty of the task, he lobbied in 1993 for the creation of peace enforcement units that would allow the United Nations to deploy troops quickly to enforce ceasefires by taking coercive actions against violators. As with UN peacekeeping forces employed during the Cold War, the secretary-general recommended that these rapid deployment units be established by the voluntary contribution of member states, act when authorized by the Security Council, and serve under the command of the secretary-general. In contrast to traditional peacekeeping operations, however, their use could be ordered without the express consent of the disputants, and they would be trained and equipped to use force if necessary.

Despite Boutros-Ghali's energetic quest, the creation of a large, easily mobilized, multilateral contingency force positioned to manage disputes never really got off the ground. The Clinton administration, fearing a possible loss of control

---

[9]Leslie H. Gelb, "Tailoring a U.S. Role at the U.N.," *International Herald Tribune* (January 2–3, 1993), p. 4.
[10] *Wall Street Journal,* December 17, 1992, p. A1.

and a backlash from isolationist members of the Republican Party, vetoed contributing U.S. military units to a permanent UN standby force in its Presidential Decision Directive 13 of 1993. Without active support in Washington, the other great powers' enthusiasm to release command authority of their military units to the United Nations dissipated, and the capacity of the United Nations to organize collective responses to threats to peace is much in doubt.

The Organization for Security and Cooperation in Europe (OSCE) offers a second option for a new concert-based security architecture. Although the Helsinki process has established principles supportive of a two-tier formula that gives the great powers incentives to share costs and responsibilities for security without reducing the lesser powers to second-class citizens, the OSCE has not yet proven itself up to the challenge of providing the foundation for a concert-based global collective security mechanism. To begin with, transforming this regional security organization into a body that includes Japan, China, and other affected states must be considered. Furthermore, the organization must devise a decision-making formula grounded in majority rule rather than in the unanimous consent of such a large, diverse membership of 55 sovereign states. The security document approved by consensus at the December 1996 OSCE summit in Lisbon did not, revealingly, strengthen the OSCE's capacity to lead; the new security model instead affirmed the right of every country to develop its own security alliances, over the objections of Russia, which unsuccessfully lobbied for the OSCE to play a major role in defining European security. Although the OSCE is equipped with the means to intervene in regions of conflict, its past record does not inspire confidence in its capacity for preventive peacekeeping. Its contribution remains restricted to diplomatic activities and the building of peace-respecting democratic civil societies.

The North Atlantic Treaty Organization (NATO) represents a third possible mooring for international security. For some people, however, NATO is more an anachronism than an anchor. The utility of any alliance tends to diminish when the common external threat that brought it together disappears. Without a Soviet or Russian threat, NATO must enlarge its membership and the geographical definition of its responsibilities if it is to play a major security role in the 21st century.

Yet for all the speculation about a broadened, reconfigured NATO, its future remains uncertain. Fractures traverse NATO's membership. Until very recently, there was little evidence that NATO was prepared to take a bold step away from its original mission. With the creation of the North Atlantic Cooperation Council and the implementation of the Clinton administration's "Partnership for Peace" plan to enlarge NATO's membership by including some of the former Warsaw Pact members, the alliance has extended its outreach into central and eastern Europe. But this expansion has greatly exacerbated the fears of Russia and some of Moscow's former Warsaw Pact allies, who vehemently voiced their opposition to an enlarged NATO that threatened to perpetuate their exclusion. To reduce these fears, NATO's Reinforcement Concept continues to express satisfaction with backing the conflict-prevention efforts initiated by other multilateral institutions, and its Strategic Concept eschews leadership in favor of shared risks and roles. Still, unless NATO reconstitutes itself to deal seriously with out-of-area operations, and to cope more decisively with threats that come not from power blocs but internal divisions and nationalism, it will likely go out of existence.

To survive, NATO must redefine its mission to serve as the organizational home for a concert-based collective security mechanism that can deal with the kinds of ethno-nationalist clashes that are likely to most undermine security and order in the future. Even more critically in the long run, it must concentrate its energies on relieving the fears of ostracism and containment by the other powers outside NATO's traditional zone of influence and operation. Russia, in particular, cannot be excluded—a principle U.S. President Clinton recognized when he declared at the January 1994 Brussels summit that his aim was ultimately "a security based not on Europe's division but on the potential of its integration." Simply put, the Partnership for Peace must be extended and enlarged in a way that reassures Moscow that NATO's expansion will not threaten Russia.[11] Otherwise, the possibility that ultranationalist forces in Russia will seek to reassert their nation's imperial sway over its lost empire in the "near abroad" remains a serious concern. At issue is whether NATO's 1997 pledge to neither base nuclear weapons nor substantial foreign troops on new members' territory, and its energized efforts to reassure Moscow by proposing a new "Atlantic Partnership Council" that would bring Russia and other states not in the alliance into a consultive partnership based on consensus decision making, will provide the level of confidence that is required.

Similarly, an excluded China and Japan are unlikely to look favorably to an enlarged NATO that defines its purpose as their containment. Exclusion is the match that historically has ignited revanchist fires. Restricting security protection to only the full-fledged members of NATO effectively denies it to the others and thus does nothing to prevent the organization from remaining a symbol of division. The "associate status" granted to the east and central European states under the Partnership for Peace plan does not go far enough; it leaves them without a guarantee of assistance if they are attacked.

---

[11]U.S.-Russian negotiations in May 1997 to forge a NATO-Russian "charter" were in response to the need to ease the anxieties many Russians feel about a perceived hostile alliance moving closer to their shrunken borders. An exercise in post–Cold-War cooperation, the Albright-Primakov talks on the charter agreement to alleviate Russian fears were also a U.S. reaction of alarm about the May 1997 Sino-Russian strategic agreement to stand together on international issues, including, symptomatically, their joint opposition to American attempts to "monopolize" international affairs and "to expand and strengthen military blocs" like NATO. See "NATO-Russia Charter," *International Herald Tribune,* May 7, 1997, p. 8; Sherman Garnett, "Russia, China Bury the Hatchet—But How Far?" The *Christian Science Monitor,* May 7, 1997, p. 19.

A transformed NATO accommodating the security concerns of *every* great power is the best antidote to a return to the days of a world divided in separate blocs, each seeking to contain the expansion of the other. Such a restructuring is not yet on the horizon, however, and the U.S. half-measure of "separable but not separate" membership can easily invite the very kind of polarization into competing alliances that it seeks to avoid. Filling the security vacuum around Russia (and China?) could revive the East-West division that followed Yalta— to no one's benefit.

Finally, some people have suggested that the Group of Seven (G-7) should become the focal point for collective peacekeeping activities in the 21st century. Two reasons typically underpin such arguments. First, G-7 members are democracies, and disputes between democracies rarely escalate to war because each side shares a common set of norms regarding popular sovereignty and civil liberties, respects the other's legitimacy, and can expect the other industrialized liberal democracies to rely on peaceful means of conflict resolution. Second, because they are connected by a web of economic linkages, the G-7 countries have material incentives to avoid policies that will rupture profitable business transactions.

These reasons notwithstanding, the drawback of the G-7 as a security mechanism is that it functions like an exclusive club whose formal membership does not include Russia or China. While shared democratic values may lay the groundwork for cooperation among members of the club, economic friction can and demonstrably has limited the scope of the club's activities. Trading relationships involve both costs and benefits. The rewarding aspects of commerce may be offset by fierce competition, resulting in irritation, disputes, and hostility. In view of the differential growth rates among the great powers and their anxiety about trade competitiveness in an interdependent global marketplace, the major battles of the future may be clashes on the economic front rather than armed combat among soldiers. And even in the event that political solidarity overrides economic rivalry, the G-7 is ill-equipped to orchestrate peacekeeping missions. Its business is managing business, not warfare.

In sum, the United Nations, NATO, OSCE, and the G-7 all have limitations. Nevertheless, they will play prominent roles in the coming years if only because they are the major structures that already exist. Indeed, it is highly probable that any concert-based collective security architecture that emerges in the near future will consist of an *ad hoc* combination of regional bodies tied together by the interlocking membership of great powers. This security framework would be predicated on the avoidance of hierarchical authority and the creation of "a pattern of interlocking mutually reinforcing organizations" like the collaborative system proposed for consideration at the July 1997 NATO summit.[12] Under such a

---

[12]Klaus Kinkel, "Working Together to Build Europe's New Security Framework," *International Herald Tribune,* December 24–25, 1996, p. 8.

concert-led interinstitutional conference mechanism, responsibility would be centered in those security organizations located in the most threatened flash points. For example, the Eurasian land mass might have NATO or the OSCE anchoring its western flank, some kind of an Organization for Security and Cooperation in the Pacific devised for the eastern flank, with relevant great powers holding memberships in both organizations and meeting regularly under the auspices of the UN Security Council. A full-fledged, comprehensive global collective security system, dedicated to containing aggression anywhere at any time, may be too ambitious and doomed to failure. But a restricted, concert-based collective security mechanism could bring a modicum of order in a fragile and disorderly new multipolar system.

SECURITY STRUCTURES FOR THE FUTURE

The impending structural shift to multipolarity rivets our attention on the historical preoccupation of contending great powers with the goal of gaining power relative to that of the others. They appear to be natural competitors, relentlessly striving for position with one another in the global hierarchy. Whereas few powers seek to rule the world, all are averse to subservient status—for no great power wants equality with their inferiors, only with their superiors.

The diffusion of military and economic capabilities among states that invariably have divergent interests raises serious obstacles for maintaining order and solving transnational problems. Multilateralism, with its emphasis on consultative, shared decision making, provides an opportunity for great powers to recognize their common security threats and avoid the potentially bitter confrontations that otherwise would engender hostile, inflexible blocs. Not all international conflict is amenable to multilateral resolution, but by promoting mutual responsibility and multiple advocacy, multilateralism creates a legitimacy for policy initiatives that is lacking in unilateralism and special bilateral partnerships.

Whether the actions taken by any concert-based collective security organization retain their legitimacy hinges on how such a body is perceived. Will it be seen as an agent of peaceful change, or as a bulwark of the status quo? Great-power consensus on the rules of a security regime can reduce the probability that disputes will escalate to a new Cold War and possible aggression, but it is no guarantee of international justice. Unless concert-based collective security is regarded as a mechanism for ensuring that desirable change can occur without coercive means, its long-term prospects will be disappointing. As political scientist E. H. Carr reminds us, establishing a mechanism for peaceful change in a ruthlessly competitive state system is "the fundamental problem" of international politics.[13]

---

[13]E.H. Carr, *The Twenty Years' Crisis, 1919–1939,* 2nd ed. (London: Macmillan, 1946), p. 222.

14

BUILDING PEACE IN PIECES: THE PROMISE OF EUROPEAN UNITY

Donald J. Puchala

This essay traces the evolutionary process by which the economic and political consolidation of the formerly independent states of Europe led to the creation of the European Union. Drawing on the expectations and vision after World War II that inspired European leaders to construct a security community, Puchala evaluates, in light of integration theory and recent developments and policy initiatives, the progress, pitfalls, and promise of achieving even greater European unity through the cooperative pooling of sovereignty in the 21st century. Puchala is Charles L. Jacobson Professor of Public Affairs and Director of the Walker Institute of International Studies at the University of South Carolina. His many publications include (with Emek Uçarer) *Immigration into Western Societies: Problems and Policies* (1997).

The story of Western Europe's movement toward supranational unity should be familiar to anyone who keeps abreast of current events. Both the vanquished and the victors in Europe were devastated by World War II, even more horribly than they were devastated one generation before by World War I. From these tragic

This essay was written especially for this book.

experiences emerged an awareness among Europeans that if their system of warring sovereign states were not somehow transformed, Europe's future might very well be like its past. There also emerged in Western Europe after 1945 an imaginative plan to build a lasting peace by organizing international relations at a level beyond the nation state. At this "supranational" level sovereignty would be constrained, differing interests would be bargained and adjudicated rather than fought over, and common interests could be elevated and acted upon. A united and peaceful Europe had been the dream of philosophers for centuries. But for farsighted European statesmen of the immediate post–World War II generation—Jean Monnet, Robert Schuman, Konrad Adenauer, Alcide de Gasperi, Paul-Henri Spaak, and others—uniting Europe became an imperative. It was the key to peace.

Since the early 1950s, Western Europe has been uniting, in small and large institutional steps, in fits and starts, and in political and economic leaps forward followed by slides backward. But, for those countries involved, the predominant course of their relations has been toward incrementally more international cooperation and supranational authority and incrementally less national autonomy. Postwar intra-European international economic cooperation began in the late 1940s under the incentives of the American-initiated Marshall Plan.[1] The first supranational experiment was the European Coal and Steel Community in 1952. Six countries—France, West Germany, Italy, the Netherlands, Belgium, and Luxembourg—turned the regulation of their coal and steel industries over to a European High Authority and simultaneously opened their borders to the free movement of goods, money, and labor in these industries. By 1958, the Six were able to form the European Economic Community (EEC), which opened borders to free economic movement in all economic sectors and established the EEC as a single entity in economic dealings with the outside world.

Institutionally, a European Commission, headquartered in Brussels, was created to design common economic policies for the six member states and to oversee their administration. However, a Council of Ministers, representing the governments of the member states, retained final authority in the European policy-making process. A European Parliament, representing public opinion and political parties, functioned from the beginning of the movement toward European unity, though initially this body was appointed rather than elected and it had very little power. A European Court of Justice, charged with adjudicating claims and conflicts among and between governments and the newly established institutions, also functioned from the beginning. Both the Parliament and the Court were to grow in prominence as the unity movement progressed.

---

[1]M. Margaret Ball, *NATO and the European Union Movement* (New York: Frederick A. Praeger, 1959), pp. 217–252; Jacques Freymond, *Western Europe Since the War: A Short Political History* (New York: Frederick A. Praeger, 1964), p. 41.

There were, of course, problems along the way toward greater Western European unity, since national sovereignty is never easily relinquished and opposition to international cooperation is never entirely absent. Formulating and administering a common agricultural policy affecting all EEC member countries, for example, proved to be a major challenge, as did formulating and administering a common system of indirect taxation, a common policy regarding transport, and a common fisheries policy. Tensions persisted, and still persist, over how far and how fast Europe ought to move toward government beyond the nation state, over how large the European Union ought to be, over the balance of initiative and authority among the central institutions, and about how the benefits and burdens of forging greater unity ought to be distributed.

Still, the most pronounced 50-year trend in intra-European international relations has been the broadening and deepening of cooperation among governments along with the relegation of ever more authority to institutions and processes operating at the supranational level. The European Economic Community of the Six—alternatively called the European Community, the European Communities, the Common Market, or simply "Brussels"—is today a European Union (EU) of 15 countries. A first expansion in the early 1970s brought in the United Kingdom, Ireland, and Denmark, followed in the early 1980s by Greece, Spain, and Portugal, followed again in the 1990s by the accession of Austria, Sweden and Finland. By the late 1990s the European Union was on the threshold of a bold, new enlargement that may eventually encompass all of the former communist countries of Central Europe as well as the island states of Malta and Cyprus.

While the union was expanding geographically, the functional breadth of its policy making was also broadening. As it turned out, creating a common market among countries involved a good deal more than simply opening borders and freeing trade. Legislation and regulations pertaining to all aspects of economic intercourse needed to be harmonized across countries. Product standards needed to be standardized. Government contracting needed to be competitively opened to nonnationals. Cartels needed to be similarly constrained from country to country, and so too countless other liberalizing, standardizing, and harmonizing actions had to be taken to guarantee that the European Economic Community would be in fact a common market. A major thrust in the direction of completing the common market, and thus harmonizing much of European economic life, was made between 1985 and 1992, driven by the Single European Act (SEA) and pursued under the slogan "Europe 1992."

Making common foreign economic policies with respect to trade and development had been the prerogative of the central institutions of the EEC since their inception. But during the 1980s, under the rubric of Political Cooperation, European Community members began to seek common positions on a range of political issues on the world agenda, such as Middle Eastern and Central American questions. They also began to coordinate their activities within the United Nations and other world organizations. With the signing of the Maastricht Treaties, which transformed the European Communities into the European Union in 1993, seeking common European foreign and security policies (CFSP) became a constitutional prerogative, and the groundwork was thus laid for the emergence of "Europe" as a world political actor. Maastricht also opened the way for common European policy making through an institution called Justice and Home Affairs, which coordinates transnational programs that combat criminal and antiterrorist activities, and which will deal with immigration matters all along the European Union's extensive external frontiers. Maastricht also pointed the way toward the eventual harmonization of social policies pertaining to working conditions, pensions and benefits, health insurance, and the like across all member countries. Most importantly, the Maastricht agreements committed the members of the European Union to entering into an Economic and Monetary Union (EMU), with a common currency, a central bank, and a common monetary policy, by the first decade of the 21st century. EMU, the first phases of which are scheduled for 1999, will move monetary decision making from the member states to central European institutions. Hence, it represents a dramatic step beyond national sovereignty.

Subtly, but unmistakably, while the European Union broadened geographically and deepened functionally, its institutions began to look and to operate increasingly like an embryonic central government. The European Commission, which had supranational authority from the outset, protected its prerogatives over time, and succeeded in inserting itself into areas of policy, like CFSP, where national governments were loath to surrender sovereignty. The Council of Ministers has remained the bastion of national governments, national sovereignty, and national interests. Nevertheless, over time, requirements for decisions by unanimity (giving each member state a veto) have been relaxed, and today many important questions before the Council are decided by majority vote. Meanwhile, the European Parliament, now directly elected, has expanded its consultative role rather dramatically and even gained some genuine legislative authority. For its part, the European Court of Justice has evolved into a constitutional court for the European Union with a penchant for enforcing the superiority of European law over national laws.

Where the European unity movement may be headed remains an open question that will be considered later in this essay. But what the movement has thus far accomplished is quite clear. In the course of a half century intra-European international relations have been transformed. Western Europe is no longer a system of warring sovereign states. In fact, it is not entirely accurate to describe the European Union as a system of sovereign states at all. Today a level of governance exists within the European Union that functions above constituent states and commands mandatory compliance with supranationally formulated legislation. There are also supranational political, judicial, and administrative enforcement procedures, which are continually employed and reasonably effective. Most importantly, when the original peace-building objectives of the European unity movement are recalled, it is quite evident that Western Europe has become a zone of peace. Any possibility that this situation can or will change for the foreseeable future is remote.

EXPLAINING EUROPEAN UNITY

Because patterns of intra-European international relations since 1945 are not readily explainable in traditional ways, interpreting the movement toward European unity has posed an intellectual challenge. The early consensus among scholars was to label what was happening in postwar Western Europe "international integration." Though several more precise and technical definitions were offered by scholars studying it, most would agree that international integration fundamentally has to do with the peaceful coming together of states and peoples, and this, in the most general way, is what has been happening in postwar Western Europe. Beginning in the early 1950s those who were closely watching European events made efforts to generalize about the hows and whys of international integration, and they embodied their insights and formulations in a variety of so-called *integration theories.*

Theorists disagreed about the nature, causes, and conditions of international integration. But, they agreed initially on one issue: what international integration *is not.* It is not traditional power politics, or anything like the kind of international relations depicted by exponents of political realism.[2] International relations as understood by the political realists is a realm of behavior occupied by sovereign states, where each competes with all others for domain, prestige, greater power, or whatever the ingredients of national security turn out to be in particular cases. In this realm, power, usually military, makes the crucial difference in bringing about outcomes and thus determines winners and losers. According to the realists' understanding, international issues of significance are those that governments are willing to go to war to settle. Other matters, such as trade issues and similar pursuits after welfare, are "low politics" and therefore never of central importance in foreign policy or of great consequence for the fate of nations. War is ever possible; it is always expected; it frequently occurs.[3] What does not occur in the realists' world are meaningful or lasting international cooperation (except possibly in military alliances), autonomous or consequential action by international organizations, relinquished sovereignty, important issues that are non–military-strategic in nature, or international order founded upon anything other than balanced power. It needs to be emphasized that the realists'

---

[2]Hans J Morgenthau, *Politics Among Nations: The Struggle for Power and Peace,* 4th ed. (New York: Alfred A. Knopf, 1967), pp. 3–14.; Edward Hallet Carr, *The Twenty Years' Crisis 1919–1939: An Introduction to the Study of International Relations* (New York: Harper Torchbooks, 1964), pp. 63–95.

[3]Raymond Aron, *Peace and War: A Theory of International Relations,* tr. Richard Howard and Annette Baker Fox (Garden City, N.Y.: Doubleday & Company, 1966), pp. 8–17.

"power politics" vision of international relations is not inaccurate. Historically it has been highly accurate, and in the emerging Cold War system of the 1950s it explained well the fundamental structure and dynamics of crucial aspects of world affairs. But, *it did not explain what has been happening in Western Europe since 1945.*

Analysts studying international integration in Western Europe observed and described a kind of international relations that differed from traditional power politics in a variety of ways. As they looked at postwar Western Europe, these analysts observed that:

1. Sovereign states are not the only consequential actors in international relations. Indeed, some outcomes in international relations can be understood only in terms of the motives, behavior, or impacts of international public organizations and bureaucracies, formal and *ad hoc* coalitions of transnationally grouped officials, organized nongovernmental associations, multinational business enterprises, international social classes, and other actors traditionally deemed inconsequential.

2. Issues of national security and war and peace are not the only kinds of foreign policy concerns that governments deem highly important. In fact, some governments allot their most serious attention and efforts to foreign policies directed toward enhancing national welfare defined in terms of per capita income, employment, human security, and the general well-being of their citizens. The importance that governments attach to such welfare goals and the domestic penalties and rewards surrounding their attainment or sacrifice make economic and social issues into "high politics" concerns.

3. International relations can be fundamentally collaborative processes played out to positive-sum conclusions where all participants "win." Significant outcomes take the form of realizing and distributing rewards among collaborating actors or coalitions. Cooperation, not competition, is the international mode.

4. Influence in international relations follows from forging and manipulating bonds of interdependence among actors, and not necessarily from threatening or exerting physical force. Bargaining and persuasion, not compulsion, are the modal means to international influence.

5. Ordered international relations result as readily from adherence to, or compliance with, norms, rules and laws as from balanced power. International law can be an effective ordering force in international relations.

While students of international integration in Western Europe could agree that they were observing a qualitatively new and different kind of international relations on the Old Continent, they could not agree upon exactly what is was that was driving the states and peoples toward ever broadening and deepening unity. Important, though very different, explanations of European integration followed from the seminal work of the American scholars Karl W. Deutsch and Ernst B. Haas, who, in the late 1950s, laid the intellectual groundwork for theories of international integration that later came to be called International Community Formation and Neo-Functionalism.[4] These theories, elaborated and tested by other scholars, retain considerable explanatory power even today.[5]

International Community Formation

In explaining the dynamics of European unity, Karl Deutsch distinguished between the coming together of peoples, which he called "integration," and the merger of states or governments, which he called "amalgamation."[6] For Deutsch, a community is a population whose members, because of a host of recognized commonalities, identify with one another and distinguish between themselves and others. Integration is essentially community formation, and when it occurs across nations it becomes international community formation. Community formation (that is, integration) is essentially a social-psychological process during which people come to trust and value one another, to spontaneously respond to one another's needs, to emphasize their similarities and dismiss their differences, and ultimately to distinguish between themselves collectively and others whom they perceive as being members of alien communities. In ways too complex to deal with in this short essay, the community formation process is driven by quantities and qualities of communications or transactions among peoples, which result in learning experiences, and accumulate, under particular conditions, to become the merging of identities.[7]

What turns out to be crucially important for the Deutschian analysis is that at some point in the community formation process, those involved come to recognize and accept that there is no longer any danger that differences and disagreements among them will result in wars. On the contrary almost universally shared expectations that conflicts can and will be peacefully resolved emerge. When

---

[4]In the social science literature Karl Deutsch's approach, which is here called international community formation, is referred to as transactionalism, reflecting the fact that communications or transactions among peoples purportedly caused the social-psychological changes that Deutsch studied. Deutsch, however, never used the term "transactionalism," but rather described what he was analyzing as "community formation."

[5]Some of the more imaginative elaborations on integration theory include Leon N. Linberg and Stuart A, Scheingold, *Europe's Would-Be Polity: Patterns of Change in the European Community* (Englewood Cliffs, N.J.: Prentice-Hall, 1970); Joseph S. Nye, Jr., *Peace in Parts: Integration and Conflict in Regional Organizations* (Boston: Little, Brown, 1971), pp. 21–107; Bruce M. Russett, *Community and Contention: Britain and America in the Twentieth Century* (Cambridge, Mass.: M.I.T. Press, 1963); Karl W. Deutsch, et al., *France, Germany and the Western Alliance: A Study of Elite Attitudes and European Integration* (New York: Charles Scribner's Sons, 1967).

[6]Karl W Deutsch, et al., *Political Community and the North Atlantic Area: International Organization in the Light of Historical Experience* (Princeton, N.J.: Princeton University Press, 1957).

[7]Donald J Puchala, "International Transactions and Regional Integration," *International Organization* no. 4 (Autumn 1970), pp. 732–764.

such social-psychological conditions prevail within an emergent international community, Deutsch claims that a "security community" has come into being.[8]

In the Deutschian scheme, community formation or the coming together of peoples must occur, both logically and practically, before amalgamation or the merger of states or governments. It is the new international community that decides to make itself into a new political entity and to signal and protect its integrity and autonomy by establishing institutions of government. Furthermore, it is the new international community that renders itself governable by allotting legitimacy to the newly established institutions of government.

From the Deutschian perspective, what had to be happening in Western Europe from the 1950s onward was the emergence of an international community, a "supranationality" as it were, whose needs for collective action internally and autonomy vis-à-vis the outside world were both making imperative and legitimizing international amalgamation in the form of overarching institutions and common public policies. If community formation came first, political amalgamation could follow. Empirically, there was some evidence that international community formation was occurring in postwar Western Europe.[9] However, the "supranationality" that Deutsch and his colleagues were looking for never fully materialized, and even today, more than 50 years after the launching of the European unity movement, only a very superficial "European" identification exists and there is no really strong indication that Frenchmen, Germans, Italians, or any of the others have exchanged their national self-identifications for European ones. Yet, as the opening passages of this essay made clear, political amalgamation in the form of overarching institutions and expanding supranational prerogatives has been progressing rather impressively, so it would appear that there was no apparent linkage between prior community formation and subsequent amalgamation in the Western European experience.

The apparent failure of the causal connection between integration and amalgamation in Deutsch's theory led some to dismiss his formulation as an explanation for Western Europe's movement toward unity. But, this may have been tantamount to intellectually throwing the baby out with the bathwater, because empirical investigations disclosed that, by the mid-1960s, a security community had emerged in Western Europe. This was particularly evident in the changing attitudes of Frenchmen and Germans who eventually stopped looking upon each another as potential enemies and stopped expecting that they would fight again in the future.[10] Other significant changes in attitudes among Western Europeans also

---

[8]The concept "security community" was introduced by Richard W. Van Wagenen in his *Research in the International Organization Field* (Princeton, N.J.: Center for Research on World Political Institutions, 1952).

[9]See, Deutsch, et al., *France, Germany and the Western Alliance.*

[10]Puchala, "International Transactions and Regional Integration," pp. 744–746.

occurred during the early postwar decades that suggested generally rising levels of mutual trust, confidence, and amity, particularly evident among the educated, professionals, and young.[11] Even though no full-blown international community emerged among Western Europeans, there was nevertheless an emergent social-psychological foundation—or permissive environment—underpinning the cooperative diplomacy and the institution building that marked the amalgamative dimension of the movement toward European unity. This foundation was probably a necessary condition for initiating productive international cooperation, especially since the countries involved were democratic and public sentiments therefore counted politically. There is every indication that this supportive attitudinal environment has persisted over time.

Neo-Functionalism

Ernst Haas was influenced by the early work of the British scholar David Mitrany, who, in a formulation that he called "Functionalism," proposed to the post–World War II world that the path to lasting peace required organization and governance beyond the nation state.[12] Meaningful international cooperation could take place, Mitrany said, if "functions" generally performed by national governments—providing for the well-being of citizens, regulating commerce, protecting the environment, and the like—were assigned to supranational agencies and treated as universal human interests rather than separate national interests. But, whereas Mitrany's Functionalism was a plan for global action, Haas' Neo-Functionalism was a scheme for analyzing international integration. He was most interested in what happens *after* functions are in fact supranationalized. With specific regard to Western Europe, Haas wanted to know what happened after the regulation and administration of economic sectors were assigned to supranational authorities, and in his first integration study, *The Uniting of Europe,* he closely observed the results of the creation of the European Coal and Steel Community.[13] What Haas discovered, and what became the core of Neo-Functionalism, is that supranationalizing particular functions or policy sectors tends to unleash a dynamic that almost makes imperative the supranationalizing of additional ones. International integration builds upon itself step by step; it "spills over" until something like a full-blown government emerges at the international level. This happens because each functional step toward expanded international authority sets in motion political processes that generate demands for

---

[11]Donald J Puchala, "Integration and Disintegration in Franco-German Relations, 1954–1963, *International Organization* no. 2 (1970), pp. 183–208; Karl W. Deutsch, et al., *France, Germany and the Western Alliance.*

[12]David Mitrany, *A Working Peace System* (Chicago: Quadrangle Books, 1966).

[13]Ernst B Haas, *The Uniting of Europe: Political Social and Economic Forces* (Stanford: Stanford University Press, 1958); see also, Haas, "International Integration: The European Process and the Universal," *International Organization* 15, no. 3 (Summer 1961), pp. 366–392.

further steps. At each step, and in the face of demands for new ones, national governments are forced to choose between surrendering additional autonomy and diluting sovereignty or refusing to do so and risking the collapse of their initial efforts at sector amalgamation. Neo-Functionalism posits that, other things being equal, political pressures mounted at key decision points will cause governments to choose to move toward greater amalgamation.

Spillover follows from several causes, all having to do with the politicization of issues in pluralistic societies. First, because modern industrial societies are internally highly interdependent, it is impossible to internationalize one functional sector, say, steel production, without affecting numerous other sectors, for example, mining, transport, and labor organization and representation. Because other sectors are affected and because elites within them are organized to exert pressure on national governments, their concerns become subjects of international discussion and questions arise about granting further authority to international agencies to handle matters in affected cognate sectors. At such points governments must decide to either grant the expanded international authority or court failure in the initial sector amalgamation. If the balance of perceived rewards and penalties favors moving toward greater amalgamation, as it frequently does, governments will grant expanded authority to international agencies. Sometimes spillover also follows from failures to appreciate the true magnitude or implications of tasks assigned to international agencies—initial conservative grants of authority prove unfeasible and must be extended. It is frequently discovered, for example, that international authorities are unable to perform their assigned tasks within initially imposed jurisdictional limits, so that either assigned tasks have to be abandoned or jurisdictional limits have to be extended.

The great strength of Haas' work was his accurate portrayal of international integration as an intensely political phenomenon. Integration involves numerous political actors, pursuing their own interests, pressuring governments, or, if they are governments, pressuring one another to negotiate toward international policies that are collectively beneficial because they are individually beneficial for all concerned. Like politics more generally, the politics of international integration is a game of bargaining that eventuates in generally acceptable public policies—*common European* policies in the case of the European Union.

The weakness of the neo-functional analysis of international integration is that since it begins by looking at the results of initial efforts at supranationalization, it offers little insight into how or why decisions are made to engage in sectoral integration in the first place. Neo-functionalism as applied to Western European integration also tended to assume too much automaticity in the spillover dynamic and therefore could not account for the intermittent slowing down or halting of the movement toward unity that occurred several times. Still, as a description of what has been happening within, and to, postwar Western Europe, neo-functionalism paints a very reliable picture. It also explains in a candidly political and empirically accurate way why the picture has taken the form it has taken.

Integration has proceeded from functional sector to functional sector. The logic of spillover, for example, is much in evidence in the political imperatives that drove the movement from the sectoral amalgamation in coal and steel in 1952, to a comprehensive common market in 1958, to the completion of the common market in 1992. Similar spillover dynamics are today driving Europe toward economic and monetary union after 1999.

EUROPEAN INTEGRATION: RETROSPECT AND PROSPECT

If our understanding of Western European integration were informed only from newspaper accounts, we would have to conclude that the European experiment with unity has actually been an interminable series of crises. It appears from the newspapers that the union is almost always on the verge of breaking apart, that one member country or another, more often than not the United Kingdom, is always obstructing cooperation, that the European Commission is always overstepping the bounds of its supranational authority and provoking criticism, or that the next integrative step—be it monetary union, a common defense policy, a common immigration policy, or another enlargement of membership—cannot possibly be taken in the face of opposition and complexities. As noted earlier, there has been no shortage of problems along the way to greater European unity, and there certainly have been major crises that have slowed international cooperation and raised doubts about the future. French President Charles DeGaulle, for example, forced the EEC to a standstill in 1966 over questions of majority voting in the Council of Ministers. The energy crisis and global inflation of the 1970s threw the European Communities into disarray as different member states were differently affected by world economic conditions. Margaret Thatcher held up European movement in the 1980s over budgetary questions. The Danes initially rejected the Maastricht Treaty, and the French very nearly defeated it too. The British brought the European Union to a halt in 1996 by escalating the "Mad Cow Crisis." The European Union is poised in 1997 on the threshold of a new enlargement, which pundits say it cannot digest; it is preparing to implement monetary union, which critics say is unnecessary and unwise; it is taking up the rest of the Maastricht agenda, which journalists say is too ambitious; it is contending with British ambivalence, which Europeans in the street say is intolerable and destructive; and it is confronted with an economic recession that persists despite diligent efforts to end it. The European Union today is preoccupying the European press and once again evoking the prophets of doom.

Though the movement toward Western European unity may appear perennially precarious when examined close up in any short-term time frame, the longer-run, and more reliably assessable, European experience looks quite different. Historically, the course of intra-European international relations in the context of the European Community and its institutional progeny is best seen as a series of problems constructively solved and a congeries of crises constructively weathered. To date, almost every crisis in Community affairs has resulted in broadened or deepened integration or both. The characteristic pattern of international interaction during European integration has been dialectical: movements toward greater unity invariably provoke opposition, which generates confrontations, which engender negotiations, which eventuate in compromises, which reaffirm unity. Political phases in working out the integrative dialectic are frequently long, drawn out, tension-filled, exhausting to those immediately involved, and worrisome to those following the media. But, with each succeeding synthesis Community unity tends to be strengthened. Moreover, almost every major goal (and countless minor ones as well) in the course of European integration to which Community members have committed themselves—for example, establishing the customs union, formulating the common agricultural policy, enlarging in phases, implementing the value-added tax, completing the common market, introducing direct parliamentary elections, moving to majority voting, empowering the parliament, and so on—has eventually been accomplished. This has not always accorded with optimistic timetables, but eventually, and usually later rather than sooner, the goals get accomplished nonetheless. Though member governments in the European Union have differing images of where European integration is, or should be, heading, they have displayed an almost unremitting political will to always move in the direction of greater unity. In historical context then, the future would appear to favor those who favor greater European unity.

Integration theory likewise points to further integration and amalgamation within the European Union. The permissive social-psychological environment of mitigated alienation, mutual confidence, amity, and community that Karl Deutsch sought among Europeans is more in evidence today than it was at the time of Deutsch's studies. There is also rather strong public endorsement for the notion of European unity, and notable public approval for the institutions of the EU. Also in everyday evidence are the political forces and processes pressing for institutional spillover and further supranationalization that Ernst Haas identified as the dynamics of integration. Monetary union will be a product of these dynamics, as will a common European immigration policy, and eventually the politics of spillover will also yield a common European foreign and security policy. The outside world is already demanding a common foreign policy from the European Union, and, once further enlargement finally establishes the Union's geographic boundaries, the altered strategic environment of the post–Cold War world will likely impel a common European security policy.

In the autumn of 1972, when Andrew Shonfield, Director of London's Royal Institute of International Affairs, was invited to deliver the prestigious Reith Lectures over the BBC, he chose for his subject *Europe: Journey to an Unknown*

Destination.[14] His subject remains as perplexing in 1997 as it was in 1972. It is still unclear when European integration will end and what the end product will look like. Some believe that the European Union will evolve into a federation—a United States of Europe. Others envisage a looser kind of confederation wherein the member states will retain considerable autonomy—*L'Europe des États.* Still others foresee that Europe, structurally, will not look much different in the future from how it looks today, though they expect that the central institutions—Commission, Council, Parliament and Court—will become increasingly authoritative, and certainly more involved with common policy making as times goes on. It is more than likely that the eventual institutional framework for continuing European cooperation will be *sui generis*; it will not resemble traditional models, like federation or confederation; it will be tailored to meet European needs under 21st century conditions. Few expect that Europe in the future will be less unified than Europe today.

Admittedly, there is no way to say with any assurance where Europe is heading. To date, European integration has been a process, not a product. This process has yielded peace, and has led, over the span of a half century, to incrementally intensifying cooperation among an expanding group of states and peoples. It is continuing.

---

[14]Andrew Shonfield, *Europe: Journey to an Unknown Destination* (London: Penguin Books, 1973).

15

COMMUNAL CONFLICTS AND GLOBAL SECURITY

Ted Robert Gurr

Most of the countries in the world are multiethnic societies, such as in the former Yogoslavia. Within them, communal conflicts are common, many of which, exacerbated by ethno-national grievances, threaten to escalate to wars of independence. This essay describes the character of the issues relating to this growing global problem as well as the approaches the international community might pursue to protect minorities' rights and sustain global security. Its author, Ted Robert Gurr, is Distinguished University Professor of Government and Politics and Distinguished Scholar at the university's Center for International Development and Conflict Management. He is senior author of *Minorities at Risk: A Global View of Ethnonational Conflicts* (1993).

From "Communal Conflicts and Global Security" by Ted Robert Gurr, *Current History*. The essay is a revision of Chapter 11 in Ted Robert Gurr, with Barbara Harff, Monty G. Marshall, and James R. Scarritt, *Minorities at Risk: A Global View of Ethnopolitical Conflicts* (Washington, D.C.: United States Institute of Peace Press, 1993). It incorporates updated information from the 1990s phase of the Minorities at Risk project, funded by the National Science Foundation, the United States Institute of Peace, and the Korea Foundation. Footnotes have been deleted. Reprinted with permission from *Current History* Magazine, May 1995. Copyright © 1995, Current History, Inc.

Since the end of the Cold War, conflicts between communal groups and states have been recognized as the major challenges to domestic and international security in most parts of the world. Minority peoples are now the principal victims of gross human rights violations. In 1993 more than 25 million refugees fled from communal conflicts, including 3 percent of the population of sub-Saharan Africa. Communal conflict has devastated the former Yugoslavia and East-Central Africa, and threatens the stability of most of the former republics of the Soviet Union. This century's longest conflicts are still being fought over ethnonational issues in the Middle East and Southeast Asia. Communal conflict is also ascendant in the West: ethnic tensions and inequalities drive the most divisive conflicts in the United States in the 1990s, and Quebec is edging toward secession from Canada. Virtually every country in western Europe is beset by growing public antagonism toward immigrant groups of third world origin.

Before now, there was no firm basis for generalizing about the nature of communal conflicts beyond the groups or region examined in specific case studies. However, the Minorities at Risk project, an ongoing study of the status, demands, and conflicts of virtually all politically active communal groups throughout the world during the 1980s and 1990s, has found that some generalizations can be made.

The 292 communal groups that this study examines differ widely in their defining traits, political status, and aspirations. Many of the comparisons that follow distinguish between national peoples and minority peoples. National peoples are regionally concentrated groups that have lost their autonomy to expansionist states but still preserve culturally distinct features and desire some degree of political separation. Minority peoples, by contrast, have a defined socioeconomic or political status within a larger society—based on some combination of their ethnicity, immigrant origin, economic roles, and religion—and are concerned about protecting or improving that status. Table 15-1 makes distinctions between these two general types.

Global analysis suggests answers to 11 general questions about politically active communal groups:

1.   *What proportion of the world's population identifies with politically assertive communal groups? Where are they most numerous?*

In 1994 about one-sixth the global population (989 million people) belonged to 292 groups whose members either have experienced systematic discrimination or have taken political action to assert their collective interests against the states that claim to govern them. Not everyone in each group agrees about their common identities and interests; most minorities are divided by crosscutting loyalties to different clans, localities, classes, or political movements. Therefore the aggregate numbers represent the outer bounds of the populations that might be mobilized for collective action on behalf of communal interests. Shared adversity and conflict with dominant groups almost invariably sharpen the sense of common interest and build support for political action.

TABLE 15-1
TYPES OF POLITICALLY ACTIVE COMMUNAL GROUPS

National peoples

Ethnonationalists	Large, regionally concentrated peoples with a history of organized political autonomy, who have pursued separatist objectives of some time during the last 50 years.
Indigenous peoples	Conquered descendants of the original inhabitants of a region who typically live in peripheral regions, practice subsistence agriculture for herding, and have cultures sharply distinct from dominant groups.

Minority peoples

Ethnoclasses	Ethnically or culturally distinct peoples, usually descended from slaves or immigrants, with special economic roles, usually of low status.
Militant sects	Communal groups whose political status and activities are centered on the defense of their religious beliefs.
Communal contenders	Culturally distinct peoples, tribes, or clans in heterogeneous societies who hold or seek a share in state power.

Of the world's 190 countries, 120 have politically significant minorities. Table 15-2 shows that sub-Saharan Africa has the greatest concentration of minorities at risk—81 groups whose people constitute more than 50 percent of the regional population. Before the breakup of the Soviet Union and Yugoslavia, eastern Europe had the second largest percentage of minorities at 35 percent. However, while the number of politically salient minorities in the region has nearly doubled, from 32 to 59, they comprise only 14 percent of the region's total population. Asia, Latin America, and the Western democracies have had the smallest proportions, between 11 percent and 13 percent each.

2. Which communal minorities in which world regions are most seriously disadvantaged?

Ethnoclasses, such as Maghrebins in France, people of color in the Americas, and immigrant Chinese communities in Asian countries, experience on average greater political and economic inequalities and discrimination than other groups. Indigenous peoples face disadvantages nearly as great, and are threatened by severe ecological pressures on their traditional lands and resources as well. Ethnonationalists and communal contenders are less likely to be economically disadvantaged than other types of groups, but they usually face substantial political restrictions, often because their political aspirations are seen as a threat by state elites.

At the end of the 1980s, inequalities and discriminatory barriers overall were markedly lower in eastern Europe, the Soviet Union, and the industrial democracies

TABLE 15-2
MINORITIES AT RISK IN 1994, BY REGION

World region	Number of countries with minorities at risk	Population of minorities (1994 estimates)		
		Number of minorities at risk	Total	Percent of regional population
Western democracies and Japan (28 countries)	15	31	94,291,000	12
Eastern Europe and Soviet successor states (27 countries)	25	59	59,671,000	14
East, Southeast, and South Asia (34 countries)	21	62	397,474,000	13
North Africa and the Middle East (19 countries)	11	27	89,840,000	26
Africa south of the Sahara (48 countries)	30	81	294,460,000	51
Latin America and the Caribbean (34 countries)	18	32	52,965,000	11
Total (190 countries)	120	292	988,701,000	18

than in other world regions. But in the 1990s most Soviet successor states have imposed discriminatory restrictions on nontitular nationalities, erasing most of the Soviet regime's socially engineered equality of status and opportunity for national minorities. The rump Yugoslavia, Croatia, and Romania also pursue discriminatory policies toward national minorities; most other eastern and central European states have followed the Western democratic precedent.

In Africa and Asia, inequalities and discrimination against communal minorities have remained relatively high, though the new Asian democracies have been notably successful in reducing historical patterns of discrimination. Indigenous and Afro-American minorities in Latin America, though proportionally small in numbers, experienced the greatest economic differentials and most severe economic discrimination observed in any world region. Communal minorities in the Middle East and North Africa have been subject to the most severe political restrictions.

3. *Are ethno-political grievances and demands mainly the result of inequalities and discrimination?*

Two different dynamics underlie the demands and strategies of activist communal groups. First, contemporary movements for secession or regional autonomy are strongly motivated by a desire to protect and assert group identity. These autonomy demands are concentrated among ethnonationalists and indigenous peoples with a tradition of political independence and sharp cultural differences from dominant groups. The second dynamic is that ethnoclasses, communal contenders, and militant sects usually have more tangible concerns. Their strongest demands are for greater rights within societies, not to exit from them. Discrimination motivates demands for greater political and economic rights, while cultural differences prompt demands for protection of the group's social and cultural rights.

4. *How much has ethno-political conflict increased?*

Every form of ethno-political conflict increased sharply from the 1950s through the early 1990s. Nonviolent political action by communal groups more than doubled between 1950 and 1990, and both violent protest and rebellion quadrupled. Trends differ widely among regions and types of groups, however. In the democracies communal conflict peaked in the early 1970s and declined through the end of the 1980s. In contrast, ethnic protest and rebellion in eastern Europe and the Soviet Union were low for most of the postwar period but began to escalate in the early 1980s, even before perestroika and glasnost. Nonviolent protest and rebellion steadily increased in Asia and the Middle East from the 1950s onward. The decline of some communal conflicts in these regions since 1990—for example by the Kurds and non-Burmese nationalists in Myanmar—have been offset by intensified communal conflicts in India, Afghanistan, and Pakistan. Communal conflict in Africa was shaped by decolonization and its consequences. Protest reached a peak in the decade before 1960, when most African countries gained independence, but since then a pronounced shift from protest to rebellion has occurred. Africa now has the most intense ethno-political conflicts of any world region. Latin America has the lowest levels of communal conflict. Disputes there are mainly nonviolent protest by indigenous activists that reached a climacteric in the late 1970s and early 1980s; since 1990, however, there has been a fresh upsurge of activism among indigenous Latin Americans.

Worldwide comparisons show that indigenous groups have seen the greatest proportional increase in conflict, a testimony to the influence of the global indigenous rights movement that was established in the 1970s. The long-term global increase in rebellion is mainly attributable to autonomy movements by ethno-nationalists, whose magnitudes of rebellion increased fivefold between the early 1950s and the 1980s. Communal contenders, a group type found mainly in sub-Saharan Africa, have shifted from nonviolent protest to rebellion. Ethnoclasses, most of whom live in Western democracies and Latin America, have mainly relied on nonviolent protest; this escalated into sporadic episodes of rioting and terrorism from the late 1960s to the early 1980s.

5. *How serious is religiously based communal conflict?*

Religious cleavages are usually a contributing factor in communal conflict but seldom the root cause. Only 8 of the 49 militant sects in the study are defined solely or mainly by their religious beliefs. An example of these are the politically mobilized Shiite communities in Iraq and Lebanon, whose goals are political rights and recognition, not the propagation of their faith. Other sectarian minorities also have class identifications, such as the Catholics of Northern Ireland and Turkish immigrants in Germany, or nationalist objectives, such as the Palestinians in Israel's occupied territories and the Moros in the Philippines. The driving force behind the most serious and protracted communal conflicts in the Middle East is not militant Islam but the unsatisfied nationalist aspirations of the Kurds and Palestinians.

Religiously inspired political conflict was uncommon anywhere in the world until the 1960s. It doubled in magnitude from then through the end of the 1980s, but its rate of increase was outpaced by rebellion by other kinds of groups, especially ethno-nationalists. Overall, groups defined wholly or partly by sectarian differences from dominant groups accounted for one-quarter of rebellions in the 1980s.

6. *Is the trend in ethno-political activism moving toward protest or rebellion?*

Since 1945, nonviolent political action has been far more common among minorities in Western societies, including Latin America, than violent ethno-political protest and rebellion. This was also the case in eastern Europe and the Soviet Union until 1990. Deadly communal conflicts in the former Yugoslavia and the Caucasus distract attention from a significantly larger phenomenon: the breakup of the Soviet Union into five independent countries was accomplished without protracted civil wars or communal rebellions. Ethnic relations in most of the new countries are thus far fractious but seldom deadly; the exceptions have been Moldova, Georgia, Azerbaijan, and Tajikistan. Communal conflicts in the first three were in remission in early 1995; Tajikistan's civil war is a consequence of political rivalries, not communal ones.

The protagonists in the most persistent communal rebellions of the last 50 years have been ethno-nationalists such as the Tibetans, the Eritreans, southern Sudanese, the Palestinians, the Kurds, the Basques, the Karen and Kachin in Burma, and the Nagas and Tripuras in India. Eighty guerrilla and civil wars were fought by these and other communal rebels between 1945 and 1989: 26 were in Asia, 25 in sub-Saharan Africa, 22 in the Middle East and North Africa, 4 in Eastern Europe and the Soviet Union, and 2 in Latin America. A look at 33 ethno-political wars and militarized conflicts in 1993–1994 shows proportional increases in sub-Saharan Africa and the former Soviet sphere, but declines elsewhere. Twelve of the 33 were in sub-Saharan Africa, 7 in eastern Europe and the

Soviet successor states, 9 in Asia, 3 in the Middle East and North Africa, and 2 in Latin America.

7. *Do reformist responses to ethnic demands lead toward accommodation or escalation of communal conflict?*

Most communal conflicts begin with acts of protest that escalate into violent conflict. In authoritarian, third world regimes the escalation usually happens very quickly, in part because official responses are more likely to be repressive than reformist. In democracies, however, escalation to violence is usually limited and based on the actions of small, militant factions. All 24 minorities in the Western democracies and Japan used nonviolent political tactics at some time between 1945 and 1989; half resorted to violent protest, and half had militant factions that engaged in terrorism. Setting aside two movements that used violence from the onset (the Irish Republican Army and Puerto Rican nationalist groups), an average of 13 years elapsed between the establishment of political movements representing communal interests in the Western democracies and the first occurrence of violence. This gave societies ample time to respond to communal grievances while conflict was muted. Moreover, the fact that most democratic regimes have attempted reforms helps explain why communal violence in Western societies, once it did occur, is usually limited.

8. *Does regional autonomy lead to escalating wars of independence?*

Ethno-nationalist civil wars have been the most protracted and deadly conflicts of the late 20th century. They are fought with great intensity because communal demands for independence imply the breakup of existing states. Until the Soviet Union's dissolution, the only ethno-nationalists since 1945 who had won independence from existing states were the Bangladeshis, whose independence was bought at the price of political mass murder and India's intervention. Since then a revolutionary coalition has overthrown the Ethiopian regime, which paved the way for Eritrean independence.

Many political leaders on both sides of such struggles have been willing to consider autonomy arrangements that do not grant total independence. When the outcomes of 28 civil wars fought since 1950 in which one of the protagonists sought independence or autonomy are compared, the ledger is almost evenly balanced between winners and losers. On the positive side are four groups in Ethiopia that have won effective autonomy and seven national peoples elsewhere that secured autonomy agreements largely ending open conflict. Outcomes in four cases are under negotiation. On the negative side are nine national movements that were suppressed without significant gains; in four cases serious conflict continues.

Autonomy agreements have helped dampen rebellions by the Basques, the Moros, the Miskitos in Nicaragua, the Nagas and Tripuras, the people of Bangladesh's Chittagong Hill Tracts, and the Afars of Ethiopia. They failed to do so in Sudan and Sri Lanka, and have been aborted elsewhere. The success of autonomy arrangements in ending or preempting civil wars lies in the details and implementation of the powers and responsibilities between the contending parties; successful agreements have required a delicate balancing of communal and state interests, arrived at through protracted negotiations. The challenge for implementation is that both parties must honor the agreements and not defect—even in the face of political challenges and the continuation of violence by militant factions.

9. *What approaches work to balance the interests of contending groups within states?*

Most politically assertive minorities want access to political and economic opportunities, and protection of their rights in existing societies and states. Can any general lessons be drawn about how to accommodate their demands and deflect violent conflict? The answers depend on the cultural and political context.

Western democracies: Public policy toward minorities in Western democracies has evolved during the past half century from segregation to assimilation to pluralism and, in some countries, power sharing. Pluralism (multiculturalism, as it is known in North America) means arrangements that guarantee communal groups equal individual and collective rights, including the right to separate and coexisting identities. A shift toward pluralism, coupled with the devolution of power to peripheral regions and indigenous peoples, was mainly responsible for the decrease in communal conflicts in France, the United States, and other Western societies in the 1970s and 1980s. The liability is that pluralism and power sharing, if vigorously promoted, can trigger a backlash from dominant groups. Whether pluralist approaches to the growing concentrations of third world immigrants and refugees in Western countries can overcome the political and cultural resistance of dominant majorities, is an especially important question.

Africa South of the Sahara: At the other end of the spectrum of development, most African societies are heterogeneous, poor, and ruled by weak governments composed of unstable multiethnic coalitions. With a few exceptions—Nigeria and Zambia for example—they lack the capacity to suppress or fully incorporate all their diverse peoples. There are two keys to managing communal conflict in these societies. One is to strengthen and stabilize political parties to ensure that all communal groups have a fair chance at joining governing coalitions—if not now, then in the future. The second is to devolve power to local governments to ensure citizen participation and to protect the local power base of those who lose their place in national coalitions. Both steps are consistent with the trends toward democratization that are evident in much of Africa. In a general way, they also resemble the policies of pluralism and devolution that have dampened communal conflicts in Western societies.

Middle East and North Africa: Communal conflicts in the Middle East are more intractable, especially civil wars centered on Palestinian and Kurdish claims for statehood. Inequalities between dominant groups and minorities in the

Middle East are greater than in Western societies or Africa; sectarian cleavages have deeper historical roots, and ethno-conflict has been more intense and protracted. There are several examples of the accommodation of contending communal interests in the region: governments in the Maghreb have made significant concessions to Berber culture, and the Egyptian government has sustained largely successful efforts to protect the Coptic minority against discrimination and attacks by Islamic militants.

Elsewhere, however, the role of outside powers is vital for the management of communal conflicts. Progress toward settlement of the Palestinian-Israeli conflict hinges on continued United States involvement in the peace process as well as on internal politics in Israel. The Lebanese civil war ended only after the establishment of Syrian hegemony in central and northern Lebanon and Israel's withdrawal from the south. The outcome of the Persian Gulf War and allied protection of Iraqi Kurds provided the Kurds a rare opportunity to establish a fragile autonomy—one that is not likely to survive the eventual lifting of international sanctions against the Iraqi government. And the Iranian government's desire to rebuild the economy and reestablish Iran's leading role in the region has made Iran susceptible to international pressures to moderate its repressive policies toward the Bahais.

Eastern Europe and the Soviet Successor States: The collapse of the Soviet Union and its hegemony in Eastern Europe has transformed communal conflict in the region. Half the Soviet Union's population before the breakup was non-Russian and 40 percent of the total was at risk. Now the sources of communal demands are the new minorities of the Soviet successor states who constitute as many as 60 percent (in Kazakhstan) of the population. In the aggregate, the new minorities are 25 percent of the former republics' populations, and many are pressing their own claims against new regimes. But thus far most are doing so with the strategies found in democratic societies (that is, mass mobilization and civil protest), not the classic forms of armed rebellion.

Most of the new regimes of eastern Europe are also responding democratically: the Czechoslovakian government negotiated Slovakia's independence; the Bulgarian government aims at the pluralistic incorporation of its Muslim and Turkish minority. Only the authoritarian communist regime of Serbia continues to play by Stalinist rules. Its policies of hegemonical nationalism and repression are unlikely to be restrained without international sanctions and military intervention, or reversed except by a democratic revolution from within.

10. *Where are ethno-political conflicts most likely to escalate in the 1990s?*

The potential for escalating ethno-political conflict remains high in the Soviet successor states. However, in the Slavic states most conflicts will be settled democratically. The prospects for rebellion, civil war, and deadly intercommunal conflict are considerably greater in the Caucasian and Central Asian regions. The botched Russian effort to end Chechnya's secession by force conveys two lessons: to the Russians that they must resume their reliance on compromise in such disputes, and to restive national minorities that they must choose cautious political strategies. Nonetheless, if Russian democracy survives, civil and multi-cultural societies are likely to prevail in most of the region by the year 2000.

The western European and North American democracies will see a resurgence of ethnic conflict. Some conflicts will be based on regional claims by people like the Quebecois and the Scots, but most will be a consequence of class and communal tensions between dominant groups and minorities of Third World origin. The virtues of democratic politics are that they allow the expression of minority interests and encourage accommodation. The vice is that they are susceptible to the politics of ethnocentric reaction. The norms of democratic accommodation will likely prevail and by the year 2000 various kinds of pluralist arrangements will be in place in the Western societies that do not have them now.

Indigenous activism is also likely to escalate throughout the Americas, especially in the Latin American societies that have been most resistant to the claims of native peoples. Positive responses will be seen in democratic societies in the region, but within limits: indigenous demands for control of land and resources are not likely to be met if they constrain the economic development Latin American leaders regard as essential to political stability. Eight Central and South American societies also have significant Afro-American minorities, most of whom are seriously disadvantaged; except in Brazil, they probably will remain politically quiescent.

In the Third World, South Asia will suffer the most severe escalation of communal conflicts in the 1990s. Long-standing regional conflicts in India—in Assam, Punjab, and Kashmir—have intensified in the early 1990s, prompting communal demands by other peoples. Religio-political tensions are increasing between Muslim and Hindu communities in most countries in the region. Settlers from Bangladesh's densely crowded lowlands continue to push into the uplands, where they are embroiled in violent communal conflict with tribal peoples. Pakistani politics is rent by communal divisions among Pashtuns, Sindhis, Baluchis, and smaller minorities. In the aftermath of Afghanistan's failed communist revolution, communal rivalries have intensified among the once-dominant Pashtuns and Tajiks, Uzbeks, Hazaris, and others. The only deescalating communal conflict in the subcontinent is between Tamils and the Sinhalese-dominated state in Sri Lanka, and its decline is the result of repression more than accommodation.

Forecasting the future of communal conflict elsewhere in the third world is even more speculative. Most of the Middle East's conflicts are already under way, but few are likely to be settled decisively in the near future. Some ethno-political wars in Southeast Asia are winding down but others may intensify. In Africa the bitter communal conflicts in Ethiopia and South Africa are being worked out in the political arena, but others continue in Sudan and Somalia. In 1993–1994 stunning violence erupted in Burundi and Rwanda and is very likely to flare again in Burundi. The potential for communal warfare in Nigeria and Zaire is equally threatening.

11. *What is the functional place of communal groups in the global system of states?*

The most radical proposal for resolving conflicts between states and peoples is to reconstruct the state system so that territorial boundaries correspond more closely to the social and cultural boundaries among peoples. But such a strategy would leave unsatisfied the aspirations of many nonterritorial communal groups. For most others it would create as many problems as it resolved. The most likely means taken toward achieving such an objective are destructive civil wars, such as those in the former Yugoslavia, Ethiopia, Chechnya, and Georgia. Even if political reconstruction is achieved peacefully, it is likely to create or intensify new communal conflicts. Few ethno-nationalist regions are homogeneous, and the leaders of new states are at risk of being trapped in new communal dilemmas.

A more constructive and open-ended answer is to recognize and strengthen communal groups within the existing state system. Elise Boulding contends that devolving authority to communal groups will help resolve the fundamental structural problems of modern states: most are too large in scale and too far removed from many of their citizens to understand or deal with local concerns.

Progress toward the objective of a more pluralist world system requires that the international community accept a common obligation to protect collective rights within such an emergent system. Communal groups should have protected rights to individual and collective existence and to cultural self-expression without fear of political repression. The counterpart of such rights is the obligation not to impose cultural standards or political agendas on other peoples. This applies with special force to situations in which the international community supports the establishment of new states as a way of resolving conflicts within multiethnic societies, as in the former Yugoslavia. No new claims to statehood or autonomy ought to be recognized internationally unless the claimants assume the obligation, under pain of sanctions, to respect the rights of minorities within their borders.

16

SOUTHERN PERSPECTIVES ON WORLD ORDER

Shahram Chubin

Shahram Chubin traces the key issues that now divide the developing countries of the South from the wealthy countries of the North. Arguing that "there are still good reasons to pay attention to the South," he warns that "the end of the Cold War has freed the North to indulge its basic antipathy toward the South, to dictate to it without delicacy or dialogue." To avert a new era of North-South hostility, Chubin argues that North and South must recognize the benefits of communication and compromise. Chubin is a specialist in Middle East politics and security studies. His books include *Germany and the Middle East: Patterns and Prospects* (1992).

The international system of the last 50 years, one dominated and framed by the bipolar superpower rivalry, has been replaced by something more regionally fragmented and multifaceted, more plural and varied. Within this new system, the perspectives, interests, and security needs of the states of the South play an

From "The South and the New World Order," by Shahram Chubin, *The Washington Quarterly,* Vol. 16, Aut 1993, retitled "Southern Perspectives on World Order." Copyright © 1993 by the Center for Strategic and International Studies (CSIS) and the Massachusetts Institute of Technology. Reprinted by permission. Footnotes have been deleted.

increasingly significant role. For lack of a better term, the "South" is used here to describe that diverse collection of countries in varying degrees developing, nonaligned, and heretofore peripheral to the centers of world politics. Whether they will contribute toward the emergence of a new order, or reinforce the drift toward anarchy, remains to be seen. The developed world is ill-prepared for this fact, both conceptually and as a matter of policy.

This [essay] surveys the perspectives and attitudes of leaders in states of the South concerning the emerging international agenda. It is an explication, not a defense, and a partial one at best. There is no such thing as a coherent worldview of the South. But the failure to understand the South and to translate such understanding into effective diplomatic, economic, political, and military strategies will have profound consequences. Partnership between North and South remains a possibility, although arguably an improbable one. Antipathy and confrontation are also possible, and made more likely by Northern complacency.

The [essay] begins with a review of the state of the South in the 1990s, evaluating the problems of security and development faced by these countries and the changing international context in which leaders of these states make choices. The analysis then turns to the key issues of world order on the North-South agenda, namely proliferation, arms control, and collective security. . . .

THE STATE OF THE SOUTH

Most scholars in the North appreciate that the South faces large challenges of economic development. But this is hardly enough. . . . The South faces, in fact, a daunting set of interconnected problems in the economic, political, social, and security domains. Many Southern countries are also corrupt, unrepresentative, and repressive. Because these problems coexist with rapidly rising expectations, these countries cannot develop at the more leisurely pace enjoyed by the now developed world, where progress toward the current level of development is measured in centuries, not decades. Thus, in some fundamental sense, the circumstances of the South are without precedent. Moreover, the South is under siege—from an international community impatient to meddle in its affairs. States of the South are losing their sovereignty, which in many cases was only recently or tentatively acquired.

The problems of development confronting the South do not require recitation here. The large gap in living standards between South and North is well known. Less well known is the fact that in many parts of the South population pressures, chronic misgovernment, political insecurity, and conceptual poverty combine to drive countries backward, not forward—so the gap widens. The revolution of expectations, both political and economic, is putting governments under new stresses to perform and to direct the myriad processes of change.

Northerners are now engaged in a debate about whether the essence of power is military or political, but for most Southern states this debate is immaterial—they are unable to achieve either. The rentier states of the Persian Gulf after two decades of respectable oil revenues have been unable to achieve sustained development, transform their economies to guarantee results without oil, cooperate meaningfully on regional security, or move toward democracy, which some of them deny to be compatible with their traditions. As for military power, the accumulation of arms has been an empty and futile policy gesture except as a means of buying into Western security by recycling oil money to the West—a modern form of subvention. . . .

In an era of growing global interdependence states of the South remain more vulnerable than their counterparts in the North and more sensitive to forces beyond their borders. Consider the sliding commodity prices over the past decade, or even the much weakened position of oil producers, a relatively privileged group. Consider, too, the issue of the environment, where Southern states are being asked to meet standards and to consider the question cooperatively and in terms of interdependence. Yet as Maurice Strong, former director general of the United Nations (UN) Environment Program, has said: "The absorptive capacity of the eco-system is being preempted by the North," which should accept the responsibility of "making space" for the others.

Furthermore, in much of the South, states and frontiers are relatively artificial, and the forces keeping them intact have weakened. The end of the Cold War and bipolarity undermined a framework that had favored the territorial status quo and made international intervention difficult. The end of the Communist empire has set off fissiparous tendencies long latent in the multinational composite bloc and simultaneously sapped and delegitimized authoritarianism everywhere.

Moreover, the developing states are undergoing change at a time of maximum exposure to political pressures. . . . It is no comfort to these countries that sovereignty has been, or is being, redefined in the home of the nation-state, with a turn toward smaller communities and intermediate institutions between government (the market) and the individual. . . .

The North's weakening commitment to the sovereignty of states of the South is evident in the increased concern about human rights as an international rather than strictly domestic concern, and the concomitant increased willingness to intervene in a state's internal affairs in defense of ostensibly international standards. This has made leaders of states of the South fearful. Their fear grows even more sharp when well-meaning analysts argue that as an antidote to the excesses and disintegrative tendencies of self-determination, minority (communitarian) or individual human rights should be stressed. . . .

To be sure, . . . criteria have been defined whereby intervention will occur only if human rights violations constitute a threat to international security. Nonetheless, it is easy to see that a right to intervention is an implicit challenge to states if not a direct threat, especially if broadened as an excuse for intervention to unravel and make over states. What the Islamic Republic of Iran disarmingly calls "international arrogance" can be precisely that. On these issues its views are not far from those of India . . . and many other states of the South. Few are sufficiently homogenous or confident of their policies toward their minorities to be unaffected by the cultivation of the right or duty to intervene that has been promulgated in recent years.

Advocates of the right of intervention would do well to note that despite all the global forces promoting cultural convergence or standardization, homogenization has not (yet) been achieved. Regrettably or not, nations remain different and determined to pursue their own ideas about politics, the role of the state, religion, independence, equality, and cultural liberation. . . .

In a multicultural world, life may be richer but disputes harder to resolve. Combined with inequalities and political resentments, cultural differences and incomprehension can exacerbate North-South relations in a profoundly negative way.

During the Cold War, the states of the South were able to partially compensate for their weaknesses by banding together under the rubric of nonalignment. But this political device is now lost to them. Nonalignment died with the Cold War. More than that, the way the East-West rivalry ended, with the values and systems of the West vindicated and triumphant, undermined the very basis of the nonaligned movement, which had adopted as its foundation a moral neutrality between the two blocs.

For the erstwhile nonaligned, the end of the Cold War has had cataclysmic results. The old uncertainties of the cold war structure, which tended to nurture the status quo and play to the strengths of authoritarian regimes, have given way to a more fluid world in which the assets of the South, whether individually or collectively, are transformed. No longer proxies, clients, and strategic bases, these states are judged by their adherence to standards, values, and procedures that are now generally and unabashedly seen as full international responsibilities. These states now face strong pressures to adhere to various norms (human rights and democratic procedures) and policies (adherence to nonproliferation of nuclear and other mass destruction weapons and limitations on military spending), which some may find difficult or undesirable.

On the other hand, the end of the Cold War has freed the North to indulge its basic antipathy toward the poorer South, to dictate to it without delicacy or dialogue, and to dispense with the appearance of soliciting its views or the pretense of equality. Given today's domestic preoccupations of the North, it may be difficult to generate sympathy for a South that seems mired in problems attributable to bad governance, corrupt elites, and docile and work-shy populaces more eager to resort to rhetoric, excuses, and feuds than to build the foundations for a better future. Indeed it is not clear that the South or the developing countries generally merit sympathy. They exploited the Cold War, used it as an excuse, pampered bloated armed forces, and in some cases acted as clandestine proliferators and shameless regional predators.

However much the postindustrial world may wish it, insulation from this other, more populous and turbulent world is simply not possible. These worlds intersect most obviously in the former USSR, where the fate of Russia and its neighbors could weigh heavily in the balance between North and South. In other respects, too, the fate of the South inexorably impinges on that of the North. Due to the globalization of economies and the growth of interdependence (including the rise of transnational issues) areas cannot simply be insulated from the rest of the world. This is most evident with respect to political instabilities, in the presence of which uncertainty, repression, or persecution can give rise to large-scale migration into adjacent areas, perhaps disturbing the ethnic or national balance in the host country. It is even more clear when "domestic" issues like ethnic balance or policy toward minorities may give rise to civil wars spilling over into neighboring states and increasing the risks of "interstate war" and "outside" power intervention. (The very categories appear archaic and forced.) In the most obvious case, interstate conflicts spur migration and damage the economic prospects of belligerent states.

There are still other reasons to pay attention to the South. At the most obvious level, population pressures compel attention. Moreover, many of the new security issues such as environment and migration directly concern the South, and its fate and policies in this respect will inevitably affect those of the North. In much of the South the wave of democratization, however dimly sensed or remote from traditional culture, is welcomed by the populace and provides hope for their future. Furthermore, any world order, whether it is underpinned by balance of power, collective security, or unilateral or ad hoc interventions, must, if it is to become durable, eventually be seen to be legitimate. For this it must solicit the support of the widest number of states possible.

The United States will be a principal determinant of the character of North-South relations on these issues in the new international system. This fact alone has generated concern in the South. . . . The United States has translated its episodic interest in the external world and in the South into new pressure on those states to adhere not just to existing standards of international politics but to higher ones. It has enshrined human rights as a centerpiece of its global engagement, and in postwar Iraq it has used military force to partially dismember a state that failed to meet the new norm.

It has also enshrined nonproliferation. States of the South are now expected to exercise restraint in arms expenditures, to imitate the North (Europe and the superpowers) in arms control and disarmament, cultivate transparency, and practice "cooperative security." Whether or not they feel their security has been enhanced by the end of Cold War, they are being told to get into step with the North or else risk a cutback in development assistance. In emphasizing weapons proliferation as a new priority the United States appears to be targeting an issue that it feels can generate domestic concern and consensus; but it is arguably a false or exaggerated issue, and a crusading policy style that tends to unilateralism is the exact reverse of what is called for if the aim is to establish meaningful restraints rather than temporary obstacles to the spread of these weapons.

Thus, the South struggles not only with its own problems of political and economic development, domestic stability, and regional antagonisms, but also with a changing international system that promises it little in the way of assistance or relief. On the contrary, the South faces many international pressures well beyond its control, not least the actions of some leading actors in the international system to define and enforce new standards of behavior for which a common basis of international understanding does not exist. Unless North and South are able to arrive jointly at ordering concepts for the new international system, the possibility of conflict between them grows more likely. This is a shame, because it is avoidable and unnecessary.

WORLD ORDER: A VIEW FROM THE SOUTH

Whatever else the new world order portends, it does not mean the end of international hierarchies or a new age of equality. Nor is it clear, whatever its shape, how—or whether—it will incorporate the needs and demands of the South into its priorities or agenda. What is the new order? From the South, it looks like a new form of Western dominance, only more explicit and interventionist than in the past. In some Western states a shrillness is detectable when the South is discussed, as if the enemy has shifted there. Consider the following:

• New rationales for intervention appear to be minted daily—human rights, democracy, drugs, environment, and weapons proliferation. . . .

• Armed forces structures and sizes are being configured and geared to contingencies in the South.

• The North Atlantic Treaty Organization (NATO) has designated a rapid-reaction force for "out-of-area" contingencies.

• An antitactical ballistic missile (ATBM) system against limited strikes—GPALS, or Global Protection Against Limited Strikes—has an explicitly Southern orientation and it is on these terms that it has been offered to and considered by Russia.

• Even nuclear targeting is being reassessed, justified, and recalibrated for contingencies involving Southern states.

• The Coordinating Committee for Multilateral Export Controls (COCOM) is being reconfigured for use and application against the South.

• A host of regimes to control and restrain suppliers are in place or soon will be, all designed to deny certain technologies to Southern states (the London Club or Nuclear Suppliers Group, the Australia Group in chemicals, the Permanent Five [P-5] of the UN Security Council on conventional arms transfer registers, the Missile Technology Control Regime [MTCR] on missile technology).

• Arms-control initiatives, whether nuclear, chemical, biological or conventional, strategic or tactical/theater, are now planned and assessed for their impact on the South. Consideration of a total nuclear test ban (CTB), verification mechanisms, reduced reliance on nuclear weapons, elimination of missiles of a certain range, and possible missile test bans are now all considered in terms of their impact on the South. The Strategic Arms Reduction Treaty (START) is now presented as an important nonproliferation tool.

The North makes no apologies about being more demanding and is not timid about asserting its values since their vindication by the outcome of the Cold War. Illustrative is the North's increasing tendency to insist that there is a definite positive connection between democracy and economic development and democracy and international stability.

Economic assistance is being tied to reduced expenditure on arms. Barber Conable (president of the World Bank 1986–1991) argues that when military expenditures are above 5 percent or in excess of health and education combined "it is hard to see the good sense of lending to such countries." Robert McNamara argues that the West should link economic aid to the former Soviet republics with progress in shifting priorities from military to economic development. The recipient states (the G-24) have been reluctant to accept conditions imposed by the International Monetary Fund and World Bank that would establish a certain ceiling for military expenditures above which no aid would be forthcoming.

Such proposals appear to the South as earnest cant. Money is of course fungible. It is also arguable whether defense is the business of the Bretton Woods institutions. Military spending is simply another excuse, after human rights and the environment, not to transfer resources to poorer countries, to avoid a candid admission that the poorer countries are no longer of strategic interest.

Military spending in the South appears especially wasteful to Americans and Europeans now destroying, transferring, or converting arms. The costliness and futility of the past arms race appears to them all too apparent. Yet it is significant that there is no consensus on the role of arms and especially nuclear weapons in the Cold War: Did they deter a Soviet conventional attack? Were they instrumental in keeping the peace on the Continent? Would deterrence have been as effective at much lower levels of nuclear weapons? Were nuclear weapons essential? Without serious evaluation of the past role of nuclear weapons in the North it seems premature to deride their utility elsewhere. Also it may be noted by the states of the South that even in this phase of enthusiasm for arms control in the North, although some suggest a minimum deterrent posture, scarcely anyone suggests complete nuclear disarmament. Even nuclear weapons still retain a role in the security of the North, however residual. Why, it may be asked, can they not play a similar role in the South?

The fluidity of the current period has not made predictions any easier, yet it is evident that the hierarchy of power has been blurred as other forms of power have become more relevant. Although this blurring may have led to the "obsolescence of major war" in the North, as some suggest, this is less evidently the case elsewhere. Even in an interdependent world competition and rivalry will drive an interest in relative as opposed to absolute standing. States will still be concerned about their relative power positions. Traditionally war has been the means by which power and status have been defined and change has occurred. Choices about war and peace will depend on the alternatives and these choices are not always the same in the South as in the North. The South lacks a security community as a nucleus for order that is present in the North. The mechanisms for peaceful change in the South are not yet designed or constructed.

WEAPONS TRANSFERS AND PROLIFERATION

. . . As the risks of proliferation of new arms have become more apparent, Northern states have begun to consider ways of limiting arms and technology transfers to the South. As the developing countries now account for some 75 percent of arms traded, their military expenditures have grown at three times the pace of that of the North and now account for between two to three times their expenditures on health, education, and welfare. Apart from the distortion to their societies, such spending constitutes a potential threat to neighbors as well as the more distant North.

This Northern concern is, however, selective. Where states are poor and unable to pay for arms, Northern states advocate reduced military spending. Where there is a large market for arms, Northern suppliers compete to get orders for their shrinking defense industries (as in the Persian Gulf and East Asia). Little systematic consideration has been given to the types of arms that are particularly destructive, whether stabilizing or destabilizing; often this distinction corresponds to what you are selling as opposed to what your competitor is selling. The issue is difficult enough without commercial competition and hypocrisy, because all too often such definitions depend as much on the recipient's military doctrine as on the intrinsic characteristics of the weapon systems.

Equally little thought has been given to the relationships among various categories of arms and the reasons for proliferation. Focusing on particular weapon systems like missiles makes little sense out of context. In terms of destructive power and practical military effectiveness missiles do not (yet?) compare to advanced strike aircraft. Nor does an attempt to ban missiles treat the question of motivation in its context. Iran's quest for missiles, for example, came as a result of an inability to acquire parts for its air force (due to the embargo) and its need to counter the much larger and more varied stock of missiles of its adversary (Iraq). For Syria and others, missiles are a psychological comfort or equalizer, guaranteeing some penetration against a foe with a much superior air force.

Nonetheless, in the fight against weapons proliferation the United States in particular has singled out missiles and weapons of mass destruction. Concern about them seems to focus on the following: Under certain conditions they could increase incentives for preemption. Given their relative inaccuracy, population centers may be targeted; moreover, low accuracy may lead to a preference for mass destruction weapons over conventional ones. Some categories of unconventional weapon systems, like chemical weapons, that may be intended to deter an opponent's nuclear arms may complicate deterrence and blur thresholds. Missiles also to some extent decouple a capacity to damage or destroy an opponent from underlying industrial and societal sources of military power.

These concerns are too simplistic. Mating unconventional warheads to ballistic missiles is not easy. The effects of biological warheads are difficult to predict. [The Chemical Weapons Convention] banning chemical weapons should make the deployment and use of these particular weapons more difficult. In any case, the effort to ban only missiles with specified range and weight (300 kilometers and 500 kilograms) tends to obscure the problem of improving accuracies. Even missiles with ranges shorter than 300 kilometers, if forward-deployed and capable of delivering a strike against an opponent's military arsenal, increase the incentive to strike preemptively. As accuracies increase, more missiles may be used for counterforce strikes, and as ranges increase, they could pull into conflict a wider circle of states.

The direct military threat of these and other weapons to the North is as yet remote. But the potential threat is significant as delivery ranges increase. By one [1992] report, by the end of this decade, eight states of the South will have the ability to produce nuclear weapons, while six will have an intercontinental ballistic missile (ICBM) capability, presumably capable of reaching the United States. A larger number of countries will have the ability to build or acquire chemical and biological weapons and other missiles—perhaps as many as 50 states. Of course, the North faces a more immediate although more remote threat in terms of its access to certain regions or the possibility that regional conflicts will erupt under the nuclear umbrella it extends to a few allies in the South.

In a world where distances are shrinking while the capacity to wreak devastation is dispersing, it is not surprising that the Northern states should be inclined to do something. This impulse has translated into energetic efforts to restrict the trade and transfer of technologies that might increase these military capabilities. But this approach runs counter to much of the liberal and open exchange of information and the spread of technology that is part of the modern world. It also risks seeking to restrict dual-use technology for which Southern states may have legitimate commercial or developmental needs. . . .

NUCLEAR PROLIFERATION

After the end of the Cold War no issue appears to threaten global stability more or evokes as immediate a response as the prospect of nuclear proliferation. It conjures up images of direct attacks on the homeland of states of the North as well as a kind of global anarchy. Nuclear nonproliferation has been rediscovered with an intensity and vigor that suggest either blind neglect in the past or frenzied displacement of energy at present, for it cannot be justified by any evidence that more states are energetically looking toward nuclear weapons. It is also an issue around which the inchoate fears of the threat from the South can coalesce. . . .

Although there are many good reasons to suspect that more nuclear weapon states would contribute to global insecurity, these and other arguments do not fully satisfy skeptics, largely in the South. The recently revived crusade against proliferation suggests to some not a new threat, but a new need to focus on a threat—any threat—preferably one in the guise of an Islamic foe. In general, the poorer states find it difficult to stomach the patronizing, rueful air surrounding the subject of nuclear weapons. Despite McGeorge Bundy's conclusion that "in the long run, possessing nuclear weapons is hard work and in the absence of a threat, these weapons have little or no day-to-day value," the original nuclear powers are fated, it seems, to keep theirs because "they can't be disinvented." So the nuclear states of the North modernize their nuclear forces, even as the threats for which they were constructed have disappeared, while also pressing the South on the nuclear nonproliferation agenda.

The Southern skeptic asks why the argument of France and Britain that nuclear weapons are important for the "seat at the table" they ensure is not equally valid and just for nuclear-capable states of the developing world. They also ask why the North pursues a policy of "selective" proliferation rather than nonproliferation. Some Southerners find it difficult to understand why their major security threats cannot be met by nuclear weapons when they have little capacity to provide for a sophisticated conventional defense or deterrent. Skeptics also take issue with the argument that stable deterrence cannot emerge outside of the "civilized" North. . . .

Concern about possible nuclear weapons use in the South is also difficult to understand for those who have endured many years of war on their territory. If conventional deterrence is less effective than nuclear deterrence, and the threat of nuclear war can deter conventional attacks, then, it is argued, perhaps nuclear deterrence might rid the South of repeated wars. As for irresponsibility, it is difficult to imagine a more dangerous policy than the "extended deterrence" that was the cornerstone of the Western alliance; prudent states would be reluctant to seek to widen the utility of nuclear weapons in this fashion.

None of this means that countries of the South are queuing up for nuclear weapons, or that the benefits of nuclear status are uppermost in their minds. Wars, conflict, and instability regrettably have been the lot of many of these states. Many have not had the means to assure their security unilaterally or through access to arms or alliances. Nor have they been able to fashion a diplomatic compromise.

Moreover, their security has not automatically been improved by the passing of the Cold War. Regional concerns persist. Yet these states are usually only noticed, or taken seriously, if they look as if they are interested in nuclear weapons. Otherwise they are ignored or marginalized. . . .

Nuclear weapons will continue to hold a fascination for states in an insecure and fluid world. Whether as shortcuts, equalizers, status symbols, or simply as "options" to be kept against the possibility of need at a future date, they will be sought by states anxious about their security and/or keen to play a role in international affairs. States poor in resources or technical manpower will find it hard to acquire nuclear weapons and may not even consider them. Those states in a security environment that does not dictate their consideration, such as Latin America, may pass them by. Still others may find the original motivation for them reduced (e.g., South Africa). This will leave a number of states of some wealth, incentive, or capability that, whether from ambition, security, status incentives, or considerations of prudence, will want either to develop nuclear weapons or maintain the option of developing them quickly later.

If arms-control responses are to be found to this strategic reality, they must strive for universal, equal obligations. The extension of positive security guarantees for those states renouncing nuclear weapons that might come under nuclear threat should be considered. . . . Political incentives for nuclear weapons seem to be given shorter shrift these days when the focus is on denial of technology.

Technology- and weapons-denial strategies are not only morally unsustainable; they can scarcely be counted upon as a long-term solution. The nature of the world—technologically, scientifically, and economically—is such as to make diffusion inevitable. The real question is whether the time bought by such measures is well used to erect more effective barriers against the use of weapons of concern. . . . Technology-denial regimes such as the MTCR are one-way arrangements in which the South has to like it or lump it. This is hardly the stuff of a consensual world order.

The case of North Korea is illustrative. Here is a state with few resources, no allies, and a dim future. Neither the threat of sanctions nor a military strike is an adequate or plausible response. It may be too late for technology denial as well. A policy that combines engagement, dialogue, and positive inducements stands a greater chance of success. . . .

COLLECTIVE SECURITY

If one primary element of the new world order agenda relates to the proliferation of advanced military capability, another relates to the rules and norms governing the use of force in international affairs. The term "collective security" has been used over most of the last half century to encompass the state of thinking about these matters that emerged at the end of World War II. Today, much hope is being placed by the North in a reinvigorated UN system, released from the fetters of the Cold War, to achieve the benefits of concerted international responses to aggression.

Unfortunately, the renovation of the UN system and of collective security is taking place in a haphazard and ill-defined way. Improvisation has perforce been the dominant motif. The risks of mistakes, incompetence, overload, and disappointment are real. Little effort has been made to clarify the criteria for UN intervention, whether to make, keep, or enforce the peace. This issue is especially salient for the states of the South—the likely target, after all, of such intervention. On the face of it, such matters are by definition under the jurisdiction of the Security Council, where the South has little or no say. . . .

Ambiguity is the stuff of international politics, and it is far from clear how ambiguous circumstances in the South will be evaluated by the great powers of the North. Within the South, there is considerable skepticism that its interests will be taken into account. An obvious example is the fate of Bosnia's Muslims. In the former Yugoslavia, the complexities of peacekeeping are great, the parallels with Kuwait few, and the potential for spillover of conflict into Western Europe quite real, but it is nonetheless striking how many Islamic states have felt it necessary to suggest that UN reluctance to act stems from a double standard concerning the fate of Muslims. . . .

A related concern of states of the South is that the Security Council today disproportionately reflects U.S. power. One need not agree with Mu'ammar Qadhafi that the UN Security Council risks becoming an extension of NATO to note that, with Russia in its present condition, the United States and its allies dominate the Security Council to an extraordinary degree. Moreover, talk among these countries of reforming the membership of the Council tends to focus on adding membership for Germany or Japan, and not any Southern state, except as a bogey or argument against reform. . . .

Talk of revitalizing the UN Security Council assumes a degree of consensus about the role of the United States that may not be present in today's still culturally diverse world. Collective security will continue to be defined selectively and unequally, reflecting limited resources among the great powers, different priorities among nations generally, and uneven commitment to underlying international norms. . . .

CONCLUSION

The issues dividing North from South today are numerous, ranging from the proliferation of nuclear, chemical, and biological weapons and missiles, to technology transfer, population growth, developmental inequality, migration, and environmental issues. None of them will be dealt with productively if conceived of, and treated as, North-South security issues. They are more accurately global security issues, requiring dialogue, compromise, and grand bargains.

The system of global order centered on the UN Security Council was based on the premise of great power collaboration. It languished for 45 years and now is being revived. That revival must go very far indeed—well beyond what the existing great powers now envisage—if it is to have a meaningful impact on the security agenda of the future.

As [political scientist] Hedley Bull observed, no international order sustained by the great powers can provide equal justice for all states, but much can be done to alleviate this perhaps necessary and inevitable inequality. To provide "central direction in international affairs," the major powers need to "explain, prepare, negotiate, coordinate and create a consensus with other states . . . to involve [them] directly in the defense of the existing distribution of power." Bull argued that the fact that great power management of the international order may not "afford equal justice" to all did not necessarily make it intolerable because the great powers might have a greater stake in that international order of which they became guardians. But these same powers "do, however, have a permanent problem of securing and preserving the consent of other states to the special role they play in the system."

This managerial role, Bull believed, is only possible "if these functions are accepted clearly enough by a large enough proportion of the society of states to command legitimacy." Inter alia, great powers should "seek to satisfy some of the demands for just change being expressed in the world," which include economic justice and nuclear justice among others. Where the demand cannot be met, great powers need to go through the motions of considering them: "A great power hoping to be accepted as a legitimate managerial power cannot ignore these demands or adopt a contrary position."

The states of the North, with only one-fifth of the world's population and a dynamic two-thirds of the global economy, have a long-term interest in framing a new order that is acceptable to the majority of the world's populace. A world of diffuse discontent surely cannot be an orderly one. In a world where nuclear proliferation cannot be frozen permanently and where science and technology spread quickly, it is important to involve all states in elaborating norms and to give them a stake in the more plural world order that is at once desirable and inevitable.

17

THE COMING CLASH OF CIVILIZATIONS OR, THE WEST AGAINST THE REST

Samuel P. Huntington

Viewing the post–Cold-War landscape and its prospects, Samuel P. Huntington predicts that in the future global conflict will be primarily cultural—a clash of civilizations—along the borders where different cultures come into contact. He explains why hypernationalism is on the rise and why the impending clash of cultures will pit Western civilization against the other major world civilizations. Huntington is Albert J. Weatherhead III University Professor, chairman of the Harvard Academy for International and Area Studies, and director of the Olin Institute for Strategic Studies at Harvard University. His books include *The Clash of Civilizations and the Remaking of World Order* (1996).

World politics is entering a new phase in which the fundamental source of conflict will be neither ideological nor economic. The great divisions among mankind and the dominating source of conflict will be cultural. The principal conflicts of global politics will occur between nations, and groups of different civilizations. The clash of civilizations will dominate global politics.

During the Cold War, the world was divided into the first, second, and third worlds. Those divisions are no longer relevant. It is far more meaningful to group countries not in terms of their political or economic systems or their level of economic development but in terms of their culture and civilization.

A civilization is the highest cultural grouping of people and the broadest level of cultural identity people have, short of that which distinguishes humans from other species.

Civilizations obviously blend and overlap and may include subcivilizations. Western civilization has two major variants, European and North American, and Islam has its Arab, Turkic, and Malay subdivisions. But while the lines between them are seldom sharp, civilizations are real. They rise and fall; they divide and merge. And as any student of history knows, civilizations disappear.

Westerners tend to think of nation–states as the principal actors in global affairs. They have been that for only a few centuries. The broader reaches of history have been the history of civilizations. It is to this pattern that the world returns.

Civilization identity will be increasingly important and the world will be shaped in large measure by the interactions among seven or eight major civilizations. These include the Western, Confucian, Japanese, Islamic, Hindu, Slavic-Orthodox, Latin American, and possibly African civilizations. The most important and bloody conflicts will occur along the borders separating these cultures. The fault lines between civilizations will be the battle lines of the future.

Why? First, differences among civilizations are basic, involving history, language, culture, tradition and, most importantly, religion. Different civilizations have different views on the relations between God and man, the citizen and the state, parents and children, liberty and authority, equality and hierarchy. These differences are the product of centuries. They will not soon disappear.

Second, the world is becoming smaller. The interactions between peoples of different civilizations are increasing. These interactions intensify civilization consciousness: awareness of differences between civilizations and commonalities within civilizations. For example, Americans react far more negatively to Japanese investment than to larger investments from Canada and European countries.

Third, economic and social changes are separating people from long-standing local identities. In much of the world, religion has moved in to fill this gap, often in the form of movements labeled fundamentalist. Such movements are found in Western Christianity, Judaism, Buddhism, Hinduism, and Islam. The "unsecularization of the world," the social [philosopher] George Weigel has remarked, "is one of the dominant social facts of life in the late 20th century."

Fourth, the growth of civilization consciousness is enhanced by the fact that, at the moment that the West is at the peak of its power, a return-to-the-roots phenomenon is occurring among non-Western civilizations—the "Asianization" in Japan, the end of the Nehru legacy and the "Hinduization" of India, the failure of Western ideas of socialism and nationalism and, hence, the "re-Islamization" of the Middle East, and now a debate over Westernization versus Russianization in Boris Yeltsin's country.

More importantly, the efforts of the West to promote its values of democracy and liberalism as universal values, to maintain its military predominance, and to advance its economic interests engender countering responses from other civilizations.

The central axis of world politics is likely to be the conflict between "the West and the rest" and the responses of non-Western civilizations to Western power and values. The most prominent example of anti-Western cooperation is the connection between Confucian and Islamic states that are challenging Western values and power.

Fifth, cultural characteristics and differences are less mutable and hence less easily compromised and resolved than political and economic ones. In the former Soviet Union, Communists can become democrats, the rich can become poor and the poor rich, but Russians cannot become Estonians. A person can be half-French and half-Arab and even a citizen of two countries. It is more difficult to be half-Catholic and half-Muslim.

Finally, economic regionalism is increasing. Successful economic regionalism will reinforce civilization consciousness. On the other hand, economic regionalism may succeed only when it is rooted in a common civilization. The European [Union] rests on the shared foundation of European culture and Western Christianity. Japan, in contrast, faces difficulties in creating a comparable economic entity in East Asia because it is a society and civilization unique to itself.

As the ideological division of Europe has disappeared, the cultural division of Europe between Western Christianity and Orthodox Christianity and Islam has reemerged. Conflict along the fault line between Western and Islamic civilizations has been going on for 1,300 years. This centuries-old military interaction is unlikely to decline. Historically, the other great antagonistic interaction of Arab Islamic civilization has been with the pagan, animist and now, increasingly, Christian black peoples to the south. On the northern border of Islam, conflict has increasingly erupted between Orthodox and Muslim peoples, including the carnage of Bosnia and Sarajevo, the simmering violence between Serbs and Albanians, the tenuous relations between Bulgarians and their Turkish minority, the violence between Ossetians and Ingush, the unremitting slaughter of each other by Armenians and Azeris and the tense relations between Russians and Muslims in Central Asia.

The historic clash between Muslims and Hindus in the subcontinent manifests itself not only in the rivalry between Pakistan and India but also in intensifying religious strife in India between increasingly militant Hindu groups and the substantial Muslim minority.

Groups or states belonging to one civilization that become involved in war with people from a different civilization naturally try to rally support from other members of their own civilization. Decreasingly able to mobilize support and form coalitions on the basis of ideology, governments and groups will increasingly attempt to mobilize support by appealing to common religion and civilization identity. As the conflicts in the Persian Gulf, the Caucasus, and Bosnia continued, the positions of nations and the cleavages between them increasingly were along civilizational lines. Populist politicians, religious leaders, and the media have found it a potent means of arousing mass support and of pressuring hesitant governments. In the coming years, the local conflicts most likely to escalate into major wars will be those, as in Bosnia and the Caucasus, along the fault lines between civilizations. The next world war, if there is one, will be a war between civilizations.

If these hypotheses are plausible, it is necessary to consider their implications for Western policy. These implications should be divided between short-term advantage and long-term accommodation. In the short term, it is clearly in the interest of the West to promote greater cooperation and unity in its own civilization, particularly between its European and North American components; to incorporate into the West those societies in Eastern Europe and Latin America whose cultures are close to those of the West; to maintain close relations with Russia and Japan; to support in other civilizations groups sympathetic to Western values and interests; and to strengthen international institutions that reflect and legitimate Western interests and values. The West must also limit the expansion of the military strength of potentially hostile civilizations, principally Confucian and Islamic civilizations, and exploit differences and conflicts among Confucian and Islamic states. This will require a moderation in the reduction of Western military capabilities, and, in particular, the maintenance of American military superiority in East and Southwest Asia.

In the longer term, other measures would be called for. Western civilization is modern. Non-Western civilizations have attempted to become modern without becoming Western. To date, only Japan has fully succeeded in this quest. Non-Western civilizations will continue to attempt to acquire the wealth, technology, skills, machines, and weapons that are part of being modern. They will attempt to reconcile this modernity with their traditional culture and values. Their economic and military strength relative to the West will increase.

Hence, the West will increasingly have to accommodate these non-Western modern civilizations, whose power approaches that of the West but whose values and interests differ significantly from those of the West. This will require the West to develop a much more profound understanding of the basic religious and philosophical assumptions underlying other civilizations and the ways in which people in those civilizations see their interests. It will require an effort to identify elements of commonality among Western and other civilizations. For the relevant future, there will be no universal civilization but instead a world of different civilizations, each of which will have to learn to coexist with others.

18

ISLAM AND LIBERAL DEMOCRACY: MUSLIM PERCEPTIONS AND WESTERN REACTIONS

Bernard Lewis

Many observers fear that the Muslim world is braced for conflict with the West. The reasons why the Islamic countries harbor deep resentments toward the West and, in particular, its liberal values and democratic institutions are explored by Bernard Lewis, who warns that Western attempts to pressure Muslim governments for human rights and democratic reforms could intensify Islamic rage and escalate into a new epoch of bitter conflict. Lewis is professor emeritus of Near Eastern studies at Princeton University and author of *Cultures in Conflict: Christians, Muslims, and Jews in the Age of Discovery* (1995).

There has been much discussion of late, both inside and outside the Islamic world, about those elements in the Islamic past and those factors in the Muslim present that are favorable and unfavorable to the development of liberal democracy. From a historical perspective it would seem that of all the non-Western civilizations in the world, Islam offers the best prospects for Western-style democracy.

Abridged from the article "Islam and Liberal Democracy," *The Atlantic* 272 (February 1, 1993), pp. 89–98. *The Atlantic* article was drawn from a longer paper prepared for a colloquium on "The Expansion of Liberal Society," sponsored by the Institute for Human Sciences in Vienna. The resulting volume was published in German.

Historically, culturally, religiously, it is the closest to the West, sharing much—though by no means all—of the Judeo-Christian and Greco-Roman heritage that helped to form our modern civilization. From a political perspective, however, Islam seems to offer the worst prospects for liberal democracy. Of the more than 50 sovereign states that make up the international Islamic Conference, only one, the Turkish Republic, can be described as a democracy in Western terms, and even there the path to freedom has been beset by obstacles. Of the remainder, some have never tried democracy; others have tried it and failed; a few, more recently, have experimented with the idea of sharing, though not of relinquishing, power.

Can liberal democracy work in a society inspired by Islamic beliefs and principles and shaped by Islamic experience and tradition? It is of course for Muslims, primarily and perhaps exclusively, to interpret and reinterpret the pristine original message of their faith, and to decide how much to retain, and in what form, of the rich accumulated heritage of 14 centuries of Islamic history and culture. Not all Muslims give the same answers to the question posed above, but much will depend on the answer that prevails. . . .

FUNDAMENTALISTS AND DEMOCRATS

There are many who see no need for any . . . change and would prefer to retain the existing systems, whether radical dictatorships or traditional autocracies, with perhaps some improvement in the latter. This preference for things as they are is obviously shared by those who rule under the present system and those who otherwise benefit, including foreign powers who are willing to accept and even support existing regimes as long as their own interests are safeguarded. But there are others who feel that the present systems are both evil and doomed and that new institutions must be devised and installed.

Proponents of radical change fall into two main groups—the Islamic fundamentalists and the democrats. Each group includes a wide range of sometimes contending ideologies.

The term "fundamentalism" derives from a series of Protestant tracts, *The Fundamentals,* published in the United States around 1910, and was used first in America and then in other predominantly Protestant countries to designate certain groups that diverge from the mainstream churches in their rejection of liberal theology and biblical criticism and their insistence on the literal divinity and inerrancy of the biblical text. The use of the term to designate Muslim movements is therefore at best a loose analogy and can be very misleading. Reformist theology has at times in the past been an issue among Muslims; it is not now, and it is very far from the primary concerns of those who are called Muslim fundamentalists.

Those concerns are less with scripture and theology than with society, law, and government. As the Muslim fundamentalists see it, the community of Islam has been led into error by foreign infidels and Muslim apostates, the latter being the more dangerous and destructive. Under their guidance or constraint Muslims abandoned the laws and principles of their faith and instead adopted secular—that is to say, pagan—laws and values. All the foreign ideologies—liberalism, socialism, even nationalism—that set Muslim against Muslim are evil, and the Muslim world is now suffering the inevitable consequences of forsaking the God-given law and way of life that were vouchsafed to it. The answer is the old Muslim obligation of jihad: to wage holy war first at home, against the pseudo-Muslim apostates who rule, and then, having ousted them and re-Islamized society, to resume the greater role of Islam in the world. The return to roots, to authenticity, will always be attractive. It will be doubly appealing to those who daily suffer the consequences of the failed foreign innovations that were foisted on them.

For Islamic fundamentalists, democracy is obviously an irrelevance, and unlike the communist totalitarians, they rarely use or even misuse the word. They are, however, willing to demand and exploit the opportunities that a self-proclaimed democratic system by its own logic is bound to offer them. At the same time, they make no secret of their contempt for democratic political procedures and their intention to govern by Islamic rules if they gain power. . . .

Those who plead or fight for democratic reform in the Arab and other Islamic lands claim to represent a more effective, more authentic democracy than that of their failed predecessors, not restricted or distorted by some intrusive adjective, not nullified by *a priori* religious or ideological imperatives, not misappropriated by regional or sectarian or other sectional interests. In part their movement is an extension to the Middle East of the wave of democratic change that has already transformed the governments of many countries in Southern Europe and Latin America; in part it is a response to the collapse of the Soviet Union and the new affirmation of democratic superiority through victory in the Cold War. To no small extent it is also a consequence of the growing impact of the U.S. democracy and of American popular culture in the Islamic lands. . . .

It is precisely the catholicity, the assimilative power and attraction, of American culture that make it an object of fear and hatred among the self-proclaimed custodians of pristine, authentic Islam. For such as they, it is a far more deadly threat than any of its predecessors to the old values that they hold dear and to the power and influence those values give them. In the last chapter of the Koran, which ranks with the first among the best known and most frequently cited, the believer is urged to seek refuge with God "from the mischief of the insidious Whisperer who whispers in people's hearts. . . ." Satan in the Koran is the adversary, the deceiver, above all the inciter and tempter who seeks to entice mankind away from the true faith. It is surely in this sense that the Ayatollah Khomeini called America the great Satan: Satan as enemy, but—more especially and certainly more plausibly for his people—also as source of enticement and temptation.

In these times of discontent and disappointment, of anger and frustration, the older appeals of nationalism and socialism and national socialism—the gifts of 19th- and 20th-century Europe—have lost much of their power. Today only the democrats and the Islamic fundamentalists appeal to something more than personal or sectional loyalties. Both have achieved some limited success, partly by infiltrating the existing regimes, more often by frightening them into making some preemptive concessions. Successes have in the main been limited to the more traditional authoritarian regimes, which have made some symbolic gestures toward the democrats or the fundamentalists or both. Even the radical dictatorships, while admitting no compromise with liberal democracy, have in times of stress tried to appease and even to use Islamic sentiment.

There is an agonizing question at the heart of the present debate about democracy in the Islamic world: Is liberal democracy basically compatible with Islam, or is some measure of respect for law, some tolerance of criticism, the most that can be expected from autocratic governments? The democratic world contains many different forms of government—republics and monarchies, presidential and parliamentary regimes, secular states and established churches, and a wide range of electoral systems—but all of them share certain basic assumptions and practices that mark the distinction between democratic and undemocratic governments. Is it possible for the Islamic peoples to evolve a form of government that will be compatible with their own historical, cultural, and religious traditions and yet will bring individual freedom and human rights to the governed as these terms are understood in the free societies of the West? . . .

The question . . . is not whether liberal democracy is compatible with Islamic fundamentalism—clearly it is not—but whether it is compatible with Islam itself. Liberal democracy, however far it may have traveled, however much it may have been transformed, is in its origins a product of the West—shaped by a thousand years of European history, and beyond that by Europe's double heritage: Judeo-Christian religion and ethics; Greco-Roman statecraft and law. No such system has originated in any other cultural tradition; it remains to be seen whether such a system, transplanted and adapted in another culture, can long survive. . . .

Traditional obstacles to democracy have in many ways been reinforced by the processes of modernization and by recent developments in the region. . . . [The] power of the state to dominate and terrorize the people has been vastly increased by modern methods. The philosophy of authoritarian rule has been sharpened and strengthened by imported totalitarian ideologies, which have served a double purpose—to sanctify rulers and leaders and to fanaticize their subjects and followers. The so-called Islamic fundamentalists are no exception in this respect.

Self-criticism in the West—a procedure until recently rarely practiced and little understood in the Middle East—provided useful ammunition. This use of the West against itself is particularly striking among the fundamentalists. Western democracy for them is part of the hated West, and that hatred is central to the ideas by which they define themselves, as in the past the free world defined itself first against Nazism and then against communism.

The changes wrought by modernization are by no means entirely negative. Some, indeed, are extremely positive. One such improvement is the emancipation of women. Though this still has a long way to go before it reaches Western levels, irreversible changes have already taken place. These changes are indispensable: a society can hardly aspire realistically to create and operate free institutions as long as it keeps half its members in a state of permanent subordination and the other half see themselves as domestic autocrats. Economic and social development has also brought new economic and social elements of profound importance—a literate middle class, commercial, managerial, and professional, that is very different from the military, bureaucratic, and religious elites that between them dominated the old order. These new groups are creating their own associations and organizations, and modifying the law to accommodate them. They are an indispensable component of civil society—previously lacking, yet essential to any kind of democratic polity.

There are also older elements in the Islamic tradition, older factors in Middle Eastern history, that are not hostile to democracy and that, in favorable circumstances, could even help in its development. Of special importance among these is the classical Islamic concept of supreme sovereignty—elective, contractual, in a sense even consensual and revocable. The Islamic caliphate, as prescribed and regulated by the holy law, may be an autocracy; it is in no sense a despotism. According to Sunni doctrine, the Caliph was to be elected by those qualified to make a choice. The electorate was never defined, nor was any procedure of election ever devised or operated, but the elective principle remains central to Sunni religious jurisprudence, and that is not unimportant. . . .

This doctrine marks one of the essential differences between Islamic and other autocracies. An Islamic ruler is not above the law. He is subject to it, no less than the humblest of his servants. If he commands something that is contrary to the law, the duty of obedience lapses and is replaced not by the right but by the duty of disobedience.

Muslim spokesmen, particularly those who sought to find Islamic roots for Western practices, made much of the Islamic principle of consultation, according to which a ruler should not make arbitrary decisions by himself but should act only after consulting with suitably qualified advisers. This principle rests on two somewhat enigmatic passages in the Koran and on a number of treatises, mainly by ulama and statesmen, urging consultation with ulama or with statesmen. This principle has never been institutionalized, or even formulated in the treatises of the holy law, though naturally rulers have from time to time consulted with their senior officials, more particularly in Ottoman times.

Of far greater importance was the acceptance of pluralism in Islamic law and practice. Almost from the beginning the Islamic world has shown an astonishing diversity. Extending over three continents, it embraced a wide variety of races, creeds, and cultures, which lived side by side in reasonable if intermittent harmony. Sectarian strife and religious persecution are not unknown in Islamic history, but they are rare and atypical, and never reached the level of intensity of the great religious wars and persecutions in Christendom.

Traditional Islam has no doctrine of human rights, the very notion of which might seem an impiety. Only God has rights—human beings have duties. But in practice the duty owed by one human being to another—more specifically, by a ruler to his subjects—may amount to what Westerners would call a right, particularly when the discharge of this duty is a requirement of holy law.

TWO TEMPTATIONS

It may be—and has been—argued that these legal and religious principles have scant effect. The doctrine of elective and contractual sovereignty has been tacitly ignored since the days of the early caliphate. The supremacy of the law has been flouted. Tolerance of pluralism and diversity has dwindled or disappeared in an age of heightened religious, ethnic, and social tensions. Consultation, as far as it ever existed, is restricted to the ruler and his inner circle, while personal dignity has been degraded by tyrants who feel that they must torture and humiliate, not just kill, their opponents.

And yet, despite all these difficulties and obstacles, the democratic ideal is steadily gaining force in the region, and increasing numbers of Arabs have come to the conclusion that it is the best, perhaps the only, hope for the solution of their economic, social, and political problems.

What can we in the democratic world do to encourage the development of democracy in the Islamic Middle East—and what should we do to avoid impeding or subverting it? There are two temptations to which Western governments have all too often succumbed, with damaging results. They might be called the temptation of the right and the temptation of the left. The temptation of the right is to accept, and even to embrace, the most odious of dictatorships as long as they are acquiescent in our own requirements, and as long as their policies seem to accord with the protection of our own national interests. The spectacle of the great democracies of the West in comfortable association with tyrants and dictators can only discourage and demoralize the democratic opposition in these countries.

The more insidious temptation, that of the left, is to press Muslim regimes for concessions on human rights and related matters. Since ruthless dictatorships are impervious to such pressures, and are indeed rarely subjected to them, the brunt of such well-intentioned intervention falls on the more moderate autocracies, which are often in the process of reforming themselves in a manner and at a pace determined by their own conditions and needs. The pressure for premature democratization can fatally weaken such regimes and lead to their overthrow, not by democratic opposition but by other forces that then proceed to establish a more ferocious and determined dictatorship.

All in all, considering the difficulties that Middle Eastern countries have inherited and the problems that they confront, the prospects for Middle Eastern democracy are not good. But they are better than they have ever been before. Most of these countries face grave economic problems. If they fail to cope with these problems, then the existing regimes, both dictatorial and authoritarian, are likely to be overthrown and replaced, probably by one variety or another of Islamic fundamentalists. It has been remarked in more than one country that the fundamentalists are popular because they are out of power and cannot be held responsible for the present troubles. If they acquired power, and with it responsibility, they would soon lose that popularity. But this would not matter to them, since once in power they would not need popularity to stay there, and would continue to govern—some with and some without oil revenues to mitigate the economic consequences of their methods. In time even the fundamentalist regimes, despite their ruthless hold on power, would be either transformed or overthrown, but by then they would have done immense, perhaps irreversible, damage to the cause of freedom.

But their victory is by no means inevitable. There is always the possibility that democrats may form governments, or governments learn democracy. The increasing desire for freedom, and the better understanding of what it means, are hopeful signs. Now that the Cold War has ended and the Middle East is no longer a battlefield for rival power blocs, the peoples of the Middle East will have the chance—if they can take it—to make their own decisions and find their own solutions. No one else will have the ability or even the desire to do it for them. Today—for the first time in centuries—the choice is their own.

19

THE INSTITUTIONAL PILLARS OF GLOBAL ORDER: THE NATION–STATE IS DEAD; LONG LIVE THE NATION–STATE

The Economist

Since the Treaty of Westphalia ended the Thirty Years War of religious conflict in 1648, the international system has primarily relied on the sovereign nation–state as an institutional unit with which to organize international life and keep order in it. Many observers doubt that the nation–state will survive. This essay questions the accuracy of that prediction. In it, the editors of *The Economist* identify the main arguments underlying prophecies of the nation–state's impending death, critique them, and explain why the nation–state is likely to remain the key mechanism for containing violence in the coming millennium.

The nation–state is not what it used to be. Ignored by the global money markets, condescended to by great multinational corporations, at the mercy of intercontinental missiles, the poor thing can only look back with nostalgia to its days of glory, a century ago, when everybody knew what John Bull and Marianne and Germania and Uncle Sam stood for. It seems inconceivable that so diminished a creature can much longer continue to be the basic unit of international relations, the entity that signs treaties, joins alliances, defies enemies, goes to war. Surely the nation–state is in the process of being dissolved into something larger, more powerful, more capable of coping with the consequences of modern technology: something that will be the new, stronger, basic unit of tomorrow's world?

No, wait; hold on a minute. As Bertie Wooster said, in telling a tangled story it is fatal to begin by assuming that the customers know how matters got where they are. They will simply raise their eyebrows, and walk out on you. The current argument about the role of the nation–state in world affairs is an excellent example of the danger Bertie was pointing to.

WHY IT ISN'T WHAT IT WAS

For most people, the world is made up of 185 nation–states, on the current count in 1997 of the United Nations: some huge, some tiny, some of them democracies, most of them not, but all equal in the eye of the world's law. In fact, a majority of these 185 places are not nation–states in the strict meaning of the term, but survivals of older, cruder forms of political life. Nevertheless, all 185 share two vital characteristics. They each cover separate portions of the earth's surface; and each has a government whose claim to speak for it is recognized by most governments of the other portions of the earth's surface. These are the basic units of geopolitics, the pieces on the international chessboard, the essential components of the fearsome game known as foreign policy.

The trouble is that, over the past half-century or so, these basic units have all, big or small, become less dominant, less independent and, in a way, less separate than they were in their prime. This is because of the arrival in the world of new forces, created by the technological discoveries of the 20th century, which have the power to move things visible and invisible from one part of the globe to another whether any nation–state likes it or not. These forces take three main forms, all of which have to some extent eroded the nation–state's autonomy.

In economics, the growing ease and cheapness of moving goods from one place to another has demolished any lingering belief in national self-sufficiency. Almost every country now buys from abroad a larger proportion of what it consumes than it did 50 years ago, and a far bigger share of the world's capital is owned by multinational companies operating freely across national borders. This process has been accelerated by what electronics has done to the movement of money. The markets' ability to transfer cash anywhere at the push of a button has changed the rules for policy-making, introducing what sometimes seems like a sort of direct international democracy: when a government makes a false move, markets vote against it with ruthless speed.

A more globalized economy is in many ways a more efficient one. Most people in most countries are richer now than their ancestors ever were; and the faster discipline of today's international financial markets makes national governments more careful in the handling of their economies. But, for this article's purpose, that is not the point. The point is that the rise of new global forces has noticeably tamed the nation–state's old feeling of confident independence.

In military matters the change has been even more dramatic. Until about 60 years ago, the only way in which one country could successfully use force to impose its will on another was to defeat its soldiers on the ground. Between two countries of even approximately equal strength, that could be a long and hazardous business.

The little Heinkels and Dorniers that flew slowly over the English Channel to drop their tiny bomb-loads on Britain in 1940 were the messengers of a radical change in the nature of war. The use of force was no longer two-dimensional; the third dimension had become available. Only a few years later, the means of imposing defeat from the air had moved from aeroplanes to missiles, and their cargo had changed from a bomb that would knock down a house to one that could obliterate a city.

For at least the first part of the coming century, very few countries—perhaps only America, plus anybody who can shelter under America's protection—will have even the remotest technological hope of acquiring antimissile defenses that can ward off the missiles with nuclear (or chemical or bacteriological) warheads that an enemy can aim at you from anywhere in the globe. Otherwise, the nation–state will be naked to such attacks.

The third technology-based challenge to the old picture of the nation–state is the information revolution. People in different countries now have the means to know far more about each other. They can see on television how others entertain themselves, or argue about politics, or kill their neighbors; and on the internet, or on ever-cheaper telephones, they can then exchange opinions about it all. Even if the number of people who make active use of the information revolution is still fairly small, as the skeptics claim, this is a startling contrast with what most Englishmen and Germans knew about each other in the 1930s, let alone most Frenchmen and Englishmen in the 1790s.

Like the new forces of global economics, the globalization of knowledge is in general an excellent thing. It is always better to know than to be ignorant. But, like those economic forces, this change blurs the sense of national separateness. The similarities between people, as well as the differences, become more apparent; the supposed distinctiveness of nations grows less sharp-edged; one day, perhaps, it may even become harder for tomorrow's equivalent of Serb politicians to persuade their people that tomorrow's Bosnian Muslims are an inferior breed.

Between them, these three challenges to the nation–state look pretty powerful. So is the nation–state, as the tongue-in-cheek first paragraph of this article suggested, inevitably about to be replaced as the basic unit of global politics? The answer is no, for two reasons. None of the possible replacements, when you take a closer look at them, seems to have much real solidity. And the nation–state may have more durability than people realize, because it is still the sole possessor of what is needed to be that basic unit. Take the two points in turn.

WHY THE ALTERNATIVES WON'T WORK

One dreamy successor to the nation–state is certainly not going to happen. The disappearance of communism has not opened the door to the emergence of a one-world system. Until the final failure of the "world community" in Bosnia in 1995, many people still clung to the belief that, after the Cold War, the "end of history"—in Francis Fukuyama's misleading phrase—was at hand. Such people reckoned that most countries would no longer have any serious differences of opinion with each other about politics and economics; that they could therefore, seeing things in broadly the same way, use the United Nations as their instrument for solving minor disputes and so keeping the world tidy; and that in this way the foundations would be laid of an eventual system of global government.

It could not be. Countries have long quarreled, and will continue to quarrel, about many things besides ideology. Anyway, the end of the Cold War's particular clash of ideas was not the end of all ideological argument; consult any ardent Muslim, or any earnest exponent of "Asian values." The world remains explosively divided.

By the end of 1995, almost everybody had come to understand this. That fond post-Cold-War illusion was the result of a failure to look clearly either at the lessons of history or at today's observable facts.

Ah, says a sharper-eyed band of optimists, but surely the recent progress towards freer trade, under the aegis of the new World Trade Organization, shows that the nation–state can indeed be persuaded to obey a global set of rules. That is true; but only up to a clearly defined point.

Most countries accept the discipline of a free-trade system because they recognize that free trade is beneficial to everybody (which does not stop them bargaining ferociously over the distribution of those benefits). But, in general, countries draw a line between this pooling of economic autonomy and the pooling of political and military power. They want to hold on to the means of being able to decide for themselves, in the last resort, what suits them—including whether it suits them to go on obeying free-trade rules. That is why even the most miraculously smooth-running free-trade regime will not inevitably glide forward into a global political unity.

Nor is there much plausibility in a second suggested alternative to the nation–state. This is the idea that various groups of today's nation–states, wanting to belong to something stronger, will gather together into big new entities, each speaking for the culture or civilization of its component parts. The most lucid and provocative version of the theory has been set out by Samuel Huntington of Harvard University, who has worryingly talked of a future "clash of civilizations."

This idea, unlike the one-world dream, does rest on a basis of observable fact. Countries that belong to the same "culture-area"—meaning that they have grown out of a shared body of religious or philosophical beliefs, and a shared experience of history—often behave in similar ways long after the event that originally shaped their culture has passed into history.

The ex-communist countries in the Orthodox Christian part of Europe, for instance, seem to find it harder to become free-market democracies than those in the Protestant-Catholic part, perhaps because the Orthodox area never fully digested the Reformation, that great shaper of western civilization. And the advocates of "Asian values," with their special respect for authority, almost all come from the background of the Confucian culture. It may well be that, as the world works itself into a new, post–Cold-War shape, these cultural connections will be the basis of some formidable alliances; and that the competition between these alliances will be a large element in the geopolitics of the 21st century.

But alliances are alliances, not single units of power. The problem with the civilization-unit theory is not just that Mr. Huntington's list of civilizations includes some rather implausible candidates—does Africa, or Latin America, really seem likely to become an actor on the world stage?—but that the component parts of even the more plausible ones are still profoundly reluctant to surrender their separate identities.

It is striking that the new wave of self-awareness in the Muslim world has not produced any serious move towards a merger of Muslim states. Even the Arab subsection of the Muslim world, with the advantage of a common language, has, after a series of abortive "unification" schemes, come up with nothing grander than the reunion of the two Yemens. In the Orthodox Christian part of the world, another arguably distinct culture-zone, the recent tendency has been for things to fall apart, not come together; this area now contains more separate states than it did a decade ago.

All the other culture-zones look equally unpromising, with one possible exception. Only in Western Europe is there any seriously conceived plan to dissolve existing nation–states into something bigger—and even this European experiment may now be running into the sands. The world does not, in short, seem to be heading for that fearful-sounding "clash of civilizations."

The only other sort of glue that might bind nation–states together, if the cultural glue proves too weak, is ideology. That may seem an odd thing to say while the dust still swirls from the stunning collapse of the communist edifice. But communism's fall does not mean that ideology has ceased to exist. What demolished the communist idea was the superior strength of a rival body of ideas, free-market democracy, which was powerful enough to hold together the 16 countries of the West's alliance through all the alarms and rigors of the Cold War.

Free-market democracy won that fight, but free-market democracy is in turn now challenged by two self-proclaimed rivals. One part of the back-to-basics movement that is sweeping through the Muslim world seems to accept the free-market bit, but believes that democracy is a denial of the principle that God decides what should happen in the world. And the East Asian politicians who talk about "Asian values," though they say they accept democracy, want to run it like a family—with themselves, naturally, as the firm but kindly father—so that it does not succumb to the anarchy they think is caused by too much Western individualism.

It is not yet clear whether either of these challenges to the West's picture of the future will endure. The Muslim one is already under attack from more open-minded Islamic revivalists, who insist that there should be a democratic way of deciding what God wants for the world. Advocates of Asian values may come to be judged, by their fellow Asians, as just a bunch of politicians trying to hold on to the pleasures of power. But for now it is plain that arguments of ideology are still helping to shape the world. They pull people into rival camps and give them more precise reasons for disagreeing with each other than the mere fact of belonging to different "civilizations."

Unfortunately, ideologies suffer from exactly the same difficulty as culture-zones when they offer themselves as a substitute for the nation–state. Nobody seems to want to join the proposed substitute.

The proponents of Asian values happily go on working inside their existing countries, because that is where they wield the authority they want to preserve. The Islamic antidemocrats in various Muslim countries have made no progress in breaking down the frontiers between those countries; indeed, they do not even seem to talk to each other very much. And, when the communist ideology collapsed, it became painfully clear that its component parts had been kept together by mere force, not by the vigor of an idea.

So the late 21st century's maps will not show a handful of sprawling superstates with names like Democratia, Islamia, and Leekuanyewia. Their dotted lines will continue to reveal large numbers of those boringly familiar places, nation–states.

WHY IT STUMBLES ON

Why is the nation–state so durable, for all the battering it has taken from 20th-century technology? Partly because, in its true meaning, it is a pretty recent arrival on the political scene and has the resilience of youth; but mostly because it is still the sole possessor of the magic formula without which it is hard, in today's world, to hold any sort of political structure together.

It was little more than 200 years ago, a blink of history's eye, that men invented the nation–state as a better way of organizing the business of government than any way previously available. Before that, the state—a recognizable chunk of territory, recognizably under somebody's control—had generally been one or the other of two things: call them the brute-force state, and the justification-by-good-works state.

A brute-force state came into existence when some tough took power by strength of arms and stayed in power by killing or otherwise silencing those who objected. That was how government began in most places, and the species is by no means extinct. You could hardly have a better example of such a state than Saddam Hussein's Iraq.

The trouble with relying on brute force, though, is that however ruthless the ruler may be there will in the end usually be somebody angry and desperate enough to put a sword or a bullet through him. This most primitive form of state-system therefore evolved, except in the unluckiest places, into one in which those who controlled power sought to justify their control of it. The rulers did not ask the ruled for their consent to being ruled. But they did try to keep them happy—or just happy enough—by providing for some of their essential needs.

In the arid empires of the Old Testament world, from Babylon to Persia, one essential need was the provision of a reliable flow of water. Later the Romans, having built their empire by force, sought to justify it by providing the rule of law and a sense of order (the British did much the same in India 1,800 years later). By the Middle Ages, the implicit bargain between governors and governed had become a complicated network of mutual obligations between king, barons, and the lower orders.

It was not perfect, but it was better than plain thuggery or chaos. Even now, the world contains many examples of this second system. The Chinese government still seeks to justify its one-party grip on power by a claim to have produced order and good economic statistics; so, less convincingly, do the rulers of assorted Arab countries.

What this system still lacks, of course, is any organic link between government and people. Even the most conscientious prince of the pre–nation–state era assumed power by right of inheritance, not by the will of those he governed. "I am the state," said Louis XIV, that most *de-haut-en-bas* specimen of the old order. A century later, the inventors of the nation–state set out to provide an alternative to the lofty arrogance of his first person singular. As they saw it, a government should be able to say: "The state gives us our authority."

A nation–state is a place where people feel a natural connection with each other because they share a language, a religion, or something else strong enough to bind them together and make them feel different from others: "we", not "they." The nation–state is the politics of the first person plural. Its government can speak for its people because it is part of the "we." It emerges out of the nation.

There can be arguments about how the government does its emerging, by election or by some more obscure process. At many times in the 200-year history of the nation–state ambitious or obsessed men—Hitler was the worst of all—have claimed the right to power because they said they knew better than anybody else what their nation wanted. But even they were different from Louis XIV. They claimed their authority, truthfully or not, from the will of their people. One way or another, in the past couple of centuries the connection between people and government has become organic. The concept of the nation–state shakes hands with the concept of government by consent.

The sense of being "we" can come from a shared language, as it unitingly does in most European countries, but divisively in places like Quebec; or from a shared religion, as in Ireland or Pakistan; or from the proud ownership of some special political idea, such as direct democracy in four-language Switzerland or the "American idea" in the multiethnic United States; or from the memory of a shared horror, as in Israel. Sometimes it comes from a mixture of these things. The hatreds of Bosnia are rooted both in differences of religion and in the memories of long-ago frontier wars between different culture-areas.

However it comes about, it is the necessary foundation for any durable political system. No government, unless it is prepared to rely entirely on brute force, can do its job properly in the modern world if the people it governs do not have a clear-cut sense of identity that they share with the government—unless, in other words, they are both part of the "we."

And it still seems that only the nation–state possesses this necessary sense of identity. It is nice to learn that you belong to such-and-such a civilization, or are a believer in this ideology or that; but learning this is not enough, it appears, to pull people across the familiar boundaries of the nation–state and into the creation of some new, bigger sort of political entity.

This may not remain true forever. There was a time when Prussians and Bavarians did not smoothly think of themselves as "we Germans," or Tuscans and Sicilians as "we Italians"; but they got round to it in the end. Perhaps, in the end, Muslims will smoothly be able to think of themselves as citizens of a wider Islamic state; or Chinese-speakers will salute a neo-Confucian flag fluttering over Beijing or Singapore; or, who knows, some pan-African power may rise out of that continent's present rubble. But it is not happening yet; and, until and unless it does happen, nation–states will be the only pieces on the geopolitical chessboard.

SO WATCH EUROPE

The chief test of whether this might change will take place in Europe over the next few years. The countries of the European Union have come very close to the line that separates the pooling of their economic life from the merging of their politics. They will soon have to decide whether or not they want to cross that line. To cross it, they would need to be reasonably sure that the new Europe passes the first-person-plural test. They would have to be confident that its people now think of themselves in some serious way not chiefly as Germans or French, or whatever, but as "we Europeans."

Twice in history, Europe, or a large part of it, has felt itself to be such a single place; and on both occasions there were solid grounds for such a sense of identity. The first time was when the Roman empire hammered much of Europe into a single entity that shared the blessings of Roman law, the Latin language, and the peace of the legions. This was unquestionably a culture-zone: to the first-person-plural question, its people could reply, *Cives Romani sumus.*

The second time began when Charlemagne was crowned as "Emperor of the Catholic Church of Europe" in Rome on Christmas Day 800. The political unity of the Europe created by Charlemagne did not long survive his death. Yet, for another six centuries after Charlemagne, Europeans went on believing, as Muslims believe today, that there ought in principle to be no distinction between God's business and man's business, and that politics should come under God's guidance; and for most of that time they kept in existence institutions that tried to put this principle into practice. This was an ideological Europe. To the question of what "we Europeans" stood for, Charlemagne's descendants would have replied, *Credimus in unum Deum.*

The problem for today's unifiers of Europe is not just that Germany, France, and Britain want different things out of a European union. It is that none of their versions of a united Europe would be rooted in a distinctive ideology. The political and economic ideas by which Europe lives are much the same as America's, and indeed America was ahead of most of Europe in making itself a democracy. Nor would it be a unique culture-zone. Europe and America come from the same cultural background; they are, with minor variations, subdivisions of a single civilization.

The underlying argument of those who now pursue a separate European unity is that Europe either does not want to be, or does not think it can be, part of a wider union with its cultural and ideological cousin across the Atlantic. This is an argument of geography, and a circular one at that. Its answer to the "we" question is: We are Europeans because we are Europeans.

That need not rule it out. Tuscans and Sicilians joined each other to become Italians even though the Italy they created in 1862 had much in common with the rest of Europe. People sometimes band together simply to be stronger than they were separately. The desire to be strong is a powerful force in politics. But not as powerful as the feeling that "we" are different from "them." That is one reason why a growing question mark floats over Europe.

The nation–state will last longer than most people had thought. Only in one part of the world, Europe, is there a possibility that it may give way to a bigger post–nation–state system; and even that possibility now looks fainter than it did a few years ago. Like the natural world, the world of geopolitics does not easily change its species. The coming century will still be the home of recognizable beasts: muscular lions and fearful deer, lumbering rhinos and cunning jackals. That may be a pity; but the inhabitants of the jungle have to live with it.

20

A COMMUNITY OF PEACE: DEMOCRACY, INTERDEPENDENCE, AND INTERNATIONAL ORGANIZATION

Bruce Russett

Disputes invariably arise among states in an anarchical international system, but when they do, democracies cooperate by bargaining for compromises at the negotiating table. More than that, democracies almost never go to war with one another. This essay traces three principles embedded in "liberal democratic international theory"—free governments, free markets, and economic independence and international organizations—that explain why and how they contribute to international cooperation and security and can fundamentally change the past patterns of conflict among nations. Its author, Bruce Russett, is Dean Acheson Professor of International Relations and Director of United Nations Studies at Yale University. He edits the *Journal of Conflict Resolution* and is the author most recently of *Grasping the Democratic Peace: Principles for a Post–Cold War World* (1993), and *The Once and Future Security Council* (1997).

This essay was prepared especially for this book. It has been adapted from an article, in Polish, in David Bobrow, Edward Halizak, and Ryszard Zieba, eds., *National and International Security in the Late XX Century* (Warsaw: Wydawnictowo Naukove Scholar, 1997). Reprinted with permission of the author.

For nearly half a century the United States and its allies carried out a policy of containment, to prevent the spread of Communist ideology and Soviet power. That policy ultimately succeeded, spectacularly. Now it must be replaced by another policy, one designed to consolidate the new acceptability of free institutions around the world. The post–Cold-War era presents more than just the passing of a particular adversarial relationship; it offers a chance for fundamentally changed relations among nations.

THREE PRINCIPLES FOR A PEACEFUL INTERNATIONAL ORDER

Containment in practice meant far more than just building a strong military establishment; it used trade, economic assistance, foreign investment, and cultural instruments like the BBC and Radio Free Europe. A key feature of containment was that it was not a unilateralist policy, but multilateralist. Its multilateral instruments ranged far beyond NATO and the rest of the alliance system, to depend heavily on regional trade arrangements like the OECD, the Bretton Woods financial institutions (the World Bank and the International Monetary Fund), GATT, and many UN specialized agencies. Central UN institutions were also vital, such as the Security Council for endorsing peace enforcement action in Korea and for managing dangerous confrontations like the 1956 Suez War or keeping the Soviet-U.S. rivalry at arms length from some regional conflicts.

Contemporary policy needs a similar central organizing principle. To promote its acceptance, that principle would be best rooted in the earlier containment experience. It should build on the principles that underlay the rhetoric and much of the practice of containment, principles rooted in beliefs about the success of free political and economic systems. Those principles are democracy, free markets—especially given the argument that economic interdependence promotes peace as well as prosperity—and international law and organization. Each makes a contribution to peace, and in many instances they reinforce each other (and are themselves reinforced by peace) in "virtuous circles" or feedback loops.

Consider a puzzle about the end of the Cold War. The question is not simply why did the Cold War end, but rather, why did it end before the drastic change in the bipolar distribution of power, and why did it end peacefully? In November 1988 Margaret Thatcher proclaimed, as did other Europeans, that "the Cold War is over." By spring 1989 the U.S. State Department stopped making official reference to the Soviet Union as the enemy. The fundamental patterns of East-West behavior had changed, on both sides, beginning even before the circumvention of the Berlin Wall and then its destruction in October 1989. All of this preceded the unification of Germany (October 1990) and the dissolution of the Warsaw Pact (July 1991). Even after these latter events, the military power of the Soviet Union itself remained intact until the dissolution of the USSR at the end of December 1991. None of these events was resisted militarily.

Any understanding of the change in the Soviet Union's international behavior, before its political fragmentation, and in time reciprocated by the West, demands attention to the operation of the three principles:

1. Substantial political liberalization and movement toward democracy in the Soviet Union, with consequent improvements in free expression and the treatment of dissidents at home, in the East European satellites, and in behavior toward Western Europe and the United States.

2. The desire for economic interdependence with the West, impelled by the impending collapse of the Soviet economy and the consequent perceived need for access to Western markets, goods, technology, and capital, which in turn required a change in Soviet military and diplomatic policy.

3. The influence of international law and organizations, as manifested in the Conference on Security and Cooperation in Europe (CSCE, now OSCE) and the human rights basket of the Helsinki accords and their legitimation and support of dissent in the communist states. Also important were the various international nongovernmental organizations (INGOs) devoted to human rights.

A vision of a peace among democratically governed states has long been invoked as part of a larger structure of institutions and practices to promote peace among nation-states. In 1795 Immanuel Kant spoke of perpetual peace based partially upon states sharing "republican constitutions." His meaning was compatible with basic contemporary understandings of democracy. As the elements of such a constitution he identified freedom, with legal equality of subjects, representative government, and separation of powers. The other key elements of his perpetual peace were "cosmopolitan law," embodying ties of international commerce and free trade, and a "pacific union" established by treaty in international law among republics.

Woodrow Wilson expressed the same vision for the 20th century. His Fourteen Points sound as though Kant were guiding Wilson's writing hand. They included Kant's cosmopolitan law and pacific union. Point three demanded "removal, so far as possible, of all economic barriers and the establishment of an equality of trade conditions among all the nations consenting to the peace and associating themselves for its maintenance." The 14th point was "A general association of nations must be formed under specific covenants for the purpose of affording mutual guarantees of political independence and territorial integrity to great and small states alike." He did not explicitly invoke the need for universal democracy, since not all of America's war allies were democratic. But this meaning is clear if one considers the domestic political conditions necessary for his first point: "Open covenants of peace, openly arrived at, after which there shall be no private international understandings of any kind but diplomacy shall proceed always frankly and in the public view." His 1917 war message to Congress asserted that "a steadfast concert of peace can never be maintained except by a partnership of democratic nations." This vision emerged again after World

War II, animating the founders of what became the European Union. Now, at the end of the 20th century, it is newly plausible.

DEMOCRACIES RARELY FIGHT EACH OTHER

This chapter concentrates chiefly on the relationship between democracy and peace, referring more briefly to the other two principles. Democratization is key for two reasons. First, democracy is a desirable form of government on its own merit. It both recognizes and promotes human dignity. Democracy is not perfect, and should not be forced upon peoples who do not wish it. But for many countries it is better than the alternatives they have tried and from which they have suffered.

Second, we now have solid evidence that democracies do not make war on each other. Much of it can be found in my book, *Grasping the Democratic Peace: Principles for a Post–Cold War World.*[1] In the contemporary era, "democracy" denotes a country in which nearly everyone can vote, elections are freely contested, and the chief executive is chosen by popular vote or by an elected parliament, and civil rights and civil liberties are substantially guaranteed. Democracies may not be especially peaceful in general—we all know the history of democracies in colonialism, covert intervention, and other excesses of power. Democracies are nearly as violence-prone in their relations with authoritarian states as authoritarian states are toward each other. But the relations between stable democracies are qualitatively different.

Democracies are unlikely to engage in any kind of militarized disputes *with each other* or to let any such disputes escalate into war. In fact, they rarely even skirmish. Since 1946 pairs of democratic states have been only one-eighth as likely as other kinds of states to threaten to use force against each other, and only one-tenth as likely actually to do so. Established democracies fought *no wars* against one another during the entire 20th century. Although Finland took the Axis side against the Soviet Union in World War II, it engaged in no combat with the democracies.

The more democratic each state is, the more peaceful their relations are likely to be. Democracies are more likely to employ "democratic" means of peaceful conflict resolution. They are readier to reciprocate each other's behavior, to accept third-party mediation or good offices in settling disputes, and to accept

---

[1](Princeton, NJ: Princeton University Press, 1993). There is an enormous amount of more recent scholarship on this matter, largely confirming or extending the principle, but some of it critical. I review much of it in Bruce Russett, "Counterfactuals about War and Its Absence," in Philip Tetlock and Aaron Belkin, eds., *Counterfactual Thought Experiments in World Politics* (Princeton, NJ: Princeton University Press, 1996).

binding third-party arbitration and adjudication.[2] Careful statistical analyses of countries' behavior have shown that democracies' relatively peaceful relations toward each other are not spuriously caused by some other influence such as sharing high levels of wealth, or rapid growth, or ties of alliance. The phenomenon of peace between democracies is not limited just to the rich industrialized states of the global North. It was not maintained simply by pressure from a common adversary in the Cold War, and it has outlasted that threat.

The phenomenon of democratic peace can be explained by the pervasiveness of normative restraints on conflict between democracies. That explanation extends to the international arena the cultural norms of live-and-let-live and peaceful conflict resolution that operate within democracies. The phenomenon of democratic peace can also be explained by the role of institutional restraints on democracies' decisions to go to war. Those restraints insure that any state in a conflict of interest with another democracy can expect ample time for conflict-resolution processes to be effective, and that the risk of incurring surprise attack is virtually nil. These two influences reinforce each other. The spread of democratic norms and practices in the world, if consolidated, should reduce the frequency of violent conflict and war. Where normative restraints are weak, democratic institutions may provide the necessary additional restraints on the use of violence against other democratic states.

To the degree that countries once ruled by autocratic systems become democratic, the absence of war among democracies comes to bear on any discussion of the future of international relations. The statement that in the modern international system democracies have almost never fought each other represents a complex phenomenon: (1) Democracies rarely fight each other (an empirical statement) because (2) they have other means of resolving conflicts between them and therefore don't need to fight each other (a prudential cost-benefit statement), and (3) they perceive that democracies should not fight each other (a normative statement about principles of right behavior), which reinforces the empirical statement. By this reasoning, the more democracies there are in the world, the fewer potential adversaries democracies will have and the wider the zone of peace.

The *possibility* of a widespread zone of democratic peace in the contemporary world exists. To turn that possibility into a policy to promote democratic peace two fundamental problems must be addressed: the problem of consolidating democratic stability, and the prospects for changing basic patterns of international behavior.

---

[2]Russell Leng, "Reciprocating Influence Strategies and Success in Interstate Bargaining," *Journal of Conflict Resolution* 37, no. 1 (March 1993), pp. 3–41; William Dixon, "Democracy and the Peaceful Settlement of International Disputes," *American Political Science Review* 88, no. 1 (March 1994), pp. 14–32; Gregory Raymond, "Democracies, Disputes, and Third-Party Intermediaries," *Journal of Conflict Resolution* 38, no. 1 (March 1994), pp. 24–42.

STRENGTHENING DEMOCRACY AND ITS NORMS

The literature on the "prerequisites" of democracy is vast and often deeply flawed because it is ethnocentric and too enamored with economic preconditions. Yet much has been learned. Samuel Huntington's book, *The Third Wave: Democratization in the Late Twentieth Century*[3] reviews and synthesizes much of the earlier literature. Among developments in the world that played significant parts in *producing* the latest wave of recent transitions to democracy he identifies changes in the policies of other states and international organizations that promote human rights and democracy, and "snowballing" or demonstration effects, enhanced by international communication, as transitions to democracy in some states served as models for their neighbors. Among conditions that favor the *consolidation* of new democracies he lists a favorable international political environment, with outside assistance.

Probably most of the conditions affecting the success of democratization arise from circumstances internal to any particular state. But this list of possible conditions from outside is impressive also. Favorable international conditions may not be essential in every case, but they can make a difference, and sometimes a crucial one, when the internal influences are mixed.

With economic conditions so grim in much of the developing world, eastern Europe, and the former Soviet Union, and the consequent dangers to the legitimacy of new democratic governments, external assistance—technical and financial— is especially important. New democracies will not survive without some material improvement in their citizens' lives. As a stick, aid can surely be denied to governments that regularly violate human rights, for example the rights of ethnic minorities. Clear antidemocratic acts, such as a military coup or an aborted election, can be punished by suspending aid. As to the carrot of extending aid on a conditional basis, broader goals of developing democratic institutions require creation of a civil society, and are less easily made conditional. Recipients may see multilateral aid, with conditions of democratic reform attached, as a less blatant invasion of their sovereignty than aid from a single country.

Without exaggerating the prospects for success, it would be a terrible loss if the richer and older democracies did not make serious efforts. It would be a loss, to themselves as well as to the peoples of the struggling democracies. Any solution requires external assistance and protection to aid and speed transitions to democracy. It also requires attention to devising institutions and nurturing norms and practices of democratic government with respect for minority rights. The creation of institutions, norms, and practices to protect minorities has never been easy. But it presents the fundamental challenge of world political development in this era. It is worth remembering that the most terrible acts of genocide in this century (from Turkey's slaughter of the Armenians through Hitler, Stalin, Pol

---

[3](Norman, OK: University of Oklahoma Press, 1991).

Pot, and others) have been carried out by authoritarian or totalitarian governments, not democratic ones.[4]

Understanding that democracies rarely fight each other, and why, has great consequence for policy in the contemporary world. It should affect the kinds of military preparations believed to be necessary, and the costs one would be willing to pay to make them. It should encourage peaceful efforts to assist the emergence and consolidation of democracy. But a misunderstanding of it could encourage war making against authoritarian regimes and efforts to overturn them—with all the costly implications of preventive or hegemonic military activity such a policy might imply.

Recollection of the post-1945 success with defeated adversaries can be both instructive and misleading. It is instructive in showing that democracy could supplant a thoroughly discredited totalitarian regime. It can be misleading if one forgets how expensive it was (Marshall Plan aid for Germany and Italy and important economic concessions to Japan), and especially if one misinterprets the political conditions of military defeat. The allies utterly defeated the Axis coalition. Then, to solidify democratic government they conducted vast (if incomplete) efforts to remove the former elites from positions of authority. But they had something to build on, in the form of individuals and institutions from previous experiences with democracy. The model of "fight them, beat them, and then make them democratic" is no model for contemporary action. It probably would not work anyway, and no one is prepared to make the kind of effort that would be required. Not all authoritarian states are inherently aggressive. Indeed, at any particular time the majority are not. A militarized crusade for democracy is not in order.

External military intervention, even against the most odious dictators, is a dangerous way to try to produce a "democratic world order." Sometimes, with a cautious cost-benefit analysis and with the certainty of substantial and legitimate internal support, it might be worthwhile—that is, under conditions when rapid military success is likely *and* the will of the people at issue is clear. Even so, any time an outside power supplants any existing government the problem of legitimacy is paramount. The very democratic norms to be instilled may be compromised. At the least, intervention cannot be unilateral. It must be approved, publicly and willingly, by an international body like the United Nations or the Organization of American States. When an election has been held under UN auspices and certified as fair—as happened in Haiti—the United Nations has a special responsibility, even a duty, to see that the democratic government it helped create is not destroyed.

Under most circumstances, international bodies are better used as vehicles to promote democratic processes at times when the relevant domestic parties are

---

[4]R. J. Rummel, *Death by Government: Genocide and Mass Murder in the Twentieth Century* (New Brunswick, NJ: Transaction, 1994).

ready. Peacekeeping operations to help provide the conditions for free elections, monitor those elections, and advise on the building of democratic institutions are usually far more promising and less costly for all concerned than is military intervention.

With the end of the Cold War, the United Nations has experienced highly publicized troubles in Somalia and the former Yugoslavia as it tries to cope with a range of challenges not previously part of its mandate. Nonetheless, its successes, though receiving less attention, outnumber the failures. It emerged as a major facilitator of peaceful transitions and democratic elections in such places as Cambodia, El Salvador, Eritrea, and Namibia. Its Electoral Assistance Unit has provided election monitoring, technical assistance, or other aid to free electoral processes in more than 70 states.[5]

ECONOMIC INTERDEPENDENCE AND INTERNATIONAL ORGANIZATIONS

Ties of economic interdependence—international trade and investment—form an important supplement to shared democracy in promoting peace. During the post–World War II era, the same analyses that show how rarely democracies used or threatened to use military force against each other show a similar effect for states that trade heavily with each other. The effect of economic interdependence does not supplant, but rather supplements, the effect of democracy, and like democracy its effect remains even when alliance, wealth, and economic growth rates are controlled for in the analysis.[6]

Here then is the second element of the Kantian/Wilsonian vision, representing the role of free trade and a high level of commercial exchange. Economic interdependence gives countries a stake in each others' well-being. War would mean destruction, in the other country, of one's own markets, industrial plants, and sources of imports. If my investments are in your country, bombing your industry means, in effect, bombing my own factories. Economic interdependence also serves as a channel of information about each other's perspectives, interests, and desires on a broad range of matters not the subject of the economic exchange. These communications form an important channel for conflict management. Interdependence, however, is the key word—mutual dependence, not one-sided dominance.

The end of the Cold War represents a surrender to the force of values of economic as well as political freedom. Democracies trade more heavily with each other than do other kinds of states, even after taking into account the standard

[5]The scope of these efforts is evident in Boutros Boutros-Ghali, *An Agenda for Democratization* (New York: United Nations, 1996).

[6]John Oneal and Bruce Russett, "The Classical Liberals Were Right: Democracy, Interdependence, and Conflict, 1950–1985," *Internatinal Studies Quarterly* 41, no. 2 (June 1997).

kinds of economically-driven market calculations.[7] Moreover, trade and peace form a mutually reinforcing relationship. Not only does trade promote peace, peace promotes trade, as traders and governments develop greater confidence in the stability of political relationships.[8] International organizations promoting free trade and stable economic conditions (for example, the IMF, the United Nations Development Programme, and the World Trade Organization) thus make an indirect contribution to peace, as well as to development.

The role of international law and institutions, and the need for strengthening them, constitutes the third element of the Kantian/Wilsonian vision. As expressed in Secretary-General Boutros Ghali's *An Agenda for Peace,*[9] the United Nations has a new mission of "peace building," attending to democratization, development, and the protection of human rights. It is newly strengthened and, paradoxically, also newly and enormously burdened. The United Nations and other international organizations promote democratization and peace directly as well as indirectly. As noted above, democracies are much more likely to use international institutions for peacefully resolving disputes among themselves than are dictatorships.

Large-scale statistical analyses of the effect of international organization memberships have also been carried out. For example, the more intergovernmental organizations (IGOs) that any pair of states belongs to, the less likely they are to use or threaten violence in their relations with each other. Again, this effect is in addition to that of democracy and economic interdependence, and holds even when alliances, wealth, and other factors are controlled for.[10] International organizations promote the flow of information to help settle conflicts, provide institutions to mediate disagreements, help establish norms for behavior, and promote some sense of common identity among peoples and countries.

CAN A WIDER DEMOCRATIC PEACE BE BUILT?

New democracies should be supported financially, politically, and morally. Successful transitions to democracy in some countries can supply a model for others. Simple understanding the sources of the democratic peace can have the effect of a self-fulfilling prophecy. In a world where democracy has become widespread, understanding the fact of the "democratic peace" proposition will help to make it true.

---

[7]Harry Bliss and Bruce Russett, "Democratic Trading Partners: the Liberal Connection," manuscript, Yale University, New Haven, CT: 1996.

[8]Soo Yeon Kim, *Bilateral Conflict and Trade, 1946–1986: An Inquiry into Causality and Its Direction.* Ph.D. Dissertation. New Haven, CT: Yale University, 1997.

[9](New York: United Nations, 1993), paragraph 81.

[10]Bruce Russett and John Oneal, "The Third Leg of the Kantian Tripod for Peace: International Organizations also Matter," paper presented at the annual meeting of the International Studies Association, Toronto, March 1997.

A stable and less menacing international system can permit the emergence and consolidation of democratic governments. International threats—real or only perceived—strengthen the forces of secrecy and authoritarianism in the domestic politics of states involved in protracted conflict. Relaxation of international threats to peace and security reduces the need, and the excuse, for repressing democratic dissent.

Democracy and the expectation of international peace can feed on each other. An evolutionary process may even be at work. Because of the visible nature and public costs of breaking commitments, democratic leaders may be better able to persuade leaders of other states that they will keep the agreements they do enter into. Democratic states are able to signal their intentions in bargaining with greater credibility than autocratic states. Democracies more often win their wars than do authoritarian states (80 percent of the time; remember that the coin-flip odds would be only 50–50). Perhaps they are more prudent about what wars they get into. In war they seem to be more effective in marshaling their resources, and with free speech and debate they are more accurate and efficient information processors. Authoritarian governments that lose wars are often overthrown subsequently, and may be replaced by democratic regimes. States with competitive elections generally have lower military expenditures, which in relations with other democracies promotes cooperation; as democracies' politically relevant international environment becomes composed of more democratic and internally stable states, democracies tend to reduce their military allocations and conflict involvement.[11]

The modern international system is commonly traced to the Treaty of Westphalia and the principles of sovereignty affirmed by it. The treaty, made by princes who ruled as autocrats, affirmed the anarchy of the system, without a superior authority to ensure order. Our understanding of the modern anarchic state system risks conflating the effects of anarchy with those stemming from the political organization of its component units. When most states are ruled autocratically—as in 1648 and throughout virtually all of history since—playing by the rules of autocracy may be the only way for any state, democracy or not, to survive in Hobbesian anarchy.

The anarchic security dilemma of threat and counterthreat drove the pessimism of "realists" like Hans Morgenthau. But the emergence of new democracies with the end of the Cold War presents an opening for change in the international system

[11]James Fearon, "Domestic Political Audiences and the Escalation of International Disputes," *American Political Science Review* 88, no. 3 (September 1994), pp. 577–92; David Lake, "Powerful Pacifists: Democratic States and War," *American Political Science Review* 86, no. 1 (March 1992), pp. 24–37; Bruce Bueno de Mesquita, Randolph Siverson, and Garry Woller, "War and the Fate of Regimes: A Comparative Survey," *American Political Science Review* 86, no. 3 (1992), pp. 639–46; Michelle Garfinkel, "Domestic Politics and International Conflict," *American Economic Review* 84, no. 5 (December 1994), pp. 1294–1309; Zeev Maoz, *Domestic Sources of Global Change* (Ann Arbor: University of Michigan Press, 1996).

more fundamental even than at the end of other big wars—World Wars I and II and the Napoleonic Wars. For the first time ever, in 1992 a virtual majority of states (91 of 183) approximated the standards for democracy that I employed earlier. Another 35 were in some form of transition to democracy. Democracy in many of these states may not prove stable. A subsequent report notes some backsliding in the number of people living in democracies, though still an increase in the number of democratic governments.[12] But states probably can become democratic faster than they can become rich. This global democratic wave may crest and fall back, as earlier ones have done. Perhaps enlargement of the zone of democracy now sounds too ambitious; if so, consolidation is the very least we should settle for. If the chance for wide democratization can be grasped and held, world politics might be transformed.

The Kantian peace would be sustained by an interacting and mutually supporting combination of democratic government, economic interdependence, and international law and organization. Such an international system—an international society as well as a collection of sovereign states—might reflect very different behavior than did the previous one composed predominantly of autocracies. The West won the Cold War, at immense cost. If we should now let slip this marvelous but brief window of opportunity to solidify basic change in the international order at much lower cost, our children will wonder. Some autocratically governed states will surely remain in the system. In their relations with states where democracy is unstable, or where democratization is not begun at all, democracies must continue to be vigilant and concerned with the need for military deterrence. But if enough states do become stably democratic in the next century, then among them we will have a chance to reconstruct the norms and rules of the international order. A system created by autocracies centuries ago might now be recreated by a critical mass of democratic states.

---

[12]R. Bruce McColm et al., *Freedom in the World: Political Rights and Civil Liberties 1991–1992* (New York: Freedom House, 1992), p. 47; R. Bruce McColm et al., *Freedom in the World: Political Rights and Civil Liberties 1994–1995* (New York: Freedom House, 1995).

21

THE REALITY
AND RELEVANCE
OF INTERNATIONAL LAW
IN THE 21ST CENTURY

Christopher C. Joyner

International law reflects the need for order, predictability, and stability in international relations. The functions and impact of international law are analyzed by Christopher C. Joyner, who emphasizes both the strengths and limitations of legal norms as instruments for managing conflicts and promoting collaboration in world politics. Joyner is professor of government at Georgetown University. He is the author of *Antarctica and the Law of the Sea* (1992) and *Eagle Over the Ice: The U.S. in the Antarctic* (1997) and editor of *The United Nations and International Law* (1997).

The 1990s reinvigorated the relevance and reality of modern international law. Resort to military force by an international coalition to oust Iraq from Kuwait; implementation of a Middle East peace process between Israel and the Palestinian Liberation Organization; convening the Rio "Earth Summit" on global environment and development issues; entry into force of a new regime for governing the world's oceans, as well as the General Agreement on Tariffs and Trade/World Trade Organization arrangement for regulating international commerce; actions taken by the United Nations to end violence in Somalia, Bosnia,

---

This essay was written especially for this book.

Cambodia, and Haiti; establishment of international tribunals to try persons accused of "ethnic cleansing" and genocidal atrocities in the former Yugoslvia and Rwanda; and successful negotiation of the Dayton Peace Accords to end the war in Bosnia—these events among many others are clearly anchored by international legal implications. Yet, students of international relations rightly continue to ask certain fundamental questions about the nature and purpose of international law. Is international law really "law?" Or is it nothing more than "positive morality?" How can international law work in a modern state system dictated by considerations of national interests and power politics? Is international law more of a restraint on national policy, or is it merely a policy instrument wielded by governments to further their own ad hoc purposes to gain legitimacy? In sum, what is the reality and relevance of international law to contemporary world politics? This essay seeks to address these inquiries and in the process to explore the role of international law in international affairs on the eve of the 21st century.

THE CONCEPTUAL FOUNDATIONS OF INTERNATIONAL LAW

International law, often described as public international law or the law of nations, refers to the system of law that governs relations between states. States traditionally were the only subjects with rights and duties under international law. In the modern era, however, the ambit of international law has been greatly expanded to where it now encompasses many actors other than states, among them international organizations, multinational corporations, and even individual persons. Nevertheless, states remain the primary concern and focus of international law in world politics.[1]

It is important at the outset to note that the initial reaction of many students and laypeople alike to the notion of international law is one of skepticism. A prevalent view holds that national governments have scant respect for international law, and therefore they have little or no incentive to obey it, given the absence of a supranational system armed with sanctions capable of being enforced against a lawbreaker. In short, a popular belief is that international law is not really law.

However, the reality as demonstrated through their behavior is that states do accept international law as law and, even more significant, in the vast majority of instances they usually obey it. Though it is certainly true that international law is sometimes disobeyed with impunity, the same observation is equally true of any domestic legal system. For example, do local laws prevent traffic violations from

---

[1]See generally Alan James, *Sovereign Statehood: The Basis of International Society* (London: Allen and Unwin, 1986); Gene Lyons and Michael Mastanduno, eds., *Beyond Westphalia? State Sovereignty and International Intervention* (Baltimore: Johns Hopkins University Press, 1995); and Hendrik Spruyt, *The Sovereign State and Its Competitors* (Princeton: Princeton University Press,1995).

occurring? Do municipal (i.e., domestic) laws against murder, rape, burglary, or assault and battery prevent those crimes from being committed? Put simply, does the presence of "enforced" law *ipso facto* ensure compliance or even apprehension and prosecution? Clearly, in the real world, the answer is no. Richard Falk put it well when he observed,

> The success of domestic law does not rest in its capacity to solicit the respect of its subjects; the incidence of homicide and civil violence, and even of rebellion, is high. International law is a weak legal system not because it is often or easily flouted by powerful states, but because certain violations, however infrequent, are highly destructive and far-reaching in their implications.[2]

International law is not violated more often, or to a higher degree, than the law of other legal systems. Yet why does the contrary misconception persist? Two general reasons may offer much of the explanation. First, there is sensationalism; people tend to hear only about international law when blatant violations make the news. When states attack each other (or, for that matter, when a person is murdered), it becomes a newsworthy event. If the law is obeyed, and international relations between states proceed uninterrupted by violence, those affairs usually go unreported. The second reason for the misimpression that international law is frequently violated is the tendency of many people to presume that the mere existence of a transnational dispute automatically signifies that some law has been breached. This, of course, is not true; the fact that a dispute between states has arisen ought not to be taken to mean that a breach of international law has occurred, just as a civil dispute involving two individuals is not necessarily indicative of a breach in municipal law. Disputes between states may arise over many concerns, none of which may involve violations of law. For example, there may exist a genuine uncertainty about the facts of a case or uncertainty about the law itself; there may be need for new law to meet changing international conditions; or there may even occur the resort to unfriendly but legal acts (called retorsion) by one state against another. While these situations may be unfortunate and perhaps in some instances regrettable, they do not perforce constitute violations of the law.

Most criticism about international law can be generally categorized. First, there are those who view the law of nations as something that can never work and is therefore ignored by states, groups, or individuals. Law, in effect, becomes an "orphan" within the international community. On the other hand, there is the group that sees international law as an instrument of purpose, a "harlot" as it were, to be used, abused, or discounted in accord with one's own moment of convenience, interest, or capability. Still other critics perceive the law as not having any "teeth" or power of enforcement. The absence of an executive authority

---

[2]Richard A. Falk, *The Status of Law in International Society* (Princeton, N.J.: Princeton University Press, 1970), p. 29.

or international policeman thereby renders all values, norms, and rules subject to mere voluntary accession. International law in this instance becomes a "jailer." Perhaps more cynical is the view that international law does not exist and that it cannot exist until either all states agree to cooperate and coordinate the creation of mutually acceptable legal codes or this condition is imposed upon them. In this scenario, international law must assume the role of a "magician." Prevalent in the hard-line realist school of international politics, this perception suggests that international law provides nothing more than a utopian dream. That is, governments that place heavy emphasis upon inserting morality in foreign policy considerations live in a world of idealism, naively hoping for the mythical attainment in international affairs where law will govern supremely and people will be saved from a system of international anarchy. For these critics, proponents of international law thus represent a "never-never land" school of thought.[3]

The reality of international law does not fit either neatly or aptly into any of these perceptions. John Austin, who dominated jurisprudential thinking in Great Britain during the 19th century, contributed much in the way of theory suggesting the frailties of international law. Austin reasoned that for a legal system to exist in fact, three indispensable elements were essential: (1) There had to exist a clearly identifiable superior, or sovereign, who was capable of issuing (2) orders or commands for managing society, and (3) there had to be punitive sanctions capable of enforcing those commands. For Austin, law thus was defined as the general command emanating from a sovereign, supported by the threat of real sanctions. Since international law had neither a sovereign nor the requisite enforcement authority, Austin concluded that it was not really "law"; international law, he believed, ought to be considered merely as "positive morality."[4] The Austinian concept involves the relatively uncomplicated contention that genuine law has its rules laid down by a superior power (the executive), and that they are enforced by another superior power (the police). At first blush, this line of thinking may seem logically attractive. However, in the real world, it becomes intellectually simplistic to assume that law exists only when and where formal structures exist; moreover, it is likewise faulty to confuse characteristics of a legal system as being those prerequisites necessary to define law's existence. The remainder of this essay addresses these contentions.

THE NATURE OF INTERNATIONAL LAW

Generally speaking, the function of law is to preserve order. That is, law embodies a system of sanctioned regularity, a certain order in itself, which conveys the

---

[3]These schools critical of international law are proposed in John H. E. Fried, "International Law—Neither Orphan Nor Harlot, Neither Jailer Nor Never-Never Land," in Karl Deutsch and Stanley Hoffmann, eds., *The Relevance of International Law* (New York: Doubleday, 1971), pp. 124–176.

[4]John Austin, *The Province of Jurisprudence Determined and the Uses of the Study of Jurisprudence* (London: Weidenfeld and Nicolson, 1954), pp. 121–6, 137–144.

notion of expectations. Law provides for the regularity of activities that can be discerned, forecast, and anticipated in a society. Through law, the attempt is made to regulate behavior in order to insure harmony and maintain a society's values and institutions.[5]

In this connection, a system of law should have three basic characteristics. First, a statement of a prescribed pattern of behavior must be evident. Second, an obligational basis approved by the society must be present. And third, some process for punishing unlawful conduct in the society must be available. As essential facets, the measure of how well these elements interact will in large part determine the effectiveness of the legal system as a whole as well as the extent of its actual existence and performance.

Given these general observations, what significance can be attached to the nature of international law? Expressed in an Austinian sense, can a bona fide legal system that fulfills these objectives exist in the absence of a formal government structure, that is, without a centralized system of law creation, law application, and law enforcement? The answer clearly is yes. International law does qualify as a legal system, albeit a somewhat primitive and imperfect one. International law consists of a set of norms that prescribe international behavior, although those patterns may at times seem vaguely defined. International law furnishes a principled foundation for policy decisions, albeit adherence to principle often becomes justifiable if it can be shown to be practical. Relatedly, reasons do exist for states to obey international law; in other words, an obligatory basis does in fact exist to support international law's operation in world affairs. Finally, a system of sanctions is available in international law, and it contributes to coercive enforcement of the law. To appreciate these observations more fully, it is worthwhile to examine the evolutionary nature and sources of international law, the obligational basis for its operation, and the enforcement process available for punishing illegal behavior in the international community.

THE SOURCES OF INTERNATIONAL LAW

No legal system flashes into existence fully panoplied. All orders of law, from the most primitive to the most sophisticated, have their roots in the society they govern. International law is no different. The modern law of nations has undergone a process of evolution as old as the nation-state system itself, owing its direct origins to the Treaty of Westphalia in 1648. Importantly in this regard, over the past three centuries, specific sources for the creation of new international law have become widely acknowledged in and accepted by the international community.[6]

---

[5]For a thoughtful compendium on the evolution of law in international society, see Robert J. Beck, Anthony Clark Arend, and Robert D. Vander Lugt, eds., *International Rules: Approaches form International Law and International Relations* (Oxford: Oxford University Press, 1996).

[6]See generally Clive Parry, *The Sources and Evidences of International Law* (Dobbs Ferry, N.Y.: Oceana, 1965). The following enumeration of sources is based upon the priority set out in Article 38 of the Statute of the International Court of Justice, appended to the Charter of the United Nations.

Foremost among the sources of international law are international conventions and treaties.[7] When ratified by a substantial number of states, some multilateral conventions may be deemed tantamount to an international legal statute and are aptly labeled "lawmaking" treaties. Examples of these types of treaties include the four 1949 Geneva Conventions on the Law of War, the 1961 Vienna Convention on Diplomatic Relations, the 1967 Outer Space Treaty, the 1982 UN Convention on the Law of the Sea, the 1989 UN Convention on the Rights of the Child, and the 1992 UN Conventions on Biodiversity and Climate Change. Also, general multilateral treaties can create the organizational machinery through which new international law can be developed. For example, specialized agencies of the United Nations, such as the World Health Organization, International Civil Aviation Organization, Universal Postal Union, and International Telecommunication Union—all of which were created by specific international treaties—have themselves become sources of rules and regulations throughout the international community. Thus international organizations that were created by international law contribute to the growth of additional law through the purpose of their functional operation.[8]

The second major source of international law is custom. In the 18th and 19th centuries, when interaction among states was relatively sporadic and less complex than today, certain habitual patterns of behavior often emerged to form obligatory rules. That is, through widespread adherence and repeated use, certain customary practices by governments became accepted as law, with normatively binding constraints.[9] Prominent among laws evolving from customary state practice were those pertaining to the law of the sea, in particular those regulations establishing the three-mile territorial limit, the definition of piracy, and proper division of the spoils of war. Today, however, due to the increasing interdependence and complexity of modern international relations coupled with the spread of the traditional Eurocentric legal system beyond the borders of the Western world, custom as a body of unwritten though clearly recognized norms seems to be diminishing as a source of international law. Much of customary international law developed

---

[7]T. O. Elias, *The Modern Law of Treaties* (Leiden: Sijhoff, 1974); I. M. Sinclair, *The Vienna Convention on the Law of Treaties,* 2nd ed. (Dobbs Ferry, N.Y.: Oceana, 1984); Shabati Rosenne, *The Law of Treaties: A Guide to the Legislative History of the Vienna Convention* (Dobbs Ferry, N.Y.: Oceana, 1971); and Paul Reuter, *Introduction to the Law of Treaties* (New York: Columbia University Press, 1989).

[8]See generally Oscar Schachter and Christopher C. Joyner, eds., *United Nations Legal Order* (Cambridge: Cambridge University Press, 1995) and Rosalyn Higgins, *The Development of International Law through the Political Organs of the United Nations* (London: Oxford University Press, 1963). Significantly, however, resolutions adopted by the United Nations General Assembly are deemed only to be recommendations and are not lawfully binding upon the membership. See Christopher C. Joyner, "The U.N. General Assembly Resolutions and International Law: Rethinking the Contemporary Dynamics of Norm-Creation," *California Western International Law Journal* 11, no. 3 (Summer 1981), pp. 445–78.

[9]See Anthony A. D'Amato, *The Concept of Custom in International Law* (Ithaca, N.Y.: Cornell University Press, 1971); and H. W. A. Thirlway, *International Customary Law and Codification* (Leiden: Sijhoff, 1972).

in the era of 19th century colonialism. Largely for this reason, it is now viewed with suspicion or held in disrepute by many of the newly independent states in the Third World. Another critical weakness of custom as a contemporary source of law is couched in the traditional requirement that customary law must grow into acceptance slowly, through a gradual, evolutionary process over many decades, perhaps even hundreds of years. This requisite for gradual evolution and slow acceptance of an emergent customary norm leaves that rule vulnerable to becoming archaic or anachronistic even before it can become accepted as law. This likelihood undoubtedly is at work today as rapid advances in technology play havoc with traditional legal parameters and jurisdictional designs—a reality that makes imperative the constant need for international law to keep pace with technological developments.

The third primary source of international law is the general principles of law recognized by civilized nations.[10] Often general principles are associated with the Roman notion of *jus gentium,* the law of peoples. These principles of law, derived largely from municipal experience, hold relevant legal connotations for the international realm; consequently, they have been assimilated into the corpus of international law. General principles of law—which include notions such as "equity" (justice by right), "comity" (voluntary courtesy), and *pacta sunt servanda* ("pacts made in good faith are binding," the underpinning precept for treaty agreement)—serve as sources by analogy for the creation and perfection of international legal norms. Yet general principles of international law are encumbered by the difficulty of being framed as sources of law in terms of morality and justice. "Morality" and "justice" remain highly subjective concepts, susceptible to disparate interpretations; thus, in their application, general principles may be vulnerable to vagaries perceived in the situation or the particular context in which they are set.

The final source of modern international law is twofold and deemed to be secondary and indirect as compared to treaties, custom, and general principles. This source, first, encompasses judicial decisions of courts—both national and international—and, second, teachings and writings of the most qualified jurists and publicists. Two important points merit mention here. The first is that for international law, court decisions are principally employed as guidelines; they cannot set precedents. There is no *stare decisis in* the law of nations; accordingly, a decision by any court or tribunal, inclusive of the International Court of Justice, cannot be held as binding authority for subsequent judicial decisions. The second point is that while writings by scholars and jurists supply a rich seedbed for

---

[10]See generally Wolfgang Friedmann, "The Uses of 'General Principles' in the Development of International Law," *American Journal of International Law* 57 (April 1963), pp. 279–299; Arnold McNair, "The General Principles of Law Recognized by Civilized Nations," *British Yearbook of International Law* 33 (1957), pp. 1–19; and Georg Schwarzenberger, *The Dynamics of International Law* (South Hackensack, N.J.: Rothman, 1976).

opinions on the law, they too carry no binding legal authority. Text writers by themselves cannot create or codify international law; however, their importance as sources of the law may become amplified to the extent that governments may adopt suggestions and interpretations in the application of international law to foreign policy.[11]

International law is broad in scope and far-reaching in content; for convenience, it may be divided into laws of peace and laws of war. Under the realm of peace, international law provides norms for stipulating its subjects and sets out the process of recognition for states and governments: the rights and duties of states, how title to territory is acquired, how national boundaries are determined, and various regulations for use of ocean, air, and outer space. Also in this respect is the international law pertinent to individuals. It not only encompasses rules affecting nationality, diplomatic agents, resident aliens, and extradition but also more recent norms pertaining to international criminal law, refugees, and the protection of human rights. Within the ambit of laws relating to war, much ground is likewise covered. Included here are those laws and procedures promoting peaceful settlement of disputes; techniques available for self-help short of war; the legal nature of and requirements for belligerency; the laws of armed conflict on land, on sea, and in the air; conditions for neutrality; and the treatment and definition of war crimes.[12] Important to remember here is that these international legal considerations have been integrated into states' national laws, usually by treaty but also through specific legislation, judicial decisions, or executive fiat. This realization, however, should not imply that international law is thus rendered subservient to domestic laws. It is not, either in theory or in factual application.[13]

Though made up of a wide-ranging body of norms, international law has no specific codes or statutes. The closest approximations to municipal legal codes are called digests in international law. These digests, each of which usually entails a series of several volumes, are compendia containing selections from court decisions, international treaties, foreign policy statements, government memoranda, juridical opinions, scholarly publications, and other like materials that

---

[11]See, e.g., *Restatement (Third) of the Foreign Relations Law of the United States* (St. Paul, Minn.: American Law Institute Publications, 1987).

[12]The texts on international law are manifold. For representative samples, see Barry E. Carter and Phillip R. Trimble, *International Law* (Little, Brown & Co., 1991); Mark Janis, *An Introduction to International Law,* 2nd ed. (Boston, Little, Brown & Co., 1993); Louis Henkin, Richard C. Pugh, Oscar Schachter and Hans Smit, *International Law: Cases and Materials,* 3rd ed. (St. Paul, West Publishing, 1993); Covey T. Oliver, Edwin Firmage, Christopher L. Blakesley, Richard F. Scott and Sharon A. Williams, eds., *the International Legal System,* 4th ed. (Westbury, NY: Foundation Press, 1995); and Gerhard von Glahn, *Law Among Nations: An Introduction to Public International Law,* 7th ed. (New York: Allyn & Bacon, 1996). The classic modern treatise on international law is Robert Jennings and Arthur Watts, eds., *Oppenheim's International Law,* 9th ed. (London: Longmans, 1992).

[13]At least one prominent scholar of international law has cogently argued to the contrary, namely that the law of nations in fact represents a higher order than domestic or national law. See Hans Kelsen, *Principles of International Law,* 2nd ed. (New York: Holt, Rinehart & Winston, 1966).

furnish detailed views on international legal matters. While held as important comments on the law, digests are not regarded in and of themselves to be definitively authoritative or legally binding in their contents.[14]

Notwithstanding doubts and skepticism, then, the unmistakable fact remains that international law has definite sources and exists as a body, a reality that mirrors the fundamental conviction by states that such law is necessary. The law of nations has evolved over nearly four centuries into a body of treaty-based and customary rules, undergirded by general principles of law and explicated through judicial decisions as well as in the writings of prominent jurists and publicists. Intimately connected to this are the attendant realizations that an obligatory basis exists for international law and that, in substantial measure, the law is obeyed.

BASIS OF OBLIGATION IN INTERNATIONAL LAW

Perhaps the archfiction of international law is the notion of absolute sovereignty. Such sovereignty embodies the idea of totality and completeness; as a legal creation, sovereignty consequently becomes a paradox, if not an impossibility, when placed into the interdependent complexities of the modern state system. More significantly, unlimited sovereignty has become unacceptable today as the preeminent attribute of states, a fact which national governments have increasingly recognized as more and more of their sovereignty has been relinquished to international commitments. For example, traditionally in international law, absolute, unfettered sovereignty allowed for states to exercise free national will in deciding whether or not to resort to war. Given the incredible power of military capability today, the costs of this license could literally lead to destruction of the entire international community; as a consequence, through international legal instruments promoting arms control and national restraint, such sovereignty has been diminished by states themselves for the sake of international security. Recent examples clearly demonstrating this trend include the 1991 and 1993 Strategic Arms Reduction Talks Treaties (START I and II) between the United States and former Soviet Republics, the 1993 Convention on the Prohibition of Chemical Weapons, the renewal in 1995 of the Nuclear Nonproliferation Treaty, and agreement in 1996 on a Comprehensive Test Ban Treaty.

The above observations prompt the obvious question concerning why states should obey international law. That is, what is the obligatory basis upon which

---

[14]For examples, see the following: Green H. Hackworth, *Digest of International Law,* 8 vols. (Washington, D.C.: U.S. Government Printing Office, 1940–1944); John Bassett Moore, *A Digest of International Law,* 8 vols. (Washington, D.C.: U.S. Government Printing Office, 1906); and Marjorie M. Whiteman, *Digest of International Law,* 15 vols. (Washington, D.C.: U.S. Government Printing Office, 1963–1973).

the rule of law is founded in contemporary world affairs? The answer is plain and undeniable: It is in the states' fundamental interest to do so. States are the lawgivers in the international community. Agreement upon a legal norm and the effectiveness of its application clearly rest in how it affects each state's own national interests. Consent therefore remains the keystone to international law's efficacy because it appeases the desire of states to maintain their relative freedom of action in the name of national sovereignty. In short, states obey international law because they agree to do so. But why should they? Several plausible reasons may be proffered: National governments recognize the utility of the law; they prefer some degree of order and expectation over unpredictable anarchy; obedience is less costly than disobedience; a certain sense of justice may motivate their willingness to obey; or, habit and customary practice in international dealings over many years have operated to promote obedience.

More significant than any of these explanations, however, is the recognition that reciprocity contributes to the efficacy of international law and, correspondingly, to more regularized patterns of behavior in the international system. Put simply, states accept and obey international law because governments find it in their national interest to do so. It serves a state's national interest to accept international legal norms if other states also accept these norms, and this reciprocal process can give rise to predictive patterns of interstate conduct in international relations. States, like individual persons, have discovered that consent to be bound by and obligated to certain rules can serve to facilitate, promote, and enhance their welfare and opportunities in the society. Contemporary international law consequently has come to embody a consensus of common interests—a consensus that plainly indicates that international law works efficiently and most often when it is in the national interest of states to make it work.[15]

ENFORCEMENT OF INTERNATIONAL LAW

The third critical consideration in determining the effectiveness of international law—the quality of its enforcement—is still left hanging: What happens when states fail to obey the law, when they violate the agreed-upon norms? How is the law to be enforced or, put differently, how are violators of international law to be punished? International law does supply means for both sanction and enforcement, although, to be sure, these means are primitive in comparison to municipal procedures. Despite development over the past 70 years of relatively sophisticated, universalistic, sanctions-equipped international organizations—namely,

---

[15]See generally Thomas M. Franck, *The Power of Legitimacy Among Nations* (Oxford: Oxford University Press, 1991); Oscar Schachter, *International Law in Theory and Practice* (Martinus Nijhoff, 1991); and Rosalyn Higgins, *Problems and Process: International Law and How We Use It* (Oxford: Clarendon Press, 1994).

the League of Nations[16] and the United Nations[17]—the world community still relies primarily upon the principle of self-help to enforce international legal sanctions.

The principle of self-help permits sanctions to be applied by one party in reaction to perceived illegal conduct committed by another party. Self-help has emerged as the major means for effecting sanctions in the international community.[18] Not only must states perceive when their rights have been violated; they must also confront the state that allegedly has committed that illegal act and must compel the state to make restitution for its wrongdoing. Techniques for applying self-help range from diplomatic protest to economic boycott to embargo to war. Consequently, in international law, states literally *must* take the law into their own hands to protect their legal rights and to get the law enforced. It is not surprising, then, that international law is often characterized as being primitive.

In assessing the sanctions process in international law, it is fair to conclude that as international disputes become more serious and are viewed by governments as placing national prestige or survival increasingly at risk, the principle of limited self-help as a sanctioning process is likely to make the legal system correspondingly less effective. Absent a centralized agency for approving and supervising the sanctioning action, self-help may be rendered subject to prevalent conditions in the environment. In sum, self-help's prominent role in international law places a major limitation upon that legal system's effectiveness. As revealed in the international legal order, resort to self-help for law enforcement represents a necessary but limiting compromise between a sanctioning process required by international law and the desires by states to retain their independence, that is, their sovereignty. Self-help thus highlights the observation that international law is a relatively weak, decentralized, and primitive legal system. The fact remains, however, that international law still enjoys the status of being a legal system—one that works effectively nearly all the time and for nearly all situations when its participant member states want it to do so.

---

[16]The League of Nations Covenant, which was incorporated as Part I of the Treaty of Versailles (1919), contained in Article 16 sanction provisions that would subject a member "who committed an act of war" against another member to "the severance of all trade or financial relations, the prohibition of all intercourse between their nationals and the nationals of the Covenant-breaking State, and the prevention of all financial, commercial or personal intercourse between the nationals of the Covenant-breaking State and the nationals of any other State, whether members of the League or not."

[17]After determining "the existence of any threat to the peace, breach of the peace or act of aggression" as authorized in Article 39 of the United Nations Charter, the Security Council is empowered under Article 42 to "take such action by air, sea, or land forces as may be necessary to maintain or restore international peace and security. Such action may include demonstrations, blockade, and other operations by air, sea, or land forces of Members of the United Nations."

[18]Even so, specific legal limitations have been set on the use of force, that is, the degree and kind of "self-help" exercised. See, for example, Anthony C. Arend and Robert J. Beck, *International Law and the Use of Force* (New York: Routledge, 1993); Charles W. Kegley, Jr. and Gregory A. Raymond, *A Multipolar Peace? Great-Power Politics in the Twenty-First Century* (New York: St. Martin's Press, 1994); and Louis Henkin, Stanley Hoffmann, Jeane J. Kirkpatrick and Allan Gerson, William D. Rogers, David J. Scheffer, *Might v. Right: International Law and the Use of Force* 2nd. ed. (New York: Council on Foreign Relations, 1991); and *Ethics & International Affairs* 10 (1996).

On balance, the performance of international law is hampered by disabilities within those very elements that generally contribute to the effectiveness of legal systems. First, there is a lack of international institutions for clarifying and communicating legal norms; that is, modern international law is still characterized by an imperfect process of norm creation. Second, there is no central, generally recognized belief system to serve as an obligatory authority for international law. The obligatory basis for international law lies with the states themselves. Third, and perhaps most debilitating, international law is without an efficient, corporate process for perceiving and punishing illegal behavior in the world community. Resort by states to self-help remains the principal means for sanctioning international wrongdoing.

Yet, what appears really faulty with international law does not stem from these weaknesses in the international legal process. Rather, it derives from the decentralized international community that the law is attempting to regulate. In short, that the operation of contemporary international law may be less than wholly effective can be attributed mainly to the condition that there does not presently exist sufficient international consensus among states to demand that the law be made more effective in its application.

All this should not be inferred to mean that international law is either surrealistic or irrelevant in the contemporary world. It certainly is neither. To rush to the conclusion that international law's frailties leave it with little real function in international relations today would be not only superficial but also shortsighted. It would overlook the hundreds of decisions made by national and international tribunals aimed at settling claims and setting arbitration awards. It ignores the thousands of international law cases affecting contractual relations between corporations and governments. It fails to account for the constant, pervasive process of international intercourse that goes on involving states, organizations, and individual persons. In a modern age of satellite telecommunications, worldwide transportation, and interdependent global commerce, international law has become indispensable. Setting frequencies for telecommunication broadcasts, flight routes for aircraft, conditions for international postage and media communication, monetary exchange rates, navigation transit by ocean vessels carrying goods in trade—all these activities and myriad others are made possible only through the channels afforded by international legal agreement, that is, through international law. International law codifies ongoing solutions for persistent international problems. The law of nations has become in effect the lubricant that permits transnational commerce, communication, transportation, and travel to operate smoothly and on course in the global community.[19]

---

[19]Importantly in this regard, the United Nations since 1945 has generated a tremendous volume of international law to meet new global needs and facilitate international intercourse. See Christopher C. Joyner, "Conclusion: The United Nations as International Law-Giver," in Christopher C. Joyner, ed., *The United Nations and International Law* (Cambridge: Cambridge University Press, 1997), pp. 432–56.

CONCLUSION

Law prescribes the conduct of a society's members and makes coexistence and the survival of that society possible. Not surprisingly, then, the law of nations is pervasive and fundamental. It not only seeks to regulate or lessen possibilities for conflict but also works to promote international exchange and cooperation on a broad, multifaceted scale. International law is man-made; governments of states in the international society can in large part determine the nature of that society and formulate laws to meet those ends. Hence, the ingredients of international law are neither preordained nor immutable.

International law is law. It is not some form of diplomatic maneuvering or rhetorical camouflage. International law has form and substance: there exists a clearly identifiable corpus of rules and regulations that have been generally accepted by states in their dealings with one another. International law has specific sources from which legal norms can be derived, and self-imposed sanctions are available to states to punish illegal behavior. Yet international law should not be construed as being pure law; in other words, it is not apolitical, nor is it wholly comprised of normativism or legalism. International law cannot be so because the very components of that legal system—states—are highly politicized actors in their own right.[20]

International law is crafted not accidentally or capriciously but carefully and intentionally by the states themselves. The law of nations is a product of the times and of the national governments that operate in the international milieu. It can change, adapt, and evolve. International law is not static; it is a dynamic and evolutionary process that is shaped by events and influences events. Contemporary international law reflects the nature of the changing world because it must be responsive to that evolving reality. Flexibility therefore remains one of international law's chief strengths. Even so, ironically, it is sometimes blamed for fostering one of the law's greatest weaknesses: namely, the lack of a centralized, formal structure for codifying international norms, an omission that invites distortions in legal interpretation as well as self-serving policy positions.

International law must not be regarded as a panacea for prohibiting unlawful international conduct or as a brake on incorrigible governments. It does, however, provide internationally acceptable ways and means of dealing with these situations. Modern international law may not satisfy all national governments all of the time, nor can it supply every answer for all the international community's ills. Nevertheless, it remains far preferable to the alternative of no law at all and, similarly, it is far wiser for national governments to appreciate the existence and function of this international legal system than to overlook the mutual

---

[20]On this theme, see Francis Anthony Boyle, *World Politics and International Law* (Durham: Duke University Press, 1985) and Anne-Marie Slaughter Burley, "International Law and International Relations Theory: A Dual Agenda," *American Journal of International Law* 87 (April 1993), pp. 205–239.

advantages it affords. International law remains the best touchstone and only consistent guide for state conduct in a complex, multicultural world.[21]

On the eve of the 21st century, grave global problems have emerged as foci for serious international concern. The Third World development crisis, the disintegration of states through ethnoseparatism, forced migrations and millions of displaced refugees, transnational terrorism, overpopulation, air and water transboundary pollution, global warming, AIDS, depletion of the ozone layer, drug trafficking, proliferation of weapons of mass destruction—none of these issues are amenable to domestic or unilateral resolution. If politically viable solutions are to be reached, international cooperation is essential. The law of nations supplies proven ways and means to facilitate these collaborative international efforts. Indeed, in the search for global solutions to global problems, international law supplies the best opportunities for accommodating national interests with international priorities.

In the final analysis, international law does not fail in contemporary world society. Instead, it is the states themselves that fail the law whenever they choose not to adhere to its basic norms. Thus the need to surmount this fundamental obstacle of self-serving, sovereign-state interests must remain as the preeminent challenge on international law's global agenda in the next century. To be sure, given the profound lessons of state conduct in the past, it will not be an easy task.

[21]For discussion on this point, see Christopher C. Joyner and John C. Dettling, "Bridging the Cultural Chasm: Cultural Relativism and the Future of International Law," *California Western International Law Journal* 20, no. 2 (1989–1990), pp. 275–314.

PART THREE

POLITICS AND MARKETS

Today's global agenda embraces a broad array of international economic issues, ranging from trade protectionism and monetary stability to balance-of-payments adjustments and debt repayments. These have been matched by comparable issues on the domestic agendas of many states as they struggle with economic stagnation, unemployment, budget deficits, and productivity declines. The two sets of issues are not unrelated. Under conditions of global interdependence, defined as a state of *mutual sensitivity* and *mutual vulnerability,* decisions made in one state often have important implications and consequences for other states. Efforts to control inflation in one country, for example, can affect the value of others' currencies and hence influence the direction of their international trade and capital flows. This in turn may affect still other states' trade and payments balances, which chart their imports, exports, and other financial transactions with the rest of the world. Changes in states' economic fortunes often also affect their imperviousness or vulnerability to external political influences. Thus politics—the exercise of power and influence—and economics—the distribution of material wealth—are often tightly interconnected.

The term "political economy" highlights the intersection of politics and economics, which has had a long heritage of importance in world politics. A combination of political and economic considerations gave rise to the state system more than three centuries ago and has helped to shape patterns of dominance and dependence ever since. Today the term highlights the extensive interdependent relationships between states that knit national and global welfare into a single tapestry. Political economy thus comprises an analytical perspective that accommodates the complex realities of the contemporary global system.

By blurring the distinctions between foreign and domestic policy and between political power and economic well-being, the political economy of interdependence raises important questions about the problems that have long dominated world politics. Traditionally, issues relating to economics and other welfare matters were regarded as matters of *low politics*. While the *high politics* of peace and security issues engaged the attention of states' policy-making elites, the low politics of more routinized international economic affairs could be left in the hands of lower-level bureaucrats.

The distinction between high and low politics has always been overdrawn, perhaps, but the complexity and urgency of political economy issues are now more apparent than ever. Today, as controversies over the distribution of wealth and the processes and institutions that govern it affect everyone, transnational economic issues—fueled by the expansion of world trade since World War II and the globalization of production and finance—are among the most important political issues on the global agenda and often command the utmost attention of policy-making elites. Indeed, in the wake of the Cold War it has become commonplace to argue that geoeconomics now rivals geopolitics as the motive force behind states' struggle for preeminence in the world political system. Competition for market share, not political-military allies, now animates relations among nations. And commercial advantage, not military might, often determines who exercises influence over whom and who feels threatened and who secure.

As this brief overview suggests, insights from political economy are necessary to answer the classic questions of politics: Who gets what, when, and how? Robert Gilpin points us in the direction of important answers in the first essay in Part Three. He summarizes and critically analyzes "Three Ideologies of Political Economy": the liberal, nationalist (sometimes called mercantilist), and Marxist paradigms. The three are regarded as ideologies because they purport "to provide scientific descriptions of how the world *does* work while they also constitute normative positions regarding how the world *should* work." Their importance derives from their impact on both scholarship and national and international affairs for centuries.

The differences among the three ideologies turn on their "conceptions of the relationships among society, state, and market." Liberalism directs attention to "the market and the price mechanism as the most efficacious means for organizing domestic and international economic relations." Thus economics and politics should be completely separated into distinct spheres. This viewpoint has long dominated policy thinking throughout the Global North, that is, the industrial world in which democratic capitalism is the preferred form of domestic political economy. It also was the guiding principle underlying the international economic system created after World War II under U.S. hegemony (leadership), whose interests liberalism served.

Unlike liberalism, the central idea in the nationalist (mercantilist) ideology "is that economic activities are and should be subordinate to the goal of state building and the interests of the state. All nationalists ascribe to the primacy of the state, of national security, and of military power in the organization and functioning of the international system." Because they see interdependence as a source of conflict and insecurity, economic nationalists are concerned not only with *absolute gains* in their material well-being but also with how they fare in comparison with others, their *relative gains.* Thus economic nationalism as an ideology of political economy bears a striking resemblance to the doctrine of political realism as applied to international politics.

The 1990s have witnessed a surge of privatization and other efforts to unleash market forces throughout the world, as democratic capitalism is now the preferred pattern of domestic political economy nearly everywhere. Moreover, the liberal principle of nondiscrimination and free trade continues to dominate thinking internationally. Still, economic nationalism is a potent force in the world. It underlies much of the protectionist sentiment toward trade issues rife throughout the Global North and South (the developing countries). It also rationalizes the appeal of *strategic trade theory,* a form of industrial policy that seeks to create comparative advantages by targeting government subsidies toward particular industries. Gilpin notes that whatever its shortcomings, "economic nationalism is likely to be a significant influence in international relations as long as the state system exists."

The appeal of Marxism, on the other hand, is much diminished. Marxism-Leninism has been repudiated in the former Soviet Union and throughout eastern Europe and is on the wane in Cuba and Vietnam. Although Marxism-Leninism (communism) remains the official ideology in China, even here the forces of liberalism are evident as Chinese leaders not only accept but actively encourage the development of private enterprise. Nonetheless, in the history of ideas that have animated world politics during the past two centuries Marxism and Marxism-Leninism still command attention.

Like economic nationalism, Marxism places economic issues at the center of political life. But whereas nationalists are concerned primarily with the international distribution of wealth, Marxism focuses on both the domestic and international forces that affect the distribution of wealth. The ideology also focuses on international political change. "Whereas neither liberalism nor nationalism has a comprehensive theory of social change," Gilpin observes, "Marxism emphasizes the role of economic and technological developments in explaining the dynamics of the international system."

Lenin's reformulation of Marxist doctrine in his famous treatise *Imperialism* focuses particular attention on the role that differential rates of growth in power play in promoting international conflict and political change. For Marx, class struggle over the distribution of wealth was the central force of political change. For Lenin, international political relations among capitalist states was more important. He argued that "intensification of economic and political competition between declining and rising capitalist powers leads to economic conflict, imperial rivalries, and eventually war. He asserted that this had been the fate of the British-centered liberal world economy of the 19th century." Gilpin conjectures that "today [Lenin] would undoubtedly argue that . . . a similar fate threatens the 20th-century liberal world economy, centered on the United States."

Gilpin assesses the strengths and limitations of the three political economy perspectives. Because of the ideological character of each it is impossible to determine which one is "right." Nonetheless, all continue to make important contributions to political economy theory and practice. Liberalism and nationalism/ mercantilism in particular compete for the attention of policy makers and analysts today, as many of the remaining essays in Part Three of *The Global Agenda* demonstrate.

As noted, the liberal vision guided policy makers during and after World War II as they sought to create trade and monetary systems that would avoid repetition of the economic collapse of the 1930s, to which aggressive economic nationalism was believed to have contributed measurably. The tremendous growth in international trade since the 1940s, which has fueled an unprecedented expansion of global welfare, is a measure of the success of liberalism. Now, however, the globalization of the world political economy through trade and transnational investment is threatening the political autonomy and decision-making authority of the world's preeminent capitalist centers, the United States, Japan, and the European Union. Ironically, therefore, liberalism is now encouraging mercantilism.

The tension between liberalism and mercantilism is the focus of Erik R. Peterson's chapter, "Looming Collision of Capitalisms?" Peterson argues that "accelerating global economic competition is bringing national economic policies into sharper competition." As manifest in the temptation to pursue "defensive strategies by supporting national 'strategic' industries," he worries that the major capitalist centers will increasingly "succumb to the . . . tendency to 'pursue relative gains at the expense of mutual gains [and] political power at the expense of economic welfare.' "

The continuing growth of world trade and capital flows is among the forces leading to the acceleration of global economic integration. As Peterson notes, there are many others: "Advances in communication and information technologies, the pursuit by multinational enterprises (MNEs) of complex cross-border strategies, the formation and development of regional trading blocs, the GATT [General Agreement on Tariffs and Trade] (now the World Trade Organization [WTO]) process, economic liberalization undertaken in a host of developing economies, and ongoing efforts at marketization in former command economies are metamorphosing the international economic and financial system."

The description is nothing less than a menu of the forces propelling a dramatic restructuring of the world political economy. Given these developments, states increasingly find that existing international institutions are insufficiently able to cope with the challenges they now face, as the "integration of politics is lagging behind [the] integration of markets." In response, the principal economic powers in particular are "more and more . . . finding the answer in drawing lines beyond which they will resort to defense strategies grounded in parochial interests. The result is the development of political conditions that encourage the outbreak of economic nationalism."

Peter F. Drucker also surveys recent developments in the world political economy in "Trade Lessons from the World Economy." He argues that an increasing proportion of international trade occurs not in traditional items of merchandise—washing machines, shoes, and the like—but in services—stocks and insurance, for example. Furthermore, multinational business practices such as "transfer pricing" and the use of "alliances" ("joint ventures, partnerships, knowledge agreements, and out-sourcing arrangements") are becoming more ubiquitous. In both cases there is little difference between foreign and domestic partners.

The erosion of the distinction between the international economy and national economies described by Drucker carries with it important policy implications. Drucker finds little in the historical record to suggest that policy makers are able to steer their economies effectively through the boom and bust of typical business cycles. He is also critical of the kinds of strategic trade strategies that Peterson sees increasingly likely in the years ahead. Instead—and in the tradition of economic liberalism as well as on the basis of some states' experience—Drucker urges policy makers to give priority to the international over the domestic economy: "Managed trade is a delusion of grandeur. Outright protectionism can only do harm. . . . What is needed is a deliberate and active—indeed, aggressive—policy that gives the demands, opportunities, and dynamics of the external environment priority over domestic policy demands and priorities."

Eugene R. Wittkopf and Charles W. Kegley, Jr., the editors of *The Global Agenda,* further develop the themes underlying the transformation of the world political economy by focusing on the economic dimensions of the rapid globalization now engulfing the world. In "Vanishing Borders: The Globalization of Politics and Markets," they explain that "globalization" refers to "the intensification of economic, political, social, and cultural relations across [state] borders." Symbolized by the Internet and fueled by the revolution in computers and telecommunications, its most visible manifestations are found in the global reach of Coca-Cola and McDonald's, of shopping centers that look the same whether they are in London or Hong Kong, Chicago or Rio de Janeiro, of rock music and designer jeans that know no political boundaries, contributing to the development of a global culture in which national identities are often submerged. In the process, the state system itself is being challenged.

Wittkopf and Kegley describe how the globalization of finance and production act as the primary engines of economic globalization and the challenge it poses. Although international trade flows have grown dramatically in recent decades, financial globalization has accelerated even more. Furthermore, existing trade patterns are themselves undergoing rapid changes. Increasingly those who benefit from international trade—which includes many states that have given priority to the international economy over their domestic economies—engage in the production of high-technology electronic goods. Those who remain wedded, by necessity or design, to commodity exports, which includes many African states, find themselves losers in the globalization process.

Multinational corporations (MNCs) are the principal engines underlying the globalization of production. Long shunned by many states in the Global South, their investments are now actively encouraged, as foreign direct investment is accompanied by technology, managerial expertise, and employment opportunities. However, as the centers of global production shift, labor, which is less mobile than capital, may suffer. Workers in the Global North in particular believe they have been victimized by the "export" of jobs to the lower-wage Global South that has accompanied the globalization of production. Thus globalization challenges the sanctity of states' borders, but it also invites nationalist economic responses to the forces sweeping the world.

One response popular in Europe and the United States is the drive to increase "competitiveness" in the global marketplace. Often this encourages resort to the neomercantilist practices of economic nationalism, including the strategic trade practices that worry Peterson. In our next selection, "Competitiveness: A Dangerous Obsession," the prominent trade theorist Paul Krugman challenges policy makers' concern with competitiveness, calling it an unwarranted "obsession."

Krugman is a vocal critic of the proposition that income growth in the United States has lagged because of many U.S. firms' inability to sell in world markets. He supports his arguments with evidence that a decline in domestic productivity explains almost all of the decline in U.S. living standards between 1973 and 1990. The same is true in Europe and Japan: "In each case, the growth rate of living standards essentially equals the growth rate of domestic productivity—not productivity relative to competitors, but simply domestic productivity." Thus, even as world trade grows, "as a practical, empirical matter the major nations of the world are not to any significant degree in economic competition with each other. Of course, there is already rivalry for status and power—countries that grow faster will see their political rank rise. So it is always interesting to *compare* countries. But asserting that Japanese growth diminishes U.S. status is very different from saying that it reduces the U.S. standard of living—and it is the latter that the rhetoric of competitiveness asserts."

China has enjoyed spectacular economic growth in recent years. Indeed, it is commonplace to argue that China will likely emerge as the world's largest economy early in the next century. Its standard of living, as measured by per capita income, will continue to remain low, of course, due to its enormous population. Still, China's political rank is clearly on the rise as its economic productivity increases and its share of world export markets expands.

How to integrate China's rapidly growing political economy into the Liberal International Economic Order (LIEO) created and maintained after World War II by the United States and the other major industrial powers has become a difficult and contentious political issue. The World Trade Organization (WTO), the successor to GATT, the General Agreements on Tariffs and Trade first negotiated in the late 1940s, is the major international institution charged with protecting the principle of nondiscrimination and free trade central to the LIEO. China had hoped to become a charter member of the WTO when it opened shop in 1995, but the United States thwarted that ambition and continues to insist that China make substantial domestic reforms designed to ensure its ability to comply with WTO rules and standards. The wisdom of the U.S. position is challenged by Robert S. Ross and defended by Greg Mastel in our next two selections.

In "Enter the Dragon: China in the World Political Eocnomy," Ross argues that bringing China into the WTO fold offers the best chance to avert a repetition of the unfair trade practices Japan commonly engaged in after World War II. He recognizes that China's current practices, often carried out by state-owned enterprises rather than private entrepreneurs, "are at wide variance with the WTO obligations assumed by the world's major trading powers." Widespread corruption and the failure of the Chinese government to protect the rights of foreign businesses also are endemic problems. Still, Ross believes that ensuring China's compliance with international community standards is more likely if China is brought into the WTO now, before it achieves the economic clout that will permit it to defy external pressures. "Whether China today meets WTO standards is less important than adopting policies to promote the development of a Chinese economy compatible with the WTO. Practical pursuit of interest, rather than rigid adherence to principle, will best serve U.S. [and other industrial countries'] interest."

Mastel disagrees with Ross, as he explains in "Counterpoint: Keeping Beijing at Bay." Worrying that a Cold War mentality that places security and political concerns above economics motivates many advocates of China's early entry into the WTO, Mastel counters that "this viewpoint is dated and out of touch with current realities. China is an important player in the global economy. It is already one of the world's top 10 exporters and is expected to be the world's largest economy early in the next century. As a result, economic and trade issues with China are at least as important as security and political issues."

Against this backdrop, Mastel argues that several factors militate against China's admission to the WTO club: its current restrictive trade practices, the absence of a reliable rule of law, and a persistent totalitarian government. Mastel concludes that "The Chinese government's influence over its economy may be so pervasive that the WTO trading rules will prove inadequate to create a 'level playing field.' Simply put, China retains too many features of the communist system to be easily married with the WTO."

China's ability to resist demands that its economic practices conform with those of the rest of the international community stands in sharp contrast with the experience of many other Global South countries. For them, there is a dark side to globalization that too often smacks of their colonial past. Indeed, Martin Khor argues in "Colonialism Redux: The Dark Side of Globalization" that "colonialism is making a comeback." While military power in the past ensured the economic domination of poor countries by the rich, "little-noticed revisions of global trade rules . . . are today's weapons for restoring some of the economic underpinnings of colonialsm." Particularly important are rule revisions encouraging foreign direct investment by multinationals that also have the effect of undermining the ability of local companies to compete with foreign ones. Khor also blames MNCs (and the Global North generally) for other practices that drain resources from the South, often exacting heavy environmental tolls in the process. Free trade rules promoted by the WTO and its chief supporters may rationalize these practices, but, Khor warns, "under free trade the weaker nations will continue to suffer. . . . [Free trade] may be good among equal partners, but in today's global economy some countries are more equal than others."

The sometimes-positive, sometimes-untoward effects of MNCs on Global South economies cause us to wonder about the best path to development that will ensure a rising standard of living and quality of life for the world's burgeoning billions, many of whom continue to live in squalor and abject poverty. The newly industrializing economies (NIEs)—most notably Hong Kong, Singapore, South Korea, and Taiwan, and now Malaysia and Thailand—have enjoyed an unusual degree of economic growth in recent decades by pursuing a neomercantilist, export-led path to economic development that is the envy of others. But how many can emulate their success? Indeed, does economic growth ensure not only economic but also human development?

For several years the United Nations Development Programme (UNDP) has published its now authoritative *Human Development Report* designed to assess humanity's progress toward a better life across a spectrum of economic and social dimensions. Its *human development index (HDI)* seeks to measure societies' ability to improve the well-being of their own citizens. The concept is based on the belief that the real purpose of development "should be to enlarge people's choices." Economic growth is not the only component of human development, but it is critical. As the UNDP has repeatedly stated, "Growth is not the end of development, but the absence of growth often is."

The UNDP concludes that the record of human development leaves much to be desired. As described in our next selection from the *Human Development*

Report 1996, "Growth for Human Development," the economic gap between the world's rich and poor nations continues to widen, as "growth has been failing over much of the past 15 years in about 100 countries, with almost a third of the world's people." The report adds that "the links between growth and human development are failing [even] for people in many countries with lopsided development—with either good growth but little human development or good human development but little or no growth." The Global North is not immune from these processes, as "jobless growth" has often accompanied renewed economic activity since the recession years of the early 1990s.

The UNDP report cites a host of pluses and minuses experienced during recent years. It also turns our attention again to the opportunities globalization has provided many Global South countries, noting, however, that "While globalization has often helped growth in the strong countries, it has bypassed the weak." Its policy agenda includes "a major international priority . . . to move all countries to at least medium levels of human development in the next 10 years, laying a human foundation for accelerating growth, reducing poverty, and achieving more equitable development in the 21st century."

Even as globalization sweeps the world, another principal change in the world economy to which many analysts allude is its growing regionalization. Today the three "economic superpowers"—the United States, Japan, and the European Union—are the principal nodes around which global economic activities revolve. Some (most?) analysts regard this development with alarm, seeing it as a threat to global liberalism, a possible precursor to geoeconomic conflict and, perhaps, to geopolitical conflict. In our final selection in Part Three, "Mercantilism and Global Security," by Michael Borrus, Steve Weber, and John Zysman, with Joseph Willihnganz, the authors are concerned with the security implications of regionalism and the kinds of international security systems that are likely to be associated with alternative configurations of economic power.

Borrus, Weber, Zysman, and Willihnganz begin with the (admittedly controversial) premise that a relative decline of American power during recent decades sets the stage for new patterns of political economy. "For the moment, the United States still leads," they argue, "but more by default than from strength. . . . Its technological and economic position is declining relative to the other industrialized nations. As a result, the government's ability to exact compliance or exercise leverage in the international system is diminished." Thus the United States, despite being the world's "sole remaining superpower," will not be able to shape the post–Cold-War world political economy in the same way that it shaped the post–World-War-II world.

The authors outline several visions of how a triangular world political economy "will set the parameters within which security issues are resolved." They conclude that "bitter economic rivalry" is a likely outcome because of fear that "there can be *enduring* national winners and losers from trade competition," which is the logic underlying strategic trade theory. Strategic trade practices combined with the way technology develops and the changing relationship between civilian and military research and development will tempt states to "'grab' key technologies and markets before others can: doing so would guarantee domestic availability of the industrial resources needed to field state-of-the-art military forces and eliminate the need to make unacceptable concessions." The result would be mercantile rivalry among the world's principal trading blocs in which "fear of one another" may be the only force binding them together.

What are the security implications of such a system? "If regions come to view trade as a zero-sum game in which one region's gain is another's loss," Borrus, Weber, Zysman, and Willihnganz conclude, "they could start to regard each other as rivals competing not just for one-time gains in wealth, but for long-term growth and welfare. . . . Existing international institutions would be hard pressed to cope with the instability that would result."

22

THREE IDEOLOGIES OF POLITICAL ECONOMY

Robert Gilpin

Robert Gilpin summarizes and critically analyzes three "ideologies" of political economy: liberalism, nationalism (mercantilism), and Marxism. Each ideology alleges "to provide scientific descriptions of how the world _does_ work, while they also constitute normative positions regarding how the world _should_ work." Together the three ideologies have had a profound impact on world affairs. Gilpin is Dwight D. Eisenhower Professor of International Affairs at Princeton University. His books include _War and Change in World Politics_ (1981).

Over the past century and a half, the ideologies of liberalism, nationalism, and Marxism have divided humanity. . . . The conflict among these three moral and intellectual positions has revolved around the role and significance of the market in the organization of society and economic affairs. . . .

These three ideologies are fundamentally different in their conceptions of the relationships among society, state, and market, and it may not be an exaggeration to say that every controversy in the field of international political economy is ultimately reducible to differing conceptions of these relationships. . . .

It is important to understand the nature and content of these contrasting "ideologies" of political economy. The term "ideology" is used rather than "theory" because each position entails a total belief system concerning the nature of human beings and society. . . . These commitments or ideologies allege to provide scientific descriptions of how the world *does* work while they also constitute normative positions regarding how the world *should* work.

Although scholars have produced a number of "theories" to explain the relationship of economics and politics, these three stand out and have had a profound influence on scholarship and political affairs. In highly oversimplified terms, economic nationalism (or, as it was originally called, mercantilism), which developed from the practice of statesmen in the early modern period, assumes and advocates the primacy of politics over economics. It is essentially a doctrine of state building and asserts that the market should be subordinate to the pursuit of state interests. It argues that political factors do, or at least should, determine economic relations. Liberalism, which emerged from the Enlightenment in the writings of Adam Smith and others, was a reaction to mercantilism and has become embodied in orthodox economics. It assumes that politics and economics exist, at least ideally, in separate spheres; it argues that markets—in the interest of efficiency, growth, and consumer choice—should be free from political interference. Marxism, which appeared in the mid-19th century as a reaction against liberalism and classical economics, holds that economics drives politics. Political conflict arises from struggle among classes over the distribution of wealth. Hence, political conflict will cease with the elimination of the market and of a society of classes. . . . Both nationalism and Marxism in the modern era . . . developed largely in reaction to the tenets of liberal economics. . . .

THE LIBERAL PERSPECTIVE

Some scholars assert that there is no such thing as a liberal theory of political economy because liberalism separates economics and politics from one another and assumes that each sphere operates according to particular rules and a logic of its own.[1] This view is itself, however, an ideological position and liberal theorists do in fact concern themselves with both political and economic affairs. Whether it is made explicit in their writings or is merely implicit, one can speak of a liberal theory of political economy.

---

[1] The term "liberal" is used . . . in its European connotation, that is, a commitment to individualism, free market, and private property. This is the dominant perspective of most American economists and of economics as taught in American universities. . . .

There is a set of values from which liberal theories of economics and of politics arise; in the modern world these political and economic values have tended to appear together. . . . Liberal economic theory is committed to free markets and minimal state intervention, although . . . the relative emphasis on one or the other may differ. Liberal political theory is committed to individual equality and liberty, although again the emphasis may differ. . . .

The liberal perspective on political economy is embodied in the discipline of economics as it has developed in Great Britain, the United States, and Western Europe. From Adam Smith to its contemporary proponents, liberal thinkers . . . are committed to the market and the price mechanism as the most efficacious means for organizing domestic and international economic relations. Liberalism may, in fact, be defined as a doctrine and set of principles for organizing and managing a market economy in order to achieve maximum efficiency, economic growth, and individual welfare.

Economic liberalism assumes that a market arises spontaneously in order to satisfy human needs and that, once it is in operation, it functions in accordance with its own internal logic. Human beings are by nature economic animals, and therefore markets evolve naturally without central direction. As Adam Smith put it, it is inherent in mankind to "truck, barter, and exchange." To facilitate exchange and improve their well-being, people create markets, money, and economic institutions. . . .

The rationale for a market system is that it increases economic efficiency, maximizes economic growth, and thereby improves human welfare. Although liberals believe that economic activity also enhances the power and security of the state, they argue that the primary objective of economic activity is to benefit individual consumers. Their ultimate defense of free trade and open markets is that they increase the range of goods and services available to the consumer.

The fundamental premise of liberalism is that the individual consumer, firm, or household is the basis of society. Individuals behave rationally and attempt to maximize or satisfy certain values at the lowest possible cost to themselves. Rationality applies only to endeavor, not to outcome. Thus, failure to achieve an objective due to ignorance or some other cause does not, according to liberals, invalidate their premise that individuals act on the basis of a cost/benefit or means/ends calculus. Finally, liberalism argues that an individual will seek to acquire an objective until a market equilibrium is reached, that is, until the costs associated with achieving the objective are equal to the benefits. Liberal economists attempt to explain economic and, in some cases, all human behavior on the basis of these individualistic and rationalistic assumptions. . . .

Liberalism also assumes that a market exists in which individuals have complete information and are thus enabled to select the most beneficial course of action. Individual producers and consumers will be highly responsive to price signals, and this will create a flexible economy in which any change in relative prices will elicit a corresponding change in patterns of production, consumption, and economic institutions; the latter are conceived ultimately to be the product rather than the cause of economic behavior. . . . Further, in a truly competitive market, the terms of exchange are determined solely by considerations of supply and demand rather than by the exercise of power and coercion. If exchange is voluntary, both parties benefit. In colloquial terms, a "free exchange is no robbery."

Economics, or rather the economics taught in most American universities (what Marxists call orthodox or bourgeois economics), is assumed to be an empirical science of maximizing behavior. Behavior is believed to be governed by a set of economic "laws" that are impersonal and politically neutral; therefore, economics and politics should and can be separated into distinct spheres. Governments should not intervene in the market except where a "market failure" exists . . . or in order to provide a so-called public or collective good. . . .

A market economy is governed principally by the law of demand. . . . This "law" (or, if one prefers, assumption) holds that people will buy more of a good if the relative price falls and less if it rises; people will also tend to buy more of a good as their relative income rises and less as it falls. Any development that changes the relative price of a good or the relative income of an actor will create an incentive or disincentive to acquire (or produce) more or less of the good; this law in turn has profound ramifications throughout the society. Although certain exceptions to this simple concept exist, it is fundamental to the operation and success of a market system of economic exchange.

On the supply side of the economy, liberal economics assumes that individuals pursue their interests in a world of scarcity and resource constraints. This is a fundamental and inescapable condition of human existence. Every decision involves an opportunity cost, a tradeoff among alternative uses of available resources. . . . The basic lesson of liberal economics is that "there is no such thing as a free lunch"; to get something one must be willing to give up something else.

Liberalism also assumes that a market economy exhibits a powerful tendency toward equilibrium and inherent stability, at least over the long term. This "concept of a self-operating and self-correcting equilibrium achieved by a balance of forces in a rational universe" is a crucial one for the economists' belief in the operation of markets and the laws that are believed to govern them.[2] If a market is thrown into a state of disequilibrium due to some external (exogenous) factor such as a change in consumer tastes or productive technology, the operation of the price mechanism will eventually return it to a new state of equilibrium. . . .

An additional liberal assumption is that a basic long-term harmony of interests underlies the market competition of producers and consumers, a harmony

---

[2]J.B. Condliffe, *The Commerce of Nations* (New York: W.W. Norton, 1950), p. 112.

that will supercede any temporary conflict of interest. Individual pursuit of self-interest in the market increases social well-being because it leads to the maximization of efficiency, and the resulting economic growth eventually benefits all. Consequently, everyone will gain in accordance with his or her contribution to the whole, but, it should be added, not everyone will gain equally because individual productivities differ. Under free exchange, society as a whole will be more wealthy, but individuals will be rewarded in terms of their marginal productivity and relative contribution to the overall social product.

Finally, most present-day liberal economists believe in progress, defined most frequently as an increase in wealth per capita. They assert that the growth of a properly functioning economy is linear, gradual, and continuous. . . . Although political or other events—wars, revolution, or natural disasters—can dramatically disrupt this growth path, the economy will return eventually to a stable pattern of growth that is determined principally by increases in population, resources, and productivity. Moreover, liberals see no necessary connection between the process of economic growth and political developments such as war and imperialism; these political evils affect and may be affected by economic activities, but they are essentially caused by political and not by economic factors. For example, liberals do not believe that any causal relationship existed between the advance of capitalism in the late 19th century and the upheavals of imperialism after 1870 and the outbreak of the First World War. Liberals believe economics is progressive and politics is retrogressive. Thus they conceive of progress as divorced from politics and based on the evolution of the market.

. . . Today, the conditions necessary for the operation of a market economy exist, and the normative commitment to the market has spread from its birthplace in Western civilization to embrace an increasingly large portion of the globe. Despite setbacks, the modern world has moved in the direction of the market economy and of increasing global economic interdependence precisely because markets *are* more efficient than other forms of economic organization. . . .

In essence, liberals believe that trade and economic intercourse are a source of peaceful relations among nations because the mutual benefits of trade and expanding interdependence among national economies will tend to foster cooperative relations. Whereas politics tends to divide, economics tends to unite peoples. A liberal international economy will have a moderating influence on international politics as it creates bonds of mutual interests and a commitment to the status quo. However, it is important to emphasize again that although everyone will, or at least can, be better off in "absolute" terms under free exchange, the "relative" gains will differ. It is precisely this issue of relative gains and the distribution of the wealth generated by the market system that has given rise to economic nationalism and Marxism as rival doctrines.

THE NATIONALIST PERSPECTIVE

Economic nationalism, like economic liberalism, has undergone several meta-morphoses over the past several centuries. Its labels have also changed: mercantilism, statism, protectionism, the German Historical School, and, recently, New Protectionism. Throughout all these manifestations, however, runs a set of themes or attitudes rather than a coherent and systematic body of economic or political theory. Its central idea is that economic activities are and should be subordinate to the goal of state building and the interests of the state. All nationalists ascribe to the primacy of the state, of national security, and of military power in the organization and functioning of the international system. . . .

Although economic nationalism should be viewed as a general commitment to state building, the precise objectives pursued and the policies advocated have differed in different times and in different places. Yet, as Jacob Viner has cogently argued in an often-quoted passage, economic nationalist (or what he calls mercantilist) writers share convictions concerning the relationship of wealth and power:

> I believe that practically all mercantilists, whatever the period, country, or status of the particular individual, would have subscribed to all of the following propositions: (1) wealth is an absolutely essential means to power, whether for security or for aggression; (2) power is essential or valuable as a means to the acquisition or retention of wealth; (3) wealth and power are each proper ultimate ends of national policy; (4) there is long-run harmony between these ends, although in particular circumstances it may be necessary for a time to make economic sacrifices in the interest of military security and therefore also of long-run prosperity.[3]

Whereas liberal writers generally view the pursuit of power and wealth, that is, the choice between "guns and butter," as involving a tradeoff, nationalists tend to regard the two goals as being complementary. . . .

Economic nationalists stress the role of economic factors in international relations and view the struggle among states—capitalist, socialist, or whatever—for economic resources as pervasive and indeed inherent in the nature of the international system itself. As one writer has put it, since economic resources are necessary for national power, every conflict is at once both economic and political.[4] States, at least over the long run, simultaneously pursue wealth and national power.

As it evolved in the early modern era, economic nationalism responded to and reflected the political, economic, and military developments of the 16th, 17th, and 18th centuries: the emergence of strong national states in constant competition, the rise of a middle class devoted at first to commerce and increasingly to

---

[3]Jacob Viner, *The Long View and the Short: Studies in Economic Theory and Policy* (New York: Free Press, 1958), p. 286.

[4]Ralph G. Hawtrey, *Economic Aspects of Sovereignty* (London: Longmans, 1952).

manufacturing, and the quickening pace of economic activities due to changes within Europe and the discovery of the New World and its resources. The evolution of a monetarized market economy and the wide range of changes in the nature of warfare that have been characterized as the "Military Revolution" were also critically important.[5] Nationalists (or "mercantilists," as they were then called) had good cause to identify a favorable balance of trade with national security.

For several reasons, the foremost objective of nationalists is industrialization. . . . In the first place, nationalists believe that industry has spillover effects (externalities) throughout the economy and leads to its overall development. Second, they associate the possession of industry with economic self-sufficiency and political autonomy. Third, and most important, industry is prized because it is the basis of military power and central to national security in the modern world. In almost every society, including liberal ones, governments pursue policies favorable to industrial development. As the mercantilist theorist of American economic development, Alexander Hamilton, wrote: "not only the wealth but the independence and security of a country appear to be materially connected to the prosperity of manufactures"; . . . no contemporary dependency theorist has put it better. This nationalist objective of industrialization . . . is itself a major source of economic conflict.

Economic nationalism, both in the early modern era and today, arises in part from the tendency of markets to concentrate wealth and to establish dependency or power relations between the strong and the weak economies. . . .

In a world of competing states, the nationalist considers relative gain to be more important than mutual gain. Thus nations continually try to change the rules or regimes governing international economic relations in order to benefit themselves disproportionately with respect to other economic powers. As Adam Smith shrewdly pointed out, everyone wants to be a monopolist and will attempt to be one unless prevented by competitors. Therefore, a liberal international economy cannot develop unless it is supported by the dominant economic states whose own interests are consistent with its preservation.

Whereas liberals stress the mutual benefits of international commerce, nationalists as well as Marxists regard these relations as basically conflictual. Although this does not rule out international economic cooperation and the pursuit of liberal policies, economic interdependence is never symmetrical; indeed, it constitutes a source of continuous conflict and insecurity. Nationalist writers from Alexander Hamilton to contemporary dependency theorists thus emphasize national self-sufficiency rather than economic interdependence. The desire for power and independence have been the overriding concern of economic nationalists.

---

[5]Michael Roberts, *The Military Revolution, 1560–1600* (Belfast: Boyd, 1956).

Whatever its relative strengths and weaknesses as an ideology or theory of international political economy, the nationalist emphasis on the geographic location and the distribution of economic activities provides it with powerful appeal. Throughout modern history, states have pursued policies promoting the development of industry, advanced technology, and those economic activities with the highest profitability and generation of employment within their own borders. As far as they can, states try to create an international division of labor favorable to their political and economic interests. Indeed, economic nationalism is likely to be a significant influence in international relations as long as the state system exists.

THE MARXIST PERSPECTIVE

Like liberalism and nationalism, Marxism has evolved in significant ways since its basic ideas were set forth by Karl Marx and Friedrich Engels in the middle of the 19th century. Marx's own thinking changed during his lifetime, and his theories have always been subject to conflicting interpretations. Although Marx viewed capitalism as a global economy, he did not develop a systematic set of ideas on international relations; this responsibility fell upon the succeeding generation of Marxist writers. The Soviet Union and China, furthermore, having adopted Marxism as their official ideology, . . . reshaped it when necessary to serve their own national interests. . . .

Marxism characterizes capitalism as the private ownership of the means of production and the existence of wage labor. It believes that capitalism is driven by capitalists striving for profits and capital accumulation in a competitive market economy. Labor has been dispossessed and has become a commodity that is subject to the price mechanism. In Marx's view these two key characteristics of capitalism are responsible for its dynamic nature and make it the most productive economic mechanism yet. Although its historic mission is to develop and unify the globe, the very success of capitalism will hasten its passing. The origin, evolution, and eventual demise of the capitalist mode of production are, according to Marx, governed by three inevitable economic laws.

The first law, the law of disproportionality, entails a denial of Say's law, which (in oversimplified terms) holds that supply creates its own demand so that supply and demand will always be, except for brief moments, in balance. . . . Say's law maintains that an equilibrating process makes overproduction impossible in a capitalist or market economy. Marx, like John Maynard Keynes, denied that this tendency toward equilibrium existed and argued that capitalist economies tend to overproduce particular types of goods. There is, Marx argued, an inherent contradiction in capitalism between its capacity to produce goods and the capacity of consumers (wage earners) to purchase those goods, so that the constantly recurring disproportionality between production and consumption due to the "anarchy" of the market causes periodic depressions and economic fluctuations. He predicted that these recurring economic crises would become increasingly severe and in time would impel the suffering proletariat to rebel against the system.

The second law propelling the development of a capitalist system, according to Marxism, is the law of the concentration (or accumulation) of capital. The motive force of capitalism is the drive for profits and the consequent necessity for the individual capitalist to accumulate and invest. Competition forces the capitalists to increase their efficiency and capital investment or risk extinction. As a result, the evolution of capitalism is toward increasing concentrations of wealth in the hands of the efficient few and the growing impoverishment of the many. With the petite bourgeoisie being pushed down into the swelling ranks of the impoverished proletariat, the reserve army of the unemployed increases, labor's wages decline, and the capitalist society becomes ripe for social revolution.

The third law of capitalism is that of the falling rate of profit. As capital accumulates and becomes more abundant, the rate of return declines, thereby decreasing the incentive to invest. Although classical liberal economists had recognized this possibility, they believed that a solution could be found through such countervailing devices as the export of capital and manufactured goods and the import of cheap food. . . . Marx, on the other hand, believed that the tendency for profits to decline was inescapable. As the pressure of competition forces capitalists to increase efficiency and productivity through investment in new labor-saving and more productive technology, the level of unemployment will increase and the rate of profit or surplus value will decrease. Capitalists will thereby lose their incentive to invest in productive ventures and to create employment. This will result in economic stagnation, increasing unemployment, and the "immiser-ization" of the proletariat. In time, the ever-increasing intensity and depth of the business cycle will cause the workers to rebel and destroy the capitalist economic system.

The core of the Marxist critique of capitalism is that although the individual capitalist is rational (as liberals assume), the capitalist system itself is irrational. The competitive market necessitates that the individual capitalist must save, invest, and accumulate. If the desire for profits is the fuel of capitalism, then investment is the motor and accumulation is the result. In the aggregate, however, this accumulating capital of individual capitalists leads to the periodic overproduction of goods, surplus capital, and the disappearance of investment incentives. In time, the increasing severity of the downturns in the business cycle and the long-term trend toward economic stagnation will cause the proletariat to overthrow the system through revolutionary violence. Thus, the inherent contradiction of capitalism is that, with capital accumulation, capitalism sows the seeds of its own destruction and is replaced by the socialist economic system.

Marx believed that in the mid-19th century, the maturing of capitalism in Europe and the drawing of the global periphery into the market economy had set the stage for the proletarian revolution and the end of the capitalist economy.

When this did not happen, Marx's followers, such as Rudolf Hilferding and Rosa Luxemburg, became concerned over the continuing vitality of capitalism and its refusal to disappear. The strength of nationalism, the economic successes of capitalism, and the advent of imperialism led to a metamorphosis of Marxist thought that culminated in Lenin's *Imperialism,* first published in 1917.[6] Written against the backdrop of the First World War and drawing heavily upon the writings of other Marxists, *Imperialism* was both a polemic against his ideological enemies and a synthesis of Marxist critiques of a capitalist world economy. In staking out his own position, Lenin in effect converted Marxism from essentially a theory of domestic economy to a theory of international political relations among capitalist states. . . .

In the years between Marx and Lenin, capitalism had experienced a profound transformation. Marx had written about a capitalism largely confined to Western Europe, a closed economy in which the growth impulse would one day cease as it collided with various constraints. Between 1870 and 1914, however, capitalism had become a vibrant, technological, and increasingly global and open system. In Marx's day, the primary nexus of the slowly developing world economy was trade. After 1870, however, the massive export of capital by Great Britain and subsequently by other developed economies had significantly changed the world economy—foreign investment and international finance had profoundly altered the economic and political relations among societies. Furthermore, Marx's capitalism had been composed mainly of small, competitive, industrial firms. By the time of Lenin, however, capitalist economies were dominated by immense industrial combines that in turn, according to Lenin, were controlled by the great banking houses *(haut finance).* For Lenin, the control of capital by capital, that is, of industrial capital by financial capital, represented the pristine and highest stage of capitalist development.

Capitalism, he argued, had escaped its three laws of motion through overseas imperialism. The acquisition of colonies had enabled the capitalist economies to dispose of their unconsumed goods, to acquire cheap resources, and to vent their surplus capital. The exploitation of these colonies further provided an economic surplus with which the capitalists could buy off the leadership ("labor aristocracy") of their own proletariat. Colonial imperialism, he argued, had become a necessary feature of advanced capitalism. As its productive forces developed and matured, a capitalist economy had to expand abroad, capture colonies, or else suffer economic stagnation and internal revolution. Lenin identified this necessary expansion as the cause of the eventual destruction of the international capitalist system.

The essence of Lenin's argument is that a capitalist international economy does develop the world, but does not develop it evenly. Individual capitalist

---

[6] V. I. Lenin. *Imperialism: The Highest Stage of Capitalism* (New York: International Publishers, 1939 [1917]).

economies grow at different rates and this differential growth of national power is ultimately responsible for imperialism, war, and international political change. Responding to Kautsky's argument that capitalists were too rational to fight over colonies and would ally themselves in the joint exploitation of colonial peoples (the doctrine of "ultra-imperialism"), Lenin stated that this was impossible because of what has become known as the "law of uneven development." . . .

In effect, . . . Lenin added a fourth law to the original three Marxist laws of capitalism. The law is that, as capitalist economies mature, as capital accumulates, and as profit rates fall, the capitalist economies are compelled to seize colonies and create dependencies to serve as markets, investment outlets, and sources of food and raw materials. In competition with one another, they divide up the colonial world in accordance with their relative strengths. Thus, the most advanced capitalist economy, namely Great Britain, had appropriated the largest share of colonies. As other capitalist economies advanced, however, they sought a redivision of colonies. This imperialist conflict inevitably led to armed conflict among the rising and declining imperial powers. The First World War, according to this analysis, was a war of territorial redivision between a declining Great Britain and other rising capitalist powers. Such wars of colonial division and redivision would continue, he argued, until the industrializing colonies and the proletariat of the capitalist countries revolted against the system.

In more general terms, Lenin reasoned that because capitalist economies grow and accumulate capital at differential rates, a capitalist international system can never be stable for longer than very short periods of time. In opposition to Kautsky's doctrine of ultra-imperialism, Lenin argued that all capitalist alliances were temporary and reflected momentary balances of power among the capitalist states that would inevitably be undermined by the process of uneven development. As this occurred, it would lead to intracapitalist conflicts over colonial territories. . . .

Lenin's internationalization of Marxist theory represented a subtle but significant reformulation. In Marx's critique of capitalism, the causes of its downfall were economic; capitalism would fail for economic reasons as the proletariat revolted against its impoverishment. Furthermore, Marx had defined the actors in this drama as social classes. Lenin, however, substituted a political critique of capitalism in which the principal actors in effect became competing mercantilistic nation-states driven by economic necessity. Although international capitalism was economically successful, Lenin argued that it was politically unstable and constituted a war-system. The workers or the labor aristocracy in the developed capitalist countries temporarily shared in the exploitation of colonial peoples but ultimately would pay for these economic gains on the battlefield. Lenin believed that the inherent contradiction of capitalism resided in the consequent struggle of nations rather than in the class struggle. Capitalism would end due to a revolt against its inherent bellicosity and political consequences.

In summary, Lenin argued that the inherent contradiction of capitalism is that it develops the world and plants the political seeds of its own destruction as it diffuses technology, industry, and military power. It creates foreign competitors with lower wages and standards of living who can outcompete the previously dominant economy on the battlefield of world markets. Intensification of economic and political competition between declining and rising capitalist powers leads to economic conflicts, imperial rivalries, and eventually war. He asserted that this had been the fate of the British-centered liberal world economy of the 19th century. Today he would undoubtedly argue that, as the U.S. economy declines, a similar fate threatens the 20th-century liberal world economy, centered in the United States. . . .

A CRITIQUE OF THE PERSPECTIVES

As we have seen, liberalism, nationalism, and Marxism make different assumptions and reach conflicting conclusions regarding the nature and consequences of a world market economy or (as Marxists prefer) a world capitalist economy. . . . Each of the three perspectives has strengths and weaknesses, to be further explored below. Although no perspective provides a complete and satisfactory understanding of the nature and dynamism of the international political economy, together they provide useful insights. . . .

Critique of Economic Liberalism

Liberalism embodies a set of analytical tools and policy prescriptions that enable a society to maximize its return from scarce resources; its commitment to efficiency and the maximization of total wealth provides much of its strength. The market constitutes the most effective means for organizing economic relations, and the price mechanism operates to ensure that mutual gain and hence aggregate social benefit tend to result from economic exchange. In effect, liberal economics says to a society, whether domestic or international, "if you wish to be wealthy, this is what you must do." . . .

. . . Liberal economics can be criticized in several important respects. As a means to understand society and especially its dynamics, economics is limited; it cannot serve as a comprehensive approach to political economy. Yet liberal economists have tended to forget this inherent limitation, to regard economics as the master social science, and to permit economics to become imperialistic. When this occurs, the nature and basic assumptions of the discipline can lead the economist astray and limit its utility as a theory of political economy.

The first of these limitations is that economics artificially separates the economy from other aspects of society and accepts the existing sociopolitical framework as a given, including the distribution of power and property rights; the resource and other endowments of individuals, groups, and national societies; and the framework of social, political, and cultural institutions. The liberal world is viewed as one of homogeneous, rational, and equal individuals living in a world free from political boundaries and social constraints. Its "laws" prescribe a set of maximizing rules for economic actors regardless of where and with what they start; yet in real life, one's starting point most frequently determines where one finishes. . . .

Another limitation of liberal economics as a theory is a tendency to disregard the justice or equity of the outcome of economic activities. Despite heroic efforts to fashion an "objective" welfare economics, the distribution of wealth within and among societies lies outside the primary concern of liberal economics. . . .

Liberalism is also limited by its assumption that exchange is always free and occurs in a competitive market between equals who possess full information and are thus enabled to gain mutually if they choose to exchange one value for another. Unfortunately, as Charles Lindblom has argued, exchange is seldom free and equal.[7] Instead, the terms of an exchange can be profoundly affected by coercion, differences in bargaining power (monopoly or monopsony), and other essentially political factors. In effect, because it neglects both the effects of noneconomic factors on exchange and the effects of exchange on politics, liberalism lacks a true "political economy."

A further limitation of liberal economics is that its analysis tends to be static. At least in the short run, the array of consumer demands, the institutional framework, and the technological environment are accepted as constants. They are regarded as a set of constraints and opportunities within which economic decisions and tradeoffs are made. . . . Liberal economists are incrementalists who believe that social structures tend to change slowly in response to price signals. Although liberal economists have attempted to develop theories of economic and technological change, the crucial social, political, and technological variables affecting change are considered to be exogenous and beyond the realm of economic analysis. As Marxists charge, liberalism lacks a theory of the dynamics of international political economy and tends to assume the stability and the virtues of the economic status quo.

Liberal economics, with its laws for maximizing behavior, is based on a set of highly restrictive assumptions. No society has ever or could ever be composed of the true "economic man" of liberal theory. A functioning society requires affective ties and the subordination of individual self-interest to larger social values; if this were not the case the society would fly apart. . . . Yet Western society has gone far in harnessing for social and economic betterment a basic tendency in human beings toward self-aggrandizement. . . . Through release of the market mechanism from social and political constraints, Western civilization has reached a level of unprecedented affluence and has set an example that other civilizations

---

[7] Charles E. Lindblom, *Politics and Markets: The World's Political-Economic Systems* (New York: Basic Books, 1977), pp. 40–50.

wish to emulate. It has done so, however, at the cost of other values. As liberal economics teaches, nothing is ever achieved without a cost.

Critique of Economic Nationalism

The foremost strength of economic nationalism is its focus on the state as the predominant actor in international relations and as an instrument of economic development. Although many have argued that modern economic and technological developments have made the nation-state an anachronism, at the end of the 20th century the system of nation-states is actually expanding; societies throughout the world are seeking to create strong states capable of organizing and managing national economies, and the number of states in the world is increasing. Even in older states, the spirit of nationalist sentiments can easily be inflamed. . . . Although other actors such as transnational and international organizations do exist and do influence international relations, the economic and military efficiency of the state makes it preeminent over all these other actors.

The second strength of nationalism is its stress on the importance of security and political interests in the organization and conduct of international economic relations. One need not accept the nationalist emphasis on the primacy of security considerations to appreciate that the security of the state is a necessary precondition for its economic and political well-being in an anarchic and competitive state system. A state that fails to provide for its own security ceases to be independent. . . .

The third strength of nationalism is its emphasis on the political framework of economic activities, its recognition that markets must function in a world of competitive groups and states. The political relations among these political actors affect the operation of markets just as markets affect the political relations. In fact, the international political system constitutes one of the most important constraints on and determinants of markets. Since states seek to influence markets to their own individual advantage, the role of power is crucial in creating and sustaining market relations; even Ricardo's classic example of the exchange of British woolens for Portuguese wine was not free from the exercise of state power. . . . Indeed, as Carr has argued, every economic system must rest on a secure political base.[8]

One weakness of nationalism is its tendency to believe that international economic relations constitute solely and at all times a zero-sum game, that is, that one state's gain must of necessity be another's loss. Trade, investment, and all other economic relations are viewed by the nationalist primarily in conflictual and distributive terms. Yet, if cooperation occurs, markets *can* bring mutual (albeit not necessarily equal) gain, as the liberal insists. The possibility of benefit

---

[8] Edward Hallett Carr, *The Twenty Years' Crisis, 1919–1939.* 2d ed. (London: Macmillan, 1951 [1939]).

for all is the basis of the international market economy. Another weakness of nationalism is due to the fact that the pursuit of power and the pursuit of wealth usually do conflict, at least in the short run. The amassing and exercising of military and other forms of power entail costs to the society, costs that can undercut its economic efficiency. Thus, as Adam Smith argued, the mercantilist policies of 18th-century states that identified money with wealth were detrimental to the growth of the real wealth created by productivity increases; he demonstrated that the wealth of nations would have been better served by policies of free trade. Similarly, the tendency today to identify industry with power can weaken the economy of a state. Development of industries without regard to market considerations or comparative advantage can weaken a society economically. Although states in a situation of conflict must on occasion pursue mercantilistic goals and policies, over the long term, pursuit of these policies can be self-defeating.

In addition, nationalism lacks a satisfactory theory of domestic society, the state, and foreign policy. It tends to assume that society and state form a unitary entity and that foreign policy is determined by an objective national interest. Yet, as liberals correctly stress, society is pluralistic and consists of individuals and groups (coalitions of individuals) that try to capture the apparatus of the state and make it serve their own political and economic interests. Although states possess varying degrees of social autonomy and independence in the making of policy, foreign policy (including foreign economic policy) is in large measure the outcome of the conflicts among dominant groups within each society. Trade protectionism and most other nationalist policies result from attempts by one factor of production or another (capital, labor, or land) to acquire a monopoly position and thereby to increase its share of the economic rents. Nationalist policies are most frequently designed to redistribute income from consumers and society as a whole to producer interests.

Nationalism can thus be interpreted as either a theory of state building or a cloak for the interests of particular producer groups that are in a position to influence national policy. In their failure to appreciate fully or distinguish between the two possible meanings of economic nationalism, nationalists can be faulted for not applying, both to the domestic level and to the determination of foreign policy, their assumption that the political framework influences economic outcomes. They fail to take sufficient account of the fact that domestic political groups frequently use a nationalist rationale, especially that of national security, to promote their own interests. . . .

The validity of nationalists' emphasis on protectionism and industrialization is more difficult to ascertain. It is true that all great industrial powers have had strong states that protected and promoted their industries in the early stages of industrialization and that without such protectionism, the "infant" industries of developing economies probably would not have survived the competition of powerful firms in more advanced economies. Yet it is also the case that high levels of protectionism in many countries have led to the establishment of inefficient industries and even retarded economic development. . . . In the final quarter of the 20th century, economies like those of Taiwan and South Korea, which have limited protectionism while favoring competitive export industries, have performed better than those less developed countries that have attempted to industrialize behind high tariff walls while pursuing a strategy of import substitution.

The nationalist's bias toward industry over agriculture also must get a mixed review. It is true that industry can have certain advantages over agriculture and that the introduction of industrial technology into a society has spillover effects that tend to transform and modernize all aspects of the economy as it upgrades the quality of the labor force and increases the profitability of capital. Yet one must remember that few societies have developed without a prior agricultural revolution and a high level of agricultural productivity. . . . In fact, certain of the most prosperous economies of the world, for example, Denmark, the American farm belt, and western Canada, are based on efficient agriculture. . . . In all these societies, moreover, the state has promoted agricultural development.

One may conclude that the nationalists are essentially correct in their belief that the state must play an important role in economic development. A strong state is required to promote and, in some cases, to protect industry as well as to foster an efficient agriculture. Yet this active role of the state, though a necessary condition, is not a sufficient condition. A strong and interventionist state does not guarantee economic development; indeed, it might retard it. The sufficient condition for economic development is an efficient economic organization of agriculture and industry, and in most cases this is achieved through the operation of the market. Both of these political and economic conditions have characterized the developed economies and the rapidly industrializing countries of the contemporary international system.

It is important to realize that, whatever its relative merits or deficiencies, economic nationalism has a persistent appeal. Throughout modern history, the international location of economic activities has been a leading concern of states. From the 17th century on, states have pursued conscious policies of industrial and technological development. Both to achieve stable military power and in the belief that industry provides a higher "value added" . . . than agriculture, the modern nation-state has had as one of its major objectives the establishment and protection of industrial power. As long as a conflictual international system exists, economic nationalism will retain its strong attraction.

Critique of Marxist Theory

Marxism correctly places the economic problem—the production and distribution of material wealth—where it belongs, at or near the center of political life. Whereas liberals tend to ignore the issue of distribution and nationalists are concerned primarily with the *international* distribution of wealth, Marxists focus on both the domestic and the international effects of a market economy on the distribution of wealth. They call attention to the ways in which the rules or regimes governing trade, investment, and other international economic relations affect the distribution of wealth among groups and states. . . .

Another contribution of Marxism is its emphasis on the nature and structure of the division of labor at both the domestic and international levels. As Marx and Engels correctly pointed out in *The German Ideology,* every division of labor implies dependence and therefore a political relationship. . . . In a market economy the economic nexus among groups and states becomes of critical importance in determining their welfare and their political relations. The Marxist analysis, however, is too limited, because economic interdependence is not the only or even the most important set of interstate relations. The political and strategic relations among political actors are of equal or greater significance and cannot be reduced to merely economic considerations, at least not as Marxists define economics.

The Marxist theory of international political economy is also valuable in its focus on international political change. Whereas neither liberalism nor nationalism has a comprehensive theory of social change, Marxism emphasizes the role of economic and technological developments in explaining the dynamics of the international system. As embodied in Lenin's law of uneven development, the differential growth of power among states constitutes an underlying cause of international political change. Lenin was at least partially correct in attributing the First World War to the uneven economic growth of power among industrial states and to conflict over the division of territory. There can be little doubt that the uneven growth of the several European powers and the consequent effects on the balance of power contributed to their collective insecurity. Competition for markets and empires did aggravate interstate relations. Furthermore, the average person's growing awareness of the effects on personal welfare and security of the vicissitudes of the world market and the economic behavior of other states also became a significant element in the arousal of nationalistic antagonisms. For nations and citizens alike, the growth of economic interdependence brought with it a new sense of insecurity, vulnerability, and resentment against foreign political and economic rivals.

Marxists are no doubt also correct in attributing to capitalist economies, at least as we have known them historically, a powerful impulse to expand through trade and especially through the export of capital. . . . Capitalists desire access to foreign economies for export of goods and capital; exports have a Keynesian demand effect in stimulating economic activity in capitalist economies, and capital exports serve to raise the overall rate of profit. Closure of foreign markets and capital outlets would be detrimental to capitalism, and a closed capitalist economy would probably result in a dramatic decline in economic growth. There is reason to believe that the capitalist system (certainly as we have known it) could not survive in the absence of an open world economy. The essential character of capitalism, as Marx pointed out, is cosmopolitan; the capitalist's ideology is international. Capitalism in just one state would undoubtedly be an impossibility.

In the 19th and 20th centuries the dominant capitalist states, Great Britain and the United States, employed their power to promote and maintain an open world economy. They used their influence to remove the barriers to the free flow of goods and capital. Where necessary, in the words of Simon Kuznets, "the greater power of the developed nations imposed upon the reluctant partners the opportunities of international trade and division of labor." [9] In pursuit of their own interests, they created international law to protect the property rights of private traders and investors. . . . And when the great trading nations became unable or unwilling to enforce the rules of free trade, the liberal system began its steady retreat. Up to this point, therefore, the Marxists are correct in their identification of capitalism and modern imperialism.

The principal weakness of Marxism as a theory of international political economy results from its failure to appreciate the role of political and strategic factors in international relations. . . . Although competition for markets and for capital outlets can certainly be a cause of tension and one factor causing imperialism and war, this does not provide an adequate explanation for the foreign policy behavior of capitalist states.

The historical evidence, for example, does not support Lenin's attribution of the First World War to the logic of capitalism and the market system. The most important territorial disputes among the European powers, which precipitated the war, were not those about overseas colonies, as Lenin argued, but lay within Europe itself. The principal conflict leading to the war involved redistribution of the Balkan territories of the decaying Ottoman Empire. And insofar as the source of this conflict was economic, it lay in the desire of the Russian state for access to the Mediterranean. . . . Marxism cannot explain the fact that the three major imperial rivals—Great Britain, France, and Russia—were in fact on the same side in the ensuing conflict and that they fought against a Germany that had few foreign policy interests outside Europe itself.

In addition, Lenin was wrong in tracing the basic motive force of imperialism to the internal workings of the capitalist system. As Benjamin J. Cohen has pointed out in his analysis of the Marxist theory of imperialism, the political and strategic conflicts of the European powers were more important; it was at least in part the stalemate on the Continent among the Great Powers that forced their interstate competition into the colonial world.[10] Every one of these colonial conflicts (if one excludes the Boer War) was in fact settled through diplomatic means. And, finally, the overseas colonies of the European powers were simply

---

[9] Simon Kuznets, *Modern Economic Growth: Rate, Structure, and Spread* (New Haven: Yale University Press, 1966), p. 335.

[10] Benjamin J. Cohen, *The Question of Imperialism: The Political Economy of Dominance and Dependence* (New York: Basic Books, 1973).

of little economic consequence. As Lenin's own data show, almost all European overseas investment was directed to the "lands of recent settlement" (the United States, Canada, Australia, South Africa, Argentina, and the like) rather than to the dependent colonies in what today we call the Third World.[11] In fact, contrary to Lenin's view that politics follows investment, international finance during this period was largely a servant of foreign policy, as was also the case with French loans to Czarist Russia. Thus, despite its proper focus on political change, Marxism is seriously flawed as a theory of political economy.

[11]Lenin, *Imperialism,* p. 64.

23

LOOMING COLLISION
OF CAPITALISMS?

Erik R. Peterson

Global economic integration is accelerating at a rapid economic pace, but, argues Erik R. Peterson, the "integration of policies is lagging behind integration of markets." Rapid globalization thus threatens to bring the major centers of capitalism into conflict with one another as they pursue "defensive strategies grounded in parochial interests . . . that encourage the outbreak of economic nationalism." Peterson is vice president and director of studies at the Center for Strategic and International Studies in Washington, D.C. He is co-editor of the CSIS monograph series on "East Asia Economic and Financial Outlook."

Accelerating global economic integration is bringing national economic policies into sharper competition, especially among the advanced capitalist economies. How these competing domestic policies are managed through the turn of the century and beyond will have profound implications not only for the international economy but also for broader international security and political

From "Looming Collision of Capitalism?" by Erik R. Peterson, *The Washington Quarterly,* 17:2 (Spring, 1994). Copyright © 1994 by the Center for Strategic and International Studies (CSIS) and the Massachusetts Institute of Technology. Reprinted by permission. Some footnotes have been deleted.

relations. The risk is that increasingly nationalist economic policies, fanned by deteriorating economic conditions and social pressures, will propel the preeminent economic powers—and the rest of the world with them—into an era of *"realeconomik"* in which parochial economic interests drive governments to pursue marginal advantage in an international system marked by growing interdependencies.

The conclusion in December 1993 of the General Agreement on Tariffs and Trade (GATT) Uruguay Round, the culmination of seven years of tortuous negotiation by governments to strip away more of their own policy prerogatives, refuted the proposition that the major economic powers—the United States, the European Union (EU), and Japan—were leading the collective effort to break down traditional trade barriers and trade-distorting domestic policies globally. Although it culminated in agreement, the process revealed the extent to which those powers were disinclined to do the "heavy lifting" in liberalizing their policies that many of the less prominent economies had already done to advance the round. In effect, the protracted negotiations highlighted the thresholds of national tolerance among the predominant economies beyond which the political costs for the respective governments were unacceptably high.

There is little doubt that the current economic troubles confronting Washington, Brussels, and Tokyo were a major factor in limiting the scope of the final GATT agreement. Those troubles have also elevated the levels of economic nationalism and unilateralism, both of which can be expected to intensify further as longer-term structural problems in all three economies generate additional political and economic dislocations in the years ahead.

Because of the increasingly binding constraints placed on national economic policy making by the process of global economic integration, the temptation for the major economies to engage in defensive strategies by supporting national "strategic" industries—especially high-technology industries—could bring the major capitalisms into collision. The operative question is whether the governments concerned will succumb to the growing tendency to "pursue relative gains at the expense of mutual gains [and] political power at the expense of economic welfare,"[1] or whether they will be able to devise a system of rules and an appropriate institutional vehicle to defuse the potential for escalating economic clashes between respective "national champions."

ACCELERATING ECONOMIC GLOBALIZATION

It has long been recognized that the traditional line of demarcation between domestic and international economic policy making is fading. Economic shocks ranging from the oil embargo by the Organization of Petroleum Exporting

[1]Theodore H. Moran, "An Economics Agenda for Neorealists," *International Security* 18 (Fall 1993), p. 211.

Countries to the "Black Monday" international stock market crash in October 1987 have underlined the susceptibility of national markets to developments abroad. For governments worldwide, the internationalization of the world economy has also meant the progressive deterioration of their capacity to manage their economies. Macroeconomic policies have been increasingly undermined by the offsetting effects of international responses; an increase in interest rates to decelerate economic growth, for example, is more likely than ever before to be countered by an increase in interest-sensitive capital flows from abroad.

But international trade and investment linkages have expanded to such an extent that sensitivities of economies to decision making in other economies are now substantially more pronounced. Advances in communication and information technologies, the pursuit by multinational enterprises (MNEs) of complex cross-border strategies, the formation and development of regional trading blocs, the GATT process, economic liberalization undertaken in a host of developing economies, and ongoing efforts at marketization in former command economies are metamorphosing the international economic and financial system. As these elements bring about higher levels of global integration, constraints on national economic policy making will continue to grow—and with them the potential for wider conflict over national policies.

The real-time capabilities offered by new communication and information technologies have already had a tremendous impact on international capital flows. Daily global capital movements have increased to well over $1 trillion in 1992. The implications of these movements for national macroeconomic policy making are profound. Alan Greenspan, chairman of the Federal Reserve, noted in August 1993 that the internationalization of finance and the reduction in constraints on international capital flows "expose national economies to shocks from new and unexpected sources, with little if any lag." As a result, he stressed the importance central banks should attach to developing new ways of assessing and limiting risk. But those ways remain to be identified.

Nowhere has the impact on policy making of these cross-border capital flows been more obvious recently than in the EU, where international speculative pressures played a significant role in the partial collapse in the European Monetary System in 1992. Those forces contributed to the circumstances that led London and Rome to withdraw from the semifixed exchange rates under the Exchange Rate Mechanism (ERM); since the British and Italian withdrawal, they have also forced the Spanish to devalue the peseta and brought the Belgian franc under extreme stress. As the *Economist* noted in October 1993, "[t]he financial markets have discovered, in a way they are unlikely to forget for years, their power to crack the system."[2] In short, we have entered a new stage in the development of international finance in which financial markets—and even some individuals— can dramatically influence the outcome of policy decisions by states.

---

[2]"Europe's Monetary Future: From here to EMU," *Economist,* October 23, 1993, p. 25.

MNEs are another major driver of global economic integration. By virtue of increasingly complex strategies involving multi-tier networks of firms that are geographically dispersed and through strategic alliances with other firms, MNEs are establishing unprecedented linkages among economies worldwide. According to the United Nations Conference on Trade and Development (UNCTAD), the strategies of MNEs have generally moved beyond a "simple integration" approach involving strengthened links with their foreign affiliates and with independent firms serving as subcontractors or licensees; the new strategy, which UNCTAD characterizes as "complex integration," provides for heightened geographical distribution of the value-added chain.[3] That MNEs account for a staggering one-third of world private productive assets suggests how important the ramifications of such a shift of strategy are.

According to UNCTAD, sales by MNEs outside their countries of origin were $5.5 trillion in 1992—as opposed to total world exports for the same year of about $4.0 trillion; furthermore, the stock of foreign direct investment (FDI) worldwide reached $2 trillion in 1992, as opposed to one-half that amount in 1987.[4] These data reflect the substantial role that MNEs are playing in integrating the world economy and suggest the extent to which private-sector forces have become a factor in national economic decision making. As discussed in greater detail below, a number of countries with policies that were previously anathema to MNEs have refashioned their approaches so that attraction of foreign investment is a key component of their economic development strategies.

The development of regional trading blocs has also generated higher levels of economic interdependence and by definition represents the voluntary acceptance by the respective member states of constraints on national policy prerogatives. Because the EU, the North American Free Trade Agreement (NAFTA), and the emerging trading framework in Asia are based on political as well as economic considerations, the trend toward regionalism transcends the surrender of policy prerogatives for purely economic reasons. Nevertheless, the impact is to advance economic integration between member states. In the case of the EU, where the impact of German monetary policy clearly transcends the national economic challenges inherent in reunification, the linkages may be more pronounced than some member states would want.

The GATT process, of course, has also steadily broken down barriers between international and domestic policy making. The GATT is no longer the vehicle through which only tariff barriers are broken down; the nontariff barriers that were the focus of the Tokyo Round and the issues at the fore of the Uruguay Round—trade in services, trade-related investment measures, intellectual property protection, price supports and subsidies, countervailing duties, dumping, and

---

[3]UNCTAD, *World Investment Report 1993: Transnational Corporations and Integrated International Production* (New York, N.Y.: United Nations, 1993), pp. 4–5, 115–133.
[4]*Ibid.*, pp. 13–14.

dispute settlement—have exposed the nerves of national economic interests as never before. The demonstrations from Brussels to Tokyo attested to the degree to which GATT negotiations have become (and should be) a major domestic political issue. By definition, the GATT process and the Uruguay Round . . . represent "another stake in the heart of the idea that governments can direct economies."[5]

Economic and financial liberalization in developing economies represents another stimulus to growing integration. A select number of developing countries with liberalized investment environments are now primary targets of portfolio and foreign direct investment flows.[6] Over the past 10 years, international portfolio investment in developing countries has mushroomed. Market capitalization has grown by a factor of 11, from $67 billion in 1982 to $770 billion in 1992. As a percentage of world equity market capitalization, developing countries increased their share over this period from 2.5 to 7 percent. The trend can be expected to continue as secondary markets in developing countries widen and deepen. . . . The key reason for this rapid growth in developing-country capital markets is profitability. . . . Over the past eight years emerging markets as a group have significantly outperformed their counterparts in developed countries.

The pattern of FDI [foreign direct invesment] to developing countries has been no less extraordinary. According to UNCTAD, FDI flows to developing countries increased from $25 billion in 1991 to $40 billion in 1992; if high growth is sustained in Asia and Latin America, annual flows could double in real terms to $80 billion by the end of the century. What is behind this trend? Simply put, economic liberalization has replaced statism, trade liberalization has followed protectionism, and privatization has replaced nationalization. For these countries, the necessity of conforming their national economic decision making to the realities of the international system is now a matter of record. In many cases, those adjustments have extended beyond actions to attract FDI inflows to include fundamental policy shifts such as imposing discipline on fiscal deficits, developing clear legal and commercial systems, streamlining bureaucracies, simplifying taxation systems, and liberalizing trade policies.

Although they are not yet as fully integrated into the world economic system, the former command economies that are seeking to marketize their systems are another driver of international integration. For the first time since the beginning of the century, they are opening their economies to the world economic system and enacting national policies designed to encourage the development of market forces.

---

[5]"The World Wins One," *Wall Street Journal,* December 15, 1993, p. A-16.

[6]Argentina, Brazil, the People's Republic of China, Egypt, Hong Kong, Mexico, Nigeria, Singapore, Taiwan, and Thailand. See UNCTAD, *World Investment Report.*

INTEGRATING MARKETS VERSUS INTEGRATING POLICIES

It should be stressed that there are fundamental differences among these forces driving international economic integration. Some can be referred to as "organic" integration—the private cross-border flows of capital, goods and services, technology, and information driven in large part by MNEs. Others promote "inorganic" integration—the formal and politically oriented trade agreements forged among countries to reduce tariff and nontariff barriers and harmonize trade-relevant domestic economic policies.

Organic integration is the result of strategies enacted by international private-sector actors to maximize the efficiency of their operations in the light of increasing global competition. As noted above, to an ever greater extent MNEs are distributing their operations internationally regardless of political institutions and frameworks to seek innovation or to achieve cost savings at various stages in the value-added chain. Although the pattern of this distribution of economic activity may be (and often is) influenced by regional economic blocs such as the EU and the NAFTA, it will be influenced only to the extent that such frameworks can be incorporated into prevailing global strategies. Increasingly, however, that activity is falling outside the regional blocs and generating higher levels of more global economic integration in the process.

These kinds of private-sector-driven economic dependencies must be differentiated from the "inorganic" or formalized efforts at economic cooperation undertaken among and between states. Such arrangements are based by definition on perceived mutual gains from economic cooperation, but generally they also represent a mixture of economic and political concern. The EU is clearly grounded in political and security objectives advanced in the period immediately after World War II; for its part, the NAFTA also has a strong political character. As a result, the inorganic integration fostered by regional blocs may not necessarily reflect the market fundamentals that are driving the interdependence now created by the private sector. Furthermore, the political nature of regional blocs suggests the possibility that they might be tempted to engage in aggressive trade policies that could generate a protectionist equivalent of an arms race. They could ultimately become the means by which organic integration is resisted.

Together, these organic and inorganic forces driving economies into heightened interdependence . . . progressively limit the area in which national economic policy making is feasible. It follows that governments are likely to resist the restrictions this kind of global convergence places on their policy prerogatives, especially when they are facing acute short-term economic challenges or when the adjustments forced by growing integration entail profound economic or social change. In short, integration of policies is lagging behind integration of markets.

CAPITALISMS IN COLLISION?

The salient question is how governments can protect their national economic interests in an increasingly integrated global economic and financial framework. More and more, the preeminent economic powers in particular are finding the answer in drawing lines beyond which they will resort to defensive strategies grounded in parochial interests. The result is the development of political conditions that encourage the outbreak of economic nationalism.

The current political and economic environments in the United States, Europe, and Japan do not augur well for the level of cooperation necessary to avoid the neomercantilist confrontation that could flow from competing national policies. The overarching security concerns generated by the common threat from the erstwhile Soviet Union are a thing of the past, and immediate economic concerns now overshadow residual security ties. It is a time of fundamental redefinition of security, political, and economic relations—but the process of redefinition is proceeding in the absence of the international leadership and corresponding institutions necessary to meet the challenges of escalating economic rivalry.

The trauma that Washington experienced in fall 1993 in deciding on whether to adopt a free-trade agreement with Mexico—an economy only 4 percent of the U.S. gross national product and with a $5.5 billion trade deficit—amounted to a highly visible demonstration of U.S. attitudes about trade. Although of course the NAFTA was adopted, the emotional and sometimes vacuous debate served to highlight the extent to which economic nationalism threatens the historic role of the United States as leader of the global economic system. But apart from the NAFTA debate, there are other symptoms of this uncertainty. Regular calls in the U.S. Congress and elsewhere for unilateralist approaches to trade and foreign investment issues suggest that the concepts of "fair" rather than "free" trade and "reciprocal treatment" rather than "national treatment" in international capital flows are steadily gaining ground.

These warning signs are the result of the growing perception in the United States that new approaches are necessary to ensure fair access for trade and investment by U.S. firms. The perception is grounded in the view that what was recently referred to as "unilateralist national treatment"[7]—namely, the position on international investment that Washington has maintained for decades—is not being reciprocated by many of its investment partners. Of course, the recent domestic economic difficulties have thrown fuel on the fire.

In Europe, where the economic problems at present are even more pronounced, where the partial collapse of the ERM has generated profound doubts

---

[7]See Office for Technology Assessment, *Multinationals and the National Interest: Playing by Different Rules* (Washington, D.C.: OTA, 1993).

about the outlook for a single European currency, and where the tenuous ratification process of the Maastricht agreement has left leaders searching for ways to advance the integration agenda, attention is predominantly inward. The seriousness of the challenge was underlined in October 1993 when the president of the European Commission, Jacques Delors, warned that the then European Community was drifting toward becoming a free-trade zone that could break up in as little as 15 years. The EU is clearly in a period of intense consolidation and restructuring.

Japan is also engaged in political and economic soul-searching. The Hosokawa coalition . . . embarked on a program of political reform with potentially important longer-term implications for Tokyo's position in the international economic system. The outcome, however, is by no means assured. . . . The government must continue to pass through the political thicket of its own eight-party coalition before contesting with the opposing Liberal Democratic Party to push through its initiatives. It must also do so against the backdrop of stagnating or declining growth, severe volatility in the financial markets, less than promising longer-term growth projections, and a highly resistant bureaucracy. [Prime Minister Hasokawa and his successor, Tsutomu Hata, both resigned prematurely amid continuing domestic turmoil in Japan. In early 1996 premier Tomiichi Murayama also resigned amid Japan's languishing economy and a severe banking crisis. He was replaced by the Liberal Democrat Ryutoro Hashimoto—eds.]

When considered together, these developments in the United States, Europe, and Japan have led some analysts to revisit arguments advanced in the 1970s about the ungovernability of democracies.[8] But there is also reason to question whether relations between the capitalist countries themselves will be governable. It is no exaggeration to suggest that the political agendas in all three major economic powers are predominantly inward-looking and focus primarily on reviving national economic growth and employment. All three are engaged in economic triage. Evidence of economic parochialism in the pursuit of those objectives appears to be growing on a day-by-day basis. In short, they could be on a course that suggests the potential for the rise of neomercantilism.

"STRATEGIC" TRADE AT ISSUE

In particular, there is the possibility of an escalation of industrial policies that would bring "national champions" and "strategic" industries—especially those in

---

[8]See, for example, the articles on ungovernability by Michel Crozier, Samuel P. Huntington, and Joji Watanuki in *American Enterprise* 4 (November-December 1993), pp. 28–41. The three authors originally addressed the issue in a research effort in the early 1970s sponsored by the Trilateral Commission, chaired by Zbigniew Brzezinski, which culminated in the book entitled *The Crisis of Democracy* (New York, N.Y.: New York University Press, 1975).

high technology—into sharper conflict. The magnitude of the threat has been set out by the Organization for Economic Cooperation and Development (OECD):

> Government support for economically strategic industries could become a major source of international dispute in the 1990s. The move over the last decade towards subsidies and other forms of state assistance for important technologically advanced sectors is set to accelerate. The proliferation of such policies, which affect a relatively narrow band of often identical sectors, could well develop into a keenly competitive "subsidy race," with harmful and far-reaching implications for the international system of trade, investment and technology.[9]

Despite the predominately unfavorable—or, at best, mixed—experience with allocating government resources in support of strategic industries, the temptation for governments is to engage in "picking winners" because of the political benefits they engender and the rationale under "strategic trade" theory that "technology trajectories" have a clustering effect of positive externalities extending throughout a wider part of the economy.[10] Some advocates of this theory suggest that such interventionist national policies can be advanced without undermining the pursuit of an open, integrated world economy.[11] Others point to the impending competition for "national futures."[12] That this new genre of thought on competition theory is predicated on results with pronounced sensitivities to changes in assumptions has not prevented it from assuming rising political currency.[13] Nor have the new political advocates of strategic trade been deterred by steadily mounting empirical evidence suggesting that protection and subsidization of industries can actually weaken their competitive position.

Whatever the underlying explanations, from the standpoint of competing national policies the advancement of strategic trade objectives can be achieved through a wide array of policy measures—including but not limited to trade-related policies such as "orderly marketing agreements"; industrial and technology policies that provide subsidy, research and development support, and other "cover"; discriminatory procurement practices; and exemption of relevant sectors from antitrust law.

Assuming such strategic trade policies are adopted more fully by all three major world economic powers, it follows that competition between the respective "beggar-thy-neighbor" approaches could mount quickly because they are based on zero-sum thinking. As Michael Porter has noted,

---

[9]OECD, *Strategic Industries in a Global Economy: Policy Issues for the 1990s* (Paris: OECD Publications, 1991).

[10]Wayne Sandholtz, Michael Borrus, John Zysman, Jay Stowsky, Ken Conca, Steven Vogel, and Steve Weber, *The Highest Stakes: The Economic Foundations of the Next Security System* (New York, N.Y.: Oxford University Press, 1992).

[11]See Peter F. Cowhey and Jonathan D. Aronson, *Managing the World Economy: The Consequences of Corporate Alliances* (New York, N.Y.: Council on Foreign Relations Press, 1993).

[12]Sandholtz, *Highest Stakes*, p. 182.

[13]Michael E. Porter, *The Competitive Advantage of Nations* (New York, N.Y.: The Free Press, 1990), p. 812, n. 46.

[i]f the rate of innovation slows because an "us versus them" attitude leads to subsidy, protection, and consolidation that blunts incentives, the consequences for advanced and less advanced nations alike are severe.[14]

Government intervention in a host of sectors has been a long-established practice in the EU. From ESPRIT to EUREKA, from Concorde to Airbus, from the TGV rail initiative in France to aircraft production in the Netherlands, industrial policy is already a part of the European economic topography. In Japan, where the connection between the government and the private sector is also well established, decision makers have a less visible but nevertheless significant role in promoting industries through a variety of policies. And in the United States, where sector support has been less prevalent, momentum is mounting for a shift to a higher profile for the government in selected strategic industries. The shift is in response to the perception that "our competitors close off their markets to American firms while looking for ways to tap into our rich market . . . and we let them."[15] A senior Clinton administration official recently put it this way: "If no one else wants to play the game [our way], we'd look pretty silly [doing nothing] while they clean our clock."[16]

These divergent positions on industrial policy serve to highlight the more general differences between the capitalisms of the United States, the EU, and Japan. At issue is the differing relationship between government and business in each of the major economic powers and how those relations translate into national policies that have international repercussions. At one end of the spectrum is the consumer-oriented system of capitalism in the United States, where linkages between government and business have been loose and sometimes at odds as a result of the tradition of limiting the extent to which market concentrations occur; at the other end is Japan, which by fostering a producers-oriented form of capitalism is marked by substantially closer ties between the public and private sectors; and in the middle is the EU, where government intervention—traditionally based on social welfare criteria—is more pronounced than in the United States.

A MULTILATERAL RESPONSE?

A common approach by the three preeminent economies to defining acceptable limits to industrial policy is necessary if spiraling competition for marginal advantage is to be averted. The prospect for the negotiation of multilateral rules governing industrial policy is, however, remote at best. No international framework is in sight that could represent a release valve for the emerging pressures associated

[14]Porter, *The Competitive Advantage,* p. 682.

[15]Scott Gibson and Saul Goldstein, "The Plane Truth: How European Deals Are Killing U.S. Jobs," *Washington Post,* October 10, 1993.

[16]Hobart Rowen, "A Little Boost from Washington," *Washington Post,* October 7, 1993, p. A-23. Rowen was quoting President Bill Clinton's science adviser, John H. Gibbons.

with these competing policies. The Group of Seven (G-7) falls substantially short of representing a forum through which a detailed agreement could be reached. Despite its past attention to the issue, the OECD is not likely to become the forum for the United States, the EU, and Japan to seek to reconcile their differences because of the large membership involved, although the OECD could take an active role in defining more specifically how the highly industrialized economies might proceed more generally in fashioning an approach to the issue. The experience of the Uruguay Round suggests that the next stage of negotiations under the [World] Trade Organization will be equally if not more arduous as differences in competition and investment policies come to the fore.

Furthermore, no single economic power seems predisposed to spearhead an effort to defuse the potential of conflicting industrial policies. In the meantime, "competition between governments [is progressively replacing] competition between companies as industrial activities become more and more global."[17]

It is an irony that at this critical historical juncture—when many of the former command economies are embarking on transitions to market systems and a number of developing countries have substantially liberalized their economies after decades of failed statist policies—the highly industrialized powers are in economic distress and embroiled in efforts to reinvigorate their domestic economies. If, as expected, the macroeconomic difficulties in the United States, Europe, and Japan persist or intensify, the attempt at integration into the world economy by significant parts of the second and third worlds—a historically unprecedented development that for decades has been the lodestar of the highly industrialized states themselves—will have been unassisted by the major global economic players and in some ways impeded by their paralysis.

Another fundamental irony of the immediate post–Cold War period is that with the decline of the threat from Moscow, the emphasis is shifting from the clash between capitalism and communism to the differences between the "capitalisms" of the highly industrialized economies. The threat is that traditional political and security linkages will be recast as subordinate features of a competition for industrial advantage—or supremacy.

In the face of rising domestic economic problems and accelerating global economic integration, the manner in which the major economic powers manage their relations through the turn of the century and beyond will have an enormous impact on the world economy. A descent into a period of *realeconomik,* pitting government against government in a global competition for markets, would have a deleterious effect on the capacity of those same governments to meet future national and international economic challenges. Such a descent would also threaten the integrity of political and security relations in a highly uncertain period. To

---

[17]Candice Stevens, "Industrial Internationalisation and Trade Friction," *OECD Observer,* no. 173 (December 1991–January 1992), p. 30.

avoid this outcome, policy makers need to heed the advice of Akio Morita, who in an open letter to the G-7 heads of state in June 1993 argued:

> You, as political leaders, have the power to take the steps necessary to make the increasing de facto globalization of business the most creative, positive, and beneficial force it can be, rather than the source of new international conflict.[18]

[18]Akio Morita, "Toward a New World Economic Order," *Atlantic Monthly* (June 1993), pp. 88–89.

24

TRADE LESSONS FROM
THE WORLD ECONOMY

Peter F. Drucker

**Peter F. Drucker argues that in recent years profound changes have occurred
in the structure and processes of the world economy that have important if
often-ignored policy implications. "What is needed," he argues, "is a deliberate and active—indeed, aggressive—policy that gives the demands, opportunities, and dynamics of the external economy priority over domestic
policy demands and problems." Drucker is Clarke Professor of Social Science
and Management at the Claremont Graduate School. *Post-Capitalist Society*
(1993) is among his many books.**

ALL ECONOMICS IS INTERNATIONAL

In recent years the economies of all developed nations have been stagnant, yet
the world economy has still expanded at a good clip. And it has been growing
faster for the past 40 years than at any time since modern economies and the discipline of economics emerged in the 18th century. From this seeming paradox
there are lessons to be learned, and they are quite different from what practically

everyone asserts, whether they be free traders, managed traders or protectionists. Too many economists, politicians, and segments of the public treat the external economy as something separate and safely ignored when they make policy for the domestic economy. Contrary lessons emerge from a proper understanding of the profound changes in four areas: the structure of the world economy, the changed meaning of trade and investment, the relationship between world and domestic economies, and the difference between workable and unworkable trade policies. . . .

WHAT TRADE DEFICIT?

For practically everyone international trade means merchandise trade, the import and export of manufactured goods, farm products, and raw materials. But international trade is increasingly services trade—little reported and largely unnoticed. The United States has the largest share of the trade in services among developed countries, followed by the United Kingdom. Japan is at the bottom of the list. The services trade of all developed countries is growing fast, and it may equal or overtake their merchandise trade within 10 years. Knowledge is the basis of most service exports and imports. As a result, most service trade is based on long-term commitments, which makes it—excluding tourism—impervious to foreign exchange fluctuations and changes in labor costs.

Even merchandise trade is no longer confined to the sale and purchase of individual goods. Increasingly it is a relationship in which a transaction is only a shipment and an accounting entry. More and more merchandise trade is becoming "structural" and thereby impervious to short-term (and even long-term) changes in the traditional economic factors. Automobile production is a good example. Plant location decisions by manufacturers and suppliers are made at the time of product design. Until the model is redesigned, say in 10 years, the plants and the countries specified in the original design are locked in. There will be change only in the event of a catastrophe such as a war or fire that destroys a plant. Or take the case of a Swiss pharmaceutical company's Irish plant. Rather than sell a product, it ships chemical intermediates to the company's finished-product plants in 19 countries on both sides of the Atlantic. For this the company charges a "transfer" price, which is a pure accounting convention having as much to do with taxes as with production costs. The traditional factors of production are also largely irrelevant to what might be called "institutional" trade, in which businesses, whether manufacturers or large retailers, buy machinery, equipment, and supplies for new plants or stores, wherever located, from the suppliers of their existing plants, that is, those in their home countries.

Markets and knowledge are important in these types of structural and institutional trade decisions; labor costs, capital costs and foreign exchange rates are restraints rather than determinants. More important, neither type of trade is foreign trade, except in a legal sense, even when it is trade across national boundaries.

For the individual business—the automobile manufacturer, the Swiss pharmaceutical company, the retailer—these are transactions within its own system.

Accounting for these developments, U.S. trading activity is more or less in balance. The trade deficit bewailed in the media and by public and private officials is in merchandise trade, caused primarily by an appalling waste of petroleum and a steady decline in the volume and prices of farm exports. The services trade account has a large surplus. According to little-read official figures, published every three months, the services trade surplus amounts to two-thirds of the merchandise trade deficit. Moreover, government statisticians acknowledge gross underreporting of service exports, perhaps by as much as 50 percent.

THE COMING OF ALLIANCES

Traditional direct investment abroad to start or acquire businesses continues to grow. Since the 1980s direct investment in the United States by Europeans, Japanese, Canadians, and Mexicans has grown explosively. But the action is rapidly shifting to alliances such as joint ventures, partnerships, knowledge agreements, and outsourcing arrangements. In alliances, investment is secondary, if there is any at all. A recent example is the dividing up of design and production of an advanced microchip between Intel, a U.S.–based microchip *designer,* and Sharp, the Japanese electronics *manufacturer.* Both will share the final product. There are alliances between scores of university research labs and businesses—pharmaceutical, electronic, engineering, food processing, and computer firms. There are alliances in which organizations outsource support activities; a number of American hospitals, and some in the United Kingdom and Japan, let independent suppliers do their maintenance, housekeeping, billing, and data processing, and increasingly let them run the labs and the physical therapy and diagnostic centers. Computer makers now outsource the data processing for their own businesses to contractors. . . . They are also entering alliances with small, independent software designers. Commercial banks are entering alliances with producers and managers of mutual funds. Small and medium-sized colleges are entering alliances with one another to do paperwork jointly.

Some of these alliances involve substantial capital investment, as in the joint ventures of the 1960s and 1970s between Japanese and U.S. companies to produce American-designed goods in Japan for the Japanese market. But even then the basis of the alliance was not capital but complementary knowledge—technical and manufacturing knowledge supplied by the Americans, marketing knowledge and management supplied by the Japanese. More and more, investment of whatever size is symbolic—a minority share in each other's business is regarded as "bonding" between partners. In many alliances there is no financial relationship between the partners. (There is apparently none between Intel and Sharp.)

Alliances, formal and informal, are becoming the dominant form of economic integration in the world economy. Some major companies, such as Toshiba, the

Japanese electronics giant, and Corning Glass, the world's leading maker of high-engineered glass, may each have more than 100 alliances all over the world. Integration in the Common Market is proceeding far more through alliances than through mergers and acquisitions, especially among the middle-sized companies that dominate most European economies. As with structural and institutional trade, businesses make little distinction between domestic and foreign partners in their alliances. An alliance creates a relationship in which it does not matter whether one partner speaks Japanese, another English, and a third German or Finnish. And while alliances increasingly generate both trade and investment, they are based on neither. They pool knowledge.

THE VITAL LINK

For developed economies, the distinction between the domestic and international economy has ceased to be a reality, however much political, cultural, or psychological strength remains in the idea. An unambiguous lesson of the last 40 years is that increased participation in the world economy has become the key to domestic economic growth and prosperity. Since 1950 there has been a close correlation between a country's domestic economic performance and its participation in the world economy. The two major countries whose economies have grown the fastest in the world economy, Japan and South Korea, are also the two countries whose domestic economies have grown the fastest. The same correlation applies to the two European countries that have done best in the world economy in the last 40 years, West Germany and Sweden. The countries that have retreated from the world economy (most notably the United Kingdom) have consistently done worse domestically. In the two major countries that have maintained their participation rate in the world economy within a fairly narrow range—the United States and France—the domestic economy has put in an average performance, neither doing exceptionally well nor suffering persistent malaise and crisis like the United Kingdom.

The same correlation holds true for major segments within a developed economy. In the United States, for instance, services have tremendously increased their world economy participation in the last 15 years; finance, higher education, and information are examples. American agriculture, which has consistently shrunk in terms of world economy participation, has been in continual depression and crisis, masked only by ever-growing subsidies.

Conversely, there is little correlation between economic performance and policies to stimulate the domestic economy. The record shows that a government can harm its domestic economy by driving up inflation. But there is not the slightest evidence that any government policy to stimulate the economy has an impact, whether it be Keynesian, monetarist, supply-side, or neoclassical. . . . The evidence not only suggests that government policies to stimulate the economy in the short term are ineffectual, but also something far more surprising:

they are largely irrelevant. Government, the evidence shows clearly, cannot control the economic weather.

The evidence of the past four decades does show convincingly that participation in the world economy has become the controlling factor in the domestic economic performance of developed countries. For example, a sharp increase in manufacturing and service exports kept the U.S. economy from slipping into deep recession in 1992, and unemployment rates for adult men and women never reached the highs of earlier post–World War II recessions. Similarly, Japan's sharply increased exports have kept its current recession from producing unemployment figures at European levels of 8 to 10 percent.

WHAT WORKS, WHAT DOES NOT

The evidence is crystal clear that both advocates of managed trade and conventional free traders are wrong in their prescriptions for economic growth. Japan's industrial policy of attempting to select and support "winning" business sectors is by now a well-known failure. Practically all the industries the Japanese Ministry of International Trade and Industry (MITI) picked—such as supercomputers and pharmaceuticals—have been at best also-rans. The Japanese businesses that succeeded, like Sony and the automobile companies, were opposed or ignored by MITI. Trying to pick winners requires a fortune-teller, and the world economy has become far too complex to be outguessed. Japan's economy benefited from a competency—an extraordinary ability to miniaturize products—that was virtually unknown to MITI. Pivotal economic events often take place long before we notice their occurrence. The available data simply do not report important developments such as the growth of the service trade, of structural and institutional trade, of alliances.

Still, the outstanding overall performance of Japan and other Asian countries cannot be explained away as merely a triumph of conventional free trade. Two common economic policies emerge from a recent World Bank study of eight East Asian "superstars": Japan, South Korea, Hong Kong, Taiwan, Singapore, Malaysia, Thailand, and Indonesia. First, they do not try to manage short-term fluctuations in their domestic economies—they do not try to control the economic weather. Moreover, not one of the East Asian economies took off until it had given up attempts to manage domestic short-term fluctuations. All eight countries focus instead on creating the right economic climate. They keep inflation low. They invest heavily in education and training. They reward savings and investment and penalize consumption. The eight started modernizing their economies at very different times, but once they got going, all have shown similar growth in both their domestic and international economies. Together they now account for 21 percent of the world's manufactured goods exports, versus 9 percent 30 years ago. Five percent of their populations live below the poverty line, compared with about 40 percent in 1960, and four of them—Japan,

Hong Kong, Taiwan, and Singapore—rank among the world's richest countries. Yet the eight are totally different in their culture, history, political systems, and tax policies. They range from laissez-faire Hong Kong to interventionist Singapore to statist Indonesia.

The second major finding of the World Bank study is that these eight countries pursue policies to enhance the competitiveness of their industries in the world economy with only secondary attention to domestic effect. These countries then foster and promote their proven successes in the world economy. Though MITI neither anticipated nor much encouraged Japan's world market successes, the whole Japanese system is geared to running with them. Japan offers its exporters substantial tax benefits and credits, which remain scarce and expensive for domestic businesses, and it deliberately keeps prices and profits high in a protected domestic market in order to generate cash for overseas investment and market penetration.

The same lessons were being taught until recently by the two countries in the West that showed similar growth: West Germany and Sweden. These countries, too, have very different domestic policies. But both created and maintained an economic growth climate, and through the same measures: control of inflation, high investment in education and training, a high savings rate obtained by high taxes on consumption, and fairly low taxes on savings and investment. Both also gave priority to the world economy in governmental and business decisions. The moment they forgot this—when the trade unions a few years back began to subordinate Germany's competitive standing to their wage demands, and the Swedes subordinated their industries' competitive standing to ever-larger welfare spending—their domestic economies went into stagnation.

An additional lesson of the world economy is that investment abroad creates jobs at home. In both the 1960s and the 1980s, expanded U.S. business investments overseas spurred rapid domestic job creation. The same correlation held for Japan and Sweden, both of which invested heavily in overseas plants to produce goods for their home markets. In manufacturing—and in many services, such as retailing—investment per worker in the machinery, tools, and equipment of a new facility is three to five times annual production. Most of this productive equipment comes from institutional trade (that is, from the home country of the investor), and most of it is produced by high-wage labor. The initial employment generated to get the new facility into production is substantially larger than the annual output and employment during its first few years of operation.

The last 40 years also taught that protection does not protect. In fact, the evidence shows quite clearly that protection hastens decline. Less-protected U.S. farm products—soybeans, fruit, beef, and poultry—have fared a good deal better on world markets than have the more subsidized traditional crops, such as corn, wheat, and cotton. Equally persuasive evidence suggests that the American automobile industry's share of its domestic market went into a precipitous decline as soon as the U.S. government forced the Japanese into "voluntary" export restraints. That protection breeds complacency, inefficiency, and cartels has been known since before Adam Smith. The counterargument has always been that it protects jobs, but the evidence of the last 40 years strongly suggests that it does not even do that.

FREE TRADE IS NOT ENOUGH

The world economy has become too important for a country not to have a world-economy policy. Managed trade is a delusion of grandeur. Outright protectionism can only do harm, but simply trying to thwart protectionism is not enough. What is needed is a deliberate and active—indeed, aggressive—policy that gives the demands, opportunities, and dynamics of the external economy priority over domestic policy demands and problems. For the United States and a number of other countries, it means abandoning ways of thinking that have dominated American economics perhaps since 1933, and certainly since 1945. We still see the demands and opportunities of the world economy as externalities. We usually do not ask whether domestic decisions will hurt American competitiveness, participation, and standing in the world economy. The reverse must become the rule: will a proposed domestic move advance American competitiveness and participation in the world economy? The answer to this question determines what are the right domestic economic policy and business decisions. The lessons of the last 40 years teach us that integration is the only basis for an international trade policy that can work, the only way to rapidly revive a domestic economy in turbulence and chronic recession.

25

VANISHING BORDERS: THE GLOBALIZATION OF POLITICS AND MARKETS

Eugene R. Wittkopf and Charles W. Kegley, Jr.

Globalization **captures the intensification of interdependence now engulfing the world economically, culturally, socially, and ecologically. Eugene R. Wittkopf and Charles W. Kegley, Jr., examine the uneven spread of economic globalization and ask about its implications for states' ability to control the globalizing forces they themselves have helped to create. Wittkopf is R. Downs Poindexter Professor of Political Science at Louisiana State University. Kegley is Pearce Professor of International Relations at the University of South Carolina. Together they have authored** *World Politics: Trend and Transformation* **(1997), from which this essay is adapted.**

Integration and disintegration, nationalism and globalism are simultaneous but divergent trends that underlie the transformation of contemporary world politics. They portend very different futures, however. In one scenario, sovereignty is at bay as the globalization of markets and culture transcends the boundaries of the contemporary geopolitical world and erodes the meaning of national identity. In the other, nations and states sometimes compete with one another, although their goals are essentially the same: to attain or retain the trappings of independence from and control over the homogenizing forces now sweeping the world.

Globalization may be defined as "the intensification of economic, political, social, and cultural relations across borders."[1] It stems from "the onrush of economic and ecological forces that demand integration and uniformity and that mesmerize the world with fast music, fast computers, and fast food—with MTV, Macintosh, and McDonald's pressing nations into one commercially homogenous global network: one McWorld tied together by technology, ecology, communications, and commerce."[2] A critical characteristic of these cross-border interactions is that national governments do not originate them. Indeed, governments increasingly are challenged by transforming trends in which borders are becoming transparent.

The economic side of globalization dominates the headlines of financial pages and computer trade journals. It is found in "that loose combination of free-trade agreements, the Internet, and the integration of financial markets that is erasing borders and uniting the world into a single, lucrative, but brutally competitive, marketplace."[3] Because even the most powerful states cannot escape these forces, globalization implies nothing less than a redistribution of global economic power, which may also translate into a redistribution of political power.

In this chapter we examine the globalization of finance, trade, production, and labor. We will show that "globalization is uneven. It unites but it also divides, creating winners here and losers there."[4] We conclude by asking about the implications for the future of the state in a global system of vanishing borders.

THE GLOBALIZATION OF FINANCE

Global finance encompasses "all types of cross-border portfolio-type transactions—borrowing and lending, trading of currencies or other financial claims, and the provision of commercial banking or other financial services. It also includes capital flows associated with foreign direct investment—transactions involving significant control of producing enterprises."[5] The *globalization of finance* refers to the increasing transnationalization of financial markets. Its central characteristic is that the emerging system of financial arrangements is not centered on a single state. Thus globalization implies the growth of a single, unified, world market. While

---

[1]Hans-Henrik Holm and Georg Sørensen, "Introduction: What Has Changed?" in *Whose World Order, Uneven Globalization and the End of the Cold War* Hans-Henrik Holm and Georg Sørensen, eds. (Boulder, Colo.: Westview, 1995), p. 1.

[2]Benjamin R. Barber, "Jihad vs. McWorld," *Atlantic Monthly* 269 (March 1992), pp. 53–63.

[3]Thomas Friedman, "Answers Needed to Globalization Dissent," *Houston Chronicle,* February 8, 1996, p. 30.

[4]Georg Sørensen, "Four Futures," *Bulletin of the Atomic Scientists* 51 (July–August 1995), p. 72.

[5]Benjamin J. Cohen, "Phoenix Risen: The Resurrection of Global Finance," *World Politics* 48 (January 1996), p. 269.

telecommunications specialists talk about the "death of distance," financial specialists talk about the "end of geography," which "refers to a state of economic development where geographic location no longer matters in finance."[6]

Evidence of financial globalization abounds. Although trade has grown dramatically since World War II, the volume of cross-border capital flows has increased even more. Financial flows now exceed trade in merchandise by 20 to 40 times, and the gap continues to widen.[7] Further evidence is found in foreign exchange markets, where currency traders—often exchanging more than $1 trillion daily—make profits on the basis of minute shifts in the value of states' currencies.

Securities markets reveal the globalization of finance as well. Foreign investors' activities in U.S. stock markets during the 1980s increased by more than $300 billion. They also set new records in Japan, growing from 4.6 billion yen in 1980 to more than 54 billion in 1987. Between 1980 and 1990 the market value of shares (known as "capitalization") on world stock markets increased from $2.5 to $8.2 trillion. "New York's capitalization doubled, London's more than tripled, and Tokyo's increased tenfold."[8] In addition, new financial instruments have emerged, leading to new markets in which they are bought and sold. "Derivatives" are one example. These are complex financial instruments that combine speculation in "options" and "futures" designed to hedge against volatility in financial markets, but they require no actual buying of the underlying securities (stocks and bonds). Derivatives now account for trillions of dollars in cross-border transactions and "are rapidly becoming one of the most globalized financial markets."[9]

As these data suggest, markets are being transformed profoundly by the rapid acceleration of financial globalization. We may not yet have experienced the end of geography, but clearly financial globalization "has put governments distinctly on the defensive, eroding much of the authority of the contemporary sovereign state."[10] What explains these changes?

Analysts generally agree that at least three developments account for the globalization of finance. First, the oil crisis of 1973–1974 and the OPEC decade that followed unleashed a rapid increase in global financial flows. New patterns of global investments and new tools of financial management followed.

Second, beginning in the 1970s and accelerating in the 1980s, basic changes began to take place in the philosophy governing the regulation of national financial markets and capital movements. Washington and London

[6]Richard O'Brien, *Global Financial Integration: The End of Geography* (New York: Council on Foreign Relations Press, 1992), p. 1.

[7]Philip G. Cerny, "The Dynamics of Financial Globalization: Technology, Market Structure, and Policy Response," *Policy Sciences* 27, no. 4 (1994), p. 324.

[8]Andrew C. Sobel, *Domestic Choices, International Markets: Dismantling National Barriers and Liberalizing Securities Markets* (Ann Arbor, Mich.: University of Michigan Press, 1994), pp. 50–1.

[9]Cerny, "The Dynamics of Financial Globalization," pp. 331, 334.

[10]Cohen, "Phoenix Risen," p. 270.

("Reaganism" and "Thatcherism") played key roles in deregulating markets, choosing to emphasize the principles of classic economic liberalism, which say that markets operate best when free of government interference. As private-market actors became more sophisticated in evading national markets where regulations impeded their access, states responded by lowering their regulatory standards. This stimulated others to do the same as the competitive pressures on states to attract foreign capital multiplied.

Third, technological innovations spurred the globalization of finance. As one analyst has written, "To a great extent the end-of-geography story is a technology story, the story of the computerization of finance."[11] Another argues that "the development and impact of technology [do] not involve merely the machinery of . . . financial transactions—the electronic equivalent of nuts and bolts—but also the culture of production, competition, and innovation in the financial sector and, indeed, in all of the other sectors of economy and society, which are inextricably intertwined with finance."[12] Still, global finance is different from many other markets in that no physical goods need actually be exchanged in the transaction. Instead, numbers are changed on a computer screen, formally concluding agreements in an instant.

What are the consequences of the globalization of finance? Many economists see the increased mobility of capital as proof that markets become more efficient as they are widened. From this perspective, the exploding volume of international finance encourages further deregulation and liberalization of markets throughout the world and the convergence of monetary and fiscal policies, particularly among states in the Global North.

The mobility of capital has also changed the global political context. Because financial markets are no longer centered in a single state, the financial system is not subject to regulation by anyone in particular. Instead, it has taken on a life of its own, constraining states' policy choices in the economic arena much as political realists argue that the distribution of power constrains their choices in the political-military arena. In effect, the mobility of capital now systematically constrains state behavior by rewarding some actors and punishing others much as military power once did.

The "imperatives of international competitiveness" explain the costs and benefits that now encourage states effectively to undermine their ability to determine their own fates. States compete not only for shares of the global markets, but also for the benefits that flow from a world in which markets have become increasingly interconnected. By encouraging the globalization of finance, however, states now find that they have difficulty controlling their own shares of global markets.

---

[11]O'Brien, *Global Financial Integration,* p. 8.
[12]Cerny, "The Dynamics of Financial Globalization," p. 326.

THE GLOBALIZATION OF TRADE

Growing international trade has propelled widespread advances in global welfare during the past half-century. Its expansion in this decade has been particularly rapid. The gains from trade are uneven, however. As a result, domestic protectionist measures designed to cushion or curtail the unfavorable effects of the rapid globalization of trade abound. The Global North often instigates these measures, usually targeting the rapidly growing economies in the Global South, particularly in Asia. For the newly industrialized economies (NIEs) in Asia and other emerging markets, however, the globalization of trade has become the preferred route to economic advancement.

Trade integration is the difference between growth rates in trade and gross domestic (or gross world) product. As trade integration grows, so does interdependence. As the data in Figure 25–1 show, the 1990s have witnessed not only growth in trade integration but also a spectacular increase in the *speed* of integration, as growth in trade has consistently outpaced growth in production. The speed of integration has been sharply higher in the Global South than in the North, reflecting the Global South's increasing contribution to trade growth—a trend expected to continue. Eastern Europe, Central Asia, and East Asia have

FIGURE 25–1
GROWTH OF WORLD OUTPUT AND TRADE, 1981–1996
Source: *World Economic and Social Survey 1995* (1995), p. 35.

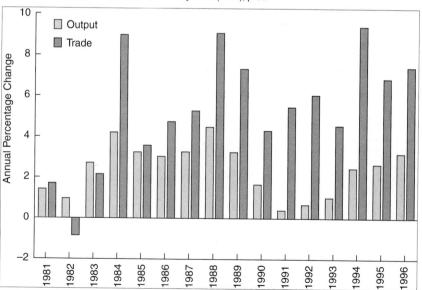

experienced the most rapid integration into the world political economy. North Africa, sub-Saharan Africa, and the Middle East lag far behind. The differences among these groups reflect their historical experiences and the different strategies of development each has chosen. They also reflect changes in technology and consumer demands in a globalizing world political economy.

New Products

High-technology electronic goods (data-processing equipment, telecommunications equipment, and semiconductors and microprocessors) make up an increasing proportion of trade in manufactured goods.[13] The Global North is the major supplier of high-technology goods, accounting for nearly 75 percent of new-product exports in 1993. The United States and Japan lead the pack, followed by western Europe. But these patterns are changing rapidly, creating winners not only in products but also among producers as dramatic changes in export markets focused on Asia unfold.

The Global South's share of world trade, both now and projected into the future, is growing. Its share of manufactured-product exports is growing as well, but its share of total exports of the new products has grown even more. This is the area where Asia surpasses all others. Table 25–1 shows the percentage share of

[13]Our discussion of the production and trade in new products draws on the chapter "International Trade in 'New' Manufactured Products," in the United Nations' *World Economic and Social Survey 1995* (New York: United Nations, 1995), pp. 171–8.

TABLE 25–1
SHARE OF NEW PRODUCTS IN MANUFACTURED EXPORTS,
SELECTED COUNTRIES, 1980–1993 (PERCENTAGES)

	1980	1985	1990	1993
Global South	14	13	18	23
Asian NIEs	16	18	28	32
Hong Kong	13	14	17	19
South Korea	11	13	24	24
Singapore	33	36	51	56
Taiwan	16	16	23	25
Other Asian countries				
Malaysia	46	53	52	54
Thailand	1	2	24	25
Global North	8	11	11	13
United States	11	17	17	17
Japan	15	22	24	25

Source: Adapted from *World Economic and Social Survey 1995* (New York: United Nations, 1995), p. 74.

new products in the manufactured exports of selected countries and economic groups. The six Asian countries listed account for nearly two-thirds of all developing country exports of the new products. New products comprise nearly one-third of their total output of manufactured goods—twice the level of the United States.

The emergence of Asia as a primary supplier of high-tech manufactured-product exports has resulted from a relocation of production centers during the past two decades. The determination of the four Asia Tigers and now the new "cubs" (Malaysia and Thailand) to pursue an export-led path to development—including a determination to specialize in high-technology electronic products—has contributed to their success in the production of the new manufactured products. Another important factor is the growing worldwide specialization in the manufacture of these products stemming from "outsourcing" the production of less technologically sophisticated components to countries where wages are lower. As this happens, other investments and technology follow, with the final products being exported back to many of the same countries where the investments originated. The rapid technological upgrading of exports has enabled the Asian NIEs and emerging markets to join in this process. In short, they have been winners. At the same time, however, many workers in the Global North believe they have been victimized as investment capital and production centers have shifted.

Trade in services also promises to make new winners. Because the United States enjoys comparative advantages in this area, it has been a strong advocate of bringing services under the liberalizing rules of the World Trade Organization. Trade in services already has expanded more than threefold since 1980, with the Global North reaping most of the benefits. Interestingly, however, the Global South has increased its share of this growing trade even more rapidly. The spread of information technology and the comparatively lower wage costs in developing economies are among the reasons. In the case of services, then, it appears that—at least for the time being—North and South are both reaping the profits of the globalization of trade.

Commodities

The "new" international division of labor is reflected in the role of the Asian NIEs in the rapidly expanding trade in new, high-tech products. The "old" division of labor, born of the colonial era, also describes the structure of international trade. Many countries in the Global South continue to depend heavily on export earnings from raw materials and agricultural products, such as oil, copper, cocoa, and coffee. Many Northern nations also export large quantities of minerals and agricultural products. The United States and Canada, for example, were long described as the "breadbasket of the world." Their dependence on primary products is comparatively small, however. Not so for the oil-producing countries in the Middle East or the producers of non-oil primary products throughout the Global South. For them, developments in the global commodities marketplace are critically important. For the most part, though, commodity trends over the past several decades have been harmful to their development objectives.

The pattern of trade that developed during the colonial and imperial periods of the past made developing economies the principal source of primary-product exports to the colonial powers. They, in turn, made sure their colonies were the principal buyers of their manufactured goods. That pattern persisted even after the states that now comprise the Global South gained their sovereignty. The rapidly developing economies of Asia have managed to break out of this pattern, but many others—particularly in Africa—have not. Thus they continue to be subject to the vagaries of the world market for commodities.

Much evidence supports the argument that the price of commodities since World War II has been erratic in the short term and downward turning in the long run. More importantly from the viewpoint of the globalization of trade, the industrial economies of the Global North increasingly have become uncoupled from the primary-product economies of the Global South. Consider the following: "The seminal product of the 1920s was the automobile, which was 60 percent energy and raw materials and 40 percent skills and knowledge; the seminal product of the 1990s is the computer chip, which is 2 percent energy and raw materials and 98 percent ideas, skills, and knowledge."[14] As the information age spreads beyond the North to those in the South that are technologically innovative, primary-product producers will be the losers. Large numbers of them are in Africa south of the Sahara.

THE GLOBALIZATION OF PRODUCTION

In the early 1990s Ford Motor Company launched a program called Ford 2000. Its purpose is to transform the world's second-largest industrial firm into its first truly international corporation. Management control will no longer be centered in Dearborn, Michigan, but rather dispersed throughout the world. Already Ford's chairman Alex Trotman—himself from Scotland—proudly proclaims that "there's not an American in charge of any of our national companies in Europe." Ford anticipates changes in its product line as well. Unlike most multinational corporations today, which manufacture and sell products tailored for particular regional markets (such as the Toyota corporation), Ford intends to develop manufacturing capabilities that reduce duplication in different national settings. This also will permit greater standardization and move it along the path toward a "world car." Reduced costs and greater efficiency are the goals.

Ford's plan to develop a truly international corporation is arguably the "highest stage" of corporate development. According to Harvard University's

---

[14]Ray Marshall, "The Global Jobs Crisis," *Foreign Policy* 100 (Fall 1995), p. 55.

Christopher Bartlett, multinational corporations evolved through four stages. The initial period was one of corporate colonialism, when European MNCs directed their investments toward the nation's colonies. This was followed, after World War II, by the nationalistic period, in which U.S. companies dominated the manufacture of goods and sold them in foreign markets. Today, as noted, most multinationals are in a regional phase, manufacturing and selling products tailored for particular regional markets. From a management point of view, MNCs' overseas operations are "appendages" of a centralized hub. Ford's plans to move into the fourth stage of MNC development would disperse the hub, much as production facilities themselves are now spread worldwide.

As the multinational corporation has evolved, it has been the primary agent of the globalization of production, propelling as well the extraordinary growth in trade and capital mobility witnessed during the past half-century. Today there are more than 38,500 multinational parent companies. The outward flow of foreign direct investment (FDI) stock attributable to their more than 250,000 foreign affiliates stood at an estimated $2.4 trillion at the end of 1994.[15] Most of these stocks are located in the Global North, which is also the primary source and target of the outward flow of FDI.

The reason for the concentration of FDI in the North is clear: Profits are MNCs' primary motivations, and their investment returns are likely to be greatest in the Global North, where a combination of affluence and political stability reduces investment risks. Still, the Global South is the host of considerable FDI. Although the amounts fluctuate on a yearly basis, the 1990s generally have seen a return to the patterns of the early 1980s, when a growing number of developing countries were viewed as targets of opportunity. Today, those opportunities are in Asia.

The impact of foreign direct investment extends beyond money. With it comes technology, managerial expertise, and employment opportunities. Champions of MNCs view these as contributions to the development of less developed economies. Not surprisingly, nations in the Global South often actively seek MNC investment capital and the other perquisites that flow from it. MNCs are especially important to those who seek to emulate the economic success of the newly industrializing economies, which depend on an ability to sustain growth in exports. Foreign capital is critical in this process.

Foreign investment is not without costs, however. With it comes political influence, for example, which sometimes skews the political process in questionable directions. Critics of MNCs also worry that the presumed economic benefits of FDI gloss over their adverse economic consequences. "They see these giant corporations not as needed agents of economic change but more as vehicles of antidevelopment. Multinationals, they argue, reinforce dualistic economic

---

[15]*World Investment Report 1995* (New York: United Nations, 1995), p. 9.

structures and exacerbate domestic inequalities with wrong products and inappropriate technology."[16]

Critics contend that MNCs exact a cost not only on the Global South but also on the Global North. They note that while corporate executives often have a "broad vision and understanding of global issues," they have little appreciation of, or concern for, "the long-term social or political consequences of what their companies make or what they do."[17] These allegedly include a host of maladies, including environmental degradation, a maldistribution of global resources, and social disintegration. Beyond this, critics worry that MNCs are beyond the control of national political leaders. "More and more, they must conform to the demands of the outside world because the outsiders are already inside the gates. Business enterprises that routinely operate across borders are linking far-flung pieces of territory into a new world economy that bypasses all sorts of established political arrangements and conventions."[18] Still, some corporate visionaries extol multinational corporations' transnational virtues. "There are no longer any national flag carriers," in the words of Kenichi Ohmae, a Japanese management consultant. "Corporations must serve their customers, not governments."

LABOR'S PLACE IN THE GLOBALIZATION PROCESS

In his manifesto on the evils of capitalism, Karl Marx urged the workers of the world to unite, throwing off the bondages imposed by the oppressive owners of capital. Marx assumed that workers everywhere shared a common purpose and vision, but that has long since been proven untrue. Moreover, as the liberalization of markets throughout the world and their rapid integration proceeds globally, labor markets will be profoundly affected. Competition—not solidarity—has intensified. Indeed, as workers in the formerly centralized economies of the Soviet Union, Europe, and others, including India, are integrated into the global labor market through the elimination of restrictive trade barriers and the regulation of capital markets elsewhere, the world will experience a dramatic increase in the number of workers exposed to the vagaries of a world political economy increasingly oblivious to national borders.

Accommodating the influx of new workers will be difficult. Already "the world is experiencing the worst employment crisis since the 1930s," according to a former secretary of the U.S. Department of Labor. "Almost one-third of the Earth's 2.8 billion workers are either jobless or underemployed, and many of those who are employed work for very low wages with little prospect for

[16]Michael P. Todaro, *Economic Development in the Third World,* 5th ed. (New York: Longman, 1994), p. 535.

[17]Richard J. Barnet and John Cavanagh, *Global Dreams: Imperial Corporations and the New World Order* (New York: Simon & Schuster, 1994), p. 18.

[18]Ibid., p. 19.

advancement."[19] Europe suffers chronic unemployment, with as much as 12 percent of the labor force idled. Unemployment rates are lower in the United States, but the real wages of most U.S. workers have fallen over the past two decades. Mass unemployment characterizes conditions in many of the economies in transition, while in much of the Global South employment growth has slowed and wage rates have fallen. The costs of the deteriorating employment picture are high.

> High levels of joblessness result not only in an enormous waste of resources but also in human suffering and hopelessness, rising inequality within and between countries, and a host of ills. The conditions threaten social cohesion and undermine democratic institutions—or make them much more difficult to establish. And growing global interdependence causes such problems in one country to affect others negatively as well.[20]

Multinational corporations have been a primary vehicle of growing global interdependence. This often has been made possible by moving manufacturing sites and technical know-how to developing countries, where labor is cheap. Of the 8 million jobs created by MNCs between 1985 and 1992, 5 million were in the Global South. In countries as diverse as Argentina, Barbados, Botswana, Indonesia, Malaysia, Mauritius, Mexico, the Philippines, Singapore, and Sri Lanka, multinationals account for one-fifth of the manufacturing-sector employment.[21] Thus workers have benefited from new job opportunities. In a world of highly mobile capital, however, this also makes them vulnerable.

Such fears, born of experience, are all too real in the Global North. Workers there fear losing their jobs due to cheap imports made possible by lower-cost production in the Global South or because the companies they work for will relocate abroad. The irony is that economic growth has been rekindled since the recession of the early 1990s. For many, however, this has been a time of "jobless growth." And even if they keep their jobs, employees often blame cheap foreign labor for their own lack of pay hikes, resulting in stagnating living standards.

Wage rates differ widely throughout the world (see Figure 25–2). It is difficult to assess the impact of wage rates in different countries on one another, because labor trends are affected not only by trade but also by technological developments, trends in labor productivity, and migration. However, economic theory does predict that, as a result of international trade, the wage rates in poor countries will be pulled up somewhat. Meanwhile wage rates in rich countries will come down, at least for unskilled workers. "The logic behind this is that trade affects the relative rewards of factors of production by changing the relative price of goods. Opening up to trade increases the price of labor-intensive goods in

[19]Marshall, "The Global Jobs Crisis," p. 50.
[20]Ibid.
[21]*World Development Report 1995* (New York: Oxford University Press, 1995), p. 62.

FIGURE 25–2

SAME WORK, DIFFERENT PAY

Source: Ishac Diwan and Ana Revenga, "Wages, Inequity, and International Integration," *Finance & Development* 32 (September 1995), p. 8.

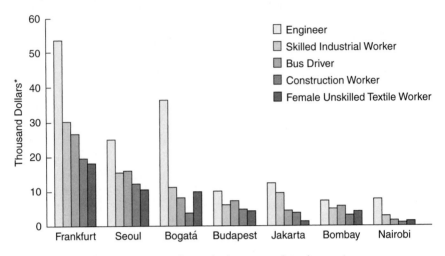

*Thousand dollars per year, converted at purchasing power parity exchange rates.

poor, labor-rich countries, which, as a consequence, shift their resources to the production of labor-intensive goods. This, in turn, raises demand for labor in poor countries, and hence raises relative wages. As relative prices of goods converge in rich and poor countries, so do wages."[22] In short, as a consequence of trade, wage rates should tend toward convergence. For some, this means a gain in welfare; for others, it means lost income.

With protectionist sentiments already widespread in the Global North, countries in the Global South worry that their own hopes for economic advancement cannot be realized unless and until the Global North relaxes its multitude of restrictive trade barriers. Interestingly, however, concern for the impact of low wage rates is no longer confined to the Global North. Faced with the prospect of huge numbers of low-wage Chinese workers entering the work force, some Global South nations now also feel threatened. This is leading them, too, to embrace protectionist trade practices. Thus the challenge of globalization promises to shape the global political agenda well into the next century.

[22]Ishac Diwan and Ana Revenga, "Wages, Inequality, and International Integration," *Finance & Development* 32 (September 1995), p.8.

THE STATE AND GLOBALIZATION:
SYSTEM STRESS OR TRANSFORMATION?

Rapid globalization, fueled in large measure by the revolution in microelectronics, is a process unlikely to be forestalled. Analysts differ on whether globalization is desirable or despicable, however, depending in part on the scenarios about the future world order that globalization will help create and the political perspectives that inform their world views. Some focus on the benefits of globalization for economic well-being, others on its unevenness and the prospects for marginalizing large numbers of peoples and states. Some focus on the challenge globalization poses to an international system founded on the state; others are more sanguine about the state's resilience and the prospects for global governance to cope with the challenge of globalization.

Globalization, as the term itself suggests, has been a worldwide phenomenon, but it has been uneven. The intensification of interdependence has been most pronounced among the nations of the Global North and the emerging economies of East Asia, which have reaped its economic benefits. But because it is uneven, globalization also threatens to widen the gulf between the world's rich and poor countries. This is true even within the Global South, which already stands at some distance from the high-consumption societies of the North.

> If the borderless world rewards entrepreneurs, designers, brokers, patent owners, lawyers, and dealers in high-value services, then East Asia's commitment to education, science, and technology can only increase its lead over other developing economies. By contrast, their relative lack of capital, high technology, scientists, and skilled workers, and export-oriented industry makes it difficult for poorer countries to partake in the communications and financial revolution. . . . Some grimmer forecasts suggest the developing world may become more marginalized, partly because of the dematerialization of labor, raw materials, and foodstuffs, partly because the advanced economies may concentrate upon greater knowledge-based commerce among themselves. . . .
>
> As we move into the next century the developed economies appear to have all the trump cards in their hands—capital, technology, control of communications, surplus foodstuffs, powerful multinational companies—and, if anything, their advantages are *growing* because technology is eroding the value of labor and materials, the chief assets of developing countries.[23]

But is technology also eroding the ability of even the rich states to control their economic and political fortunes? Certainly a world of vanishing borders challenges the territorial state, but states still establish the political framework

---

[23]Paul Kennedy, *Preparing for the Twenty-First Century* (New York: Random House, 1993), pp. 223–25.

governing the world political economy. State power thus retains its relevance in shaping outcomes even in a world political economy undergoing rapid change. International regimes like those that evolved after World War II to promote global governance in monetary and trade affairs may also prove effective as management strategies for coping with the globalization challenge. A key issue is whether states can find a focal point, a norm, around which cooperation could emerge. Liberal theorists in both politics and economics, who focus on the mutual gains stemming from international cooperation, are optimistic about the possibilities. Political realists and neomercantilists, who are concerned more with relative gains than absolute gains, are more pessimistic.

26

COMPETITIVENESS: A DANGEROUS OBSESSION

Paul Krugman

Increasingly policy makers have worried about their nations' competitiveness in the global marketplace and have embraced domestic and foreign economic policies they believe will enhance their national fortunes. Economic trade theorist Paul Krugman chastises those seemingly obsessed with competitiveness, arguing that it "is a meaningless word when applied to national economies." Krugman is professor of economics at the Massachusetts Institute of Technology. His numerous books include *Peddling Prosperity: Economic Sense and Nonsense in the Age of Diminished Expectations* **(1994).**

THE HYPOTHESIS IS WRONG

In June 1993, Jacques Delors made a special presentation to the leaders of the nations of the European Community, meeting in Copenhagen, on the growing problem of European unemployment. Economists who study the European situation were curious to see what Delors, president of the EC Commission, would say. Most of them share more or less the same diagnosis of the European problem: the taxes and regulations imposed by Europe's elaborate welfare states have made employers reluctant to create new jobs, while the relatively generous level of unemployment benefits has made workers unwilling to accept the kinds of low-wage jobs that help keep unemployment comparatively low in the United States. The monetary difficulties associated with preserving the European Monetary System in the face of the costs of German reunification have reinforced this structural problem.

It is a persuasive diagnosis, but a politically explosive one, and everyone wanted to see how Delors would handle it. Would he dare tell European leaders that their efforts to pursue economic justice have produced unemployment as an unintended by-product? Would he admit that the EMS could be sustained only at the cost of a recession and face the implications of that admission for European monetary union?

Guess what? Delors didn't confront the problems of either the welfare state or the EMS. He explained that the root cause of European unemployment was a lack of competitiveness with the United States and Japan and that the solution was a program of investment in infrastructure and high technology.

It was a disappointing evasion, but not a surprising one. After all, the rhetoric of competitiveness—the view that, in the words of President Clinton, each nation is "like a big corporation competing in the global marketplace"—has become pervasive among opinion leaders throughout the world. People who believe themselves to be sophisticated about the subject take it for granted that the economic problem facing any modern nation is essentially one of competing on world markets—that the United States and Japan are competitors in the same sense that Coca-Cola competes with Pepsi—and are unaware that anyone might seriously question that proposition. Every few months a new best-seller warns the American public of the dire consequences of losing the "race" for the 21st century. A whole industry of councils on competitiveness, "geoeconomists," and managed trade theorists has sprung up in Washington. Many of these people, having diagnosed America's economic problems in much the same terms as Delors did Europe's, are now . . . formulating economic and trade policy for the United States. So Delors was using a language that was not only convenient but comfortable for him and a wide audience on both sides of the Atlantic.

Unfortunately, his diagnosis was deeply misleading as a guide to what ails Europe, and similar diagnoses in the United States are equally misleading. The idea that a country's economic fortunes are largely determined by its success on world markets is a hypothesis, not a necessary truth; and as a practical, empirical matter, that hypothesis is flatly wrong. That is, it is simply not the case that the world's leading nations are to any important degree in economic competition with each other, or that any of their major economic problems can be attributed to failures to compete on world markets. The growing obsession in most advanced nations with international competitiveness should be seen, not as a well-founded concern, but as a view held in the face of overwhelming contrary evidence. . . . Thinking in terms of competitiveness leads, directly and indirectly, to bad economic policies on a wide range of issues, domestic and foreign, whether it be in health care or trade.

MINDLESS COMPETITION

Most people who use the term "competitiveness" do so without a second thought. It seems obvious to them that the analogy between a country and a corporation is reasonable and that to ask whether the United States is competitive in the world market is no different in principle from asking whether General Motors is competitive in the North American minivan market.

In fact, however, trying to define the competitiveness of a nation is much more problematic than defining that of a corporation. The bottom line for a corporation is literally its bottom line: if a corporation cannot afford to pay its workers, suppliers, and bondholders, it will go out of business. So when we say that a corporation is uncompetitive, we mean that its market position is unsustainable—that unless it improves its performance, it will cease to exist. Countries, on the other hand, do not go out of business. They may be happy or unhappy with their economic performance, but they have no well-defined bottom line. As a result, the concept of national competitiveness is elusive.

One might suppose, naively, that the bottom line of a national economy is simply its trade balance, that competitiveness can be measured by the ability of a country to sell more abroad than it buys. But in both theory and practice a trade surplus may be a sign of national weakness, a deficit a sign of strength. For example, Mexico was forced to run huge trade surpluses in the 1980s in order to pay the interest on its foreign debt since international investors refused to lend it any more money; it began to run large trade deficits after 1990 as foreign investors recovered confidence and began to pour in new funds. Would anyone want to describe Mexico as a highly competitive nation during the debt crisis era or describe what has happened since 1990 as a loss in competitiveness?

Most writers who worry about the issue at all have therefore tried to define competitiveness as the combination of favorable trade performance and something else. In particular, the most popular definition of competitiveness nowadays runs along the lines of the one given in [former U.S.] Council of Economic Advisors Chairman Laura D'Andrea Tyson's *Who's Bashing Whom?:* competitiveness is "our ability to produce goods and services that meet the test of international competition while our citizens enjoy a standard of living that is both rising and sustainable." This sounds reasonable. If you think about it, however, and test your thoughts against the facts, you will find out that there is much less to this definition than meets the eye.

Consider, for a moment, what the definition would mean for an economy that conducted very little international trade, like the United States in the 1950s. For such an economy, the ability to balance its trade is mostly a matter of getting the exchange rate right. But because trade is such a small factor in the economy, the level of the exchange rate is a minor influence on the standard of living. So in an economy with very little international trade, the growth in living standards—and thus "competitiveness" according to Tyson's definition—would be determined almost entirely by domestic factors, primarily the rate of productivity growth. That's domestic productivity growth, period—not productivity growth relative to other countries. In other words, for an economy with very little international trade, "competitiveness" would turn out to be a funny way of saying "productivity" and would have nothing to do with international competition.

But surely this changes when trade becomes more important, as indeed it has for all major economies? It certainly could change. Suppose that a country finds that although its productivity is steadily rising, it can succeed in exporting only if it repeatedly devalues its currency, selling its exports ever more cheaply on world markets. Then its standard of living, which depends on its purchasing power over imports as well as domestically produced goods, might actually decline. In the jargon of economists, domestic growth might be outweighed by deteriorating terms of trade. So "competitiveness" could turn out really to be about international competition after all.

There is no reason, however, to leave this as a pure speculation; it can easily be checked against the data. Have deteriorating terms of trade in fact been a major drag on the U.S. standard of living? Or has the rate of growth of U.S. real income continued essentially to equal the rate of domestic productivity growth, even though trade is a larger share of income than it used to be?

To answer this question, one need only look at the national income accounts data the [U.S.] Commerce Department publishes regularly in the *Survey of Current Business.* The standard measure of economic growth in the United States is, of course, real GNP—a measure that divides the value of goods and services produced in the United States by appropriate price indexes to come up with an estimate of real national output. The Commerce Department also, however, publishes something called "command GNP." This is similar to real GNP except that it divides U.S. exports not by the export price index, but by the price index for U.S. imports. That is, exports are valued by what Americans can buy with the money exports bring. Command GNP therefore measures the volume of goods and services the U.S. economy can "command"—the nation's purchasing power—rather than the volume it produces. And as we have just seen, "competitiveness" means something different from "productivity" if and only if purchasing power grows significantly more slowly than output.

Well, here are the numbers. Over the period 1959–73, a period of vigorous growth in U.S. living standards and few concerns about international competition, real GNP per worker-hour grew 1.85 percent annually, while command GNP per hour grew a bit faster, 1.87 percent. From 1973 to 1990, a period of stagnating living standards, command GNP growth per hour slowed to 0.65 percent. Almost all

(91 percent) of that slowdown, however, was explained by a decline in domestic productivity growth: real GNP per hour grew only 0.73 percent.

Similar calculations for the European Community and Japan yield similar results. In each case, the growth rate of living standards essentially equals the growth rate of domestic productivity—not productivity relative to competitors, but simply domestic productivity. Even though world trade is larger than ever before, national living standards are overwhelmingly determined by domestic factors rather than by some competition for world markets.

How can this be in our interdependent world? Part of the answer is that the world is not as interdependent as you might think: countries are nothing at all like corporations. Even today, U.S. exports are only 10 percent of the value-added in the economy (which is equal to GNP). That is, the United States is still almost 90 percent an economy that produces goods and services for its own use. By contrast, even the largest corporation sells hardly any of its output to its own workers; the "exports" of General Motors—its sales to people who do not work there—are virtually all of its sales, which are more than 2.5 times the corporation's value-added.

Moreover, countries do not compete with each other the way corporations do. Coke and Pepsi are almost purely rivals: only a negligible fraction of Coca-Cola's sales go to Pepsi workers, only a negligible fraction of the goods Coca-Cola workers buy are Pepsi products. So if Pepsi is successful, it tends to be at Coke's expense. But the major industrial countries, while they sell products that compete with each other, are also each other's main export markets and each other's main suppliers of useful imports. If the European economy does well, it need not be at U.S. expense; indeed, if anything a successful European economy is likely to help the U.S. economy by providing it with larger markets and selling its goods of superior quality at lower prices.

International trade, then, is not a zero-sum game. When productivity rises in Japan, the main result is a rise in Japanese real wages; American or European wages are in principle at least as likely to rise as to fall, and in practice seem to be virtually unaffected.

It would be possible to belabor the point, but the moral is clear: while competitive problems could arise in principle, as a practical, empirical matter the major nations of the world are not to any significant degree in economic competition with each other. Of course, there is always a rivalry for status and power—countries that grow faster will see their political rank rise. So it is always interesting to *compare* countries. But asserting that Japanese growth diminishes U.S. status is very different from saying that it reduces the U.S. standard of living—and it is the latter that the rhetoric of competitiveness asserts. . . .

THE THRILL OF COMPETITION

The competitive metaphor—the image of countries competing with each other in world markets in the same way that corporations do—derives much of its attractiveness from its seeming comprehensibility. Tell a group of businessmen that a country is like a corporation writ large, and you give them the comfort of feeling that they already understand the basics. Try to tell them about economic concepts like comparative advantage, and you are asking them to learn something new. It should not be surprising if many prefer a doctrine that offers the gain of apparent sophistication without the pain of hard thinking. The rhetoric of competitiveness has become so widespread, however, for three deeper reasons.

First, competitive images are exciting, and thrills sell tickets. The subtitle of Lester Thurow's huge best-seller, *Head to Head,* is "The Coming Economic Battle among Japan, Europe, and America"; the jacket proclaims that "the decisive war of the century has begun . . . and America may already have decided to lose." Suppose that the subtitle had described the real situation: "The coming struggle in which each big economy will succeed or fail based on its own efforts, pretty much independently of how well the others do." Would Thurow have sold a tenth as many books?

Second, the idea that U.S. economic difficulties hinge crucially on our failures in international competition somewhat paradoxically makes those difficulties seem easier to solve. The productivity of the average American worker is determined by a complex array of factors, most of them unreachable by any likely government policy. So if you accept the reality that our "competitive" problem is really a domestic productivity problem pure and simple, you are unlikely to be optimistic about any dramatic turnaround. But if you can convince yourself that the problem is really one of failures in international competition—that imports are pushing workers out of high-wage jobs, or subsidized foreign competition is driving the United States out of the high value-added sectors—then the answers to economic malaise may seem to you to involve simple things like subsidizing high technology and being tough on Japan.

Finally, many of the world's leaders have found the competitive metaphor extremely useful as a political device. The rhetoric of competitiveness turns out to provide a good way either to justify hard choices or to avoid them. The example of Delors in Copenhagen shows the usefulness of competitive metaphors as an evasion. Delors had to say something at the EC summit; yet to say anything that addressed the real roots of European unemployment would have involved huge political risks. By turning the discussion to essentially irrelevant but plausible-sounding questions of competitiveness, he bought himself some time to come up with a better answer. . . .

By contrast, the well-received presentation of [President] Bill Clinton's initial economic program in February 1993 showed the usefulness of competitive rhetoric as a motivation for tough policies. Clinton proposed a set of painful spending cuts and tax increases to reduce the Federal deficit. Why? The real reasons for cutting the deficit are disappointingly undramatic: the deficit siphons off funds that might otherwise have been productively invested, and thereby exerts a steady if small drag on U.S. economic growth. But Clinton was able instead to offer a stirring patriotic appeal, calling on the nation to act now in order to make the economy competitive in the global market—with the implication that dire economic consequences would follow if the United States does not.

Many people who know that "competitiveness" is a largely meaningless concept have been willing to indulge competitive rhetoric precisely because they believe they can harness it in the service of good policies. An overblown fear of the Soviet Union was used in the 1950s to justify the building of the interstate highway system and the expansion of math and science education. Cannot the unjustified fears about foreign competition similarly be turned to good, used to justify serious efforts to reduce the budget deficit, rebuild infrastructure, and so on?

A few years ago this was a reasonable hope. At this point, however, the obsession with competitiveness has reached the point where it has already begun dangerously to distort economic policies.

THE DANGERS OF OBSESSION

Thinking and speaking in terms of competitiveness poses three real dangers. First, it could result in the wasteful spending of government money supposedly to enhance [national] competitiveness. Second, it could lead to protectionism and trade wars. Finally, and most important, it could result in bad public policy on a spectrum of important issues.

During the 1950s, fear of the Soviet Union induced the U.S. government to spend money on useful things like highways and science education. It also, however, led to considerable spending on more doubtful items like bomb shelters. The most obvious if least worrisome danger of the growing obsession with competitiveness is that it might lead to a similar misallocation of resources. To take an example, recent guidelines for government research funding have stressed the importance of supporting research that can improve U.S. international competitiveness. This exerts at least some bias toward inventions that can help manufacturing firms, which generally compete on international markets, rather than service producers, which generally do not. Yet most [U.S.] employment and value-added is now in services, and lagging productivity in services rather than manufactures has been the single most important factor in the stagnation of U.S. living standards.

A much more serious risk is that the obsession with competitiveness will lead to trade conflict, perhaps even to a world trade war. Most of those who have preached the doctrine of competitiveness have not been old-fashioned protectionists. They want their countries to win the global trade game, not drop out. But what if, despite its best efforts, a country does not seem to be winning, or lacks confidence that it can? Then the competitive diagnosis inevitably suggests that to close the borders is better than to risk having foreigners take away high-wage jobs and high-value sectors. At the very least, the focus on the supposedly competitive nature of international economic relations greases the rails for those who want confrontational if not frankly protectionist policies.

We can already see this process at work, in both the United States and Europe. In the United States, it was remarkable how quickly the sophisticated interventionist arguments advanced by Laura Tyson in her published work gave way to the simple-minded claim by U.S. Trade Representative Mickey Kantor that Japan's bilateral trade surplus was costing the United States millions of jobs. And the trade rhetoric of President Clinton, who stresses the supposed creation of high-wage jobs rather than the gains from specialization, left his administration in a weak position when it tried to argue with the claims of NAFTA foes that competition from cheap Mexican labor will destroy the U.S. manufacturing base.

Perhaps the most serious risk from the obsession with competitiveness, however, is its subtle indirect effect on the quality of economic discussion and policy making. If top government officials are strongly committed to a particular economic doctrine, their commitment inevitably sets the tone for policy making on all issues, even those that may seem to have nothing to do with that doctrine. And if an economic doctrine is flatly, completely, and demonstrably wrong, the insistence that discussion adhere to that doctrine inevitably blurs the focus and diminishes the quality of policy discussion across a broad range of issues, including some that are very far from trade policy per se. . . .

To make a harsh but not entirely unjustified analogy, a government wedded to the ideology of competitiveness is as unlikely to make good economic policy as a government committed to creationism is to make good science policy, even in areas that have no direct relationship to the theory of evolution. . . .

So let's start telling the truth: competitiveness is a meaningless word when applied to national economies. And the obsession with competitiveness is both wrong and dangerous.

27

ENTER THE DRAGON: CHINA IN THE WORLD POLITICAL ECONOMY

Robert S. Ross

Robert S. Ross argues that bringing China into the World Trade Organization offers the best prospect for easing Chinese trade protectionism and assuring China's eventual full participation in the rule-based liberal international trade regime. Author of *Negotiating Cooperation: U.S.–China Relations, 1969–1989* **(1995), Ross teaches political science at Boston College and is a research associate at the John King Fairbank Center for East Asian Research at Harvard University.**

The completion of the Uruguay Round of the General Agreement on Tariffs and Trade (GATT) and the establishment of the World Trade Organization (WTO) were truly major accomplishments. Together, they are helping to construct an international economic order characterized by liberal trade norms and dispute-settlement procedures that follow agreed-upon rules.

Challenges to the stability of this trade order could nonetheless arise from many sources. Economic factors such as unequal rates of growth and national recessions could elicit counterproductive foreign economic policies. Challenges could also come from powerful countries that refuse to play by the established rules of the WTO liberal trade regime and thus lead to destructive countervailing protectionist measures from their economic partners.

The post–World War II trade system faced such a challenge from Japan, whose effective export-promotion policies undermined the domestic industries of the advanced industrial economies, while its protectionist import restrictions prevented these industries from competing in the Japanese domestic market. Unfair Japanese trade practices brought about growing protectionism from Japan's major trading partners, including the United States and the European Union. Although Japan and its competitors have been able to contain the impact of their protectionist measures, Japanese protectionism has been a major factor contributing to the recent regionalization of the international economy and the emergence of trading zones characterized by special privileges for select WTO members.

THE CHALLENGE OF A RISING CHINA

Japan remains the country with the world's largest trade surplus, and its economic system remains mostly impenetrable. Nonetheless, the openness of the world economy may well be facing an even greater challenge from China's emergence as an economic power. If China's economy continues to grow at current annual rates of 8 to 10 percent, and if it acquires advanced-technology capabilities, China's impact on the international economic system will dwarf that of Japan, even considering Japan's most influential period, during the 1970s and 1980s. With favorable domestic economies of scale and a nearly unlimited supply of cheap labor, China could become a major export power capable of prevailing in the domestic markets of its economic competitors. If China simultaneously were to fail to offer opportunities for participation in its own domestic market, its policies could lead to destabilizing responses by all of the major economic powers.

Clearly, the challenge for the international community is to incorporate China into the global economy so that its behavior reinforces the contemporary trend toward trade liberalization. What is in dispute is the means by which this can be achieved. Chinese membership in the WTO is at the center of this debate. Correct management of China's application would have considerable implications for Chinese economic policy, for the role of the WTO in managing a liberal trade order, and for global economic stability. The dilemma is that there is no easy response to China's application.

Current Chinese trade practices are at wide variance with the WTO obligations assumed by the world's major trading powers. China's state-owned enterprises, which contributed approximately 31 percent to China's total industrial output in 1995 and control strategic sectors of the economy, receive big subsidies and enjoy preferential access to government investment projects. Equally important, high tariffs and nontransparent government regulations protect China's private, collective, and state-owned manufacturers of consumer and industrial goods, further interfering with free trade. China's economic reforms and trade liberalization process have a long way to go before its economic policies meet WTO standards.

An equally important factor is the central government's failure to enforce a range of domestic policies meant to protect the rights of foreign businesses. China's ineffective protection of intellectual property rights is only the most obvious failure. Pervasive corruption throughout China and the absence of an effective central regulatory system weaken the government's ability to enforce international economic obligations on local governments and businesses. The absence of an effective legal system enforced by an independent judiciary compounds these problems, insofar as judicial recourse often is not an available remedy for injured parties. Corruption rather than law often determines the outcome of economic disputes in China.

China's growing economic power and its detrimental economic practices present the international community with a clear-cut policy objective: to persuade China to abandon its current practices for an economic system that complements the WTO's rule-based order. Moreover, if this process is delayed, China will develop sufficient economic power to resist pressures for reform. The United States faced this situation in its relations with Japan. By the time Washington actively sought change in Japan's trading system in the 1980s, Japan had developed the economic power to resist U.S. pressure. Washington failed to act when it had maximum leverage.

THE FAILURE OF CURRENT U.S. POLICY

The United States and its economic partners seek Chinese compliance with the WTO guidelines applicable to the major economic powers. Chinese membership in the WTO should be evaluated in terms of its contribution to this important agenda. Uncompromising adherence to rules and legal norms is a prerequisite to domestic order, but it is inappropriate for achieving interests in a world of states. Whether China today meets WTO standards is less important than adopting policies to promote the development of a Chinese economy compatible with the WTO. Practical pursuit of interest, rather than rigid adherence to principle, will best serve U.S. interests.

While it is in the interest of the United States and other industrial countries that China establish a liberal economic system as soon as possible, it is in China's interest to prolong its current policies. Although China has succeeded in expanding exports, the long-term expansion of its industrial base requires the use of the protectionist measures that Indonesia, Japan, South Korea, and Taiwan employed to assist their nascent industrial systems prior to liberalization.

There is a conflict of interest between China and the global trading system that requires negotiation. Mere insistence that China abide by the rules before it is admitted to the WTO will not lead to a negotiated settlement. On the contrary,

Chinese foreign trade officials argue that the U.S. price for Chinese admission into the WTO—rapid compliance with the trading rules applicable to the other major economic powers and a weakened industrial base—is too high. They have thus decided that China should remain outside of the WTO until the entry requirements are eased.

It is clear that WTO membership provides insufficient benefits to persuade China to liberalize its economy prematurely. Most-favored-nation (MFN) trade status assures China continued access to global markets. Although WTO textile regulations will eventually prove more advantageous than those of the Multi-Fibre Textile Agreement, the changing structure of Chinese trade is reducing the importance of textile exports to the Chinese economy. Equally important, improved access to international textile markets will not compensate China for a weakened industrial base. Given China's current ability to access markets, the benefit of WTO membership is primarily prestige. Beijing has determined that prestige is of little use in making China strong or in raising the standard of living of the Chinese people.

In this respect, contemporary China is different from the Japan of the 1960s. Whereas the United States had significant leverage over Japan in the early years of its post–World-War-II development, it lacks comparable leverage over China at a similar stage in China's development. The reason is that China has a far more open economy than Japan had at a similar stage of its development. Whereas Japan's trading partners could not sell to the Japanese market, China's trading partners have developed a significant interest in maintaining their access to the lucrative Chinese markets in consumer goods, aircraft, and infrastructure projects. This is not to say that the advanced industrial countries have no leverage over China, but that they have less leverage to compel China to open its markets fully. The result is a failed effort to use the prospect of Chinese membership in the WTO as an incentive for Beijing to liberalize its foreign economic policies.

The most profound implication of U.S. policy intransigence will be for China's future economic behavior. Not only has China *not* made the concessions demanded by Washington, but U.S. policy will merely encourage Beijing to persist in its current policies. Chinese isolation from the WTO and the resulting Chinese resentment of the major trading powers will likely enhance Beijing's proclivity to pursue mercantilist policies for national power rather than merely short-term protectionist policies for economic development.

Denial of Chinese membership in the WTO will not minimize the global impact of Chinese protectionism. China will affect the world trade system through its bilateral relationships: WTO member countries will seek bilateral accommodations with China in order to profit from its vast market, thus weakening the liberal trading order. This was the impact of U.S. and European bilateral arrangements with Japan. Denying China membership in the WTO may reflect principled adherence to the rules of trade and allow America to hold the moral high ground, but it will not realize American interests or the interests of America's major trading allies in maintaining a stable liberal economic order. Keeping China out of the WTO provides only the illusion of isolating the problem; it will not solve the problem.

A NEW DIRECTION

. . . One of the great missed opportunities of U.S. China policy was its failure to achieve Chinese membership in the GATT on terms negotiated by the Bush administration in 1989. If China had entered the GATT in 1989, it would be committed to a far more open trade system than is currently the case. Following the June 4, 1989, suppression of the Chinese democracy movement, Washington withdrew support for the agreement. Now China is under no obligation to conform to any GATT/WTO guidelines.

Moreover, the longer the agreement is delayed, the longer the actual period of adjustment will be. The clock for Chinese adherence to WTO regulations does not start ticking until China joins the WTO. In addition, the longer China's entrance is postponed, the more powerful it will become, thus diminishing the organization's ultimate leverage. It is in the interest of the major economic powers to get the WTO clock ticking as soon as possible.

Chinese membership in the WTO will increase international leverage over China. Current efforts to coerce China to reform its economic system depend entirely on U.S. efforts. One of the reasons that U.S. negotiations with China for market access have failed is that the United States lacks support from its allies. By conducting negotiations within the multilateral setting of the WTO, the likelihood of maintaining a "united front" would be far greater, and the pressure on Beijing to compromise, more compelling. In addition, it would be politically easier for Chinese leaders to bow to WTO pressures than to unilateral U.S. insistence.

For any international regime to succeed, it must reflect the interests of its most important members. The United States acknowledged this fact throughout the Cold War when it allowed significant protectionism for its NATO allies and Japan in numerous economic sectors. It continued to do so during the Uruguay Round when it made concessions to Japan and France over agricultural products. While those compromises resulted in a less liberal trade agreement than the United States would have liked, they have enabled Europe and Japan to contribute to the integrity of the overall regime. As a result, the WTO may well be more stable and enduring. Accommodating Chinese interests may require concessions similar to those offered to Europe and Japan. But failure to include China in WTO negotiations will only ensure that the regime will develop in a direction inimical to Chinese interests. Asian countries understand this point. They have admitted China into the Association of Southeast Asian Nations Regional Forum and the Asia-Pacific Economic Cooperation forum because they understand that a Chinese commitment to these institutions requires a Chinese voice in their development. The same truth holds for the WTO. By incorporating China, the WTO will develop in a direction that reflects a consensus of all the major powers. This is the prerequisite to global economic stability. The alternative is a trade regime that encourages Chinese policies that are likely to destabilize a system that does not reflect its interests.

Chinese membership in the WTO will also strengthen the hand of Chinese policy makers who want to promote a more liberal Chinese trading system. Prior to Chinese membership in the World Bank and the International Monetary Fund, many analysts argued that China would be a destructive force—that its communist bureaucrats would undermine these institutions' commitments to international norms. Just the opposite occurred. Not only did China become a constructive member of these institutions, but its membership has allowed implicit alliances to develop between the institutions and pro-reform policy makers, strengthening their hand within China. Chinese membership in the WTO could create similar partnerships.

Finally, Chinese membership in the WTO would serve American bilateral interests with China. The United States has assumed the burden of obtaining Chinese compliance with international economic norms. This is the case in intellectual property rights negotiations. The primary causes of Chinese intellectual property rights violations are the political and economic decentralization of post-Mao China, the lack of an effective legal system to enforce government regulations, and the corruption of those authorities who participate in the piracy of intellectual property. Copyright infringement is rampant in China, affecting domestic producers of cigarettes, drugs, and food products as well as the profits of China's own software and entertainment industries, and the regime's legitimacy has suffered. By all appearances, the Chinese government would like to end much of the piracy in the Chinese economy. It simply lacks the authority.

There seems to be little that U.S. policy makers can do to fundamentally improve Chinese enforcement of intellectual property rights violations—foreign economic sanctions will not enhance central Chinese government authority over local activities. The threat of sanctions has only encouraged Chinese leaders to commit to improved intellectual property protection by local officials who are not susceptible to government policy, creating periodic crises with Washington when agreements are not fulfilled. Moreover, when Beijing shuts down factories that pirate intellectual property, they often quickly reopen elsewhere in connivance with corrupt local officials. The economics of piracy almost guarantees it; the cost of new duplicating facilities is significantly less than the potential profit. Focusing on Chinese policy toward these high-profile factories merely creates the illusion that rapid progress is possible and heightens American acrimony when expectations are unmet.

As with Chinese protectionism, the issue is how to encourage constructive Chinese behavior. Current U.S. policy has failed. Multilateral WTO sanctions would impose costs on the central government for its failure to control localities, while removing the burden on Sino–U.S. relations for inevitable Chinese infractions. Moreover, the WTO would be an effective channel for technical assistance in developing a Chinese system for regulating intellectual property. Over the long run, a better Chinese regulatory and legal system will do the most to promote global interests.

Without doubt, Chinese foreign economic practices will remain troubling for many years to come. The evolution of the Chinese political and economic systems will primarily reflect long-term domestic trends—a growing respect for law and the institutionalization of political authority. International pressures will not fundamentally affect the pace of change. Whether or not China is admitted into the WTO, it will remain a problematic trading partner.

In these circumstances, foreign policies can only help to ameliorate a difficult situation; they cannot resolve it. Moreover, Chinese membership in the WTO entails some risk—allowing a blatant violator of international economic norms to join the WTO may well erode the organization's credibility. Nonetheless, Chinese membership in the WTO sooner rather than later remains the best option for improving a difficult situation.

China's admission to the WTO will subject it to multilateral pressures for adherence to a self-imposed agreement to adopt liberal trading practices within a specified time. Currently, China has not agreed to any multilateral commitments to reform its trading system. Isolating China will not compel China to change nor will it protect the international economic system from counterproductive Chinese trade practices. Rather, it will ensure that China's gap with WTO standards will grow, along with Chinese resentment and the incentive to adopt destabilizing trade policies. . . .

28

COUNTERPOINT: KEEPING BEIJING AT BAY

Greg Mastel

Greg Mastel challenges the wisdom of admitting China to the World Trade Organization without first insisting on significant prior legal and economic reform. According to Mastel, "China retains too many features of the communist system to be easily married with the WTO." Mastel is vice president for policy planning and administration at the Economic Strategy Institute in Washington, D.C.

With the Sino-American relationship under much stress, many "China hands" have viewed China's application to join the World Trade Organization (WTO) as an issue on which the United States could compromise in order to keep the peace. The United States, with the support of other major countries, has been delaying China's entry into the WTO until China commits to sufficient trade and market reforms. Arguing, however, that the Clinton administration is too legalistic in its approach to China's application, some China experts have urged that the administration put aside its concerns and support China's immediate entry into the WTO.

From "Beijing at Bay," by Greg Mastel. Reprinted with permission from *Foreign Policy* 104, Fall, 1996. Copyright © 1996 by the Carnegie Endowment for International Peace.

This view places political and security concerns above economic concerns. It has the ring of classic U.S. Cold War foreign policy decision making, a paradigm that has dominated U.S. policy toward China for decades. This viewpoint is dated and out of touch with current realities. China is an important player in the global economy. It is already one of the world's top 10 exporters and is expected to be the world's largest economy early in the next century. As a result, economic and trade issues with China are at least as important as security and political issues.

More importantly, the integrity of the WTO would be severely damaged if China were admitted without significant legal and economic reform. The WTO is more than a simple club of trading partners. The WTO—originally the General Agreement on Tariffs and Trade (GATT)—is a postwar institution founded to establish and promote the principles of free markets and free trade. Thus, simply being a big player in international commerce does not warrant WTO membership. The acceptance of key market principles—even if they are not always rigorously applied—should be the key test for WTO membership. Viewed in this light, China's compatibility with the WTO is open to question. In fact, there are three basic reasons to question China's current compatibility with the organization.

CHINESE TRADE BARRIERS

The most visible impediments to China's membership in the WTO are its formal trade barriers, including tariffs, import licenses, and subsidies. In recent years, these formal trade barriers have been lowered; however, others have appeared, and China still has considerably more formal trade barriers that are inconsistent with WTO membership than any other major country. . . .

RULE OF LAW

The formal trade barriers . . . are only the tip of the iceberg. It is very difficult to ensure that any trade agreement will translate into changes in Chinese policy. China simply does not yet have a reliable rule of law. . . . This issue may seem initially to have little to do with international trade negotiations, but China's lack of a rule of law presents almost insurmountable problems for WTO membership. In China, trade regulations and tariffs are set by national policy, but their implementation in different provinces and ports is inconsistent. Officials often are open to bribes, a practice that results in further inconsistency. Some laws are simply not enforced, particularly if it is profitable not to enforce them. . . .

The lack of a reliable rule of law governing Chinese behavior in international commerce raises serious concerns about China's readiness for WTO membership. After all, it does little good to negotiate trade agreements with a government that, by its own admission, is unable or unwilling to live by the agreements it negotiates. Before China can be considered a serious applicant for WTO membership, it must establish a reliable rule of law, at least in relation to trade and investment.

THE COMMUNIST SYSTEM

Another difficulty, closely related to the lack of a rule of law, is the presence of a still nearly totalitarian government. One of the issues that illustrates the problem . . . is the issue of "trading rights." Essentially, trading rights are granted to private enterprises to enable them to engage in foreign commerce without governmental approval. But Chinese citizens, or enterprises operating in China, do not automatically enjoy these rights. In WTO negotiations, China has proposed granting these rights, in a limited sense, to foreign entities operating in China but has been silent on extending similar rights to Chinese citizens. This issue highlights the expansive role of the Chinese government in commercial decision making. After all, if consumers do not have the right to purchase imports, what sense does it make to negotiate on tariffs and quotas?

The WTO, like the GATT before it, normally ignores the degree of political freedom a government permits: A number of WTO members have authoritarian governments. But now there is an increasing focus on the link between social freedom and the potential for conducting normal commerce. In the debate over congressional approval of the North American Free Trade Agreement, [U.S.] Senator Patrick Moynihan . . . posed the question, "How can you have free trade with a country that is not free?" In his argument, Moynihan focused on the absence of both an independent judiciary and a corruption-free government to enforce trade and commercial regulations in Mexico, but an even more compelling argument can be made with regard to China.

There are several problems caused by the expansive powers and influence of the Chinese government. The first and most obvious is the continuing role of government planning in the Chinese economy. Since the late 1970s, China has undertaken considerable economic reforms and has moved toward creating a more market-oriented economy. Yet China is still—and intends to remain— largely a centrally planned economy. Although China is undertaking reforms, state-run industries are still responsible for a significant portion of China's gross domestic product, and they employ an enormous number of people and provide a major source of exports. China recently adopted another five-year economic plan and maintains extensive plans to support what it calls "pillar industries." Reaching beyond those industries directly owned by the state, new sectoral guidelines have been issued for the automotive and pharmaceutical industries, and there is reportedly a similar blueprint for the electronics industry.

These plans contain many policy elements inconsistent with the WTO, including import-substitution directives, local-content requirements, onerous investment requirements, and foreign-exchange balancing requirements. Even more troubling is the fact that the Chinese government clearly has no intention of ending the issuance of industrial guidelines. Despite assurances that future plans would be WTO-consistent, there is no evidence that recent industrial plans are moving in that direction.

Beyond the formal role of central planning, the pervasive presence of the government in Chinese society raises serious questions about the possibility of establishing a normal trading relationship with China. A large percentage of trading decisions, particularly with regard to infrastructure projects and agriculture, are made directly by government agencies, and the Chinese government has explicitly used foreign purchases and business deals as tools to promote foreign policy objectives.

Where the government's role in commercial decisions is direct, perhaps WTO provisions regulating government procurement and state trading could be of some help in regulating Chinese trading decisions. The Chinese government, however, has innumerable opportunities to tilt regulatory decisions in favor of, or against, any enterprise. The opportunities to harass foreign businesses are numerous and the opportunities for WTO policing are limited because there is rarely any formal paper trail, and there is often no formal decision.

More difficult still is moderating the informal role the government plays throughout society. The official Chinese press has been pounding away regularly at the United States on a variety of foreign policy issues, accusing the United States of seeking to "contain" China. In such a political environment, and given the need for government approval to thrive and even survive, can any Chinese citizen ignore government rhetoric when selecting business partners? With memories of the Cultural Revolution and Tiananmen Square very much in mind, the answer is almost certainly "no."

Historically, the GATT/WTO was conceived in part as an organization of market economies convened to assist the market world in its competition with the nonmarket world. Viewed in this context, the problem presented by the fact of the world's largest nonmarket economy seeking to join the WTO comes into focus. The Chinese government's influence over its economy may be so pervasive that the WTO trading rules will prove inadequate to create a "level playing field." Simply put, China retains too many features of the communist system to be easily married with the WTO. . . .

Most of the "China hands" who suggest that China be allowed immediate entry into the WTO unfortunately are not "WTO hands," or even "trade hands." The more one understands the cost of such a gesture, the clearer it becomes that it would amount to granting an enormous trade concession in order to achieve ill-defined political benefits. . . . Sacrificing a sound economic and trade relationship in the hope of achieving some temporary gains in other areas would be unwise policy. China should become a full-fledged member of the world trading system, but it should do so in a way that strengthens the system instead of undermining it.

29

COLONIALISM REDUX: THE DARK SIDE OF GLOBALIZATION

Martin Khor

Martin Khor examines how free trade and related rules, supported by the industrial societies of the Global North and promulgated by the World Trade Organization and other international institutions, threaten the economic sovereignty of the Global South. He concludes that free trade "may be good among equal partners, but in today's global economy some countries are more equal than others." Khor is director of the Third World Network and editor of the magazines *Third World Resurgence* and *Third World Economics*.

Colonialism is making a comeback. For centuries, the governments and corporations of the industrial nations, backed by military power, exploited the resources and markets of the poorer countries. The determination of these countries to recapture control of their resources and impose policies that favored domestic over foreign interests spurred the anticolonial struggles that culminated in independence for much of Latin America, Africa, and Asia. Now the

From "Colonialism Redux," (ABRIDGEMENT) by Martin Khor. Reprinted with permission from the July 15/22, 1996 issue of *The Nation* magazine.

former colonial powers are in the process of regaining the right of transnational companies to dominate the economies of their former colonies, this time through trade agreements.

Some little-noticed revisions of global trade rules, as well as a series of proposed new rules, are today's weapons for restoring some of the economic underpinnings of colonialism. The new proposals . . . from the European nations, backed by the United States and Japan, . . . would guarantee global corporations "national treatment," meaning that national governments could not impose any measures that favor local companies or discriminate against foreign ones. As a result, a wide array of restrictions in nations all over the world that prohibit foreign corporations from opening branches or buying property, and that limit the share of local businesses foreigners may own, would be swept away.

For developing nations, the new rules have profound implications. Many countries have adopted policies that favor the growth of local companies. Some give them tax breaks and preference in government contracts; indigenous banks are offered protections not available to foreign ones. Governments justify such policies in the name of national development. Many would argue that because foreign firms were given preference during the colonial era, local companies need special treatment for a period of time so that they can better compete with foreign ones.

Malaysia's New Economic Policy, for example, was formulated to increase Malaysians' equity ownership in several sectors of the economy by placing limits on foreign holdings. As a result, the foreign share of Malaysia's total equity has fallen from 70 percent in 1970 to about 30 percent in 1996. Malaysian policies that restrict foreign ownership of land and property and limit the scope of foreign banks have likewise helped build a domestic economy that is the engine of the country's development.

The proposals the industrial powers now push in the World Trade Organization (WTO) build on a history of postcolonial economic arrangements that rig the global economy against the interests of poorer countries. Despite the well-publicized cases of Western economic and humanitarian aid to Third World countries, there is a far greater net outflow of economic resources from South to North. Take raw materials. Only 20 percent of the world's industrial wood comes from tropical forests, yet more than half of that is exported to the richer nations. Most of it is used for furniture, housing, packing material, even matchsticks. The wood that is exported from the South—mainly for wasteful uses in the North—is lost to Southern peoples, who now have difficulty obtaining wood for essential uses such as houses, furniture, and boats.

Even worse, the processes of extracting Third World resources cause economic loss through environmental degradation such as deforestation, soil erosion and desertification, and the pollution of water supplies. Soils required for food production become infertile; forests that are the habitats of indigenous peoples are overlogged or flooded out; wood used for fuel disappears as whole forests are felled; and water from rivers and wells is clogged from the silt that washes down from denuded hills.

There is also a net loss of financial resources. Prices of Southern commodities have been plummeting while the prices of manufactured goods imported from the North continue to rise. According to the United Nations, the prices of commodities other than oil fell by an average of 52 percent between 1980 and 1992. The impact has been particularly severe in the sub-Saharan African countries, whose dependence on commodity exports is greatest. In the period from 1986 to 1989, sub-Saharan Africa suffered a total loss of $56 billion due to the decline in the purchasing power of its exports.

The external debt crisis, which originated in the 1970s, has been another major source of financial drain on the South. To this day, many of the "development projects" designed to encourage the export of natural resources are financed by foreign loans. It is rare for these projects to generate sufficient returns to repay the debts, so the money must be raised either through an increase in exports or through new taxes, which in Third World countries invariably hit poor people hardest.

Another source of the drain from the South is the dominance by multinational corporations of international transport, trade, and distribution of commodities exported by the South. These companies siphon off an overwhelming share of the final price of the commodities. Third World countries have to pay large amounts for freight, insurance, packing, and marketing of their exported and imported goods. Many studies have shown that Third World countries receive only 10 to 15 percent of the final retail price of their commodities when sold to Northern consumers. In the case of bananas, three global corporations control 70 percent of total exports and retailing; Third World growers gross only 11.5 percent of the retail price in the consuming countries.

The 80s and the first half of the 90s have been particularly brutal on the South. The debt crisis escalated in 1982 as interest rates skyrocketed. That led to austerity imposed by the structural adjustment policies of the World Bank and International Monetary Fund. In the area of trade, commodity prices dipped to their lowest levels. Aid has collapsed. In the area of technology, a proposed U.N. code of conduct on technology transfer to help Third World countries build up their own technological capabilities was scuttled, and in its place the trade-related intellectual property rights of global companies were given greater protections under [the General Agreement on Tariffs and Trade (GATT), the WTO's predecessor]. These new rules give Southern countries very little opportunity to learn from the North and build their own technological capacity in order to compete on an equal footing.

Nor can Third World countries expect much help form international organizations in curbing restrictive business practices and monopolies by global corporations. The code of conduct on transnational corporations that had been negotiated for more than a decade at the UN Center on Transnational Corporations was abandoned, and the center was transformed into an agency that promotes foreign investment.

The growing gap between South and North was exacerbated by the Uruguay Round of the General Agreement on Tariffs and Trade, which expanded GATT's powers to include eliminating barriers to the rapidly growing trade in such services as banking, insurance, information, the media, and professional services such as law, medicine, tourism, accounting, and advertising.

In banking, a number of Southern countries have long restricted the participation of foreign banks to a limited range of activities. To preserve local banks some countries prohibited foreign banks from setting up branches in small towns. Now, under the new GATT rules, the marginalization of local banks, financial, and other professional services will accelerate.

The Uruguay Round of GATT also threatens to affect health conditions in the South drastically. The private health care industry and insurance companies of Northern countries have launched a drive to commercialize health care services in the South. They are beginning to buy up hospitals and bring about the privatization of health care, which will make it inaccessible to the vast bulk of the people.

Even some of the newer environmental initiatives in the South are endangered. Indonesia, for example, recently proposed to ban the export of rattan, an important forest product that is becoming scarce. Immediately, the United States and the European Community protested that the export ban violated the principle of free trade, and threatened retaliation against Indonesian exports.

The Uruguay Round of GATT and the . . . WTO investment rules have led many Southern governments and groups to conclude that colonialism is being reimposed, that the economies of the South are being subordinated in new ways to the corporate interests of the North. Northern countries, finding that the UN General Assembly is often hostile because the majority of its members fight for Southern interests, have sought to shift more and more of the social and economic aspects of the UN to the World Bank, the International Monetary Fund (IMF), and the WTO.

The WTO cloaks its work in the principle that all nations should be treated equally. But under free trade the weaker nations will continue to suffer. That is why so many in the South oppose free trade: It may be good among equal partners, but in today's global economy some countries are more equal than others.

30

GROWTH FOR DEVELOPMENT?

United Nations Development Programme

Some countries have experienced spectacular economic advances since the early 1980s, but many others have not, resulting in a widening gap between the world's rich and poor countries. Furthermore, the United Nations Development Programme (UNDP) concludes that "the links between [economic] growth and human development are failing for people in many countries with lopsided development—with either good growth but little human development or good human development but little or no growth." The chapter is from the 1996 edition of the United Nations agency's widely acclaimed annual *Human Development Report* .

Human development is the end—economic growth a means. So, the purpose of growth should be to enrich people's lives. But far too often it does not. The recent decades show all too clearly that there is no automatic link between growth and human development. And even when links are established, they may gradually be eroded—unless regularly fortified by skillful and intelligent policy management.

. . . Growth has been failing over much of the past 15 years in about 100 countries, with almost a third of the world's people. And the links between growth and human development are failing for people in the many countries with lopsided development—with either good growth but little human development or good human development but little or no growth. . . .

[M]ore economic growth, not less, will generally be needed as the world enters the 21st century. But more attention must go to the structure and quality of that growth to ensure that it is directed to supporting human development, reducing poverty, protecting the environment, and ensuring sustainability.

Since 1980 there has been a dramatic surge in economic growth in some 15 countries, bringing rapidly rising incomes to many of their 1.5 billion people, more than a quarter of the world's population.

Over much of this period, however, economic decline or stagnation has affected 100 countries, reducing the incomes of 1.6 billion people—again, more than a quarter of the world's population. In 70 of these countries average incomes are less than they were in 1980—and in 43 countries less than they were in 1970. Over 1990–93 alone, average incomes fell by a fifth or more in 21 countries, mostly in Eastern Europe and among the [Commonwealth of Independent States] (CIS) countries.

Although many are aware of this economic stagnation and decline, the full extent and gravity are too often obscured because of the stunning success of the fast-growing countries, because most of the richer countries have maintained their growth, and because of repeated hopes that many of the economies with falling incomes are poised to resume growth. After 15 years of such disappointing performance, international policy makers need to question whether that optimism is warranted.

The advances have often been at rates exceeding anything seen since the start of the industrial revolution some two centuries ago. The declines have also been unprecedented, far exceeding in duration, and sometimes in depth, the declines of the Great Depression of the 1930s in the industrial countries.

In much of this success and disaster, many of the poor have missed out, and even the better off have often been left vulnerable to unemployment and downsizing—to cutbacks in health and welfare services. Although per capita incomes in the [Organization for Economic Cooperation and Development] (OECD) countries now average $20,000, surveys reveal growing insecurity and considerable dissatisfaction.

The world has become more polarized, and the gulf between the poor and rich of the world has widened even further. Of the $23 trillion global GDP in 1993, $18 trillion is in the industrial countries—only $5 trillion in the developing countries, even though they have nearly 80 percent of the world's people.

- The poorest 20 percent of the world's people saw their share of global income decline from 2.3 percent to 1.4 percent in the past 30 years. Meanwhile, the share of the richest 20 percent rose from 70 percent to 85 percent. That doubled the ratio of the shares of the richest and the poorest—from 30 to 1 to 61 to 1.
- The assets of the world's 358 billionaires exceed the combined annual incomes of countries with 45 percent of the world's people.
- During the past three decades the proportion of people enjoying per capita income growth of at least 5 percent a year more than doubled, from 12 percent to 27 percent, while the proportion of those experiencing negative growth more than tripled, from 5 percent to 18 percent.
- The gap in per capita income between the industrial and developing worlds tripled, from $5,700 in 1960 to $15,400 in 1993.

Increasing polarization is reflected in the growing contrasts in regional performance. Most of Asia, with more than half the world's people, experienced accelerating and often spectacular per capita income growth over the 1980s. OECD countries generally maintained slow but steady growth in per capita income. But failed growth was the dominant experience in four groups of countries:

- In sub-Saharan Africa declines mostly began in the late 1970s. Many reform efforts have been launched, often spurring recoveries, but 20 countries are still below their per capita incomes of 20 years ago.
- Among the Latin American and Caribbean countries, several began to recover slowly in the late 1980s, but 18 of them are still below their per capita incomes of 10 years ago.
- Eastern Europe and the CIS countries maintained at least slow growth over most of the 1980s, but then suffered steep declines in per capita income—which fell on average by a third from the peaks in the mid-1980s.
- Many Arab states also suffered sharp declines in income in the 1980s, with falling oil prices and other setbacks in the world economy.

Although very rapid population growth explains part of the negative per capita income growth, blaming population growth for all or even most of the decline is too simple. Even with lower fertility and slower population growth, per capita incomes would have fallen in many countries.

Policy makers are often mesmerized by the quantity of growth. They need to be more concerned with its structure and quality. Unless governments take timely corrective action, economic growth can become lopsided and flawed. Determined efforts are needed to avoid growth that is jobless, ruthless, voiceless, rootless, and futureless.

Jobless growth is where the overall economy grows but does not expand the opportunities for employment. In the OECD countries in 1993 the average unemployment rate was 8 percent—ranging from 2.5 percent in Japan to 10 percent in the United Kingdom, 18 percent in Finland, and 23 percent in Spain. In

FIGURE 30–1

GROWTH HAS FAILED FOR MORE THAN A QUARTER OF THE WORLD'S PEOPLE

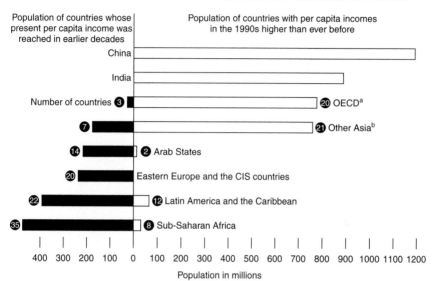

Population of countries whose present per capita income was reached in earlier decades

Population of countries with per capita incomes in the 1990s higher than ever before

Population in millions

the developing countries too, jobless growth has meant long hours and very low incomes for the hundreds of millions of people in low-productivity work in agriculture and the informal sector.

Ruthless growth is where the fruits of economic growth mostly benefit the rich, leaving millions of people struggling in ever-deepening poverty. During 1970–85 global GNP increased by 40 percent, yet the number of poor increased by 17 percent. While 200 million people saw their per capita incomes fall during 1965–80, more than 1 billion people did in 1980–93.

Voiceless growth is where growth in the economy has not been accompanied by an extension of democracy or empowerment. Political repression and authoritarian controls have silenced alternative voices and stifled demands for greater social and economic participation.

Policy makers once debated whether they should choose economic growth or extensive participation, assuming that these were mutually exclusive. That debate is dead. People do not want one or the other—they want both. But too many people are still denied even the most basic forms of democracy, and many of the world's people are in the grip of repressive regimes.

Voiceless growth can also be growth that gives women only a minor role in an economy's management and direction. As *Human Development Report 1995* showed, human development, if not engendered, is endangered.

Rootless growth . . . causes people's cultural identity to wither. There are thought to be about 10,000 distinct cultures, but many risk being marginalized or eliminated. In some cases minority cultures are being swamped by dominant cultures whose power has been amplified with growth. In other cases governments have deliberately imposed uniformity in the pursuit of nation building— say, with a national language.

This can be dangerous. The violence in the former Soviet Union and in the Balkan states of former Yugoslavia is a tragic legacy of culturally repressive governance. The nations that have held together best, from Switzerland to Malaysia, are often those that have recognized cultural diversity and decentralized economic and political governance to try to meet the aspirations of all their people.

Futureless growth is where the present generation squanders resources needed by future generations. Rampant and uncontrolled economic growth in many countries is laying waste to forests, polluting rivers, destroying biodiversity, and depleting natural resources.

This damage and destruction is increasing, driven overwhelmingly by demand in the rich countries, inadequate conservation in the developing countries, and the pressure of poor people pushed onto marginal lands in poor countries. On past trends, global production will triple by about 2030. Unless serious conservation and pollution controls are in place soon, production will be long past the point of sustainability.

In sum, development that perpetuates today's inequalities is neither sustainable nor worth sustaining.

Despite the economic downturns and difficulties, key indicators of human development have advanced in almost all developing countries. Indeed, developing countries have made much more progress in human development than in income. Between 1960 and 1993 the North-South gap in life expectancy was more than halved, from 23 years to 11 years.

Human progress has nevertheless been very slow in some regions, and in some cases it even deteriorated. In the past 15 years the primary enrollment ratio stagnated in sub-Saharan Africa as a whole, and in 17 countries it declined by 37–50 percent. And while the human development index (HDI) of most regions has improved, in Eastern Europe and the CIS countries it has declined sharply.

Overall, countries already in the high human development category (with an HDI of more than 0.800) have been able to reduce their HDI shortfall (the difference between the maximum possible HDI of 1 and the value achieved) by nearly 2.7 percent a year. For low human development countries (with an HDI of less than 0.500) the reduction was only 0.9 percent a year. So, there was a clear widening of the gap in human development as well.

Countries with similar levels of income and growth can have very different rates of advance in human development. During the past three decades both Tunisia and Congo enjoyed the same economic growth from similar starting points of income and human development. But Tunisia reduced its HDI shortfall by 60 percent; Congo by only 16 percent.

This record contains a warning. Unless economic growth is restored for countries in decline, their gains in human development may be ever more difficult to sustain—and present disparities will grow. At present rates of progress, it will take a century or more for the low human development countries to reach high human development. . . .

Improvements in human development have clearly been possible even in times of economic setback. But such advances can be sustained over a long time only if supported by economic growth. At the same time, for economic growth to be sustained, it must be constantly nourished by human development. Human development and economic growth should move together, strongly linked.

The record of economic growth and human development over the past 30 years shows that no country can follow a course of lopsided development for such a long time—where economic growth is not matched by advances in human development, or vice versa. Lopsided development can last for a decade or so, but it then shifts to rapid rises in both incomes and human development, or falls into slow improvements in both human development and incomes. Countries follow one of four patterns:

• *Slow economic growth and fast human development.* Countries achieving human development with only slow economic growth in one decade either increased economic growth in the next (the Republic of Korea in the 1960s and China and Indonesia in the 1970s) or slipped back into poor economic growth and slow human development (Cameroon, Sierra Leone, and others in the 1980s).

• *Fast economic growth and slow human development.* Lopsided development tilted against human development is a dead end, with economic growth petering out after a decade or so of fast growth (such as Brazil and Egypt in the 1980s). No country with fast growth and slow human development maintained fast growth and accelerated human development.

• *Mutually reinforcing growth and human development.* Some countries enjoyed rapid improvements in both human development and incomes, sustained over three decades, in a mutually reinforcing virtuous circle.

• *Mutually stifling growth and human development.* Other countries suffered slow advances in human development and slow economic growth.

The traditional view that economic growth in the early stages is inevitably associated with deteriorating income distribution has been proved false. The new insight is that an equitable distribution of public and private resources can enhance the prospects for further growth.

The assertion that the benefits of growth in the early stages would inevitably be skewed towards the rich rested on two principal arguments. The first came from Nobel laureate Simon Kuznets, who said that inequality would first rise, as workers left agriculture for industry, and then fall as industrial production became more widespread. The second was advanced by Nicholas Kaldor, who emphasized the importance of savings. He argued that the only way to finance growth would be by channeling the initial benefits into the pockets of rich capitalists. Since they have a higher propensity to save, only they could provide the funds for investment.

These hypotheses have been disproved by recent evidence of a positive correlation between economic growth and income equality (as represented by the share of the poorest 60 percent of the population). Japan and East Asia pioneered this form of equitable development, and China, Malaysia, and Mauritius have been following a similar route more recently.

The discovery of this reinforcing relationship between equity and growth has far-reaching implications for policy makers. Well-developed human capabilities and well-distributed opportunities can ensure that growth is not lopsided and that its benefits are equitably shared. They can also help in getting the most growth.

To ensure that these links work efficiently and effectively in both directions, policy makers need to understand how the links connect. Some of the most important issues determining how growth contributes to human development [include these]:

- *Equity*—The more equally GNP and economic opportunities are distributed, the more likely that they will be translated into improved human well-being.

- *Job opportunities*—Economic growth is translated into people's lives when they are offered productive and well-paid work. An important way to achieve this is to aim for patterns of growth that are heavily labor-intensive.

- *Access to productive assets*—Many people find their economic opportunities stifled by a lack of access to productive assets—particularly land, physical infrastructure, and financial credit. The state can do much in all these areas by stepping in and leveling the playing fields.

- *Social spending*—Governments and communities can greatly influence human development by channeling a major part of public revenue into high-priority social expenditure—particularly by providing basic social services for all.

- *Gender equality*—Fairer opportunities for women and better access to education, child care, credit, and employment contribute to their human development. They also contribute to the human development of other family members and to economic growth. Investing in women's capabilities and empowering them to exercise their choices is the surest way to contribute to economic growth and overall development.

- *Population policy*—Education, reproductive health, and child survival all help lower fertility, thus creating the conditions for slower population growth and lower education and health costs in the longer run.

- *Good governance*—When those in power give high priority to the needs of the whole population, and when people participate in decision making at many levels, the links between economic growth and human well-being are likely to be stronger and more durable.

• *An active civil society*—Nongovernmental organizations and community groups also play a vital part in enhancing human development. They not only supplement government services, extending them to people and groups who would otherwise remain unserved. They also play a vital advocacy role, mobilizing public opinion and community action and helping shape human development priorities.

A determined effort to expand human capabilities—through improved education, health, and nutrition—can help transform the prospects for economic growth, especially in the low-human-development, low-income countries. A World Bank study of 192 countries concluded that only 16 percent of growth is explained by physical capital (machinery, buildings, and physical infrastructure), while 20 percent comes from natural capital. But no less than 64 percent can be attributed to human and social capital. An extensive analysis of earlier experience in the Asian industrializing tigers, including Japan, comes to similar conclusions.

Without growth, it is difficult to create jobs and increase wages. With growth, job opportunities normally expand. But again, the process is not automatic. Witness several recent periods of "jobless growth." And even when jobs have been created, they have not met the aspirations of people in search of job security, remunerative work, or creative work. They have also bypassed whole groups of society—including women, young adults, the uneducated, the unskilled, and people with disabilities.

To forge a strong link between economic growth and employment requires employment-generating growth strategies. The experience of the fast-growing Asian economies—Hong Kong, the Republic of Korea, Singapore, and Taiwan (province of China)—shows how sustained long-term growth can expand employment (by 2–6 percent a year), reduce unemployment (down to less than 2.5 percent) and raise productivity and wages. This in turn reduced inequality and poverty. Such growth was led by small-scale agriculture in Taiwan (province of China) and by labor-intensive export-oriented manufacturing in Hong Kong, the Republic of Korea, and Singapore.

The Latin American experience stands in stark contrast. During the 1960s and 1970s the average annual growth in per capita income was more than 4 percent in Brazil, 3.5 percent in Mexico, and 2.5 percent in Costa Rica. But this growth was not accompanied by the creation of enough jobs to absorb the growing labor force or by increases in productivity. The region's productivity growth during the past three decades was only 0.5 percent a year, an eighth that of the Asian tigers' 4 percent. Growth was concentrated in capital-intensive activities—mining and import-substitution industries. Employment expanded, but mostly in the service sectors and without a sustained increase in productivity.

A strategy for economic growth that emphasizes people and their productive potential is the only way to open opportunities. Although most of the action must be taken at the country level, it is increasingly clear that new international measures are also needed to encourage and support national strategies for employment creation and human development.

Some of the specifics:

• *A political commitment to full employment*—The countries achieving the greatest success in employment have generally been those that deliberately set out to do so. Rather than assuming that employment would materialize automatically, they have publicly identified it as a central policy objective.

• *Enhancing human capabilities*—High-employment economies have generally invested heavily in the development of human capabilities—particularly education, health, and skills. They also have constantly upgraded technical skills to enable workers to adapt to rapidly changing international conditions. The Republic of Korea invests $160 per person a year in health and education, Malaysia $150. India, by contrast, invests only $14, Pakistan $10, and Bangladesh $5.

• *Strengthening small-scale and informal sector production*—In many countries such production has demonstrated the potential for generating employment and incomes for millions of people while providing a wide range of the basic goods and services needed in daily life. It needs to be encouraged and supported, not restricted. Some countries have increased opportunities for employment—particularly self-employment—by extending access to credit. There are many encouraging examples among small farmers, microenterprises, and poor and marginal communities. And extension services and other mechanisms to enable small-scale producers to get better and quicker access to technology and information can often make a big difference in their productivity.

• *Broader and more egalitarian access to land*—Numerous studies show that small farmers achieve higher output per hectare than large farmers. So, providing greater access to land can increase productivity, employment, and growth while reducing poverty and easing the pressure on scarce resources.

• *Research and development*—Another part of successful employment strategies is intensive investment in research and development for labor-intensive technology, including the adaptation of imported capital-intensive technologies to fit local needs.

The imbalances in economic growth over the past 15 years are clear enough. But if allowed to continue well into the next century, they will produce a world gargantuan in its excesses and grotesque in its human and economic inequalities:

• Poverty in sub-Saharan African and other least developed countries would deepen, with per capita income falling to $325 by 2030.

• Meanwhile, per capita income in the OECD countries would rise to nearly $40,000.

• Although East Asia would catch up to the incomes of the OECD countries in 15–25 years, it would take China about 50 years, and India a century or more.

Such scenarios do not pretend to be a forecast. They simply suggest what could happen if current trends continued, to emphasize the need for purposeful action—both national and international. Much attention is now given to the rapid rates of population growth. Equal attention needs to be given to the much larger and more rapidly growing imbalances in the growth of consumption and resource use.

Globalization is one of the most dramatic developments of recent years. During 1965–90 world merchandise trade tripled, and global trade in services increased more than fourteenfold. Meanwhile, financial flows have reached unimaginable dimensions. More than a trillion dollars roam the world every 24 hours, restlessly seeking the highest return. This flow of capital is not just offering unprecedented opportunities for profit (and loss). It has opened the world to the operation of a global financial market that leaves even the strongest countries with limited autonomy over interest rates, exchange rates, or other financial policies.

Many developing countries have seized globalization as an opportunity. Countries that combine low wages with high-technology skills have outcompeted more established countries. In just 10 years India has expanded its software development industry, centered on "Silicon Bangalore," to become the world's second largest software exporter. Other developing countries need to escape their debilitating dependence on exports of low-value primary products by combining their natural resources with their human capital. In the 21st century rapid strides in technology and communications will open the prospect of "leapfrogging" several decades of development—but only for the poor countries that can master the new skills and compete.

While globalization has often helped growth in the strong countries, it has bypassed the weak. The poorest countries, with 20 percent of the world's people, have seen their share of world trade fall between 1960 and 1990—from 4 percent to less than 1 percent. And they receive a meagre 0.2 percent of the world's commercial lending. Although private investment flows to developing countries increased between 1970 and 1994 from $5 billion to $173 billion, three-quarters of this went to just 10 countries, mostly in East and Southeast Asia and Latin America. Countries elsewhere, particularly in sub-Saharan Africa, have been left behind.

The agenda to achieve the new patterns of growth for human development would have four priorities:

First, three groups of countries need faster economic growth, especially after the declines of the 1980s.

• *The low human development countries*—With nearly 2 billion people, these countries must accelerate their human development, backed by rapid economic growth. A massive expansion of education and health must be at the core, especially when half the population often lacks these most basic requirements. Each of these countries has to revamp its domestic social and economic policies, with stronger priorities for human development, economic growth, and poverty reduction. And most will also need a new level of long-term international commitment for debt relief, more and better-focused financial assistance, and actions to open export markets and move to sustained economic growth. All the least-developed countries need to reach a minimum annual economic growth rate of 3 percent per capita, with a higher rate in countries still below their per capita incomes of a decade or more ago.

• *The formerly socialist countries, now in transition*—With their per capita incomes having fallen by about a third since 1990, these countries must restart growth and sustain it for several decades. Domestic reforms backed by loans and other international economic and social support can help achieve this and end the free fall of many of these economies.

• *The middle range of developing countries*—Most countries in Latin America, the Middle East, North Africa, and South and Southeast Asia need an acceleration in growth to support human development.

Second, in two groups of countries the priority is to improve the quality of growth and to sustain—rather than increase—the rate of growth.

• *The fast-growing developing countries*—For China and the countries of East and Southeast Asia the challenge is not so much to accelerate growth further. It is to ensure the long-term sustainability of this growth and to give more attention to poverty reduction and human development.

• *The OECD countries*—With very high incomes and growth averaging about 2 percent per capita during the 1980s, the human development challenge for the OECD countries is to move to new approaches to employment, equity, and satisfying lifestyles in ways consistent with steady growth. Another part of that challenge is to provide support for health care, pensions, and other social services—for children, the working poor, and the growing numbers in their post-retirement years.

The limits to growth and material consumption will become more obvious as countries reach higher levels of income—but there are no limits to human creativity, human compassion and the human spirit.

Third, global action is needed to support national efforts to expand employment opportunities. Both developing and industrial countries need international support if their national efforts towards full employment are to succeed. New forms of international action are required, and the United Nations and the Bretton Woods organizations should work together to devise them. This report recommends:

• New measures to support countries in reversing downward employment trends, including more effective multilateral and bilateral debt relief, reformed development assistance backed by concessional resources, and access to export markets, often through trade preferences.

• A global commission to study and propose international measures for national policy and action for full employment.

Fourth, a global safety net should be created to move all countries with low levels of human development to medium levels in the next 10 years. National and international efforts for human development may have continued over time—but those supporting it with economic growth and resources have too often failed. A major international priority must be to move all countries to at least medium levels of human development in the next 10 years—laying a human foundation for accelerating growth, reducing poverty, and achieving more equitable development in the 21st century.

• High-profile monitoring and reporting on the situation of the poorest and least-developed countries, at least until rapid growth in human development and incomes is achieved.

• Serious and sustained support for any least-developed country that has a plan for widespread and solid human development.

Often this assistance needs to be accompanied by a radical overhaul of the domestic management of their economies. But not always. A good number of the poorer and weaker economies have already taken far-reaching measures to reform and restructure their economies, but with little growth to show for their efforts.

Richer countries need to provide greater support—with an international safety net, fashioned perhaps through compacts between poor and rich nations. The poor nations can demonstrate their willingness to invest in their people and in their economies. The rich nations can offer a package of resources (through aid, debt relief, and trade concessions) sufficient to generate a respectable rate of growth and to provide universal coverage of basic social services. This will strengthen the link between economic growth and human development, both nationally and internationally.

In a fast-changing global economy there are no simple answers, no easy rides. And . . . inertia is not an option. Economic growth should lead to fuller choices for all people—rather than few choices for most people or many choices for a few. But it is never enough to wait for economic growth automatically to trickle down to the poor. Instead, human development and poverty reduction must be moved to the top of the agenda for political and economic policy making. And even when links between economic growth and human development have been painstakingly established, they must be protected against being blown apart by sudden shifts in political power or market forces.

31

MERCANTILISM AND GLOBAL SECURITY

Michael Borrus, Steve Weber, and John Zysman, with Joseph Willihnganz

Michael Borrus, Steve Weber, John Zysman, and Joseph Willihnganz probe the security implications of the tripolar world political economy that is emerging in the wake of the decline of American economic power and prowess. They worry in particular about the "powerful intellectual, political, and technological forces that could push the world into . . . mercantile rivalry" and the likely inability of existing international institutions "to cope with the instability that would result." Borrus, Weber, and Zysman teach at the University of California, Berkeley. They are co-authors of *The Highest Stakes: The Economic Foundations of the Next Security System* (1992), a product of the Berkeley Roundtable on the International Economy (BRIE), co-directed by Borrus and Zysman. Willihnganz is an editor at BRIE.

For the third time this century the United States faces a new world. It looks in many ways like the world that America has for 40 years struggled to create, a

Reprinted with permission © *The National Interest*, no. 29, Washington, D.C. Footnotes have been deleted.

world it hardly dared hope for. But even so it poses new and difficult questions about the international system and America's place in it. American competitive troubles, Asian industrial might, and continuing European integration create the basis for a wholly new system of relations among the major powers that will substantially reduce American influence. For the moment, the United States still leads, but more by default than from strength.

For over four decades the postwar security system presumed a Soviet enemy, a U.S. military umbrella over allies in Western Europe and Asia, and a system of free trade and stable finance dominated and coordinated by the United States. This system of trade and finance, established within GATT [the General Agreement on Tariffs and Trade], Bretton Woods, and successor agreements, rested on American industrial and technological leadership. That foundation of power made it possible for the United States to support the rebuilding of Europe and Japan, establish for itself favorable terms of trade, and channel compliance with its security aims.

But now the United States is slipping. Its technological and economic position is declining relative to the other industrialized nations. As a result, the government's ability to exact compliance or exercise leverage in the international system is diminished. . . . Having lost its technological and industrial hegemony, the United States will be increasingly subject to the kinds of constraints that it used to impose on others. . . .

. . . Shifts in America's industrial, financial, and technological position have been complemented by the rapid emergence of powerful new capabilities in Japan and Europe that go beyond mere catch-up. During the postwar years, while the United States held fast to the tried-and-true formula of mass production and consumption, other countries began to innovate more rapidly. [Its] most successful competitors, in particular Germany and Japan, undertook new approaches in two critical domains: policy and production.

In the policy realm, both states made smart use of the fact that their defense burden was relatively light and chose to emphasize investment over consumption, which created excellent macroeconomic conditions for rapid growth. Both governments also encouraged the rapid adoption and widespread diffusion of technology acquired abroad and helped provide for a well-trained workforce ready to use it. In Japan, government went a step further by closing through formal and informal means its domestic market to foreign firms, reserving growth in domestic demand for Japanese producers. These kinds of policies helped build strong industries by sheltering them from foreign competition, guaranteeing domestic demand, and encouraging continuous rounds of reinvestment, which in time led to real innovations in production. Government policy in effect "created" competitive advantage for domestic firms and "comparative" advantage for the nation in higher wage industries.

But it is innovation in production and production organization that has increasingly separated the United States and its competitors. New methods of manufacturing and technology development, emerging in countries as diverse as Japan, Italy, and Germany, are quickly giving leading firms a competitive edge in technology-intensive, high value-added industries. . . . The U.S. economy retains the advantage of being the world's largest; its technological and scientific resources are still broader and deeper than those of its competitors. But rapidly expanding capabilities in Europe and Asia now permit a serious challenge to American economic leadership and create the potential for autonomy where there was once U.S.-imposed constraint. Indeed, it is America's autonomy that is now threatened as it risks substantial dependence in industry, finance, and critical segments of technology.

Such a realignment of economic capabilities will have political consequences. At a minimum, the balance of constraints and opportunities facing states will shift dramatically. In 1956 the United States threatened a run on the pound to constrain British, French, and Israeli foreign policy. Today Japan and Germany have the financial leverage to influence the American exchange rate and monetary policy. Again, consider what happened when the United States wanted to punish Toshiba for having sold precision military technology to the Soviet Union. The U.S. government sought to ban Toshiba products from the U.S. market, but could not—too many major U.S. customers depend on Toshiba for critical components and technologies. Such examples demonstrate that America's ability to exact compliance through its position in trade and finance has been deeply eroded, leaving it without the array of foreign policy levers it enjoyed in the past and with vulnerabilities it has not had to cope with until now.

In sum, a radical realignment of economic capabilities, combined with the end of the Cold War, creates the possibility of fundamentally new relationships among great powers, and the regions that they dominate. The certainties of the bipolar world are gone, and the bonds that were a part of that world are loosening.

THREE REGIONS

The security system that develops over the next decade will reflect a world that is slowly dividing itself into three powerful trading groups: Asia, North America, and Europe. Though the world may be "globalizing," its major components are these three regions. Multinational corporations and financial institutions roam the globe, but each has a home—a country that necessarily shapes its character, and both constrains and directs its choices. And though the three major regions are interconnected (in part by the activities of these firms), each also commands an independent industrial and technological base, vast financial resources, and a developed domestic market capable of sustaining steady growth. This provides each with the economic foundations for independent action.

Consider first the Japan-centered Asian trade and investment region. Since 1985, trade within Asia has grown substantially faster than between Asia and other regions. The major source of imports for each Asian economy is usually another Asian economy, most often Japan. By almost any significant measure Japan, rather than the United States, is now the dominant economic player in Asia. Japan is the region's technology leader, its primary supplier of capital goods, its dominant exporter, and its largest foreign direct investor and foreign aid supplier. Financial ties further reinforce intra-Asian trends. From 1984 to 1989, for example, there was as much Japanese investment in Asia as in the previous 33 years, doubling the cumulative total. The result of such trade and investment is a network of producers across Asia, generally controlled by Japanese firms, that diffuses technology and production know-how to other firms in the Japanese periphery. As other Asian nations absorb production knowledge and emulate the Japanese model of success, innovations in policy and manufacturing spread throughout the region much more quickly and effectively than they do to either Europe or North America. The presence of such broad economic strength across Asia guarantees the region increasing autonomy.

Next, consider Europe. Trade within the European Community [now the European Union] has grown faster than trade between the region and the rest of the world since the establishment of the EC in 1958. Intra-[EU] trade is now the dominant proportion of each member-state's trade. Discounting intra-European trade, Europe's percentage of world exports and imports drops dramatically: exports from 44.6 percent to 13.8 percent, and imports from 42.6 percent to 11 percent. Trade within Europe will only increase further with the creation of a single market and possibly a single currency. And, as in Asia, financial ties reinforce trade ties. Like Japan and the rest of Asia, Europe appears to have both an industrial/technological base capable of providing for itself and an emerging political will to develop and maintain that capability, and to respond more effectively to external constraints. Though Europe (like Asia) is by no means a single political actor, European governments increasingly cooperate to create regional economic capabilities and policy. Today Europe is in a position to court autonomy.

The United States, with the largest economy in the world, sits at the center of the North American region, which is also strengthening internal trade and financial ties. Canada and the United States are already each other's largest trading partners. The North American Free Trade Agreement . . . will expand that trade further and bring Mexico—America's third largest trading partner—fully into the fold. The Free Trade Agreement may also spawn de facto trade barriers to goods and services coming from outside the region, thus insulating it from the two other groups and reinforcing the drive toward autonomy.

COMPETING VISIONS

Economic relations among these three trading regions will set the parameters within which security issues are resolved. There are several visions of what the emerging system could be like.

The most attractive vision is an extension of the present system of free trade. Though trade in the industrialized world is rarely wholly "free," the unrestricted flow of goods, services, and capital among regions, as within them, would remain the overarching goal of such a system. Governments would continue to act on the belief that progressively freer trade benefits everyone in the end, even given the painful costs of domestic adjustments to competition. Governments would primarily negotiate the rules of trade, not trade outcomes, and they would continue to make use of the framework for these negotiations established in the postwar multilateral institutions like [the World Trade Organization]. The system would be managed by a loose alliance of the three regions' principal powers. A consensus on shared goals for the world economy would replace a hegemonic distribution of power as the foundation for cooperation and stability. There might be relative shifts in position among the three centers of power. Some countries might get rich more quickly, but all would get richer over time, and the significance of those differences would be submerged in the shared goal of peaceful economic expansion. The security system that would emerge from such an order could be built around collaboration and cooperation among the advanced countries, something approximating a latter-day (but global) concert of Europe. We call this kind of world "true multilateral cooperation." In it, the United States would continue to be *primus inter pares.*

A less desirable vision begins with the economic regions fending off trade competition from one another as a way of avoiding most of the painful domestic adjustments. Each region would concentrate on its own internal development and would try to avoid the strains of direct competition by protecting markets. Round after round of "defensive protectionism" would disengage further the three economies and transform the world by steps into three nearly independent subeconomies. Trade would continue to become more concentrated within each group and perhaps decrease among them. Each group would work to limit its exposure to and dependence on the others, and whatever unavoidable links were left between them would be managed by agreement, rather than by markets. In this world of economic regions each group would command its own currency, industrial and technological base, and its own financial system—all insulated from those of the others. The result in economic terms would be three relatively autonomous trading groups with low levels of sensitivity to each other's choices and even lower levels of vulnerability to each other's actions. There might be some shift in relative position in this scenario as well, but all would be wealthy—though, having given up the benefits of global free trade, not as wealthy as they could be.

What kind of security system could we expect from such an economic arrangement? Three large, inwardly oriented groups could coexist comfortably—in principle—so long as there was mutual recognition that the drive for regional autonomy and political stability within each group was defensively motivated and posed no threat to similar arrangements outside. With internal growth and autonomy assured at home, disputes between regions could be marginal in this live-and-let-live world of regional coexistence.

Security arrangements in this relatively benign world could, however, look very different from what we have become accustomed to in the postwar world. In fact, this might not be a security "system" at all. Certainly, low levels of interdependence would make conflict among the regions unlikely. Would there be much cooperation? The optimistic view is that there would probably not be formal, institutionalized cooperation (as there was in NATO, where an attack on one was an attack on all), but that would not necessarily be a bad thing. As security threats in the new world will be more diffuse than in the past, regions, or countries, would cooperate on an ad hoc basis, with like-minded countries forming coalitions around specific challenges—a "Persian Gulf" coalition, or a "Sarajevo" coalition, for example. In a world without hegemony, "security cooperation ála carte" sounds practical, cheap (compared to supporting institutions like NATO) and fairly stable. In security debates this vision has become something approaching conventional wisdom as a "second-best" solution in the post–Cold War world.

What's wrong with this picture? Many would say the only real downside is that the gains from inter-regional free trade would be lost. While this loss would be unfortunate, it is maintained, the only real "threat" it poses is moderately lower income levels for all. The real trouble, however, is that this vision of regional coexistence rests on outdated arguments. Regional coexistence is not likely to be stable in the 21st century because of new patterns of technology development and new ideas that have evolved to explain and interpret the competition that results. Powerful material and intellectual forces exist that could tilt this peaceful world into mercantile rivalry and unpredictable conflict.

THE CULT OF THE ECONOMIC OFFENSIVE

The principal force that could propel the regions into bitter economic rivalry is the possibility that there can be *enduring* national winners and losers from trade competition. This possibility is grounded in provocative new theories of trade and technology that undermine the basic intellectual premises of free trade and confirm recent experiences in high-technology competition.

Strategic trade theory, as it is often called, proposes that governments can by unilateral action permanently alter the competitive balance of trade in critical industries. By providing subsidies or protection, governments can give domestic firms—or entire industries—resources to build an improved global market position. If other countries do not similarly support their firms, the first country will have "created" advantage. If the industries selected for this special treatment serve as catalysts for the rest of the economy, their improved welfare benefits the entire economy. By promoting these key sectors governments can, in effect, secure permanent gains for the nation as a whole.

The trouble is that these gains come at the expense of other nations and possibly at their permanent expense. As one state's firms capture increasing market share, another state's firms suffer; and since the firms suffering are in the same critical catalyst position in their own economy, the whole economy suffers. Moreover, if the industries in question are natural oligopolies because of high investment or technological barriers to entry (as with the aircraft or semiconductor industries), the "created" advantage one firm enjoys might be enough to drive other firms permanently from the market. This generates serious consequences for other national economies, which find themselves suddenly dependent on critical components and technologies they can no longer produce at home. The promise of autonomy becomes, instead, a threat of dependence.

When we combine strategic trade arguments with an understanding of how technology develops and how strongly that development affects the evolution of modern industrial economies, the implications become even sharper. The clearest way to think about how technology develops is to picture each nation moving along a technology "trajectory." Industrial technologies are not like pure science in that they do not come in a universal language with open and equal access to everyone. Production technologies accrue locally in networks of shared knowledge, learning, and experience—in firm-supplier links, skilled workers, and the like. This kind of knowledge is rarely traded among nations (except as partially embodied in products and technology licenses). This means that technological innovation tends to build up local assets within national borders and place states on distinct trajectories, or paths, that powerfully shape possibilities for future growth. If a nation's markets and firms are organized in such a way that these innovations spread easily, a few critical industries can strongly influence how an economy fares.

Together, strategic trade and technology theories open up the possibility that nations or regions could come to see themselves competing in a win-or-lose, zero-sum game for their economic futures. But can promotional policies really affect competition as profoundly as these theories suggest? Can governments really pick winners over losers? The answer is that it may not matter whether they can or not. It only matters whether nations *believe* they can. And if one government plays the strategic trade game, other governments will have trouble standing aside. In fact, nations or regions might feel provoked to develop strategic trade policies simply out of the fear that others might be doing the same.

Governments will find it difficult to deny themselves the tools of strategic trade. Strategic trade is based on the notion of a "first mover advantage." This advantage can prove decisive in capturing markets and particularly in generating a cycle of reinvestment and learning that creates enduring advantage in high-technology competition. For these reasons, it is not a viable policy to sit back and watch while others move ahead. In fact, it can be seen as potentially devastating if governments believe that markets and technologies critical to supporting further economic development at home will be lost to those who moved first.

The dynamic is reminiscent of "the cult of the offensive" among European military organizations prior to World War I. In that case, a group of states set up and trained their armies according to the idea that military offense was dominant over defense—which led to the conclusion that a tremendous advantage came to the side that struck first. They turned out to be wrong about the nature of war in 1914—in fact the defense turned out to have the advantage—but "the cult of the offensive," as wrong as it was, nevertheless changed the character of relationships among the European states. On the strength of the idea, states that prepared their armies for quick decisive strikes forced their neighbors to do the same rather than plan for defense. In a world where offense was believed dominant, even states that preferred the status quo had to protect themselves against the possibility that others would launch preemptive strikes—and the only way to do that seemed to be by preparing to do the same thing themselves. Readying armies to preempt became a prudent policy even if the advantages of doing so were uncertain, because what was clear was that it would certainly be much worse *not* to act while somebody else did. The logic of strategic trade coupled with the notion of technology trajectories has similar implications for economic competitors. Nations or regions may be provoked to develop strategic trade policies in an effort to seize a first mover advantage, or simply out of fear that others might be doing the same. In either case even the appearance or suspicion that other governments might be attempting to do this could be sufficient to tip benign regionalism into mercantile rivalry.

This tendency will be reinforced by a new dynamic developing between military and commercial technology. In the Cold War system technologies "spun-off" from military to commercial applications because military technologies were frequently more sophisticated than those available in the civilian sector. The classic example is integrated circuit technology, which was developed first for military and aerospace application. Now, because of the new industrial capabilities mentioned earlier, the dynamic is frequently reversed—that is, advanced commercial technologies "spin-on" into military applications.

What does this portend for security cooperation? The advent of spin-on has already prompted governments to regard many commercial technologies as militarily sensitive and therefore warranting secrecy orders. But this is not the most significant implication. More important, spin-on implies that nations that cede commercial markets may also sacrifice the ability to develop critical military systems. Lacking the supply base of resident skills, knowledge, process, and subsystems know-how of related commercial industries, it may not be possible to maintain leading-edge military capability. This creates a whole new level of security vulnerability for the control that trade rivals have over militarily relevant commercial technologies can be used to extract concessions or impose constraints in return for granting access to technology. Taken together, these dangers reinforce the temptation to "grab" key technologies and markets before others can—doing so would guarantee domestic availability of the industrial resources needed to field state-of-the-art military forces and eliminate the need to make unacceptable concessions.

The prospects for mercantile rivalry between three large economic regions, each with a market large enough to influence global competition and large enough to capture most scale economies, are real. If they are unconnected by intimate ties of trade and investment, free from any common threat, standing in relative autonomy, one must ask of these three regions: What will bind them together? The only answer may be this: fear—fear of one another.

IDEAS MATTER

The next security system could be defined by true multilateral cooperation, by peaceful regional coexistence, or, most dangerously, by mercantilist regional rivalry. The risk is that if regions come to view trade as a zero-sum game in which one region's gain is another's loss, they could start to regard each other as rivals competing not just for one-time gains in wealth, but for long-term growth and welfare. There are powerful intellectual, political, and technological forces that could push the world into this kind of mercantile rivalry. Existing international institutions would be hard pressed to cope with the instability that would result. . . .

Relationships are based not only on the distribution of power but also on ideas and the institutions that are connected to them. The security system that emerges over the next decade will reflect the new realities of economic power but it will also be shaped by the visions brought to it by the major actors. This was true even within the demanding constraints of a bipolar world. At the end of World War II, the United States and the Soviet Union both moved to construct security systems to balance the power of the other, but they chose to do so in very different ways according to different sets of ideas. The Soviet Union put together a network of bilateral treaties that connected Moscow to each of the Eastern European states but kept those states separate from each other—the organizing principle was "divide and conquer" and its success lay in making each Warsaw Pact nation individually dependent on Stalin for security and economic intercourse. The United States could have done the same and there would have been concrete advantages to doing so. But Washington chose a different model, the model that became NATO, where the allies were bound together in a system of indivisible security and each was protected equally by an American military umbrella. Security in the West became what economists call a "nonexcludable good"—which was at the root of the burden-sharing or free-riding complaints that the United States frequently leveled at its allies. But it did so only because the United States chose to fashion its alliance relationships in that way.

The point is that this choice was not determined by the distribution of power, but was based on a distinctive set of American ideas about world order, ideas that were firmed up by American diagnoses of the failures of international arrangements during the interwar years. The United States sought to avoid the discriminatory bilateral trade deals with Eastern Europe that contributed to Nazi power and the "checkerboard" system of weak guarantees in Western Europe that gave way so easily to aggression. Americans also believed that pluralistic and democratic states that traded freely could live together peacefully and grow economically, without threatening each other's vital interests.

The two sets of ideas were brought together in the multilateral institutions of the postwar Western world. Peace, prosperity, and democracy might not have been shared equally within those institutions, but they were to be shared by all. What emerged from this design did not match perfectly the American conception, but it came remarkably close. Economic and military power certainly helped the United States induce or compel sometimes reluctant nations to join the fold and comply with the bargains. But the substance of the bargains was as much a product of American vision as it was a product of economic strength.

Today a new basis for security relationships is forming. Hegemonies are gone, economic power is dispersed, and new ideas—about trade, security, development, and order—are emerging from new centers of power. These ideas will help to shape the relationships that in turn will determine the quality of life in the international system for both the most powerful states and their smaller neighbors. There are more strong voices on the world stage today than fifty years ago, and each has different things to say. The United States will have to listen. It must also shape the script.

THE CHALLENGE

It is possible for the United States to be effective without being dominant, but this will require a clear presentation of the kind of world [Americans] want to live in 10 years hence and a program for getting from here to there. Mercantilist rivalry is not a necessary consequence of the new distribution of power, but it could arrive by default. To avoid it, the United States must act from strength at home and with multilateral cooperation abroad.

The first priority is to reestablish American economic strength. Neither external agreements nor combative trade policy can compensate for what [Americans] fail to do for [themselves]. Only [the United States] can provide the kind of macroeconomic environment, human and physical infrastructure, and mechanisms for the domestic development and diffusion of technologies that make it possible to be one of the winners in the big leagues of global economic competition.

The trick will be to re-establish American economic strength while avoiding beggar-thy-neighbor trade and technology practices that could push the world into mercantilist rivalry. That is where multilateral cooperation comes in: America's own economic redevelopment agenda provides the opportunity to establish new multilateral agreements to contain mercantilist behavior.

Achieving such multilateral cooperation will require several new actions. The United States and its allies need to agree to a set of principles that endorses reciprocal access to regional markets, investment opportunities, and supply-base technologies. Reciprocity of access permits as much openness as each regional economy can tolerate politically and forces compromises in domestic practices that impede access whenever domestic industries seek foreign market opportunities. Effective reciprocity will in turn depend upon some degree of consensus about what domestic and business practices are appropriate. Some code of behavior will be needed to eliminate the most extreme and disruptive practices. To make up for the inevitable gaps and loopholes in that code, states will have to negotiate specific bargains.

The complex arrangements needed to achieve these goals will be difficult to negotiate in large multilateral forums like [the WTO]. . . . Indeed, most of what will be accomplished will be on a bilateral basis. Consequently, it is crucial that bilateral negotiations take place in a multilateral context with rules of procedure and sufficient transparency to ensure that those who are not direct participants can make their needs and interests felt. The agenda for cooperation is daunting, but no more daunting than the GATT [predecessor to the WTO] agenda must have looked to statesmen at the end of the 1940s.

The stakes may be as high now as when the GATT was conceived. Now, as then, real wealth and power are at stake. Then it was concentrated in U.S. hands; now it is regionally dispersed. Then [Americans] expected the system would benefit U.S. interests; now the United States has no such confidence. Hegemony is long gone, and a new world beckons. Now America needs to act not from the belief that [it is] and can remain dominant, but from an understanding of how [it] can be effective in circumstances in which [it] no longer [is].

PART FOUR

FOUR

ECOLOGY AND
POLITICS

Some years ago T. S. Eliot lamented poetically that the world would end not with a bang but with a whimper. For decades the nuclear sword of Damocles hung by the slenderest of threads, threatening a fiery and shattering apocalypse. The quest for security continues, and the nuclear threat, while sharply diminished, remains. Still, the end of the Cold War signals a dramatic change. Since 1947, the *Bulletin of the Atomic Scientists* has used the hands of a clock—with the hour hand pointed toward midnight and the minute hand moving seemingly inexorably toward it—to symbolize how close humankind stands to the nuclear precipice. In 1988, for the first time in 16 years, the minute hand was moved away from the witching hour, not toward it—from three to six minutes to midnight. In April 1990 the clock was again reset, this time at 10 minutes to midnight. And in December 1991, when the editors concluded that "the world has entered a new era," the hands were moved to 17 minutes from 12, off the scale of danger. Only later, in December 1995, following a poll of interested people that included a "hearing" on the Internet, did the editors conclude they had moved the hands too far, inching them back to 14 minutes before midnight. "The world is still a very dangerous place, and trends are in the wrong direction," they reasoned.

Even as the threat of a nuclear apocalypse recedes, numerous challenges broadly conceived as *ecological* threaten that the final cataclysm may still occur. Though now more by accretion or accident than by design, the consequences of an ecological catastrophe would be no less fatal than a nuclear one. Whether the world's political leaders and others touched by environmental challenges will cope effectively is problematic.

Part Four of *The Global Agenda* examines the politics of the ecological agenda. *Ecology* in this context refers to the relationship between humans and their physical and biological environments. The importance of the environmental issues on the global ecological agenda derives from the combination of world population growth and extant consumption patterns that strain the earth's delicate life-support systems. Food and resource scarcities have plagued the ecopolitical landscape from time to time in recent years as world population continues to grow inexorably, but it is a series of other environmental challenges—including acid rain, depletion of the stratospheric ozone layer, destruction of tropical rainforests, and global climate change—that has captured worldwide attention, pushing the ecological problematique to the forefront of the global agenda as Cold War tensions recede.

Environmental stresses result from human efforts to stretch the global habitat's ability to sustain ever higher living standards for ever larger numbers of people. Technological innovations are especially important, as they permit newer and sometimes more efficient uses of existing resources. But they also result in pollution and other forms of environmental degradation of waterways, landmasses, and the atmosphere that threaten the environment future generations will inherit. The global commons—resources such as the oceans, the seabed, the radio spectrum, and outer space—previously regarded as the common heritage of humankind, are now able to be exploited by the technologically sophisticated, who may seek to deny them to others.

Environmental issues sometimes bear directly on issues of war and peace, as scarcities of renewable and nonrenewable resources may invite the classic kinds of interstate conflict that once characterized competition over territory. Water shortages in the Middle East, for example, threaten economic and political instability in an already politically volatile region, as access to water supples by downstream countries along the region's major rivers may be constrained by the decisions of nations farther upstream. Even comparatively abundant but unevenly distributed resources may create global conflicts if they lead to a level of dependence on foreign suppliers perceived as a threat to national security. Fear that Iraq's Saddam Hussein might gain control over a significant portion of world oil supplies following his invasion of Kuwait was certainly a primary motivation underlying the 1991 Persian Gulf War. If population growth and resource scarcities also portend, as some have argued, that there are "limits to growth" and that the consumption patterns of the past necessary to support the standards of living to which at least the industrial world has become accustomed must be curtailed in the future, questions of equity and justice, already so prominent on the North-South axis of the global agenda, will be magnified. The future of all people and states is thus affected by how these issues are addressed, and the world that our children and their children inherit will be profoundly affected by the choices made today.

States, acting alone, may be the appropriate vehicles for dealing with some environmental issues, but for most they are not. Acid rain and other transboundary pollutants know no limits. Nuclear contamination of the atmosphere poses threats far beyond its origins. Climatological changes induced by fossil fuel consumption and destruction of the protective ozone layer caused by other abuses imperil all. Concerted international collaborative efforts are required to deal with these and many of the other ecological issues on the global agenda.

As this brief menu suggests, the range of global political issues encompassed by the ecological agenda is broad and, like issues of peace and security and economic interactions, complex. Until recently, however, the critical importance of ecological issues has been less well recognized. For most people ecological issues are typically remote. Unless we are touched directly by something like the disposal of toxic chemical waste or spent nuclear fuel, atmospheric contamination in the form of acid rain, soil erosion due to strip mining or deforestation, or life-threatening drought caused by excessive heat, ecological issues seem too distant to be of little immediate relevance or concern. Despite this, there is a growing awareness worldwide—supported by survey data in the Global North and South alike—that people perceive environmental concerns as central to the quality of life they now enjoy and that their children will inherit.

The Earth Summit, which took place in June 1992 in Rio de Janeiro, Brazil, was an important milestone in the development of public consciousness. Formally known as the United Nations Conference on Environment and Development (UNCED), the summit brought together more than 150 governments, 1,400 nongovernmental organizations, and some 8,000 journalists. UNCED Secretary-General Maurice F. Strong characterized the work of the summit as "a new beginning," the "first steps on a new pathway to our common future." Earth Summit participants agreed on statements of principles relating to the environment and development and to the management of the earth's forests, conventions on climate change and biodiversity, and a program of action—*Agenda 21*—that embodies a political commitment to the realization of a broad range of environmental and development goals.

Prior to the Earth Summit the environment and development had been treated separately—and often regarded as in conflict with one another because development frequently imperils and degrades the environment. During the Earth Summit itself the concept *sustainable development* was used to galvanize a simultaneous treatment of environmental and development issues. The concept was first articulated in *Our Common Future,* the 1987 report of the World Commission on Environment and Development, popularly known as the Brundtland Commission after the Norwegian Prime Minister who was its chair. The commission defined a sustainable society in timeless fashion: It is one that "meets the needs of the present without compromising the ability of future generations to meet their own needs."

Because "sustainability" means living off the Earth's interest without encroaching on its capital, it draws attention to problems of intra- and intergenerational equity. At issue is how current needs can be met without depriving future generations of the resources necessary for their own prosperity and survival. Literally hundreds of books and articles have asked in one way or another how this ambitious goal might be achieved. A common thread throughout them is that sustainability cannot be achieved without dramatic changes in the social, economic, and political fabric of the world as we now know it.

Our first essay in Part Four of *The Global Agenda,* "An Ecological Approach to International Relations" by Dennis Pirages, introduces a way of thinking about international political issues that stresses the interrelatedness of human populations with other organisms and the environment. Pirages identifies four elements in the ecological approach to international relations. The first includes a concern with the relationship between "the size and distribution of human populations and the sustaining capabilities of the physical environment." Here Pirages directs attention to the growth in world population and shows how it relates to such environmental problems as the depletion of the protective ozone layer and global climate change caused by the burning of fossil fuels. He notes that "preserving a balance between population growth, industrialization, and the future integrity of the global economy obviously requires new approaches to development." Hence the importance of the concept *sustainable development.*

The second element deals with the relationship between human populations and the state system, which often means populations in conflict. Here the focus is on the relationship between environmental scarcity and various forms of intra- and interstate conflict, including pressures for legal and illegal migration among states. The third element draws attention to human populations in interaction with other species, and the fourth deals with interactions between humans and pathogenic microorganisms. The former heightens our sensitivities to the impact of humans on nature's delicate ecological balance, and the latter reminds us that, even "in the face of an ongoing biomedical revolution, traditional diseases are making a comeback . . . to challenge human immune systems." Collectively the four dimensions of an ecological approach to international relations identify the many strands of environmental challenges humanity now faces, as discussed in the remaining essays in this part of *The Global Agenda.*

The remainder of our tour begins with "The Stork and the Plow: How Many is Too Many?" by the well-known human ecologists Paul R. Ehrlich, Anne H. Ehrlich, and Gretchen C. Daily. The authors begin by noting that "the struggle merely to support today's population at today's standards of living is causing environmental destruction on a scale and at a pace unprecedented in human history." "How long," they ask, "can we go on this way?"

To probe the answer they draw on the ecological concept *carrying capacity*: "the maximum population size of any organism that an area can support, without reducing its ability to support the same species in the future." Although easily defined, carrying capacity is not some fixed number, immutable in all times and places. Instead, it depends on complex interactions among biological, social, economic, and technological forces, which often have the effect of mitigating or postponing nature's constraints. Still, the authors emphatically deny that human ingenuity has stretched the global carrying capacity sufficiently. "The current population is being maintained only through the exhaustion and dispersion of a one-time inheritance of natural capital through rapid draining of the bank account. Worse yet, there is no way of replenishing critical, nonsubstitutable elements of Earth's natural capital on any time scale of interest." Only a dramatic increase in *efficiency* and *equity* promises substantial growth of the current carrying capacity, but "increasing efficiency and equity seems anathema to the dominant, consumption-oriented culture" that now dominates the world.

As noted, the concept of sustainable development, which challenges the now-dominant consumption-oriented culture, figured prominently in the deliberations of policy makers and the agreements they reached at the Earth Summit. But to what effect? Christopher Flavin addresses that question in "Rio Retrospective: The Earth Summit Then and Now." His conclusions are disheartening. Population growth marches on, emissions of carbon dioxide remain unabated, biological riches continue to be ravished, and millions of people fall farther behind their rich counterparts, with governments unable to provide an adequate social safety net.

Flavin acknowledges that his five-year retrospective on the Earth Summit is hardly sufficient time to permit realization of the summit's ambitious goals. Still, he concludes that "one lesson is clear: Although substantial progress has been made on specific environmental problems, the world has so far failed to meet the broader challenge of integrating environmental strategies into economic policy." Flavin concludes with a brief look at the road from Rio, which finds that important international and national institutions have been put into place along with significant new agreements and strengthened older ones. However, a shortfall in the resources necessary to address the Earth Summit's challenge remains.

Population growth and rampant consumption are the principal roadblocks standing in the way of sustainability. People in the Global North are especially prone to see population growth in the Global South as the major stumbling block. There is merit in that viewpoint because rising population in the world's poorest countries propels shortages not only of basic commodities, such as fuelwood, but also rapid urban growth with all its attendant demands for educational facilities, other social services, and jobs. Meanwhile, waste levels and pollution soar. As Janet Welsh Brown points out in "Population, Consumption, and the Path to Sustainability," no government is prepared to meet these challenges.

Despite the impact of population growth in the South, consumption patterns in the North have an even more devastating impact on the global environment.

The 20 percent of world population that comprises the world's wealthy countries, for example, consume "80 percent of its paper, iron, and steel; 75 percent of its timber and energy; 60 percent of its meat, fertilizer, and cement; and half of its fish and grain. . . . Historically, the highly industrialized countries are responsible for as much as 75 percent of total world consumption." Noteworthy in this respect—and disturbingly so in the eyes of some—is that the share of resources consumed by the Global South is increasing, as rising affluence combines with population growth to place even greater demands on the global carrying capacity. Thus the world faces a dilemma: "Poor countries need to 'grow' out of poverty, just as the United States and Europe and Japan seek to 'grow' their economies to provide jobs and services expected by the citizenry. But growth on the American model, or even on that of the more materials-efficient European and Japanese economies, cannot alone forestall an environmental day of reckoning." What is required is a comprehensive effort at both national and international levels to move toward sustainable development. Welsh concludes optimistically that many governments, including the United States, which is the largest consumer of world resources, already have taken steps to ameliorate some of their most deleterious environmental practices.

The preceding essays are "neo-Malthusian" in orientation. The term comes from the writing of the Reverend Thomas Malthus, an early "growth pessimist" who in 1798 wrote a classic *Essay on the Principle of Population* in which he predicted that world population growth would eventually outstrip its ability to feed itself. Today, neo-Malthusians, as we have already seen, believe that world population is pushing against the earth's resources, straining its ability to meet the needs of this generation and the next. Some among them continue to focus specifically on world food supplies and on the strains that population growth and rising affluence place on global food resources and the international community norm of ensuring food security for all people. Under the leadership of its president, Lester Brown, the Washington-based Worldwatch Institute has been particularly vigorous as both a monitor of trends in global food resources and an advocate of changes necessary to avert a neo-Malthusian disaster.

Worldwatch associate Gary Gardner is author of our next essay, "Dependent Development? Losing Ground in Asia." His analysis builds on the demonstrable fact that rising affluence is typically accompanied by rising consumption. In the case of Asia, rapid economic development in combination with population growth is rapidly undermining the region's ability to provide for its own food needs. Indeed, policy makers in some Asian land-poor countries have consciously decided to reduce their cropland to pave the way for rapid industrial development. Inevitably this means their economies will become increasingly dependent on foreign agricultural imports to meet critical domestic needs. While this development may provide important diplomatic leverage to some grain-exporting states, Gardner worries that it may also "saddle them with serious responsibilities: political instability in importing nations could rest in part on exporters' ability to keep the grain pipeline open. In a leaner world, such a commitment may be difficult to keep." Whether Asia's experience foretells developments elsewhere is difficult to predict with precision, but neo-Malthusians remain pessimistic as they contemplate the strains population growth and rising affluence will place on global agricultural systems in the new millennium.

Population growth and rising affluence exert pressure on nonhuman species as well as croplands. As Pirages pointed out in the introductory essay in this section, the expansion of human populations into previously unsettled territory often threatens other species with extinction. Today, the preservation of biodiversity encapsulates this concern. "Biodiversity" is an umbrella term that refers to the earth's variety of life. As a practical matter, public attention to biodiversity until recently has been focused almost exclusively on preserving species diversity. Efforts to protect endangered species from extinction and conservation programs designed to protect old-growth forests, tall-grass prairies, wetlands, coastal habitats, coral reefs, and similar areas are illustrative. Globally, protecting tropical forests, home to countless species of animals and plants, many of which remain unknown, has garnered special attention.

Some analysts argue that guarding against the loss of biodiversity is the most serious challenge facing humanity, as its consequences are irreversible. Among them is Peter Raven, whose essay "Catastrophic Extinction" explains both the threat—"we are losing plant and animal species at between 1,000 and 10,000 times the natural rate"—and "Why"—for both ethical and economic reasons—"Biodiversity Matters." Noteworthy is his widely shared view that tropical forests are home to thousands of as-yet unknown species with potential therapeutic value in the treatment of human diseases. He also notes the "essential services" the floras and faunas of natural ecosystems provide in protecting watersheds, regulating local climates, and maintaining atmospheric quality. The Earth Summit recorded states' sensitivity to biodiversity as an issue on the global agenda, but, as with other ecopolitical matters, little systematic progress has been made in protecting the Earth's genetic heritage.

Like biodiversity, global climate change figured prominently at Rio, but progress in dealing with that issue also remains slow. Negotiators did reach agreement on a Framework Convention on Climate Change whose purpose is to address the human causes of climate change by reducing emissions of carbon dioxide and other "greenhouse" gases, but the agreement imposed few obligations on the signatory parties, reducing their incentives to comply with agreed-upon targets and complicating the politics of climate change policy in a global context.

For years scientists had warned that global warming—the gradual rise in world temperatures—would cause dramatic changes in world climatological patterns, stimulating widespread changes in the world's political and economic systems and relationships. Many also believed that an increase in human-made gases released into the atmosphere—principally carbon dioxide caused by burning fossil fuels—was the primary climate change culprit, altering the natural "greenhouse" effect of the atmosphere when it traps heat from the earth that would otherwise escape into outer space.

Critics of the thesis that human activity causes global warming countered that the observable rise in global temperature during the past century is part of the cyclical pattern of temperature changes the world has experienced for tens of thousands of years. That view is increasingly discredited, however. Since 1988, hundreds of scientists from around the world have been organized as a team, known as the Intergovernmental Panel on Climate Change (IPCC), which has the purpose of assessing the evidence of climate change and its causes. In 1995, the IPCC for the first time stated conclusively its belief that global climate trends are "unlikely to be entirely due to natural causes." Instead, "the balance of evidence . . . suggests a discernible human influence on global climate." Without significant efforts to reduce the emission of greenhouse gases, the IPCC concluded, dramatic global temperature rises over the next century could exceed those that ended the last ice age. Already the world has entered a period of climatic instability likely to cause, as the IPCC put it, "widespread economic, social, and environmental dislocation over the next century."

If the scientific community is now comparatively united in its assessments of the causes and consequences of global climate change, the world's political leaders remain in disarray as they assess policy choices for dealing with it. Differences between the Global North and South are especially acute, reflecting in part the vast differences in their economies and the role of energy resources—past, present, and future—in fueling economic advancement. Robert M. White examines these differences in his essay, "Climate Science and National Interests: Coping with Global Climate Change." White notes that while the scientific community is increasingly united around the central propositions driving climate change, there also has been "a hardening of political positions among the developed and developing countries." Today the fault line separating the world's rich and poor nations on this issue "is almost irreparable." "On one side of the fault line are the developing nations that are committed to the view that it has been the industrialized nations who have up until now caused the global increases of greenhouse gas concentrations in the atmosphere. The developing countries are now industrializing and need greater amounts of energy, largely from fossil fuels; they do not intend to let their economic growth be slowed by restrictions on energy use."

White examines the multiple interests that underlie the positions of the North and South and explores the variant impulses that arise from the science and politics of global climate change. What is refreshing about his analysis compared with many previous inquiries into global climate change possibilities is the belief that in many scenarios only slight adaptations in human behavior may be necessary. In other scenarios, however, more radical adaptations will be required. In either case, the scientific evidence is now clear: humanity will face the prospect of a changing climate, and policy makers throughout the world cannot escape that inevitability.

A recurring message in the preceding essays is that world population growth is a primary stimulus underlying the broad array of environmental challenges that now dot the global agenda. Neo-Malthusians, as we have seen, are especially concerned about the impact of population growth on the global carrying capacity. In contrast, growth optimists, often called *cornucopians,* place greater faith in the ability of humankind to cope with ecopolitical challenges. For them, the magic of the marketplace is the adjustment mechanism that ultimately will balance the size and distribution of the human population and the sustaining capabilities of the physical, social, and economic environments. Economists steeped in the tradition of economic liberalism are often among the chief advocates of the cornucopian viewpoint. Though not beyond challenge, their perspective is a useful antidote to the pessimism of neo-Malthusians, who too often leave us with the impression that little can be done to ameliorate the global environmental adversities that humankind now faces.

Eugene Wittkopf and Charles Kegley, editors of *The Global Agenda,* compare the competing perspectives of neo-Malthusians and cornucopians in Essay 39 (Optimists and Pessimists: Competing Perspectives on Global Population Growth and Its Consequences"). They note the trends in global population already in place and assess how they affect prospects for economic development, global food security, and environmental protection. They reach no judgment about the policy prescriptions that flow naturally from cornucopian and neo-Malthusian assessments of global population trends and their consequences, but they do surmise that "an interdependent and rapidly globalizing world promises that none will be immune to the population trends and dynamics that now engulf the world."

As the world undergoes rapid demographic and economic change, new challenges seem to appear in rapid succession. Surprisingly, one of them is the threat to humans from microorganisms once thought to have largely been conquered. As Laurie Garrett explains in "Encroaching Plagues: The Return of Infectious Disease," microbes have proven to be remarkably adaptable, thus challenging the belief widespread since World War II that the world's public health community could leave "the age of infectious disease permanently behind."

The mobility of people in a world undergoing rapid globalization sharpens the threat of encroaching plagues: "Every week one million people cross an international border. One million a week travel between the industrial and developing worlds. And as people move, unwanted microbial hitchhikers tag along. . . . In the age of jet travel . . . a person incubating a disease such as Ebola can board a plane, travel 12,000 miles, pass unnoticed through customs and immigration, take a domestic carrier to a remote destination, and still not develop symptoms for several days, infecting many other people before his condition is noticeable."

Rapid urbanization throughout the world, much of it related to overpopulation in the Global South as people migrate from rural areas to cities in search of economic opportunity, is also a major contributing factor. "These new centers of urbanization typically lack sewage systems, paved roads, housing, safe drinking water, medical facilities, and schools adequate to serve even the most affluent residents. They are squalid sites of destitution where hundreds of thousands live much as they would in poor villages, yet so jammed together as to ensure astronomical transmission rates for airborne, waterborne, sexually transmitted, and contract-transmission microbes."

Garrett worries about the national security implications of the return of infectious diseases, including what she sees as the threat of biological warfare. In a larger sense, however, the microbial threat grows out of the complex man-milieu relationships that intertwine humankind with its biological and physical environments without regard to the political borders that separate peoples. If Garrett's analysis is correct, political leaders and public health officials alike will be tested as they seek to cope with the epidemiological challenges of a borderless world.

The national security implications of ecological challenges range beyond the threat posed by the return of infectious disease, as we noted earlier. War itself often precipitates enormous desecration of the environment. Rome sowed salt on a defeated Carthage to prevent its resurgence. The Dutch breached their own dikes to allow ocean saltwater to flood fertile farmlands in an effort to stop the advancing Germans during World War II. The United States used defoliants on the dense jungles in Vietnam in an effort to expose enemy guerrillas. And Iraq engaged in acts of "environmental terrorism" when it released millions of gallons of oil into the Persian Gulf during the war over Kuwait. But is the reverse true? Does descrecration of the environment precipitate violent conflict?

On the surface the answer would appear to be yes, but this may be too facile a conclusion. Systematic inquiry by Thomas F. Homer-Dixon and his associates into the relationship between scarcities of critical environmental resources and violent conflict in Africa, Asia, and elsewhere leads to the conclusion that environmental scarcities "do not cause wars between countries, [but] they do sometimes sharply aggravate stresses within countries, helping stimulate ethnic clashes, urban unrest, and insurgencies."

Scarcity takes various forms, as Homer-Dixon explains in "Environmental Scarcity and Violent Conflict: Global Implications." How differences in scarcities interact with one another complicates our understanding of the relationship between environmental factors and violent conflict, but they also lead us to be cautious in predicting the outcome of potential environmental conflicts. Homer-Dixon nonetheless predicts that international stability, particularly among a group of "pivotal states," will be challenged by the "chronic and diffuse subnational strife that environmental scarcity helps generate"—and for which conventional military responses are inadequate. Homer-Dixon concludes pessimistically that "We can expect an increasing bifurcation of the world into those societies that can adjust to population growth and scarcity—thus avoiding turmoil—and those that cannot. If several pivotal states fall on the wrong side of this divide, humanity's overall prospects will change dramatically for the worse."

The environmental scarcities of concern to Homer-Dixon are primarily those that fall within states' borders. Common property resources are different. When resources are held in common, individual actors have an incentive to exploit them to their maximum because the collectivity must bear the costs of exploitation, but they alone realize the benefits. The metaphor of the tragedy of the commons, a stock concept in environmental politics, helps explain this typical national response to the global commons. Marvin S. Soroos examines the applicability of the metaphor in our next selection, "The Tragedy of the Commons in Global Perspective," and uses it as a springboard to probe several environmental issues and strategies for avoiding environmental tragedies. Importantly, he relates these strategies to values (conservation, production, equity, and freedom), the realization of which necessarily often entails tough political choices as states seek to cope with ecological exigencies. Soroos concludes that "remarkable progress has been made in establishing the institutional infrastructure needed to preserve the natural environment." Even as he wonders about the ability of sovereign states to cooperate effectively to cope with their common environmental challenges, his analysis of the many areas in which states have already proven an ability to strike bargains to protect their mutual interests makes us optimistic that a global tragedy of the commons may be averted.

Part Four of *The Global Agenda* is concluded on another positive note. It comes from Julian L. Simon in his essay on "The State of Humanity: A Cornucopian Appraisal." Well-known for his criticism of neo-Malthusian logic, Simon's embrace of the equilibrating mechanisms of the free market over the long-haul of history leads to the conclusion not only that things are better now than they have been, but that the future is bright indeed. Whereas neo-Malthusians are concerned that the human prospect is diminished by the population surge that threatens other basic values, Simon sees people as "the ultimate resource," contributing not only to the problems the world faces but also to their solutions.

32

AN ECOLOGICAL
APPROACH TO
INTERNATIONAL RELATIONS

Dennis Pirages

Dennis Pirages describes the way human populations intertwine with technological developments and with their biological and physical environments to form the building blocks of an ecological approach to international relations. Pirages is professor of government and director of the Harrison Program on the Future Global Agenda at the University of Maryland. He is editor of *Building Sustainable Societies: A Blueprint for a Post-Industrial World* (1996).

Nearly 30 years ago Harold and Margaret Sprout introduced a new perspective into the study of international relations with publication of their book *Toward a Politics of the Planet Earth*.[1] Building a bridge between their early work on man-milieu relationships and the field of ecology, the Sprouts advanced innovative ideas that have now become an important part of an ecological approach to understanding emerging issues in international relations.

This essay was written specifically for this book.
[1]Harold Sprout and Margaret Sprout, *Toward a Politics of the Planet Earth* (New York: Van Nostrand Reinhold, 1971).

This ecological approach is anchored in an evolutionary perspective that emphasizes interactions between human populations, other organisms, and the physical environment. Human beings, social institutions, and value systems have shaped and been shaped by interaction with the physical environment. Rapid changes in these relationships on a relatively finite planet are now creating numerous international and global issues ranging from starvation and malnutrition to global warming.

ELEMENTS OF AN ECOLOGICAL APPROACH

An ecological approach to international relations begins with the observation that *Homo sapiens* is but one species among millions sharing a global ecosystem. Like most species, *Homo sapiens* live in basic units called populations. Biologists define a population as a "dynamic system of interacting individuals that are potentially capable of interbreeding with each other."[2] While this strict biological definition can be applied to human beings, it is much more useful to think of human populations as being demarcated by common languages and cultures. These populations can then be defined by "marked gaps in efficiency of communications." These gaps both maintain and are maintained by differences in language, values, beliefs, and other aspects of culture.[3]

The thousands of individual populations that once roamed the Earth's surface are now consolidated within the confines of states. Sometimes human populations are congruent with state borders, but, due to historical reasons, often they are not. Thus, two or more populations often share the same political territory (Rwanda) or a population can be spread across several states (Kurds in the Middle East). Political instability or even violence and bloodshed frequently result from situations where populations and borders do not match.

Human populations are subject to biological and ecological imperatives similar to those governing other species. These include a tendency to grow in numbers and material affluence until the limits of territorial carrying-capacity are reached. When food and other necessary resources have been abundant, human populations have expanded, only to be trimmed back by environmental and resource changes resulting in famine and pestilence. If needed resources cannot be obtained at home, and if capabilities exist to get them elsewhere, "lateral pressure" develops to obtain them from neighbors.[4]

An ecological approach to international relations focuses on changes in population-environment relationships and the impact of these changes on the evolution of four key relationships:

---

[2]Kenneth E. F. Watt, *Principles of Environmental Science* (New York: McGraw Hill, 1973), p. 1.
[3]Karl W. Deutsch, *Nationalism and Social Communication* (Cambridge: MIT Press, 1964), p. 100.
[4]Nazli Choucri and Robert North, *Nations in Conflict* (San Francisco: W. H. Freeman, 1975).

- Between the size and distribution of the human population and the sustaining capabilities of the physical environment.
- Between different human populations and the state system.
- Between human populations and those of other species.
- Between human populations and pathogenic microorganisms.

Various kinds of insecurities can result from destabilizing any of these relationships. For example, rapid population growth stresses the natural systems that sustain human life, leading to various kinds of environmental degradation. Or significant changes in human behavior can increase vulnerability to various pathogenic microorganisms.

FROM GROWING LIMITS TO SUSTAINABLE GROWTH

The shared global ecosystem provides natural resources that are essential for the survival of all life forms. Energy, water, food, and other raw materials are basic to the welfare of all human beings. But beyond these basic resources, all creatures rely on the environmental services provided by the shared atmosphere and hydrosphere. These constantly moving systems of air and water provide gasses, liquids, and nutrients that are required to sustain life. The hydrosphere and atmosphere also disperse pollutants created by industrial processes, being particularly important in moving pollutants away from densely populated urban areas.

The rapid growth of human populations and the surging demands of industrialization are now destabilizing the relationship between them and the environment. Various societies at different times and in different places have encountered local sustainability crises as demands on nature have exceeded carrying-capacity. But it has only been recently that population growth and industrialization have threatened the integrity of the entire global ecosystem. As recently as 1650, there were only about 500 million people on the Earth. But this number quickly doubled and by 1850 there were more than 1 billion. Only 80 years were required for the next doubling and by 1930 there were 2 billion people on the Earth. The next doubling was accomplished in only 40 years—by 1970 4 billion people were pressed together on a much more crowded planet. Although population growth rates have slowed somewhat over the past decade due to family planning efforts, the present world population of 5.8 billion people is expected to grow to 8.2 billion by the year 2025, and 85 percent of it will be living in the presently less industrialized countries.[5]

Visible academic and policy concerns over the long-term sustainability of population increase and related industrial growth on a finite planet have been readily apparent for less than 30 years. Growing demographic and environmental problems provided a catalyst for the publication of *The Limits to Growth* study

[5]Population Reference Bureau, "World Population Data Sheet 1996" (Washington: Population Reference Bureau, 1996).

in 1972.[6] Using a complex computer model of developmental trends, the study called attention to nonsustainable growth patterns in global population, resource consumption, and pollution. The authors came to the conclusion that without significant reductions in rates of population growth and new resource efficiencies in industrial production, some sort of devastating ecological crisis would be inevitable. Publication of the study, the 1972 Stockholm Conference on the Human Environment, and the first energy crisis all raised awareness of the importance of ecological issues in international politics and sparked extended policy debates over growth-related issues.

More recent discoveries linking human activities to the deterioration of the atmosphere have confirmed the importance of protecting the shared global ecosystem. Nearly two decades ago scientists began speculating that chlorofluorocarbons (CFCs), used primarily in cooling and industrial processes, were being released into the atmosphere with serious consequences for the Earth's protective ozone layer. Ozone is actually distributed in small quantities throughout the stratosphere and protects all life forms from intense ultraviolet solar radiation. The CFCs and close relatives slowly break down in the stratosphere and release chlorine atoms that eventually break apart ozone molecules. Measurements have confirmed a significant reduction of stratospheric ozone. A 1987 international agreement, the Protocol on Substances that Deplete the Ozone Layer (better known as the Montreal Protocol), has been put in place to prevent future atmospheric releases of CFCs.

The global spread of fossil-fuel based industrialization has created another significant atmospheric problem that has become the subject of international diplomacy. As early as 1896 Svante Arrhenius theorized that human activities, such as burning fossil fuels, release carbon dioxide and other "greenhouse gasses" into the atmosphere. As the concentration of these gases increases, the long-wavelength infrared radiation from the Earth's surface increasingly is impeded from passing through the atmosphere and into outer space. This leads to a gradual warming of the Earth. The greenhouse warming issue is much more contentious than ozone, however, since significant restrictions on worldwide production of greenhouses gases would hobble future industrialization plans in the less-developed parts of the world.

Preserving a balance between population growth, industrialization, and the future integrity of the global ecosystem obviously requires new approaches to development. In 1987, the World Commission on Environment and Development (the Brundtland Commission) met to consider the future implications of growth limitations. The commission concluded that future development must be sustainable; that is, it must be "development that meets the needs of the present

---

[6]Donella H. Meadows, Dennis L. Meadows, Jørgen Randers, and William W. Behrens, III, *The Limits to Growth* (New York: Universe Books, 1972).

without compromising the ability of future generations to meet their own needs."[7] This statement marked a major departure in international development thinking in two ways. First, it focused on the necessity of meeting growing basic human needs on a finite planet instead of simply catering to human wants. Second, it abandoned a long-cherished assumption that technology would naturally make successive generations better off than their predecessors. The commissioners concluded that pressure on natural resources has changed prospects for traditional forms of development, and that therefore greater concern for social equity between and within generations was required.

The sustainablity movement in international relations has continued to gather political momentum in the 1990s. The 1992 United Nations Conference on Environment and Development (UNCED), held in Brazil, produced "Agenda 21," a 40-chapter action plan for shaping sustainability policies into the next century. And, in international diplomacy, environmental issues, which used to be considered "low politics," have displaced many of the "high politics" issues that used to be at the top of the diplomatic agenda.

POPULATIONS IN CONFLICT

Rapid and uneven growth of populations can often cause conflicts within and among states. Pressures of population growth tend to force people to move from ecologically devastated areas to those with lower population growth and greater opportunity. When two or more human populations coexist within the confines of a state, differential rates of population growth and resulting quarrels over control of land and other resources can be a source of ethnic conflict, civil disorder, or even massacres. Thus, tribal strife in Rwanda, communal strife in India, or even ethnic clashes in Bosnia have resulted in various kinds of conflict and turmoil.

Empirical research indicates that rapidly growing populations can cause environmental degradation, which in turn can lead to problems of agricultural production, economic decline, population displacement, and the disruption of institutions and social relations.[8] While the causes of scarcity conflicts between states are complex and relationships are not direct, there is much evidence that environmental scarcity leads to population movements, identity conflicts, and civil strife.[9]

Differential patterns of population growth also create pressures for legal and illegal migration among states. In the contemporary demographically divided world, there are "demographic fault lines" separating high and low population

---

[7]World Commission on Environment and Development, *Our Common Future* (New York: Oxford University Press), 1987, p. 43.

[8]Thomas F. Homer-Dixon, "On the Threshold: Environmental Changes as Causes of Acute Conflict," *International Security* 16, no. 2 (1991), p. 91.

[9]Thomas F. Homer-Dixon, "Environmental Scarcities and Violent Conflict: Evidence from Cases," *International Security* 19, no. 1 (1994).

growth countries, and migrants use various methods to cross them. Thus, a major fault line runs through the Mediterranean separating rapidly growing North African populations from the nearly stable populations of Europe. At present, there are 164 million people in North Africa and the number is expected to grow to 272 million by 2025. During this period, the population of Europe is expected to remain stable.[10] Given its historical ties to North Africa, France has been most directly affected by a surge of legal and illegal migrants. The right-wing party headed by Jean-Marie Le Pen has capitalized on public discontent and garnered an increasing portion of the national and regional vote while suggesting that all immigrants should be repatriated to their countries of origin. In Germany, immigrants have received harsh treatment ranging from discrimination to murder.

Differences in population growth rates will continue to alter demographics on a global scale. By the year 2025, there will be six people living on the less industrialized side of the demographic divide for each person living on the industrialized side. The burgeoning populations in the less-affluent world are likely to mount new kinds of migration, as well as ideological and even military challenges to the stable and graying populations in the industrial world.

ENDANGERED SPECIES

Expansion of human activities into previously unsettled territory is leading to the extinction of significant numbers of other species. While this represents a direct threat to animal security, it can also redound to the detriment of human beings.[11] Human beings share the global habitat with other species and are often in direct resource competition with them. Thus, periodic rampages by elephants and tigers in recently "humanized" parts of India or the destruction brought about by deer and bears in American suburbs are examples of territorial conflicts between human beings and beasts. Biblical plagues of locusts, as well as the contemporary activities of the California Medfly, illustrate the intense competition for food resources in the shared global habitat.

Although steps taken to protect vanishing species are often controversial, good arguments can be made for preserving this aspect of ecological balance. Human beings and other species are tightly locked in a web of interdependence that is incompletely understood. Accidentally removing some of the components of that web could have unforeseen consequences for the entire global ecosystem.

POPULATIONS AND PLAGUES

Perhaps the greatest potential threat to human security in the next century is the disruption of the balance between human populations and the pathogenic

---

[10]Population Reference Bureau, "World Population Data Sheet 1996."

[11]See Paul R. Ehrlich and Anne H. Ehrlich, *Extinction: The Causes and Consequences of the Disappearance of Species* (New York: Random House, 1981).

microorganisms that cause various kinds of diseases. Threats from microorganisms are certainly not new, and history is littered with the remains of civilizations that have been devastated by their attacks. Populations of *Homo sapiens* and a large variety of microorganisms have coevolved over time in an ever-changing shared environment. For the most part, a delicate equilibrium has been maintained between them. But pathogenic microbes have temporarily gained an upper hand at various times and have influenced the course of history by wiping out large numbers of human beings.[12]

It is somewhat ironic that, in the face of an ongoing biomedical revolution, traditional diseases are making a comeback and new microbes are evolving to challenge human immune systems. The World Health Organization estimates that one-quarter of the world's population is subject to chronic intestinal parasitic infections. Of the nearly twenty million annual deaths due to communicable diseases, resurgent tuberculosis kills three million people annually, malaria two million, and hepatitis one million.[13] In addition, the AIDS virus, estimated to have infected more than 750,000 people in North America, has infected between 13 and 15 million people worldwide. More than eight million are infected in Sub-Saharan Africa, and in South Africa one-fifth of the adult population will be HIV positive by the year 2000.[14]

Many of the bacteria and viruses that pose threats for the next century have coexisted with *Homo sapiens* for long periods of time. But population growth, changes in human behavior, changes in patterns of residence, poverty, and a revolution in transportation are altering the balance between human beings and microbes.[15] In the words of Nobel Laureate Joshua Lederberg, "Some people think that I am being hysterical, but there are catastrophes ahead. We live in evolutionary competition with microbes—bacteria and viruses. There is no guarantee that we will be the survivors."[16]

CONCLUSION

An ecological approach to understanding international relations has gathered considerable momentum over the last decade in both academic and policy communities. But some view the development of this approach with suspicion, on the grounds that it emphasizes environmental limits rather than technological possibilities. Indeed, some optimists see the forces of technology to be liberating human populations from environmental constraints. Thus Julian Simon, an

---

[12]William H. McNeill, *Plagues and Peoples* (Garden City, NY: Anchor Press/Doubleday, 1976).

[13]World Health Organization, *The World Health Report 1995* (Geneva: World Health Organization, 1995).

[14]*Ibid.,* p.30; Lynne Duke, "Opening S. Africa Brings Rapid Advance of AIDS," *Washington Post,* July 23, 1995, p. A16.

[15]Dennis Pirages, "Microsecurity: Disease Organisms and Human Well-Being," *The Washington Quarterly* 18, no. 4 (1995).

[16]"Emerging Viruses, Emerging Threat," *Science* (January 19, 1990).

advocate of population growth, has declared it to be the ultimate resource and "that population growth, along with lengthening of human life is a moral and material triumph."[17] But these technological and population "optimists" live, for the most part, in relative comfort in the industrialized countries where they can easily ignore the plight of the ecologically disadvantaged in the less-affluent neighborhoods of an ecologically interdependent global village.

In an era in which academic and political initiatives are often lacking, there is some hesitance to embrace an ecological perspective because of a misplaced fear of environmental determinism. But if human values, institutions, and patterns of behavior are to a considerable extent driven and constrained by biological and ecological factors, it is better to understand them and make policies based upon them, rather than to pretend that nature's constraints do not exist.

---

[17]Julian L. Simon, *The Ultimate Resource* (Princeton: Princeton University Press, 1981), p. 9.

33

THE STORK AND THE PLOW: HOW MANY IS TOO MANY?

Paul R. Ehrlich, Anne H. Ehrlich, and Gretchen C. Daily

Carrying capacity is a key concept in ecological analysis. The authors of this essay recognize that carrying capacity is "not some fixed number of people," as "the problems of population, social and economic equity, and environmental deterioration" are "completely intertwined." Still, they worry that global life-support systems are now vulnerable to collapse. Paul R. Ehrlich is Bing professor of population studies at Stanford University; Anne H. Ehrlich is a senior research associate in biology and policy coordinator of the Center for Conservation Biology at Stanford University; and Gretchen C. Daily is an interdisciplinary research associate at the Stanford Center for Conservation Biology. The Ehrlichs are the authors of many books about population growth and the environment, including *Healing the Planet: Strategies for Resolving the Environmental Crisis* (1991).

As the 20th century draws to a close, humanity faces the daunting prospect of supporting its population without inducing catastrophic and irreversible destruction on

From *The Stork and the Plow,* by Paul R. Ehrlich, Anne H. Ehrlich, and Gretchen C. Daily. Reprinted by permission of The Putnam Publishing Group and the authors. Copyright © 1995 by Paul R. Ehrlich, Anne H. Ehrlich, and Gretchen C. Daily. Footnotes have been deleted.

Earth's life-support systems. Human and agricultural fertility are on a collision course—the stork is threatening to overtake the plow. By 1999, the human population will surge past 6 billion in number and will still be skyrocketing. United Nations demographers project continuing expansion for another century or so to nearly 12 billion. While roughly a billion people in industrialized nations live in comfort undreamed of in centuries past, another billion suffer extremes of poverty and violence that the rich can hardly imagine. The rest are concentrated near the low end of the standard of living continuum.

The struggle merely to support today's population at today's standards of living is causing environmental destruction on a scale and at a pace unprecedented in human history. Accelerating degradation and deforestation of land, depletion of groundwater, toxic pollution, biodiversity loss, and massive atmospheric disruption are wrecking the planet's machinery for producing the basic material ingredients of human well-being.

Alarm in the international scientific community regarding the seriousness of this dilemma is widespread and mounting. Yet the very existence of the dilemma is largely unappreciated by the general public and the politically oriented and ecologically ignorant pundits of the TV/radio talk-show circuit. A student can get all the way through a major university and still not be aware of its existence. Presidents and prime ministers overlook it. Vatican policies and the exhortations of fundamentalists of various religions make it worse.

This set of circumstances prompted over 600 of the world's most distinguished scientists, including a majority of the living Nobel laureates in the sciences, to issue the *World Scientists' Warning to Humanity* in 1993. It reads, in part:

> The earth is finite. Its ability to provide for growing numbers of people is finite. And we are fast approaching many of the earth's limits. Current economic practices which damage the environment, in both developed and underdeveloped nations, cannot be continued without the risk that vital global systems will be damaged beyond repair. . . .
>
> Pressures resulting from unrestrained population growth put demands on the natural world that can overwhelm any efforts to achieve a sustainable future. If we are to halt the destruction of our environment, we must accept limits to that growth. . . .
>
> No more than one or a few decades remain before the chance to avert the threats we now confront will be lost and the prospects for humanity immeasurably diminished. . . . A great change in our stewardship of the earth and the life on it is required, if vast human misery is to be avoided and our global home on this planet is not to be irretrievably mutilated.
>
> The developed nations are the largest polluters in the world today. They must greatly reduce their overconsumption, if we are to reduce pressures on resources and the global environment. The developed nations have the obligation to provide aid and support to developing nations, because only the developed nations have the financial resources and technical skills for these tasks.
>
> Acting on this recognition is not altruism, but enlightened self-interest: whether industrialized or not, we all have but one lifeboat.

This was followed a year later by a similar statement issued by the world's scientific academies. The scientific evidence behind these statements is overwhelming. Yet we're like the profligate offspring who inherits a fortune, puts it into a checking account, and spends it as if there were no tomorrow. We keep writing bigger and bigger checks, struggling to fend off ever-growing problems, while paying no attention to the increasingly rapid decline in the remaining balance.

Hundreds of millions of individual decisions are made each year about having or not having children. These individual decisions seem to have nothing to do with the size of the global population and everything to do with the lives, aspirations, and well-being of the women and men who make them. But the futures of their children and grandchildren will be shaped by the sum of all these decisions in the most profound way, as the seemingly inexorable demographic future unfolds. The likely outcome thus raises questions for the world community that are seldom considered by prospective parents.

How long can we go on this way? Can 8, 10, 12, or 14 billion human beings even be supported on our fragile planet? Under what conditions? What environmental costs would be incurred in the process? How will population growth ultimately end, as it must? What limiting factors will come into play first? How familiar will the Four Horsemen of the Apocalypse—famine, pestilence, war, and death—become as resource scarcities intensify? What social choices and trade-offs will humanity face in the struggle to support such huge numbers of people? How will women, in particular, be affected, and what crucial roles may women play in resolving the human dilemma? Can equity—between the sexes, between children and adults, between rich and poor—be increased in the face of population growth? Indeed, can rapid population growth be humanely ended and reversed *without* greater equity? Most important of all, can human beings, with their self-avowed intelligence, engineer and carry through a transition to a sustainable world? How?

Approaching these questions requires an understanding of the carrying capacity of Earth for human life. *Carrying capacity* has a rather daunting ring to it, but it's basically a down-to-earth idea that's becoming more and more central to our lives—a concept we can ill afford to go on ignoring. Biologists define carrying capacity as the maximum population size of any organism that an area can support, without reducing its ability to support the same species in the future. Carrying capacity is determined by characteristics of both the area and the organism. For example, a larger or richer area will, all else being equal, have a higher carrying capacity. Similarly, an area can support more rabbits eating vegetation than it can support coyotes eating rabbits.

Although carrying capacity is easily defined, calculating it precisely—even for nonhuman organisms—can be very difficult since it does not remain constant. Carrying capacity may fluctuate with climate or other forces that affect the abundance of resources. Assuming no large-scale alterations in the environment, however, major changes in carrying capacity only occur as fast as organisms evolve different resource requirements.

For human beings, the matter is complicated by three factors. First, people vary tremendously in the types and quantities of resources they consume. For the most part, one rabbit is like any other rabbit in terms of resource use; however, an average Kenyan is nothing like an average American in this regard. Second, trade enables human populations to exceed local carrying capacities. The population of the Netherlands uses roughly 17 times more land than there is within the country for food and energy alone. The Netherlands is effectively importing carrying capacity from other parts of the globe. Third, human beings may undergo extremely rapid cultural (including technological) evolution in the array and amounts of resources consumed. Just consider how much American resource use has changed since pioneer days.

Carrying capacity therefore is not some fixed number of people; rather, it depends heavily on the cultural and economic characteristics of the population in question. Earth can support a larger population of cooperative, far-sighted, vegetarian pacifist saints than of competitive, myopic, meat-eating, war-making, typical human beings. All else being equal, Earth can hold more people if they have relatively equal access to the requisites of a decent life than if the few are able to monopolize resources and the many must largely do without. The problems of population, social and economic inequity, and environmental deterioration are thus completely intertwined.

This makes it useful to distinguish between *biophysical carrying capacity*—the maximum population size that could be sustained under given technological capabilities—and *social carrying capacity*—the maximum that could be sustained under a given social system and its associated patterns of resource consumption. In the end, regardless of humanity's technological accomplishments, biophysical constraints will limit the number of people that can be supported without destroying Earth's future capacity to support people. Social forces, however, will always come into play to limit a population before absolute biophysical constraints do. Human beings are prone to error and greed, making resource use both inefficient and inequitable. Social carrying capacity is also smaller than biophysical carrying capacity because the latter implies a standard of living—a battery-chicken lifestyle for people—that would be universally undesirable.

Human ingenuity has greatly increased both biophysical and social carrying capacities, and the potential exists for further increases. But has that ingenuity made today's population sustainable? The answer to this question is clearly no, by a simple standard. The current population is being maintained only through the exhaustion and dispersion of a one-time inheritance of natural capital—through rapid draining of the bank account. Worse yet, there is no way of replenishing critical, nonsubstitutable elements of Earth's natural capital on any time scale of interest. For instance, it typically takes thousands of years to form enough fertile soil to support agriculture; once it has eroded away, that's it. And soil is only one of several types of natural capital being depleted. In effect, human activity is diminishing Earth's biophysical carrying capacity just as the need for it is greatly intensifying.

Human activity needs to be *sustainable* in order for its population to remain within Earth's carrying capacity. A sustainable population is one whose activities and well-being can be maintained without interrupting, weakening, or losing valued qualities. A sustainable population would pass on its inheritance of natural capital, not unchanged but undiminished in potential to support future generations. The oft-cited Brundtland Report in 1987 defined "sustainable development" as ensuring that development "meets the needs of the present without compromising the ability of future generations to meet their own needs."

The world population and food situation beautifully illustrates both the superficial simplicity and the underlying complexity of humanity's ties to the laws and limits of nature. No human activity causes as much direct environmental damage as agriculture, yet no other activity is more dependent for its success on environmental integrity. No lack of the material ingredients of well-being causes as much human suffering as lack of food. And no index so plainly measures failure of a population to remain within its carrying capacity as the extent of hunger-related disease and death.

Still, extensive environmental damage and hunger do not arise simply from ignoring nature's constraints. They are produced by a complex and often self-reinforcing interplay of social, economic, political, and natural forces operating at all scales—from rural villages to global trade agreements. As its population continues to expand, humanity must consider manipulation of these social, economic, and political forces as a means of commensurately expanding social carrying capacity.

In the past, enormous increases in carrying capacity have been wrought by pushing back intellectual frontiers—the boundaries of human knowledge and understanding. Sequential augmentation of carrying capacity occurred as newly developed physical and intellectual tools spread across territorial frontiers—regions not yet subject to the resource exploitation regime associated with the new tools (such as agriculture or minerals exploitation). New is not always better, though, and carrying capacity has also sometimes been reduced through misappropriation and misapplication of technologies. At this stage in the game, as the scientific community warns, we cannot prudently count on intellectual innovation to resolve the human dilemma in time.

The greatest promise for inducing a sufficiently rapid increase in carrying capacity today lies in pushing back cultural frontiers—converting the world's nations to a new regime of resource distribution. Any hope for providing the projected population of 8 to 12 billion people with decent lives lies in becoming more resource-efficient and, especially, more equitable than most human societies have been in a very long time. *Efficiency,* broadly speaking, is the amount of satisfaction derived per unit resource. *Equity* is the similarity of people's access to sociopolitical rights, adequate food and other material resources, health, education, and other ingredients of well-being. Increasing efficiency and equity seems anathema to the dominant, consumption-oriented culture. Yet it is now within the power of either the rich or the poor, independently, to bring the global life-support system to collapse. Perhaps this possibility of mutually assured destruction will finally motivate those on both sides to pursue efficiency and equity as matters of self-interest. . . .

34

RIO RETROSPECTIVE: THE EARTH SUMMIT THEN AND NOW

Christopher Flavin

The 1992 Earth Summit in Rio de Janeiro laid out an ambitious agenda designed to achieve an environmentally sustainable global economy. Christopher Flavin summarizes the record of achievements and failures five years later, concluding that "the Earth Summit set a standard for itself that was almost certain to lead to disappointment." Flavin is vice president for research at the Worldwatch Institute and co-author of *Power Surge: Guide to the Coming Energy Revolution* (1994).

Five years after the historic U.N. Conference on Environment and Development in Rio de Janeiro, the world is falling well short of achieving its central goal—an environmentally sustainable global economy. Since the Earth Summit in 1992, human numbers have grown by roughly 450 million, which exceeds the combined populations of the United States and Russia. Annual emissions of carbon, which produce carbon dioxide, the leading greenhouse gas, have climbed to a new high, altering the very composition of the atmosphere and the earth's heat balance.

During these past five years the earth's biological riches have also been rapidly and irreversibly diminished. Huge areas of old-growth forests have been degraded or cleared—in temperate as well as tropical regions—eliminating thousands of species of plants and animals. Biologically rich wetlands and coral reefs are suffering similar fates. Despite a surge in economic growth in developing countries, an estimated 1.3 billion people are so poor that they cannot meet their basic needs for food or shelter.

In its vast scope and ambitious record, the Earth Summit set a standard for itself that was almost certain to lead to disappointment. Of course, the failure to reverse in only five years trends that have been under way for decades is not surprising. Unfortunately, few governments have even begun the policy changes that will be needed to put the world on an environmentally sustainable path. Only a half-dozen countries, for example, have levied environmental taxes to discourage the unsustainable use of materials and energy. And many nations continue to subsidize clear-cutting of forests, inefficient energy and water use, and mining.

One of the signal accomplishments of Rio was the official linking of environment and development issues, including an explicit recognition that poverty itself is a driving force behind a large share of environmental degradation. Although many think of development in simple economic terms, it can be better thought of as an increase in the options available to people—for meeting their basic needs for food, shelter, and education, for example. As biological and cultural diversity are diminished, those options are reduced.

In the years since Rio, millions of poor people have fallen even further behind, and governments have been either unable or unwilling to provide an adequate safety net. In many countries, environmental and social problems are exacerbating ethnic tension, creating millions of refugees and sometimes leading to violent conflict. Yet most governments still pursue economic growth as an end in itself, neglecting the long-term sustainability of the course they chart. In many developing countries, rapid growth has led to a sharp deterioration in air and water quality in the 90s, and undermined the natural resources on which people depend.

Five years is not long enough to judge Rio's full legacy, but one lesson is clear: Although substantial progress has been made on specific environmental problems, the world has so far failed to meet the broader challenge of integrating environmental strategies into economic policy. Until finance ministers, and even prime ministers, take these problems as seriously as environmental officials do, we will continue to undermine the natural resource base and ecosystems on which the human economy depends.

If the economy is to be put on a sustainable footing in the 21st century, it is unlikely to be the result of a top-down, centralized plan; the answer is more likely to lie in an eclectic mix of international agreements, sensible government policies, efficient use of private resources, and bold initiatives by grassroots organizations and local governments. In fact, Rio may have been a last hurrah for those who hope for vast "Marshall Plans" to solve world problems. National governments have generally failed to meet even the minimal financial commitments made in Rio. If the long-term viability of human society is to be assured, we all have to get involved.

THE ROAD FROM RIO

The broad goals of the Earth Summit were laid out in Agenda 21, the 40-chapter plan of action for achieving sustainable development that was signed by the leaders gathered in Rio. This landmark document concludes that "an environmental policy that focuses mainly on the conservation and protection of resources without consideration of the livelihoods of those who depend on the resources is unlikely to succeed."

The goals included in Agenda 21 range from protecting wetlands and deserts to reducing air and water pollution, improving energy and agricultural technologies, managing toxic chemicals and radioactive wastes more effectively, and reducing the incidence of disease and malnutrition. By embracing a broad range of environmental and social aims, Agenda 21 reflects the scope of the challenges the world now faces. But its very ambition has weakened its effectiveness—by straining the limited capacities of governments and international agencies.

The most important institution to emerge from the Earth Summit was the United Nations Commission on Sustainable Development (CSD), set up to review national implementation of Agenda 21 and to provide high-level coordination among various U.N. environment and development programs. At annual ministerial-level meetings in New York, the CSD has focused on a range of disparate environmental goals—from protecting mountains and grasslands to phasing lead out of gasoline and developing environmental indicators. The CSD has been a useful discussion forum and has launched some promising initiatives, including the Intergovernmental Panel on Forests, which is now meeting regularly to craft stronger efforts to protect the world's woodlands. The commission lacks regulatory powers and a budget of its own, however, so it can only cajole other U.N. programs and agencies into taking its pronouncements seriously.

Under Agenda 21, governments are required to prepare national sustainable development strategies. By 1996, 117 governments had formed national commissions to develop these strategies—most of them made up of a diverse array of industry and nongovernmental organization (NGO) representatives as well as government officials. Unfortunately, most reports prepared so far are broad, rhetorical, self-congratulatory documents that describe existing environment and development programs but do little to redirect them. Too many of the strategies treat environmental issues as separate concerns to be addressed by environment ministries rather than as problems that are woven into the very fabric of the world economy.

Nevertheless, in the five years since the Earth Summit, the international community has begun to embrace the concept of sustainable development and to use that notion to shift the priorities of existing agencies and programs. Governments have also adopted a number of specific agreements, including guidelines for safety in biotechnology and an agreement to protect fish that straddle the boundaries of national waters. In addition, a new Desertification Convention has been negotiated and signed. The Basel Convention has been strengthened to ban many exports of hazardous wastes to developing countries, and a program of action for the protection of the marine environment from land-based pollution has been adopted. Meanwhile, a treaty to control persistent organic pollutants is being negotiated.

The speeches of the more than 100 world leaders at the Earth Summit were marked by bold rhetoric about the need to channel billions of dollars toward the new challenge of environmentally sustainable development. The Conference Secretariat, led by Canadian industrialist Maurice Strong, prepared a report concluding that developing countries alone would need to invest an additional $600 billion annually during the 90s to achieve Agenda 21's goals, and that $125 billion of this would need to be in the form of aid from industrial countries—more than double the total foreign aid being received by developing countries in the early 90s.

Very little new money has been forthcoming since Rio. To the contrary, the last five years have been marked by major economic and political changes that diverted attention away from the challenge of sustainable development. The end of the cold war has seen the collapse of economies throughout Central Europe, and has added nations such as Russia and Ukraine to the list of leading foreign aid recipients—a kind of negative "peace dividend."

During the 90s, economic and social pressures have made "rich" countries feel poor, leading them to cut back on domestic social programs and, in some cases, to slash their foreign aid commitments. In Agenda 21, these countries reaffirmed earlier promises to raise annual foreign aid contributions to 0.7 percent of their gross national products (GNP). Instead, overall assistance levels have fallen to their lowest level since 1973 and now average just 0.3 percent of GNP. The steepest falloff was in the United States, where official development assistance declined from $11.7 billion in 1992 to $7.3 billion in 1995; by then, Japan was providing twice as much development assistance as the United States.

Similar cutbacks have undermined the budgets of agencies that many nations had been counting on to promote sustainable development, including the United Nations Environment Programme (UNEP) and the United Nations Development Programme (UNDP), which saw their annual budgets stagnate at $106 million and $1.4 billion respectively in 1995. (By way of comparison, a company must have revenues of $8.9 billion just to make the Fortune Global 500 list.) Effective U.N. programs such as the International Register of Potentially Toxic Chemicals and the Global Environment Monitoring System have been starved for funds, as have programs to help developing countries craft new environment and development strategies.

The one major financial initiative dedicated to the Rio agenda is the Global Environment Facility (GEF), a specialized fund managed by the World Bank, UNEP, and UNDP. Started in pilot form in 1991, the GEF was envisioned in Agenda 21 as a means to support developing-country projects that mitigate global environmental problems. Since Rio, the GEF has also become the interim funding arm of the climate and biodiversity conventions.

Following these mandates, the GEF has provided support for several dozen worthwhile projects, including efforts to set up national parks, protect endangered species, and promote solar energy, energy efficiency, and other alternatives to fossil fuels. But it has been hampered by feuding member governments and by a management structure that is complex even by the byzantine standards of the United Nations. The $315 million approved for GEF funding in 1996 is actually slightly smaller than the $322 million approved in 1992.

The World Bank, which loans roughly $20 billion to developing countries each year, has a far greater impact on environmental trends around the world. Since Rio, the Bank has strengthened its environmental review process and has withdrawn support from some high-profile environmental projects that critics denounced as wasteful or destructive, such as the Arun Dam in Nepal. James Wolfensohn, who became President of the 50-year-old Bank in 1995, has publicly embraced the challenge of sustainable development, a commitment that is backed up by a Vice President for Environmentally Sustainable Development— Ismail Serageldin.

These symbolic changes have highlighted a growing gulf between the new environmentally concerned senior management and the hundreds of task managers and country directors that wield the Bank's real power. These individuals remain focused on narrow financial goals, and so far the Bank has failed even to develop an adequate environmental screening process for their loans, according to internal assessments. Consequently, it continues to lend large sums for projects that add to global carbon emissions, destroy natural ecosystems, and undermine the livelihoods of poor people, say outside critics, while the broader vision of a more sustainable economy is largely ignored.

The failure to fulfill the legacy of Rio during these past five years can be attributed in part to the inevitable time lags that mark any new policy initiatives— particularly at the international level. In fact, the fastest progress is now occurring on those issues that were first identified decades ago. In most industrial countries, for example, air and water pollution are now less severe than they were during the Stockholm Conference on the Human Environment in 1972. And many developing countries have begun to implement stringent air pollution laws and to phase lead out of gasoline. At the global level, efforts to end production of the chemicals that deplete the atmosphere's protective ozone layer are already well under way, and have led to a 76 percent reduction in the manufacture of the most damaging ones.

In other areas, the world still seems to be moving in reverse. Lack of clean water, for example, has permitted a resurgence of infectious disease in many developing nations, while human and animal immune and reproductive systems are being disrupted by chlorine-based chemicals that have become ubiquitous in ecosystems. More seriously, three global problems still stand in the way of achieving a sustainable world: human-induced climate change, the loss of biodiversity, and expanding human population and consumption levels. As recognized in three separate agreements—the 1992 Framework Convention on Climate Change, the 1992 Convention on Biological Diversity, and the 1994 Population Plan of Action—a stable atmosphere, a rich biological world, and a steady human population are essential to humanity's future prospects. Failure to achieve these goals would complicate a range of other problems and lead to an almost inevitable decline in the human condition.

35

POPULATION, CONSUMPTION, AND THE PATH TO SUSTAINABILITY

Janet Welsh Brown

Achieving the goal of sustainable development requires not only keeping population in check in the Global South but also—and arguably more importantly—stemming rampant consumption in the Global North. Sustainability cannot be achieved, argues Janet Welsh Brown, if current patterns of population growth and consumption persist. Brown is a senior fellow at the World Resources Institute and co-author of _Global Environmental Politics_ (1996).

Is world population growth a problem? Most Americans would answer yes, though they do not think of the United States as being part of the problem. The technological optimists among us claim that, theoretically at least, the planet can feed, clothe, and house 10 billion people. But rapid population growth multiplies poverty and environmental degradation, and a laissez-faire attitude about a world population that will double in the next 50 years will assure that for the poor the world over, life will remain harsh.

Does this mean that rapid population growth is a security problem? Not if one equates security with the traditional struggle of major military powers over scarce resources. But if the world pursues the American model of development, with its high levels of consumption, air and water pollution, and damage to the natural resource base, and extrapolates these effects and population growth to 2025 and 2050, some basic physical and biological systems could be at risk of collapse. Less apocalyptic but just as loaded with the potential for human misery is the possibility that in many countries on the upswing, such as Mexico, Egypt, Kenya, or the Philippines, a downward spiral of population growth, debt, inequality, and loss of soil and agricultural production could lead to economic decline and widespread political instability.

There is time—but not a lot—to control pollution and prevent degradation of the natural resource base. Collectively, countries know better ways of assuring development, and a population stabilizing at 10 billion or 11 billion should be able to live humanely on the planet's resources if governments take the difficult steps required to curb excessive consumption and manage resources sustainably—and if the United States takes the lead.

POPULATION GROWTH NORTH AND SOUTH . . .

Between the Second World War and the 1990s, the world's population increased from 2.5 billion to 5 billion, and the global economy grew fourfold. Most of the population growth occurred in the developing countries, where 80 percent of the world's people live today. Economic activity exploded commensurately, but with the most impressive advances seen in the highly industrialized states of the Organization for Economic Cooperation and Development (OECD). On a tide of postwar, postindependence economic growth and great reductions in mortality, the quality of life of most people everywhere improved—a fact easily forgotten as headlines of wars and natural disasters repeat themselves.

Using a medium-growth scenario, United Nations population projections promise a world of 8.5 billion people in 2025 and around 10 billion in 2050. Ninety-five percent of the growth will be in developing countries, most of it in the very poorest. The populations of some countries, such as Somalia, Pakistan, Nicaragua, and Honduras, will double in as little as 22 or 23 years. Others— Mexico and Egypt, for instance—will double in 30 years. Even China, which has achieved a remarkable decline in fertility and reached replacement-only levels in the early 1990s, will see 17 million people added to its population each year, assuring growth from its current 1.2 billion to 1.5 billion by 2025. India, the second-largest country with 905 million people in 1994, will surpass China in population soon after 2025 because its population is still increasing at 1.9 percent per year. Bangladesh and the Philippines are growing at more than 2 percent annually. (In the next century, half the world's people will live in Asia.) Growth is also rapid in sub-Saharan Africa and the Arab countries. Most population increases in developing countries will take place in cities, and the ranks of the young will swell throughout these countries. Already 45 percent of all Africans are under the age of 15.

What demands does such growth in the developing world put on economies and ecosystems? Food production must more than double in the next 50 years, and the demand for wood, the main fuel in the poorest communities, will also double. (Even now, some cities in African countries are ringed with deforested areas, and in India demand for fuelwood is six times the sustainable yield of India's forests.) Governments must build twice as many schools and clinics, train twice as many teachers and health-care workers, and scramble desperately to keep from slipping backward in the provision of drinking water and sanitation. Twice as many jobs will be needed, just to stay even with population growth. Pressure on land, air, and water everywhere will double, and waste and pollution levels will soar.

No government is adequately prepared for these tasks—especially in the poorer developing countries of Asia, Africa, and Latin America, where rapidly growing populations, poverty, and environmental degradation feed on one another. The poor, who are both victims and agents of environmental deterioration, press upon fragile lands, contributing to a cycle of deforestation, soil erosion, periodic flooding, loss of productivity, and further poverty. With few or no educational and health services, poor sanitation, and low status and meager opportunities for women, the populations of poor countries swell. Despite high infant and maternal mortality, the numbers of the poor will increase and feed migration to the cities, where life is only marginally better and where people face a new set of environmental problems—water and air pollution of debilitating intensity. Some developing countries have broken the cycle. South Korea and China represent two different models for development: they have produced stunning economic growth and reduced poverty and fertility rates, but both are paying dearly in pollution and resource degradation.

The population of the former communist countries is likely to increase only slightly by 2025. In the same period the highly industrialized countries will increase from 1.2 billion to 1.4 billion, and most of that growth will be in the United States. Without immigration, the United States is growing at the rate of 0.7 percent annually, compared with 0.2 percent for Europe and 0.38 percent for Japan. Each year the United States adds 2 million people in births over deaths, plus another million through immigration. This is the equivalent of adding another California every 10 years. And alone among all the highly industrialized countries, the United States has seen its fertility rate rise in the 1990s to two children per woman, after hovering between 1.7 and 1.8 for 17 years.

In the United States, a 1 percent population growth rate means adding almost 3 million people to the population each year. It means further suburban sprawl, longer commutes to work, more pollution, and fewer open spaces. Even though these are real problems, few Americans perceive population growth as a domestic issue. Indeed, only when the differing rates at which societies consume materials and energy are taken into account, and when the relative impacts on the environment of different levels of development, wealth, and technology are calculated, does the seriousness of population growth become clear.

. . . AND CONSUMPTION NORTH AND SOUTH

Relative rates of resource consumption have become an issue internationally only since the North-South negotiations that led to the United Nations Conference on Environment and Development (UNCED) in Rio de Janeiro in 1992 at the "Earth Summit." The 180 nations represented at the conference signed a declaration and work plan that acknowledged the links between economic growth and environmental protection and the need for sustainable development. The OECD countries insisted that population growth be addressed, while developing countries charged that the North's extraordinary per capita consumption of energy and natural resources—including many from the South—drives global environmental problems. As a result, both population and consumption concerns found their way into Agenda 21, the conference's blueprint for a sustainable world.

After UNCED, consumption was examined in relation to resource depletion, environmental degradation, and such global environmental problems as atmospheric warming, destruction of the ozone layer, fisheries depletion, and biodiversity loss. The postconference studies have made it clear that the environmental effects of population growth and increasing consumption rates can be tempered by technological improvements that make production, distribution, and disposal more efficient, by incentives to invest and trade, and by taxes and regulations. Examples include reduction of subsidies to resource-hungry industries and tax revisions that make polluters pay and provide incentives for more efficient resource use. Tools such as these are gaining acceptance as countries begin fulfilling their UNCED commitments, though not as rapidly as population is growing or certain resources deteriorating.

Current income and consumption disparities stem from a long history of economic domination of Africa, Asia, and Latin America by Europe, the United States, and Japan. Today there is a great divide . . . between the average per capita GDP of the OECD countries and that of the developing countries. . . . Hope of quickly closing the gap is dim, since the new technologies promising greater efficiency and substitutes for scarce materials are owned mostly by northern enterprises.

The rich and the poor take their toll on the environment in different ways: the rich through their high per capita consumption and production of wastes, and the poor through their pressure on fragile lands. In most poor countries a growing upper class consumes on a level comparable to that of citizens of the OECD countries. While the OECD countries have had the greater impact—contributing mightily to global warming and destruction of the ozone layer with their heavy use of fossil fuels and chemicals—the developing countries' production of food and fiber, mining and processing, and disposal of wastes have had mostly local impacts on soils, forests, biodiversity, and water.

Thirty years ago, environmentalists such as the authors of *Limits to Growth,* were mainly worried about the depletion of nonrenewable resources (fossil fuels, metals, and other minerals). Technology has since decreased dependence on natural resources by providing new materials and making use of resources more efficient. Today it is clear that it is the so-called renewable resources—soil, forests, fisheries, biological diversity, air, and water—that human society is despoiling and using at unsustainable rates. In the worst cases, the depletion of the resource base may exceed its ability to regenerate, perhaps leading to ecosystem collapse.

Consumption, according to the [U.S.] President's Council on Sustainable Development (PCSD) . . . , includes the "end-products, their ingredients and by-products, and all wastes generated throughout the life of a product, from raw materials extraction through disposal. It also means resource use by all kinds of consumers—industries, commercial firms, governments, nongovernmental organizations and individuals." Not surprisingly, consumption rates differ starkly between the industrialized and developing countries.

The 20 percent of the world's population that lives in the highly industrialized countries consumes an inordinate share of the world's resources: 80 percent of its paper, iron, and steel; 75 percent of its timber and energy; 60 percent of its meat, fertilizer, and cement; and half of its fish and grain. Per capita consumption comparisons are even more dramatic: in the OECD nations, each person uses 20 times as much aluminum and 17 times as much copper as a person in the developing countries. As for fossil fuels, so central to development and key to global warming, the industrialized countries use almost 50 percent of the total, which is nine times the average per capita consumption in the developing countries. Historically, the highly industrialized countries are responsible for as much as 75 percent of total world consumption, but the developing countries' share of consumption of most materials and energy is slowly rising and will continue to do so.

The United States, with the world's largest economy, is also the largest consumer of natural resources and the largest producer of wastes. In the last 20 years, personal consumption of goods and services in the United States has risen 45 percent. The country is an especially heavy user of plastics and petroleum feedstocks, synthetic fabrics, aluminum and copper, potash, and gravel and cement. With a few exceptions, most notably oil, 70 percent of the minerals the United States uses are produced domestically, so the primary environmental consequences of production, transportation, and use are also felt there. The United States, with barely 5 percent of the world's population, is the leading contributor of greenhouse gases (about 19 percent) and probably the largest producer of toxic wastes. Although per capita consumption in the United States of most materials is decreasing slightly (the exceptions are paper and plastics), overall consumption continues to rise as population grows. For example, per capita energy consumption declined between 1980 and 1993, but total consumption rose 10 percent with the addition of 32 million to the population.

IMPLEMENTING SUSTAINABILITY

Although it is not politically popular to admit it, American patterns of production and consumption—admired and imitated by most of the world—are not sustainable. The environmental effects of high natural resources consumption will be multiplied as the developing countries' economic development requires an increasing share of the earth's largesse. And larger populations in both the industrialized and developing worlds constitute another formidable multiplier. The world faces a dilemma—poor countries need to "grow" out of poverty, just as the United States and Europe and Japan seek to "grow" their economies to provide jobs and services expected by the citizenry.

But growth on the American model, or even on that of the more materials-efficient European and Japanese economies, cannot alone forestall an environmental day of reckoning. Remaining tropical forests and all the diversity they house are disappearing at an annual rate of 0.9 percent—equivalent to the loss of a territory the size of the state of Washington annually. According to the UN Food and Agriculture Organization, all 17 major ocean fisheries have reached or exceeded their limits, mainly from overfishing, and 9 are in serious decline. Stabilizing atmospheric concentrations of greenhouse gases will require as much as a 60 percent reduction in emissions worldwide. Current emission levels, even without the growth required in energy use in developing countries, will result in a doubling and eventually a quadrupling of greenhouse gases—bringing long-term global warming, changes in precipitation, and sea-level rise.

If a new kind of security threat is to be avoided and these trends diverted, then a more sustainable model of development is clearly required. As was noted earlier, in 1992 at UNCED, nations from around the world produced Agenda 21, their blueprint for sustainable development. Although loaded with political compromises, the 294-page document is instructive in its detail and comprehensivness. It includes chapters on energy and marine management, as well as on the status of women and the role of nongovernmental organizations in development. . . .

Sustainable development, by definition, means that each nation has to work out its own plan for economically and environmentally sensible development. Among the highly industrialized nations, the Netherlands has moved with greatest determination, ordering a radical reduction of toxic agricultural chemicals and negotiating long-term agreements between major industries and government that set ambitious goals for improving energy efficiency. By setting an example at home, and promoting sustainable development in its bilateral aid program, the Dutch have exerted leadership both in the European Union and in worldwide environmental negotiations that is extraordinary for so small a country.

Not all countries waited for UNCED before tackling their unsustainable development practices. Brazil, in the late 1980s, reversed the policies that had encouraged cattle ranching over tropical forest protection. And the Philippines halted logging subsidies that had encouraged transforming steep uplands from forest to farmland, with all the attendant problems. The transition to sustainable development is as difficult in developing countries as anywhere else, as entrenched political elites defend the old models of development that have benefited them. Further changes in the developing countries will depend largely on the policies and practices of the international financial institutions—the World Bank and the IMF—which so far have been reluctant partners in the push for sustainable development.

Equally important is the example set by the highly industrialized countries, which must demonstrate that the transition to sustainable development is technically feasible, affordable, and politically possible. The United States, as the largest economic power, consumer, and polluter, is the key country that skeptics are watching. At present the United States is at a difficult point of transition. The nation has taken many steps to control pollution and degradation over the last 25 years, but few politicians are willing seriously to challenge such sacred cows as America's national addiction to the automobile, its extensive subsidies of water and energy, and its unsustainable harvest of public forests and catch from the seas.

The United States does, however, have many tools and experience in using them. In the early 1980s, state and federal legislation stemmed the loss of coastal wetlands, in part by cutting off construction and insurance subsidies for more than 150 undeveloped barrier islands. States like Florida, faced with a huge influx of retirees and tourists in the 1970s and 1980s, enacted land-use management to control development. Along with the federal government and private conservation organizations, states have also purchased sensitive and wilderness areas to protect them from development. The Clean Air Act provided the incentives for rapidly developing such pollution-control technologies as scrubbers, cleaner coal, and fluidized-bed combustion—advances that the energy industry had claimed would be difficult and costly when the legislation was first proposed.

Prices can also trigger technological improvement. The 1970s oil crisis, precipitated by price hikes by the Organization of Petroleum Exporting Countries, led to major savings in fuel costs when airlines invested in more efficient engines. Banning harmful materials—phosphates from detergents, asbestos, chlorofluorocarbons (CFCS)—has also been achieved at both the national and international levels, despite strong opposition from affected industries.

Unlike in some European countries, fiscal measures have not been effectively used in the United States to restrain the use of private automobiles and subsidize public transport. The only serious gasoline tax proposals ever made in the United States were quickly shot down in 1993, although modest measures such as taxes on petroleum and mineral extraction, recycling incentives, and user fees for waste disposal have been employed at state and local levels for conservation purposes. . . .

In the past, policy makers in the United States have often been jolted into action by catastrophes. Severe drought-driven crop failure in the southeast in 1988 riveted Congress' attention for the first time on the dangers of global warming, even though the drought could not be directly attributed to it. Hurricanes and the 1993 flooding of the Missouri and Mississippi Rivers revived the national debate on limits on federal disaster insurance. The United States can count on more such crises—a major crop failure, disease, or destruction associated with the weather, or an unmanageable threat to petroleum supplies from abroad—that will crank up the legislative and policy machinery and provide the impetus for a national shift to sustainable development. But American political leaders could also act before avoidable tragedy strikes again and could govern with the ecological and environmental security of future generations in mind.

36

DEPENDENT DEVELOPMENT? LOSING GROUND IN ASIA

Gary Gardner

Asia's rapid economic development in combination with its large and growing population is straining its capacity to produce enough food, causing it to turn increasingly to foreign producers for agricultural imports. Gary Gardner explores the dynamics underlying pressures on Asia's croplands and what its emerging import dependence portends for global food security. He concludes that "tough economic, political, and ethical issues . . . are likely to arise in a world of food scarcity." Gardner is a research associate at the Worldwatch Institute and a contributor to its annual series on the *State of the World.*

In 1994, the government of Taiwan decided to break a social rule that is probably as old as civilization. Eager to maximize industrial output, but hindered by labor shortages and lack of space for factory expansions, political leaders ordered the conversion of 18 percent of the country's farmland to factories and housing over 10 years. They also decided to transfer 75 percent of Taiwanese farm laborers into industrial jobs. Taiwan is probably the first society in history to make the shrinking of its agricultural base a matter of policy.

From "Losing Ground in Asia," by Gary Gardner, *World Watch* 9, November/December 1996. Reprinted by permission of Worldwatch Institute.

That decision would be less remarkable if the country's farmers were awash in surpluses. But Taiwan already imports more than 80 percent of its grain. Nor is the farm labor pool oversupplied—Taiwan's farmers are aging, and few young people choose a career in agriculture. But rather than preserving all its remaining farms, Taiwan is gambling that it can import all the grain it needs—indefinitely.

Yet in an Asian context, Taiwan is unusual only because it is *deliberately* stripping away its agriculture. All across the continent, feverish industrialization is devouring cropland. And as the farms disappear, dependence on imported food is growing—a trend that worries many Asian leaders. The other two Asian countries already high on the growth curve—South Korea and Japan—are roughly as land-poor as Taiwan, and import more than 70 percent of their grain. Countries newer to the game—Vietnam, Indonesia, China, Thailand, and India—have slightly larger cropland bases, reckoned in per capita terms, but their farmland is also shrinking fast. Throughout the continent, cropland loss is one of the most pervasive and least noticed costs of industrialization.

While that cost may seem acceptable now, it is not likely to remain so. The world may be entering an era of agricultural scarcity, in which our demand for grain—humanity's basic food—begins to edge ahead of our ability to produce it. Over the past several years, population growth and sagging production have virtually eliminated the global grain surpluses that have shaped agricultural markets since the 1950s. The world's surplus grain stocks dropped in seven of the past nine years; in 1995 reserves reached their lowest levels on record. And food demand will soar in the next 25 years, as world population surges, and as rising incomes in many developing countries allow growing numbers of people to move to richer diets.

Food problems in Asia could mean a brisk business for major grain exporting nations, and it may offer them some important diplomatic leverage. But it would also saddle them with serious responsibilities: political stability in importing nations could rest in part on exporters' ability to keep the grain pipeline open. In a leaner world, such a commitment may be difficult to keep. Suppliers will face tricky ethical questions as they weigh the demands of Asian nations—many of them major trading partners—against the grain needs of other, less wealthy countries. And as tighter grain markets tend to push food prices up everywhere, suppliers will have to decide whether to let this inflationary pressure into their own economies or to try to reduce it through grain export restrictions. Importing and exporting nations alike have an interest in preventing more Asian cropland from being whittled away.

ANCIENT TREND, MODERN THREAT

Loss of cropland is as old as agriculture itself—and many societies have prospered in the face of it. But on the eve of the 21st century, several converging realities are about to magnify this ancient problem greatly. First, the world is on the brink of the largest increase in food demand in history. Global population is expected to grow by some 2 billion people over the next 25 years, with most of the increase coming in developing countries. Many of these countries are also growing wealthier: as their incomes increase, hundreds of millions of people will be able to diversify their diets by eating more meat, eggs, milk, cheese, butter, and other foods that require large amounts of grain to produce. (Using grain in livestock feeds is much less efficient than consuming it directly.) Increasing demand for fruits, vegetables, and cooking oil—made from land-intensive oilseeds—will cut further into grain production.

In its effort to meet this unprecedented need for food, however, agriculture will be handicapped by a second trend: it is running out of space. In earlier eras, cropland loss could be offset by cultivating virgin land, but today nearly all of the world's good arable land is already in use. It is true that tropical forests are still being cut and burned in the quest for cropland—at terrible ecological cost—but the cleared land is usually too poor to support crops for more than a couple of years, without extensive fallowing. In much of the rest of the world, lack of water or extreme temperatures prevent farmers from bringing more land under the plow. After 10,000 years of global expansion, grain area peaked in 1981, and has fallen more than 5 percent since then. Together with population growth, cropland loss is pushing down an important agricultural index: the amount of cropland available for each of the world's 5.2 billion people. Today, global per capita grain area stands at only 0.12 hectares, about one-sixth of a soccer field, and roughly half its 1950 level.

Agriculture is losing steam on another front as well. Over the past several decades, annual growth in yield—in the amount of grain that can be harvested from an area of cropland—had come to seem as inevitable as the spring rains. Farmers have used several methods to increase their harvests: they have applied more fertilizer, for example, expanded irrigation, and planted new "miracle" crop strains such as those introduced during the Green Revolution of the 1960s and 1970s. These techniques will continue to boost yields here and there, but on a global basis, their effect seems largely to have played itself out. Major crop producers are now curtailing fertilizer use as their returns diminish; global irrigated area may have begun to shrink; and there's no sign of a second Green Revolution. In 1990, world grain harvest peaked at 1,780 million tons and has since been in decline; the 1995 harvest was down 100 million tons from the 1990 level—a drop of more than 5 percent.

This confluence of pressures is especially intense in Asia. Demand for food there is rising rapidly: Asia is home to more than half of the world's people, and more than half of the global population increase over the next 25 years will take place there. Economic growth on the continent averaged 8 percent annually over the past four years (excluding Japan, which was suffering a recession), and has allowed millions of people to shift to richer diets. At the same time, growth in grain yields has slowed dramatically in most Asian countries—even in high-tech Japan, which invests heavily in rice breeding. Expanding irrigation has been a key Asian strategy for boosting yields, but natural or economic constraints may prevent the taps from opening much farther. China, for example, already irrigates 60 percent of its cropland, but water tables are dropping under some 10 percent of its cultivated area. Most other Asian countries irrigate less than 30 percent of their cropland and probably could not afford to extend that percentage significantly, even where water is available.

And in per capita terms, Asia is especially poor in cropland—so poor that Asian farm area per person is more conveniently expressed in square meters than in hectares. Asia has just 850 square meters (0.085 hectares) of grainland for each of its people. That's equivalent to an eighth of a soccer field. And the most developed Asian nations—Japan, South Korea, and Taiwan—have only 220 square meters per person, which is less than the area of a tennis court.

THE PATH TO IMPORT DEPENDENCY

Asia's crowded conditions, rapid economic growth, and shrinking cropland base have prompted a steady rise in grain imports over the years, from 6 million tons in 1950 to nearly 90 million tons in 1995. Even so, most Asian countries have thus far managed to keep their import dependence relatively low: three-quarters of Asia's people live in countries that import 10 percent or less of their grain. But that is likely to change as more and more countries follow Japan, Taiwan, and South Korea down the asphalt path of conventional development. Once en route, agriculture can be very difficult to preserve: Japan and South Korea have long sought to minimize imports of rice, the grain of choice in those countries, but their overall reliance on grain imports continues to climb. (See Figure 36-1.) Today a new wave of development is sweeping over the entire continent, and a host of industrializing nations—including China, India, Vietnam, Indonesia, Malaysia, and Thailand—is sacrificing cropland to development:

- In Indonesia, brisk economic growth in the 1980s caused the population of greater Jakarta to balloon by 44 percent, and office space to multiply 19 times. Growth continued into the 1990s, leading to cropland loss in 1994 alone of some 20,000 hectares—enough area to meet the rice needs of 330,000 Indonesians.
- In Vietnam, an aggressive policy of economic expansion has produced an annual growth rate of more than 7 percent over the past six years. In 1994, the country's cropland losses came to 20,000 hectares—on a par with Indonesia's. Continued losses at that rate would strip the country of more than 7 percent of its grainland in the next 25 years, even as its population increases by some 40 percent.
- In China, farmers lost some 3.9 million hectares between 1986 and 1992— some 3 percent of the country's total cropland and an area large enough to feed 45 million people. Losses were especially high in southern China, where factories are eliminating rice paddies that support two or even three harvests a year. Post-1992 figures are not available but the country's continuing economic boom is almost certainly accelerating the trend.

FIGURE 36-1

JAPAN, SOUTH KOREA, AND TAIWAN GHA/CAPITA AND IMPORTS AS SHARE OF CONSUMPTION

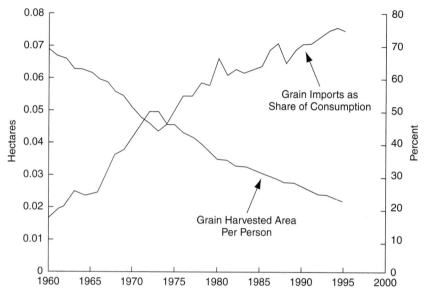

Not all Asian leaders view such events with the equanimity of their Taiwanese colleagues. Some even advocate farmland preservation. "All citizens in China must treasure and protect every inch of arable land," Chinese premier Li Peng said in a nationwide television address in June [1996]. "With economic growth and the growing population, the conflict between humans and the land will become even more acute in China." But as that comment suggests, it is proving difficult to reconcile the preservation ideal with the pressures for conventional development. In May 1996, China's State Council proposed limits on urban growth in order to save farmland from being "swallowed up by city expansion." But the same month, China's Vice Minister of Construction spoke expansively of the need to build 600 *new* cities by 2010—a near doubling of China's urban areas in only 15 years—to accommodate the country's booming urban population.

Or consider the case of Vietnam, where Prime Minister Vo Van Kiet banned the conversion of rice land to nonfarm uses in March 1995. But within a week of the decree, he had issued an exemption that allowed construction of an auto assembly plant on paddy land. Three months later, the prime minister hedged again, this time for construction of a golf resort.

The bureaucratic confusion in China illustrates the clashing interests of farmers and developers in a crowded country: large-scale industrial and urban expansion will inevitably consume cropland. But the Vietnamese case shows that some development paths are more costly to cropland than others, and that careful policy choices can save farmland even as they promote economic growth. For example, Vietnam could reconsider its commitment to the world's most land-intensive mode of transport: the private automobile. Buses carry about four times as many people per unit of road area as cars do; a subway is nine times more land-efficient. Yet Vietnam has begun to encourage car ownership: the country's import quotas for cars were tripled in 1996, and car and truck sales are projected to increase sixfold between 1995 and 2000. Many other Asian governments are building a substantial automotive sector as well. The number of cars in China is expected to jump from 2 million in 1995 to 22 million in 2010. Vehicle sales and registrations are also surging in India, Indonesia, Malaysia, and Thailand.

Recreation is another urban activity whose toll on land can be controlled. By allowing a golf course to be built on rice land, Vietnam's Prime Minister chose one of the most land-intensive recreational uses possible. But Vietnam is not alone. Between 1989 and 1994, Thailand built 160 golf courses—a new one every 11 days. Ranging in size from160 to 320 hectares each, the courses probably displaced between 17,000 and 34,000 hectares of farmland, an area that could have fed up to a quarter million Thais. South Korea had 86 operating golf courses by 1994, and another 400 under construction or awaiting approval. Japan had more than 2,000 courses by that time—enough to cover an area larger than metropolitan Tokyo—and another 395 in planning.

As development eliminates cropland in crowded Asian countries, the prosperity it brings is continually increasing the demand for grain. Growth in China's roaring economy, for example, has spawned a huge demand for meat, which has increased feedgrain consumption fivefold since 1978. The domestic market for beer—another grain-intensive product—has risen by 15 percent annually since the early 1980s. And surging demand for nongrain crops is a further constraint on grain production. The amount of land in vegetable production, for example, more than doubled between 1980 and 1993. Elsewhere in Asia, the picture is much the same. India's poultry production tripled between 1983 and 1993; per capita grain consumption in Vietnam is up 16 percent since 1990. This growth in consumption is unlikely to create agricultural markets powerful enough to resist land-hungry development, but it does tie improvements in the standard of living ever more tightly to the fate of cropland.

CROSSING THE LINE

There is a simple formula that can be used to chart a society's growing inability to feed itself: a decline in the amount of grain area per person will eventually trigger a substantial rise in grain imports. Of course, "substantial" can be defined in a number of ways, but 20 percent of consumption is a useful benchmark. Very few countries outside of Asia import more than 20 percent of their grain—only a few nations in Africa and the Mideast do so regularly. A country importing at that level can fairly be called import dependent. For Asia's first industrializing

FIGURE 36-2

GRAIN HARVESTED AREA PER PERSON IN 1995

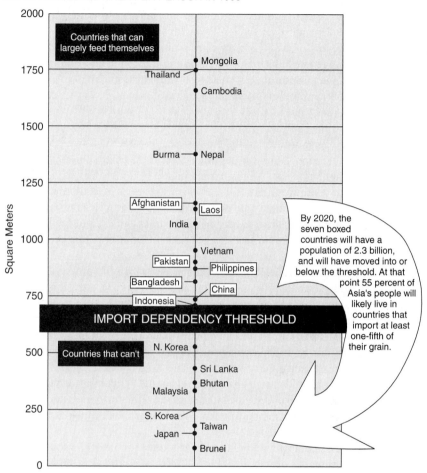

nations, grain imports hit the 20 percent level at roughly similar per capita grain areas: 600 square meters for Japan (around 1950), 750 square meters for South Korea (in 1967), and 610 square meters for Taiwan (in 1967). For these three countries, the 600 to 750 square meter per person range constituted a sort of "import dependency threshold," at which land loss began to translate into serious importing. If 600 to 700 square meters is taken as today's threshold, then the club of heavy grain importers in Asia is on the verge of expanding dramatically.

Today, a large group of Asian countries sits just above that threshold. (See Figure 36-2.) By 2020, seven of these will drop below the threshold and into the zone of major import dependency, joining the eight already there. When this happens, the share of Asia's population within the zone will skyrocket, from the current 7 percent to more than 61 percent. Once India joins the importers, probably by 2030, more than 90 percent of Asians will likely rely on imports for 20 percent or more of their grain consumption. Said another way, roughly half the world could be dependent on foreign grain for at least 20 percent of its staple foods within 35 years. Continued loss of cropland in Asia is setting the stage for a wholesale change in food supply conditions on the continent—and in the relations between Asian nations and grain exporting countries. . . .

WHEN NATIONS CAN NO LONGER FEED THEMSELVES

Economists have long trumpeted the gains made possible by a free exchange of goods between nations. If Asians buy their food from other countries, where it can be produced more cheaply, both parties should be better off—so goes the argument. But this reasoning ignores the political dynamics of trade, and it fails to distinguish between essential commodities like food—for which there is no substitute—and less vital goods, like cars or VCRs. In an era of tight food supplies, the politics of scarcity may affect the behavior of both importer and exporter alike.

If competition for exported grain becomes the norm in coming decades, a handful of major grain suppliers—the United States, Canada, Argentina, France, and Australia—could stand to gain. These five countries account for more than 80 percent of the world's grain exports, a supply concentration that could translate into substantial diplomatic leverage. How that leverage might be used is unclear, but grain has been embargoed for political reasons before: in 1980, the United States restricted sales of wheat to the Soviet Union, after it invaded Afghanistan. The United States alone controls some 40 percent of world grain exports; a coalition of the United States, Canada, and Australia would control more than half. For nations importing more than 20 percent of their grain, such a coalition would pack formidable clout.

Political pressure, however, will not be the only problem confronting grain importers. The sluggish growth in yields is affecting exporting nations as well—a trend that may eventually prevent them from meeting the full global demand for grain. In the United States, for example, yield increases have slowed each decade, from 45 percent in the 1950s to only 10 percent in the 1980s. By the 1990s, growth in yields barely matched the growth in U.S. population. With production increases just covering the growth in U.S. demand, there is little room to boost the country's exports. Indeed, shipments from the five major grain-exporting nations have been flat for years. (See Figure 36-3.) Previously, slack demand helped keep exports from growing but in this decade, the major constraint is the slow growth in yields.

Year-to-year fluctuations in the harvest could also threaten Asian grain imports. The United States has seen corn exports oscillate between 31 and 60 million tons over the past decade, due to the uncertainties of rain-fed production.

FIGURE 36-3

GRAIN EXPORTS, TOP FIVE EXPORTERS 1960–96

Because 75 percent of global corn exports come from the United States, the world grain markets are in large measure at the mercy of the weather in the U.S. corn belt. From around 1960 to 1990, when global grain surpluses were the norms, the impact of a bad year could be cushioned by drawing down grain reserves or putting idled land back into production. But today, these back-up options are largely unavailable. There is no immediate prospect of recovery from the record-breaking drop in grain reserves, and cropland is no longer set aside in the United States except for conservation purposes. With so little slack on the production side, another bad harvest in the major grain exporters could already pose a serious global problem.

But it's unlikely that the problem would be confined to the importing countries. In one way or another, exporting countries would probably also feel the effects of a shortage. Japan, Taiwan, South Korea, and increasingly, China are major economic powers, and would doubtless use their economic leverage to reduce any threats to their food supply. Japan, for instance, has already experienced the sting of withdrawn food supplies and has shown itself capable of reacting. In 1973, a U.S. embargo on soybean exports hit the country hard, and led it to invest heavily in Brazilian soybean production, in order to diversify its suppliers. Today, there are few such untapped agricultural frontiers, but perhaps Japan or other wealthy Asian countries may one day consider heavier investments in the agricultural machinery of the major grain producers—with an eye to greater influence over the product.

Even if no such attempt is made, serious trouble in importing nations is likely to spill over their borders. Increasing prices could well lead to political instability, as happened in Jordan [in 1996], when an increase in bread prices sparked food riots. Severe shortages could lead to an exodus of refugees. By becoming the source of a major portion of Asian food, supplier nations will take on increasing responsibility for the continents' political stability.

Supplier nations may also face ethical dilemmas. In a grain-tight world, prices will likely rise globally, and consumers in supplier countries may clamor for protection from the price hikes. Would suppliers be justified in limiting exports in order to dampen inflationary pressures at home? . . . [In 1996], the European Union answered that question in the affirmative by imposing an export tax on wheat in response to rising bread prices in Europe. The move shielded European consumers from inflation of food prices—but only by increasing the inflation burden on importers, who were left to compete for the reduced pool of supplies on the international market. If grain markets tighten substantially, grain producers would probably not be able to insulate themselves fully from the inflationary effects, but the more important issue may be: When does such protectionism become immoral? How much of a right do wealthy populations have to protect themselves from food price hikes if the embargoes begin to increase the price of feeding the world's poor?

The dilemma is sharpest not in Asia, but in Africa. Few African nations could compete with the major Asian countries in a bidding war for grain. How should the world economy best compensate for the greater Asian purchasing power? Does Africa have a greater moral claim to any surplus food because it uses imported grain more efficiently—for direct human consumption—while Asians feed much of their imports to livestock? And if efficient use *is* a moral issue, doesn't the United States, with one of the world's highest levels of meat consumption per person, have a moral obligation to cut its grain consumption first? These are among the tough economic, political, and ethical issues that are likely to arise in a world of food scarcity. . . .

37

CATASTROPHIC EXTINCTION: WHY BIODIVERSITY MATTERS

Peter Raven

The loss of biodiversity is regarded by some analysts as the most serious ecological problem, as its consequences are irreversible. Peter Raven summarizes the dimensions of species extinction now evident and explains why preservation should be a global priority. Raven is director of the Missouri Botanical Gardens in St. Louis, Missouri.

We are confronting an episode of species extinction greater than anything the world has experienced for the past 65 million years. Of all the global problems that confront us, this is the one that is moving the most rapidly and the one that will have the most serious consequences. Unlike other global ecological problems, these extinctions—and the loss of our biodiversity—are completely irreversible.

THE IMPACT OF HUMANITY

The Earth, our planetary home, is truly finite. Economic formulas, developed over the past 200 years to keep track of the values involved in human transactions,

From "A Time of Catastrophic Extinction," by Peter Raven, *The Futurist,* No. 29, September/October 1995. Used with permission from the World Future Society, Bethesda, Maryland.

cannot make the planet any larger. Nor can they give us any more of the productive systems and commodities on which we depend. No matter how clever we may be, the earth remains the same. We can use it and its systems sustainably, or we will destroy them.

Our species first appeared about 500,000 years ago, at the very last instant of the planet's 4.5-billion-year history. As our hunter-gatherer ancestors began to move over the face of the earth, they also began to exterminate many of the large animals and birds that they killed for food. When agriculture was invented independently in eastern Asia, the eastern Mediterranean, Mexico, and Peru some 8,000 to 11,000 years ago, there were perhaps as few as 5 million people throughout the world. But this population then began to grow quickly, and the extensive land clearing and grazing that characterized early agriculture caused rapidly increasing extinctions. . . .

Human beings—just one of about 10 million species on the planet—are currently estimated to be consuming, wasting, or diverting 40 percent of net photosynthetic production on land. Our impact on forests and other biologically rich communities is already so intense around the world that we are losing plant and animal species at between 1,000 and 10,000 times the natural rate that occurred before our ancestors first appeared on earth. Judged from the fossil record, the average life span of a species is about 4 million years. So, if there are about 10 million species in the world, the normal rate of extinction can be calculated at about four species a year. In contrast to this historical level, and at a moderate estimate, we are now likely to lose around 50,000 species a year over the next few decades. . . .

If we lose two-thirds of all living species over the course of the next century, this will be more or less equivalent to the proportion that disappeared at the end of the Cretaceous Period, 65 million years ago—one of several great extinctions in Earth's history. It took more than 5 million years for the world to regain equilibrium after that. This is a sobering period of time to contemplate, because it is more than five times as long as the history of our own species.

BIODIVERSITY AS A PRIORITY

Why does biodiversity matter? There are three classes of reason for concern. The first is ethical and aesthetic. As . . . population expert Paul Ehrlich put it in 1990, "Because *Homo sapiens* is the dominant species on Earth, we and many others think that people have an absolute moral responsibility to protect what are our only known living companions in the universe. Human responsibility in this respect is deep, beyond measure, beyond conventional science for the moment, but urgent nonetheless."

The second class of reason is economic. We use organisms for food, medicines, chemicals, fiber, clothing, structural materials, energy, and many other purposes. Only about 100 kinds of plants provide the great majority of the world's food. They are precious, and their genetic diversity should be preserved and enhanced. There are also tens of thousands of other plants, especially in the tropics, that have edible parts and might be used more extensively for food if we knew them better. But overconcentration on the 20 or so best-known food plants tends to lead us to neglect the others.

Plants and other organisms are natural biochemical factories. More than 60 percent of the world's people depend directly on plants for their medicines. For example, the Chinese use more than 5,000 of the estimated 30,000 species of plants in their country for medicinal purposes.

Moreover, the great majority of Western medicines owe their existence to research on the natural products that organisms produce. For example, natural products played a role in the derivation of each of the top 20 pharmaceutical products sold in the United States in 1988. Relatively few of the 250,000 known kinds of plants in the world have been fully examined, so it stands to reason that the remaining species may contain unknown compounds of probable therapeutic importance. . . .

For example, artemesin is the only drug effective against all of the strains of the *Plasmodium* organisms that cause malaria, which afflicts 250 million people a year. Its chemical structure is totally different from quinine and the other chemicals that have been used against the disease over the past two centuries. Neither its existence nor its effectiveness could have been predicted had the Chinese not traditionally been using an extract of natural wormwood, *Artemisia annua,* to treat malaria.

Taxol, the only drug that shows promise against breast and ovarian cancer, was initially found in the western yew by a U.S. government program randomly screening plants for anticancer activities. Its molecule is structurally unique, and there is no way it could have been visualized had it not been discovered in nature.

A novel compound from the African vine *Ancistrocladus korupensis,* Michellamine B, shows a remarkable range of anti-HIV activity. It does not work in the same way as ATZ and other anti-HIV drugs. When its method of action is understood, it may well assist in the discovery of other drugs that will be effective against AIDS.

Against this background, it is easy to understand why the major pharmaceutical firms are expanding their programs of exploration for new, naturally occurring molecules with useful properties. What is almost impossible to understand is why the world's nations have not already united in a major effort to explore and conserve the biodiversity on which so much of our common future will so clearly depend.

The third class of reason for being concerned about the loss of biodiversity centers on the array of essential services provided by natural ecosystems, such as:

- Protecting watersheds.
- Regulating local climates.

- Maintaining atmospheric quality.
- Absorbing pollution.
- Generating and maintaining soils.

Ecosystems, functioning properly, are responsible for the earth's ability to capture energy from the sun and transform it into chemical bonds to provide the energy necessary for the life processes of all species, including ourselves.

MODELS FOR PRESERVING BIODIVERSITY

Clearly, much of the quality of ecosystem services will be lost if the present episode of extinction is allowed to run unbridled for much longer. And the rebuilding of these systems, in which our descendants will be engaged, is likely to be seriously impaired by our neglect.

The preservation of biodiversity can only be accomplished as part of an overall strategy to promote global stability. The first prerequisite of a sustainable world is to attain a stable human population. But this will not in itself allow the attainment of a stable world. For this the problems of poverty and social justice must be addressed much more effectively throughout the world. More than four-fifths of the world's resources are consumed by the rapidly shrinking fraction of the global population (now less than a quarter of the total) that lives in industrialized countries. This overconsumption must be brought under control.

If the problems of population and poverty in the developing world (and over-consumption in industrialized nations) could be addressed adequately, there are a number of strategies that could be employed for managing biodiversity, such as conserving a reasonable sample of the species that exist today. For instance, a worldwide system of protected areas ought to be established and maintained, based perhaps on the UNESCO Biosphere Reserve and the Man and the Biosphere Reserve programs. Areas should be selected systematically in order to include the greatest possible proportion of the existing global biodiversity.

These protected areas must also be managed in a regional context, taking into account modified and partly natural ecosystems, as well as human interactions of all kinds. It will clearly not be possible to protect all of the world's biodiversity by preserving samples of pristine ecosystems permanently in their original condition. This will happen only with the full participation of the peoples of developing countries, and assisted strongly by the industrialized world, which must provide the bulk of the financial resources. The Global Environment Facility, an interim financial mechanism adopted by the Convention on Biological Diversity, offers a model of how the funding for such programs might be organized. . . .

Developing countries contain at least four-fifths of global biodiversity—and more than three-quarters of the world's population—but are home to only about 6 percent of the world's scientists and engineers. Developing strong scientific communities in these countries is critical. Their scientific infrastructure must be strengthened as rapidly as possible by providing funds for adequate library resources, computer facilities, and inexpensive and rapid communication and by encouraging collaboration between scientists from countries with adjacent biomes. . . .

All nations should have access to the relevant biotechnology. Its intelligent use—helping to make possible the incorporation of biodiversity into everyday living and thus the stimulation of economic growth—leads directly to reduced pressures on natural ecosystems. Young scientists in the developing world should be encouraged to master the principles of biotechnology and to apply them to indigenous organisms. By applying these principles, scientists could use hundreds of additional tropical species appropriately at a commercial level. In addition, the knowledge possessed by indigenous and other rural peoples must be viewed as a precious and rapidly vanishing field of information—one we must learn about while there is still time.

Steps ought to be taken, for both scientific and economic reasons, to try to sample the diversity that exists now, because the next few decades can only be a time of catastrophic extinction. In many ways, we now have an opportunity comparable to that of living in the final decades of the Cretaceous Period 65 million years ago. We have opportunities to sample the full range of biodiversity with which we coexist—opportunities that may never occur again.

38

CLIMATE SCIENCE AND NATIONAL INTERESTS: COPING WITH GLOBAL CLIMATE CHANGE

Robert M. White

The scientific community is increasingly united in its view that human activity is in part responsible for global climate change, but political leaders remain sharply divided in their assessments of the appropriate policies that should be followed. As Robert M. White explains, perceptions of national interests in the Global North and South will shape policy makers' responses to the accumulating evidence of global climate change. White is president emeritus of the National Academy of Engineering and a senior fellow at the University Corporation for Atmospheric Research and the Heinz Center for Science, Economics, and the Environment. He is a former administrator of the U.S. National Oceanic and Atmospheric Administration.

Scientific developments and a change in U.S. policy have shifted the terms of the discussions that will take place in Kyoto, Japan, in December 1997 at the conference of parties to the Framework Convention on Climate Change. Growing scientific confidence about the role of human activity in global climate change and the willingness of the United States to consider binding reductions in

From "Climate Science and National Interests," by Robert M. White, *Issues in Science and Technology*, 13, Fall 1996. Reprinted by permission of the author.

greenhouse gas emissions will force the conference participants to address the issue of climate change more directly and to consider immediate and far-reaching measures. But this is not a problem that can be solved by science alone. Reaching agreement on targets for greenhouse gas emission reductions for the period beyond the turn of the century will be difficult because of the deep-seated differences between rich and poor nations, between coastal countries and fossil-fuel rich nations, and between various other factions.

When the participating nations [involved in negotiating the Framework Convention on Climate Control] met in Berlin in March-April 1995, they agreed on emissions limitations for the decade 1990–2000 that would limit global greenhouse gas emissions in the year 2000 to the level that prevailed in 1990. However, all signs indicate that the world will miss its goal by a wide margin. In fact, U.S. officials believe that only the United Kingdom and Germany are on track to meet their targets.

What's more, all parties recognize that even if they were to reach their goal for the year 2000, it would not stabilize the climate but only stabilize the rate of increase of atmospheric carbon dioxide concentrations and presumably, to a reasonable approximation, the rate of increase of the average surface temperature. At the levels of greenhouse gas emissions of 1990, some 6 billion tons of carbon would be emitted to the atmosphere each year, increasing the carbon dioxide concentration in the atmosphere annually and thus adding to the radiative forcing and presumably to the continuing rise in global temperature.

Stabilization of the climate in its present state, as expressed by the global surface temperature, would require reductions of 60 to 80 percent in greenhouse gas emissions—an unrealistic goal for a global economy that is fundamentally dependent on coal, oil, and gas for its viability in the foreseeable future. . . . [Policy makers negotiating future climate-control agreements] must plot a course that recognizes the growing certainty among most scientists that human actions are changing the global climate, as well as the political divisions that threaten to unravel any attempt at coordinated action. And once they confront the limits of what can be done to slow global climate change, they must face the challenge of what to do next.

NEW SCIENCE

The . . . policy debate will be particularly contentious because negotiators will have to deal with the fact that scientific understanding of the climate warming process has changed significantly since the 1990 international assessment by the International Panel on Climate Change (IPCC) of the World Meteorological Organization and the United Nations Environment Program. The scientific findings reflected in the 1996 report . . . necessitate changes in the negotiating positions of many countries. Although a scientific debate still rages about it, the most important new finding in the summary report is that comparisons between the forecast and observed patterns of global surface temperature convinced the panel that "the balance of evidence suggests that there is a discernible human influence on global climate." This is a significant change in conclusions.

Until [the IPCC's 1996 report], there [had] been a reluctance on the part of the scientific community to claim that the temperature rise observed over the past century is due in part to human activity. The prevailing view has been that the observed global surface temperature rise was within the limits of natural climate variability. Some scientists not involved in the IPCC process still maintain that there is not enough evidence to support such a statement, and an international group of dissenting scientists has warned against premature action on global warming. But the clear implication of the IPCC conclusion is that serious consideration must be given to actions that influence human activities so that global reductions of greenhouse gas emissions can be achieved.

The [1996] report also devotes more attention to long-term projections of temperature changes to be expected by the year 2100. Although the 1990 report also made projections for the end of the next century, it was principally concerned with the temperature around 2030, the year in which greenhouse gas concentrations are projected to be double the present levels. The 1996 IPCC report expects smaller global average temperature increases than were being projected five years ago. The best estimate for the year 2100 is for a global surface average temperature increase of 2 degrees centigrade, with a range of 1 to 3.5 degrees centigrade. The 1990 report projected a 3-degree-centigrade increase with a range of 1.5 to 4.5 degrees centigrade. In short, new projections indicate more gradual and smaller increases in temperature. . . .

A future important change in the most recent scientific results is that a much closer correspondence between the temperature increase over the past century and that reproduced by the newest and more complete mathematical models of the global atmosphere and oceans has been achieved. The models, which are the basis for projections of climate change that have been developed during the past half decade, give much more realistic simulations of atmospheric conditions. Previously, mathematical models yielded projections of temperature that were much higher than the observed temperature rise. . . .

The new element that changed the nature of the calculations was the incorporation into the mathematical models of the effects of aerosols. Aerosols are small solid or liquid particles that form in many ways—most importantly as sulfates formed from sulfur dioxide emissions in the burning of fossil fuels but also from volcanoes and dust. Unlike carbon dioxide, aerosols are not evenly distributed throughout the global atmosphere but are concentrated over industrial areas and deserts. As particles, however, they act in an opposite manner from greenhouse gases. They tend to cool the atmosphere by reflecting sunlight into space. When the effects of aerosols are introduced into the mathematical models, as they have been in those considered in the 1996 report, they partially counteract the warming effects of greenhouse gases and thus result in predicted rates of warming that are lower and slower than those of previous mathematical models. . . .

A debate still continues among scientists about the reality of this aerosol effect.

SAME OLD POLITICS

As consensus is building in the science underlying . . . policies . . . there has been a hardening of political positions among the developed and developing countries. Island nations and some coastal nations, fearing that their territories may be inundated by the rise in sea level associated with global climate warming, are understandably strongly in favor of immediate action. They seek agreements on emission caps and timetables. Countries dependent on fossil fuel production and use, such as the oil-rich Persian Gulf states and coal-dependent countries such as China and India are opposed to such agreements.

This Balkanization of political interests . . . is superimposed on the long-standing difference of views between the industrialized and developing nations on how to proceed. This fault line . . . is almost irreparable. Only vast economic and resource concessions to the third world by the industrialized countries can bridge this discontinuity. On one side of the fault line are the developing nations that are committed to the view that it has been the industrialized nations who have up until now caused the global increases in greenhouse gas concentrations in the atmosphere. The developing countries are now industrializing and need greater amounts of energy, largely from fossil sources; they do not intend to let their economic growth be slowed by restrictions on energy use.

But all projections of economic and population growth and associated increases in energy usage conclude that any realistic approach to constrain greenhouse gas emissions must focus on the developing world because that is where the largest increases are expected to occur. The [current] negotiating position of the industrialized countries, which are prepared to accept restrictions on energy use, stems from the credence that they place in scientific assessments that the projected temperature changes have a good probability of being on the high side of expected ranges.

In the view of the developing world, the industrialized North owes the industrializing South an "ecodebt," which should be paid in two ways: The North should bear most of the burden of greenhouse gas reductions, and it should transfer environmental and energy technology to the South on favorable terms so that the energy efficiency of their economies can be increased, thus reducing the emissions of greenhouse gases from their territories. In fact, one of the major achievements of the 1992 UN Conference on Environment and Development in Rio was the agreement to create the Global Environmental Facility to provide funding from the industrialized countries to enable the developing countries to acquire and introduce environmentally advantageous technologies. Pledges of resources have been substantial but have fallen far short of the aspirations of the developing countries.

Accommodating all these varied interests will not be easy. Strategies that will achieve global emission goals without impeding the economic growth of developing nations abound, but all involve severe penalties on one or another of the parties to the convention. The various strategies are based on models of the evolution and growth of the economies of the world's countries, assumptions about technological trajectories, estimates of rates of population growth, and alternative modes of accommodating all parties. What emerges from the various studies employing such models are scenarios of possible futures that depend fundamentally on the fraction of the total global energy supply that will be met with fossil fuels of various kinds and assumptions about the role that will be played in the energy supply system by renewable and nuclear sources. Assumptions are also made about the rate of increase in the efficiency of energy supply and demand technologies.

The dilemma is now being resolved largely in the political arena. In countries with politically strong "green" movements, governments favor emission caps and timetables for achieving them. They are buttressed by the results of the IPCC assessments. In the United States, . . . there is a vocal dissenting scientific community and political differences on this issue between the Republican and Democratic parties. . . . Other nations . . . face similar internal debates. . . .

The outcome of [these debates] will vitally affect not only the energy supply and demand industries but other industries and businesses as well, to say nothing of the effects on agriculture and water resources. The implications go further, for if the threat of an unacceptable climate cannot be addressed, we will certainly be unable to achieve an environmentally sustainable global economy.

An interesting development has taken place within the industrial community. . . . Some parts of the international insurance industry have come to believe that the weather anomalies of the past several years that have caused an estimated $25 billion to $30 billion in global annual losses are out of line with normal climatological expectations. In the United States, Hurricane Andrew alone accounted for $15.5 billion in insurance claims. The suggestion that anomalous weather phenomena that have caused great insurance industry losses may be related to climate warming has been implied by some U.S. scientists and publicized in the press. It is not surprising, therefore, that the insurance industry is supporting efforts to arrest the rise in global temperatures. The fossil energy industries, including producers such as the oil, gas, and petroleum companies and users such as the automobile interests, have always argued for caution before implementing policies to limit fossil fuel use, with some questioning the scientific validity of the climate warming concept.

In this confusing confluence of scientific and political interests, little is understood about the distribution of the climatic and economic effects that must be of central concern to negotiators. The global average surface temperature is but a surrogate measure for the intensity of the climate-warming phenomenon. Any particular global average surface temperature will give rise to nonuniform geographic distributions of high and low temperatures.

Mathematical models are as yet not able to portray the regional and national distributions of temperature or precipitation with any certainty. Negotiators therefore do not know, except to a crude approximation, what the effects of global climate warming will be on their territories. Sea level rises are exceptions because the effects of global climate warming are essentially uniform throughout the world oceans. But these effects are now projected to be smaller than previously thought. In the 1990 report, the IPCC projected approximately a 2-foot rise in sea level by 2100; in its 1996 report, the sea level rise is estimated at about 1.5 feet for the same period. Yet the 1996 estimates have a wide range, from 0.5 feet to more than 3 feet. Again, at the lower end of the range the rise is unlikely to be troublesome for most regions, whereas at the high end of the range the effects would be devastating.

We know little about other distributional effects except on the grossest scale. All projections are for greater warming in the polar than in the equatorial latitudes. This suggests that nations located at higher latitudes will undergo a greater warming at the surface than those in midlatitudes and in equatorial regions. Because the intensity of the global circulation is driven by temperature differences between polar and equatorial regions, the implication is for a less intense global circulation, which is more typical of warmer seasons in midlatitudes. Even slight changes in climate can significantly affect climatically marginal regions, but it is not clear, for example, whether arid regions will be exposed to more precipitation or increased desiccation.

THE NEGOTIATIONS

Unlike other negotiations where national interests are clear, government representatives [must negotiate in the face of] unknown consequences for their countries. . . . Their goal [is] the stabilization of the present distribution of climate with its advantages and disadvantages for the nations of the world. Climate can be regarded as a resource, conferring advantages on some nations and disadvantages on others. The current climate is advantageous for U.S. agriculture and disastrous for Mongolian farmers. No negotiation, except perhaps for those related to preventing nuclear conflicts, has the potential for such broad societal impacts.

The economic effects are similarly uncertain. These will depend on the way economic development evolves. Many different scenarios and options are portrayed by mathematical models of the global economy. Even more than the mathematical models that project the physical state of the atmosphere and the oceans, economic models of the global economy are shot through with assumptions and simplifications concerning the course of economic growth. Whereas refinement of mathematical models of the physical environment can be expected to continue to reduce uncertainties, models of the evolution of the global economy may be so distorted by political and economic events as to be projecting the unknowable.

Assumptions are made in the economic models about the trajectories of technological development in moving from fossil to nonfossil fuels and about the growth of population. When these economic and population models are joined with physical models of the atmosphere, oceans, and biosphere, it becomes possible to project the characteristics of future climates. Although these models provide important information on possible futures, they tell us little about how economic effects will be distributed among nations and individuals.

The weakness of the economic models helps explain why even when nations can agree on greenhouse-gas abatement goals, negotiators will find it extremely difficult to agree on how to achieve them. An international regime with the power to promulgate policies and regulations and enforce them would be out of the question. . . . Few nations would agree to such an international authority, especially in the face of the uncertain consequences for their economies.

Whatever approaches individual countries adopt, from free market incentives to command-and-control regulatory systems, there would still be the need to allocate greenhouse-gas emission quotas to individual nations. Many policy makers favor the market-based approach of tradable emission permits, which the United States uses to control sulfur dioxide emissions. When working properly, this system provides tremendous flexibility to those responsible for reducing emissions and takes advantage of market forces to achieve the lowest possible cost of attainment. However, the success of such a concept depends on the initial allocation of emission caps to various countries. Would they be allocated on the basis of population, gross national product, the geographical extent of territory, or some combination of these? Arriving at an equitable formula for allocation of greenhouse gas emission caps would be an extremely difficult task, if doable at all.

Furthermore, because it is the cumulative amount of carbon dioxide emissions over time that governs their effects on climate, negotiators can play with emission limits that vary with time. For example, it has been suggested that emissions in the near term could be allowed to grow rapidly, with serious emission restrictions reserved for the future. . . . This might seem to be a rational approach because it would provide time to verify that the climate is indeed changing before more drastic action is taken. Finally, assuming that . . . agreement on allocation of greenhouse gas emission caps and schedules to each nation, . . . individual governments would face the equally difficult task of allocating such caps within their territory and among economic sectors.

TOOLS FOR CHANGE

The likelihood is that no matter how successful the international negotiations [may be], humanity will still be faced with the prospect of a changing climate. If the actual temperature increases are at the low end of the projected temperature range, traditional modes of adaptation are feasible, In fact, the actions taken by nations today in the face of existing climate variability would need to be extended only slightly for people to adapt. Human beings live in the most extreme polar and desert regions. Throughout history, humans have adapted to climate variability by planting crops that thrive in different climates, building dams to store water, building coastal defenses against inundations, and adapting clothing and modes of shelter to enable them to exist in almost all climates. Extraordinary changes in these strategies would probably not be needed.

Even if the temperature regime and the implied changes in precipitation occur at the higher end of the projected range, adaptation is still a key way to cope with climate change as its regional and distribution effects become apparent. International assistance could be invoked to deal with the most egregious of these conditions, as indeed it is today in the face of persistent droughts or floods. . . .

Central to reducing greenhouse gas emissions are changes in the global energy system. Options are needed for moving to nonfossil energy sources, should this be necessary. Research and development in a wide range of alternative technologies is under way in many countries, and international collaboration has already begun on some of them, such as the development of nuclear fusion through the International Thermonuclear Experimental Reactor.

However, more needs to be done. Many of the promising energy options are sufficiently far from commercialization that international collaborative actions might advance their availability. For transportation, the development of hydrogen as a safe fuel appears feasible. For other uses, more efficient energy production by photovoltaics, biomass, wind, and fuel cells seems promising. In addition, the outlook for inherently safe and politically acceptable nuclear power systems is becoming more favorable. The fact is that absent efficient new energy technologies to achieve greenhouse emission goals, [policy makers] simply will not have the tools necessary to address the problems associated with global climate change.

39

OPTIMISTS AND PESSIMISTS: COMPETING PERSPECTIVES ON GLOBAL POPULATION GROWTH AND ITS CONSEQUENCES

Eugene R. Wittkopf and Charles W. Kegley, Jr.

Ours has become a demographically divided world, as the bulk of the world's population now lives in the Global South, which continues to experience population growth, and a minority lives in the Global North, which is approaching zero population growth. Eugene R. Wittkopf and Charles W. Kegley, Jr., examine the correlates of rapid population growth and the competing perspectives embraced by neo-Malthusians and cornucopians for coping with it. Wittkopf is R. Downs Poindexter Professor of Political Science at Louisiana State University. Kegley is Pearce Professor of International Relations at the University of South Carolina. They are co-authors of *American Foreign Policy: Pattern and Process* (1996). This essay is adapted from their book *World Politics: Trend and Transformation* (1997).

GLOBAL DEMOGRAPHIC TRENDS

The dramatic growth in world population in the twentieth century is historically unprecedented. It took two million years before world population reached 1 billion in 1804; 2 billion was reached in 1927. Since then, additional billions have

This essay was prepared especially for this book.

FIGURE 39-1

WORLD POPULATION GROWTH, 1750–1995 AND PROJECTED TO 2150
Source: Adapted from United Nations, *World Population Prospects: The 1994 Revision*
(New York: United Nations, 1995), pp. 101, 226–227, 234–235, 242–243.

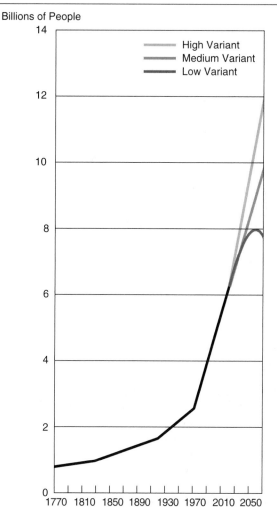

been added even more rapidly: 3 billion was reached by 1960, 4 billion in 1974, and 5 billion in 1987. The sixth billion will be added before the end of this century (see Figure 39-1). How is this possible? Because world population grows by nearly ten thousand *each hour of every day.* In fact, more people will be added to the world's population in the last fifth of the twentieth century than at any other time in history. If present trends continue uninterrupted, world population will grow to 7.5 billion in 2015, stand at 9.8 billion in 2050, andreach 10 billion only a few years later—about the time most of today's college students in the Global North will be drawing on their retirement benefits. Indeed, most of those reading this chapter will have witnessed the largest population surge ever to have occurred in a single generation—theirs.

The rapid growth of world population after reaching 2 billion early in this century is described by a simple mathematical principle articulated in 1798 by the Reverend Thomas Malthus in his classic *Essay on the Principle of Population:* Unchecked, population increases in a geometric or exponential ratio. When population increases at such an accelerating rate, the compound effect can be staggering. Consider, for example, how money deposited in a savings account grows as it earns interest not only on the original investment but also on the interest payments. If each of our ancestors had put a mere ten dollars in the bank for us 200 years ago, and it accrued a steady 6 percent annual interest, today we would all be millionaires! Population grows in the same way: It is a function of increases in the original number of people plus those accruing from past population growth. Thus a population growing at a 1 percent rate will double in 69 years, while a population growing at a 2 percent rate will double in only 35 years.

Worldwide, the rate of population growth peaked at just over 2 percent in the late 1960s and then declined to just under 1.6 percent by the mid-1990s. Hence world population in 2050 will be far less than once thought, but not all countries will share equally in the phenomenon. In fact, rapid population growth in the Global South is the most striking demographic development in the post-World War II era, and its consequences will continue to be felt well into the future. During the next fifty years the developed and the developing worlds alike will experience declining population growth rates, but the incremental contributions of the Global South to expanding world population will actually increase. By the middle of the twenty-first century all of the net population growth in the world will arise in the less developed regions, as the populations in the Global North will decline in absolute numbers. Ours has become, and will remain, a demographically divided world.

POPULATION DYNAMICS

The surge in the Global South's population is easily explained. It resulted from a combination of high birth rates and rapidly falling death rates, particularly since World War II. But to understand the population surge projected for the next century—when birth rates throughout the world will decline—we have to understand the force of *population momentum,* the continued growth of population for decades into the future because of the large numbers of people now entering their childbearing years. Like the inertia of a descending airliner when it first touches down on the runway, population growth simply cannot be halted even with an immediate, full application of the brakes. Instead, many years of high fertility mean that more women will be entering their reproductive years than in the past. Not until the size of the generation giving birth to children is no larger than the generation among which deaths are occurring will the population "airplane" come to a halt.

The population pyramids for Western Europe and Sub-Saharan Africa depicted in Figure 39-2 illustrate the force of population momentum. Africa's age and sex profile is one of rapid population growth, as each new age group (cohort) contains more people than the one before it. Thus, even if individual African couples choose to have fewer children than their parents, Africa's population will continue to grow because there are now more men and women of childbearing age than ever before. In contrast, Europe's population profile is one of slow growth, as recent cohorts have been smaller than preceding ones. Europe in fact has moved beyond replacement-level fertility to become a "declining" population, described by low birth rates and a growing number of people who survive middle age. A product of an extended period of low birth rates, low death rates, and increased longevity, Europe's age structure is best described as that of a "mature" or "old" society.

As the Global North generally, like Europe, ages, much of the Global South continues to mirror the Sub-Saharan African profile. Because each cohort is typically larger than the one before it, the number of young men and women entering their reproductive years will also grow. Figure 39-3 projects into the future the consequences of the Global South's now proportionately larger fertile age groups and shows why the demographic momentum already in place will produce quite different population profiles in the developed and the developing worlds.

COMPETING PERSPECTIVES: NEO-MALTHUSIANS VERSUS CORNUCOPIANS

The momentum set in motion by prior population growth explains why world population will continue to grow for many decades into the future. The consequences of this dramatic growth, already set in motion, has long been of concern as analysts contemplate the economic, political, and social consequences of a seemingly ever-expanding population. Two broadly defined groups of analysts approach these issues quite differently. Taking their name and orientation from Malthus' classic population essay, *neo-Malthusians* believe that world population is pushing against the earth's resources, straining its ability to meet the needs of this generation and the next. Neo-Malthusians—many of whom are human ecologists sometimes called "growth pessimists"—routinely point to a host of uncomfortable facts about the present global condition: "Since Malthus wrote, the human population has grown by a factor of six, and total human energy use by a factor of one hundred or so. . . . The forest cover of the earth has been cut by a third and the area of undisturbed wetlands by half. The composition of the atmosphere has been altered by human-generated pollution. Hundreds

FIGURE 39-2
PATTERNS OF POPULATION CHANGE: POPULATION PYRAMIDS FOR EUROPE AND SUB-SAHARAN AFRICA, 1995.
Source: Adapted from United Nations, Sex and Age Distribution of the World Populations: The 1994 Revision (New York: United Nations, 1994), pp. 25, 73.

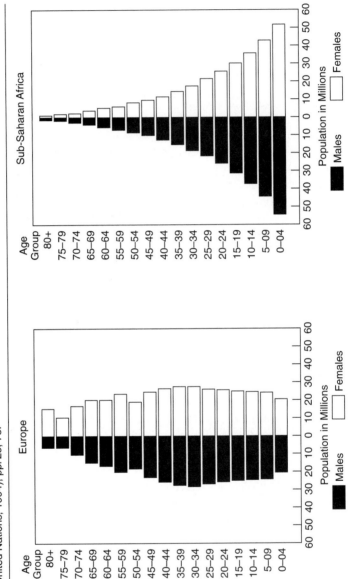

FIGURE 39-3

THE FUTURE: POPULATION PYRAMIDS FOR THE GLOBAL NORTH AND SOUTH, 1995 AND 2050

Source: Adapted from United Nations, *Sex and Age Distribution of the World Populations: The 1994 Revision* (New York: United Nations, 1994), pp. 25, 73.

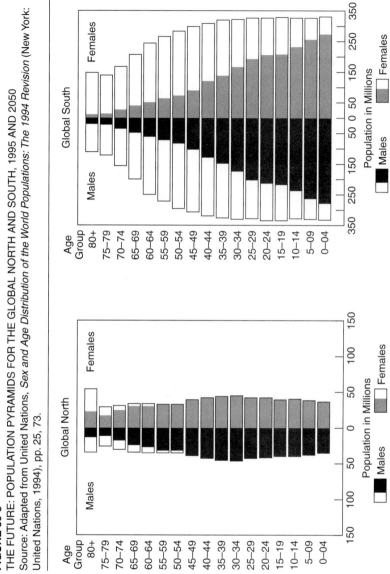

of millions of people have starved to death; thousands of species have gone extinct."[1]

In contrast with the pessimism of neo-Malthusians, *cornucopians*—many of whom are economists and otherwise known as "growth optimists"—emphasize quite different global trends:

* Global life expectancy more than doubled this century from thirty to sixty-four years, while global infant mortality fell from 170 infant deaths per 1,000 births in 1950 to just 60 in 1990. Rapid population growth has occurred not because human beings suddenly started breeding like rabbits but because they finally stopped dropping like flies.

* Despite a tripling of the world's population in this century, global health and productivity have exploded. Today human beings eat better, produce more, and consume more than ever. . . .

* "Overpopulation" is a problem that has been misidentified and misdefined. The term has no scientific definition or clear meaning. The problems typically associated with overpopulation (hungry families, squalid and overcrowded living conditions) are more properly understood as issues of poverty. . . .

* Although some blame dwindling natural resources for the reversals and catastrophes that have recently befallen heavily populated low-income countries, such episodes are directly traceable to the policies or practices of presiding governments.[2]

Compelling as the neo-Malthusian and cornucopian perspectives may be, determining which perspective is "right" is difficult, as history does not provide a clear answer. For example, the absolute gap in income between North and South continues but the gap in human development between rich and poor countries has narrowed. Moreover, the relative economic position of many countries within the Global South has improved with time, as their gross economic products have grown more rapidly than their populations, but the total number of people living in absolute poverty also continues to grow. Even in Sub-Saharan Africa—which in the last decade has experienced sharp declines in economic growth coupled with the world's most rapid population growth—it is too facile to attribute the former to the latter. Instead, a host of economic and political factors provide a more complete explanation of African ills. These include "the subversion of democracy and the rise of combative military rulers, often encouraged by the cold war (with Africa providing client states—from Somalia and Ethiopia to Angola and Zaire—for the superpowers, particularly from the 1960s onward)." More generally, "Sub-Saharan Africa lags behind other developing regions in economic security, in health care, in life expectancy, in basic education, and in political and economic stability. It should be no great surprise that it lags

---

[1]Donella H. Meadows, "Seeing the Population Issue Whole," *The World & I,* June 1993, p. 397.

[2]Nicholas Eberstadt, "Population, Food, and Income: Global Trends in the Twentieth Century," in *The True State of the Planet,* ed. Ronald Bailey (New York: Free Press, 1995), p. 8.

behind in family planning as well. To dissociate the task of population control from the politics and economics of Africa would be a great mistake and would seriously mislead public policy."[3]

What applies in Africa applies elsewhere: Population alone is not the cause of current ills; instead, it is an accomplice that aggravates other problems, including ill-advised government policies, political instability, unsustainable resource consumption, and inadequate technology. We can better appreciate these interactions by examining how population dynamics affect economic development, food security, and environmental preservation.

The Demography of Development

Dependent children (those younger than fifteen) in the Global South typically make up about 35 percent of the total population (compared with 20 percent in the developed world). This means there are fewer than two working-age adults for each child under the age of 15 in developing countries compared with more than three in the Global North. Such a large proportion of dependent children burdens public services, particularly the educational system. It also encourages the immediate consumption of economic resources rather than their reinvestment in social infrastructure to promote future economic growth.

As the children mature, the demands for new jobs, housing, and other human needs multiply. However, the resources to meet them are typically scarce and inadequate. On a global scale, as many as 1.3 billion people will be added to the work force in the Global South between 1995 and 2020. In places like Mexico this means that 1 million new jobs must be created every year to absorb the wave of young people entering the labor market. Failure to do so worries political leaders not only in Mexico but also elsewhere, notably the United States. As one Mexican leader warned, "The consequences of not creating [at least] 15 million jobs in the next fifteen years are unthinkable. The youths who do not find them will have only three options: the United States, the streets, and revolution."[4]

The search for jobs is a major factor stimulating international migration, which has reached historic proportions in recent years. It also propels internal migration, contributing to the rapid urbanization occurring throughout the world, but especially in the Global South. By the turn of the century half of the world's 6 billion people will live in cities, three-fourths of them in the developing countries. New York, London, and Shanghai were the only cities with populations of 10 million or more in 1950. By the mid-1990s the number had grown to fifteen—eleven of them in the Global South—with even larger "megacities" and

---

[3]Amartya Sen, "Population: Delusion and Reality," *New York Review of Books* 41 (September 22, 1994), pp. 65–66.

[4] George D. Moffett, *Critical Masses: The Global Population Challenge* (New York: Viking, 1994), p. 20.

"supercities" on the horizon. Lagos, Nigeria, an "urban agglomeration" of 9.7 million in 1994, will increase to more than 24 million by 2015; São Paulo, Brazil, with 16 million will grow to 21 million; and Bombay, India, will increase its rank from the world's sixth largest urban agglomeration to the second (behind Tokyo)as it nearly doubles in size to 27.4 million between 1994 and 2015. Increasingly, the fate of these and other exploding cities in the Global South will determine the fate of nations and whole regions.[5]

The growth of urban areas in itself is not necessarily bad, but the speed of today's urbanization often is, as it overwhelms the capacity of local governments to keep pace with the multiple demands that accompany urban growth. Today, millions of urban dwellers live in crowded, cramped hovels in sprawling shanty-towns and squatter settlements amid mounting garbage dumps, without adequate water or sanitation, without access to adequate health care or education and other social services, but in the constant shadow of pervasive crime and violence. And the environmental and health hazards multiply. Cars, for example, are proliferating more rapidly than people in many cities in the Global South and promise to add dramatically to the pollution of urban areas worldwide. So crushing are the burdens of urban life in many developing countries that one analyst described it as "a close approximation of hell on earth."[6]

The untoward consequences of urbanization are not confined to city dwellers. Urbanization increases pressures on local agricultural systems as well, because there are fewer hands in the countryside to feed the growing number of mouths in the city. Furthermore, food prices in urban areas are often purposely depressed by governing elites. This has the dual effect of diminishing farmers' incentives to produce while also encouraging them to abandon their lands in search of a better future in the city. Pressures to import food follow. By 2030 only ten Global South countries (India, Bangladesh, Indonesia, Iran, Pakistan, Egypt, Ethiopia and Eritrea, Nigeria, Brazil, and Mexico) are expected to require some 190 million tons of imported grains—an amount equal to nearly all of world grain exports in 1994.[7] All ten have rapidly growing urban agglomerations which in many cases will be three or four times as large in 2030 as now.

As fertility rates in the Global South decline, the number of children under fifteen will also steadily decline. If the experience of Europe, North America, and especially Japan is a guide, this should lead to economic gains. Ironically, however, the demographic life cycle also portends that the countries now most burdened by a rapid population growth among young people also will be those with an increasing number of older dependents, as today's youth grow to maturity and old age fifty years hence—effectively turning the population pyramid

---

[5] Eugene Linden, "The Exploding Cities of the Developing World," *Foreign Affairs* 75 (January/February 1996), pp. 52–65.

[6] Frances Cairncross, "Environmental Pragmatism," *Foreign Policy* 95 (Summer 1994), p. 39.

[7] Lester R. Brown, *Who Will Feed China? Wake-Up Call for a Small Planet* (New York: Norton, 1995), p. 115.

shown in Figure 39–3 upside down. As birth rates decline and longevity increases, the "dependency ratio"—those no longer economically productive and thus dependent on others in the work force—will shift away from younger people toward the elderly. Urbanization will further increase the social burdens of the world's growing number of elderly people by breaking down the extended families that in traditional societies provide social security for older people. The experience of the Global North demonstrates the untoward effects of this long-term demographic change, as demands for social services, particularly expensive health care, will multiply, burdening the Global South in yet another way.

The aging of the population in the Global North is especially striking in Japan, where the demographic transition (discussed below) began later than elsewhere but was completed more rapidly. While Sweden today is the "oldest" nation, with nearly one-fifth of its citizens sixty-five or older, Japan is the most rapidly aging, with the highest life expectancy in the world. Elderly persons are expected to comprise one-fourth of Japan's population by 2025. Already most Japanese workers are over forty.

As Japan continues to age, it will confront troublesome questions about its ability to continue the vigorous economic productivity and high domestic savings rates that have stimulated the projection of its economic power abroad. The Japanese term "child shock" dramatizes the growing crisis forecast by the decline in workers and growth in pensioners. The Japanese government and private-sector groups have joined forces to promote pronatalist attitudes among the Japanese people to raise fertility rates. However, unlike similar efforts undertaken during the 1930s (when war between Japan and the United States loomed on the horizon), the response to these contemporary efforts to stimulate birth rates has been unenthusiastic.

Providing for the increasing number of dependent elderly people relative to the number of productive workers is also a political concern elsewhere in the Global North. In western Europe the wisdom of pursuing pronatalist policies to reverse the projected decline in its overall population has been intensely debated. Much of the dialogue has turned on questions of individual versus collective welfare. Advocates of pronatalist measures are concerned with the "continued vitality of national populations that do not replace themselves: No children, no future, is the key phrase." National pride, concern for the country's place among the world powers, and the prominence of European culture in a world where non-European countries grow much faster also propel pronatalists. Opponents of pronatalist measures, on the other hand, question whether it makes sense to stimulate births when Europe already suffers from chronic high unemployment. "With modern technology eliminating jobs, workers are encouraged to work shorter hours, part-time, or retire early, and immigration is halted," the argument continues, "so why should we have more people?"[8]

[8] Dirk J. van de Kaa, "Europe's Second Demographic Transition," *Population Bulletin* 42 (no. 1 1987), 48.

The Demography of Global Food Security

The gloomiest of Malthus' predictions made two centuries ago is that the world's population will eventually outstrip its capacity to produce enough food to sustain its growing numbers. Malthus based his prognosis on what he regarded as the simple mathematical fact that, while population grows exponentially, agricultural output grows only arithmetically. He did not foresee that agricultural output would also grow at an increasing rate due to technological innovations.

Increases in the world's food output have been especially remarkable since World War II, far outstripping the largest-ever expansion of world population. The greatest gains occurred as a result of the increased productivity of farmers in the Global North. However, the South also scored impressive results by expanding the acreage devoted to agriculture and, later, by introducing new high-yield strains of wheat and rice—what we now call the "Green Revolution." By the 1980s Indonesia, once a massive importer of food, had largely been removed from the import market; and India, once regarded as a permanent candidate for the international dole, had actually become a modest grain exporter.

Continued growth in world food production is uncertain, yet it is necessary if output is to keep pace with an expanding world population and improved living standards. A former secretary of the U.S. Department of Agriculture describes the challenge in dramatic terms: "In the next two to four generations, world agriculture will be called on to produce as much food as has been produced in the entire 12,000-year history of agriculture."[9] Cornucopians, who point with pride to the continued growth of food production since the 1980s, confidently predict the challenge be met, believing that technology will continue to improve agricultural productivity. They argue that continued advances can be expected as current resources are used more efficiently and high-yield farming practices continue to spread. A case in point is that China's and Vietnam's shedding of the communist agricultural regimen in favor of market-based systems has enabled both to score dramatic per-capita food production gains—ranging from 30 percent to more than 50 percent since the early 1980s—even in the face of rapidly rising populations. Growth optimists also believe biotechnology contains the seeds of dramatic new breakthroughs now only dimly perceived; already it has produced impressive yields with promise not only for food production but also preservation of the environment and biodiversity.[10]

Neo-Malthusians are decidedly less sanguine. They worry that agricultural and other biological systems like ocean fisheries will be unable to sustain rising demand, jeopardizing realization of the goal of global *food security* (continued

[9] Orville L. Freeman, "Meeting the Needs of the Coming Decade: Agriculture Vs. the Environment," *Futurist* 24 (November-December 1990), p. 16.

[10] Dennis Avery, "Saving the Planet with Pesticides," in *The True State of the Planet,* ed. Ronald Bailey (New York: Free Press, 1995), pp. 67–68.

access by all people to enough food for an active, healthy life). They point to several disturbing trends to illustrate their concern.

- Although food production has increased steadily, per-capita production has generally stagnated.
- The world's fish catch peaked at 100 million tons in 1989—a level believed to be near the maximum sustainable yield of ocean fisheries—and has since grown little, with most increased output attributed to aquaculture (fish farming).[11] The world's rangelands are under similar pressure, as they are grazed beyond their capacity to regenerate themselves.
- The world's carryover stocks of grain ("the amount in the bin when the new harvest begins"), which in effect provide the world with a food-security buffer during lean years, has dropped to levels not seen since the 1970s, when grain prices doubled in the face of a global food crisis.[12]

Neo-Malthusians point to other developments that suggest a less-than-rosy future, including the impact of rising affluence on global food supplies and the resources required to provide them. As wealth increases, people move up the "food ladder," shifting their preferences from beans and rice to steak and chicken, asparagus and apricots. The culinary preferences of more-affluent people also translate into proportionately higher demands on agricultural lands and water resources. Still, ascending the food ladder is the shape of things to come.

China's meat consumption is currently rising by 3 million tons (and 10 percent) per year. Chinese meat consumption has traditionally been very low, but rising per-capita incomes are putting more meat within the reach of many more consumers. Indians do not eat much meat because of their predominant Hindu religion, but the demand for dairy products is rising by 2 million tons per year. Indonesia is Islamic, so its residents do not eat pork, and it has no extensive grazing lands for beef, but poultry consumption is rising at double-digit rates. All told, Asia's diet upgrading is the biggest surge in farm resource demand the world has ever seen. . . . And each ton of added protein demand will require three to five added tons of grain and oilseed production to provide feed to produce the additional animal protein.[13]

Thus, even as world population growth begins to level off, pressures on world food systems will continue their forward momentum.

Can the world's food-producing systems sustain the growing demand stimulated by population growth and rising affluence? Lester Brown, a prominent neo-Malthusian and his associates at the Worldwatch Institute, warn that the earth's carrying capacity is limited and that its limits are rapidly approaching. They argue that diminishing returns from fertilizer applications combined with

---

[11] Lester R. Brown, Nicholas Lenssen and Hal Kane, *Vital Signs 1995* (New York: Norton, 1995), pp. 32–33.

[12] Lester R. Brown, et al., *State of the World 1996* (New York: Norton, 1996), p. 8.

[13] Avery, "Saving the Planet with Pesticides," pp. 51–52.

soil erosion, growing water scarcity, and other environmental stresses already undermine the ability of national agricultural systems to provide for a growing world population. China—which accounts for more than one-fifth of humanity—is especially worrisome. Drawing on the experience of Japan, South Korea, and Taiwan, Brown argues that the transformation of China from an agricultural to an industrial society will cause its food consumption to quickly outrace production (see also Chapter 36 in this book). Increasingly, then, China will have to turn to the world marketplace to feed its billion-plus residents.

Africa's experience already seems to vindicate neo-Malthusians' pessimism. The continent's food production increased by less than 2 percent annually during the 1970s, but its population grew by nearly 3 percent. Starvation and death became daily occurrences in broad stretches of the Sahel, ranging from Ethiopia in the east to Mauritania in the west. The situation was repeated a decade later when, in Ethiopia in particular, the world witnessed the tragic specter of tens of thousands suffering and dying from malnutrition and famine at a time of unprecedented food surpluses worldwide.

Growth optimists reject the Malthusian analogy as applied to Africa, particularly the prophecy that excessive population growth causes food deficits. They point out that civil strife, ethnic bloodletting, and war have characterized postcolonial Africa, as conflicts affecting tens of millions of people have ravaged one-third or more of the countries in the region since the 1970s. In some cases, as in Ethiopia, Somalia, and the Sudan, food was actively used as a political weapon. The UN/U.S. humanitarian intervention in Somalia in 1992–1994 sought to curb these practices, but with limited success. Thus war is not the *consequence* but the *cause* of famine, malnutrition, and starvation, cornucopians argue. "Famines come about when political systems fail to encourage agriculture and distribution successfully. And those political failures have a pattern: They occur in centralized, authoritarian systems. Free-market economics do not produce famines."[14]

Asia's recent experience also seems to vindicate cornucopian logic. The continent's per-capita food production has outstripped all other world regions since the early 1980s, with China and Vietnam leading the pack as each moved toward market-based agricultural systems—and this despite dramatic population increases.

Still, millions go hungry each day. The World Resources Institute[15] estimates that at the beginning of the 1990s nearly 800 million people in Africa, Asia, Latin America, and the Middle East—representing 20 percent of humanity—suffered chronic undernutrition. Neo-Malthusians urge that, on moral grounds alone, population growth must be stemmed so that those who now suffer most can be relieved. In practice, however, the issue is not a lack of food but its maldistribution, as the repeated African tragedies show. According to the microeconomic

[14] Avery, "Saving the Planet with Pesticides," p. 54.
[15] World Resources Institute, *World Resources 1994–95* (New York: Oxford University Press, 1994), p. 108.

principle known as Engel's law, poorer families typically spend a much higher percentage of their budget on food than do higher-income groups. Yet the ability to acquire more food depends on having the income necessary to buy it. Most people stop eating because they no longer grow it themselves and cannot buy it from others, not because insufficient food is grown. From this perspective, poverty—not overpopulation—is the cause of the food deficits so many countries and people experience.

But what causes poverty? And what are its cures? Neo-Malthusians and cornucopians both speak to the ills, and both offer prescriptions for dealing with the disease. But who is right?

The Demography of Environmental Preservation

Neo-Malthusians stress environmental degradation in assessing the adverse consequences of population growth. Excessive consumption in the Global North also falls under their indictment (see also Chapter 35 in this book). Unless both are curbed, they argue, "ecological overshoot"—exceeding the earth's carrying capacity—will surely follow. Thus the environmental toll of population growth and rising affluence seemingly binds humanity in a common fate. Still, not everyone will share the costs equally. Herein lies what many describe as the "planetary predicament," as the costs of environmental stress affect the Global North and South quite differently.

Soil erosion, desertification, and deforestation are worldwide phenomena, but they are often most acute where population growth and poverty are most evident. The search for fuelwood is a major source of deforestation and a primary occupation in developing countries. Deforestation and soil erosion also occur when growing populations without access to farmland push cultivation into hillsides and tropical forests ill-suited to farming. In the Sahel area of Africa, growing populations of livestock as well as humans hastened the destruction of productive land, producing a desert which led to famine, a graphic illustration of what ecologists call "the tragedy of the commons," which occurs when individuals pursing private gain cause destruction of resources from which all of them benefit (also see Chapter 42 in this book).

Where population growth rates remain high a kind of "ecological transition" occurs, whose end result is typically disastrous. "In the first stage, expanding human demands are well within the sustainable yield of the biological support system. In the second, they are in excess of the sustainable yield but still expanding as the biological resource itself is being consumed. And in the final stage, human consumption is forcibly reduced as the biological system collapses."[16] Tragically, an ecological transition applies to much of the Global South.

[16] Lester R. Brown, et al., *State of the World 1987* (New York: Norton, 1987), p. 27.

Logic suggests that excessive population growth exacerbates environmental stress. Cornucopians recognize this, but they differ from neo-Malthusians in identifying the causal agents, seeing population pressures as only one among many. "Many other factors (government policies, the legal system, access to capital and technology, the efficiency of industrial production, inequity in the distribution of land and resources, poverty in the South, and conspicuous consumption in the North) may work separately or together to buffer or increase humankind's impact on the environment." That conclusion has important policy implications, suggesting that "the potential for reducing the effect of population growth depends largely on altering factors such as these that compound the environmental impact of human activity.[17]

POPULATION POLICIES

Can the momentum of population growth be slowed, even stalled? By what means? The questions are simple, but the answers are complex, raising a host of policy-relevant questions not easily answered. Should individual couples have the right to make their own reproduction decisions without outside interference, regardless of the social and economic consequences of large families? Should governments embrace coercive practices, including forced sterilization and other restrictive policies, to stem population growth if the social and economic costs of a large and growing population are deemed excessive? Even though answers to these difficult questions are not easily found, we do know that economic and social development profoundly affect individuals' reproductive decisions. The demographic transition theory and the role of women in society illustrate this.

The *demographic transition* describes the change that Europe and later North America experienced between 1750 and 1930, when a condition of high birth rates combined with high death rates was replaced by low birth rates and low death rates. The transition started when death rates began to fall—presumably due to economic growth, rising living standards, and improved disease control. Although the potential for substantial population growth was high, birth rates soon began to decline as well. The demographic transition is now underway virtually everywhere in the world. The experience of the Global South, however, differs from that of Europe and North America. Death rates declined precipitously following World War II rather than mirroring the slow, long-term declines of the Global North, largely as a result of more effective "death-control" measures introduced by the outside world. A population explosion inevitably followed.

There are two ways to explain the changes in birth and death rates that occur with the demographic transition. One argument says that the decline in death

---

[17] World Resources Institute, *World Resources 1994–95*, pp. 27–28.

rates itself stimulates a decline in birth rates. This implies that societies eventually reach an "equilibrium" in their mortality and fertility rates.

When death rates fall because of advances in medicine and better living conditions, the equilibrium is disturbed. The population grows unless birth rates adjust to the new mortality conditions and also decline. The fact that it may take many years after mortality falls for fertility to fall is explained as a perception lag—that is, the time it takes couples to realize that more of their children will live to adulthood, and therefore, to feel secure that they can have fewer births and still achieve their desired number of surviving children.[18]

A second explanation of the demographic transition holds that "modernization" produces declines in both mortality and fertility. According to this argument, birth rates decline because economic growth alters people's preferred family size. In traditional societies children are economic bonuses; as modernization proceeds, they become economic burdens, inhibiting social mobility and capital accumulation. The move from large to small families, with the associated decline in fertility, is therefore usually exhibited when modernization takes place. Eventually birth and death rates both reach very low levels. With fertility rates near the replacement level, low population growth (or none at all) follows.

The "equilibrium" and "modernization" explanations of demographic transitions are not mutually exclusive. They may in fact be at work simultaneously in much of the Global South, where declines in death and birth rates have often occurred in tandem. Both, then, contain the seeds of population policies that may help push the world fertility rate farther along the path toward the replacement level.

The role of women in society, and especially their education, also have an important influence on preferences toward family size.

Having an education usually means that women delay marriage, seek wage-paying jobs, learn about and have more favorable attitudes toward family planning, and have better communication with their husbands when they marry. Educated women have fewer infant deaths; high infant mortality is associated with high fertility. Similarly, when women have wage-paying jobs, they tend to have fewer children (and conversely, women with fewer children find it easier to work).[19]

Still, women throughout the world continue to be disadvantaged relative to men across a broad spectrum of educational statistics, such as literacy rates, school and college enrollments, and targeted educational resources. Women also enjoy less access to advanced study and training in professional fields, such as

---

[18] Wolfgang Lutz, "The Future of World Population," *Population Bulletin* 49 (June 1994), p. 8.

[19] Population Reference Bureau, *World Population: Toward the Next Century* (Washington, D.C.: Population Reference Bureau, 1981), p. 5.

science, engineering, law, and business. In addition, within occupational groups, they are almost always in less-prestigious jobs, they face formidable barriers against involvement in politics, and everywhere they receive less pay than men. Although these and other gender differences have narrowed in recent years, in most countries the complex social, cultural, economic, and political forces that underlie gender inequalities remain firmly rooted.

Addressing women's rights is difficult because the issues touch deeply entrenched as well as widely divergent religious and cultural beliefs. In many Islamic countries, for example, women must hide their faces with veils in public, and women and men are often completely separated in social and religious activities. These traditions are difficult to understand in many western countries. On the other hand, western conceptions of feminism and women's rights, typically focused on social, political, and economic equality of the sexes, are foreign to women elsewhere, where the issues are personal and the goals pragmatic: "access to capital, the right of inheritance, basic education for girls, a voice in the political establishment and medical systems that let them make choices, especially in reproductive health."[20]

The world community has become increasingly sensitive to the status of women and their role in social development and population stabilization. The third United Nations population conference, held in Cairo in 1994, noted that "in all parts of the world, women are facing threats to their lives, health, and well-being as a result of being overburdened with work and of their lack of power and influence." The principles embraced by the conference called for "the elimination of all kinds of violence against women," and its Programme of Action called for comprehensive national and international programs directed at child survival and women's health needs; the need to advance the rights and economic, political, and social roles of women; improving the education of girls and women; and increasing male responsibility in family planning and child rearing. The Programme of Action also set out specific goals to be achieved by 2015 which deal with access to primary school education, family-planning services, reproductive health, infant and under-five mortality, maternal mortality, and life expectancy.

The proposals contained in the Programme of Action are only recommendations and thus not binding on governments. Indeed, few could be expected to act on all of them, particularly given the enormous resources their realization demands. By the end of this century the expenditures on family planning alone are expected to balloon to $10 billion, nearly double the amount spent in the early 1990s. Even greater sums would be required to meet the goals of increased access to primary education and to health care (including that required by the growing number of HIV/AIDS patients). Global South countries cannot be expected to meet these demands by themselves, and others—meaning governments

---

[20] Barbara Crossette, "The Second Sex in the Third World," *New York Times,* September 10, 1995, p. E1.

in the Global North—will be asked to supplement their resources. However, domestic political support for foreign aid among donor countries has virtually disappeared. Mounting a sustained effort to stem the growth of world population thus remains a formidable challenge.

A PRESCRIPTION FOR OPTIMISM OR PESSIMISM?

Neo-Malthusians and cornucopians paint quite different visions of our future. Might both be right? Rapidly expanding populations stress environmental systems, exacerbate poverty, and encourage reproduction to hedge against the future. Economic and social development, on the other hand, discourage large families, stimulating reduced birthrates and hence declining population growth rates. So, too, do government family-planning policies. Still, competing policy prescriptions often flow from these alternative viewpoints. Neo-Malthusians are typically proactive in their choice of instruments to blunt population growth. Cornucopians are more content to let individuals and market mechanisms adjust imbalances in population growth and its consequences. Our perceptual lens will help frame our preferred policy prescriptions for coping with a demographically divided world. Meanwhile, an interdependent and rapidly globalizing world promises that none will be immune to the population trends and dynamics that now engulf the world.

40

ENCROACHING PLAGUES: THE RETURN OF INFECTIOUS DISEASE

Laurie Garrett

Rapid globalization has opened political borders to biological as well as economic penetration. Laurie Garrett worries that the biological evolution of microbes in combination with an increasingly borderless world exposes peoples and states to threats once thought conquered. Garrett is a medical and science reporter for the newspaper *Newsday* **and author of** *The Coming Plague: Newly Emerging Diseases in a World Out of Balance* **(1994).**

THE POST-ANTIBIOTIC ERA

Since World War II, public health strategy has focused on the eradication of microbes. Using powerful medical weaponry developed during the postwar period—antibiotics, antimalarials, and vaccines—political and scientific leaders in the United States and around the world pursued a military-style campaign to obliterate viral, bacterial, and parasitic enemies. The goal was nothing less than pushing humanity through what was termed the "health transition," leaving the age of infectious disease permanently behind. By the turn of the century, it was thought, most of the world's population would live long lives ended only by the "chronics"—cancer, heart disease, and Alzheimer's.

The optimism culminated in 1978 when the member states of the United Nations signed the "Health for All, 2000" accord. The agreement set ambitious goals for the eradication of disease, predicting that even the poorest nations would undergo a health transition before the millennium, with life expectancies rising markedly. It was certainly reasonable in 1978 to take a rosy view of Homo sapiens' ancient struggle with the microbes; antibiotics, pesticides, chloroquine and other powerful antimicrobials, vaccines, and striking improvements in water treatment and food preparation technologies had provided what seemed an imposing armamentarium. The year before, the World Health Organization (WHO) had announced that the last known case of smallpox had been tracked down in Ethiopia and cured.

The grandiose optimism rested on two false assumptions: that microbes were biologically stationary targets and that diseases could be geographically sequestered. Each contributed to the smug sense of immunity from infectious diseases that characterized health professionals in North America and Europe.

Anything but stationary, microbes and the insects, rodents, and other animals that transmit them are in a constant state of biological flux and evolution. Darwin noted that certain genetic mutations allow plants and animals to better adapt to environmental conditions and so produce more offspring; this process of natural selection, he argued, was the mechanism of evolution. Less than a decade after the U.S. military first supplied penicillin to its field physicians in the Pacific theater, geneticist Joshua Lederberg demonstrated that natural selection was operating in the bacterial world. Strains of staphylococcus and streptococcus that happened to carry genes for resistance to the drugs arose and flourished where drug-susceptible strains had been driven out. Use of antibiotics was selecting for ever-more-resistant bugs.

More recently scientists have witnessed an alarming mechanism of microbial adaptation and change—one less dependent on random inherited genetic advantage. The genetic blueprints of some microbes contain DNA and RNA codes that command mutation under stress, offer escapes from antibiotics and other drugs, marshal collective behaviors conducive to group survival, and allow the microbes and their progeny to scour their environments for potentially useful genetic material. Such material is present in stable rings or pieces of DNA and RNA, known as plasmids and transposons, that move freely among microorganisms, even jumping between species of bacteria, fungi, and parasites. Some plasmids carry the genes for resistance to five or more different families of antibiotics, or dozens of individual drugs. Others confer greater powers of infectivity, virulence, resistance to disinfectants or chlorine, even such subtly important characteristics as the ability to tolerate higher temperatures or more acidic conditions. Microbes have appeared that can grow on a bar of soap, swim unabashed in bleach, and ignore doses of penicillin logarithmically larger than those effective in 1950.

In the microbial soup, then, is a vast, constantly changing lending library of genetic material that offers humanity's minute predators myriad ways to outmaneuver the drug arsenal. And the arsenal, large as it might seem, is limited. In 1994, the [U.S.] Food and Drug Administration licensed only three new antimicrobial drugs, two of them for the treatment of AIDS and one an antibacterial. Research and development has ground to a near halt now that the easy approaches to killing viruses, bacteria, fungi, and parasites—those that mimic the ways competing microbes kill one another in their endless tiny battles throughout the human gastrointestinal tract—have been exploited. Researchers have run out of ideas for countering many microbial scourges, and the lack of profitability has stifled the development of drugs to combat organisms that are currently found predominantly in poor countries. "The pipeline is dry. We really have a global crisis," James Hughes, director of the [U.S.] National Center for Infectious Diseases at the Centers for Disease Control and Prevention (CDC) in Atlanta, said recently.

DISEASES WITHOUT BORDERS

During the 1960s, 1970s, and 1980s, the World Bank and the International Monetary Fund devised investment policies based on the assumption that economic modernization should come first and improved health would naturally follow. Today the World Bank recognizes that a nation in which more than 10 percent of the working-age population is chronically ill cannot be expected to reach higher levels of development without investment in health infrastructure. Furthermore, the bank acknowledges that few societies spend health care dollars effectively for the poor, among whom the potential for the outbreak of infectious disease is greatest. Most of the achievements in infectious disease control have resulted from grand international efforts such as the expanded program for childhood immunization mounted by the United Nations Children's Emergency Fund and WHO's smallpox eradication drive. At the local level, particularly in politically unstable poor countries, few genuine successes can be cited.

Geographic sequestration was crucial in all postwar health planning, but diseases can no longer be expected to remain in their country or region of origin. Even before commercial air travel, swine flu in 1918–19 managed to circumnavigate the planet five times in 18 months, killing 22 million people, 500,000 in the United States. How many more victims could a similarly lethal strain of influenza claim [now] when some half a billion passengers will board airline flights?

Every day 1 million people cross an international border. One million a week travel between the industrial and developing worlds. And as people move, unwanted microbial hitchhikers tag along. In the 19th century most diseases and infections that travelers carried manifested themselves during the long sea voyages that were the primary means of covering great distances. Recognizing the symptoms, the authorities at ports of entry could quarantine contagious individuals or take other action. In the age of jet travel, however, a person incubating a disease such as Ebola can board a plane, travel 12,000 miles, pass unnoticed through customs and immigration, take a domestic carrier to a remote destination, and still not develop symptoms for several days, infecting many other people before his condition is noticeable.

Surveillance at airports has proved grossly inadequate and is often biologically irrational, given that incubation periods for many incurable contagious diseases may exceed 21 days. And when a recent traveler's symptoms become apparent, days or weeks after his journey, the task of identifying fellow passengers, locating them, and bringing them to the authorities for medical examination is costly and sometimes impossible. The British and U.S. governments both spent millions of dollars in 1976 trying to track down 522 people exposed during a flight from Sierra Leone to Washington, D.C., to a Peace Corps volunteer infected with the Lassa virus, an organism that produces gruesome hemorrhagic disease in its victims. . . .

In the fall of 1994 the New York City Department of Health and the U.S. Immigration and Naturalization Service took steps to prevent plague-infected passengers from India from disembarking at New York's John F. Kennedy International Airport. All airport and federal personnel who had direct contact with passengers were trained to recognize symptoms of *Yersinia pestis* infection. Potential plague carriers were, if possible, to be identified while still on the tarmac, so fellow passengers could be examined. Of 10 putative carriers identified in New York, only two were disocvered at the airport; the majority had long since entered the community. Fortunately, none of the 10 proved to have plague. Health authorities came away with the lesson that airport-based screening is expensive and does not work.

Humanity is on the move worldwide, fleeing impoverishment, religious and ethnic intolerance, and high-intensity localized warfare that targets civilians. People are abandoning their homes for new destinations on an unprecedented scale, both in terms of absolute numbers and as a percentage of population. In 1994 at least 110 million people immigrated, another 30 million moved from rural to urban areas within their own country, and 23 million more were displaced by war or social unrest, according to the U.N. High Commissioner for Refugees and the Worldwatch Institute. This human mobility affords microbes greatly increased opportunities for movement.

THE CITY AS VECTOR

Population expansion raises the statistical probability that pathogens will be transmitted, whether from person to person or vector—insect, rodent, or other—to person. Human density is rising rapidly worldwide. Seven countries now have overall population densities exceeding 2,000 people per square mile, and 43 have densities greater than 500 people per square mile. (The U.S. average, by contrast, is 74.)

High density need not doom a nation to epidemics and unusual outbreaks of disease if sewage and water systems, housing, and public health provisions are adequate. The Netherlands, for example, with 1,180 people per square mile, ranks among the top 20 countries for good health and life expectancy. But the areas in which density is increasing most are not those capable of providing such infrastructural support. They are, rather, the poorest on earth. Even countries with low overall density may have cities that have become focuses for extraordinary overpopulation, from the point of view of public health. Some of these urban agglomerations have only one toilet for every 750 or more people.

Most people on the move around the world come to burgeoning metropolises like India's Surat (where pneumonic plague struck in 1994) and Zaire's Kikwit (site of the 1995 Ebola epidemic) that offer few fundamental amenities. These new centers of urbanization typically lack sewage systems, paved roads, housing, safe drinking water, medical facilities, and schools adequate to serve even the most affluent residents. They are squalid sites of destitution where hundreds of thousands live much as they would in poor villages, yet so jammed together as to ensure astronomical transmission rates for airborne, waterborne, sexually transmitted, and contact-transmission microbes.

But such centers are often only staging areas for the waves of impoverished people that are drawn there. The next stop is a megacity with a population of 10 million or more. In the 19th century only two cities on earth—London and New York—even approached that size. Five years from now there will be 24 megacities, most in poor developing countries: São Paulo, Calcutta, Bombay, Istanbul, Bangkok, Tehran, Jakarta, Cairo, Mexico City, Karachi, and the like. There the woes of cities like Surat are magnified many times over. Yet even the developing world's megacities are way stations for those who most aggressively seek a better life. All paths ultimately lead these people—and the microbes they may carry—to the United States, Canada, and Western Europe.

Urbanization and global migration propel radical changes in human behavior as well as in the ecological relationship between microbes and humans. Almost invariably in large cities, sex industries arise and multiple-partner sex becomes more common, prompting rapid increases in sexually transmitted diseases. Black market access to antimicrobials is greater in urban centers, leading to overuse or outright misuse of the precious drugs and the emergence of resistant bacteria and parasites. Intravenous drug abusers' practice of sharing syringes is a ready vehicle for the transmission of microbes. Underfunded urban health facilities often become unhygienic centers for the dissemination of disease rather than its control.

THE EMBLEMATIC NEW DISEASE

All these factors played out dramatically during the 1980s, allowing an obscure organism to amplify and spread to the point that WHO estimates it has infected a cumulative total of 30 million people and become endemic to every country in the world. Genetic studies of the human immunodeficiency virus that causes AIDS indicate that it is probably more than a century old, yet HIV infected perhaps less than .001 percent of the world population until the mid-1970s. Then the virus surged because of sweeping social changes: African urbanization; American and European intravenous drug use and homosexual bathhouse activity; the Uganda-Tanzania war of 1977–79, in which rape was used as a tool of ethnic cleansing; and the growth of the American blood products industry and the international marketing of its contaminated goods. Government denial and societal prejudice everywhere in the world led to inappropriate public health interventions or plain inaction, further abetting HIV transmission and slowing research for treatment or a cure.

The estimated direct (medical) and indirect (loss of productive labor force and family-impact) costs of the disease are expected to top $500 billion by the year 2000, according to the Global AIDS Policy Coalition at Harvard University. The U.S. Agency for International Development predicts that by then some 11 percent of children under 15 in sub-Saharan Africa will be AIDS orphans and that infant mortality will soar fivefold in some African and Asian nations, due to the loss of parental care among children orphaned by AIDS and its most common opportunistic infection, tuberculosis. Life expectancy in the African and Asian nations hit hardest by AIDS will plummet to an astonishing low of 25 years by 2010, the agency forecasts.

Medical experts now recognize that any microbe, including ones previously unknown to science, can take similar advantage of conditions in human society, going from isolated cases camouflaged by generally high levels of disease to become a global threat. Furthermore, old organisms, aided by mankind's misuse of disinfectants and drugs, can take on new, more lethal forms. . . .

THE REAL THREAT OF BIOWARFARE

The world was lucky in the September 1994 pneumonic plague epidemic in Surat. Independent studies in the United States, France, and Russia revealed that the bacterial strain that caused the outbreak was unusually weak, and although the precise figures for plague cases and deaths remain a matter of debate, the numbers certainly fall below 200. Yet the epidemic vividly illustrated three crucial national security issues in disease emergence: human mobility, transparency, and tensions between states up to and including the threat of biological warfare.

When word got out that an airborne disease was loose in the city, some 500,000 residents of Surat boarded trains and within 48 hours dispersed to every corner of the subcontinent. Had the microbe that caused the plague been a virus or drug-resistant bacterium, the world would have witnessed an immediate Asian pandemic. As it was, the epidemic sparked a global panic that cost the Indian economy a minimum of $2 billion in lost sales and losses on the Bombay stock market, predominantly the result of international boycotts of Indian goods and travelers.

As the number of countries banning trade with India mounted that fall, the Hindi-language press insisted that there was no plague, accusing Pakistan of a smear campaign aimed at bringing India's economy to its knees. After international scientific investigations concluded that *Yersinia pestis* had indeed been the culprit in this bona fide epidemic, attention turned to the bacteria's origin. . . . Several Indian scientists claimed to have evidence that the bacteria in Surat had been genetically engineered for biowarfare purposes. Though no credible evidence [existed] to support it, and Indian government authorities vigorously [denied] such claims, the charge is almost impossible to disprove, particularly in a region rife with military and political tensions of long standing.

Even when allegations of biological warfare are not flying, it is often exceedingly difficult to obtain accurate information about outbreaks of disease, particularly from countries dependent on foreign investment or tourism or both. Transparency is a common problem; though there is usually no suggestion of covert action or malevolent intent, many countries are reluctant to disclose complete information about contagious illness. For example, nearly every country initially denied or covered up the presence of the HIV virus within its borders. Even now, at least 10 nations known to be in the midst of HIV epidemics refuse to cooperate with WHO, deliberately obfuscating incidence reports or declining to provide any statistics. Similarly, Egypt denies the existence of cholera bacteria in the Nile's waters; Saudi Arabia has asked WHO not to warn that travelers to Mecca may be bitten by mosquitoes carrying viruses that cause the new, superlethal dengue hemorrhagic fever; few countries report the appearance of antibiotic-resistant strains of deadly bacteria; and central authorities in Serbia recently rescinded an international epidemic alert when they learned that all the scientists WHO planned to send to the tense Kosovo region to halt a large outbreak of Crimean-Congo hemorrhagic fever were from the United States, a nation Serbia viewed with hostility.

The specter of biological warfare having raised its head, Brad Roberts of the Center for Strategic and International Studies is particularly concerned that the New Tier nations—developing states such as China, Iran, and Iraq that possess technological know-how but lack an organized civil society that might put some restraints on its use—might be tempted to employ bioweapons. The Federation of American Scientists has sought, so far in vain, a scientific solution to the acute weaknesses of verification and enforcement provisions in the 1972 Biological Weapons Convention, which most of the world's nations have signed.

That treaty's flaws, and the very real possibility of bioweapons use, stand in sharp focus today. Iraq's threat in 1990–91 to use biological weapons in the Persian Gulf conflict found allied forces in the region virtually powerless to respond: the weapons' existence was not verified in a timely manner, the only available countermeasure was a vaccine against one type of organism, and protective gear and equipment failed to stand up to windblown sand. [In] June [1996] the U.N. Security Council concluded that Iraqi stocks of bioweaponry might have been replenished after the Gulf War settlement.

More alarming were the actions of the Aum Shinrikyo cult in Japan in early 1995. In addition to releasing toxic sarin gas in the Tokyo subway on March 18, cult members were preparing vast quantities of *Clostridium difficile* bacterial spores for terrorist use. Though rarely fatal, clostridium infections often worsen as a result of improper antibiotic use, and long bouts of bloody diarrhea can lead to dangerous colon inflammations. Clostridium was a good choice for biological terrorism: the spores can survive for months and may be spread with any aerosol device, and even slight exposure can make vulnerable people (particularly children and the elderly) sick enough to cost a crowded society like Japan hundreds of millions of dollars for hospitalizations and lost productivity.

The U.S. Office of Technology Assessment has calculated what it would take to produce a spectacular terrorist bioweapon: 100 kilograms of a lethal sporulating organism such as anthrax spread over Washington, D.C., by a crop duster could cause well over 2 million deaths. Enough anthrax spores to kill five or six million people could be loaded into a taxi and pumped out its tailpipe as it meandered through Manhattan. Vulnerability to terrorist attacks, as well as to the natural emergence of disease, increases with population density.

A WORLD AT RISK

A 1995 WHO survey of global capacity to identify and respond to threats from emerging disease reached troubling conclusions. Only six laboratories in the world, the study found, met security and safety standards that would make them suitable sites for research on the world's deadliest microbes, including those that cause Ebola, Marburg, and Lassa fever. Local political instability threatens to compromise the security of the two labs in Russia, and budget cuts threaten to do the same . . . in the United States . . . and . . . in Britain. . . .

Bolstering research capacity, enhancing disease surveillance capabilities, revitalizing sagging basic public health systems, rationing powerful drugs to avoid the emergence of drug-resistant organisms, and improving infection control practices at hospitals are only stopgap measures. National security warrants bolder steps.

One priority is finding scientifically valid ways to use polymerase chain reaction (popularly known as DNA fingerprinting), field investigations, chemical and biological export records, and local legal instruments to track the development of new or reemergent lethal organisms, whether natural or bioweapons. The effort should focus not only on microbes directly dangerous to humans but also on those that could pose major threats to crops or livestock. . . .

Only three diseases–cholera, plague, and yellow fever—are subject to international regulation, permitting U.N. and national authorities to interfere as necessary in the global traffic of goods and persons to stave off cross-border epidemics. The World Health Assembly, the legislative arm of WHO, recommended at its 1995 annual meeting in Geneva that the United Nations consider both expanding the list of regulated diseases and finding new ways to monitor the broad movement of disease. The Ebola outbreak in Kikwit demon-strated that a team of international scientists can be mobilized to swiftly contain a remote, localized epidemic caused by known nonairborne agents. . . .

Nobel laureate Joshua Lederberg of Rockefeller University has characterized the solutions to the threat of disease emergence as multitudinous, largely straightforward and commonsensical, and international in scope; "the bad news," he says, "is they will cost money."

Budgets, particularly for health care, are being cut at all levels of government. Dustin Hoffman made more money . . . playing a disease control scientist in the movie *Outbreak* than the combined annual budgets for the U.S. National Center for Infectious Diseases and the UN Programme on AIDS/HIV.

41

ENVIRONMENTAL SCARCITY AND VIOLENT CONFLICT: GLOBAL IMPLICATIONS

Thomas F. Homer-Dixon

Scarcities of environmental resources are often thought to be a potential source of violent international conflict. However, research by a number of scholars organized and directed by Thomas F. Homer-Dixon leads to the conclusion that environmental scarcities "do not cause wars between countries, [but] they do sometimes sharply aggravate stresses within countries, helping stimulate ethnic clashes, urban unrest, and insurgencies." Homer-Dixon teaches political science at the University of Toronto, where he is director of the Peace and Conflict Studies program.

Scarcities of critical environmental resources—in particular cropland, freshwater, and forests—are contributing to mass violence in several areas of the world. While these "environmental scarcities" do not cause wars between countries, they do sometimes sharply aggravate stresses within countries, helping stimulate ethnic clashes, urban unrest, and insurgencies. This violence affects Western national interests by destabilizing trade and economic relations, provoking migrations, and

From "Environmental Scarcity, Mass Violence, and the Limits to Ingenuity," by Thomas F. Homer-Dixon, *Current History.* Reprinted with permission from *Current History* magazine, November 1996. Copyright © 1996, Current History, Inc.

generating complex humanitarian disasters that divert militaries and absorb huge amounts of aid.

Policy makers and citizens in the West ignore these pressures at their peril. In Chiapas, Mexico, Zapatista insurgents recently rose against land scarcity and insecure land tenure produced by long-standing inequalities in land distribution, by rapid population growth among groups with the least land, and by changes in laws governing land access. The insurgency rocked Mexico to the core, helped trigger the peso crisis, and reminded the world that Mexico remains—despite the North American Free Trade Agreement (NAFTA) and the pretenses of the country's elites—a poor and profoundly unstable developing country.

In Pakistan, shortages and the maldistribution of good land, water, and forests have encouraged the migration of huge numbers of rural poor into major cities such as Karachi and Hyderabad. The conjunction of this in-migration with high fertility rates is causing urban populations to grow at a staggering 4 to 5 percent a year, producing fierce competition and often violence among ethnic groups over land, basic services, and political and economic power. This turmoil exacts a huge cost on the national economy. It may also encourage the Pakistani regime to buttress its internal legitimacy by adopting a more belligerent foreign policy on issues such as Kashmir and nuclear proliferation.

In South Africa, severe land, water, and fuelwood scarcity in the former black homelands has helped drive millions of poor blacks into teeming squatter settlements in the major cities. The settlements are often constructed on the worst urban land, in depressions prone to flooding, on hillsides vulnerable to slides, or near heavily polluting industries. Scarcities of land, water, and fuelwood in these settlements provoke interethnic rivalry and violent feuds between settlement warlords and their followers. This strife jeopardizes the country's transition to democratic stability and prosperity.

THREE FORMS OF SCARCITY

It is easy for the 1 billion or so people living in rich countries to forget that the well-being of about half the world's population of 5.8 billion remains directly tied to local natural resources. Nearly 3 billion people rely on agriculture for their main income; perhaps 1 billion of these are subsistence farmers who survive by eating what they grow. More than 40 percent of the world's people—some 2.2 billion—use fuelwood, charcoal, straw, or cow dung as their main source of energy; 50 to 60 percent rely on these biomass fuels for at least some of their energy needs. Over 1.2 billion people lack access to clean drinking water.

The cropland, forests, and water supplies that underpin the livelihoods and well-being of these billions are renewable. Unlike nonrenewable resources such as oil and iron ore, renewables are replenished over time by natural processes. If used prudently, they should sustain an adequate standard of living indefinitely.

Unfortunately, in the majority of regions where people are highly dependent on renewable resources, these resources are being depleted or degraded faster than they are being renewed. From Gaza and the Philippines to Honduras, the evidence is stark: aquifers are being overdrawn and salinized, coastal fisheries are disappearing, and steep uplands have been stripped of their forests, leaving their thin soils to erode into the sea.

These environmental scarcities usually have complex causes. Resource depletion and degradation are a function of the physical vulnerability of the resource, the size of the resource-consuming population, and the technologies and practices this population uses. The size of the population and its technologies and practices are in turn a result of a wide array of other variables, from the status of women to the availability of human and financial capital.

Moreover, resource depletion and degradation, taken together, are only one of three sources of environmental scarcity. Depletion and degradation produce a decrease in total resource *supply*—that is, a decrease in the size of the total resource "pie." But population growth and changes in consumption behavior can also cause greater scarcity by boosting the *demand* for a resource. Thus, if a rapidly growing population depends on a fixed amount of cropland, the amount of cropland per person—the size of each person's slice of the resource pie—falls inexorably. In many countries resource availability is being squeezed by both supply and demand pressures.

The third cause of scarcity is a severe imbalance in the *distribution* of wealth and power, which results in some groups in a society receiving disproportionately large slices of the resource pie while others get slices that are too small to sustain their livelihoods. This unequal distribution, which we call structural scarcity, . . . often . . . is deeply rooted in the institutions and class and ethnic relations inherited from the colonial period. Often it is sustained and reinforced by international economic relations that trap developing countries into dependence on a few raw material exports. It can also be reinforced by heavy external debts that encourage countries to use their most productive environmental resources—such as their best croplands and forests—to generate hard currency rather than to support the most impoverished segments of their populations.

HOW SCARCITIES INTERACT

In the past, scholars and policy makers have usually addressed these three sources of scarcity independently. But supply, demand, and structural scarcities interact and reinforce each other in extraordinarily pernicious ways.

One type of interaction is resource capture. This occurs when powerful groups within a society recognize that a key resource is becoming more scarce (due to both supply and demand pressures) and use their power to shift resource access in their favor. This shift imposes severe structural scarcities on weaker groups. In Chiapas, worsening land scarcity (caused in part by rapid population growth) encouraged powerful landowners and ranchers to exploit weaknesses in the state's land laws in order to seize land from campesinos and indigenous farmers. Gradually these peasants were forced deeper into the state's lowland rain forest, further away from the state's economic heartland and further into poverty.

In the Jordan River basin, Israel's critical dependence on groundwater flowing out of the West Bank—a dependence made acute by a rising Israeli population and salinizing aquifers along the Mediterranean coast—encouraged Israel to restrict groundwater withdrawals on the West Bank during the occupation. These restrictions were far more severe for Palestinians than for Israeli settlers. They contributed to the rapid decline in Palestinian agriculture in the region, to the increasing dependence of young Palestinians on day labor within Israel and, ultimately, to rising frustrations in the Palestinian community.

Another kind of interaction, ecological marginalization, occurs when a structural imbalance in resource distribution joins with rapid population growth to drive resource-poor people into ecologically marginal areas, such as upland hillsides, areas at risk of desertificaiton, and tropical rain forests. Higher population densities in these vulnerable areas—along with a lack of the capital and knowledge needed to protect local resources—causes resource depletion, poverty, and eventually further migration, often to cities.

Ecological marginalization affects hundreds of millions of people around the world, across an extraordinary range of geographies and economic and political systems. We see the same process in the Himalayas, the Sahel, Central America, Brazil, India's Rajasthan, and Indonesia. For example, in the Philippines an extreme imbalance in cropland distribution between landowners and peasants has interacted with high population growth rates to force large numbers of landless poor into interior upland regions of the archipelago. There, the migrants use slash and burn agriculture to clear land for crops. As millions more arrive from the lowlands, new land becomes hard to find, and as population densities on the steep slopes increase, erosion, landslides, and flash floods become critical. During the 1970s and 1980s, the resulting poverty helped drive many peasants into the arms of the communist New People's Army insurgency that had a stranglehold on upland regions. Poverty drove countless others into wretched squatter settlements in cities like Manila.

Of course, many factors unique to the Filipino situation have combined with environmental and demographic stress to produce these outcomes. Environmental scarcity is never a determining or sole cause of large migrations, poverty, or violence; it always joins with other economic, political, and cultural factors to produce its effects. In the Filipino case the lack of clear property rights in upland areas encouraged migration into these regions and discouraged migrants from conserving the land once they arrived. And President Ferdinand Marcos' corrupt and authoritarian leadership reduced regime legitimacy and closed off options for democratic action by aggrieved groups.

Analysts often overlook the importance of such contextual factors and, as a result, jump from evidence of simple correlation to unwarranted conclusions about causation. Thus some commentators have asserted that rapid population growth, severe land scarcity, and the resulting food shortfalls caused the Rwandan genocide. In an editorial in August 1994, *The Washington Post* argued that while the Rwandan civil war was "military, political, and personal in its execution," a key underlying cause was "a merciless struggle for land in a peasant society whose birthrates have put an unsustainable pressure on it." Yet, while environmental scarcities in Rwanda were serious, close analysis shows that the genocide arose mainly from a conventional struggle among elites for control of the Rwandan state. Land scarcity played at most a peripheral role by reducing regime legitimacy in the countryside and restricting alternatives for elite enrichment outside the state.

Despite these caveats, in many cases environmental scarcity powerfully contributes to mass violence. Moreover, it is not possible entirely to subordinate its role to a society's particular institutions and policies. Some skeptics claim that a society can fix its environmental problems by fixing its institutional and policy mistakes; thus, they assert, environmental scarcity's contribution to conflict does not merit independent attention. . . . Research shows that such arguments are incomplete at best.

First, environmental scarcity is not only a consequence of institutions and policy; it also can reciprocally influence them in harmful ways. For example, during the 1970s and 1980s the prospect of chronic food shortages and a serious drought encouraged governments along the Senegal River to build a series of irrigation and flood-control dams. Because of critical land scarcities elsewhere in the region, land values in the basin shot up. The Mauritanian government, controlled by Moors of Arab origin, then took control of this resource by changing the laws governing land ownership and abrogating the traditional rights of black Mauritanians to farm, herd, and fish along the river.

Second, environmental scarcity should not be subordinated to institutions and policies because it is partly a function of the physical context in which a society is embedded. The original depth of soils in the Filipino uplands and the physical characteristics that make Israel's aquifers vulnerable to salt intrusion are not functions of human social institutions or behavior. And third, once environmental scarcity becomes irreversible (as when a region's vital topsoil washes into the sea), then the scarcity is, by definition, an external influence on society. Even if enlightened reform of institutions and policies removes the original political and economic causes of the scarcity, it will be a continuing burden on society.

RESOURCE SCARCITY AS A CAUSE OF INTERSTATE WAR

Scarcity-induced resource capture by Moors in Mauritania helped ignite violence over water and cropland in the Senegal River basin, producing tens of thousands of refugees. Expanding populations, land degradation, and drought spurred the rise of the Shining Path guerrillas in the southern highlands of Peru. In Haiti, forest and soil loss worsens a chronic economic crisis that generates strife and periodic waves of boat people. And land shortages in Bangladesh, exacerbated by fast population growth, have prompted millions of people to migrate to India—an influx that has, in turn, caused ethnic strife in the Indian states of Assam and Tripura.

Close examination of such cases shows that severe environmental scarcity can reduce local food production, aggravate the poverty of marginal groups, spur large migrations, enrich elites who speculate on resources, and undermine a state's moral authority and capacity to govern. These long-term stresses can slowly tear apart a poor society's social fabric, causing chronic popular unrest and violence by boosting grievances and changing the balance of power between contending social groups and the state.

The violence that results is usually chronic and diffuse, and almost always subnational, not international. There is virtually no evidence that environmental scarcity causes major interstate war. Yet among international relations scholars, it has been conventional wisdom for some time that critical scarcities of natural resources can produce international conflict. . . .

There is no doubt that some major wars in this century have been motivated in part by one country's desire to seize another's nonrenewable resources, such as fossil fuels or iron ore. For example, before and during World War II, Japan sought to secure coal, oil, and minerals in China and Southeast Asia. But the story is different for renewables like cropland, forests, fish, and freshwater. It is hard to find clear examples from this century of major war motivated mainly by scarcities of renewables.

There are two possible explanations. First, modern states cannot easily convert cropland and forests seized from a neighbor into increased state power, whereas they can quickly use nonrenewables like iron and oil to build and fuel the military machines of national aggression. Second, countries with economies highly dependent on renewables tend to be poor, and poor countries cannot easily buy large and sophisticated conventional armies to attack their neighbors. For both these reasons, the incentives and the means to launch resource wars are likely to be lower for renewables than for nonrenewables.

The exception, some might argue, is water, especially river water—adequate water supplies are needed for all aspects of national activity, including the production and use of military power, and rich countries are as dependent on water as poor countries (often they are more dependent). Moreover, about 40 percent of the world's population lives in the 214 river basins shared by more than one country. Thus at a meeting in Stockholm in August 1995, Ismail Serageldin, the World Bank's vice president for environmentally sustainable development, declared that the "wars of the next century will be over water," not oil.

The World Bank is right to focus on the water crisis. Water scarcity and pollution are already hindering economic growth in many poor countries. With global water use doubling every 20 years, these scarcities—and the subnational social stresses they cause—are going to get much worse. But Serageldin is wrong to declare that we are about to witness a surge of "water wars."

Wars between upstream and downstream neighbors over river water are likely only in a narrow set of circumstances: the downstream country must be highly dependent on the water for its national well-being; the upstream country must be able to restrict the river's flow; there must be a history of antagonism between the two countries; and, most important, the downstream country must be much stronger militarily than the upstream country.

There are very few river basins around the world where all these conditions hold. The most obvious example is the Nile. Egypt is wholly dependent on the river's water, has historically turbulent relations with its upstream neighbors, Sudan and Ethiopia, and is vastly more powerful than either. And Egypt has several times threatened to go to war to guarantee an adequate supply of Nile waters.

But more common is the situation along the Ganges, where India has constructed a huge dam—the Farakka Barrage—with harsh consequences on downstream cropland, fisheries, and villages in Bangladesh. Bangladesh is so weak that the most it can do is plead with India to release more water. There is little chance of a water war here between upstream and downstream countries (although the barrage's effects have contributed to the migrations out of Bangladesh into India). The same holds true for other river basins where alarmists speak of impending wars, including the Mekong, Indus, Paraná, and Euphrates.

PIVOTAL STATES

The chronic and diffuse subnational strife that environmental scarcity helps generate is exactly the kind of conflict that bedevils conventional military institutions. Around the world we see conventional armies pinned down and often utterly impotent in the face of interethnic violence or attacks by ragtag bands of lightly armed guerrillas and insurgents. As yet, environmental scarcity is not a major factor behind most of these conflicts. But we can expect it to become a far more powerful influence in coming decades because of larger populations and higher resource consumption rates.

The world's population is growing by 1.6 percent a year, on average, real economic product per capita is also rising by 1.5 percent a year. These increases combine to boost the earth's total economic product by about 3 percent annually. With a doubling time of approximately 23 years, the current global product of $25 trillion should exceed $50 trillion in today's dollars by 2020.

A large component of this increase will be achieved through greater consumption of the planet's natural resources. Already, as a group of geographers has noted, "transformed, managed, and utilized ecosystems constitute about half of the ice-free earth; human-mobilized material and energy flows rival those of nature."[1] Such changes are certain to grow because of the rapidly increasing scale and intensity of our economic activity.

At the level of individual countries, these changes often produce a truly daunting combination of pressures. Some of the worst-affected countries are "pivotal states"—. . . including South Africa, Mexico, India, Pakistan, and China—[that] are key to international stability in their regions. . . .

In coming decades, . . . we can expect an increasing bifurcation of the world into those societies that can adjust to population growth and scarcity—thus avoiding turmoil—and those that cannot. If several pivotal states fall on the wrong side of this divide, humanity's overall prospects will change dramatically for the worse.

[1]B. L. Turner et al., eds,. *The Earth as Transformed by Human Action: Global and Regional Changes in the Biosphere over the Past 300 Years* (Cambridge: Cambridge University Press, 1990), p. 13.

42

THE TRAGEDY OF THE COMMONS IN GLOBAL PERSPECTIVE

Marvin S. Soroos

The *tragedy of the commons* is a key concept in ecological analysis. Marvin S. Soroos describes the metaphor, relates it to many of the specific issues on the global agenda of environmental issues, and suggests strategies for averting environmental tragedies. Noteworthy is his observation that "remarkable progress has been made in recent decades to lay the international infrastructure for an assault on the wide range of environmental problems that pose significant dangers for humankind." Soroos is professor of political science and public administration at North Carolina State University and author of *The Endangered Atmosphere: Preserving a Global Commons* (1997).

THE ENVIRONMENT ON THE GLOBAL AGENDA

The convergence of 118 heads of state on Rio de Janeiro in June 1992 for the United Nations Conference on the Environment and Development (UNCED), otherwise known as the Earth Summit, confirmed the rise of the deteriorating state of the global environment to a prominent position on international agendas.

This essay was written specifically for this book.

The environment is a relatively new issue, having received substantial attention from policy makers and publics for only about three decades. While certain specific ecological problems were addressed considerably earlier, they were not viewed as part of a much larger crisis in the relationship between a rapidly growing and industrializing world population and the natural order upon which it depends for its survival and economic well-being.

Two events took place in 1972 that were especially important in the emergence of the environment as a global issue. One was the publication of the Club of Rome's influential and controversial report entitled *The Limits to Growth.*[1] It warned of an uncontrollable collapse of modern civilization within a century if bold steps were not taken promptly to restrain exponential growth trends in population and industrial production that would otherwise overshoot the availability of food, deplete the planet's one-time endowment of nonrenewable reserves of fossil fuels and minerals, and seriously degrade the environment with pollutants. The other event was the United Nations Conference on the Human Environment, held in Stockholm in June 1972, which focused world attention on a wide range of interrelated environmental problems and led to the creation of the United Nations Environment Programme (UNEP), which has done much to stimulate national and international efforts to preserve the natural environment.

Numerous problems appear on the global environmental agenda, each of which has serious consequences in its own right. On the land areas, tropical forests are being burned or logged at an alarming rate with little concern for the resulting extinction of untold numbers of species of plants and animals, many of which remain to be recorded. Deserts are expanding in numerous parts of Africa and Asia, largely due to human activities—in particular the stripping of wooded areas for firewood, the overgrazing of livestock, and improper irrigation. Overuse and misuse of land has reduced its fertility and led to substantial erosion of topsoil; aquifers are rapidly being drawn down to provide irrigation water for expanding agricultural operations. A legacy of toxic waste dumps threatens the health of millions of people, especially in the industrialized regions of the world.

The marine environment has been badly contaminated by pollutants, especially in largely self-contained areas such as the Mediterranean Sea, the Baltic Sea, the Caribbean Sea, the Red Sea, and the Persian Gulf. The most spectacular cause of ocean pollution has been accidents involving supertankers, the best known being the groundings of the *Torrey Canyon* in 1967, the *Amoco Cadiz* in 1978, and the *Exxon Valdez* in 1989. Larger quantities of pollutants enter the oceans and seas from land-based sources, such as river systems laden with sewage, industrial effluents, and runoff from agricultural areas containing fertilizers and pesticides. The oceans have also been a repository for toxic substances ranging from chemical weapons and radioactive wastes to sludge from sewage treatment plants.

---

[1]Donnella H. Meadows, Dennis L. Meadows, Jørgen Randers, and William H. Behrens, *The Limits to Growth* (New York: Signet, 1972).

Atmospheric pollutants became the leading environmental concern during the 1980s. In the heavily industrialized regions of Europe and North America, the severe consequences of the transboundary flow of pollutants, in particular sulfur and nitrogen oxides responsible for acid precipitation, became all to apparent as aquatic life disappeared in numerous freshwater lakes and a phenomenon known as "forest death syndrome," or *waldsterben* in German, spread rapidly through forested areas. The 1986 disaster at the Chernobyl nuclear power plant in the Soviet Union exposed hundreds of millions of Europeans to potentially health-damaging levels of radioactive iodine-131 and cesium-137.

Even more alarming are the warnings of the scientific community about the loss of ozone in the stratosphere and the apparent trend toward a general warming of the atmosphere. These two problems are central to what has become known during the past decade as the "global change" problematique, which refers to a number of complex and interrelated alterations of the natural environment resulting from the growing scale of human activities.

Concern about ozone depletion rose sharply in the mid-1980s following revelations of a recurring "ozone hole" over Antarctica during the southern spring seasons and a lesser amount of ozone loss at other latitudes. Scientists have linked most of the loss of stratospheric ozone to a family of synthetic chemical compounds known as CFCs, which have been widely used in aerosol sprays, refrigerants, foam packaging and insulation, and cleaning solutions, as well as to halons used primarily in fire extinguishers. Increased exposure to the sun's intense ultraviolet (UV) radiation may contribute to human health problems including the deadly melanoma variety of skin cancer, weakened immune systems, and eye disorders such as cataracts. Scientists have linked increased amounts of UV radiation to leaf damage, lessened photosynthesis, mutations, and stunted growth in approximately half of the agricultural crops that have been studied. There is also widespread concern that ecosystems will be seriously disrupted if UV radiation kills microorganisms such as phytoplankton and zooplankton, which are the bases of food chains.

Forecasts of a general warming of the atmosphere take into account the increased concentrations of "greenhouse gases" such as carbon dioxide, methane, CFCs, and nitrous oxides. Scientists are broadly in agreement that global mean temperatures have risen between 0.3 and 0.6° C over the past century, at least partly due to human pollutants, and that a further increase of 0.8 to 3.5° C is likely by 2100 if mitigating actions are not taken. Many scientific questions remain to be answered on the consequences of a warming of this magnitude. Coastal cities, low-lying agricultural areas, and even entire small island nations may become uninhabitable if a continued warming trend causes ocean levels to rise by an anticipated 50 centimeters and triggers a significant increase in the number and intensity of tropical storms. Farming elsewhere may be disrupted by changing temperatures and rainfall patterns, and numerous ecosystems such as forests may be unable to adapt to rapidly migrating climatic zones. A weakening of ocean currents caused by a reduction of temperature contrasts between equatorial and polar regions could lead to even more fundamental changes in the planet's weather patterns.

The international community has been very active over the past 25 years in addressing many of these environmental problems. The Stockholm conference of 1972 was the first of a series of major world conferences sponsored by the United Nations, sometimes referred to as "global town meetings," that keyed on specific global problems. Among these were world conferences on population (1974 and 1984), food (1974), human settlements (1976), water (1977), desertification (1977), new and renewable sources of energy (1981), and outer space (1982). The Third United Nations Law of the Sea Conference (UNCLOS III), which was convened 12 times between 1973 and 1982, took up several environmental problems, most notably the depletion of marine fisheries and pollution of the oceans. The World Meteorological Organization (WMO) sponsored World Climate Conferences in 1979 and 1990. More recent gatherings include the Earth Summit in Rio in 1992, the International Conference on Population and Development in Cairo in 1994, and two 1996 gatherings—the Second UN Conference on Human Settlements in Istanbul and the World Food Summit in Rome.

A more significant development, however, has been the establishment of a network of international institutions that address environmental issues. The United Nations Environment Programme, which is headquartered in Nairobi, Kenya, plays a central role in stimulating and coordinating action on environmental problems both by other international agencies and by nations. The organization has taken a leading role in identifying and investigating ecological problems and in monitoring the state of many aspects of the environment through its Global Environmental Monitoring System (GEMS). Several specialized agencies affiliated with the United Nations have a longer history of concern with environmentally related problems, including the International Maritime Organization (IMO) on pollution from oceangoing vessels, the WMO on the effects of atmospheric pollutants on the weather, the World Health Organization (WHO) on the impact of pollutants on human health, the International Atomic Energy Agency (IAEA) on the dangers of radioactive substances, the Food and Agricultural Organization (FAO) on the condition of ocean fisheries and the effects of environmental degradation on food production, and the International Labor Organization (ILO) on environmental hazards in work places. Environmental problems have also occupied a prominent place on the agendas of numerous regional organizations, most notably those of the European Union.

Nongovernmental organizations (NGOs) have been active participants in efforts to address global environmental problems at both national and international levels. The Stockholm conference drew participation from 237 NGOs, and more than 6,000 are registered with the Environmental Liaison Center in Nairobi. Upwards of 7,000 NGOs participated in the official meetings of the Earth Summit or the informal, and more boisterous, Environmental Forum that took place simultaneously in the parks of downtown Rio. The World Conservation Union (formerly the International Union for the Conservation of Nature and Natural Resources) and the World Wildlife Fund (WWF) have been collaborating with UNEP on the World Conservation Strategy that was launched in 1980. The International Council of Scientific Unions (ICSU) has been called upon for much of the scientific information that has guided the formulation of international policies and regulations on environmental matters. In the mid-1980s, ICSU launched the International Geosphere-Biosphere Program, an international scientific project that has mobilized the world's scientists to conduct research on the relationships between atmospheric, marine, and terrestrial components of the Earth system and the impact of human activities on them. Public interest groups such as Greenpeace, Friends of the Earth, the European Environmental Bureau, and the Sierra Club International publicize environmental problems and prod national governments and international bodies to take action on them.

Despite the relative newness of the environment as a global policy problem, remarkable progress has been made in establishing the international institutional infrastructure needed to preserve the natural environment. There is certainly reason to wonder, however, whether sovereign states, which now number nearly 200, can achieve the level of international cooperation needed to effectively address problems of the magnitude and complexity of climate change.

GLOBAL TRAGEDIES OF THE COMMONS

Garrett Hardin's well-known parable of the "tragedy of the commons" is a useful model for analyzing the human sources of many environmental problems and the strategies by which they might be addressed.[2] The parable has applicability to all levels of political organization ranging from the smallest village to the global community of states. Let us first review Hardin's story and then consider how it applies to several of the global environmental problems mentioned in the previous section. Potential strategies for averting a "tragedy" are taken up in the next section.

We are asked to imagine an old English village that has a community pasture on which the resident herders are freely permitted to graze their individually owned cattle for their own profit. Such an arrangement, known as a "commons," works well as long as the number of cattle is small relative to the size of the pasture. But once the combined herd of the villagers reaches and exceeds the "carrying capacity" of the pasture, the grasses are gradually depleted and the undernourished cattle produce less meat and milk for their owners. If more and more cattle are added to an already overcrowded pasture, the eventual outcome is its total destruction as a

[2]Garrett Hardin, "The Tragedy of the Commons," *Science* 162 (1968), pp. 1241–8.

resource, and the villagers can no longer derive a profit from grazing cattle on it. Such an unfortunate eventuality is what Hardin refers to as a "tragedy."

Hardin contends that a tragedy is virtually inevitable when there is no legal limit on the number of cattle the villagers may graze on the pasture. Each villager can be expected to calculate that the profits derived from adding a cow to the pasture will accrue to himself exclusively. Alternatively, whatever costs arise due to what this cow contributes to an overgrazing of the pasture will be divided among all the herders of the village. Therefore, the individual villager figures that there is more to gain personally from adding a cow to the pasture than to lose from the resulting damage from overgrazing. Moreover, the logic that leads the villager to add a single cow to an already overused pasture also leads him to further additions. And what is rational behavior for one villager is also rational for others. Thus, if the villagers pursue their rational self-interest, the pasture will be destroyed by the ever-increasing herd.

Why do the village herders, upon seeing the earlier signs of the unfolding tragedy, fail to exercise restraint in adding cattle, realizing that they will all pay a heavy price if the pasture becomes badly overgrazed? The answer lies in the possibility that at least one among them will not act responsibly, but rather will continue to add cattle to the pasture. This so-called "free rider" not only takes advantage of the restraint of the other villagers for his own financial benefit but may also bring about the very tragedy they were attempting to avert. Thus, unless the villagers are confident that all will limit their herds, they become resigned to the inevitability of a tragedy and continue adding cattle to the overcrowded pasture in order to maximize their personal share of what the pasture has to offer before it is rendered useless.

Global environmental problems are obviously much more complex than the story of destruction of the common pasture in the English village. Nevertheless, distinct parallels exist between the causes of some global problems and the reasons for the tragedy in Hardin's parable. The similarity is especially notable in the case of the living resources of the ocean. Coastal populations have harvested fish in the oceans for millennia, in most cases at sustainable levels. The situation has changed dramatically in recent decades, however, both because of a rapidly growing world population that is looking more to the oceans for a source of protein and because of technological advancements that made it possible to greatly increase the catch. Schools of fish can now be located more efficiently using helicopters, radar, and sonar, while strong synthetic fibers and mechanical hauling devices allow for the use of larger nets that will hold much greater quantities of fish. Drift nets up to 30 miles in length have been widely used with a devastating impact on marine life. Perhaps the biggest change in the modern fishing industry has been the use of gigantic stern-ramped trawlers and factory ships with the capacity for on-board processing of the catch, which are often accompanied by numerous specialized support vessels. Such "fishing armadas" can stay away from their home ports for many months while intensively harvesting fisheries in distant reaches of the oceans.

Traditionally, international law has treated the oceans as a commons, the only exception being a three-mile zone of territorial waters that for centuries was recognized as being within the jurisdiction of coastal states. Beyond this narrow coastal zone, fishing boats from all lands could help themselves to the ocean's bounty for their private gain because fish became their property upon being caught. Under these rules the total world catch tripled between 1950 and 1975. "Tragedies" were apparent in some regions for species such as cod, halibut, herring, anchovy, swordfish, haddock, and the California sardine, as evidenced by a dramatic drop in catches when not enough fish were left to regenerate the stock for the future. These stocks were overfished for essentially the same reasons that the herders added cattle to an already overgrazed pasture in Hardin's village. The operators of fishing fleets received all the profits from the sale of their catch while dividing the costs associated with overfishing with all others harvesting the same fishery. Furthermore, fugitives that they are, fish passed up by one fleet in the interests of conservation are likely to turn up in the nets of others, who as free riders continue to deplete the fishery.

Pollution of the oceans and atmosphere also fits the pattern of Hardin's tragedy of the commons. But rather than taking something out of an area that is beyond the jurisdictions of nations, pollution involves its use for the disposal of unwanted substances. Few problems arose as long as the amount of pollution generated by human activities was small relative to the vastness of the mediums into which they were introduced. But as with other resources, there are limits to the amount of pollutants that can be absorbed and dispersed by the oceans and atmosphere before serious problems begin to emerge, as is now apparent in the case of the ozone-depleting and greenhouse pollutants. The task of determining harmful levels of pollution is complicated by the delay between the time that substances are introduced into the environment and the point at which the consequences become apparent.

As sinks for pollutants, the oceans and the atmosphere have also traditionally been treated as international commons. All countries have been free to make use of them for getting rid of wastes whose disposal would otherwise be expensive or inconvenient. Introducing pollution into these mediums can have considerable offsetting costs, but from the perspective of the polluters, these costs are shared very widely while the benefits of having a cheap way of discarding wastes accrue to them exclusively. Thus, strong financial incentives are present for continuing the polluting activity. Moreover, any restraint that is exercised out of concern for the quality of the environment is likely to be futile and self-defeating if other polluters, including one's competitors, do not exercise similar responsibility.

Population can also be looked upon as a "tragedy of the commons" type of problem, as Hardin does in his original essay and his later theory of "lifeboat ethics."[3] In this formulation, food and other resources correspond to the pasture of the English village, births to the addition of cattle to the pasture, and the parents of the new arrivals to the herders. Parents, it could be argued, derive significant private benefits from children, such as companionship and affection, a source of labor, and security in old age. The environmental costs associated with what their children contribute to the overpopulating of their country or the world as a whole are shared with the rest of the population. Couples may also calculate that any restraint they exercise in limiting the size of their families will have little or no beneficial impact, because others who are less ecologically responsible will continue to have large numbers of offspring. The parallel is strained by the fact that most people do not have free access to the food and resources they need for their children, but must pay for them. Hardin suggests that free access to necessities, as through welfare payments or international food assistance, in effect creates a commons and the subsequent behavior that brings about its destruction.

AVERTING ENVIRONMENTAL TRAGEDIES

Several strategies hold some promise for avoiding the tragedy that Hardin forecasts will occur if all villagers have open access to the community pasture. One is to encourage *voluntary restraint,* possibly through education about the ecological consequences of irresponsible actions and by bringing social pressures to bear on members of the community who have not moderated their actions. Hardin has little faith in voluntary restraints because of the prospect that free riders will take advantage of the situation. A second option is to adopt *regulations* that limit the number of cattle each villager can graze on the pasture. Such rules, which can take the form of limits, quotas, prohibitions, taxes, and standards, should be restrictive enough to keep the total use of a resource from exceeding its carrying capacity. For regulations to be effective, however, there must be sufficiently strong inducements for compliance, such as stiff penalties for violators.

The last two possibilities for averting a tragedy would discard the commons arrangement. The pasture could be *partitioned* into fenced-in plots that would be assigned to individual villagers. Under this setup, the villagers would not only receive all the profits from grazing cattle on their sections, but would also absorb all the costs if they allow them to become overgrazed. Thus, a built-in incentive exists for the villagers to conserve their plots, or what Hardin refers to as "intrinsic responsibility." *Community ownership* of the herd is the final alternative. Rather than allowing privately owned cattle to graze the pasture, as under the other arrangements, access would be limited to a publicly owned herd, with the profits being distributed among the villagers. Under such an arrangement, the community as a whole would not only receive all the profits, but also absorb all

---

[3]Garrett Hardin, "Living on a Lifeboat," *Bioscience* 24 (1974), pp. 561–8.

the costs of overgrazing. Thus, the managers of the community herd would have little incentive for allowing the pasture to become overgrazed.[4]

Examples of all four of these strategies can be observed in the efforts of the international community to address environmental problems. Because nations are reluctant to sacrifice any part of their sovereignty to a higher authority, it is sometimes impossible to do more than encourage them to act responsibly to minimize damage to the environment beyond their borders. In this regard, one of the most commonly cited articles of the Stockholm Declaration of 1972 sets forth the principle that "States have . . . the responsibility to ensure that activities within their jurisdiction or control do not cause damage to the environment of other States or of areas beyond the limits of national jurisdiction."

Appeals to states to act voluntarily in an ecologically responsible manner have generally not been auspicious successes. However, there has been an encouraging tendency in recent years for a number of European countries to act unilaterally in setting target years for ambitious reductions of emissions of air pollutants, such as those of sulfur and nitrogen oxides that are responsible for acid precipitation and carbon dioxide that contributes to global warming. This tendency has been especially pronounced in the case of sulfur dioxide—11 countries in the mid-1980s declared goals of reducing emissions well beyond the 30 percent cutback (from 1980 levels) mandated by an international protocol adopted in 1985. Sweden, for example, set the ambitious goal of an 80 percent reduction by 2000, which it had largely achieved by 1991. These unilateral commitments to deep reductions in air pollution are ostensibly a response to political pressures from environmentally concerned publics and an effort to set an example that other countries will hopefully follow.

More is accomplished to ameliorate environmental problems when specific obligations are written into regulations that are negotiated and adopted in international institutions. Approximately 20 international fishery commissions, the equivalents of the village government in Hardin's story, were created by fishing nations to conserve the fisheries that they harvest in common. Some of these commissions established rules that limited the annual catch at or below a scientifically determined "maximum sustainable yield" (MSY) for the fishery. One strategy was to limit fishing to a prescribed season, which would be abruptly closed when the combined efforts of the fishing operators approached the MSY. Other commissions assigned a share of the MSY to countries based on their historical proportion of the catch from a fishery.

International restrictions have also been adopted to reduce pollution of the marine environment. The landmark Convention for the Prevention of Pollution by Oil was adopted in 1954 and amended several times in the International

---

[4]Natalia Mirovitskaya and Marvin S. Soroos, "Socialism and the Tragedy of the Commons: Reflections on Environmental Practice in the Soviet Union and Russia," *Journal of Environment and Development* 4, no. 1 (1995), pp. 77–109.

Maritime Organization (IMO). Among the provisions of the treaty was a prohibition on discharges of crude and heavy fuel oils in the seas within 50 miles of coastlines. In 1973, the IMO adopted another convention, known as MARPOL '73, that covered a broader range of pollutants and extended the prohibition to the discharge of oily substances to areas deemed especially vulnerable to damage from pollution. The disposal of toxic substances in the seas is the subject of other international treaties, the most important one being the London Dumping Convention of 1972. It establishes a "black list" of highly toxic chemicals such as mercury, DDT, PCBs, persistent plastics, high-level radioactive wastes, and agents of chemical or biological warfare that may not be disposed of in the oceans and a "gray list" of less harmful wastes that may be dumped under controlled conditions. In 1993 the parties to the London Convention adopted a permanent ban on the dumping of all radioactive wastes at sea.

Compared to the oceans, the atmosphere is still a relatively underdeveloped subject of international law. The Economic Commission for Europe (ECE), which includes eastern and western European countries in addition to the United States and Canada, adopted a protocol in 1985 that committed ratifiers to a 30 percent reduction of their sulfur dioxide emissions by 1993 (based on 1980 levels). A 1988 protocol freezes nitrogen oxide emissions at 1987 levels by 1994, while a 1991 protocol limits the release of volatile organic compounds. A revised, and more sophisticated, sulfur protocol was adopted in 1994 that is based on the concept of "critical loads," the amount of acidic deposition areas can absorb without serious environmental damages. Similarly, the 1987 Montreal Protocol mandated a 30 percent reduction in the production of CFCs by 1993 and a 50 percent cutback by 1998. Subsequent amendments to the protocol were adopted in London in 1990 and Copenhagen in 1992 that provide for the complete phasing out of CFCs and most other ozone-depleting chemicals by 1996.

For international regulations to be effective, mechanisms may be needed both for detecting violations and for sanctioning the violators. Few international agencies are well equipped to perform these tasks. Certain international fishery commissions have had programs for monitoring compliance with their rules through independent on-board inspections of fishing vessels. Likewise, the ECE sponsors a network of stations known as EMEP that monitors the transboundary flow of air pollutants between its members. Sanctions are generally left to other states that have an interest in seeing to it that international rules are being followed. For example, a United States law provides that countries that violate international agreements on the protection of marine mammals will lose 50 percent of the quota of fish they would otherwise be permitted to harvest in the coastal fishery zone of the United States.

The partitioning of resources used by numbers of states is a feasible strategy for avoiding some but not all environmental problems. Pollutants introduced into the atmosphere cannot be confined within the boundaries of states because air circulates with prevailing wind currents. Likewise, ocean currents widely disperse many of the pollutants introduced into the marine environment. Ocean fisheries, most of which are located near coastlines, are more susceptible to partitioning. The Convention on the Law of the Sea, which was adopted in 1982 but did not come into force until 1994 after receiving its 60th ratification, gives coastal states jurisdiction over the resources of the oceans and seabed out to a distance of 200 nautical miles off shorelines, in what is called an "exclusive economic zone" (EEZ). Coastal states are empowered to determine the maximum catch within their EEZs and to decide who will be allowed to harvest fish up to this limit. They may reserve the fisheries for their own nationals or allow foreign operators to take part of the catch, possibly for a negotiated fee.

Such an arrangement can be an effective way of conserving fisheries consisting of localized or sedentary species provided the coastal state is diligent in managing them and has the means of enforcing the limits that it has set. Unfortunately, the experience so far has been that most coastal states exercise too little restraint on three nationals, who have been quick to increase the intensity of their harvesting, thus provoking a tragedy of their own making. As a consequence the United States and Canada have been forced to indefinitely close the once highly productive Georges Banks and Grand Bank fisheries off their east coasts, throwing tens of thousands of fishermen and processors out of work. Migratory species, such as the skipjack tuna and some species of whales, which move through the EEZs of two or more countries and the high seas as well, pose a more complicated problem because cooperation among several states is needed to prevent overharvesting. A similar problem occurs with andromous species, most notably salmon, which live most of their life spans in the high seas, where they can be harvested legally by any country, but migrate to freshwater streams to spawn. Coastal states are reluctant to invest heavily to conserve spawning habitats if the stock is likely to be overfished by other countries on the high seas. Here again, cooperative arrangements among several states are necessary if the fishery is to be conserved.

Community ownership of the means of using a resource is rare at the international level. The primary stumbling block to an international consensus on the new Law of the Sea Treaty was the provision for a commercial arm of an International Seabed Authority, to be known as the Enterprise. This international public corporation would mine the mineral-rich modules lying on the floor of the deep seas in competition with private seabed-mining firms. The private firms will be required to assist the Enterprise both by sharing the fruits of their prospecting efforts and by making mining technologies available at reasonable commercial rates. The objective behind the creation of the Enterprise would not, however, be to conserve the nodules, which are in bounteous supply. Rather it is designed to ensure that less technologically advanced countries will have an opportunity to participate in the development of a resource declared to be the "common heritage of mankind" by the General Assembly in 1970.

Of the four principal types of strategies that can be adopted to avert a tragedy, regulations appear to have the broadest applicability and the greatest potential for success. Appeals for voluntary restraint too often go unheeded and some of the most critical natural resources cannot physically be divided into self-contained sections. Moreover, a community in which sovereign states are the predominant actors is simply not ready for international public enterprises to play a major role in exploitation of natural resources. The governments of most nations, however, recognize the need for rules to preserve those aspects of the global environment that are beyond the jurisdiction of any state. This is not to say, however, that they don't often balk at agreeing to specific regulations and complying with them.

RECONCILING ALTERNATIVE VALUES

Each of the four strategies for averting an environmental tragedy outlined in the previous section has certain advantages and disadvantages. Which is the most appropriate in a specific context depends in part on the relative priority given to values such as conservation, production, equity, and freedom.

Conservation implies that the resource is neither overused nor misused, so that its future value is not substantially diminished. In the analogy of the English village, conservation means that the pasture is sustainably grazed so that there is no noticeable decline in the grass cover, which reduces the number of cattle that can be sustained. In the case of ocean fisheries, conservation implies that enough of the stock of the fish remains after the harvest to allow for a regeneration of the fishery up to its optimal levels. In regard to pollution, conservation can be interpreted to mean not allowing pollutants to reach a level at which serious harm to the environment begins to take place. For example, acid-forming precipitants would not be allowed to exceed the critical load above which there would be significant damage to forests and freshwater aquatic life.

Maximizing production is often a strong competing priority. The villagers depended upon their cattle for a livelihood and, therefore, could not accept sharp cutbacks on their herds. Their interests would be best served by an arrangement that allows them to graze as many cattle as possible without bringing about an environmentally destructive overshoot. Thus, international fishery commissions limit the catch of fish on the basis of the MSY. Requiring costly equipment for preventing pollution can have a substantial effect on industrial production, especially if a total cleanup is the objective. It should be noted that the dictates of short-term production and profit may be at odds with the same values over the longer run. Short-term gain may be achieved by ravaging the resource until it is totally destroyed, while long-term profitability depends upon careful stewardship of the resource to preserve its future value.

Equity implies fairness in whatever management strategy is adopted. What is fair, however, is subject to divergent interpretations. For example, in the village setting, does the principle of equity dictate that all the herders be allowed to graze the same number of cattle on the pasture regardless of size of family or the number of cattle they owned before limits were imposed? Likewise, if the pasture is partitioned, would it be necessary for all to have equally sized plots? If the pasture is to be used by a community-owned herd, should all households receive an equal share of the profits? Similar issues of equity have complicated the task faced by fishery commissions in dividing up the total allowable catch among member countries. To what extent should the national shares be based on factors such as geographical proximity, population size, investments in fishing fleets, and distribution of the catch historically? The fairness of the provisions for EEZs under the new ocean law has been criticized on grounds that most of the productive fisheries will come under the control of only a few states.

In the case of measures to control pollution, the fairness question arises over whether the percentage reductions in emissions should be required of all countries. Less-developed countries, which historically are responsible for a small share of the pollutants causing problems such as ozone depletion and global warming, may contend that it is their "turn to pollute" to achieve their aspirations for economic development and a higher standard of living for their populations.

From one perspective equity is a matter of all being equally free to exploit a resource even though some, by virtue of their capital and advanced technologies, may be better able to take advantage of available opportunities. From another perspective, equity is an outcome that is equally favorable to all members of the community, including the poorer, less advantaged ones. At UNCLOS III a sharp dispute arose over rules for developing the seabed between a small group of advanced states whose companies possess technologies for mining the mineral-rich nodules and the large majority of countries that would be left out of the potential mineral bonanza unless they could participate in an international enterprise.

Freedom suggests flexibility in the types of activities that are permitted. Most actors—be they states, corporations, or individuals—value freedom and are reluctant to submit to limitations on their behavior. Freedom for states is embodied in the principle of sovereignty; for corporations, in the doctrine of free enterprise; and for individuals, in the principle of human rights as expressed in documents such as the Universal Declaration of Rights of 1948. In a frontier situation, where population is sparse, a greater amount of freedom of action can be tolerated without the prospect of severe environmental degradation. As a population becomes more dense and puts heavier demands on the environment, as it has done globally in recent decades, maintaining the quality of the environment becomes a more pressing problem. It should also be kept in mind that the freedom of one party to act often impinges on the freedom of others. For example, the freedom to emit sulfur dioxide indiscriminately may negate the freedom of others to fish in freshwater lakes and enjoy healthy forests.

No single strategy can be expected to maximize the achievement of all four of these values. The steps necessary to conserve the resources of commons may require substantial compromises on freedom. Thus, preserving the ozone layer has required relinquishing the prerogative of producing and using CFCs and other chemicals that threaten atmospheric ozone. Maximizing commercial use of commons is often at odds with the dictates of equity. For example, assigning quotas equally to all members of a community, regardless of their capacity to make use of their shares, may lead to unexploited opportunities to exploit a commons, unless the quotas can be freely traded. Achieving equity may also be at odds with the goal of conservation. Allowing the developing countries to increase their emissions of greenhouse gases to the much higher levels that have prevailed in the industrial countries would thwart any prospect of minimizing climate change. Thus, developing countries have bargained for substantial amounts of technical and economic assistance as a quid pro quo for their acceptance of international rules that prevent them from substantially increasing their use of the atmosphere as a sink for these pollutants.

CONCLUSIONS

Having taken note of the emergence of the environment as a major global issue and the initiation of an international response, this essay demonstrates some ways the story of the overgrazing of the pasture of the English village parallels several of the most serious environmental problems appearing on the agendas of international institutions. Hardin's story is helpful for understanding the motivation behind a variety of environmentally destructive behaviors, even by those who are well aware of the consequences of their actions. It is also useful for identifying courses of action that have potential for averting an environmental tragedy and the problems inherent in reconciling the objective of conservation with other values, such as maximizing production, achieving equity, and allowing freedom of action.

The parable fits some environmental contexts much better than others. It is especially applicable to the exploitation of limited resources in international commons, such as the oceans, atmosphere, radio waves, and outer space. It is of less value in analyzing the use of resources that lie entirely within the boundaries of states, notably fossil fuels, minerals, forests, and agricultural land, which have not been freely accessible to users from other countries. It has been proposed, however, that some of these latter resources be considered parts of the common heritage of mankind. For example, the millions of species of plants and animals that exist on the planet have been described as the "genetic heritage of mankind," even though the specimens of many are geographically concentrated within the borders of a single state.[5] Likewise, unique human artifacts from ancient civilizations, such as temples, sculptures, and paintings, have been designated by UNESCO as the "cultural heritage of mankind." Identifying them as such confers a responsibility on the states in which they are located to preserve them for present and future generations of the world's population.

[5]Norman Myers, *The Primary Resource: Tropical Forests and Our Future* (New York: Norton, 1984).

43

THE STATE OF HUMANITY: A CORNUCOPIAN APPRAISAL

Julian L. Simon

Julian Simon embraces the cornucopian perspective on the state of humanity, arguing that the historical record "portrays extraordinary progress for the human enterprise." For Simon, the addition of more people to the global habitat is the source not only of more problems but also of more solutions, as people are "the ultimate resource." Simon, an economist, is professor of management at the University of Maryland. His books include *The Ultimate Resource* (1996).

[The historical record] portrays extraordinary progress for the human enterprise, especially in the past two centuries. Yet many people believe that conditions of life are generally worse than in the past, rather than better. We must therefore begin by discussing this perception. . . .

The choice of comparison one makes always is crucial. . . . It usually makes sense to compare our present state of affairs with *how it was before*. This is the comparison that is usually relevant for policy purposes because it measures our progress. But many private and public discussions instead compare a present state of *one group* to the present state of *other groups,* as a supposed measure of "equity," or as the basis for indignation and righteousness, or to support their political positions. Others compare the actual situation to the *best* possible, or to ideal purity, ostensibly to motivate improvement. . . . This . . . is very different from the sorts of problems that most of humanity has faced throughout most of its history. . . . Almost every absolute change, and the absolute component of almost every economic and social change or trend, points in a positive direction, as long as we view the matter over a reasonably long period of time. That is, all aspects of material human welfare are improving in the aggregate. . . .

SOME KEY MATERIAL TRENDS

Let's start with the longest and deepest trends. Surprising though they may be, please be aware that these trends . . . represent the uncontroversial settled findings of the economists and other experts who work in these fields. . . .

Length of Life

Let's begin with the all-important issue, life itself. The most important and amazing demographic fact—the greatest human achievement in history, in my view—is the decrease in the world's death rate. . . . The stylized graph in Figure 43-1 shows that it took thousands of years to increase life expectancy at birth from just over 20 years to the high 20s. Then in just the past two centuries, the length of life one could expect for a newborn in the advanced countries jumped from less than 30 years to perhaps 75 years. . . .

Starting well after World War II, length of life in the poor countries has leaped upward by perhaps 15 or even 20 years since the 1950s, caused by advances in agriculture, sanitation, and medicine. . . .

The extraordinary decline in child mortality shown in Figure 43-2 is an important element in increased life expectancy, for which every parent must give fervent thanks. But contrary to common belief, in the rich countries such as the United States the gains in life expectancy among the *oldest* cohorts have been particularly large in recent years. For example, among U.S. males aged 65–74, mortality fell 26 percent from 1970 to 1988, and among females of that age, mortality fell 29 percent and 21 percent from 1960 and 1970 to 1988, respectively.[1]

The decrease in the death rate is the root cause of there being a much larger world population nowadays than in former times. In the 19th century the planet Earth could sustain only 1 billion people. Ten thousand years ago, only 4 million could keep themselves alive. Now, more than 5 billion people are living longer and more healthily than ever before, on average. This increase in the world's population represents humanity's victory against death.

[1]*U.S. Statistical Abstract* (1990), p. 75.

FIGURE 43-1
TRENDS IN LIFE EXPECTANCY OVER THE MILLENNIA (STYLIZED)

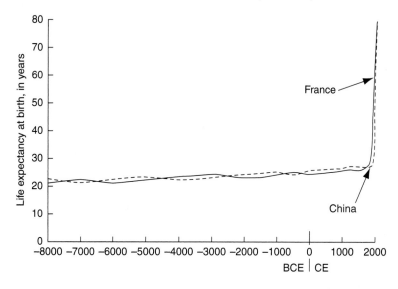

FIGURE 43-2
CHILD MORTALITY (1751 TO PRESENT)

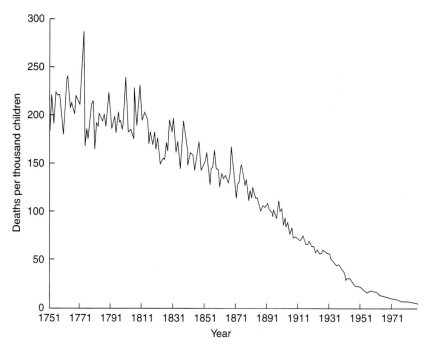

FIGURE 43-3
PERCENT OF POPULATION EMPLOYED IN AGRICULTURE, GREAT BRITAIN (1600 TO
THE PRESENT)

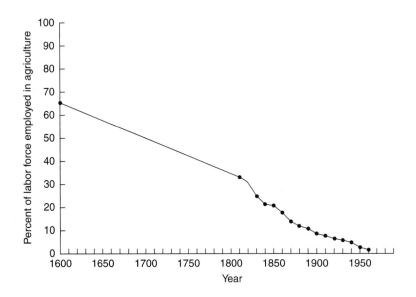

The trends in health are more complex. The decline in mortality is the most important overall indicator of health, of course. And the increase in height in the Western countries in the past century is another strong index of health and nutrition. . . . But whether the process of keeping more people alive into older age is accompanied by better or poorer health on average in those older years is in doubt. . . .

Proportion of the Labor Force in Agriculture

The best simple measure of a country's standard of living is the proportion of the labor force devoted to agriculture. When everyone must work at farming, as was the case only two centuries ago, there can be little production of nonagricultural goods. Figure 43-3 shows the astonishing decline over the centuries in the advanced countries in the proportion of the population working in agriculture, now only about 1 person in 50. This shift has enabled consumption per person to multiply by a factor of 20 or 40.

Raw Materials

People have since antiquity worried about running out of natural resources—flint, game animals, what-have-you. Yet, amazingly, all the historical evidence shows that raw materials—all of them—have become less scarce rather than more. . . . Natural resource scarcity—as measured by the economically meaningful indicator of cost or price—has been decreasing rather than increasing in the long run for all raw materials, with only temporary and local exceptions. Copper gives typical evidence that the trend of falling prices has continued throughout all of history. In Babylonia under Hammurabi—almost 4,000 years ago—the price of copper was about a thousand times its price in the United States now, relative to wages. At the time of the Roman Empire the price was a hundred times higher. And there is no reason why this trend should not continue forever.

The trend toward greater availability includes the most counterintuitive case of all—oil. . . . Concerning energy in general, there is no reason to believe that the supply of energy is finite, or that the price of energy will not continue its long-run decrease forever.

Food is an especially important resource. The evidence is particularly strong that the trend in nutrition is benign despite rising population. The long-run price of food is down sharply, even relative to consumer products, due to increased productivity. . . . And per-person food consumption is up over the last 30 years. The increase of height in the West . . . is another mark of improved nutrition.

(Africa's food production per person is down, but by the 1990s, few any longer claim that Africa's suffering has anything to do with a shortage of land or water or sun. Hunger in Africa clearly stems from civil wars and government interference with agriculture, which periodic droughts have made more murderous.)

Only one important resource has shown a trend of increasing scarcity rather than increasing abundance. It is the most important and valuable resource of all—human beings. Certainly there are more people on earth now than ever before. But if we measure the scarcity of people the same way that we measure the scarcity of other economic goods—by how much we must pay to obtain their services—we see that wages and salaries have been going up all over the world, in poor countries as well as in rich countries. The amount that one must pay to obtain the services of a barber or a professor has risen in India, jut as the price of a barber or professor has risen in the United States over the decades. This increase in the price of people's services is a clear indication that people are becoming more scarce even though there are more of us.

THE STANDARD OF LIVING

The pure purchasing-power aspect of the standard of living is difficult to measure. Consider, for example, that before the collapse of communism, the conventional-data estimate of per capita income in East Germany was 79 percent of that in West Germany, and the "purchasing power parity" estimate was fully 90 percent. It is now clear to all that these computations were misleading. And the clearest evidence comes from data on individual elements of consumption and wealth. [Available data now] show unmistakably how the standard of living has increased in the world and in the United States through the recent centuries and decades, right up through the 1980s. . . .

A related question concerns possible exploitation by the rich countries that might cause misery for the poor countries. But the distribution of the most important element of "real wealth"—life expectancy—has narrowed between rich and poor countries (as well as between the rich and poor segments of populations within countries) over previous decades. . . . The reduction in the gap between literacy rates and other measures of amount of education in rich and poor countries corroborates this convergence. . . . Data on the *absolute* gap between yearly incomes of the rich and poor countries are beside the point; widening is inevitable if all get rich at the same proportional rate, and the absolute gap can increase even if the poor improve their incomes at a faster proportional rate than the rich. Here one should notice that increased life expectancy among the poor relative to the rich reduces the gap in lifetime income, which is a more meaningful measure than yearly income.

It is important that the convergence among nations be properly interpreted as a spreading of a better standard of living to the entire world, rather than as a leveling down of the rich.

Cleanliness of the Environment

Ask an average roomful of people if our environment is becoming dirtier or cleaner, and most will say "dirtier." Yet the air in the United States and in other rich countries is irrefutably safer to breathe now than in decades past; the quantities of pollutants—especially particulates, which are the main threat to health—have been declining. And water quality has improved; the proportion of monitoring sites in the United States with water of good drinking ability has increased since the data began in 1961. More generally, the environment is increasingly healthy, with every prospect that this trend will continue. . . .

When considering the state of the environment, we should think first of the terrible pollutions that were banished in the past century or so—the typhoid that polluted such rivers as the Hudson, smallpox that humanity has finally pursued to the ends of the earth and just about eradicated, the dysentery that distressed and killed people all over the world as it still does in India, the plagues and other epidemics that trouble us much less than in generations past, or not at all. Not only are we in the rich countries free of malaria (largely due to our intensive occupation of the land), but even the mosquitoes that do no more than cause itches with their bites, are so absent from many urban areas that people no longer need screens for their homes and can have garden parties at dusk. It is a mark of our extraordinary success that these are no longer even thought of as pollutions.

The root cause of these victorious campaigns against the harshest pollutions was the nexus of increased technical capacity and increased affluence—wealth being the capacity to deal effectively with one's surroundings. . . .

SPECIES EXTINCTION

Fear is rampant about rapid rates of species extinction. The fear has little or no basis. The highest rate of observed extinctions is one species per year, in contrast to the 40,000 per year some ecologists have been forecasting for the year 2000. Species matter, and deserve thought. But the facts should matter, too, in deciding whether to spend tens of billions for research, "debt for nature" swaps, and other expensive programs. Furthermore, the new possibilities for genetic engineering, and for storage of seeds, reduce the dangers of extinctions that do occur. . . .

Population Growth

. . . There have been major changes in the intellectual status of the topic. Only two comments will be made:

1 A score of competent statistical studies, starting in 1967 with an analysis by Nobel prizewinner Simon Kuznets, agree that there is no negative statistical relationship between economic growth and population growth for periods up to a century. And there is strong reason to believe that more people have a positive effect in the longer run. That is, population growth does not lower the standard of living; it raises it in the long run.

2 There was a major turnaround in the 1980s in population economics. After decades of "Everyone knows . . ." that population growth hampers economic development, there has been a revolution in scientific thought on the matter. The consensus now is close to the position in the paragraph above, though it runs against intuitive "common sense." . . .

THE GREENHOUSE EFFECT, THE OZONE LAYER, AND ACID RAIN

What about the greenhouse effect? The ozone layer? Acid rain? The one certainty is that on all of these issues there is major scientific controversy and lack of consensus about what has happened until now, why it happened, and what might happen in the future. . . .

An important aspect of these atmospheric issues is that no threatening trend in *human welfare* has been connected to changes in these phenomena. There has been no increase in skin cancers from ozone, no damage to agriculture from a greenhouse effect, and slight or no damage to lakes from acid rain. It may even be that a greenhouse effect would benefit us on balance by warming some areas we'd like warmer and by increasing the carbon dioxide stimulus to agriculture.

Perhaps the most important aspect of these as well as the yet-unknown atmospheric scares that will surely be brought before the public is that we now have ever-increasing capacities to reverse such trends if necessary. And we can do so at costs that are manageable rather than being an insuperable constraint upon growth or an ultimate limit upon the increase of productive output or of population. . . .

OTHER ASPECTS OF HUMAN WELFARE

People alive now are living in the midst of what may be seen as the most extraordinary three or four centuries in human history—the period before us and probably the period after us as well. The Industrial Revolution and the gross material aspects of life are only a tiny part of the change.

Some advances need only to be mentioned to be assented to. Consider the amount of physically caused pain that people suffered in their lives without any help from scientific medicine. Childbirth was a nightmare for every woman; now anesthetics allow a woman to choose a level of pain that is tolerable to her. People whose limbs were injured in peace or war often had to have them amputated, with only liquor as painkiller. Those who lived long enough to die of cancer had no way to dull their agony. Nowadays, it is miraculously different.

So far only material aspects of life have been mentioned. Now let us consider some of the important nonmaterial trends.

Education and Opportunity

Consider the astounding increase since World War II in the amount of education that the youth of the world are acquiring. . . . This trend implies a vast increase in young people's opportunities to use their talents for their own and their families' benefits, and hence to the benefit of others in society as well. In my view, this trend is one of the most important, and one of the most happy, of all the trends experienced by the human enterprise. Already one can see results in the names on professors' doors in departments of computer science and chemistry, for example, in universities all over the United States and in the Nobel Prize awards—Asian and African names that would not have been seen a decade or two ago. Less and less often will people of genius and strong character live out their lives in isolated villages unable to contribute to civilization at large.

The process of providing educational opportunity will not be complete for decades, at least. One can still see children sharing rickety desks and scarce books in a Colombian fishing village—just two miles from a busy modern international airport. But even this is vastly better than the way it was just a few years ago—no school at all. And we can be confident that a century from now, scenes like that will be quite scarce.

The spread of reading material is manifest—all in the period of time since Gutenberg, so short relative to the history of humanity that it seems only an eye-blink. The recent spread may be measured by the increased amount of newsprint used in the world from decade to decade, and in the prices of advertising. . . . And though access to libraries is not yet universal, with the aid of computers and electronic communications, that day is not far away. To dramatize this progress, reflect on the childhood only two centuries ago of Abraham Lincoln, who could not afford paper and pencil. Among a world's population five times as large as it was then, there are almost no children so stricken with educational poverty.

Work, Leisure, and Boredom

Leisure is surely greater now than since our days as hunters and gatherers. . . . There is some evidence that work time has increased for some groups in the past decade or two. But for many people, work is a good in itself in the sense that its goal is not the production of additional income, which confuses the issue quantitatively; the opportunity to do this additional rewarding work is a great good in itself, rather than a bad thing. . . .

Indeed, one of the greatest boons to humanity in recent decades is the diminution in the boring factory tasks that robotized and dehumanized workers. No one who has not experienced eight-hour shifts of such mind-numbing jobs as lifting cases of beer onto or off a conveyor belt, or stacking double, triple, or quadruple sets of empty cans 11-high in a truck that requires petty arithmetic so that the worker cannot even daydream, can understand how bad the mind-torture is. (Postal workers who sort mail and move bags of it are some of the last of these sufferers in a modern society. And of course workers in poor countries still suffer this because their muscle power is cheaper than machines.)

Though I have no data to document the observation, we apparently do not suffer another of the old painful ills—leisure, boredom with nothing to do—that people experienced in earlier times. Indeed, even people who work less than 40 hours a week complain that they have too many things that they want to do.

Boredom also is dispelled by electronic entertainment. This is an extraordinary gift to the old and shut-in; anyone who has been in a hospital bed suffering too much pain even to be able to read a newspaper knows the value of taped music and books, and even junk television. . . .

Mobility and Travel

Mobility and travel speed constitute another aspect of life that shows extraordinary improvement. . . . Only two centuries ago, horse and sailing ship were the fastest modes of movement. Now there are bullet trains and supersonic flight. The 1992 price of much faster space travel is $6 million per trip, but that price is sure to fall rapidly.

These changes, along with the breathtaking gains in communications speed, are society-altering aids to the spread of human opportunity and liberty all over the world. They also ease the curse most of humanity has suffered—the boredom in isolated villages. Music was a rare pleasure only a century ago. Now there are few people on earth too poor to purchase music around the clock on a transistor radio.

QUALIFICATIONS TO THE ARGUMENT

I am not saying that all is well everywhere, and I do not predict that all will be rosy in the future. Children are hungry and sick; people live out lives of physical or intellectual poverty and lack of opportunity; irrational war (not even for economic gain) or some new pollution may finish us off. What [is true] is that for most relevant economic matters, the aggregate trends are improving rather then deteriorating.

Please note, too, that a better future does not happen "automatically" and without effort. It will happen because women and men will struggle with problems with their muscles and minds, and will probably overcome most of them—as people always have eventually overcome economic problems in the past—if the social and economic system gives them opportunity to do so. . . .

THE DOOMSAYERS' FORECASTS

Every forecast of the doomsayers has turned out to be wholly wrong. Metals, foods, and other natural resources have become more available rather than more scarce throughout the centuries. The famous *Famine 1975* forecast by the Paddock brothers—that we would see millions of famine deaths in the United States on television—was followed instead by gluts in agricultural markets. Paul Ehrlich's primal scream about "What will we do when the [gasoline] pumps run dry?" was followed by gasoline cheaper than since the 1930s. The Great Lakes are not dead; instead they offer better sport fishing than ever. The main pollutants, especially the particulates that have killed people for years, have lessened in our cities. . . .

How can it be that economic welfare grows in time along with population, rather than humanity being reduced to misery and poverty as population grows and we use more and more resources? We need some theory to explain this controversion of common sense.

The Malthusian theory of increasing scarcity based on supposedly fixed resources, which is the theory that the doomsayers rely upon, runs exactly contrary to the evidence from the long sweep of history. This is because Malthusianism and contemporary doomsters omit from their accounts the positive long-run effects of the problems induced by additional people and economic activity. Maybe neighborhood kids running over your lawn do not benefit you by causing improvements in lawn care technology. But more people putting pollutants into the air eventually lead to agitation and the search for ways to prevent and clean up pollutions, a process that eventuates in our having a cleaner environment than before the pollution began to be bad. It is this crucial adjustment mechanism—the reason England's air and water are cleaner than they have been for centuries—that is too often left out of thinking on these matters.

More generally, the process operates as follows: More people and increased income cause problems in the short run—shortages and pollutions. Short-run scarcity raises prices and pollution causes outcries. These problems present opportunity and prompt the search for solutions. In a free society, solutions are eventually found, though many people seek and fail to find solutions at cost to themselves. In the long run the new developments leave us better off than if the problems had not arisen. This theory fits the facts of history.

Technology exists now to produce in virtually inexhaustible quantities just about all the products made by nature—foodstuffs, oil, even pearls and diamonds—and make them cheaper in most cases than the cost of gathering them in the wild natural state. And the standard of living of commoners is higher today than that of royalty only two centuries ago—especially their health and life expectancy, and their mobility to all parts of the world.

Consider this prototypical example of the process by which people wind up with increasing availability rather than decreasing availability of resources. England was full of alarm in the 1600s about an impending shortage of energy due to the deforestation of the country. People feared a scarcity of wood for both heating and the iron industry. This impending scarcity led to the development of coal. . . .

. . . Because of increased demand due to population growth and increased income, the price of whale oil for lamps jumped in the 1840s, and the U.S. Civil War pushed it even higher, leading to a whale oil "crisis." This provided incentive for enterprising people to discover and produce substitutes. First came oil from rapeseed, olives, and linseed, and camphene oil from pine trees. Then inventors learned how to get coal oil from coal. Other ingenious persons produced kerosene from the rock oil that seeped to the surface, a product so desirable that its price then rose from $0.75 a gallon to $2.00. This high price stimulated enterprises to focus on the supply of oil, and finally Edwin L. Drake brought in his famous well in Titusville, Pennsylvania. Learning how to refine the oil took a while. But in a few years there were hundreds of small refiners in the United States, and soon the bottom fell out of the whale oil market, the price falling from $2.50 or more at its peak around 1866 to well below a dollar.

Here we should note that it was not the English or American government that developed coal or oil, because governments are not effective developers of new technology. Rather, it was individual entrepreneurs and inventors who sensed the need, saw opportunity, used all kinds of available information and ideas, made lots of false starts that were very costly to many of those individuals but not to others, and eventually arrived at coal and oil as viable fuels—because there were enough independent individuals investigating the matter for at least some of them to arrive at sound ideas and methods. This happened in the context of a competitive enterprise system that worked to produce what was needed by the public. And the entire process of impending shortage and new solution left us better off than if the shortage problem had never arisen.

The extent to which the political-social-economic system provides personal freedom from government coercion is a crucial element in the economics of resources and population. Skilled persons require an appropriate social and economic framework that provides incentives for working hard and taking risks, enabling their talents to flower and come to fruition. The key elements of such a framework are economic liberty, respect for property, and fair and sensible rules of the market that are enforced equally for all. . . .

CONCLUSION

The decrease in the death rate, and the attendant increase in life expectancy—more than doubling—during the last two centuries in the richer countries and in the 20th century in the poorer countries, is the most stupendous feat in human history. The decline in mortality is the cause of the rapid increases in human population during these periods. This triumph against death would seem the occasion for great rejoicing. Instead we find gloom. One reason for this peculiar outcome is focusing on short-run intergroup comparisons rather than on long-run changes for the human group as a whole.

In the short run, all resources are limited. An example of such a finite resource is the amount of time you will devote to reading this chapter. The longer run, however, is a different story. The standard of living has risen along with the size of the world's population since the beginning of recorded time. There is no convincing economic reason why these trends toward a better life should not continue indefinitely.

The key theoretical idea again: The growth of population and of income create actual and expected shortages, and hence led to price run-ups. A price increase represents an opportunity that attracts profit-minded entrepreneurs to seek new ways to satisfy the shortages. Some fail, at cost to themselves. A few succeed, and the final result is that we end up better off than if the original shortages had never arisen. . . .

Adding more people causes problems. But people are also the means to solve these problems. The main fuel to speed the world's progress is our stock of knowledge; the brakes are our lack of imagination and unsound social regulations of these activities. The ultimate resource is people—especially skilled, spirited, and hopeful young people endowed with liberty—who will exert their wills and imaginations for their own benefit, and so inevitably they will benefit the rest of us as well.